Cisco ASA, PIX, and FWSM Firewall Handbook

David Hucaby, CCIE No. 4594

Cisco Press

Cisco Press
800 East 96th Street
Indianapolis, Indiana 46240 USA

Cisco ASA, PIX, and FWSM Firewall Handbook

David Hucaby

Copyright© 2008 Cisco Systems, Inc.

Cisco Press logo is a trademark of Cisco Systems, Inc.

Published by:
Cisco Press
800 East 96th Street
Indianapolis, IN 46240 USA

Printed in the United States of America

Third Printing: August 2008

Library of Congress Cataloging-in-Publication Data

Hucaby, David.
   Cisco ASA, PIX, and FWSM firewall handbook / Dave Hucaby. --2nd ed.
        p.   cm.
   Earlier ed. published under title: Cisco ASA and PIX firewall handbook.
   ISBN 978-1-58705-457-0 (pbk.)
   1.   Computer networks--Security measures.   2.   Firewalls (Computer
security)   I. Hucaby, Dave. Cisco ASA and PIX firewall handbook.   II.
Cisco Systems, Inc.   III. Title.

   TK5105.59.H83 2007
   005.8--dc22

ISBN-13: 978-1-58705-457-0

ISBN-10: 1-58705-457-4

Warning and Disclaimer

This book is designed to provide information about configuring and using the Cisco Adaptive Security Algorithm (ASA) series and the Cisco Catalyst Firewall Services Module (FWSM). Every effort has been made to make this book as complete and accurate as possible, but no warranty or fitness is implied.

The information is provided on an "as is" basis. The authors, Cisco Press, and Cisco Systems, Inc., shall have neither liability nor responsibility to any person or entity with respect to any loss or damages arising from the information contained in this book or from the use of the discs or programs that may accompany it.

The opinions expressed in this book belong to the author and are not necessarily those of Cisco Systems, Inc.

Trademark Acknowledgments

All terms mentioned in this book that are known to be trademarks or service marks have been appropriately capitalized. Cisco Press or Cisco Systems, Inc., cannot attest to the accuracy of this information. Use of a term in this book should not be regarded as affecting the validity of any trademark or service mark.

Corporate and Government Sales

The publisher offers excellent discounts on this book when ordered in quantity for bulk purchases or special sales, which may include electronic versions and/or custom covers and content particular to your business, training goals, marketing focus, and branding interests. For more information, please contact: **U.S. Corporate and Government Sales** 1-800-382-3419 corpsales@pearsontechgroup.com. For sales outside the United States please contact: **International Sales** international@pearsoned.com

Feedback Information

At Cisco Press, our goal is to create in-depth technical books of the highest quality and value. Each book is crafted with care and precision, undergoing rigorous development that involves the unique expertise of members from the professional technical community.

Readers' feedback is a natural continuation of this process. If you have any comments regarding how we could improve the quality of this book, or otherwise alter it to better suit your needs, you can contact us through email at feedback@ciscopress.com. Please make sure to include the book title and ISBN in your message.

We greatly appreciate your assistance.

Publisher	Paul Boger
Associate Publisher	Dave Dusthimer
Cisco Representative	Anthony Wolfenden
Cisco Press Program Manager	Jeff Brady
Executive Editor	Brett Bartow
Managing Editor	Patrick Kanouse
Senior Development Editor	Christopher Cleveland
Project Editor	Mandie Frank
Copy Editor	Kevin Kent
Technical Editors	Greg Abelar, Mark Macumber
Editorial Assistant	Vanessa Evans
Designer	Louisa Adair
Composition	S4 Carlisle Publishing Services
Indexer	Tim Wright
Proofreader	Kathy Bidmen

CISCO

Americas Headquarters	Asia Pacific Headquarters	Europe Headquarters
Cisco Systems, Inc.	Cisco Systems, Inc.	Cisco Systems International BV
170 West Tasman Drive	168 Robinson Road	Haarlerbergpark
San Jose, CA 95134-1706	#28-01 Capital Tower	Haarlerbergweg 13-19
USA	Singapore 068912	1101 CH Amsterdam
www.cisco.com	www.cisco.com	The Netherlands
Tel: 408 526-4000	Tel: +65 6317 7777	www-europe.cisco.com
800 553-NETS (6387)	Fax: +65 6317 7799	Tel: +31 0 800 020 0791
Fax: 408 527-0883		Fax: +31 0 20 357 1100

Cisco has more than 200 offices worldwide. Addresses, phone numbers, and fax numbers are listed on the Cisco Website at **www.cisco.com/go/offices.**

About the Author

David Hucaby, CCIE No. 4594, is a lead network engineer for the University of Kentucky, where he works with health-care networks based on the Cisco Catalyst, ASA, FWSM, and VPN product lines. He was one of the beta reviewers of the ASA 8.0 operating system software. He has a B.S. and M.S. in electrical engineering from the University of Kentucky. He is the author of three other books from Cisco Press: *CCNP BCMSN Official Exam Certification Guide*, *Cisco Field Manual: Router Configuration*, and *Cisco Field Manual: Catalyst Switch Configuration*.

He lives in Kentucky with his wife, Marci, and two daughters.

About the Technical Reviewers

Greg Abelar has been an employee of Cisco since December 1996. He was an original member of the Cisco Technical Assistance Security team, helping to hire and train many of the engineers. He has held various positions in both the Security Architecture and Security Technical Marketing Engineering teams at Cisco. Greg is the primary founder and project manager of the Cisco written CCIE Security exam. Greg is the author of the Cisco Press title *Securing Your Business with Cisco ASA and PIX Firewalls* and coauthor of *Security Threat Mitigation and Response: Understanding Cisco Security MARS*, and has been a technical editor for various Cisco Press security books.

Visit Greg's blogs:
Internet Security for the Home—http://security1a.blogspot.com/
Enterprise Internet Security—http://security2b.blogspot.com/

Mark Macumber is a systems engineer in the field sales organization for Cisco. Mark joined Cisco in 1999 working in the Network Service Provider Sales Division on Internet Service Provider networks and with telco DSL network designs. Since 2002, Mark has served in the large enterprise customer space working through customer designs for campus switching, WAN routing, unified communications, wireless, and security. Security products and architecture are Mark's current technical focus within the enterprise space. The Enterprise Security SE team learns and delivers content on Cisco security products such as firewalls, host/network based intrusion detection/prevention systems, AAA, security information management, network admission control, and SSL/IPSec VPN.

Dedications

As always, this book is dedicated to the most important people in my life—my wife, Marci, and my two little daughters, Lauren and Kara. I would also like to dedicate the book to my parents, Reid and Doris Hucaby.

God has blessed me with a very wonderful and supportive family.

Acknowledgments

It is my pleasure to be involved in writing another Cisco Press book. Technical writing, for me, is great fun, although writing large books is hard work. The good folks at Cisco Press provided a wealth of help during the writing process. In particular, I'm very grateful to have worked with my friends Brett Bartow and Chris Cleveland yet again. They are amazing at what they do, and I'm very appreciative! I'm also grateful to Mandie Frank for managing many of the production pieces for the final product.

I would like to acknowledge the hard work and good perspective of the technical reviewers for this edition: Greg Abelar and Mark Macumber. I respect these two fellows' abilities very much, and I'm glad they agreed to wade through the book with me.

Several people have gone out of their way to help me, whether they realize it or not. Hopefully I have listed them all here.

Mark Macumber remains a valuable resource and friend on many fronts. Surely he cringes when he sees the word "favor" in the subject line of my emails!

I would also like to thank the many people on the ASA 8.0 beta team who have offered me their help and knowledge: Madhusudan Challa, Pete Davis, Matt Greene, Iqlas Ottamalika, Jeff Parker, Priyan Pathirana, Dan Qu, Nelson Rodrigues, Nancy Schmitt, Vincent Shan, Andy Teng, Mark Terrel, and Nagaraj Varadharajan.

Several people involved in the FWSM 3.2 development have been very patient and helpful, even though I arrived too late to get in on the beta program: Anne Dalecki Greene, Munawar Hossain, and Reza Saadat.

Two TAC engineers who have helped answer my questions along the way should also be acknowledged: Kureli Sankar and Kevin Tremblay.

Finally, revising this book has been an unusually difficult project for me. As always, God has given me encouragement and endurance at just the right times. I have come to appreciate the little signs that Kara makes and sticks up around the house. Two signs in particular have been right on the mark:

"Out of Time"

and

"Be Thankful"

This Book Is Safari Enabled

The Safari® Enabled icon on the cover of your favorite technology book means the book is available through Safari Bookshelf. When you buy this book, you get free access to the online edition for 45 days.

Safari Bookshelf is an electronic reference library that lets you easily search thousands of technical books, find code samples, download chapters, and access technical information whenever and wherever you need it.

To gain 45-day Safari Enabled access to this book:

- Go to http://www.ciscopress.com/safarienabled
- Complete the brief registration form
- Enter the coupon code TPF4-9KYE-YBT2-D2ED-ID66

If you have difficulty registering on Safari Bookshelf or accessing the online edition, please e-mail customer-service@safaribooksonline.com.

Contents at a Glance

Contents

Icons Used in This Book

Throughout this book, you will see a number of icons used to designate Cisco and general networking devices, peripherals, and other items. The following icon legend explains what these icons represent.

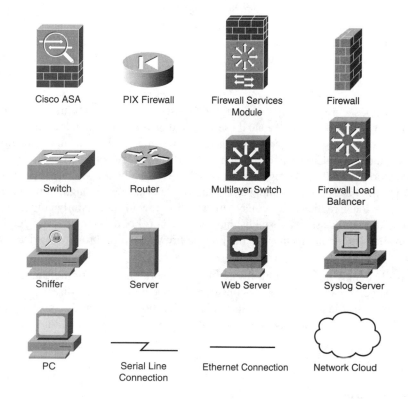

Command Syntax Conventions

The conventions used to present command syntax in this book are the same conventions used in the IOS Command Reference. The Command Reference describes these conventions as follows:

- **Boldface** indicates commands and keywords that are entered literally as shown. In actual configuration examples and output (not general command syntax), boldface indicates commands manually by the user (such as a **show** command).
- *Italics* indicates arguments for which you supply actual values.
- Vertical bars | separate alternative, mutually exclusive elements.
- Square brackets [ ] indicate optional elements.
- Braces { } indicate a required choice.
- Braces within brackets [{ }] indicate a required choice within an optional element.

Foreword

Today's networks are called upon to securely deliver data, voice, videoconferencing, wireless communication, and much more to a wide variety of users, such as employees, suppliers, partners, and customers. Securing the network has become a vital task to ensure this ubiquitous connectivity is delivered without risking unauthorized access, misuse, or attacks on the network.

While a vast number of different security technologies are now being applied to the problem of securing networks and endpoints, the long-proven and trusted firewall remains the central component to any security deployment. It is the firewall that continues to act as the primary gatekeeper, ensuring that all network traffic, from Layer 2 to Layer 7, is authorized and verified as legitimate before it transits the network.

Many books on network security and firewalls settle for a discussion focused primarily on concepts and theory. This book, however, goes well beyond these topics. It covers, in tremendous detail, the information every network and security administrator needs to know when configuring and managing market-leading firewall products from Cisco, including the PIX and ASA Security Appliances and Catalyst Firewall Services Module. As the title suggests, this book is really a handbook that provides in-depth explanations of the initial configuration and, perhaps more importantly, the ongoing management of Cisco firewalls. It provides practical, day-to-day guidance for how to successfully configure all aspects of the firewall, including topics such as establishing access control policies, authorizing end users, leveraging high availability deployments, and monitoring firewall health through a variety of management interfaces.

In addition to his role managing Cisco firewalls as a lead network engineer for the University of Kentucky, the author, David Hucaby, CCIE, spent considerable time collaborating directly with the Cisco engineering teams responsible for these products to ensure this book contains the most in-depth, useful, and up-to-date information available anywhere. Keep this book handy—you will find yourself referencing it often!

Jason W. Nolet
Vice President of Engineering
Security Technology Group
Cisco
June 2007

Introduction

This book focuses on the complete product line of Cisco firewall hardware: the PIX and ASA Security Appliance families and the Catalyst Firewall Services Module (FWSM). Of the many sources of information and documentation about Cisco firewalls, very few provide a quick and portable solution for networking professionals.

This book is designed to provide a quick and easy reference guide for all the features that can be configured on any Cisco firewall. In essence, an entire bookshelf of firewall documentation, along with other networking reference material, has been "squashed" into one handy volume.

This book covers only the features that can be used for stateful traffic inspection and overall network security. Although Cisco firewalls can also support VPN functions, those subjects are not covered here.

This book is based on the most current Cisco firewall software releases available at press time—ASA release 8.0(1) and FWSM release 3.2(1).

In the book, you will find ASA, PIX, and FWSM commands presented side-by-side for any specific task. The command syntax is shown with a label indicating the type of software that is running, according to the following convention:

- **ASA**—Refers to any platform that can run ASA release 7.0(1) or later. This can include the ASA 5500 family, as well as the PIX 500 family. For example, even though a PIX 535 can run a specific build of the ASA 8.0(1) code, the commands are still labeled "ASA" to follow the operating system being used.

- **PIX**—Refers to a PIX release 6.3.

- **FWSM**—Refers to FWSM release 3.1(1) or later.

If you are using an earlier version of software, you might find that the configuration commands differ slightly.

With the advent of the ASA platform, Cisco began using different terminology: firewalls became known as *security appliances* because of the rich security features within the software and because of the modular nature of the ASA chassis. This new terminology has been incorporated in this book where appropriate. However, the term *firewall* is still most applicable here because this book deals with both security appliances and firewalls embedded within Catalyst switch chassis. As you read this book, keep in mind that the terms *firewall* and *security appliance* are used interchangeably.

How This Book Is Organized

This book is meant to be used as a tool in your day-to-day tasks as a network or security administrator, engineer, consultant, or student. I have attempted to provide a thorough explanation of many of the more complex firewall features. When you better understand how a firewall works, you will find it much easier to configure and troubleshoot.

This book is divided into chapters that present quick facts, configuration steps, and explanations of configuration options for each Cisco firewall feature. The chapters and appendixes are as follows:

- **Chapter 1, "Firewall Overview"**—Describes how a Cisco firewall inspects traffic. It also offers concise information about the various firewall models and their performance.

- **Chapter 2, "Configuration Fundamentals"**—Discusses the Cisco firewall user interfaces, feature sets, and configuration methods.

- **Chapter 3, "Building Connectivity"**—Explains how to configure firewall interfaces, routing, IP addressing services, and IP multicast support.

- **Chapter 4, "Firewall Management"**—Explains how to configure and maintain security contexts, flash files, and configuration files; how to manage users; and how to monitor firewalls with SNMP.

- **Chapter 5, "Managing Firewall Users"**—Covers the methods you can use to authenticate, authorize, and maintain accounting records for a firewall's administrative and end users.

- **Chapter 6, "Controlling Access Through the Firewall"**—Describes the operation and configuration of the transparent and routed firewall modes, as well as address translation. Other topics include traffic shunning and threat detection.

- **Chapter 7, "Inspecting Traffic"**—Covers the Modular Policy Framework, which is used to define security policies that identify and act on various types of traffic. The chapter also discusses the application layer inspection engines that are used within security policies, as well as content filtering.

- **Chapter 8, "Increasing Firewall Availability with Failover"**—Explains firewall failover operation and configuration, offering high availability with a pair of firewalls operating in tandem.

- **Chapter 9, "Firewall Load Balancing"**—Discusses how firewall load balancing works and how it can be implemented in a production network to distribute traffic across many firewalls in a firewall farm.

- **Chapter 10, "Firewall Logging"**—Explains how to configure a firewall to generate an activity log, as well as how to analyze the log's contents.

- **Chapter 11, "Verifying Firewall Operation"**—Covers how to check a firewall's vital signs to determine its health, how to verify its connectivity, and how to observe data that is passing through it.

- **Chapter 12, "ASA Modules"**—Discusses the Security Services Modules (SSMs) that can be added into an ASA chassis, along with their basic configuration and use.

- **Appendix A, "Well-Known Protocol and Port Numbers"**—Presents lists of well-known IP protocol numbers, ICMP message types, and IP port numbers that are supported in firewall configuration commands.

- **Appendix B, "Security Appliance Logging Messages"**—Provides a quick reference to the many logging messages that can be generated from an ASA, PIX, or FWSM firewall.

How to Use This Book

The information in this book follows a quick-reference format. If you know what firewall feature or technology you want to use, you can turn right to the section that deals with it. The main sections are numbered with a quick-reference index that shows both the chapter and the section (for example, 3-3 is Chapter 3, section 3). You'll also find shaded index tabs on each page, listing the section number.

Feature Description

Each major section begins with a detailed explanation of or a bulleted list of quick facts about the feature. Refer to this information to quickly learn or review how the feature works.

Configuration Steps

Each feature that is covered in a section includes the required and optional commands used for common configuration. The difference is that the configuration steps are presented in an outline format. If you follow the outline, you can configure a complex feature or technology. If you find that you do not need a certain feature option, skip over that level in the outline.

In some sections, you will also find that each step in a configuration outline presents the commands from multiple firewall platforms side-by-side in a concise manner. You can stay in the same configuration section no matter what type or model of firewall you are dealing with.

Sample Configurations

Each section includes an example of how to implement the commands and their options. Examples occur within the configuration steps, as well as at the end of a main section. I have tried to present the examples with the commands listed in the order you would actually enter them to follow the outline.

Many times, it is more difficult to study and understand a configuration example from an actual firewall because the commands are displayed in a predefined order—not in the order you entered them. Where possible, the examples have also been trimmed to show only the commands presented in the section.

Displaying Information About a Feature

Each section includes plenty of information about the commands you can use to show information about that firewall feature. I have tried to provide examples of this output to help you interpret the same results on your firewall.

Refer to the following sections for information about these topics:

- **1-1: Overview of Firewall Operation**—Discusses the mechanisms a Cisco firewall uses to inspect and control traffic passing through it. The firewall inspection engines and algorithms are responsible for enforcing any security policies configured into the firewall.

- **1-2: Inspection Engines for ICMP, UDP, and TCP**—Describes how a firewall reacts to traffic of different IP protocols. The inspection mechanisms for the ICMP, UDP, and TCP protocols are covered.

- **1-3: Hardware and Performance**—Provides an overview and comparison of the various Cisco firewall platforms and their specifications. This information can help you decide which firewall model is best suited for your application.

- **1-4: Basic Security Policy Guidelines**—Presents a list of suggestions for configuring and maintaining firewalls in a corporate network.

CHAPTER 1

Firewall Overview

A firewall has multiple interfaces, but it isolates traffic between each one. The simplest firewall configuration has one outside and one inside interface, as shown in Figure 1-1.

Figure 1-1 *Basic Firewall with Two Interfaces*

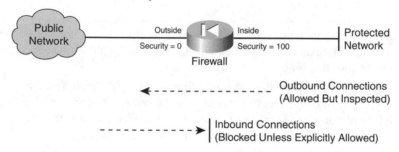

Each interface is assigned a *security level* from 0 (lowest) to 100 (highest). Multiple interfaces are each assigned an arbitrary security level, as shown in Figure 1-2.

Figure 1-2 *Basic Firewall with Several Interfaces*

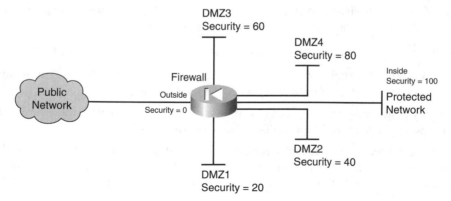

A firewall is usually represented by the symbol of a diode, an electronic component that allows current to pass in only one direction. Flow in the direction of the arrow is allowed, whereas flow against the arrow is blocked. Other symbols also are commonly used to represent firewalls. Most of those involve a brick wall with or without flames.

Likewise, a firewall has the following default behavior:

- In general, outbound connections from a higher security interface to a lower one are allowed, provided that they are permitted by any access lists that are applied to the firewall interfaces.

- All inbound connections from a lower security interface to a higher one are blocked.

The default policies can be changed so that some outbound connections can be blocked and some inbound connections can be allowed. Also, firewall interfaces can be assigned identical security levels so that traffic is allowed to pass between them.

All traffic is inspected according to a suite of stateful firewall inspection processes and algorithms. These are commonly called inspection engines or application layer protocol inspection.

NOTE   Inbound and outbound connections refer to the direction in which a connection is initiated. For example, if a host on the outside tries to initiate a connection with an inside host, that is an inbound connection.

Keep in mind that an inbound connection is entirely different from traffic that returns in the inbound direction. Return traffic is allowed inbound through the firewall only if it is in response to a previously established outbound connection. The same is true for connections and return traffic in the opposite direction.

1-1: Overview of Firewall Operation

A firewall's essential function is to isolate its interfaces from each other and to carefully control how packets are forwarded from one interface to another. In its default state, a firewall does not allow any packets to pass through it until some security policies are configured.

Before connections can form between firewall interfaces, two conditions must be met:

- An address translation policy *must* be configured between a pair of interfaces. (This requirement can be disabled with the **no-nat-control** command or Cisco firewall.)

- A security policy must be configured to allow the connection to initiate toward the destination. This is usually in the form of an access list applied to a firewall interface.

A Cisco firewall inspects traffic through a progression of functions. Figure 1-3 shows the order of these functions as a packet arrives at interface X (the left side of the figure) and exits at interface Y (the right side of the figure). The following sections describe each firewall function.

Figure 1-3 *A Cisco Firewall's Sequence of Packet Inspection Functions*

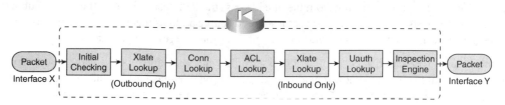

Initial Checking

As packets arrive at a firewall interface, they are checked for basic integrity. One of the most important things that can be checked is the integrity of a packet's source address. When a host sends a packet through a firewall, the firewall normally is concerned with finding a route for the destination address so that the correct egress interface can be used. The source address usually is ignored until the destination host needs to send a reply.

A malicious host can insert a bogus source IP address into the packets it sends. This is called *address spoofing*, and it is used to impersonate another host. When the malicious traffic is received, it looks like someone else sent it.

RFC 2827, "Network Ingress Filtering: Defeating Denial of Service Attacks which Employ IP Source Address Spoofing," describes a method that a firewall can use to detect when a source address is being spoofed.

NOTE   You can find all RFCs online at http://www.ietf.org/rfc/rfc*xxxx*.txt, where *xxxx* is the number of the RFC. If you do not know the RFC's number, you can try searching by topic at http://www.rfc-editor.org/cgi-bin/rfcsearch.pl.

A Cisco firewall uses this technique in its Unicast Reverse Path Forwarding (RPF) feature. When this feature is enabled on an interface, the source address in each incoming packet is inspected. The source address must be found in the firewall's table of known routes, which in turn must reference the interface on which the packet arrived. In other words, the firewall just verifies that the packet would take the same path in reverse to reach the source.

The firewall drops any packets that do not meet the RPF test, and the action is logged. If the RPF feature is enabled, you should make sure any IP subnets that can be reached on a firewall interface are also identified with a **route** command on the firewall. That way, the firewall can find those source addresses for the RPF test (as well as send packets toward those destination networks).

The outside firewall interface is a special case, however. Usually, the firewall has a default route associated with the outside interface, because most of the public network or Internet can be found on the outside. How can a firewall check for address spoofing on packets arriving at the outside interface?

If a source address cannot be found in the table of known routes, the default route is assumed to match. Therefore, packets arriving from the outside pass the RPF test as long as the source subnet or a default route exists. If an outside host uses a spoofed source address that belongs to a host or subnet on another firewall interface, however, the firewall finds that the reverse path does not match.

In other words, RPF can detect spoofed addresses only when they are spoofed *between* interfaces. To do this, the firewall has to know that a spoofed address on one interface actually exists on another interface. Only those packets are dropped. However, if a host on the outside interface spoofs the address of another outside host, the firewall cannot detect it, because the spoofing occurs on a single interface.

Xlate Lookup

A Cisco firewall maintains a translation or *xlate* table for each protected host that can participate in connections. A host's xlate entry can be statically defined before any active connections form. However, the static xlate entry is not actually created and used until the relevant traffic passes through the firewall. The host's xlate entry can also be created dynamically as a new connection is initiated.

Figure 1-4 illustrates the concept behind xlate operation. A host outside the firewall (Host A) has a registered public IP address, called a *foreign address*. A host on the inside of the firewall (Host B) has an internal IP address, called the *real* or *local address*. The internal host's address is translated through an xlate entry so that the local address appears on the outside of the firewall as a *mapped* or *global address*. Address translation is covered in greater detail in Chapter 6, "Controlling Access Through the Firewall."

Figure 1-4   *The Basic Concept Behind Xlate*

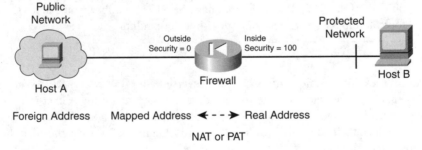

Each entry in the xlate table is maintained with the following parameters:

- Protocol used (ICMP, UDP, or TCP)
- Local and global interfaces
- Local and global IP addresses
- Local and global port numbers (if applicable; UDP and TCP only)

- Flags (type of xlate)
- Idle timer (incremented if no packets have used the xlate)
- Absolute timer (incremented since the xlate entry was created)
- Uauth bindings (originating user if user authentication or cut-through proxy is used)
- Connections using the xlate entry:
  - — Number of connections
  - — Number of embryonic (not yet fully established) connections
  - — A list of the active connections

Xlate table lookups occur at different points in the inspection process, depending on the direction of the connection. For an outbound connection (initiated from the inside), the xlate entry must be created early in the sequence of events. This is because the translated (global) address is used to build the actual connection entry and is used as the reference point for any access control list (ACL) operations. For inbound connections, the opposite is true—any connections and ACL operations must look at the untranslated (global) addresses, so xlate lookup must occur late in the game.

A firewall controls several aspects of each xlate entry:

- The number of active connections allowed to use an entry can be held to a maximum limit or can be unlimited (the default).
- The number of embryonic connections attempting to use an entry can be held to a maximum limit or can be unlimited (the default).
- An entry is aged out of the table if it has been idle for a timeout period.

Conn Lookup

A Cisco firewall examines and keeps track of the state of each connection attempting to go through it. This is often called *stateful inspection*. If a connection is allowed to form (the access list permits the traffic flow), each state change is updated in the firewall's connection or *conn* table. As soon as a connection initiates and a conn table entry is created, traffic from the source to the destination is allowed to pass. As well, the return traffic for that connection is allowed back through the firewall toward the source.

The connection state and the behavior of packets from the source and destination must follow the rules of the IP protocol being used. Any deviation from the accepted behavior causes the connection to be dropped and logged.

Each entry in the conn table is maintained with the following parameters:

- Protocol used (ICMP, UDP, or TCP)
- Local and foreign IP addresses (note that *local* addresses are used here, after the xlate lookup)
- Local and foreign port numbers (if applicable; UDP and TCP only)
- Flags for fixup type and connection state

- Idle timer (incremented if no packets have used the connection)
- Byte counter (total traffic volume using the connection)
- Local and foreign TCP sequence numbers

Conn entries are aged out of the table if they have been idle (no data passing through) for a timeout period. Conn entries can also age out after a short period if the connections are not fully established.

When Transmission Control Protocol (TCP) is used for a connection, a Cisco firewall can generate a random initial sequence number (ISN) toward the foreign host. Some hosts do not generate a truly random ISN, resulting in predictable values that can be exploited. The firewall can substitute a truly random ISN into the TCP packets when the connection is negotiated. This reduces the risk of session hijacking and is totally transparent to the local and foreign hosts.

ACL Lookup

Before a connection can be completed or actually allowed to form, its traffic must be permitted by an ACL. You can configure any number of ACLs in a firewall, but only one ACL can be applied to a firewall interface in a specific direction.

NOTE Before ASA 7.0(1), ACLs could be applied in only the inbound direction, to inspect traffic as it *enters* the interface. In later releases, ACLs can be applied in the inbound or outbound direction. All releases of FWSM support ACLs in both directions.

ACLs are not used to inspect a connection's state. Rather, they are used only to permit or deny packets in a single direction, only as connections are being initiated. For connectionless protocols such as Internet Control Message Protocol (ICMP), ACLs permit or deny all packets in the direction in which they are applied.

By default, no ACLs are configured or applied to any of a firewall's interfaces. Connections are permitted to initiate from a higher-security interface to a lower one—even with no ACL applied to the higher-security interface. One exception is the Catalyst 6500 Firewall Services Module (FWSM), which requires an ACL on any interface before permitting traffic to pass. However, no connections are allowed to initiate from a lower-security interface to a higher one until an ACL is applied to the lower-security interface.

ACL configuration and use are covered in greater detail in Section "6-3: Controlling Access with Access Lists," in Chapter 6.

Uauth Lookup

A Cisco firewall can authenticate users as they pass through to initiate connections. After a user is successfully authenticated, the firewall keeps the user credentials cached so that additional connections can be quickly approved. In other words, the firewall acts as a cut-through authentication proxy so that no further authentication is needed.

User authentication occurs by a request-reply exchange between the firewall and an authentication, authorization, and accounting (AAA) server, such as Remote Authentication Dial-In User Service (RADIUS) or Terminal Access Controller Access Control System Plus (TACACS+).

After a user is authenticated, the firewall can also request authorization information from the server. This information is used to limit users to reaching only specific resources through the firewall. The firewall can authorize users through one of the following methods:

- Retrieving a AAA attribute for the user
- Controlling the user's connections with an ACL referenced by the AAA server
- Controlling the user's connections with an ACL that has been downloaded from the AAA server

The firewall performs these functions by keeping a table of authenticated users and their user authentication (*uauth*) attributes. The uauth table records each authenticated user, along with his or her source IP address, the authorization ACL name (if any), and session timer values. In Chapter 5, "Managing Firewall Users," Section "5-5: Configuring AAA for End-User Cut-Through Proxy," covers AAA functions in greater detail.

After a user authenticates with the firewall, he can use and create new connections until his *absolute uauth timer* expires. As well, the firewall tracks to see if the user has not sent or received data on any of his connections for an *idle uauth timer* period. If the idle timer expires, that user is deleted from the uauth table, and all current connections are closed. That user is required to reauthenticate when he attempts a new connection. If the absolute timer expires, all the user's existing connections are allowed to remain open. However, the user is prompted to reauthenticate when a new connection is initiated.

Inspection Engine

The firewall inspects each connection and applies rules according to the protocol being used. This process has traditionally been called *fixup*, and more recently an *inspection engine* or application layer protocol inspection.

Some protocols are simple and have very loose guidelines about the traffic between source and destination. These are called *connectionless* protocols, and they include ICMP and UDP. Other protocols are very strict about the handshaking and packet exchange between source and destination. These are called *connection-oriented* protocols, and they include TCP.

1-2: Inspection Engines for ICMP, UDP, and TCP

The following sections outline the basic stateful inspection of each type of applicable protocol.

ICMP Inspection

ICMP is a connectionless protocol, because it allows one host to send another host a message without expecting a reply. Because of this, a firewall cannot examine or track the state of ICMP traffic between two machines. However, beginning with ASA 7.0(1) and FWSM 3.1(1), a firewall can track the state of ICMP packet exchanges, offering an approximation of a stateful inspection.

A firewall must rely on some of its basic mechanisms for inspecting ICMP traffic—the xlate table and ACLs. Note that no connections are used with ICMP, so no conn entries are created for ICMP traffic. Figure 1-5 shows how a Cisco firewall reacts when it needs to handle ICMP traffic between two hosts on different interfaces.

Figure 1-5 *How a Firewall Handles ICMP Traffic*

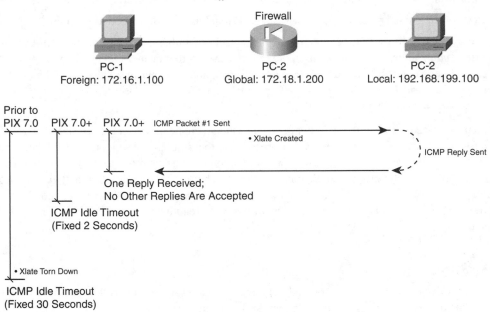

Host PC-1 sends an ICMP packet to host PC-2. The firewall needs an xlate entry for one or both of the hosts. This is created from either a static xlate or a dynamic assignment, depending on the configuration. The ICMP packet must also be permitted by any ACL that is applied to the firewall interface toward PC-1.

As an example of this process, PC-1 (foreign address 172.16.1.100) tries to ping host PC-2 (global address 172.18.1.200). PC-2 has a static xlate entry that translates global address 172.18.1.200 on the outside to local address 192.168.199.100 on the inside.

The **debug icmp trace** command reveals debugging information for all ICMP traffic passing through the firewall. Similar information could be gathered from Syslog messages generated by the firewall.

In this case, message IDs 305009, "Built static translation," and 609001, "Built local-host," might be seen. The **debug icmp trace** command output for this scenario is as follows:

```
Firewall# debug icmp trace
ICMP trace on
Warning: this may cause problems on busy networks
1: ICMP echo-request from outside:172.16.1.100 to 172.18.1.200 ID=768 seq=3328
   length=40
2: ICMP echo-request: untranslating outside:172.18.1.200 to inside:192.168.199.100
3: ICMP echo-reply from inside:192.168.199.100 to 172.16.1.100 ID=768 seq=3328
   length=40
4: ICMP echo-reply: translating inside:192.168.199.100 to outside:172.18.1.200
```

On line 1, the echo request ICMP packet is received on the outside interface. Line 2 shows the xlate entry being used which is an "untranslation" toward the inside host PC-2. Line 3 records the echo reply returning toward PC-1. Line 4 shows that the xlate entry has been used again, in the forward direction toward PC-1.

As soon as the xlate entries are in place and the ACLs permit the traffic, the two hosts are free to send ICMP packets to each other. In fact, other hosts might also be able to send ICMP packets to them too, if the xlate entry exists for the destination host and the ACL permits it.

If NAT is used, the xlate entries remain in effect for the duration of a connection or until the static NAT entry is removed from the configuration. For dynamic Port Address Translation (PAT), however, the firewall simply allows the ICMP packets to continue until a fixed 30-second idle time has expired. The following output demonstrates this scenario.

NOTE   As a part of the ICMP inspection engine, ASA releases 7.0(1) and later, as well as FWSM 3.1(1) and later, have much tighter control over ICMP activity. The firewall permits only a single reply to any ICMP request that passes through it. Although the ICMP xlate entry might remain active until the 30-second idle timer expires, any actual ICMP return traffic after the first reply packet is dropped.

If NAT is used for the xlate entry, the firewall allows the ICMP connection to remain open for 2 seconds after the one ICMP reply packet is seen. Dynamic PAT is slightly different; the ICMP connection is closed immediately after the first reply packet.

```
Firewall# show xlate local 172.21.4.2 debug
14340 in use, 34527 most used
Flags: D - DNS, d - dump, I - identity, i - inside, n - no random,
       o - outside, r - portmap, s - static
ICMP PAT from inside:172.21.4.2/1024 to outside:10.10.10.10/62204 flags r
   idle 0:00:29 timeout 0:00:30
Firewall # show xlate local 172.21.4.2 debug
14360 in use, 34527 most used
```

```
Flags: D - DNS, d - dump, I - identity, i - inside, n - no random,
       o - outside, r - portmap, s - static
Firewall #
```

A ping has created a dynamic xlate entry, and that entry has been idle for 29 seconds. Notice that the timeout value is 30 seconds, which is a fixed value for ICMP entries. One second later, the xlate entry has been deleted from the table.

A Case Study in ICMP Inspection

Without the stateful inspection of ICMP traffic, the decision to allow ICMP traffic does have its shortcomings. This is because of the nature of the ICMP protocol.

For example, it might seem natural to always expect an ICMP echo request to come first and an echo reply to be returned. After all, that is how the whole ping process works and how the ICMP inspection engine operates. Suppose ICMP inspection is disabled, as it is in releases before ASA 7.0(1) and FWSM 3.1(1), and ICMP echo packets are permitted to pass through a firewall.

You might be surprised to learn that a host on the outside can then send something odd to an inside host—unsolicited ICMP echo reply packets without any echo requests! This can happen even if the firewall is using dynamic PAT of the inside host addresses. It is all possible because ICMP has no inherent connection or state information.

The following configuration displays a capture on the firewall to briefly show that only ICMP echo reply packets are being sent toward the inside host 192.168.199.100. Chapter 11, "Verifying Firewall Operation," explains captures in more detail.

```
Firewall# show capture test
6 packets captured
23:09:21.471090 172.16.1.100 > 192.168.199.100: icmp: echo reply
23:11:01.497212 172.16.1.100 > 192.168.199.100: icmp: echo reply
23:11:01.498112 172.16.1.100 > 192.168.199.100: icmp: echo reply
23:11:01.498951 172.16.1.100 > 192.168.199.100: icmp: echo reply
23:11:01.499791 172.16.1.100 > 192.168.199.100: icmp: echo reply
23:11:01.500828 172.16.1.100 > 192.168.199.100: icmp: echo reply
6 packets shown
Firewall#
```

Now look at the following xlate and ICMP debug activity to see how the firewall reacts to the unsolicited echo replies:

```
Firewall#
67: ICMP echo-reply from outside:172.16.1.100 to 172.18.1.200 ID=0 seq=3369
  length=80
68: ICMP echo-reply: untranslating outside: 172.18.1.200 to inside:192.168.199.100
69: ICMP echo-reply from outside: 172.16.1.100 to 172.18.1.200 ID=1 seq=3369
  length=80
70: ICMP echo-reply: untranslating outside: 172.18.1.200 to inside:192.168.199.100
71: ICMP echo-reply from outside: 172.16.1.100 to 172.18.1.200 ID=2 seq=3369
  length=80
```

```
72: ICMP echo-reply: untranslating outside: 172.18.1.200 to inside:192.168.199.100
73: ICMP echo-reply from outside: 172.16.1.100 to 172.18.1.200 ID=3 seq=3369
    length=80
74: ICMP echo-reply: untranslating outside: 172.18.1.200 to inside:192.168.199.100
75: ICMP echo-reply from outside: 172.16.1.100 to 172.18.1.200 ID=4 seq=3369
    length=80
76: ICMP echo-reply: untranslating outside: 172.18.1.200 to inside:192.168.199.100
```

The reply packets are sent to the inside host, and the xlate entry is used to do it. Now imagine other possibilities in which an outside host could use various ICMP message types to annoy an inside host or communicate with a backdoor Trojan horse that has been installed. At the very least, the outside host could keep the xlate entry from ever idling out just by sending bogus ICMP packets toward the inside.

With ICMP inspection enabled, the same test case is performed. A ping is sent from an inside host toward an outside target, and the firewall creates a dynamic PAT ICMP xlate entry. The firewall accepts only a single echo reply packet and closes the ICMP connection.

The xlate entry stays active for a full 30 seconds until it idles out. During that time, an outside host attempts to send ICMP traffic to the PAT address. The firewall immediately rejects the traffic because it does not match any of the ICMP state information that was originally recorded. As well, the ICMP connection has already been closed, and a new inbound connection is not created, even though the inbound access list has an entry that permits any ICMP traffic to any inside host.

The following Syslog information demonstrates this rejection and the follow-up by the firewall.

```
Feb 22 2007 00:52:15 : %ASA-6-305011: Built dynamic ICMP translation from
    inside:192.168.198.4/33 to outside:128.163.93.131/0
Feb 22 2007 00:52:15 : %ASA-6-302020: Built ICMP connection for faddr
    128.163.93.129/0 gaddr 128.163.93.131/0 laddr 192.168.198.4/33
Feb 22 2007 00:52:15 : %ASA-6-302021: Teardown ICMP connection for faddr
    128.163.93.129/0 gaddr 128.163.93.131/0 laddr 192.168.198.4/33
Feb 22 2007 00:52:21 : %ASA-3-106014: Deny inbound icmp src outside:128.163.93.129
    dst outside:128.163.93.131 (type 8, code 0)
Feb 22 2007 00:52:45 : %ASA-6-305012: Teardown dynamic ICMP translation from
    inside:192.168.198.4/33 to outside:128.163.93.131/0 duration 0:00:30
```

Notice that the ICMP connection was built and torn down within the same second of time, immediately after the echo reply was received. The last line shows that the xlate entry stayed active until the 30-second idle timer expired.

UDP Inspection

User Datagram Protocol (UDP) is also a connectionless protocol. A host might send unsolicited UDP packets to another without expecting any reply in return. This can occur with protocols such as Real-Time Transport Protocol (RTP) for voice traffic. However, some protocols such as DNS use UDP for a two-way exchange, but no actual connection is established.

For most UDP traffic, a firewall cannot examine or track the state of the information exchange. UDP is inspected only through the use of the xlate table, ACLs, and conn table entries. Even though UDP is connectionless, a Cisco firewall creates conn entries as pairs of hosts communicate with UDP packets. Figure 1-6 shows how a firewall reacts to handle UDP traffic between two hosts on different interfaces.

Figure 1-6 *How a Firewall Handles UDP Traffic*

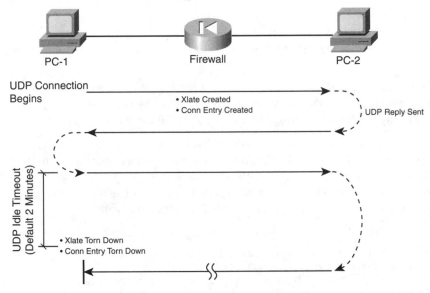

In Figure 1-6, the hosts pass messages back and forth, as if there is a connection between them. Host PC-1 begins the session by sending a UDP packet to PC-2. If the ACLs applied to the firewall interfaces permit this traffic, the firewall proceeds to define a UDP connection. To forward the traffic, the firewall needs an existing xlate table entry or needs to create one.

With the first packet in the session, the firewall creates a new connection entry in the conn table. This entry identifies the source and destination addresses and UDP ports so that all packets that pass between the pair of hosts can be identified with this specific connection.

UDP packets can now be passed back and forth between PC-1 and PC-2. The firewall allows the connection to continue as long as packets pass through that connection. If no packets have passed through the connection before the UDP idle connection timer expires, the UDP connection is closed by being deleted from the conn table. By default, a UDP connection idles out after 2 minutes.

This means that UDP connections never close by themselves, because they have no mechanism to do so. Instead, any UDP connections that are created by a firewall must just wait to idle out and close.

You should be aware of one exception a Cisco firewall makes in how it handles UDP connections: DNS traffic usually occurs as one request from a host for a name resolution and one valid response from a DNS server. Naturally, a host might send several duplicate requests to several different DNS servers, and it might get back several responses. In the end, only one reply really matters to the requesting host.

Suppose a DNS server is on the inside of a firewall, and all DNS traffic (UDP port 53) is permitted to reach it from the outside. If an outside host sends a legitimate DNS request, the firewall creates a UDP connection entry. While that connection is open to the outside host, that host might have free access to begin pestering the DNS server with bogus requests until the server becomes overwhelmed. This activity could go on and on, as long as the UDP connection never becomes idle.

Likewise, a client on the inside might send a DNS request to a DNS server on the outside. The firewall would create a UDP connection between the client and server, permitting the legitimate DNS reply. While the connection is "open," other malicious hosts on the outside could spoof the source address of the DNS server, targeting the inside client as the destination. Any number of bogus DNS replies could be sent inward, bombarding the unsuspecting client.

A Cisco firewall implements a feature called DNS Guard that prevents this from happening. The firewall observes DNS requests that pass through it over UDP connections. After a request is forwarded, the firewall allows only the *first* DNS reply to return to the requesting host. All replies after that are dropped, and the UDP connection triggered by the DNS request is immediately closed or deleted.

As a part of the UDP fixup process, a firewall also inspects and reacts differently to certain predefined UDP protocols. Individual application inspection engines are available, providing additional security over that of the generic UDP inspection engine. Section "7-3: Application Inspection," in Chapter 7, "Inspecting Traffic," describes this in further detail.

TCP Inspection

TCP is a connection-oriented protocol. Before two hosts can exchange TCP traffic, they must perform a three-way handshake to establish a TCP connection. Then, as packets are exchanged, the connection state is always updated with parameters that tell the far-end host what data to expect and how much data can be returned. To close a TCP connection, the two hosts must perform a modified three-way handshake.

Because TCP is connection-oriented, a firewall can track the exact state of the information exchange at any given time. For each TCP connection, the firewall examines source and destination address and port pairs, along with the TCP sequence number, the acknowledgment value, and the TCP flags. Packets that have unexpected values cannot be part of an existing connection, so the firewall drops them.

TCP connections are inspected through the use of the xlate table, ACLs, and conn table entries. The conn entries also have flags that reflect the current state of the TCP connections. For example, the state of the three-way handshake to initiate a connection is marked by flags that indicate which end sent the first SYN bit and which host is expecting the next SYN or SYN-ACK bit handshake. Likewise, the handshake to close a TCP connection is tracked by the state of FIN bit exchanges.

Figure 1-7 shows how a firewall handles TCP traffic between two hosts on different interfaces. Here, the packet exchange between hosts PC-1 and PC-2 is a bit more complex than ICMP or UDP because of the orderly fashion in which TCP connections must progress to maintain their states.

Figure 1-7 *How a Firewall Handles TCP Traffic*

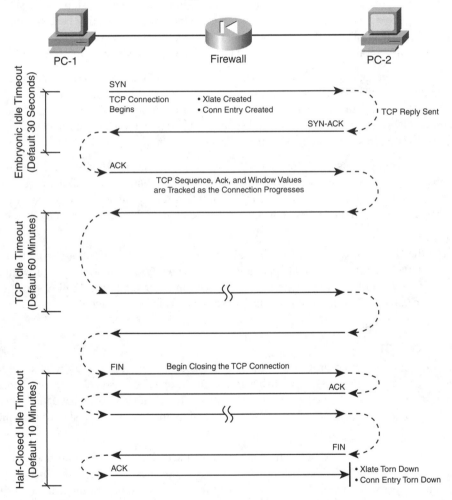

PC-1 initiates the TCP connection by sending a SYN bit in its packet to PC-2. The firewall creates a dynamic xlate entry if one does not already exist. As well, a new conn entry is created for the TCP connection between this pair of hosts. The firewall expects PC-2 to reply with a packet that has the SYN and ACK bits set.

At this point, the connection is only half-open, and it is considered an *embryonic connection* (not fully formed). If the SYN bit reply is not received within 30 seconds, the embryonic idle timer expires, and the connection is closed. Before ASA 7.0(1), the embryonic idle time was fixed at 30 seconds; in later releases, it defaults to 30 seconds but can be configured.

Finally, PC-1 must also complete the three-way handshake by sending a packet with the ACK bit set. If this handshake is properly followed, the firewall begins allowing TCP packets to flow through the connection. Each of these packets is examined to see if the TCP sequence number, acknowledgment number, and flags are being updated with the expected values.

NOTE   When a TCP connection is initiated, a host sends the first SYN packet, along with an ISN so that the far-end host knows how to respond. The ISN value is sometimes predictable, giving malicious users on the outside the ability to hijack a connection by masquerading as the actual initiating host.

A Cisco firewall intercedes on behalf of the inside host when a TCP connection is initiated. When the first TCP packet is forwarded on the outside network, the firewall generates a random ISN value. For each connection, the firewall maintains a translation between the inside sequence number and the outside sequence number. This adds a level of security, because outside hosts can never guess the true TCP ISN values that the inside hosts are using.

TCP connections can close in several ways:

- The two hosts can send FIN bits to each other in a two-way handshake. The firewall tracks this exchange to be sure that the connection is behaving correctly.

- One host can send a reset (RST) bit, requesting that the far-end host close and delete the connection immediately.

- The firewall also maintains an idle timer for each connection. If no packets have been sent through the connection before the idle timer expires, the firewall immediately closes the connection and deletes it from its conn table. By default, the idle timeout is 60 minutes.

Additional TCP Connection Controls

One host begins a TCP connection with another host by sending it a TCP packet with the SYN flag. A malicious host can begin so many TCP connections with another host that the target host can run out of memory or resources—even though none of the connections are actually established or completed. Each of the connections begins by having the SYN flag set, as if it were legitimate.

While an initial SYN packet goes unanswered with a SYN packet reply, the TCP connection is not yet established. As previously discussed, this condition is called an *embryonic,* or *half-open,* connection.

A Cisco firewall can monitor and control the number or volume of embryonic connections by watching the initial SYN packets that arrive on one interface, destined for a host on a different interface.

When the embryonic connection limit is exceeded, the firewall performs *TCP intercept* and acts as a proxy. The firewall intercepts the incoming SYN packet, and the connection state information is recorded in memory. The SYN is not actually sent to the target host; instead, the firewall answers with a SYN packet reply on the target's behalf. If the source responds with a SYN-ACK packet, indicating that the connection is legitimate, the firewall sends a copy of the original SYN packet to the target. In effect, this delays the connection's formation but allows the target to become aware of a true connection request. The TCP three-way handshake can proceed to establish the connection.

> **NOTE** For inbound connections (from a lower-security interface to a higher-security interface), the embryonic connection limit is defined, along with the static xlate entry (the **static** configuration command). This can prevent a denial-of-service attack coming from the outside.
>
> For outbound connections, the limit is defined along with the dynamic NAT or PAT xlate entry (the **nat** configuration command). This can prevent an attack coming from the inside, targeting hosts on the outside.

Finally, TCP connections that are established normally stay open until the two hosts exchange a two-way handshake of packets with the FIN flag set. If a FIN packet is sent but is not answered with another FIN packet, the TCP connection is in the *half-closed* state. A firewall can allow connections to remain in this state until the half-closed timer expires (the default is 10 minutes). After that occurs, the connection is deleted from the conn table without waiting for the handshake to complete.

TCP Normalization

Beginning with ASA 7.0(1) and FWSM 3.1(1), the TCP inspection engine can be configured to inspect and operate on several additional TCP parameters. *TCP normalization* is a feature that allows packet inspection based on configurable options defined in a modular service policy. This feature is covered in detail in Section "7-2: Defining Security Policies in a Modular Policy Framework," of Chapter 7.

You can enable the following types of TCP normalization inspection:

- Consistent retransmissions of TCP packets
- TCP checksum verification
- TCP maximum segment size (MSS) exceeded
- Misuse of TCP header reserved bits
- Packets with the SYN bit set while containing data

- Spoofed retransmission of packets dropped after time-to-live (TTL) expiration
- Handling of the TCP urgent flag
- Unexpected changes in TCP window values
- Handling of various TCP options

Other Firewall Operations

Cisco firewalls can also perform other functions while traffic is being inspected:

- **Content filtering**—A firewall can work with external servers to permit or deny users' access to web content. Section "7-1: Filtering Content," in Chapter 7 discusses this in further detail.

- **Failover**—Two physical firewalls can operate as a failover pair, in which one of the two is always active. This provides greater availability in case one of the firewalls fails. Chapter 8, "Increasing Firewall Availability with Failover," covers failover in greater detail.

- **DHCP**—A firewall can act as a DHCP client to receive dynamic IP addressing information from a service provider. It also can act as a DHCP server to provide dynamic information to a set of clients on a protected network. Section "3-3: DHCP Server Functions," in Chapter 3, "Building Connectivity," covers this topic in further detail.

- **Syslog**—A firewall can generate logging information about a wide variety of activity, to be collected by a logging server. Chapter 10, "Firewall Logging," covers Syslog functionality in greater detail.

- **Management**—You can manage a Cisco firewall in a variety of ways. You can use Simple Network Management Protocol (SNMP) to query some firewall parameters and receive notifications. Also, several GUI front-end applications are available to help you configure and monitor firewalls. Chapter 4, "Firewall Management," covers these features in further detail.

- **Packet capture**—A Cisco firewall can be configured to capture packets passing through an interface. This can be a useful troubleshooting tool or a way to examine specific traffic that is present in a network. Chapter 11 covers this and other troubleshooting tools in greater detail.

- **Emulation of multiple firewalls**—Beginning with ASA 7.0(1) and FWSM 2.2, a Cisco firewall can be configured to run multiple security contexts. Each context is an independent virtual firewall emulated on a single hardware platform. Section "4-1: Using Security Contexts to Make Virtual Firewalls," in Chapter 4 discusses multiple-context mode in detail.

1-3: Hardware and Performance

Cisco offers firewall functionality in a variety of hardware platforms, many of which are network appliances, where the firewall is contained in a standalone chassis. These include the Cisco PIX Security Appliance and Cisco Adaptive Security Appliance (ASA) platforms.

Section 1-3

The FWSM is a "blade" or module that can be used in a Catalyst 6500 switch chassis. This moves the firewall presence into an infrastructure switch itself rather than an external appliance.

Cisco also offers a firewall function as part of the Cisco IOS Software, which can be run on many router platforms. This function allows an existing router to become a firewall, too.

Table 1-1 lists the various firewall models, along with many of their specifications. This table provides a quick reference if you need to compare the capabilities or performance ratings of different models.

Table 1-1   *Cisco Firewall Specifications*

	ASA 5505	ASA 5510	ASA 5520	ASA 5540	ASA 5550	Catalyst 6500 FWSM
Operating System	ASA 7.x, 8.x	ASA 7.x, 8.x	ASA 7.x, 8.x	ASA 7.x, 8.x	ASA 7.x, 8.x	FWSM 2.x, 3.x
Memory	256 MB	256 MB	512 MB	1 GB	4 GB	1 GB
Flash (minimum)	64 MB	64 MB	64 MB	64 MB	64 GB	128 MB
Throughput	150 Mbps	300 Mbps	450 Mbps	650 Mbps	1.2 Gbps	5 Gbps
Concurrent Connections	10,000/25,000[1]	50,000/ 130,000[1]	280,000	400,000	600,000	1 million
Physical Interfaces	Eight 10/100 switch; two Power over Ethernet (PoE)	Five 10/100	Four 10/100/ 1000, one 10/ 100	Four 10/100/ 1000, one 10/100	Eight 10/100 plus 12 10/100 or nine GigabitEthernet	0
Logical Interfaces	Three (no trunking)/20 (trunking)	50/100[1]	150	200	250	100
Failover	No / Stateless Active/Standby (A/S)[1]	No / Active/ Active (A/A) and A/S	A/A and A/S	A/A and A/S	A/A and A/S	A/A and A/S[2]
AAA and Cut-Through Proxy	Yes	Yes	Yes	Yes	Yes	Yes
Command-Line Interface	Console, Telnet, Secure Shell (SSH)	Console, Telnet, SSH	Console, Telnet, SSH	Console, Telnet, SSH	Console, Telnet, SSH	Telnet, SSH
GUI	ASDM	ASDM	ASDM	ASDM	ASDM	ASDM
Routing	Static, RIP, EIGRP, OSPF	Static, RIP, EIGRP, OSPF	Static, RIP, EIGRP, OSPF	Static, RIP, EIGRP, OSPF	Static, RIP, EIGRP, OSPF	Static, RIP, OSPF

Table 1-1   *Cisco Firewall Specifications (Continued)*

	ASA 5505	ASA 5510	ASA 5520	ASA 5540	ASA 5550	Catalyst 6500 FWSM
Operating System	ASA 7.x, 8.x	ASA 7.x, 8.x	ASA 7.x, 8.x	ASA 7.x, 8.x	ASA 7.x, 8.x	FWSM 2.x, 3.x
Security Contexts	0	0 / 2, 5[1]	2, 20	2, 50	2, 50	100
VPN-Capable	Yes	Yes	Yes	Yes	Yes	No[3]

1.   Base license/Security Plus license.

2.   The FWSM supports only LAN-based failover, because it has no physical failover cable connector.

3.   The FWSM does not support any IPSec VPN features except for a 3DES tunnel that is used for management purposes.

1-4: Basic Security Policy Guidelines

As you plan your security policies and configure your firewall, you should keep several things in mind. Rather than presenting a long treatise on security policies and how to protect against vulnerabilities and attacks, this small section provides a short list of rules of thumb. If you follow these suggestions, you should be able to configure a firewall to provide the best possible protection.

- **Gather and review firewall logs regularly.**

   After a firewall is configured, you can easily test to see if it is blocking or permitting access to secured resources according to the correct security policies. However, there is no easy way to watch a denial-of-service or worm attack without seeing a record of traffic being permitted or denied.

   A firewall can generate a wealth (and a deluge) of logging information. This data should be collected by a Syslog server that is properly sized for the task. You should also review the Syslog data on a regular basis so that you can spot new malicious activity or expose the use of a vulnerable port you forgot to close.

   The most important reason to keep firewall logs is to keep an audit trail of network activity. If you experience an attack or a misuse of network resources, you can rely on the Syslog record as evidence.

- **Make inbound ACLs very specific.**

   You should tightly control traffic coming into your secured network from the public or unsecured side. If you offer public access to a corporate web or e-mail server, for example, be sure to permit only those specific protocols and ports. Otherwise, if you leave the inbound access too broad or open, you increase the chances that someone will find a way to exploit an

Section 1-4

unexpected protocol or service. In addition, best practices suggest that any inbound access should terminate only on hosts that are located on a demilitarized zone (DMZ) firewall interface—not on the inside network.

As for outbound traffic control, the internal (protected) users are usually well-known and trusted. You can leave the outbound access open, but best practices suggest that you configure outbound access lists to prevent hosts on the inside network from participating in worms or attacks aimed at DMZ or outside networks.

You might also use outbound access lists to enforce corporate policies to limit or prohibit certain activity or to control the access of unauthorized services. The firewall can also authenticate outbound users before giving them access and can work with external servers to control web content.

- **Protect the DMZ in several directions.**

  If corporate resources are offered to the public network, it is usually best to place them in a DMZ. This is a small network on a firewall interface that has a medium level of security. Users on the outside or public network are allowed to reach the servers on the DMZ using specific protocols and ports.

  Be careful how you configure the security policies on the DMZ interface. Make sure that outside users are allowed access only to the specific protocols needed. Then make sure that machines on the DMZ interface are allowed access to other inside (secured) hosts using only the protocols needed for data transfer.

  For example, suppose you have a public web server that offers information using HTTP. That web server populates its web pages by sending SQL requests to other data center servers on the inside network. For the DMZ, you should configure the firewall to allow outside access to the web server using only TCP port 80 (HTTP). In addition, the DMZ server should be allowed to send only SQL packets toward the inside data center, and nothing else. If you leave open access (any protocol or port number) between the DMZ server and the inside, the DMZ can become a "springboard" so that malicious users on the outside can compromise the DMZ server and use it to compromise others on the inside.

- **Be overly cautious about ICMP traffic.**

  ICMP packets are very useful when you need to troubleshoot access or network response time to a host. Ping (ICMP echo) packets are well known for this. However, configuring a firewall to allow open access for the ICMP protocol usually is not wise.

  Malicious users on the outside can use ICMP to detect or attack live hosts on a DMZ or inside network. Typically, best practice is to use a firewall to hide as much information as possible about the internal secured network. Outbound pings might be allowed so that your internal users can test to see if a service is alive on the public Internet. Inbound pings (echo requests) should be denied altogether, because you don't want outside users to know if your internal services are alive. The only exception might be to allow pings to reach your hosts that offer public services, but nothing else.

Best practices suggest that you allow only specific types of ICMP packets to enter your network from the outside. These include echo-reply, unreachable, and time-exceeded ICMP messages. In any event, you should configure ICMP inspection if at all possible, so that the firewall can make a best effort at tracking and controlling ICMP message exchanges.

- **Keep all firewall management traffic secured.**

  You can manage or maintain a firewall in many ways:

  — Open a management session using Telnet, SSH, ASDM, or Cisco Security Manager (CSM)

  — Copy a new operating system image or configuration file into the firewall

  — Collect Syslog information from the firewall

  — Poll firewall parameters through SNMP

  — Authenticate users through TACACS+ and RADIUS servers

Clearly, any of these methods can drastically change the firewall's behavior or operation. You should always make every effort to keep all types of management access limited to an inside or secured network. If you open any management access toward the outside, you stand a chance of letting a malicious user manage your firewall for you. At the least, someone might intercept your Syslog or SNMP traffic and learn something important about your internal network.

If you absolutely need some management access from the outside, only do so through a secure means like a virtual private network (VPN) connection or SSH with a strong authentication method. This allows management traffic to be extended only to someone who can verify his or her identity over an encrypted path.

- **Periodically review the firewall rules.**

  Cisco uses a model called the security wheel. The process of providing network security begins with developing a strong corporate security policy. This includes the following tasks:

  — Identifying the resources that will be secured

  — Identifying the "inside" users and hosts that will need access to other, less-secure network resources

  — Identifying corporate services that will be protected but will be accessible from the unsecured networks

  — Developing an authentication scheme, if needed, that can identify and grant permission for corporate and outside users

  — Developing a plan for auditing the security activities

Actually implementing and refining the policies becomes a continual process of four steps:

a. Secure the network (configure firewalls, routers, intrusion protection systems, and so on)

b. Monitor and respond to malicious activity

    c. Test existing security policies and components

    d. Manage and improve network security

Further Reading

Refer to the following recommended sources for further technical information about firewall functionality and securing a network:

Cisco's SAFE Blueprint documents at http://www.cisco.com/go/safe

Cisco ASA: All-in-One Firewall, IPS, and VPN Adaptive Security Appliance by Omar Santos and Jazib Frahim, Cisco Press, ISBN 1-58705-209-1 (978-1-58705-209-5)

Securing Your Business with Cisco ASA and PIX Firewalls by Greg Abelar, Cisco Press, ISBN 1-58705-214-8 (978-1-58705-214-9)

Firewall Fundamentals by Wes Noonan and Ido Dubrawsky, Cisco Press, ISBN 1-58705-221-0 (978-1-58705-221-7)

Network Security Principles and Practices by Saadat Malik, Cisco Press, ISBN 1-58705-025-0 (978-1-58705-025-1)

Designing Network Security, Second Edition by Merike Kaeo, Cisco Press, ISBN 1-58705-117-6 (978-1-58705-117-3)

Cisco Access Control Security: AAA Administration Services by Brandon Carroll, Cisco Press, ISBN 1-58705-124-9 (978-1-58705-124-1)

Network Security Architectures by Sean Convery, Cisco Press, ISBN 1-58705-115-X (978-1-58705-115-9)

Refer to the following sections for information about these topics:

- **2-1: User Interface**—Discusses the command-line interface (CLI) methods that an administrative user can use to connect to and interact with a firewall.

- **2-2: Firewall Features and Licenses**—Covers the license activation keys that can be used to unlock firewall functions.

- **2-3: Initial Firewall Configuration**—Presents a brief overview of the methods that can be used to start configuring a firewall.

CHAPTER 2

Configuration Fundamentals

2-1: User Interface

A Cisco firewall, like any other networking device, offers several ways for the administrative user to connect to and interact with the firewall. Users usually need to make changes to the firewall's security policies and configuration, monitor firewall activity, and troubleshoot traffic handling. All interaction with a firewall is based on a common user interface, which can be described as follows:

- A Cisco firewall supports user access by these methods:
    - Command-line interface (CLI) by an asynchronous console connection
    - CLI by a Telnet session
    - CLI by Secure Shell (SSH) version 1.x or 2 (Adaptive Security Appliance [ASA] and Firewall Services Module [FWSM])
    - Adaptive Security Device Manager (ASDM) through a web browser for ASA and FWSM platforms, and PIX Device Manager (PDM) for PIX platforms running 6.3 or earlier releases
    - Cisco Security Manager (CSM)
    - VPN/Security Management Solution (VMS) Firewall Management Center

- A firewall also provides a user interface to the ROM monitor bootstrap code when the operating system is not running.

- Users can execute commands from the *user level* or from the *privileged level*. The user level offers basic system information commands. The privileged level offers complete access to all firewall information, configuration editing, and debugging commands.

- A help system offers command syntax and command choices at any user prompt.

- A history of executed firewall commands can be kept. As well, command lines can be edited and reused.

- The output from a command can be searched and filtered so that useful information can be found quickly.

NOTE   Only the CLI itself is covered in this section. The mechanisms to reach it (Telnet, SSH, and so on) are covered in Chapter 4, "Firewall Management," Section 4-4, "Managing Administrative Sessions."

TIP   The Catalyst 6500 Firewall Services Module (FWSM) does not have an accessible console connection or other physical interface. However, you can still access an FWSM from the Catalyst 6500 native IOS CLI, as if you were connected to its console. Use the following Catalyst EXEC command to connect to the FWSM in chassis slot number *slot*:

```
Switch# session slot slot processor 1
```

User Interface Modes

The user interface of a Cisco firewall consists of several modes, each providing a different level of administrative capability and a different function. The user interface modes are as follows:

- User EXEC mode

    Administrative users can connect to a firewall via the console port, Telnet session, or SSH session. By default, the initial access to a firewall places the user in *user EXEC* mode and offers a limited set of commands. When you connect to the firewall, a *user-level password* is required. A firewall designates user EXEC mode with a prompt of this form:

```
Firewall>
```

NOTE   User-level authentication and passwords are covered in Chapter 5, "Managing Firewall Users."

- Privileged EXEC mode

    As soon as a user gains access to user EXEC mode, the **enable** command can be used to enter *privileged EXEC* or *enable* mode. Full access to all the executable commands is available. To leave privileged EXEC mode, use the **disable**, **quit**, or **exit** command. The syntax for entering privileged EXEC mode is as follows:

```
Firewall> enable
password: password
Firewall#
```

Notice that the pound, or number, sign (#) is used to designate privileged EXEC mode.

- Configuration mode

    From privileged EXEC mode, you can enter configuration mode. From this mode, you can issue firewall commands to configure any feature that is available in the operating system. In PIX 6.x, all configuration is performed in one global configuration mode. Later releases, however, offer a global configuration mode and many submodes, much like the Cisco IOS software. To leave configuration mode and return to EXEC mode, enter **exit** or press **Ctrl-z**. You can also use the **exit** command to exit a submode and return to global configuration mode.

    The syntax for entering global configuration mode is as follows:

```
Firewall# configure terminal
Firewall(config)#
```

User Interface Features

Within an administrative session, you can enter commands and get helpful information about entering commands. As well, you can filter the information that a firewall displays in a session as a result of a command. These mechanisms are discussed in the following sections.

Entering Commands

To enable a feature or parameter, enter the command and its options normally. To disable a command that is in effect, begin the command with **no**, followed by the command. You need to include enough options to identify the command uniquely, as it exists in the firewall session or configuration. For example, the following configuration commands enable and then disable the embedded HTTP server:

```
Firewall(config)# http server enable
Firewall(config)# no http server enable
```

You can see the configuration commands that are in effect by using one of the following commands:

ASA, FWSM	Firewall# **write terminal**
	or
	Firewall# **show running-config** [*command*]
PIX 6.3	Firewall# **write terminal**
	or
	Firewall# **show running-config**
	or
	Firewall# **show** *command*

Notice that the ASA and FWSM platforms allow you to specify a command keyword in the **show running-config** command. If it is included, only the related configuration commands are shown, rather than the entire configuration. PIX 6.3 shows specific configuration commands by omitting the **running-config** keyword with the **show** *command* syntax.

TIP	Some ASA and FWSM configuration commands and their options are not shown if they use their default values. To see every configuration command that is enabled or active, even if it is a default, you can use the **show running-config all** [*command*] syntax.

Commands and their options can be abbreviated with as few letters as possible without becoming ambiguous. For example, to enter configuration mode, the command **configure terminal** can be abbreviated as **conf t**.

ASA and FWSM platforms also offer a keyword completion function. If you enter a shortened or truncated keyword, you can press the **Tab** key to make the firewall complete the keyword for you. Keyword completion can be useful when you are entering keywords that are very long and hyphenated. For example, pressing the **Tab** key after entering **show ru** produces the completed command **show running-config**:

```
Firewall# show ru[Tab]
Firewall# show running-config
```

This works only if the truncated keyword is unambiguous; otherwise, the firewall cannot decide which one of several similar keywords you want. If you press **Tab** and the keyword stays the same, you know you have not entered enough characters to make it unambiguous.

You can edit a command line as you enter it by using the left and right arrow keys to move within the line. If you enter additional characters, the remainder of the line to the right is spaced over. You can use the **Backspace** and **Delete** keys to make corrections.

TIP	Sometimes the firewall might display an informational or error message while you are entering a command line. To see what you've entered so far, you can press **Ctrl-l** (lowercase L) to redisplay the line and continue editing.
	For example, suppose an administrator is trying to enter the **hostname** configuration command to set the firewall's host name. Before he or she can enter the command, the firewall displays a logging message that interrupts the command line:

```
pix-c# config t
pix-c(config)# hostnNov 15 2004 00:34:08  single_vf : %PIX-7-111009:
  User 'enable_15' executed cmd: show interface [user presses Ctrl-l here]
pix-c(config)# hostn
```

Pressing **Ctrl-l** displays the line again without all the clutter.

Command Help

You can enter a question mark (**?**) after any keyword in a command line to get additional information from the firewall. Entering the question mark alone on a command line displays all available commands for that mode (configuration or EXEC).

You can also follow a command keyword with a question mark to get more information about the command syntax. Doing this in PIX 6.3 displays the command syntax of *all* commands that use that keyword. For example, entering **arp ?** causes the firewall to show the syntax of the **arp** command, as well as the **show arp** and **clear arp** commands.

ASA and FWSM platforms offer context-based help, much like the Cisco IOS software. Entering a question mark after a keyword causes the firewall to list only the possible keywords or options. For example, entering **show arp ?** results in the following output:

```
Firewall# show arp ?
  statistics  Show arp statistics
  |           Output modifiers
  <cr>
Firewall# show arp
```

Here, **show arp** can be followed by **statistics**, a pipe symbol (I), or the Enter key (<cr>).

With an ASA platform, you can also use the question mark with a partially completed command keyword if you do not know the exact spelling or form. The firewall displays all possible keywords that can be formed from the truncated word. For example, suppose you do not remember what commands can be used to configure access lists. Entering **access?** in configuration mode reveals the possibilities:

```
Firewall(config)# access?
access-group  access-list
Firewall(config)# access
```

Notice that the truncated command keyword is displayed again, ready to be completed with more typing.

If you enter a command but use the wrong syntax, you see the following error:

```
Type help or ''?' for a list of available commands
```

ASA and FWSM platforms also display a carat (^) symbol below the command line location to point out the error. For example, suppose a user forgets and enters the command **config type** rather than **config term**:

```
Firewall# config type
              ^
ERROR: % Invalid input detected at '^' marker.
Firewall#
```

The carat points to the keyword **type**, starting at the **y**, where the syntax error begins.

Command History

The firewall keeps a history of the last 19 commands that were issued in each interactive session. You can see the entire history list for your current session with the **show history** command.

You can use the command history to recall a previous command that you want to use again. This can save you time in entering repetitive commands while allowing you to make edits or changes after you recall them.

Each press of the up arrow key (↑) or **Ctrl-p** recalls the next older or previous command. Each press of the down arrow key (↓) or **Ctrl-n** recalls the next most recent command. When you reach either end of the history cache, the firewall displays a blank command line.

When commands are recalled from the history, they can be edited as if you just entered them. You can use the left arrow key (←) or right arrow key (→) to move within the command line and begin typing to insert new characters. You can also use the **Backspace** or **Delete** key to delete characters.

NOTE   The arrow keys require the use of an American National Standards Institute (ANSI)-compatible terminal emulator (such as the VT100).

Searching and Filtering Command Output

A **show** command can generate a long output listing. If the listing contains more lines than the terminal session can display (set using the **pager** command, whose default is 24 lines), the listing is displayed a screenful at a time, with the following prompt at the bottom:

```
<---More --->
```

To see the next screen, press the spacebar. To advance one line, press the **Enter** key. To exit to the command line, press the **q** key.

You can use a regular expression (*reg-expression*) to match against lines of output. Regular expressions are made up of patterns—either simple text strings (such as *permit* or *route*) or more complex matching patterns. Typically, regular expressions are regular text words that offer a hint to a location in the output of a **show** command. You can use the following command structure to perform a regular-expression search:

```
Firewall# show command ... | {begin | include | exclude | grep [-v]} reg-expression
```

To search for a specific regular expression and start the output listing there, use the **begin** keyword. This can be useful if your firewall has a large configuration. Rather than using the spacebar to eventually find a certain configuration line, you can use **begin** to jump right to the desired line.

To display only the lines that include a regular expression, use the **include** (or **grep**) keyword. To display all lines that do not include a regular expression, use the **exclude** (or **grep -v**) keyword.

A more complex regular expression can be made up of patterns and operators. Table 2-1 lists and defines the characters that are used as operators.

Table 2-1   *Regular-Expression Operators*

Character	Description
.	Matches a single character.
*	Matches zero or more sequences of the preceding pattern.
+	Matches one or more sequences of the preceding pattern.
?	Matches zero or one occurrences of the preceding pattern.
^	Matches at the beginning of the string.
$	Matches at the end of the string.
_	Matches a comma, braces, parentheses, the beginning or end of a string, or a space.
[ ]	Defines a range of characters as a pattern.
( )	Groups characters as a pattern. If it is used around a pattern, the pattern can be recalled later in the expression using the backslash (\) and the pattern occurrence number.

For example, the following command can be used to display all the logging messages with message ID 302013 currently stored in the logging buffer:

```
Firewall# show log | include 302013
302013: Built outbound TCP connection 1788652405 for outside:69.25.38.107/80
   (69.25.38.107/80) to inside:10.1.198.156/1667 (207.246.96.46/52531)
302013: Built outbound TCP connection 1788652406 for outside:218.5.80.219/21
   (218.5.80.219/21) to inside:10.1.100.61/3528 (207.246.96.46/52532)
[output truncated]
```

Message 302013 records TCP connections built in either the inbound or outbound direction. To display only the *inbound* TCP connections recorded, the regular expression could be changed to include **302013**, any number of other characters (**.***), and the string **inbound**:

```
Firewall# show log | include 302013.*inbound
302013: Built inbound TCP connection 1788639636 for outside:216.117.177.135/54780
   (216.117.177.135/54780) to inside:10.1.3.16/25 (207.246.96.46/25)
Firewall#
```

You might also use a regular expression to display command output that contains IP addresses within a range. For example, the following command filters the output to contain only IP addresses that begin with 10.10.5, 10.10.6, and 10.10.7:

```
Firewall# show log | include 10.10.[5-7].*
```

Terminal Screen Format

By default, all output from the firewall is displayed for a terminal session screen that is 80 characters wide by 24 lines long. To change the terminal screen width, you can use the following configuration command:

```
Firewall(config)# terminal width characters
```

Here, *characters* is a value from 40 to 511. You can also specify 0, meaning the full 511-character width.

To change the screen length (the number of lines displayed when paging through a large amount of output), you can use the following configuration command:

```
Firewall(config)# pager [lines number]
```

Here, *number* can be any positive value starting at 1. If you use only the **pager** keyword, the page length returns to its default of 24 lines.

You can also disable screen paging completely by using **pager lines 0**. This action might be useful if you are capturing a large configuration or logging message output with a terminal emulator. A more efficient practice would be to let all the output scroll by into the emulator's capture buffer; otherwise, you would have to use the spacebar to page through the output and then later remove all the **<--- More --->** prompts that were captured too.

2-2: Firewall Features and Licenses

When a Cisco firewall runs an image of the operating system, it must have the proper license activation keys to unlock the required features. To see a list of features and their current availability on a firewall, you can use the following EXEC command:

```
Firewall# show version
```

Example 2-1 shows some sample output from a PIX Firewall. The **show version** command displays the current version of the firewall operating system (6.3(4) in this case), the firewall's elapsed uptime, and some information about the hardware. You can find the amount of RAM memory, Flash memory, and the MAC addresses of the physical interfaces here too. In this example, the firewall is a model PIX-525 and has 256 MB of RAM, 16 MB of Flash, two **ethernet** interfaces, and two **gb-ethernet** interfaces. (Here, **ethernet** implies a 10/100BASE-TX interface; Gigabit Ethernet interfaces are called **gb-ethernet**.)

Example 2-1   *Sample Output from the PIX 6.3 **show version** Command*

```
Firewall# show version

Cisco PIX Firewall Version 6.3(4)
Cisco PIX Device Manager Version 3.0(1)

Compiled on Wed 13-Aug-03 13:55 by morlee
```

Example 2-1 *Sample Output from the PIX 6.3 **show version** Command (Continued)*

```
Firewall up 252 days 7 hours

Hardware:   PIX-525, 256 MB RAM, CPU Pentium III 600 MHz
Flash E28F128J3 @ 0x300, 16MB
BIOS Flash AM29F400B @ 0xfffd8000, 32KB

Encryption hardware device : IRE2141 with 2048KB, HW:1.0, CGXROM:1.9, FW:6.5
0: ethernet0: address is 0030.8587.446e, irq 10
1: ethernet1: address is 0030.8587.446f, irq 11
2: gb-ethernet0: address is 0003.4725.1f97, irq 5
3: gb-ethernet1: address is 0003.4725.1e32, irq 11
Licensed Features:
Failover:                        Enabled
VPN-DES:                         Enabled
VPN-3DES-AES:                    Enabled
Maximum Physical Interfaces:     8
Maximum Interfaces:              12
Cut-through Proxy:               Enabled
Guards:                          Enabled
URL-filtering:                   Enabled
Inside Hosts:                    Unlimited
Throughput:                      Unlimited
IKE peers:                       Unlimited

This PIX has an Unrestricted (UR) license.

Serial Number: 431030631 (0x19b10167)
Running Activation Key: 0xb0751733 0xd6201f9f 0x135e15a6 0xef5e1f26
Configuration last modified by enable_15 at 22:00:46.880 EST Thu Feb 24 2005
Firewall#
```

The shaded text lists all the firewall features. This sample firewall has a valid license to operate as one of two firewalls in a failover pair. The firewall can use the DES, 3DES, and AES encryption methods and has four physical interfaces, with the capability to add more if needed.

However, notice that the firewall has a limit of 8 physical interfaces and a maximum of 12 interfaces. How is it possible to have up to 12 interfaces? Cisco firewalls can also support logical interfaces, in the form of virtual LANs (VLANs). A total of 12 interfaces, either physical or logical, can be configured for use.

For comparison, Example 2-2 shows the **show version** output from an ASA 5510 running release 8.0 of the operating system. The output format is only slightly different.

Example 2-2 *Sample Output from the ASA 8.0 **show version** Command*

```
Firewall# show version

Cisco Adaptive Security Appliance Software Version 8.0(0)235
```

continues

Example 2-2 *Sample Output from the ASA 8.0 **show version** Command (Continued)*

```
Device Manager Version 6.0(0)97


Compiled on Wed 07-Mar-07 14:37 by builders
System image file is "disk0:/asa800-235-k8.bin"
Config file at boot was "startup-config"


Firewall up 3 days 23 hours
Hardware:   ASA5510, 256 MB RAM, CPU Pentium 4 Celeron 1600 MHz
Internal ATA Compact Flash, 64MB
BIOS Flash AT49LW080 @ 0xffe00000, 1024KB


Encryption hardware device : Cisco ASA-55x0 on-board accelerator (revision
0x0)
                              Boot microcode   : CN1000-MC-BOOT-2.00
                              SSL/IKE microcode: CNLite-MC-SSLm-PLUS-2.01
                              IPSec microcode  : CNlite-MC-IPSECm-MAIN-2.04
0: Ext: Ethernet0/0 : address is 0016.c789.c8a4, irq 9
1: Ext: Ethernet0/1 : address is 0016.c789.c8a5, irq 9
2: Ext: Ethernet0/2 : address is 0016.c789.c8a6, irq 9
3: Ext: Ethernet0/3 : address is 0016.c789.c8a7, irq 9
4: Ext: Management0/0 : address is 0016.c789.c8a8, irq 11
5: Int: Internal-Data0/0 : address is 0000.0001.0002, irq 11
6: Int: Internal-Control0/0 : address is 0000.0001.0001, irq 5
Licensed features for this platform:

Maximum Physical Interfaces  : Unlimited
Maximum VLANs                : 50
Inside Hosts                 : Unlimited
Failover                     : Disabled
VPN-DES                      : Enabled
VPN-3DES-AES                 : Enabled
Security Contexts            : 0
GTP/GPRS                     : Disabled
VPN Peers                    : 250
WebVPN Peers                 : 2
Advanced Endpoint Assessment : Disabled


This platform has a Base license.

Serial Number: JMX1014K070
Running Activation Key: 0x70092e4e 0x507e4e04 0xa8f1f16c 0x85c41864
0x4917ef91
Configuration register is 0x1
Configuration last modified by enable_15 at 00:06:07.574 EDT Thu Mar 22 2007
Firewall#
```

Notice that several of the licensed features are disabled, because this firewall has a Base license.

The **show version** output from a FWSM platform is similar, listing its licensed features. Example 2-3 shows the command output.

Example 2-3   *Sample Output from the FWSM 3.2 show version Command*

```
Firewall# show version
FWSM Firewall Version 3.1(4) <system>
Compiled on Fri 08-Dec-06 16:55 by dalecki

Firewall up 16 days 14 hours
failover cluster up 40 days 20 hours

Hardware:   WS-SVC-FWM-1, 1024 MB RAM, CPU Pentium III 1000 MHz
Flash TOSHIBA THNCF128MBA @ 0xc321, 20MB

0: Int: Not licensed        : irq 5
1: Int: Not licensed        : irq 7
 2: Int: Not licensed       : irq 11

Licensed features for this platform:
Maximum Interfaces     : 1000
Inside Hosts           : Unlimited
Failover               : Active/Active
VPN-DES                : Enabled
VPN-3DES-AES           : Enabled
Cut-through Proxy      : Enabled
Guards                 : Enabled
URL Filtering          : Enabled
Security Contexts      : 20
GTP/GPRS               : Disabled
VPN Peers              : Unlimited

Serial Number: SAD0912013X
Running Activation Key: 0x2d5557af 0x85b15342 0x5cced864 0xa4e560f8
Configuration last modified by enable_1 at 04:38:10.700 EST Sun Feb 11 2007
Firewall#
```

Notice that the FWSM has a maximum of 1,000 interfaces. Because the FWSM has no physical interfaces to connect, all of the 1,000 interfaces are logical VLAN interfaces.

The maximum supported memory, number of interfaces, and number of concurrent connections vary across the family of Cisco firewalls. Table 2-2 shows how the models and their resources break down.

Table 2-2   *Firewall Models, Licenses, and Supported Resources*

Model	Memory (MB)	Physical Interfaces	Virtual Interfaces	VPN Peers	Concurrent Connections	Security Contexts (Max)
FWSM	1024	-	1,000	-	1,000,000	250

continues

Table 2-2 *Firewall Models, Licenses, and Supported Resources (Continued)*

Model	Memory (MB)	Physical Interfaces	Virtual Interfaces	VPN Peers	Concurrent Connections	Security Contexts (Max)
ASA 5540	1024	Four 10/100/1000, one 10/100	200	5,000	400,000	50
ASA5520	512	Four 10/100/1000, one 10/100	150	750	280,000	20
ASA 5510	256	Five 10/100	50^1 100^2	250	$50,000^1$ $130,000^2$	0^1 5^2
ASA 5505	256	Eight 10/100, two PoE	3 (non-trunking)[1] 20 (trunking)[2]	10^1 25^2	$10,000^1$ $25,000^2$	0^1 0^2
PIX 535	1024^3 512^4	10	150	2,000	500,000	50
PIX 525	256^3 128^4	8	100	2,000	280,000	50
PIX 515E	64^3 32^4	6	25	2,000	130,000	5
PIX 506E	32^3 0^4	2	2	25	25,000	-
PIX 501	16^3 0^4	2	-	10	7,500	-

1. Base license
2. Security Plus license
3. PIX Unrestricted license
4. PIX Restricted license

Some firewall platforms can support high availability by operating in failover pairs. One firewall can run in an active mode, while the other can run in a standby mode or an active mode. The failover pair capabilities of the FWSM, ASA, and PIX are as follows:

- The FWSM platform always allows an active/active or active/standby failover pair to be configured.

- All models of ASA allow active/active or active/standby, except for the ASA 5510 and ASA 5505. Failover is not supported with the Base license. With the Security Plus license, the ASA 5510 can run in either active/active or active/standby, while the ASA 5505 can run in active/ standby without keeping state information.

- PIX firewalls can operate in a failover pair with the Unrestricted (UR) license, but not with the Restricted (R) license. The PIX can also have a Failover (FO) license, allowing it to run in an active/standby pair, but not as a standalone firewall. The Failover-Active/Active (FO-AA) license allows a PIX to run in an active/active pair, but not as a standalone firewall.

Firewall features are unlocked by a license activation key. Beginning with ASA 7.0, the activation key is a 20-byte string consisting of five groups of eight hexadecimal digits each. Prior releases use a 16-byte string consisting of four groups of eight hexadecimal digits each.

TIP   The Catalyst 6500 FWSM comes standard with an Unrestricted license. Because of this, it does not use an activation key.

If your ASA or PIX firewall does not have the 56-bit Data Encryption Standard (DES), 168-bit Triple DES (3DES), or 256-bit Advanced Encryption Standard (AES) encryption methods enabled, you can obtain a free license activation key from Cisco.com. You need an active Cisco.com user ID to access the license request pages at http://www.cisco.com/go/license. Under the **Licenses Not Requiring a PAK** section, click on the **click here for available licenses** link.

Find the Cisco ASA or PIX listing under **Security Products** and click on the **license** link. You have to fill out an Encryption Software Export Distribution Authorization Form to get permission to legally download and use strong encryption technology from Cisco.

You can also register your firewall license and request an activation key to upgrade any of the other features. To do this, go to http://www.cisco.com/go/license and enter the Product Authorization Key (PAK).

When you request any type of license upgrade on Cisco.com, you must also enter your firewall serial number. You can find the serial number, programmed into the firewall hardware or the Flash memory at the factory, by issuing the **show version** command. The serial number is used to calculate a license activation key; therefore, the activation key works only with the firewall it was intended to support.

Upgrading a License Activation Key

A firewall keeps its activation key stored in nonvolatile Flash memory, along with an image of its operating system. The key and image are read, copied into RAM, and used when the firewall boots up.

You also can download a new key and a new operating system image to a running firewall. The new key and operating system image are immediately stored in Flash memory, because the firewall is already running from its RAM resources.

You can see the current activation key (the one copied into RAM) by issuing the following EXEC command:

```
Firewall# show activation-key
```

Example 2-4 shows a sample of the output from an ASA command. Notice that this firewall has the same key in both Flash and running (RAM) memory. This only means that the key has not been updated or changed since the firewall was booted up.

Example 2-4 *Sample Output from the **show activation-key** Command*

```
Firewall# show activation-key
Serial Number: 807243559
Running Activation Key: 0xc422440f 0x2eb1445a 0x46fb4413 0x74a344ee 0x4b33d295
Licensed features for this platform:
Maximum Physical Interfaces : 10
Maximum VLANs               : 100
Inside Hosts                : Unlimited
Failover                    : Active/Active
VPN-DES                     : Enabled
VPN-3DES-AES                : Enabled
Cut-through Proxy           : Enabled
Guards                      : Enabled
URL Filtering               : Enabled
Security Contexts           : 5
GTP/GPRS                    : Enabled
VPN Peers                   : Unlimited

This platform has an Unrestricted (UR) license.

The flash activation key is the SAME as the running key.
Firewall#
```

Before you can enter a new activation key, the firewall must be running the exact same operating system image as the one stored in Flash memory. This ensures that the features unlocked by the activation key are applicable to the most recent image present on the firewall. If the images differ, you see the following message from the **show activation-key** command:

```
The flash image is DIFFERENT from the running image.
The two images must be the same in order to examine the flash activation key.
```

In this case, the firewall must be reloaded so that the image in Flash is the one being run.

You can enter a new license activation key in one of two ways:

- **ROM monitor mode**

  After an image of the firewall operating system has been downloaded via TFTP from monitor mode, the firewall asks if a new activation key is needed. The new key is added before the image is run.

- **Configuration mode**

  ```
  Firewall# activation-key activation-key-tuples
  ```

  activation-key-tuples is a string of four groups (PIX 6.3 or FWSM) or five groups (ASA) of eight hexadecimal digits each, provided by Cisco. Each tuple or group of eight digits can begin with 0x to designate hexadecimal notation, but this is not necessary.

For example, a new activation key is entered on an ASA platform as follows:

```
Firewall# activation-key 0xcc055f66 0xd4c45b68 0x98505048 0x8a8c5890 0x4b35d295

License Features for this Platform:
Maximum Physical Interfaces : 10
Maximum VLANs               : 100
Inside Hosts                : Unlimited
Failover                    : Active/Active
VPN-DES                     : Enabled
VPN-3DES-AES                : Enabled
Cut-through Proxy           : Enabled
Guards                      : Enabled
URL Filtering               : Enabled
Security Contexts           : 5
GTP/GPRS                    : Enabled
VPN Peers                   : Unlimited

This machine has an Unrestricted (UR) license.

Both running and flash activation keys were updated with the requested key
Firewall#
```

2-3: Initial Firewall Configuration

A Cisco firewall can be configured through the CLI on the console port. You can enter configuration mode with the following privileged EXEC command:

```
Firewall# configure terminal
```

Commands can then be entered one at a time. To end configuration mode and return to EXEC mode, you can press **Ctrl-z** or enter **exit**. Chapters 3 through 10 cover all the firewall features and configuration commands.

> **TIP**   Whenever you make configuration changes to a firewall, you should always make sure the running configuration is saved to a nonvolatile location. Otherwise, if the firewall is rebooted or if power is lost, your configuration changes also are lost.
>
> You can save the running configuration to the firewall's nonvolatile Flash memory with the **write mem** command. Chapter 4 in Section 4-3, "Managing Configuration Files," discusses this procedure in more detail.

You can use a firewall management application such as ASDM, PDM, or Firewall Management Center (Firewall MC, a part of the VMS software) to make configuration changes on a firewall. If you intend to do this, you need to give the firewall a minimal "bootstrap" configuration so that the management application can communicate with and manage it.

You can use the **setup** EXEC command to start the bootstrap procedure. The firewall then prompts you for the necessary values. At a minimum, the firewall needs the following parameters that are collected by the **setup** command:

- Enable password
- Current time (Coordinated Universal Time [UTC] or Greenwich Mean Time [GMT])
- Current date
- IP address of the firewall's inside interface (where it reaches the management application)
- Firewall's host name
- Firewall's domain name (used to generate an SSL certificate for web management access)
- Management station's IP address

Refer to the following sections for information about these topics:

- **3-1: Configuring Interfaces**—Discusses how you can configure firewall interfaces to join and communicate on a network. Physical, trunk, and logical interfaces are covered, as well as priority queue operation.

- **3-2: Configuring Routing**—Explains the configuration steps needed to define static routes on a firewall, as well as the RIP, OSPF, and EIGRP dynamic routing protocols.

- **3-3: DHCP Server Functions**—Provides information about how a firewall can operate as a DHCP server and a DHCP client. These functions support dynamic addressing for the firewall and for internal hosts, without the use of a dedicated DHCP server.

- **3-4: Multicast Support**—Presents the configuration steps needed to allow a firewall to forward multicast traffic in a secure manner and to participate in multicast routing.

CHAPTER 3

Building Connectivity

A firewall must be configured with enough information to begin accepting and forwarding traffic before it can begin doing its job of securing networks. Each of its interfaces must be configured to interoperate with other network equipment and to participate in the Internet Protocol (IP) suite.

A firewall must also know how to reach other subnets and networks located outside its immediate surroundings. You can configure a firewall to use static routing information or information exchanged dynamically with other routers. You can even configure a firewall to handle IP multicast traffic, either as a proxy or as a multicast router.

You can also configure a firewall to provide various Dynamic Host Control Protocol (DHCP) services so that hosts connected to its interfaces can get their IP addresses dynamically.

This chapter discusses each of these topics in detail.

3-1: Configuring Interfaces

Every firewall has one or more interfaces that can be used to connect to a network. To pass and inspect traffic, each firewall interface must be configured with the following attributes:

- Name.

- IP address and subnet mask (IPv4; beginning with Adaptive Security Appliance (ASA) 7.0 and Firewall Services Module (FWSM) 3.1(1), IPv6 is also supported).

- Security level (a higher level is considered more secure).

By default, traffic is allowed to flow from a higher-security interface to a lower-security interface ("inside" to "outside," for example) as soon as access list, stateful inspection, and address translation requirements are met. Traffic from a lower-security interface to a higher one must pass additional inspection and filtering checks.

Firewall interfaces can be physical, where actual network media cables connect, or logical, where the interface exists internally to the firewall and is passed to a physical trunk link. Each Cisco firewall platform supports a maximum number of physical and logical interfaces. Starting with PIX OS release 6.3, trunk links are also supported. The trunk itself is a physical interface, and the

Virtual LANs (VLAN) carried over the trunk are logical VLAN interfaces. A trunk link has the following attributes:

- Firewall trunk links support only the IEEE 802.1Q trunk encapsulation method.

- As each packet is sent to a trunk link, it is tagged with its source VLAN number. As packets are removed from the trunk, the tag is examined and removed so that the packets can be forwarded to their appropriate VLANs.

- 802.1Q trunks support a native VLAN associated with the trunk link. Packets from the native VLAN are sent across the trunk *untagged*.

- A firewall does not negotiate trunk status or encapsulation with Dynamic Trunking Protocol (DTP); the trunk is either "on" or "off."

Figure 3-1 shows how a trunk link between a firewall and a switch can encapsulate or carry frames from multiple VLANs. Notice that frames from the native VLAN are sent without a tag, and frames from other VLANs have a tag added while in the trunk.

Figure 3-1 *How an IEEE 802.1Q Trunk Works on a Firewall*

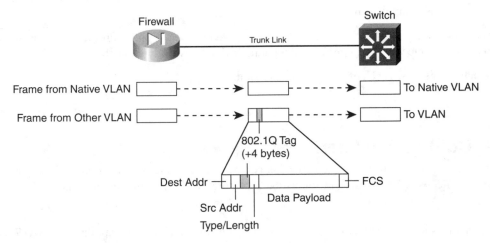

Surveying Firewall Interfaces

You can see a list of the physical firewall interfaces that are available by using the following command:

```
Firewall# show version
```

Firewall interfaces are referenced by their hardware index and their physical interface names. For example, the **show version** command on a PIX 525 running PIX release 6.3 produces the following output:

```
Firewall# show version
0: ethernet0: address is 0030.8587.546e, irq 10
1: ethernet1: address is 0030.8587.546f, irq 11
```

```
2: gb-ethernet0: address is 0003.4725.2f97, irq 5
3: gb-ethernet1: address is 0003.4725.2e32, irq 11
```

The first number is the hardware index, which indicates the order in which the interfaces were placed in the firewall backplane. Each physical interface has a hardware ID name that indicates its medium; **ethernet0** is a 10/100BASE-TX port, and **gb-ethernet0** is a Gigabit Ethernet port.

With ASA 7.0 and later, the output is slightly different:

```
Firewall# show version
0: Ext: Ethernet0          : media index  0: irq 10
1: Ext: Ethernet1          : media index  1: irq 11
2: Ext: GigabitEthernet0   : media index  0: irq 5
3: Ext: GigabitEthernet1   : media index  1: irq 11
```

TIP   On an FWSM, all interfaces are logical and have names beginning with **vlan** followed by the VLAN number. With a default configuration, the only VLAN interfaces available are the ones that have been configured from the Catalyst switch Supervisor module. These are created with the following Catalyst IOS configuration commands:

```
Switch(config)# firewall vlan-group group vlan-list
Switch(config)# firewall module mod vlan-group group
```

In the first command, an arbitrary VLAN group number, *group*, is defined to contain a list of one or more VLANs that will be internally connected to the FWSM. The second command associates the FWSM located in switch chassis slot *mod* with the VLAN group *vlan-group*. For example, the following commands can be used to provide VLANs 10, 20, and 30 to the FWSM located in slot 4:

```
Switch(config)# firewall vlan-group 1  10,20,30
Switch(config)# firewall module 4 vlan-group 1
```

Logical interfaces have a hardware ID in the form **vlan1, vlan55**, and so on. These interfaces are not available until you define them with configuration commands, so they are not shown in the **show version** output.

At this point, you should identify each of the interfaces you will use. At a minimum, you need one interface as the "inside" of the firewall and one as the "outside." By default, the firewall chooses two interfaces for the inside and outside. You can view the interface mappings with the **show nameif** EXEC command. You also can change the interface-name mappings as needed.

TIP   The **show interface** command lists each interface along with its state, MAC and IP addresses, and many counters. You can use the output to verify an interface's activity and current settings.

> The interface state is shown by two values: The configured administrative state (**up** or **administratively down**) and the line protocol state (**up** or **down**). The line protocol state indicates whether the interface is connected to a live network device.

Configuring Interface Redundancy

By default, each physical firewall interface operates independently of any other interface. The interface can be in one of two operating states: up or down. When an interface is down for some reason, the firewall cannot send or receive any data through it. The switch port where a firewall interface connects might fail, causing the interface to go down, too.

Naturally, you might want to find a way to keep a firewall interface up and active all the time. Beginning with ASA 7.3(1), you can configure physical firewall interfaces as redundant pairs.

As a redundant pair, two interfaces are set aside for the same firewall function (inside, outside, and so on) and connect to the same network. Only one of the interfaces is active; the other interface stays in a standby state. As soon as the active interface loses its link status and goes down, the standby interface becomes active and takes over passing traffic.

Both physical interfaces in a redundant pair are configured as members of a single logical "redundant" interface. In order to join two interfaces as a redundant pair, the interfaces must be of the same type (10, 100, 1000BASE-TX GigabitEthernet, for example).

The redundant interface is configured with a unique interface name, security level, and IP address—the parameters used in firewall operations.

You can use the following configuration steps to define a redundant interface:

1. Define the logical redundant interface:

   `Firewall(config)# `**`interface redundant`**` number`

   You can define up to eight redundant interfaces on an ASA. Therefore, the interface *number* can be 1 through 8.

2. Add physical interfaces as members:

   `Firewall(config-int)# `**`member-interface`**` physical_interface`

   The physical interface named *physical_interface* (gigabitethernet0/1, for example) becomes a member of the logical redundant interface. Be aware that the member interface cannot have a security level or IP address configured. In fact, as soon as you enter the **member-interface** command, the firewall automatically clears those parameters from the interface configuration.

   You can repeat this command to add a second physical interface to the redundant pair. Keep in mind that the order in which you configure the interfaces is important.

   The first physical interface added to a logical redundant interface becomes the active interface. That interface stays active until it loses its link status, causing the second or standby interface to take over. The standby interface can also take over when the active interface is administratively shut down with the **shutdown** interface configuration command.

However, the active status does not revert back to the failed interface, even when it comes back up. The two interfaces trade the active role back and forth only when one of them fails.

The redundant interface also takes on the MAC address of the first member interface that you configure. Regardless of which physical interface is active, that same MAC address is used.

As an example, interfaces ethernet0/1 and ethernet0/2 are configured to be used as logical interface redundant 1:

```
Firewall(config)# interface redundant 1
Firewall(config-if)# member-interface ethernet0/1
INFO: security-level and IP address are cleared on Ethernet0/1.
Firewall(config-if)# member-interface ethernet0/2
INFO: security-level and IP address are cleared on Ethernet0/2.
Firewall(config-if)# no shutdown
```

The redundant interface is now ready to be configured as a normal firewall. From this point on, you should not configure anything on the two physical interfaces other than the port speed and duplex.

TIP   Make sure the logical redundant interface and the two physical interfaces are enabled with the **no shutdown** command. Even though they are all logically associated, they can be manually shut down or brought up independently.

You can monitor the redundant interface status with the following command:

```
Firewall# show interface redundant number [ip [brief] | stats | detail]
```

The **ip brief** keywords provide a short summary of the redundant interface, its IP address, and its status. All of the other keyword combinations give identical output—a verbose listing of interface parameters and counters, as well as a brief redundancy status. The following example shows the status of interface redundant 1:

```
Firewall# show interface redundant 1
Interface Redundant1 "inside", is up, line protocol is up
  Hardware is i82546GB rev03, BW 100 Mbps, DLY 1000 usec
        Auto-Duplex(Full-duplex), Auto-Speed(100 Mbps)
        MAC address 0016.c789.c8a5, MTU 1500
        IP address 192.168.100.1, subnet mask 255.255.255.0
        1 packets input, 64 bytes, 0 no buffer
        Received 1 broadcasts, 0 runts, 0 giants
        0 input errors, 0 CRC, 0 frame, 0 overrun, 0 ignored, 0 abort
        0 L2 decode drops
        1 packets output, 64 bytes, 0 underruns
        0 output errors, 0 collisions, 0 interface resets
        0 babbles, 0 late collisions, 0 deferred
```

```
            0 lost carrier, 0 no carrier
            input queue (curr/max blocks): hardware (5/0) software (0/0)
            output queue (curr/max blocks): hardware (0/8) software (0/0)
    Traffic Statistics for "inside":
            0 packets input, 0 bytes
            1 packets output, 28 bytes
            0 packets dropped
          1 minute input rate 0 pkts/sec,  0 bytes/sec
          1 minute output rate 0 pkts/sec,  0 bytes/sec
          1 minute drop rate, 0 pkts/sec
          5 minute input rate 0 pkts/sec,  0 bytes/sec
          5 minute output rate 0 pkts/sec,  0 bytes/sec
          5 minute drop rate, 0 pkts/sec
  Redundancy Information:
          Member Ethernet0/1(Active), Ethernet0/2
          Last switchover at 10:32:27 EDT Mar 14 2007
Firewall#
```

Notice that physical interface Ethernet0/1 is currently the active interface, while Ethernet0/2 is not. The output also reveals the date and time of the last switchover.

When the active interface goes down, the standby interface takes over immediately. That whole process is subsecond and happens rather silently. The only record of the redundant switchover can be found in the syslog output, as in the following example:

```
Mar 14 2007 10:41:54: %ASA-4-411002: Line protocol on Interface Ethernet0/1, changed state
to down
Mar 14 2007 10:41:54: %ASA-5-425005: Interface Ethernet0/2 become active in redundant
interface Redundant1
```

You can also use the **debug redundant** {**event** | **error**} command to see redundant failover information in real time.

Basic Interface Configuration

You should follow the configuration steps in this section for each firewall interface that you intend to use. By default, interfaces are in the shutdown state and have no IP address assigned.

1. Define the interface as physical (Step a) or logical (Step b):

   a. Define a physical interface:

FWSM	—
PIX 6.3	Firewall(config)# **interface** *hardware-id* [*hardware-speed*] [**shutdown**]
ASA	Firewall(config)# **interface** *hardware-id* Firewall(config-if)# **speed** {**auto** | **10** | **100** | **nonegotiate**} Firewall(config-if)# **duplex** {**auto** | **full** | **half**} Firewall(config-if)# [**no**] **shutdown**

The interface is referenced by its *hardware-id*. For example, this could be **gb-ethernet1** in PIX 6.3 or **GigabitEthernet1** on an ASA.

In PIX 6.3, the interface medium's speed and duplex mode are given by one of the following *hardware-speed* values:

1000full	Gigabit Ethernet autonegotiation, advertising full duplex
1000full nonegotiate	Gigabit Ethernet full duplex with no autonegotiation
1000auto	Gigabit Ethernet autonegotiation
100full	100-Mbps full duplex
auto	Intel 10/100 autonegotiation
100basetx	100-Mbps half duplex
10full	10-Mbps full duplex
10baset	10-Mbps half duplex
bnc	10-Mbps half duplex with BNC
aui	10-Mbps half duplex with AUI

Beginning with ASA 7.0, the interface speed and duplex are configured with separate interface configuration commands. By default, an interface uses autodetected speed and autonegotiated duplex mode.

TIP   By default, interfaces are administratively shut down. To enable an **interface** in PIX 6.3, use the interface configuration command without the **shutdown** keyword. For PIX 7.x, use the **no shutdown** interface configuration command.

To disable or administratively shut down an interface, add the **shutdown** keyword.

---

b.   (Optional) Define a logical VLAN interface:

FWSM	Firewall(config)# **interface vlan** *vlan_id*
PIX 6.3	Firewall(config)# **interface** *hardware_id vlan_id* **logical**
ASA	Firewall(config)# **interface** *hardware_id*[*.subinterface*] Firewall(config-subif)# **vlan** *vlan_id*

Logical VLAN interfaces must be carried over a physical trunk interface, identified as *hardware_id* (**gb-ethernet0** or **GigabitEthernet0,** for example). In PIX 6.3, the VLAN interface itself is identified by *vlan_id*, a name of the form **vlan***N* (where *N* is the VLAN number, 1 to 4095). The **logical** keyword makes the VLAN interface a logical one.

On an ASA, a *subinterface* number is added to the physical interface name to create the logical interface. This is an arbitrary number that must be unique for each logical interface. The VLAN number is specified as *vlan_id* in a separate **vlan** subinterface configuration command.

Packets being sent out a logical VLAN interface are tagged with the VLAN number as they enter the physical trunk link. The VLAN number tag is stripped off at the far end of the trunk, and the packets are placed on the corresponding VLAN. The same process occurs when packets are sent toward the firewall on a VLAN.

The trunk encapsulation used is always IEEE 802.1Q, and the tagging encapsulation and unencapsulation are automatically handled at each end of the trunk. Make sure the far-end switch is configured to trunk unconditionally. For example, the following Catalyst IOS switch configuration commands could be used:

```
Switch(config)# interface gigabitethernet 0/1
Switch(config-if)# switchport
Switch(config-if)# switchport trunk encapsulation dot1q
Switch(config-if)# switchport mode trunk
```

By default, any packets that are sent out the firewall's physical interface itself are not tagged, and they appear to use the trunk's native VLAN. These packets are placed on the native VLAN number of the far-end switch port.

If you intend to use logical VLAN interfaces on a physical firewall interface that is trunking, you should never allow the trunk's native VLAN to be used. You can do this by configuring a VLAN number on the physical interface, too. After this is done, the firewall cannot send packets across the trunk untagged.

By default, Cisco switches use VLAN 1 as the native (untagged) VLAN on all trunk links. Be aware that the native VLAN can be set to any arbitrary VLAN number on a switch. Find out what native VLAN is being used, and choose a different VLAN number on the firewall's physical interface.

Also make sure that the switch is using something other than the native VLAN to send packets to and from the firewall. The idea is to use only VLANs that are defined specifically to pass data to and from the firewall while eliminating the possibility that an unexpected VLAN appears on the trunk. For example, you could use the following commands on a Catalyst switch to set a trunk's native VLAN to VLAN 7 and to allow only VLANs 100 through 105 to pass over the trunk to the firewall:

```
SwitchIconfig)# interface gigabitethernet 1/1
Switch(config-if)# switchport
Switch(config-if)# switchport trunk native vlan 7
Switch(config-if)# switchport trunk allowed vlan 100-105
Switch(config-if)# switchport mode trunk
```

You can use the following configuration command to force the firewall to tag packets on the physical firewall trunk interface, too:

FWSM	—
PIX 6.3	Firewall(config)# **interface** *hardware_id vlan_id* **physical**
ASA	—

Again, the VLAN is identified by *vlan_id*, a name of the form **vlan***N* (where *N* is the VLAN number, 1 to 4095). The physical keyword makes the logical VLAN interface overlay with the **physical** interface so that any packets passing over the interface receive a VLAN ID tag.

After a VLAN has been assigned to the physical interface, the firewall drops any untagged packets that are received over the trunk interface's native VLAN.

This step is unnecessary beginning with an ASA, because the physical interface is configured with the **no nameif** command by default, which forces all traffic to pass through one or more subinterfaces that are configured with a VLAN number, requiring a VLAN tag.

TIP   After a VLAN number has been assigned to a logical interface, it is possible to change the VLAN number. You can use this PIX 6.3 configuration command to change from the old VLAN name to a new one:

Firewall(config)# **interface** *hardware_id* **change-vlan** *old-vlan-id new-vlan-id*

---

2. (Optional) Name the interface:

FWSM	Firewall(config)# **nameif** *vlan-id if_name securitylevel*
PIX 6.3	Firewall(config)# **nameif** {*hardware-id* | *vlan-id*} *if_name securitylevel*
ASA	Firewall(config)# **interface** *hardware_id[.subinterface]* Firewall(config-if)# **nameif** *if_name* Firewall(config-if)# **security-level** *level*

Here, the physical interface is identified by its *hardware-id* (**gb-ethernet0**, for example) or *vlan-id* (**vlan5**, for example; the word **vlan** is always present). If multiple-security context mode is being used, the *vlan-id* or *hardware-id* could be an arbitrary name that has been mapped to the context by the **allocate-interface** command in the system execution space.

The interface is given the arbitrary name *if_name* (1 to 48 characters) that other firewall commands can use to refer to it. By default, the "inside" and "outside" names are predefined to two interfaces. You can change those assignments, and you can use entirely different names if you want.

A security level is also assigned to the interface as **security***level* (where *level* is a number 0 to 100, from lowest to highest). PIX 7.x is the exception, where the security level is given with the keyword **security-level**, followed by the *level* number (0 to 100). Security levels 0 and 100 are reserved for the "outside" and "inside" interfaces, respectively. Other perimeter interfaces should have levels between 1 and 99.

For example, the outside interface could be configured as follows:

FWSM	`Firewall(config)# nameif vlan10 outside security0`
PIX 6.3	`Firewall(config)# nameif gb-ethernet0 outside security0`

ASA	`Firewall(config)# interface gigabitethernet0`
	`Firewall(config-if)# nameif outside`
	`Firewall(config-if)# security-level 0`

NOTE   Security levels are used only to determine how the firewall inspects and handles traffic. For example, traffic passing from a higher-security interface toward a lower one is assumed to be going toward a less-secure area. Therefore, it is forwarded with less-stringent policies than traffic coming in toward a higher-security area.

In addition, firewall interfaces must have different security levels. The only exceptions are with ASA and FWSM 2.2+, which allow interfaces to have the same security level only if the **same-security-traffic permit inter-interface** global configuration command has been used. In that case, traffic is forwarded according to policies set by access lists, with no regard to higher or lower security levels.

---

3. Assign an IP address.

   You can assign a static IP address if one is known and available for the firewall. Otherwise, you can configure the firewall to request an address from either a DHCP server or through PPPoE. (Your ISP should provide details about obtaining an address.) Choose one of the following steps:

   a. (Optional) Assign a static address:

   `Firewall(config)# ip address if_name ip_address [netmask]`

   If you have a static IP address that the firewall can use, you can assign it here. The interface named *if_name* (**inside** or **outside**, for example) uses the IP address and subnet mask given.

   If you omit the *netmask* parameter, the firewall assumes that a classful network (Class A, B, or C) is being used.

   For example, if the first octet of the IP address is 1 through 126 (1.0.0.0 through 126.255.255.255), a Class A netmask (255.0.0.0) is assumed.

If the first octet is 128 through 191 (128.0.0.0 through 191.255.255.255), a Class B net-mask (255.255.0.0) is assumed.

If the first octet is 192 through 223 (192.0.0.0 through 223.255.255.255), a Class C net-mask (255.255.255.0) is assumed.

If you use subnetting in your network, be sure to specify the correct *netmask* rather than the classful mask (255.0.0.0, 255.255.0.0, or 255.255.255.0) that the firewall derives from the IP address.

b.   (Optional) Obtain an address via DHCP:

Firewall(config)# **ip address outside dhcp [setroute]** [**retry** *retry_cnt*]

Generally, the outside interface points toward an ISP. Therefore, the firewall can generate DHCP requests from that interface. If no reply is received, the firewall retries the request up to *retry_cnt* times (4 to 16; the default is 4).

You can also set the firewall's default route from the default gateway parameter returned in the DHCP reply. To do this, use the **setroute** keyword; otherwise, you have to explicitly configure a default route.

TIP   You can release and renew the DHCP lease for the outside interface by entering this configuration command again.

---

c.   (Optional) Obtain an address through PPPoE.

A PIX or an ASA (beginning with release 8.0) platform can use a PPPoE client to make a broadband connection to an ISP. Point-to-Point Protocol over Ethernet (PPPoE) is a practi-cal way of using the firewall's physical Ethernet interface to communicate with an ISP over traditional PPP infrastructure. PPPoE is supported only when the firewall is config-ured for single context, routed mode, without failover.

Like PPP, PPPoE requires the remote access client (the ASA, in this case) to authenticate and obtain network parameters before it can begin communicating over the link. To do this, the firewall uses a Virtual Private Dialup Network (VPDN) group. The group speci-fies the authentication method and the username and password credentials assigned by the ISP. You can use the following steps to configure the PPPoE client:

— Define a username for PPPoE authentication:

FWSM	—
PIX 6.3	Firewall(config)# **vpdn username** *username* **password** *passwd* [**store-local**]
ASA	Firewall(config)# **vpdn username** *username* **password** *passwd* [**store-local**]

The firewall authenticates itself with an ISP using a username *username* (a text string) and password *passwd* (an unencrypted text string). You can repeat this command to define multiple usernames and passwords if several ISPs are possible.

By default, the username and password are entered into the firewall configuration as a part of this command. If you use a management tool such as Cisco Security Manager (CSM) or CiscoWorks Firewall Management Center to deploy the firewall, a template configuration might overwrite a valid username and password. You can choose to store the username and password locally in the firewall's Flash memory by adding the **store-local** keyword.

— (Optional) Define a VPDN group to contain PPPoE parameters:

FWSM	—
PIX 6.3	Firewall(config)# **vpdn group** *group_name localname username*
ASA	Firewall(config)# **vpdn group** *group_name* **localname** *username*

The firewall can associate PPPoE parameters into groups such that one group is used to negotiate with one ISP. Here, the *group_name* is an arbitrary name (up to 63 characters) that points to a locally defined username *username* and password pair. This pair should already be configured with the **vpdn username** *username* command.

— Set the PPPoE authentication method:

FWSM	—
PIX 6.3	Firewall(config)# **vpdn group** *group_name* **ppp authentication** {**pap | chap | mschap**}
ASA	Firewall(config)# **vpdn group** *group_name* **ppp authentication** {**pap | chap | mschap**}

For the VPDN group, you should use the same authentication method that your ISP uses: **pap** (Password Authentication Protocol, with cleartext exchange of credentials), **chap** (Challenge Handshake Authentication Protocol, with encrypted exchange), or **mschap** (Microsoft CHAP, version 1 only).

— Enable PPPoE requests using a VPDN group:

FWSM	—
PIX 6.3	Firewall(config)# **vpdn group** *group_name* **request dialout pppoe**
ASA	Firewall(config)# **vpdn group** *group_name* **request dialout pppoe**

The firewall builds PPPoE requests using the parameters defined in VPDN group *group_name*.

— Request IP address information on the outside interface:

FWSM	—
PIX 6.3	`Firewall(config)# ip address outside pppoe [setroute]`
ASA	`Firewall(config)# interface if_name` `Firewall(config-if)# ip address pppoe [setroute]`

The firewall sends PPPoE requests on its outside interface to authenticate and obtain an IP address and subnet mask from the ISP. If the default gateway that is returned should be used as the firewall's default route, add the **setroute** keyword. Otherwise, a default route must be configured manually on the firewall.

You can renegotiate the address parameters with the ISP by entering this configuration command again.

TIP   If you already have a static IP address assigned by the ISP, you can use an alternative command:

`Firewall(config)# ip address outside ip-address netmask pppoe [setroute]`

Here, the IP address and netmask are already known. The firewall still authenticates with the ISP through PPPoE, but it uses these values rather than negotiating them.

As an example of PPPoE interface configuration, the following commands can be used to define a VPDN group for one ISP that can be used by the firewall:

```
Firewall(config)# vpdn username JohnDoe password JDsecret
Firewall(config)# vpdn group ISP1 localname JohnDoe
Firewall(config)# vpdn group ISP1 ppp authentication chap
Firewall(config)# vpdn group ISP1 request dialout pppoe
Firewall(config)# ip address outside pppoe setroute
```

4. Test the interface:

   a. Verify the IP address:

   `Firewall# show ip`

   or

   `Firewall# show ip if_name {dhcp | pppoe}`

   b. Ping the next-hop gateway address:

   `Firewall# ping [if_name] ip_address`

You can send ICMP echo requests to the next-hop gateway or a host located on the same subnet as the firewall interface. You can specify which firewall interface name to use with *if_name*, but this is not required. The target is at *ip_address*.

If ICMP replies are received, they are reported along with the round-trip time, as in this example:

```
Firewall# ping 192.168.199.4
    192.168.199.4 response received -- 0ms
    192.168.199.4 response received -- 30ms
    192.168.199.4 response received -- 0ms
Firewall#
```

c. Verify PPPoE operation:

As soon as the PPPoE client is configured and the interface is connected and is operational, the firewall automatically attempts to bring up the PPPoE connection. You can see the status with the following command:

```
Firewall# show vpdn session
```

For example, if the PPPoE client has negotiated its connection, you might see the following output:

```
Firewall# show vpdn session
PPPoE Session Information (Total tunnels=1 sessions=1)
Remote Internet Address is 192.168.11.1
Session state is SESSION_UP
Time since event change 10002 secs, interface outside
PPP interface id is 1
36 packets sent, 36 received, 1412 bytes sent, 0 received
Firewall#
```

If the PPPoE connection does not come up normally, you can use the **debug pppoe event** command to see PPPoE negotiation events as they occur.

Interface Configuration Examples

A firewall has three interfaces:

- **inside** (gb-ethernet0)
- **outside** (gb-ethernet1)
- **dmz** (gb-ethernet2)

These interfaces have IP addresses 172.16.1.1, 172.17.1.1, and 172.18.1.1, respectively. The configuration commands needed are as follows, for both PIX 6.3 and ASA releases:

PIX 6.3	ASA
```Firewall(config)# interface gb-ethernet0 1000auto Firewall(config)# interface gb-ethernet1 1000auto Firewall(config)# interface gb-ethernet2 1000auto Firewall(config)# nameif gb-ethernet0 inside security 100 Firewall(config)# nameif gb-ethernet1 outside security 0 Firewall(config)# nameif gb-ethernet2 dmz security 50 Firewall(config)# ip address inside 172.16.1.1 255.255.0.0 Firewall(config)# ip address outside 172.17.1.1 255.255.0.0 Firewall(config)# ip address dmz 172.18.1.1 255.255.0.0```	```Firewall(config)# interface gigabitethernet0 Firewall(config-if)# speed auto Firewall(config-if)# duplex auto Firewall(config-if)# nameif inside Firewall(config-if)# security-level 100 Firewall(config-if)# ip address 172.16.1.1 255.255.0.0 Firewall(config)# interface gigabitethernet1 Firewall(config-if)# speed auto Firewall(config-if)# duplex auto Firewall(config-if)# nameif outside Firewall(config-if)# security-level 0 Firewall(config-if)# ip address 172.17.1.1 255.255.0.0 Firewall(config)# interface gigabitethernet2 Firewall(config-if)# speed auto Firewall(config-if)# duplex auto Firewall(config-if)# nameif dmz Firewall(config-if)# security-level 50 Firewall(config-if)# ip address 172.18.1.1 255.255.0.0```

Now consider the same scenario with an FWSM in slot 3 of a Catalyst 6500 switch. The **inside**, **outside**, and **dmz** interfaces are all logical, as VLANs 100, 200, and 300, respectively:

```
Switch(config)# firewall vlan-group 1 100,200,300
Switch(config)# firewall module 3 vlan-group 1
Switch(config)# exit
Switch# session slot 3 processor 1

Firewall# configure terminal
Firewall(config)# nameif vlan100 inside security100
Firewall(config)# nameif vlan200 outside security0
Firewall(config)# nameif vlan300 dmz security50
Firewall(config)# ip address inside 172.16.1.1 255.255.0.0
Firewall(config)# ip address outside 172.17.1.1 255.255.0.0
Firewall(config)# ip address dmz 172.18.1.1 255.255.0.0
```

As a final example, consider an ASA or PIX Firewall in a similar scenario. Here, a single physical interface (gb-ethernet0) is configured as a trunk. The **inside**, **outside**, and **dmz** interfaces are all logical, as VLANs 100, 200, and 300, respectively. The configuration commands needed are shown as follows for both the PIX 6.3 and ASA releases:

PIX 6.3	ASA
Firewall(config)# **interface gb-ethernet0 1000auto** Firewall(config)# **interface gb-ethernet0 100 physical** Firewall(config)# **interface gb-ethernet0 200 logical** Firewall(config)# **interface gb-ethernet0 300 logical** Firewall(config)# **nameif vlan100 inside security100** Firewall(config)# **nameif vlan200 outside security0** Firewall(config)# **nameif vlan300 dmz security50** Firewall(config)# **ip address inside 172.16.1.1 255.255.0.0** Firewall(config)# **ip address outside 172.17.1.1 255.255.0.0** Firewall(config)# **ip address dmz 172.18.1.1 255.255.0.0**	Firewall(config)# **interface gigabitethernet0** Firewall(config-if)# **speed auto** Firewall(config-if)# **duplex auto** Firewall(config-if)# **no nameif** Firewall(config-if)# **interface gigabitethernet0.1** Firewall(config-if)# **vlan 100** Firewall(config-if)# **nameif inside** Firewall(config-if)# **security-level 100** Firewall(config-if)# **ip address 172.16.1.1 255.255.0.0** Firewall(config-if)# **interface gigabitethernet0.2** Firewall(config-if)# **vlan 200** Firewall(config-if)# **nameif outside** Firewall(config-if)# **security-level 0** Firewall(config-if)# **ip address 172.17.1.1 255.255.0.0** Firewall(config)# **interface gigabitethernet0.3** Firewall(config-if)# **vlan 300** Firewall(config-if)# **nameif dmz** Firewall(config-if)# **security-level 50** Firewall(config-if)# **ip address 172.18.1.1 255.255.0.0**

In the PIX 6.3 configuration, notice that VLAN 100 has been configured on the "physical" portion of the gb-ethernet0 interface. This ensures that VLAN 100 is tagged on the trunk, along with VLANs 200 and 300. In fact, nothing is sent or received untagged on the firewall's trunk.

To configure similar behavior on an ASA, the **no nameif** command is added to the physical interface (gigabitethernet0) configuration. In effect, this prevents the physical interface from becoming active, other than carrying VLAN traffic as a trunk link.

Configuring IPv6 on an Interface

Beginning with ASA 7.0, firewall interfaces can be configured with an IPv6 address in addition to a traditional IPv4 address. IPv6 addresses are 128 bits long—much longer than a 32-bit IPv4 address! As well, the IPv6 address format is very different and can be written in the following ways:

- In full hexadecimal format, the address is written as eight groups of four hexadecimal digits, with colons separating the groups. For example, 1111:2222:3333:4444:5555:6666:7777:8888 represents a single IPv6 host.

- Leading 0s can be omitted in any group. For example,
  1111:0200:0030:0004:5555:6666:7777:8888 can also be written as
  1111:200:30:4:5555:6666:7777:8888.

- Because IPv6 addresses are so long and the address space is so large, addresses with many
  embedded 0s are common. Therefore, you can abbreviate any number of contiguous 0s as a
  double colon (::), even if the 0s cross a digit group boundary. For example,
  1111:0:0:0:0:0:0:8888 could also be written as 1111::8888. This abbreviation can be used only
  once in an address, however.

- IPv6 addresses can also be shown with a network prefix. This specifies how many most-
  significant bits are used to represent a network address. This is very similar to IPv4 addresses,
  where the address and prefix values are separated by a slash (/). For IPv6, this format is also
  ipv6_address/prefix_length, where the prefix length is a value from 1 to 128 bits.

Each firewall interface can potentially have three different IPv6 addresses configured:

- **Link-local address**—An address that is unique on a network connection to other devices. This
  is used only for IPv6 neighbor discovery, address autoconfiguration, and administrative uses. A
  firewall cannot forward packets that have link-local addresses as the destination. The address
  format consists of the following components:

  — **FE80** in the 10 most-significant bits

  — 54 bits of 0s

  — 64 bits of host addressing in the modified EUI-64 format

- **Site-local address**—A unique address within the site network that cannot be routed outside the
  site. The address consists of the following components:

  — **FEC0** in the 10 most-significant bits

  — 38 bits of 0s

  — 16 bits of subnet ID addressing

  — 64 bits of host addressing

- **Global address**—A globally unique address that can be routed outside the local link and local
  network. The address consists of the following components:

  — **001** in the 3 most-significant bit positions

  — 45 bits of provider addressing (unique to each service provider)

  — 16 bits of site or subnet addressing (unique only within the local site network)

  — 64 bits of host addressing (48 bits usually come from the MAC address)

After you configure IPv6 addresses and routing information, the firewall can begin to statefully
inspect traffic using IPv6. The following inspection engines are equipped to inspect either IP version:

- ICMP
- UDP

- TCP
- FTP
- SMTP
- HTTP
- SIP (beginning with ASA 8.0)

You can follow these steps to configure IPv6 on your firewall:

1. Select a firewall interface:

   ```
   Firewall(config)# interface hardware-id
   ```

   The interface is identified by its *hardware-id*, which is the full interface type and number or an abbreviated version. For example, **GigabitEthernet 0**, **GigabitEthernet0**, and **gig0** all refer to the same interface.

2. Assign an IPv6 address to an interface.

   a. (Optional) Use autoconfiguration to derive interface addresses.

   A firewall can use stateless autoconfiguration to derive link-local and global addresses for an interface. Use the following commands to enable autoconfiguration:

   ```
   Firewall(config-if)# ipv6 address autoconfig
   Firewall(config-if)# ipv6 enable
   ```

   The firewall first creates a link-local address for the interface. This can be done without any knowledge of surrounding networks or neighboring devices. The link-local address is formed as follows, building digits from least- to most-significant (right to left):

   — The three least-significant octets are the three least-significant octets of the MAC address.

   — The three most-significant octets of the MAC address become the three next-most-significant octets of the link-local address.

   In addition, the next-to-least-significant bit of the most-significant MAC address byte is set to 1. For example, **0003.47** would become **0203.47**.

   The most-significant address digits always begin with **FE80**.

   For example, consider the following firewall interface. You can use the **show interface** command to display the interface's MAC address, which is 0003.4708.ec54. When the autoconfiguration is complete, the IPv6 link-local address can be seen with the **show**

ipv6 interface command. Here, the link-local address has become
fe80::203:47ff:fe08:ec54:

```
Firewall# show interface gigabitethernet 1.2
Interface GigabitEthernet1.2 "inside", is up, line protocol is up
        VLAN identifier 2
        MAC address 0003.4708.ec54, MTU 1500
        IP address 192.168.198.1, subnet mask 255.255.255.0
        Received 1482892 packets, 81328736 bytes
        Transmitted 311834 packets, 24639862 bytes
        Dropped 1060893 packets
Firewall#
Firewall# show ipv6 interface inside
inside is up, line protocol is up
  IPv6 is enabled, link-local address is fe80::203:47ff:fe08:ec54
  No global unicast address is configured
  Joined group address(es):
    ff02::1
    ff02::2
    ff02::1:ff08:ec54
[output omitted]
```

The global interface address has a similar form, but it begins with the prefix learned from
a neighboring router. A modified EUI-64 address is used, which includes the **ff:fe** and
MAC address portions.

After a prefix has been learned from router advertisements, you can display the global
address with the **show ipv6 interface** command, as in the following example:

```
Firewall# show ipv6 interface inside
inside is up, line protocol is up
  IPv6 is enabled, link-local address is fe80::203:47ff:fe08:ec54
  Global unicast address(es):
    1999::203:47ff:fe08:ec54, subnet is 1999::/64 [AUTOCONFIG]
      valid lifetime 2591959 preferred lifetime 604759
  Joined group address(es):
    ff02::1
    ff02::2
    ff02::1:ff08:ec54
[output omitted]
```

b. (Optional) Specify a link-local address:

```
Firewall(config-if)# ipv6 address ipv6_address link-local
```

You can assign a specific link-local address as *ipv6_address* if autoconfiguration is not
wanted.

    c. (Optional) Specify a complete global IPv6 address:

```
Firewall(config-if)# ipv6 address ipv6_address/prefix_length [eui-64]
```

You can specify the complete global address as *ipv6_address*. The *prefix_length* (1 to 128) specifies the number of most-significant address bits reserved for the network address. The global address must be unique within the IPv6 network.

You can also use the **eui-64** keyword to let the firewall build a unique modified EUI-64 address format. The *ipv6_address* value is used for the upper 64 bits. The lower 64 bits of the address are the upper three octets of the interface MAC address, **ff:fe**, and the lower three MAC address octets.

3. Use IPv6 neighbor discovery to learn about neighboring devices.

A firewall can participate in IPv6 neighbor discovery to learn about other directly connected devices. Neighbor discovery is always enabled. You can follow these steps to adjust the neighbor discovery operation:

    a. (Optional) Set the neighbor solicitation interval:

```
Firewall(config-if)# ipv6 nd ns-interval value
```

The firewall sends neighbor solicitation messages at the interval *value* (1000 to 3,600,000 milliseconds [ms]; the default is 1000 ms or 1 second).

    b. (Optional) Set the neighbor reachability time:

```
Firewall(config-if)# ipv6 nd reachable-time value
```

If the neighboring device becomes unreachable, the firewall can send neighbor solicitation messages in an attempt to get a response. The firewall waits for *value* milliseconds (0 to 3,600,000; the default is 0) before declaring the neighbor unreachable. A value of 0 means that the firewall advertises an unspecified reachability time to its neighbors and does not measure this time itself.

    c. (Optional) Adjust duplicate address detection (DAD):

```
Firewall(config-if)# ipv6 nd dad attempts value
```

A firewall attempts to check to see if another device is using its own interface link-local address. If a duplication is detected, no IPv6 data is processed on the interface.

If the link-local address is not duplicated, the firewall checks for a duplicate of its interface global IPv6 address.

The firewall sends *value* (0 to 600; the default is 1) neighbor solicitation messages to detect a duplicate address. If *value* is set to 0, no DAD is performed.

| TIP | If a directly connected IPv6 neighbor cannot be discovered automatically, you can define it as a static entry. Use the following global configuration command to define and locate the neighboring device: |

```
Firewall(config)# ipv6 neighbor ipv6_address if_name mac_address
```

The neighbor uses the local data-link address *ipv6_address* and MAC address *mac_address* (xxxx.xxxx.xxxx hex format). As well, the neighbor can be found on the firewall interface named *if_name* (**outside**, for example).

Suppose a neighboring device connected to the inside interface uses IPv6 local data-link address fe80::206:5bff:fe02:a841 and MAC address 0006.5b02.a841. You could use the following command to define a static neighbor entry:

```
Firewall(config)# ipv6 neighbor fe80::206:5bff:fe02:a841 inside
    0006.5b02.a841
```

4. Configure IPv6 router advertisements on the interface.

As a Layer 3 IPv6 device, a firewall can participate in router advertisements so that neighboring devices can dynamically learn a default router address. You can follow these steps to configure how the firewall carries out its router advertisement process:

a. (Optional) Stop sending router advertisements:

```
Firewall(config-if)# ipv6 nd suppress-ra
```

By default, a firewall acts as an IPv6 router if IPv6 is enabled and the interface has an IPv6 address. The firewall sends periodic router advertisements to neighboring IPv6 devices, announcing itself as a router.

You can use the **ipv6 nd suppress-ra** command to stop sending router advertisements. In this case, the firewall appears as a regular IPv6 neighbor or node. Neighbor discovery is active even when router advertisements are suppressed.

b. (Optional) Set the router advertisement interval:

```
Firewall(config-if)# ipv6 nd ra-interval [msec] value
```

By default, a firewall sends router advertisements out an IPv6 interface every 200 seconds. You can adjust the interval to *value* (3 to 1800 seconds, or 500 to 1,800,000 ms if the **msec** keyword is given).

c. (Optional) Adjust the lifetime of router advertisements:

```
Firewall(config-if)# ipv6 nd ra-lifetime seconds
```

By default, router advertisements are sent with a valid lifetime of 1800 seconds. Neighboring devices can expect the firewall to be a default router for the duration of the lifetime value.

You can adjust the lifetime to *seconds* (0 to 9000 seconds). A value of 0 indicates that the firewall should not be considered a default router on the advertising interface.

5. (Optional) Configure IPv6 prefixes to advertise.

   By default, a firewall advertises the prefix from any IPv6 address that is configured on an interface. The prefix advertisement can be used by neighboring devices to autoconfigure their interface addresses.

   In the commands covered in Steps 5a through 5d, you can use the **default** keyword to define lifetimes for all prefixes that are advertised. Otherwise, you can specify an IPv6 prefix as *ipv6_address/prefix_length*. The *prefix_length* is the number of the most-significant bits used as a network prefix, from 1 to 128.

   You can also add the **no-autoconfig** keyword to advertise that the prefix should not be used for autoconfiguration. By default, any prefix that is advertised is assumed to be "on link," meaning that it is used on the advertising interface. You can add the **off-link** keyword to specify a prefix that is not configured on the firewall interface.

   a. (Optional) Advertise a prefix with default lifetime values:

      ```
      Firewall(config-if)# ipv6 nd prefix {default |
      ipv6_address/prefix_length} [no-autoconfig] [off-link]
      ```

      By default, the prefix is advertised with a valid lifetime of 30 days (2,592,000 seconds) and a preferred lifetime of 7 days (604,800 seconds).

      For example, the following command causes the IPv6 prefix 1999::/64 to be advertised with the default values:

      ```
      Firewall(config)# ipv6 nd prefix 1999::/64
      ```

   b. (Optional) Advertise a prefix with predefined lifetime values:

      ```
      Firewall(config-if)# ipv6 nd prefix {default |
      ipv6_address/prefix_length} valid_lifetime preferred_lifetime
      [no-autoconfig] [off-link]
      ```

      The prefix is advertised with a valid lifetime of *valid_lifetime* (0 to 4,294,967,295 or **infinite** seconds). The prefix also is advertised as a preferred prefix lasting *preferred_lifetime* (0 to 4,294,967,295 or **infinite** seconds).

      To advertise the prefix 1999::/64 with a valid lifetime of 5 days (432,000 seconds) and a preferred lifetime of 1 day (86,400 seconds), you could use the following command:

      ```
      Firewall(config)# ipv6 nd prefix 1999::/64 432000 86400
      ```

   c. (Optional) Advertise a prefix with an expiration date:

      ```
      Firewall(config-if)# ipv6 nd prefix {default |
      ipv6_address/prefix_length} at valid_date_time preferred_date_time
      [no-autoconfig] [off-link]
      ```

      The prefix is advertised to remain valid until the specific date and time are reached. The valid lifetime is given as *valid_date_time*, and the prefix is preferred until *preferred_date_time* is reached.

Each date and time value is given in this form:

{*month day* | *day month*} *hh:mm*

The *month* is the month name, given as at least three characters. The *day* is 1 to 31. The time is always given in 24-hour format.

For example, suppose the prefix 1999::/64 is advertised to expire at 23:59 on December 31 for the valid and preferred lifetimes. You could use the following command to accomplish this:

Firewall(config)# **ipv6 nd prefix 1999::/64 dec 31 23:59 dec 31 23:59**

d. (Optional) Do not advertise a prefix:

Firewall(config-if)# **ipv6 nd prefix** {**default** |
    ipv6_address/prefix_length} **no-advertise**

The prefix given is not advertised.

Testing IPv6 Connectivity

As soon as you configure IPv6 operation on a firewall, make sure each of the respective interfaces has an IPv6 address. An interface must have a link-local address to communicate with its neighbors. An interface must also have a global address to be able to forward packets to other IPv6 destination addresses. You can display these addresses with the **show ipv6 interface** command.

You can display any other IPv6 routers that the firewall has discovered from router advertisements it has received. Confirm any entries seen with the **show ipv6 routers** command, as in the following example:

```
Firewall# show ipv6 routers
Router fe80::260:70ff:fed7:8800 on inside, last update 1 min
  Hops 64, Lifetime 1800 sec, AddrFlag=0, OtherFlag=0, MTU=1500
  Reachable time 0 msec, Retransmit time 0 msec
  Prefix 1999::/64 onlink autoconfig
    Valid lifetime 2592000, preferred lifetime 604800
Firewall#
```

From the **fe80** digits in the most-significant IPv6 address positions, you can distinguish the router address shown as a link-local address.

You can also use a form of the **ping** command to send IPv6 ICMP echo packets to a neighboring device with the following simplified syntax:

Firewall# **ping** [*if_name*] *ipv6_address*

With the preceding router example, you could ping the router's IPv6 link-local address to determine good connectivity and a working IPv6 configuration. The following example shows an attempted ping:

```
Firewall# ping fe80::260:70ff:fed7:8800
Sending 5, 100-byte ICMP Echos to fe80::260:70ff:fed7:8800, timeout is 2 seconds:
Interface must be specified for link-local or multicast address
Success rate is 0 percent (0/1)
Firewall#
```

Because a link-local address is being used as the ping target, the firewall cannot determine which of its interfaces to use. This is because link-local addresses do not include any network or route information that could be used to find a destination interface. The example is repeated with the interface information as follows, showing a series of successful ICMP echo and reply packets:

```
Firewall# ping inside fe80::260:70ff:fed7:8800
Sending 5, 100-byte ICMP Echos to fe80::260:70ff:fed7:8800, timeout is 2 seconds:
!!!!!
Success rate is 100 percent (5/5), round-trip min/avg/max = 1/1/1 ms
Firewall#
```

Configuring the ARP Cache

A firewall maintains a cache of Address Resolution Protocol (ARP) entries that are learned when it overhears ARP requests or ARP reply packets on its interfaces. ARP is used to resolve a host's MAC address based on its IP address, and vice versa.

You can use the following commands to configure ARP operations:

1. Define a static ARP entry:

    ```
    Firewall(config)# arp if_name ip_address mac_address [alias]
    ```

    ARP entries normally are created as the firewall hears responses to ARP requests on each interface. There might be times when you need to configure a static entry for hosts that do not answer ARP requests on their interfaces. Static ARP entries do not age out over time.

    Specify the firewall interface name *if_name* (**inside** or **outside**, for example) where the host can be found. The host's IP address and MAC address (in dotted-triplet format) must also be given.

    Use the **alias** keyword to create a static proxy ARP entry, where the firewall responds to ARP requests on behalf of the configured host IP address—whether or not it actually exists.

    For example, you can use the following command to configure a static ARP entry for a machine that can be found on the inside interface. Its MAC address and IP address are 0006.5b02.a841 and 192.168.1.199, respectively:

    ```
    Firewall(config)# arp inside 0006.5b02.a841 192.168.1.199
    ```

2. Set the ARP persistence timer:

    ```
    Firewall(config)# arp timeout seconds
    ```

    ARP entries dynamically collected are held in the firewall's cache for a fixed length of time. During this time, no new ARP information is added or changed for a specific cached host address. By default, ARP entries are held for 14,400 seconds (4 hours). You can set the persistence timer to *seconds* (1 to 1,215,752 seconds for PIX 6.3 or 60 to 4,294,967 seconds for ASA and FWSM).

    You can display the current ARP cache contents with the following command:

    ```
    Firewall# show arp [statistics]
    ```

For example, the following ARP entries have been created on a firewall:

```
Firewall# show arp
        stateful 192.168.199.1 0030.8587.546e
        lan-fo 192.168.198.2 0030.8587.5433
        outside 12.16.11.1 0003.4725.2f97
        outside 12.16.11.2 0005.5f93.37fc
        outside 12.16.11.3 00d0.01e6.6ffc
        inside 192.168.1.1 0003.4725.2e32
        inside 192.168.1.4 00d0.0457.3bfc
        inside 192.168.1.3 0007.0d55.a80a
Firewall#
```

Be aware that the firewall maintains ARP entries for its own interfaces too, as indicated by the gray shaded entries.

You can add the **statistics** keyword to display counters for various ARP activities. Consider the following output:

```
Firewall# show arp statistics
        Number of ARP entries:
        PIX : 11
        Dropped blocks in ARP: 10
        Maximum Queued blocks: 17
        Queued blocks: 0
        Interface collision ARPs Received: 0
        ARP-defense Gratuitous ARPS sent: 0
        Total ARP retries: 70
        Unresolved hosts: 0
        Maximum Unresolved hosts: 2
Firewall#
```

TIP   If a host's IP address changes or its network interface is replaced, an existing ARP entry can become stale and will be stuck in the firewall's ARP table until it expires. If this happens, you can clear the entire ARP cache contents by using the **clear arp** EXEC command.

If you decide to clear the ARP cache, you should do so only during a maintenance time when the network is not busy; otherwise, there might be a pause in network traffic passing through the firewall while the ARP cache is being rebuilt.

Although you cannot clear individual ARP cache entries, you can configure a static ARP entry for the IP address in question so that it is paired with a bogus MAC address. After that is done, remove the command that was just used. The bogus static ARP entry is removed, and the firewall relearns an ARP entry based on dynamic information from the host.

Configuring Interface MTU and Fragmentation

By default, any Ethernet interface has its maximum transmission unit (MTU) size set to 1500, which is the maximum and expected value for Ethernet frames. If a packet is larger than the MTU, it must be fragmented before being transmitted. You can use the following command to adjust an interface MTU:

```
Firewall(config)# mtu if_name bytes
```

If you need to, you can adjust the MTU of the interface named *if_name* to the size *bytes* (64 to 65,535 bytes). In some cases, you might need to reduce the MTU to avoid having to fragment encrypted packets where the encryption protocols add too much overhead to an already maximum-sized packet.

Cisco firewalls can participate in MTU discovery along an end-to-end IP routing path. This process follows RFC 1191, where the MTU is set to the smallest allowed MTU along the complete path.

You can display the current MTU configuration for all firewall interfaces by using the **show mtu** (PIX 6.3) or **show running-config mtu** (ASA and FWSM) command. Interface MTU settings are also displayed as a part of the **show interface** EXEC command output.

For example, the following output represents the MTU settings on a firewall's outside interface:

```
Firewall# show running-config mtu
mtu outside 1500
mtu inside 1500
mtu dmz 1500
Firewall#
Firewall# show interface
Interface GigabitEthernet0 "", is up, line protocol is up
  Hardware is i82542 rev03, BW 1000 Mbps
        (Full-duplex), Auto-Speed(1000 Mbps)
        Available but not configured via nameif
        MAC address 0003.4708.ec54, MTU not set
        IP address unassigned
        17786900 packets input, 21111200936 bytes, 0 no buffer
        Received 171 broadcasts, 0 runts, 0 giants
        0 input errors, 0 CRC, 0 frame, 0 overrun, 0 ignored, 0 abort
        131444 packets output, 89823504 bytes, 0 underruns
        0 output errors, 0 collisions
        0 late collisions, 191 deferred
        input queue (curr/max blocks): hardware (0/25) software (0/0)
        output queue (curr/max blocks): hardware (0/5) software (0/0)
Interface GigabitEthernet1.2 "outside", is up, line protocol is up
        VLAN identifier 2
        MAC address 0003.4708.ec54, MTU 1500
        IP address 10.1.1.1, subnet mask 255.0.0.0
        Received 17683308 packets, 20714401393 bytes
        Transmitted 119650 packets, 86481250 bytes
        Dropped 95017 packets
[output for other interfaces omitted]
```

Notice that the outside interface is actually a logical interface (GigabitEthernet1.2) representing a VLAN on a physical trunk interface (GigabitEthernet1). An MTU is set only when the **nameif** command has been configured for an interface, as in the case of the logical interface named **outside**.

TIP   Hosts using TCP connections can also negotiate the *maximum segment size* (MSS) that is used. This is done as a TCP connection is initiated, and it occurs on a per-connection basis. As a result, an MSS value can sometimes be chosen that is larger than the MTU being used along the path. This also results in TCP packets being fragmented so that they can be forwarded.

You can configure the firewall to govern the maximum MSS value negotiated on connections passing through it. The firewall overrides any request for an MSS value larger than its limit, and it replaces the MSS value in the TCP packet so that the negotiation is transparent to the end hosts.

You can use the following command to limit the TCP MSS size in all TCP connections:

```
Firewall(config)# sysopt connection tcpmss [minimum] bytes
```

By default, the TCP MSS must be between 48 and 1380 bytes. You can adjust the maximum MSS limit to *bytes* or the minimum MSS to **minimum** *bytes*.

When a firewall receives packets that have been fragmented, it stores each fragment in a cache and virtually reassembles the fragments so that the original packet can be inspected. This allows the firewall to verify the order and integrity of each fragment and to discover malicious exploits that use fragmentation. This process is part of the FragGuard firewall feature.

You can configure how the firewall handles the packet fragments it receives with the following steps:

1. Limit the number of fragments awaiting reassembly:

   ```
   Firewall(config)# fragment size database-limit [if_name]
   ```

   By default, a firewall reserves space for 200 fragmented packets in memory per interface, where they are stored temporarily while awaiting reassembly. You can change this to *database-limit* packets (up to 1,000,000 or the maximum number of free 1550-byte or 16,384-byte blocks). If an interface name is not specified, the limit applies to all interfaces.

   For example, the following command could be used to reserve space for 500 fragments arriving on the outside interface, awaiting virtual reassembly:

   ```
   Firewall(config)# fragment size 500 outside
   ```

TIP   You can display the current status of memory blocks with the **show block** EXEC command. Look for the **LOW** value for size 1550 and 16,384 to see the fewest free blocks that have been available in the past. In most cases, however, you should keep the reassembly database size set to a low or default value to prevent fragmentation DoS attacks from using large amounts of firewall memory.

---

2. Limit the number of fragments per packet:

    ```
    Firewall(config)# fragment chain chain-limit [if_name]
    ```

    By default, a firewall accepts up to 24 fragments of a single packet before they are discarded. You can change this limit to *chain-limit* (up to 8200 fragments per packet) on a global or per-interface basis. If you do not specify an interface, the *chain-limit* value is applied to all interfaces.

TIP   You might want to consider limiting the fragment space to 1, allowing only a single fragment to be stored—the whole packet itself. Most often, legitimate applications do not fragment packets in the first place, so the firewall should not receive any fragments. Some denial-of-service attacks, on the other hand, exploit the use of fragments. You can use the following command to minimize the fragment cache for all firewall interfaces:

```
Firewall(config)# fragment chain 1
```

Be aware that such a strict limit causes the firewall to drop packet fragments from legitimate (or desired) traffic too. You should consider increasing the fragment space if you have known applications (Network File System [NFS], for example) or tunneling protocols (GRE, L2TP, or IPSec) that could require the use of fragmentation.

---

3. Limit the time for all parts of a packet to arrive:

    ```
    Firewall(config)# fragment timeout seconds [if_name]
    ```

    By default, a firewall collects fragments as they arrive for 5 seconds. If the final fragment does not arrive by then, all the fragments are discarded, and the packet is never reassembled. You can adjust the collection time to *seconds* (up to 30 seconds) on a global or per-interface basis. If an interface name *if_name* is not specified, the limit applies to all interfaces.

    You can monitor a firewall's fragmentation activity with the **show fragment** EXEC command. For example, the firewall interface shown in the following output has the default fragment settings (database size 200 packets, chain limit 24 fragments, and timeout limit 5 seconds). The firewall has reassembled 534 packets, and two packets are awaiting reassembly:

    ```
    Firewall# show fragment outside
    Interface: outside
    ```

```
        Size: 200, Chain: 24, Timeout: 5, Threshold: 133
        Queue: 2, Assemble: 534, Fail: 1097, Overflow: 12401
Firewall#
```

You can also see that the reassembly process has failed 1097 times. This is because the timeout limit expired while waiting for all fragments to arrive. The process has also had overflow conditions, indicating that more than 24 fragments arrived on 12,401 different packets.

Configuring an Interface Priority Queue

In Cisco firewall releases before ASA 7.0, packets are inspected and forwarded in a best-effort fashion. Firewall interfaces have input and output queues or buffers that store inbound or outbound packets temporarily as they arrive at or leave an interface. Sometimes, packets cannot be processed quickly enough to keep up with the flow, so they are buffered until they can be serviced.

A simple queue structure like this makes for simple interface operation. For example, consider the output queue. The first packet put into the queue is the first one that is taken out and transmitted. There is no differentiation between types of traffic or any quality of service (QoS) requirements. Regardless of the packet contents, packets leave the queue in the same order they went into it.

This presents a problem for time-critical data that might pass through a firewall. For example, any type of streaming audio or video must be forwarded in a predictable manner so that packets are not delayed too much before they reach their destination. Those packets also need to be forwarded at a fairly regular rate; too much variation in packet-to-packet delay (jitter) results in poor-quality audio or video at the destination.

When streaming data is mixed with other types of high-volume data passing through a firewall, the nonstreaming data can starve the streaming data flow. This can happen simply because the streaming packets get lost in a sea of other packets competing for transmission time.

A Cisco ASA can support two types of output interface queues:

- **Best-Effort Queue (BEQ)**—Packets are placed in this queue in an arbitrary order and are transmitted whenever possible.

- **Low-Latency Queue (LLQ)**—Packets are placed in this queue only when they match specific criteria. Any packets in the LLQ are transmitted ahead of any packets in the BEQ, providing priority service.

In addition, the firewall uses a hardware queue to buffer packets that will be copied directly to the physical interface hardware for transmission. Packets are pulled from the LLQ first, and then the BEQ, and then they are placed in the hardware queue. As soon as the hardware queue is full, those packets are moved into the interface's own buffer for the actual transmission.

Figure 3-2 illustrates the interface queues available at each firewall interface, although only the outside interface is shown. Packets that will be sent out an interface are put in the BEQ by default. If a service policy has been configured for the interface, packets that match specific conditions in a class map can be marked for priority service. Only those packets are put into the LLQ.

If either the BEQ or LLQ fills during a time of interface congestion, any other packets destined for the queue are simply dropped. In addition, there is no crossover or fallback between queues. If the LLQ is full, subsequent priority packets are not placed in the BEQ; they are dropped instead.

Figure 3-2 *Firewall Interface Queue Structure*

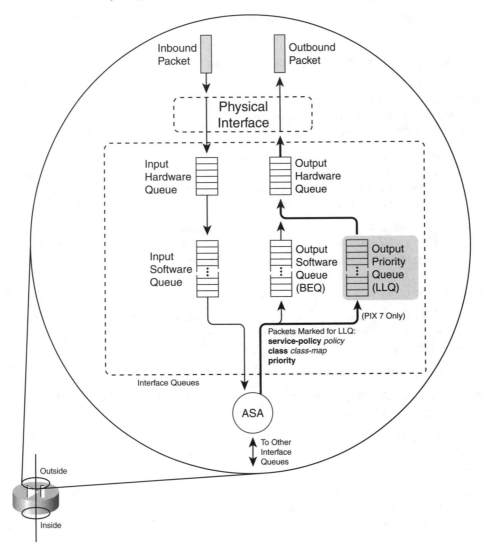

You can use the following sequence of steps to configure priority queuing:

1. Enable the priority queue on an interface:

FWSM	—
PIX 6.x	—
ASA	`Firewall(config)# priority-queue if_name`

By default, only a BEQ is enabled and used on each interface. You must specifically enable a priority queue with this command for the interface named *if_name* (**outside**, for example).

NOTE   Priority queues are supported only on physical interfaces that have been configured with the **nameif** command. Trunk interfaces and other logical interfaces are not permitted to have a priority queue. Also, priority queues are not supported in multiple-security context mode.

---

2. (Optional) Set the queue limit:

FWSM	—
PIX 6.x	—
ASA	`Firewall(priority-queue)# queue-limit packets`

You can use this command to set the depth of both the BEQ and LLQ. The depth value *packets* (1 to 2048) varies according to the firewall memory and interface speed. In addition, packets can vary in size, but the queue is always measured in generic packets, which can be up to the interface MTU (1500 bytes) bytes long.

As soon as the priority queue is enabled for the first time, the queue limit is set to a calculated default value. The limit is the number of 256-byte packets that can be transmitted on the interface over a 500-ms period. Naturally, the default value varies according to the interface speed, but it always has a maximum value of 2048 packets.

For example, the default **queue-limit** values shown in Table 3-1 are calculated for different interface speeds.

Table 3-1   *Default queue-limit Values by Interface Speed*

Interface	queue-limit in Packets
10-Mbps full duplex	488
100-Mbps full duplex	2048
1000-Mbps full duplex	2048

3. (Optional) Set the transmit queue size:

FWSM	—
PIX 6.x	—
ASA	Firewall(config)# **tx-ring-limit** *packets*

The transmit ring (**tx-ring**) is a virtual queue that represents a portion of the output hardware queue that is available to the Ethernet interface drivers. The transmit ring is measured in packets. It varies according to the efficiency and speed of the interface hardware.

As soon as the interface priority queue is enabled for the first time, the transmit ring limit is set to a calculated default value. The limit is the number of 1550-byte packets that can be transmitted on the interface in a 10-ms period. The *packets* limit has a minimum of 3 and a maximum that varies according to the interface and available memory. You can display the current maximum value through context-based help, as in the following example:

```
Firewall(config)# priority-queue outside
Firewall(priority-queue)# tx-ring-limit ?
priority-queue mode commands/options:
  <3-128>  Number of packets
Firewall(priority-queue)#
```

The default **tx-ring-limit** values shown in Table 3-2 are automatically calculated for different interface speeds.

Table 3-2   *Default tx-ring-limit Values by Interface Speed*

Interface	tx-ring-limit in Packets
10-Mbps full duplex	8
100-Mbps full duplex	80
1000-Mbps full duplex	256

TIP   By default, all packets are sent to the best-effort queue, whether or not a priority queue has been configured and enabled. To send packets to the priority queue, you must configure a service policy that matches specific traffic with a class map and then assigns that traffic to the priority queue. Section "7-2: Defining Security Policies in a Modular Policy Framework," in Chapter 7, "Inspecting Traffic," covers the configuration commands needed for this task.

For example, you should configure a modular policy that has this structure:

```
Firewall(config)# class-map class_map_name
Firewall(config-cmap)# match condition
Firewall(config-cmap)# exit
Firewall(config)# policy-map policy_map_name
Firewall(config-pmap)# class class_map_name
```

```
Firewall(config-pmap-c)# priority
Firewall(config-pmap-c)# exit
Firewall(config-pmap)# exit
Firewall(config)# service-policy policy_map_name interface if_name
```

Packets are only marked to be destined for a generic priority queue. When they are actually placed in an output queue, the firewall chooses the priority queue on the appropriate interface.

Displaying Information About the Priority Queue

You can display the current priority-queue limits with the following command:

```
Firewall# show running-config all priority-queue if_name
```

If you configure specific **queue-limit** or **tx-ring-limit** values, those are shown as part of the running configuration. However, if the priority queue uses the default values, you can see them only by displaying the default commands and parameters in the running configuration with the **show running-config all** keywords.

For example, the following output shows the outside interface queue limit values:

```
Firewall# show running-config all priority-queue outside
priority-queue outside
  queue-limit    2048
  tx-ring-limit 256
Firewall#
```

You can also get an idea about the priority queue operation on an interface with the following command:

```
Firewall# show service-policy interface if_name priority
```

You can display overall statistics for both BEQ and LLQ interface queues with the following command:

```
Firewall# show priority-queue statistics [if_name]
```

These commands are covered in more detail in "Packet Queue Status," as covered in Section "11-1: Checking Firewall Vital Signs," in Chapter 11, "Verifying Firewall Operation."

Firewall Topology Considerations

The basic principle behind using a firewall is to isolate the inside (secure) network from the outside (unsecure) network. Only through careful inspection and tightly controlled security policies are packets allowed to pass through a firewall.

Ideally, a firewall should be located between physically separate, isolated networking equipment. For example, if a firewall is used in a switched environment, its inside and outside interfaces should connect to two different switches—the inside interface to one switch and the outside interface to a different switch, as illustrated in Figure 3-3. Notice that the inside and outside interfaces are connected to two different VLANs and that it is impossible for outside traffic to pass to the inside without proper inspection by the firewall.

In some environments, the use of separate switches on each side of a firewall might be too expensive. A single switch can carry multiple VLANs, each logically isolated from the others. Why not connect several of a firewall's interfaces to just one switch, each interface assigned to a different VLAN? Along the same lines, a firewall could connect to a switch using only a single physical interface. Each logical interface could be carried over that interface as a trunk, where the VLANs are naturally isolated in the switch, as illustrated in Figure 3-4.

You can use a single switch to support multiple firewall interfaces. The inherent VLAN isolation works well with the inherent security isolation. However, you should carefully consider a few issues if you decide to connect a firewall in this fashion.

First, you should always be sure to prune any unused VLANs from trunk links that connect the firewall/switch combination to other networks. The basic idea is that no VLAN is allowed to extend from the outside, unsecure network into the inside, secure network without passing through the firewall first. If a VLAN does extend on in, there will always be the possibility that it can be exploited for a malicious attack or a compromise.

Figure 3-3 *A Simple Example of a Best-Practice Firewall Topology*

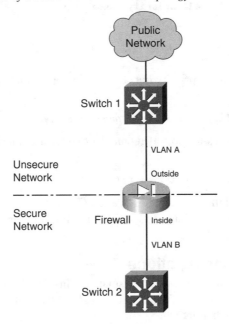

Figure 3-4 *Using a Single Switch to Support a Firewall*

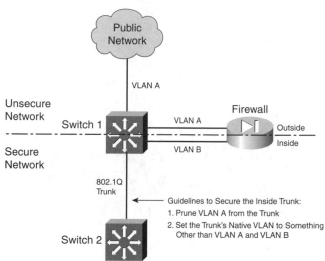

In Figure 3-4, VLAN A carries traffic to the firewall's outside interface. VLAN A should be pruned from the trunk link between Switch 1 and Switch 2 so that it is contained outside the secure internal network.

Securing Trunk Links Connected to Firewalls

Another thing to consider is the potential for an exploit called *VLAN hopping*. When a VLAN on the public side of a boundary switch extends on into the internal side as a trunk's native VLAN, it can be used to carry unexpected traffic that can "hop" over to a different VLAN. This can occur even if the native VLAN is not intended to carry any traffic into the inside network.

VLAN hopping occurs when someone can send packets on the outside VLAN as if they are encapsulated for an 802.1Q trunk. The boundary switch accepts the packets and then forwards them on the native VLAN of the inside trunk. Now, the spoofed encapsulation becomes relevant, causing other inside switches to unencapsulate the packets and send the malicious contents onto other secured VLANs. In effect, an outside user can inject packets onto VLANs that are not even visible or accessible on the outside.

Consider the network shown in Figure 3-5, where a firewall separates inside and outside networks but both networks pass through the same switch. VLAN 100 is the only VLAN allowed to extend to the outside public network. Switch 1, at the network's secure boundary, brings the inside network in over an 802.1Q trunk link. A trunk link is used because the firewall might be configured to use additional logical interfaces in the future, and those VLANs can be carried over the trunk as well.

Figure 3-5 *Example of a VLAN Hopping Exploit*

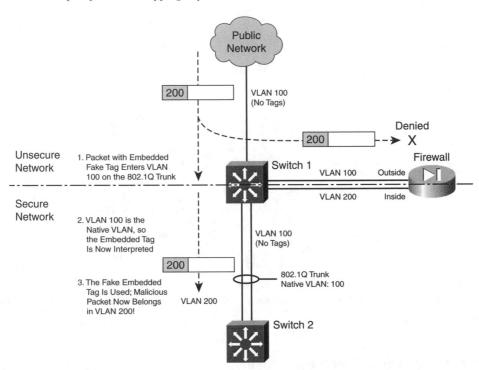

The trunk link has been configured with VLAN 100 as its native VLAN. This might have been done as an oversight, with the assumption that no other switch or host would ever connect to VLAN 100 on the inside network. However, that native VLAN is used as the springboard to get inside the secure network.

A malicious user on the outside (VLAN 100) sends a packet toward the inside. The packet is carefully crafted such that it contains an 802.1Q VLAN tag for VLAN 200—even though it is being sent over a nontrunking link that supports only a single VLAN. If the packet is a broadcast, it might be sent toward the firewall's outside interface (also on VLAN 100) when it reaches Switch 1. The firewall examines the packet and denies it entry into the inside network, as expected.

Most likely, the packet is sent as a unicast destined for an address on the internal network. When the packet reaches Switch 1, a curious thing happens. The packet originated on VLAN 100, so the switch can forward it onto VLAN 100 of the 802.1Q trunk link. VLAN 100 is the trunk's native VLAN, so the switch transmits the packet without adding its own VLAN tag. Now when the packet appears on the trunk link, the embedded fake tag is interpreted as an actual 802.1Q tag!

Downstream switches forward the packet based on its newly exposed VLAN 200 tag. Suddenly, the packet has "hopped" from VLAN 100 on the outside to VLAN 200 on the inside network.

To thwart VLAN hopping, you should always carefully configure trunk links so that the native VLANs are never used to carry legitimate traffic. In other words, set a trunk's native VLAN to an unused

VLAN. In Figure 3-5, the native VLAN of the inside trunk should be set to an unused VLAN other than VLAN A, which is present on the outside, and other than VLAN B, which is present on the inside.

Trunks on opposite sides of a boundary switch should have different unused native VLANs so that the native VLAN of one side does not pass through to the native VLAN of the other side. Figure 3-6 shows this scenario. Notice that the native VLANs on the inside and outside are set to different but unused VLAN numbers.

CAUTION   Whenever possible, you should keep the trusted and untrusted networks physically separate, carried over separate switches. Do not depend on the logical separation of VLANs within a single switch to provide inherent security. There is always a risk of misconfiguration or an exploit that would allow untrusted traffic to enter the trusted network.

Bypass Links

One last thing you should consider is the use of links to bypass a firewall. It might seem odd to secure a network with a firewall, only to open a path for traffic to go around it. Some environments must still connect other non-IP protocols between inside and outside networks, simply because a firewall can inspect only IP traffic. Still others might bypass IP multicast traffic to keep the firewall configuration simple.

Figure 3-6   *Securing Trunk Links on a Firewall Boundary Switch*

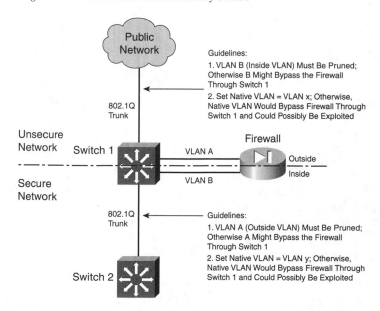

The idea behind a bypass path is that any traffic using the path is either isolated from or incompatible with traffic passing through the firewall. In fact, you might pass some IP traffic around a firewall on a VLAN that never connects to another inside network. You might support something like a wireless LAN in your network, carried over the same switches as your secured VLANs, but where wireless users are considered "outsiders." Then, you might pass a wireless VLAN around the firewall, with the intention that it connects only to networks outside the firewall.

Figure 3-7 shows a basic network that allows some traffic to bypass a firewall. In the left portion of the figure, IP traffic passes through the firewall while Novell IPX traffic passes around it over VLAN C. This is allowed only because some users on the outside map drives on IPX file servers on the inside.

TIP   At the very least, you should configure very strict IPX access lists on the Layer 3 switches at each end of the VLAN C link. If IPX traffic must be bypassed around the firewall, it should still be governed by whatever means you have available.

You should also consider using a transparent (Layer 2) firewall to handle the traffic that would otherwise flow over a link bypassing a Layer 3 firewall. For non-IP protocols, a transparent firewall can filter only according to EtherType values. However, no stateful inspection of protocols such as IPX is possible.

Figure 3-7   *Example of Risk When Bypassing a Firewall*

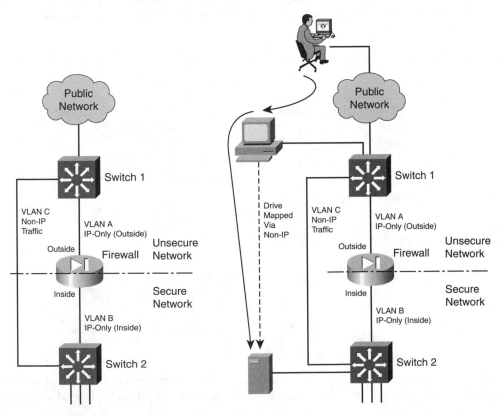

From a routing standpoint, IP and IPX are "ships in the night," coexisting on switches but not intermingling. However, consider the right portion of Figure 3-7. An outside user has managed to compromise a PC that is also on the outside. This PC has a drive mapped over IPX to a secure file server. Without passing through the firewall, the outside user has managed to gain access to data on a "secure" server on the internal network.

The solution here is to be very critical of bypassing any sort of traffic around a firewall. Even if you think you have thought of every possible angle to keep internal resources isolated, there still might be a way for someone to gain access.

3-2: Configuring Routing

A firewall is a Layer 3 device, even though it inspects packets at many layers. Packets are forwarded based on their Layer 3 destination IP addresses, so the firewall must know how to reach the various destination IP networks. (This is true unless a firewall is configured for transparent firewall mode, where it operates only on Layer 2 information.)

A firewall knows about the subnets directly connected to each of its interfaces. These are shown as routes with a **CONNECT** (PIX 6.3) or **directly connected** (ASA or FWSM) identifier in output from the **show route** command.

To exchange packets with subnets not directly connected, a firewall needs additional routing information from one of the sources listed in Table 3-3.

Table 3-3 *Routing Information Sources*

Route Type	Administrative Distance	Learning Method
Static	1	Manually configured
EIGRP summary route	5	Dynamically learned or advertised
RIP	120	Dynamically learned or advertised
EIGRP	90 (internal) 170 (external)	Dynamically learned or advertised
OSPF	110	Dynamically learned or advertised

The various routing protocols go about learning and advertising route information with different techniques. Because of this, some routing protocols are generally considered more trustworthy than others. The degree of trustworthiness is given by the *administrative distance*, an arbitrary value from 0 to 255. Routes with a distance of 0 are the most trusted, while those with a distance of 255 are the least trusted. The default values are generally accepted and are the same as those used on routers.

Administrative distance comes in handy when the same route has been learned in multiple ways. For example, suppose the route 10.10.0.0/16 has been learned by RIP (administrative distance of 120) and OSPF (administrative distance of 110). Each of the routing protocols might come up with different next-hop addresses for the route, so which one should the firewall trust? The protocol with the lowest distance value—OSPF.

Notice from Table 3-3 that static routes have a distance of 1, which makes them more trusted than any other routing protocol. If you configure a static route, chances are you are defining the most trusted information about that route. Only directly connected routes with a distance of 0, containing the subnets configured on the firewall interfaces, are more trusted.

As soon as routes are known, packets can be forwarded to other routers or gateways that in turn forward the packets toward their destinations.

A default route is useful on the firewall's outside interface, where the most general subnets and destination networks are located. Usually, the networks located on the inside and other higher-security interfaces are specific and well-known. Remember that the firewall has to learn about the inside networks through some means.

Using Routing Information to Prevent IP Address Spoofing

A packet's destination address normally is used to determine how it gets forwarded. If the destination address can be found in the routing table, the firewall can forward the packet out the appropriate interface to the destination or to a next-hop router.

Packet forwarding seems straightforward, but it makes certain assumptions about a packet and its sender. For example, the address or location of a packet's source normally is not part of the forwarding decision. That might be fine if all senders and the packets they send can be trusted implicitly. When your network is connected to a public network, full of untrusted and unknown users, however, there should be no trust at all.

A common exploit used in a denial-of-service attack involves spoofed IP addresses. A malicious user sends packets toward a target host to initiate connections or use up a resource on the target. However, the sender disguises itself by inserting a bogus source address into the packets. Either the source address does not exist, or it might be a legitimate address of some other host on some other network. The idea is to prevent any return traffic from reaching the malicious user, protecting his identity and location.

Cisco firewalls can use *Reverse Path Forwarding* (RPF) to detect spoofed source addresses in most cases. As soon as RPF is enabled, a firewall examines the source address of each packet arriving on an interface. It tries to find the reverse path, or the path back toward the source, in its routing table. In other words, the firewall acts as if it will send something back to the source to verify its location. If a route to the source address or network can be found, the outbound interface must match the interface where the packet originally arrived.

If a route cannot be found, or the reverse-path interface does not match the arriving interface, the packet is simply dropped, and a logging message is generated.

Normally, a firewall has specific routing information about all the IP networks on the inside or protected (nonpublic) interfaces, because those networks are known to exist and are controlled. Therefore, RPF checks to see whether packets sourced from a protected network are easily and accurately performed.

The outside or public network is a different story. The firewall usually cannot know about every IP network that exists in the outside world, so it makes do with a default route. The same is true of RPF on the outside interface. When a packet arrives on the outside interface, if the specific route to the source cannot be found, the firewall uses the default route to verify the reverse path.

You can enable RPF with the following configuration command:

```
Firewall(config)# ip verify reverse-path interface if_name
```

Notice that RPF is configured on a per-interface basis, only on the interface named *if_name* (**inside**, for example). You can repeat this command to enable RPF on multiple interfaces. Remember that RPF works by checking packets that *arrive* on an interface—not packets that are leaving.

NOTE   It might seem odd or inadvisable that the default route is used for RPF tests on the outside interface. After all, the majority of source address spoofing would probably be found on the outside public network. Unfortunately, this is mostly true, because a firewall cannot know everything about the outside network. The vast majority of IP addresses are found "somewhere out there" on the public Internet, on the outside interface.

However, RPF can detect when source addresses from the outside are spoofed with addresses that are used on an inside or protected interface. In other words, if someone tries to masquerade as a trusted user, using a trusted IP address, the firewall recognizes that the address is appearing on the wrong interface, and it drops the packet. This happens before a connection is formed and before any further access lists or stateful inspection are performed, preserving the firewall resources.

Figure 3-8 illustrates the RPF process. RPF has been enabled on the outside interface, to check packets arriving from the outside. The firewall's routing table is shown, providing information that RPF can use about the known inside networks. The only thing known about the outside network is the default route.

Figure 3-8   *Unicast RPF Operation*

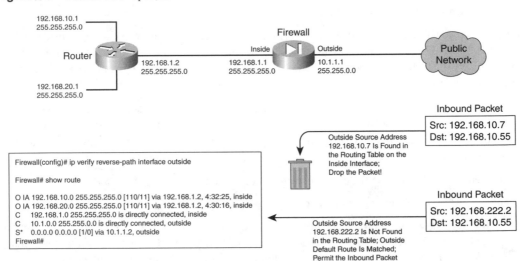

When an outside host tries to masquerade as the address 192.168.10.7, the firewall finds a matching route located on the inside network. Clearly, the outside host is spoofing that address, so the packet is dropped.

During the RPF process, each ICMP packet is examined individually. UDP and TCP packets are examined too, but only the first packet in a connection. All subsequent packets in the connection receive a quick check for the correct source interface; the route lookup and reverse path check are skipped.

You can use the following command to display RPF counters related to one or all firewall interfaces:

```
Firewall# show ip verify statistics [interface if_name]
```

For example, in the following firewall output, 3312 packets were dropped as they arrived on the inside interface because of spoofed source addresses:

```
Firewall# show ip verify statistics
interface outside: 170 unicast rpf drops
interface inside: 3312 unicast rpf drops
interface dmz: 3 unicast rpf drops
Firewall#
```

To reset the statistics counters, you can use the **clear ip verify statistics** command.

Configuring Static Routes

Static routes can be manually configured on a firewall. These routes are not learned or advertised; the routes you configure are the only routes the firewall knows unless a routing protocol is also being used.

The firewall uses static routing information, as shown in Figure 3-9.

Figure 3-9   *Static Routes Used by a Firewall*

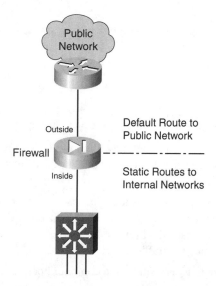

You can define static routes by following these configuration steps:

1. Define a static route to a specific subnet:

   ```
   Firewall(config)# route if_name ip_address netmask gateway_ip [distance]
   ```

   The IP subnet defined by *ip_address* and *netmask* (a standard dotted-decimal subnet mask) can be reached by forwarding packets out the firewall interface named *if_name* (**inside** or **outside**, for example). The packets are forwarded to the next-hop gateway at IP address *gateway_ip*.

   By default, a static route receives an administrative distance of 1. You can override this behavior by specifying a *distance* value (1 to 255).

TIP   You can also define the static route with the firewall's own interface IP address as the gateway address. If the next-hop gateway address is not known or if it is subject to change, you can simply have the firewall use the interface where the gateway is connected.

When packets are forwarded toward the gateway, the firewall sends ARP requests for the destination address. The next-hop router must be configured to use proxy ARP so that it responds with its own MAC address as the destination.

This is not a recommended approach, however. You should use it only in cases where the next-hop router is subject to change or is unknown. Proxy ARP is generally considered a risk, because it exposes a firewall to memory exhaustion during certain types of denial-of-service attacks.

If you have configured IPv6 operation on a firewall, you can also configure static IPv6 routes. The command syntax is very similar to the IPv4 form:

```
Firewall(config)# ipv6 route if_name ipv6_prefix/prefix_length
  ipv6_gateway [distance]
```

2. Define a default static route:

```
Firewall(config)# route if_name 0.0.0.0  0.0.0.0  gateway_ip [distance]
```

You can define a default route so that the firewall knows how to reach any network other than those specifically defined or learned. The default network and subnet mask are written as **0.0.0.0 0.0.0.0** to represent any address. They can also be given more simply as **0 0** to save typing.

The firewall assumes that the next-hop router or gateway at IP address *gateway_ip* knows how to reach the destination. You can configure up to three different default routes on a firewall. If more than one default route exists, the firewall distributes outbound traffic across the default route gateways to load balance the traffic.

You can remove a static route by repeating this command beginning with the **no** keyword.

TIP

You can verify a firewall's routing information by using the **show route** EXEC command. The output shows routes learned by any possible means, whether directly connected, static, or through a dynamic routing protocol.

Static routes are shown as routes with an **OTHER static** identifier in output from the PIX 6.3 **show route** command, or with an **S** identifier in the ASA or FWSM **show route** command. For example, the default route in the following output has been configured as a static route:

```
Firewall# show route
O IA 192.168.167.1 255.255.255.255
           [110/11] via 192.168.198.4, 82:39:36, inside
C    192.168.198.0 255.255.255.0 is directly connected, inside
C    128.163.93.128 255.255.255.128 is directly connected, outside
S*   0.0.0.0 0.0.0.0 [1/0] via 128.163.93.129, outside
Firewall#
```

Static routes and routes learned from a routing protocol are shown with square brackets containing two values. The first value is the administrative distance, and the second value is the metric derived or used by the routing protocol. For example, the OSPF route to 192.168.167.1 has **[110/11]**—OSPF uses administrative distance 110, while this specific route has an OSPF metric of 11.

Static Route Example

The following static routes are to be configured on a firewall:

- A default route points to gateway 192.168.1.1 on the outside interface.

- Network 172.21.0.0/16 can be found through gateway 192.168.254.2 on the inside interface.

- Network 172.30.146.0/24 can be found through gateway 192.168.254.10, also on the inside interface.

The static route configurations are as follows:

```
Firewall(config)# route outside 0.0.0.0 0.0.0.0 192.168.1.1 1
Firewall(config)# route inside 172.21.0.0 255.255.0.0 192.168.254.2 1
Firewall(config)# route inside 172.30.146.0 255.255.255.0 192.168.254.10 1
```

Favoring Static Routes Based on Reachability

Normally, if a static route is configured, it stays active until it is manually removed. A static route is simply an unchanging definition of a next-hop destination—regardless of whether that destination is reachable. If a single ISP is the sole means of reaching the outside world, a static default route works nicely to point all outbound traffic to the ISP's gateway address.

Suppose you had connections to two ISPs; one might be favored over the other, but the default routes to each ISP are equally weighted. In other words, the firewall tries to balance the outbound traffic equally across the connections. Even if the connection to one ISP goes down, the firewall still uses the static route that points to that ISP—effectively sending some outbound traffic into a black hole.

Beginning with ASA 7.2(1), a static route can be conditional. So, if a target address is reachable, the static route remains active; if the target is not reachable, the static route becomes inactive. This allows you to configure multiple static or default routes without worrying about whether one ISP connection is working or not.

To do this, you configure a *service level agreement (SLA) monitor* process that monitors an arbitrary target address. That process is associated with a static route so that the route tracks the reachability of the target. Use the following steps to configure static address tracking:

1. Define the SLA monitor process:

   ```
   Firewall(config)# sla monitor sla-id
   ```

   The process is known by its *sla-id*, an arbitrary number from 1 to 2,147,483,647.

2. Define the reachability test:

   ```
   Firewall(config-sla-monitor)# type echo protocol ipIcmpEcho target interface if-name
   ```

   The only test type is echo, which sends ICMP echo request packets to the *target* IP address found on firewall interface *if-name*.

You should select a target address that is a reliable indicator of a route's reachability. For example, you could use an ISP's next-hop gateway address as a target to test the ISP connection's reachability. The target address can be another router, firewall, host, and so on.

TIP   Before you configure the ICMP echo target address, you might want to manually test the target's reachability with the **ping** *target* command.

---

a. (Optional) Set the test frequency:

    `Firewall(config-sla-monitor-echo)# frequency seconds`

    By default, echo tests are run every 60 seconds. You can set a different time interval as *seconds* (1 to 604,800 seconds or 7 days).

b. (Optional) Set the number of ICMP echo packets to send:

    `Firewall(config-sla-monitor-echo)# num-packets number`

    By default, only one ICMP request packet is sent during an echo test. You can define a different number of packets as *number* (1 to 100).

c. (Optional) Set the payload size of the ICMP request:

    `Firewall(config-sla-monitor-echo)# request-data-size bytes`

    By default, each ICMP echo request packet has a payload of 28 bytes. You can set the payload size as *bytes* (0 to 16,384 bytes), although you cannot use a value less than 28. As well, you should not choose a payload size that makes the ICMP echo request packet larger than the path MTU.

d. (Optional) Set the type of service (TOS) value:

    `Firewall(config-sla-monitor-echo)# tos number`

    By default, each ICMP echo request packet sent has an IP TOS value of 0. You can choose a different value as *number* (0 to 255). This option can be handy if other routers along the path to the target are configured to enforce quality of service (QoS) policies based on the TOS byte in the IP packet headers.

e. (Optional) Set the timeout interval:

    `Firewall(config-sla-monitor-echo)# timeout milliseconds`

    By default, the firewall waits 5000 ms (5 seconds) to receive an ICMP echo reply packet in response to its echo test. If a reply packet is received within the timeout interval, the target is reachable. If not, the target is assumed to be unreachable, and the echo test fails.

You can choose a different timeout interval as milliseconds (0 to 604,000,000 millisec-onds, or 7 days). The timeout interval must be longer than the frequency defined with the frequency command.

f. (Optional) Set the test threshold:

```
Firewall(config-sla-monitor-echo)# threshold milliseconds
```

The firewall also keeps track of a test threshold, which is used as an indicator that the tar-get is getting increasingly hard to reach. The threshold is not used to decide whether the target is reachable. Instead, it can give you an idea of how realistic your choice of the tim-eout interval is.

By default, the threshold interval is set to 5000 ms (5 seconds). You can set a different threshold value as *milliseconds* (0 to 2,147,483,647 ms). Keep in mind that the threshold value must always be less than or equal to the timeout interval value.

For example, suppose you choose a timeout interval of 10,000 ms (10 seconds) and a threshold value of 5000 ms. After many echo tests are run, you can look at the test statis-tics to see how often the threshold is exceeded. If it is rarely exceeded, you might decide to reduce the timeout value to something at or below the current threshold value. If you decide to reduce the timeout value, you should also reduce the threshold value.

3. Schedule the SLA monitor test:

```
Firewall(config)# sla monitor schedule sla-id [life {forever | seconds}] [start-time
{hh:mm[:ss] [month day | day month] | pending | now | after hh:mm:ss}] [ageout seconds]
[recurring]
```

The test can begin in one of the following ways:

Starting Time	Keyword
Wait indefinitely	**pending** (the default)
At a specific time	**start-time** with time and day
Start immediately	**now**
Wait until	**after** with a time interval
Recur daily	**recurring** every day at the time given

You can specify the lifetime of the test with the **life** keyword, followed by **forever** (infinite lifetime) or *seconds*. By default, a test runs for 3600 seconds or 1 hour.

For continuing reachability tests, you should use the following command syntax:

```
Firewall(config)# sla monitor sla-id life forever now
```

The test continues to run until you manually remove it from the firewall configuration with the **no sla monitor** *sla-id* command.

4. Enable reachability tracking:

```
Firewall(config)# track track-id rtr sla-id reachability
```

The SLA monitor test identified by *sla-id* is used to track reachability information. Each track process is known by its *track-id* index, an arbitrary value from 1 to 500. You should define a unique track index for each SLA monitor test that you configure, so that each test can be tracked independently.

5. Apply tracking to a static route:

```
Firewall(config)# route if_name ip_address netmask gateway_ip [distance] track
track-id
```

The normal static route command syntax is used, along with the **track** keyword. Track process number *track-id* is used to provide reachability information for the static route. If the test target is reachable (it returns ICMP echo replies as expected), the static route remains active in the routing table.

If the target is not reachable (ICMP echo replies are not received as expected), the static route remains in the running configuration, but is not active in the routing table.

6. Monitor static route tracking:

You can monitor the status of a tracking process with any of the following EXEC commands:

```
Firewall# show track
Firewall# show route
Firewall# debug track
Firewall# debug sla monitor trace
```

Reachable Static Route Example

A firewall has two paths to the outside Internet, using two independent ISPs, as shown in Figure 3-10. The firewall can be configured with two default routes that point to the two ISP routers, 10.1.1.100 and 10.1.1.200. Outbound traffic toward the Internet is balanced across the two default routes, and across the two ISPs.

Figure 3-10   *An Example Network Using Reachability Information*

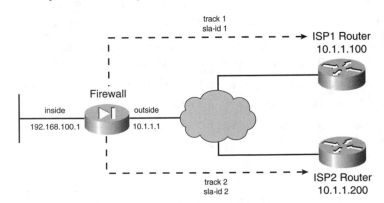

The firewall is also configured to track the reachability of each ISP, so that the appropriate static route can be deactivated if an ISP connection is down. SLA monitor test 1 is configured to perform echo tests on the ISP1 router at 10.1.1.100, while SLA test 2 checks the ISP2 router at 10.1.1.200. The following commands can be used to configure the reachability tests and static routes:

```
Firewall(config)# sla monitor 1
Firewall(config-sla-monitor)# type echo protocol ipIcmpEcho 10.1.1.100 interface outside
Firewall(config-sla-monitor-echo)# frequency 30
Firewall(config-sla-monitor-echo)# threshold 1000
Firewall(config-sla-monitor-echo)# timeout 3000
Firewall(config-sla-monitor-echo)# exit
Firewall(config-sla-monitor)# exit
Firewall(config)# sla monitor schedule 1 life forever now
!
Firewall(config)# track 1 rtr 1 reachability
!
Firewall(config)# sla monitor 2
Firewall(config-sla-monitor)# type echo protocol ipIcmpEcho 10.1.1.200 interface outside
Firewall(config-sla-monitor-echo)# frequency 30
Firewall(config-sla-monitor-echo)# threshold 1000
Firewall(config-sla-monitor-echo)# timeout 3000
Firewall(config-sla-monitor-echo)# exit
Firewall(config-sla-monitor)# exit
Firewall(config)# sla monitor schedule 2 life forever now
!
Firewall(config)# track 2 rtr 2 reachability
!
Firewall(config)# route 0.0.0.0 0.0.0.0 10.1.1.100 track 1
Firewall(config)# route 0.0.0.0 0.0.0.0 10.1.1.200 track 2
```

Notice that each static route uses a different tracking process. That means either static route can be deactivated depending on the status of its respective next-hop router. Static route tracking is a rather silent process, and the firewall will not give you any obvious signs that it is actually testing the reachability.

To see this in action, you can use the **show route** command to display the current routing table contents. If both ISP router targets are reachable, then both static routes are shown, as in the following output:

```
Firewall# show route

Codes: C - connected, S - static, I - IGRP, R - RIP, M - mobile, B - BGP
       D - EIGRP, EX - EIGRP external, O - OSPF, IA - OSPF inter area
       N1 - OSPF NSSA external type 1, N2 - OSPF NSSA external type 2
       E1 - OSPF external type 1, E2 - OSPF external type 2, E - EGP
       i - IS-IS, L1 - IS-IS level-1, L2 - IS-IS level-2, ia - IS-IS inter area
       * - candidate default, U - per-user static route, o - ODR
       P - periodic downloaded static route

Gateway of last resort is 10.1.1.100 to network 0.0.0.0

C    127.0.0.0 255.255.0.0 is directly connected, cplane
C    192.168.100.0 255.255.255.0 is directly connected, inside
S*   0.0.0.0 0.0.0.0 [1/0] via 10.1.1.100, outside
                     [1/0] via 10.1.1.200, outside
```

Here, both static routes are listed, although no indication that they are conditional is listed. You can always confirm the static route configuration with the **show run route** command:

```
Firewall# show run route
route outside 0.0.0.0 0.0.0.0 10.1.1.100 track 1
route outside 0.0.0.0 0.0.0.0 10.1.1.200 track 2
Firewall#
```

You can also see the current status of a track process with the **show track** [*track-id*] command:

```
Firewall# show track 1
Track 1
  Response Time Reporter 1 reachability
  Reachability is Up
  1 change, last change 00:01:03
  Latest operation return code: OK
  Latest RTT (millisecs) 1
  Tracked by:
    STATIC-IP-ROUTING 0
Firewall#
```

You can also enable debugging output for the tracking process. Use the **debug sla monitor trace** command to get some real-time indication of SLA probes as they are sent. However, to see messages indicating a change in reachability, you can use the **debug track** command, as in the example that follows. After each reachability change is announced, the routing table is shown for clarity. Notice how the static route to ISP2 is missing after track process 2 announces that the target is unreachable, and how the static route returns when the target comes up again.

```
Firewall# debug track
Firewall#
Firewall#
Firewall# Track: 2 Change #1 rtr 2, reachability Up->Down
Firewall# show route
Codes: C - connected, S - static, I - IGRP, R - RIP, M - mobile, B - BGP
       D - EIGRP, EX - EIGRP external, O - OSPF, IA - OSPF inter area
       N1 - OSPF NSSA external type 1, N2 - OSPF NSSA external type 2
       E1 - OSPF external type 1, E2 - OSPF external type 2, E - EGP
       i - IS-IS, L1 - IS-IS level-1, L2 - IS-IS level-2, ia - IS-IS inter area
       * - candidate default, U - per-user static route, o - ODR
       P - periodic downloaded static route

Gateway of last resort is 10.1.1.100 to network 0.0.0.0

C    127.0.0.0 255.255.0.0 is directly connected, cplane
C    192.168.100.0 255.255.255.0 is directly connected, inside
S*   0.0.0.0 0.0.0.0 [1/0] via 10.1.1.100, outside
Firewall#
Firewall#
Firewall# Track: 2 Change #2 rtr 2, reachability Down->Up
Firewall#
```

```
Firewall# show route
Codes: C - connected, S - static, I - IGRP, R - RIP, M - mobile, B - BGP
       D - EIGRP, EX - EIGRP external, O - OSPF, IA - OSPF inter area
       N1 - OSPF NSSA external type 1, N2 - OSPF NSSA external type 2
       E1 - OSPF external type 1, E2 - OSPF external type 2, E - EGP
       i - IS-IS, L1 - IS-IS level-1, L2 - IS-IS level-2, ia - IS-IS inter area
       * - candidate default, U - per-user static route, o - ODR
       P - periodic downloaded static route

Gateway of last resort is 10.1.1.100 to network 0.0.0.0

C    127.0.0.0 255.255.0.0 is directly connected, cplane
C    192.168.100.0 255.255.255.0 is directly connected, inside
S*   0.0.0.0 0.0.0.0 [1/0] via 10.1.1.100, outside
                     [1/0] via 10.1.1.200, outside
Firewall#
```

Configuring RIP to Exchange Routing Information

Cisco firewalls can passively listen to RIP updates (either version 1 or 2) to learn routing information. Routing advertisements from the firewall are limited to one type—a firewall interface as a default route. RIP can be used in either of the following versions:

- RIP version 1, which supports only classful networks. Advertisements are broadcast unencrypted.

- RIP version 2, which supports classless networks. Advertisements can be authenticated by a cryptographic function for security purposes.

RIP routing information is used by the firewall as shown in Figure 3-11.

Figure 3-11 *Firewall Using RIP for Routing Information*

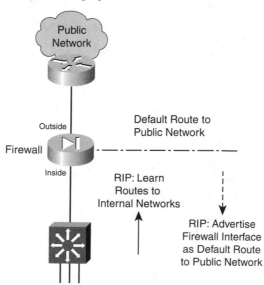

You can configure RIP on a firewall by following these configuration steps:

1. Passively listen to RIP updates from other routers.

   a. Listen to RIP version 1 updates:

   ```
   Firewall(config)# rip if_name passive [version 1]
   ```

   Any networks advertised in RIPv1 updates received on the firewall interface named *if_name* are added to the routing table. To protect information about the internal networks, the firewall does not advertise any routes to its internal or protected networks.

   b. Listen to RIP version 2 updates:

   ```
   Firewall(config)# rip if_name passive version 2 [authentication
   [text | md5 key (key_id)]]
   ```

   Any networks advertised in RIPv2 updates received on the firewall interface named *if_name* are added to the routing table.

   If RIPv2 authentication is being used by other routers, the firewall must use the same method. Advertisements can be authenticated with a cleartext **text** *key* (up to a 16-character text string) that is passed within the routing update. Naturally, having the authentication key pass across the network in the clear (unencrypted) is not very secure.

   You can also use message digest 5 (MD5) authentication. An **md5** *key* (up to a 16-character text string) can be defined on each router. The key is not sent as a part of the routing updates. Instead, it is kept hidden and is used only to validate the MD5 hash value that is computed on each routing advertisement and the key. MD5 also supports multiple keys, referenced by a *key_id* (1 to 255). Both the key ID and the key itself must match between neighboring RIPv2 routers.

2. Advertise a firewall interface as a default route:

   ```
   Firewall(config)# rip if_name default version [1 | 2] [authentication
   [text | md5 key key_id]]
   ```

   The only route that a firewall can advertise is a default route, with its own interface named *if_name* as the gateway address. The default route is advertised using RIP version **1** or **2**. An optional authentication can be used with RIPv2, as a cleartext **text** *key* or an **md5** *key*.

TIP   You can verify the RIP configuration commands that have been entered with the **show rip** [*if_name*] (PIX 6.3) or **show running-config rip** (ASA or FWSM) EXEC command.

To see RIP update activity, you can also use the **debug rip** command. In the following example, the firewall has received one route advertisement:

```
%PIX-7-711001: RIP: received packet from interface inside [pif=2]
  (192.168.198.4:520)
%PIX-7-711001: RIP: interface inside received v2 update from 192.168.198.4
%PIX-7-711001: RIP: update contains 1 routes
%PIX-7-711001: RIP: Advertise network 192.168.167.0 mask 255.255.255.0
  gateway 192.168.198.4 metric 1
```

If RIP routes do not appear in the routing table as expected, there could be a misconfiguration involving RIPv2 authentication. In this case, the debug output would show a message like this:

```
%PIX-1-107001: RIP auth failed from 192.168.198.4: version=2, type=ffff,
  mode=3, sequence=13 on interface inside
```

You can also display the current routing table to see routes that RIP has learned. Those entries are marked with an **R** indicator, as in the following example:

```
Firewall# show route
S    0.0.0.0 0.0.0.0 [1/0] via 128.163.93.129, outside
C    128.163.93.128 255.255.255.128 is directly connected, outside
R    192.168.167.0 255.255.255.0 [1/0] via 192.168.198.4, inside
C    192.168.198.0 255.255.255.0 is directly connected, inside
Firewall#
```

RIP Example

A firewall is to use RIP version 2 to learn routing information on its inside interface. The firewall also advertises its inside interface as the default gateway. MD5 authentication is being used on other internal RIPv2 routers, using key number 1, **mysecretkey**. The configuration is as follows:

```
Firewall(config)# rip inside passive version 2 authentication md5 mysecretkey 1
Firewall(config)# rip inside default version 2 authentication md5 mysecretkey 1
```

Configuring EIGRP to Exchange Routing Information

The Enhanced Interior Gateway Routing Protocol (EIGRP) is new to ASA 8.0. As its name implies, EIGRP is based on Interior Gateway Routing Protocol (IGRP), but with many enhancements. EIGRP is a distance vector routing protocol, and its routing metrics are based on a combination of delay, bandwidth, reliability, load, and MTU.

EIGRP uses a neighbor discovery mechanism that works by sending "hello" messages to directly connected neighboring routers. Neighbors can be dynamically discovered or statically configured. All EIGRP messages, including the hello protocol, are sent as multicast packets to address 224.0.0.10, the all EIGRP routers address, using IP protocol 88.

EIGRP supports variable-length subnet masks (VLSM) and route summarization, providing plenty of flexibility in its routing information. It also uses the Diffusing Update Algorithm (DUAL) to compute and maintain routing information from all of its neighbors. The ASA (or any other EIGRP router) always uses a feasible successor, or a neighboring router with the lowest cost path to a destination.

EIGRP routers do not send periodic routing updates. Rather, routing information is exchanged only when a route's metric changes, based on information from neighboring routers. If you have routers running EIGRP in your network, you might want to run EIGRP on your ASA, too, so that the ASA can benefit from dynamic routing information. You can use the following steps to configure EIGRP; if you are familiar with configuring EIGRP on a Cisco router, you should find that the ASA commands are identical.

1. Enable an EIGRP process:

    ```
    Firewall(config)# router eigrp as-num
    ```

    EIGRP routers can exchange routing information if they each belong to the same autonomous system. You can define the autonomous system number as *as-num*, a number from 1 to 65535. Make sure the autonomous system number matches that of other EIGRP routers in your network.

2. Associate a network with the EIGRP process:

    ```
    asa(config-router)# network ip-addr [mask]
    ```

    EIGRP must know which interfaces are to participate in routing updates and which interface subnets to advertise. If an interface address falls within the subnet *ip-addr* and *mask*, then EIGRP uses it in its operation.

    If you want the interface subnet to be advertised, but you do not want the interface to participate in EIGRP routing exchanges, you can use the following command:

    ```
    asa(config-router)# passive-interface if_name
    ```

3. (Optional) Use stub routing for a firewall with a single exit point:

    ```
    asa(config-router)# eigrp stub {receive-only | [connected] [redistributed] [static]
    [summary]}
    ```

    If the firewall has a single connection to the outside world through a distribution router, it can become an EIGRP stub router. As a stub, it can receive routes (usually a default route) from its neighbor, but advertises only specific routes of its own.

    With the **receive-only** keyword, the firewall receives updates but does not advertise anything. Otherwise, you can specify one or more route types to advertise. Use the **connected** keyword to advertise routes that are directly connected to the firewall, the **redistributed** keyword to advertise any routes that the firewall has redistributed into its EIGRP process, the **static** keyword to advertise static routes defined on the firewall, or the **summary** keyword to advertise summary addresses defined on the firewall.

4. (Optional) Define a specific EIGRP neighbor:

    Normally, the firewall discovers other EIGRP neighbors by exchanging multicast hello messages. If a neighbor is located across a network that does not support multicast traffic, you can statically define the neighbor. At that point, the firewall communicates with the neighbor via unicast traffic. Use the following EIGRP configuration command to define a neighbor:

    ```
    asa(config-router)# neighbor ip-addr interface if_name
    ```

    The neighbor is located at *ip-addr* over the specified interface.

5. (Optional) Filter EIGRP updates to suppress specific networks:

```
asa(config-router)# distribute-list acl {in | out} [interface if_name]
```

Routes or subnets that are permitted by access list *acl* are filtered from EIGRP updates. The **in** keyword filters the routes as they are received from other EIGRP routers, while the **out** keyword filters the routes in EIGRP advertisements from the firewall.

You can use the **interface** keyword to filter routes on a specific interface.

6. (Optional) Control route summarization:

By default, EIGRP automatically summarizes subnet routes into classful network routes when they are advertised. If you have contiguous subnets that are separated among firewall interfaces or across EIGRP routers, you should disable route summarization with the following EIGRP configuration command:

```
asa(config-router)# no auto-summary
```

Otherwise, you can configure a summary address that is advertised on an interface. This can be handy if you need a summary address that does not fall cleanly within a network boundary. In addition, if you have already disabled automatic summarization, the firewall can still advertise a summary address that is manually configured. You can configure a summary address with the following commands:

```
asa(config)# interface if_name
asa(config-if)# summary-address eigrp as-num address mask [distance]
```

The summary address given by *address mask* is advertised by EIGRP autonomous system number *as-num*. You can specify an administrative distance to override the default value of 5 for summary addresses.

7. (Optional) Redistribute routing information from other sources:

If the firewall is running other routing protocols like RIP or OSPF, you can redistribute routes learned from those methods into EIGRP. First, you should configure a route map to filter routing information from one routing protocol into EIGRP.

You can define a default metric for all routes that are redistributed into EIGRP, because metrics from the different route sources are not equivalent. Use the following EIGRP configuration command:

```
asa(config-router)# default-metric bandwidth delay reliability loading mtu
```

Specify the composite default metric as the combination of *bandwidth* (1 to 4294967295 kbps), *delay* (1 to 4294967295 in tens of microseconds), *reliability* (0 to 255, ranging from low to high), *loading* (1 to 255, ranging from low to high link usage), and *mtu* (1 to 65535 bytes).

If a default metric is not defined, you can configure a metric as a part of route redistribution.

To redistribute routes that were learned by RIP, were statically defined, or are directly connected, use the following EIGRP configuration command:

```
asa(config-router)# redistribute {rip | static | connected} [metric bandwidth delay
reliability load mtu] [route-map map_name]
```

To redistribute routes learned from OSPF, use the following EIGRP configuration command:

```
asa(config-router)# redistribute ospf pid [match {internal | external [1 | 2] | nssa-
external [1 | 2]}] [metric bandwidth delay reliability load mtu] [route-map map_name]
```

Identify the OSPF process as *pid*. You can match against OSPF **internal**, type **1** or **2** OSPF **external**, or external type **1** or **2** Not So Stubby Area (**nssa-external**) routes.

8. (Optional) Secure EIGRP updates with neighbor authentication:

```
asa(config)# interface if_name
asa(config-if)# authentication mode eigrp as-num md5
asa(config-if)# authentication key eigrp as-num key-string key-id key-id
```

The ASA can use the MD5 hash algorithm to verify a neighbor router's authentication key. Define the ASA's key as the text string *key-string*, also known as key number *key-id* (a number from 1 to 255). As soon as authentication is enabled, any EIGRP neighbors that fail to present the correct key are ignored.

9. (Optional) Adjust EIGRP timers:

By default, the firewall sends hello messages every 5 seconds and expects neighbors to hold its neighbor state if they do not receive its hello messages for 15 seconds before they consider it to be unreachable. You should adjust these timers to match the values used by neighboring routers, only if those routers are not using the default values. You can use the following interface configuration commands to adjust the timers for EIGRP autonomous system number *as-num*:

```
asa(config)# interface if_name
asa(config-if)# hello-interval eigrp as-num seconds
asa(config-if)# hold-time eigrp as-num seconds
```

10. (Optional) Adjust the interface delay used in EIGRP metric calculations:

Each firewall interface has a delay value that is used in EIGRP metric calculations. By default, the delay is set to a value that is inversely proportional to the bandwidth of the interface. You can display the current delay value with the **show interface** command, as in the following example:

```
Firewall# show interface
Interface GigabitEthernet0/0 "outside", is up, line protocol is up
Hardware is i82546GB rev03, BW 1000 Mbps, DLY 1000 usec
Auto-Duplex(Full-duplex), Auto-Speed(100 Mbps)
```

You can adjust the delay value with the following interface configuration command:

```
asa(config)# interface if_name
asa(config-if)# delay value
```

An EIGRP Configuration Example

A firewall is positioned so that its interface ethernet0/1 faces the outside public network, while ethernet0/0 faces the inside protected network. EIGRP is being used on the internal network, because of the network's size. The firewall participates in EIGRP so that it can receive dynamic updates about internal IP subnets.

Because the firewall has only a single path to the outside world, it can become an EIGRP stub router. Also, the outside interface does not need to participate in routing updates because no trusted EIGRP neighbor exists there.

You can use the following configuration commands to set up EIGRP on the firewall:

```
Firewall(config)# router eigrp 101
Firewall(config-router)# network 10.0.0.0
Firewall(config-router)# network 192.168.1.0
Firewall(config-router)# eigrp stub
Firewall(config-router)# passive-interface ethernet0/1
Firewall(config-router)# exit
Firewall(config)# route outside 0.0.0.0 0.0.0.0 10.0.1.2 1
!
Firewall(config)# interface ethernet 0/1
Firewall(config-if)# nameif outside
Firewall(config-if)# security-level 0
Firewall(config-if)# ip address 10.0.1.1 255.255.255.0
Firewall(config-if)# exit
!
Firewall(config)# interface ethernet 0/0
Firewall(config-if)# nameif inside
Firewall(config-if)# security-level 100
Firewall(config-if)# ip address 192.168.1.1 255.255.255.0
Firewall(config-if)# authentication mode eigrp 101 md5
Firewall(config-if)# authentication key eigrp 101 secret123 key-id 1
Firewall(config-if)# exit
```

Configuring OSPF to Exchange Routing Information

OSPF is a link-state routing protocol. The routing domain is partitioned into areas. Area 0 is always considered the backbone area of the OSPF domain or autonomous system.

When an OSPF router connects to two or more different areas, it is called an Area Border Router (ABR). When an OSPF router connects an area to a non-OSPF domain and it imports routing information from other sources into OSPF, it is called an Autonomous System Boundary Router (ASBR).

OSPF routers build a common database of the status of all links in the area by exchanging link-state advertisements (LSA). The routers build their routing tables by computing the shortest path first (SPF) algorithm based on that database.

Section 3-2

OSPF Routing Scenarios with a Firewall

When a firewall is configured to use OSPF, consider its role in the scenarios described in the following sections.

OSPF Used Only on the Inside

The firewall becomes an ASBR, bordering an OSPF area with a non-OSPF public network. Figure 3-12 shows this topology.

Figure 3-12 *Using OSPF Only on the Inside of the Firewall*

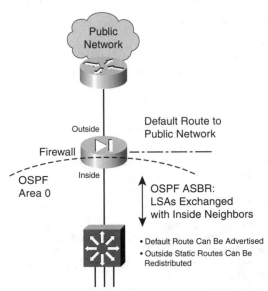

On the outside, only static routes can be configured. On the inside, OSPF LSAs are exchanged with other neighboring routers. The static routes to outside destinations can be redistributed into OSPF so that they are advertised within the inside area. There is no danger or possibility that the firewall will advertise inside to the outside (unsecure) world.

OSPF Used Only on the Outside

The firewall is an ASBR, bordering an OSPF area on the outside with a non-OSPF inside network. Figure 3-13 shows this topology.

Figure 3-13 *Using OSPF Only on the Outside of the Firewall*

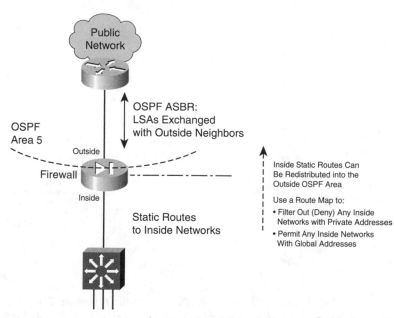

On the inside, only static routes can be configured. On the outside, OSPF LSAs are exchanged with other neighboring routers. The static routes to inside networks can be redistributed to the outside area. If you need to do that, you should carefully consider filtering the information so that no inside network details are revealed to the outside. As well, if NAT is being used at the outside firewall interface, it does not make sense to advertise inside private IP subnets.

To filter redistributed routes toward the outside, you should configure a route map on the firewall. Be sure to deny any internal network addresses and permit any global or public network addresses.

OSPF Used on Both Sides of the Firewall (Same Autonomous System)

Here, the firewall is an ABR because it borders an OSPF area with the OSPF backbone area. Because both areas are within the same autonomous system (AS), the firewall is positioned more like a traditional ABR. This situation might be needed if your organization maintains the inside and outside networks (except for the public Internet) and the firewall protects only a subset of the whole AS. Figure 3-14 shows this topology.

Figure 3-14   *Using OSPF on Both Sides of the Firewall (ABR)*

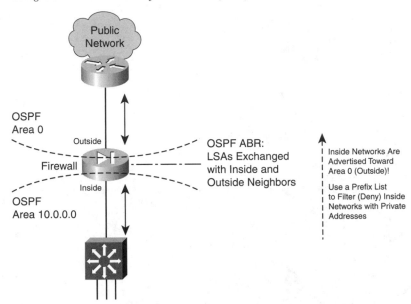

On the inside, the firewall exchanges OSPF LSAs with other inside routers in that area. On the outside, the firewall exchanges LSAs with other corporate routers in the OSPF backbone area. This topology makes it easy to maintain dynamic routing information on the routers and the firewall for a large network.

Routes from the OSPF backbone (outside) are advertised toward the inside area. This poses no real problem, because the outside networks are less secure and are expected to be known. The firewall also advertises inside routes toward the backbone area (outside).

To filter routes that are advertised toward the backbone area, you should configure a *prefix list* on the firewall. Be sure to deny any internal networks with private IP addresses and permit any others that should be known to the outside. (A prefix list is needed because the inside routes are not redistributed to the outside; rather, they are simply advertised within OSPF.)

OSPF Used on Both Sides of the Firewall (Different Autonomous Systems)

This is a unique case, because the firewall separates two distinct autonomous systems, each with its own OSPF backbone area. Now the firewall must become an ASBR for both the inside and the outside. In other words, two separate OSPF processes must run, each supporting a different AS (inside and outside). Figure 3-15 shows this topology.

Figure 3-15   *Using OSPF on Both Sides of the Firewall (ASBR)*

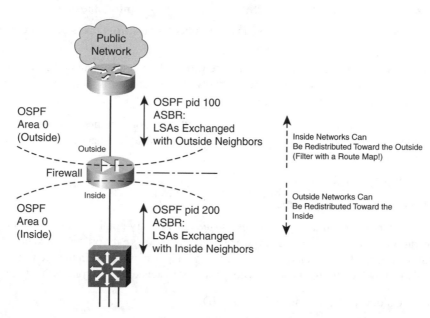

A Cisco firewall can run up to two unique OSPF processes, which makes this scenario possible. Each one runs under a different process ID or number. On the outside, LSAs are exchanged with other neighboring routers. On the inside, a different set of LSAs is exchanged with internal neighbors. By default, no routing information is advertised from the inside to the outside, and vice versa.

You can configure one OSPF process to redistribute routes from another OSPF process; however, for example, the inside process can redistribute routes from the outside process. This is usually acceptable because public routes can be freely advertised and used.

You can also redistribute routes from the inside process into the outside process. If that is necessary, you should configure a *route map* to filter any internal routing information that should not become public knowledge. Be sure to deny any internal networks with private IP addresses and permit others that should be known to the outside.

Configuring OSPF

OSPF is a complex, robust routing protocol. This also means that it is very flexible but can be tedious to configure. You should be well acquainted with OSPF as an advanced IP routing topic before you attempt to configure and use it on a firewall; however, do not be overwhelmed by the number of configuration command possibilities. Instead, try to configure OSPF according to other existing routers in your network. Break it into these basic functions:

- Configure the OSPF process. Define networks and areas.
- Configure authentication if needed.

- Configure a prefix list if the firewall will be an ABR.

- Configure summary routes, and tune OSPF only if you feel comfortable doing this.

- Configure route redistribution only if you need to inject routes from one side of the firewall to another.

In very large or complex network topologies, the firewall might connect to an OSPF stub or Not So Stubby Area (NSSA). The firewall might also be involved in a virtual link. If these situations apply, you can work through those configuration steps, too.

The configuration commands needed for each of the OSPF functions are presented in the following list. Follow them in order, skipping over the ones that are obviously not needed in your network scenario.

1. Define an OSPF process:

   ```
   Firewall(config)# router ospf pid
   ```

   The OSPF process is identified by its process ID *pid* (an arbitrary number from 1 to 65535). Up to two separate OSPF processes can be run on a firewall. This allows each process to exchange routing information independently, although a single routing table is maintained in the firewall. (The process ID is only locally significant; it is not passed or matched among routers and firewalls.)

2. (Optional) Uniquely identify the OSPF router ID:

   ```
   Firewall(config-router)# router-id ip_address
   ```

   By default, OSPF uses the numerically highest IP address defined on any firewall interface as the router ID. For example, an interface with IP address 192.168.1.2 is considered to be higher than one that uses 10.1.1.1 or even 192.168.1.1. This value identifies the "router" in any OSPF exchanges with its neighbors.

   If the highest address on your firewall is a private address (172.28.4.1, for example), you might not want to divulge the private network information to other parties. In this case, you can configure the firewall to use an interface that has a global or public IP address *ip_address*.

3. (Optional) Generate logging messages when OSPF neighbor states change:

   ```
   Firewall(config-router)# log-adj-changes [detail]
   ```

   By default, the firewall generates logging messages to indicate when an OSPF neighbor adjacency goes up or down. In other words, the **log-adj-changes** command is present in the configuration by default.

   You can add the **detail** keyword to generate logging messages for each OSPF neighbor state change, not just for neighbor up and down states. To disable adjacency logging, you can precede the command with the **no** keyword.

   For example, when adjacency logging is enabled, messages similar to the following are generated:

   ```
   %ASA-5-503001: Process 1, Nbr 192.168.167.1 on inside from FULL to DOWN,
     Neighbor Down: Dead timer expired
   ```

4. Assign and activate a network to an OSPF area:

   ```
   Firewall(config-router)# network ip_address netmask area area_id
   ```

   The OSPF process exchanges routing information on any firewall interface that falls within the address range specified here. As well, the network assigned to that interface is advertised by OSPF.

   The range of addresses is defined by *ip_address* and *netmask* (a normal dotted-decimal subnet mask, not a wildcard mask as in IOS). If an interface subnet falls within that range, it is also assigned to OSPF area *area_id* (a decimal number 0 to 4294967295, or an IP subnet written in dotted-decimal format).

TIP   An OSPF area can be referred to by a decimal number or by a subnet notation. This is possible because the area number is stored as one 32-bit number (0 to 4294967295). You might also think of the area as always having a subnet notation—a decimal area number is always preceded by three octets of 0s. For example, area 5 can also be written as 0.0.0.5, area 100 is 0.0.0.100, and area 0 is 0.0.0.0. Using subnet notation for OSPF areas is handy when you have a specific subnet by itself in one area.

Also remember that OSPF must have one backbone area, called area 0 or area 0.0.0.0.

---

5. (Optional) Authenticate OSPF exchanges with other neighbors in an area:

   ```
   Firewall(config-router)# area area_id authentication [message-digest]
   ```

   OSPF peers can authenticate information from each other using cleartext passwords (by default) or MD5 (with the **message-digest** keyword). If authentication is enabled on one device, it must be enabled on all the neighboring devices in the same area.

   In addition, the actual authentication keys are defined on each OSPF interface. This is done in Step 12b.

6. (Optional; ABR only) Keep the private network from being advertised to an outside area.

   If a firewall is configured as an ABR, it sends type 3 LSAs between the areas it touches. This means that the networks in each area are advertised into other areas. Naturally, you would not want private networks to be advertised toward the outside for security and network translation reasons.

   a. Define a prefix list for filtering routes:

   ```
   Firewall(config)# prefix-list list_name [seq seq_number] {permit | deny}
   prefix/len [ge min_value] [le max_value]
   ```

   The prefix list named *list_name* (an arbitrary text string) is defined for filtering routes. You can repeat this command to add more conditions to the list. By default, prefix list entries are automatically numbered in increments of 5, beginning with sequence number 5. Match entries are evaluated in sequence, starting with the lowest defined sequence number. By giving the sequence number *seq_number* here, you can wedge a new statement between two existing ones.

A prefix list entry can either **permit** or **deny** the advertisement of matching routes in type 3 LSAs. A prefix list entry matches an IP route address against the *prefix* (a valid IP network address) and *len* (the number of leftmost bits in the address) values. The **ge** (greater than or equal to a number of bits) and **le** (less than or equal to a number of bits) keywords can also be used to define a range of the number of prefix bits to match. A range can provide a more specific matching condition than the *prefix/len* values alone.

For example, to permit advertisements of routes with a prefix of 172.16.0.0/16 but having any mask length between 16 and 24 bits, you could use the following command:

```
Firewall(config)# prefix-list MyRoutes permit 172.16.0.0/16 ge 16 le 24
```

NOTE Prefix lists are configured in regular configuration mode first. Then, they can be applied to the OSPF process from within OSPF router configuration mode (after the **router ospf** *pid* command is entered).

---

b. Use the prefix list to filter LSAs into or out of an area:

```
Firewall(config-router)# area area_id filter-list prefix
prefix_list_name [in | out]
```

If you want to suppress advertisement of an internal network, you can apply the prefix list for LSAs going **in** or **out** of the area *area_id*. This means you can stop the advertisements from leaving a private area by applying the prefix list to the private *area_id* in the out direction. Or you can filter the advertisements on the public area *area_id* side in the in direction.

7. (Optional) Advertise a default route:

```
Firewall(config-router)# default-information originate [always]
  [metric value] [metric-type {1 | 2}] [route-map name]
```

The firewall can advertise a default route as an external route. If you use the **always** keyword, a default route is advertised even if one has not been specifically configured. The route is advertised with a **metric** of *value* (0 to 16777214; the default is 1). By default, the route is advertised as an external type 2 route (**metric-type 2**). You can also configure a route map separately and apply it with the **route-map** keyword to filter the default route that is advertised.

8. (Optional) Define a special case area.

a. (Optional) Define a stub area:

```
Firewall(config-router)# area area_id stub [no-summary]
```

If a stub area is defined, all OSPF neighbors in that area must configure it as a stub. You can include the **no-summary** keyword to create a totally stubby area; OSPF prevents the introduction of any external or interarea routes into the stub area.

or

b.   (Optional) Define an NSSA:

```
Firewall(config-router)# area area_id nssa [no-redistribution]
[default-information-originate [metric-type 1 | 2]
[metric metric_value]]
```

An NSSA is a stub area that allows external routes to be transported through. You can use the **no-redistribution** keyword on an ABR firewall if you want external routes to be redistributed only into normal areas, not into any NSSAs.

Use the **default-information-originate** keyword to generate a default route into the NSSA. If that is used, you can define the default route as an external route type **1** (route cost plus the internal OSPF metric) or **2** (route cost without the internal OSPF metric). You can also specify a default route metric as *metric_value* (0 to 16777214).

c.   (Optional) Set the default route cost:

```
Firewall(config-router)# area area_id default-cost cost
```

In a stub area or an NSSA, the firewall sends other area routers a default route in place of any external or interarea routes. You can set the cost of this default route as *cost* (0 to 65535; the default is 1).

9.   (Optional) Restore backbone area connectivity with a virtual link:

```
Firewall(config-router)# area area_id virtual-link router_id
[authentication [message-digest | null]] [hello-interval seconds]
[retransmit-interval seconds] [transmit-delay seconds]
[dead-interval seconds] [authentication-key password]
[message-digest-key id md5 password]
```

If the backbone area becomes discontiguous during a router or link failure, OSPF routers can use a virtual link to reconnect the backbone area. You can manually configure a virtual link ahead of time so that it is used as a redundant connection in case an area loses connectivity to the backbone.

Here, *area_id* is the transit area, or the area that must be crossed to reach the backbone from the firewall. The *router_id* is the IP address of the far-end router that completes the virtual link.

Because this is an extension of the backbone area, the virtual link must have many other authentication and timer values defined. These values normally are defined for the OSPF process and OSPF interfaces on the firewall. Use those values here as well as appropriate.

10. (Optional; ABR only) Summarize routes between areas:

```
Firewall(config-router)# area area_id range ip_address netmask
  [advertise | not-advertise]
```

An ABR can reduce the number of routes it sends into an area (*area_id*) by sending a summary address. The summary address is sent in place of any route that falls within the range defined by *ip_address* and *netmask*, and the **advertise** keyword is assumed (the default). If you do not want the summary address advertised, add the **not-advertise** keyword.

For example, you could use the following command to send a summary route into backbone area 0 for all hosts and subnets within 172.18.0.0/16:

```
Firewall(config)# area 0 range 172.18.0.0 255.255.0.0
```

11. (Optional) Tune OSPF.

    a. (Optional) Set the administrative distance for OSPF routes:

```
Firewall(config-router)# distance ospf [intra-area d1]
[inter-area d2] [external d3]
```

By default, all OSPF routes have an administrative distance of 110. This is consistent with Cisco routers. You can change the distance for **intra-area** routes (within an OSPF area) to *d1*. You can change the distance for **inter-area** routes (from one area to another) to *d2*. You can change the distance for **external** routes (from another routing protocol into the OSPF area) to *d3*. If you set these distances differently, the firewall can choose one type of route over another without comparing the OSPF metrics.

    b. (Optional) Change the route calculation timers:

```
Firewall(config-router)# timers {spf spf_delay spf_holdtime |
  lsa-group-pacing seconds}
```

You can configure the OSPF process to wait a delay time of *spf_delay* (0 to 65535 seconds; the default is 5) after receiving a topology change before starting the SPF calculation. The firewall waits *spf_holdtime* (0 to 65535 seconds; the default is 10) between two consecutive calculations.

You can also tune the calculation process with the **lsa-group-pacing** keyword. LSAs are gathered and processed at intervals of *seconds* (10 to 1800 seconds; the default is 240).

12. (Optional) Configure an OSPF interface.

    a. Select the OSPF interface to configure:

PIX 6.3	`Firewall(config)# routing interface if_name`
ASA, FWSM	`Firewall(config)# interface if_name`

The firewall interface named *if_name* (**inside** or **outside**, for example) is configured for OSPF parameters.

b. (Optional) Use authentication:

```
Firewall(config-if)# ospf authentication-key key
```

or

```
Firewall(config-if)# ospf message-digest-key key-id md5 key
Firewall(config-if)# ospf authentication message-digest
```

If authentication has been enabled for an OSPF area, you must also set up the authentication key on each interface in that area. For simple cleartext authentication, use the **authentication-key** keyword along with a preshared *key* (up to eight characters with no white space). This key is sent in the clear within the OSPF LSAs.

You can use the more secure MD5 method instead by using the **message-digest** keyword. MD5 keys are used to validate the MD5 hash value that is computed from each OSPF LSA and the key itself. Only the MD5 hash value is sent in the OSPF LSAs. You can define several keys by repeating the command. Each key is known by a *key-id* index (1 to 255). The actual MD5 *key* is a string of up to 16 text characters.

TIP The key string found at index *key-id* on one router or firewall must match the same key at *key-id* on all other neighboring routers or firewalls. You can change the keys periodically by defining a new key at a new *key-id* index. The old key continues to be used even though a new one has been defined. As soon as all neighboring routers have the new key too, OSPF rolls over and uses the new authentication key. At that time, you should remove the old MD5 keys with the **no ospf message-digest** *key-id* routing interface configuration command.

---

c. (Optional) Set the OSPF interface priority:

```
Firewall(config-if)# ospf priority number
```

When multiple OSPF routers are connected to a single VLAN or broadcast domain, one of them must be elected as the designated router (DR) and another as the backup designated router (BDR). This is done by comparing the interface priority values; the highest priority wins the election. By default, the priority is 1, but you can set it to *number* (0 to 255; 0 prevents the router from becoming a DR or BDR).

d. (Optional) Adjust the OSPF timers:

— Set the hello interval:

```
Firewall(config-if)# ospf hello-interval seconds
```

The time between successive hello updates is set to *seconds* (1 to 65535; the default is 10 seconds). If this is changed, the hello interval must be set identically on all neighboring OSPF routers.

— Set the dead interval:

```
Firewall(config-if)# ospf dead-interval seconds
```

If no hello updates are received from a neighboring OSPF router in *seconds* (1 to 65535 seconds; the default is 4 times the hello interval, or 40 seconds), that neighbor is declared to be down. If this is changed, the dead interval must be set identically on all neighboring OSPF routers.

— Set the retransmit interval:

```
Firewall(config-if)# ospf retransmit-interval seconds
```

— If an LSA must be retransmitted to a neighbor, the firewall waits *seconds* (1 to 65535; the default is 5 seconds) before resending the LSA.

— Set the transmit delay time:

```
Firewall(config-if)# ospf transmit-delay seconds
```

— The firewall keeps an estimate of how long it takes to send an LSA on an interface. The transmission delay is set to *seconds* (1 to 65535; the default is 1 second).

e. (Optional) Set the interface cost:

```
Firewall(config-if)# ospf cost interface_cost
```

The unitless OSPF cost for the interface becomes *interface_cost* (0 to 65535; the default is 10). The higher the interface bandwidth, the lower the cost value becomes. A firewall has a default cost of 10 for all interfaces, regardless of their speeds. This behavior is different from Cisco routers running Cisco IOS Software, where both Fast Ethernet and Gigabit Ethernet have a cost of 1.

Redistributing Routes from Another Source into OSPF

When a firewall redistributes routes from any other source into OSPF, it automatically becomes an ASBR by definition. You can (and should) use a route map to control which routes are redistributed into OSPF. To configure a route map, follow these steps:

1. Use a route map to filter redistributed routes.

a. Define the route map:

```
Firewall(config)# route-map map_tag [permit | deny] [seq_num]
```

The route map named *map_tag* (an arbitrary text string) either permits or denies a certain action. You can repeat this command if you need to define several actions for the same route map. In this case, you should assign a sequence number *seq_num* to each one.

Use the **permit** keyword to define an action that redistributes routes into OSPF. The **deny** keyword defines an action that is processed but does not redistribute routes.

b. Define one or more matching conditions.

If you configure multiple **match** statements, all of them must be met.

— Match against a firewall's next-hop outbound interface:

```
Firewall(config-route-map)# match interface interface_name
```

Routes with their next hop located out the specified firewall interface name are matched.

— Match against a route's metric:

```
Firewall(config-route-map)# match metric metric_value
```

The *metric_value* is used to match the OSPF metric of each route.

— Match against the IP address of the route itself:

```
Firewall(config-route-map)# match ip address acl_id
```

An access list named *acl_id* is used to match each route's network address. The access list must be configured separately and before this command is used. It should contain **permit** entries for source addresses that represent the IP route.

— Match against the type of route:

```
Firewall(config-route-map)# match route-type {local | internal |
  [external [type-1 | type-2]]}
```

Routes are matched according to their type: **local** (locally generated), **internal** (OSPF intra-area and interarea), **external type-1** (OSPF Type 1 external), and **external type-2** (OSPF Type 2 external).

— Match against external routes in an NSSA:

```
Firewall(config-route-map)# match nssa-external [type-1 | type-2]
```

For an NSSA, routes are matched according to OSPF external type 1 or type 2 (the default).

— Match against the IP address of the next-hop router:

```
Firewall(config-route-map)# match ip next-hop acl_id [...acl_id]
```

Routes with the next-hop router addresses that are permitted by one or more access lists are matched. If multiple access list names are listed, they are evaluated in the order given.

— Match against the IP address of the advertising router:

```
Firewall(config-route-map)# match ip route-source acl_id
  [...acl_id]
```

Routes that have been advertised by a router with IP addresses permitted by one or more access lists are matched. If multiple access list names are listed, they are evaluated in the order given.

   c. (Optional) Define attributes to be set when matched:

   — Set the next-hop IP address for a route:

   ```
   Firewall(config-route-map)# set ip next-hop ip-address
     [ip-address]
   ```

   The next-hop router address for the matched route is replaced with the IP addresses specified. These addresses correspond to adjacent or neighboring routers.

   — Set the route metric:

   ```
   Firewall(config-route-map)# set metric value
   ```

   The redistributed route is assigned the specified metric value (0 to 4294967295). You can also specify the metric value as a plus or minus sign with a number (–2147483647 to +2147483647), causing the metric to be adjusted by that value. Lower metric values signify preferred routes.

   — Set the route metric type:

   ```
   Firewall(config-route-map)# set metric-type {internal | external |
     type-1 | type-2}
   ```

   The metric type of the redistributed routes can be **internal** (internally generated), **external** (the default is OSPF type 2), **type-1** (OSPF type 1), or **type-2** (OSPF type 2).

2. (Optional) Redistribute static routes into OSPF:

```
Firewall(config-router)# redistribute {static | connected} [metric
  metric_value] [metric-type metric_type] [route-map map_name] [tag
  tag_value] [subnets]
```

Either **static** routes (configured with the **route** command) or **connected** routes (subnets directly connected to firewall interfaces) can be redistributed into the OSPF process. Use the **connected** keyword only when you have firewall interfaces that are not configured to participate in OSPF (as configured by the **network** OSPF command). Otherwise, OSPF automatically learns directly connected interfaces and their subnets from the OSPF configuration.

Routes that are redistributed can be matched and altered by the **route-map** named *map_name*. If the **route-map** keyword is omitted, all routes are distributed.

You can also set fixed values for the *metric_value* (0 to 16777214), the *metric_type* (**internal**, **external**, **type-1**, or **type-2**), and the route tag *tag_value* (an arbitrary number from 0 to 4294967295, used to match routes on other ASBRs) for all routes, not just ones matched by a route map.

By default, only routes that are not subnetted (classful routes) are redistributed into OSPF unless the **subnets** keyword is given.

3. Redistribute routes from one OSPF process into another:

```
Firewall(config-router)# redistribute ospf pid [match {internal | external
  [1 | 2] | nssa-external [1 | 2]}] [metric metric_value] [metric-type
  metric_type] [route-map map_name] [tag tag_value] [subnets]
```

Routes from the other OSPF process *ospf_pid* can be redistributed into the OSPF process being configured. You can conditionally redistribute routes by using a **route-map** named *map_name*. If you omit the **route-map** keyword, all routes are redistributed.

If you do not use a route map, you can still redistribute only routes with specific metric types by using the **match** keyword. The types include **internal** (internally generated), **external** (OSPF type **1** or **2**), and **nssa-external** (OSPF type **1** or **2** coming into an NSSA).

You can also set fixed values for the *metric_value* (0 to 16777214), *metric_type* (**internal**, **external**, **type-1**, or **type-2**), and the route tag *tag_value* (an arbitrary number 0 to 4294967295, used to match routes on other ASBRs) for all routes, not just ones matched by a route map.

By default, only routes that are not subnetted (classful routes) are redistributed into OSPF unless the **subnets** keyword is given.

OSPF Example

A firewall is situated so that it connects to OSPF area 0 on its outside interface and to OSPF area 100 on its inside interface. Therefore, the firewall is an ABR. The outside interface is 172.19.200.2/24, and the inside interface is 192.168.1.1/24. One subnet on the inside has a public IP address range 128.163.89.0/24, and all the other inside networks fall within 192.168.0.0.

Because the inside firewall interface has a higher IP address, OSPF uses that address as its router ID by default. It might be better practice to use an outside address for exchanges with OSPF neighbors on the outside backbone area. Therefore, the router ID is configured for the outside interface address.

Network 172.19.200.0/24 falls in OSPF area 0, and 192.168.0.0/16 falls in OSPF area 100 on the inside. MD5 authentication is used for both the inside and outside OSPF areas.

The internal network 192.168.0.0 has private IP addresses and probably should not be advertised toward the outside. Therefore, a prefix list named InsideFilter is configured to allow only the internal subnet 128.163.89.0/24 (a global or public address range) to be advertised. In this case, the prefix list is applied to area 0 so that it filters routing information coming *in* to that area. The configuration to accomplish this is as follows:

PIX 6.3	ASA
Firewall(config)# **ip address inside** **192.168.1.1 255.255.255.0** Firewall(config)# **ip address outside** **172.19.200.2 255.255.255.0** Firewall(config)# **prefix-list InsideFilter** **10 deny 192.168.0.0/16** Firewall(config)# **prefix-list InsideFilter** **20 permit 128.163.89.0/24** Firewall(config)# **router ospf 1** Firewall(config-router)# **router-id** **172.19.200.2** Firewall(config-router)# **network** **172.19.200.0 255.255.255.0 area 0** Firewall(config-router)# **network** **192.168.0.0 255.255.0.0 area 100** Firewall(config-router)# **area 0** **authentication message-digest** Firewall(config-router)# **area 0 filter-** **list prefix InsideFilter in** Firewall(config-router)# **area 100** **authentication message-digest** Firewall(config-router)# **exit** Firewall(config)# **routing interface** **outside** Firewall(config-routing)#**ospf message-** **digest-key 1 md5 myoutsidekey** Firewall(config)# **routing interface inside** Firewall(config-routing)#**ospf message-** **digest-key 1 md5 myinsidekey**	Firewall(config)# **interface** **gigabitethernet1** Firewall(config-if)# **nameif inside** Firewall(config-if)# **ip address** **192.168.1.1 255.255.255.0** Firewall(config)# **interface** **gigabitethernet0** Firewall(config-if)# **nameif outside** Firewall(config-if)# **ip address outside** **172.19.200.2 255.255.255.0** Firewall(config-if)# **exit** Firewall(config)# **prefix-list** **InsideFilter 10 deny 192.168.0.0/16** Firewall(config)# **prefix-list** **InsideFilter 20 permit 128.163.89.0/24** Firewall(config)# **router ospf 1** Firewall(config-router)# **router-id** **172.19.200.2** Firewall(config-router)# **network** **172.19.200.0 255.255.255.0 area 0** Firewall(config-router)# **network** **192.168.0.0 255.255.0.0 area 100** Firewall(config-router)# **area 0** **authentication message-digest** Firewall(config-router)# **area 0 filter-** **list prefix InsideFilter in** Firewall(config-router)# **area 100** **authentication message-digest** Firewall(config-router)# **exit** Firewall(config)# **interface** **gigabitethernet1** Firewall(config-if)# **ospf message-** **digest-key 1 md5 myoutsidekey** Firewall(config-if)# **interface** **gigabitethernet0** Firewall(config-if)# **ospf message-** **digest-key 1 md5 myinsidekey** Firewall(config-if)# **exit**

3-3: DHCP Server Functions

A firewall can act as a DHCP server, assigning IP addresses dynamically to requesting clients. A firewall DHCP server returns its own interface address as the client's default gateway. The interface subnet mask is returned for the client to use as well.

Cisco firewalls support up to 256 active clients at any one time. (The Cisco PIX 501 supports either 32, 128, or 256 clients, depending on the user license.)

No provisions are available for configuring static address assignments. A firewall can manage only dynamic address assignments from a pool of contiguous IP addresses.

Beginning with ASA 7.2(1), a firewall can generate dynamic DNS information based on the DHCP server. This allows DNS records to be updated dynamically, as hosts acquire an IP address. The dynamic DNS feature is covered in detail in the "Updating Dynamic DNS from a DHCP Server" section later in this chapter.

A firewall can also act as a DHCP relay, forwarding DHCP requests received on one interface to DHCP servers found on another interface. DHCP relay is similar to the **ip helper-address** command on routers and switches running Cisco IOS Software.

The DHCP relay service accepts DHCP request broadcast packets and converts them to DHCP request unicast packets. The unicasts are forwarded to the DHCP servers. After DHCP replies are received, they are relayed back to the requesting client.

Using the Firewall as a DHCP Server

Follow these steps to configure the DHCP server feature:

1. Define an address pool for host assignments:

    Firewall(config)# **dhcpd address** ip1[-ip2] if_name

    The pool of available client addresses on the firewall interface named *if_name* (**inside**, for example) goes from a lower-limit address *ip1* to an upper-limit address *ip2*. These two addresses must be separated by a hyphen and must belong to the same subnet. In addition, the pool of addresses must reside in the same IP subnet assigned to the firewall interface. In releases before PIX 6.3, only non-outside interfaces were supported. After 6.3, the outside interface can be used, too.

2. Supply clients with domain information.

    a. (Optional) Hand out dynamic information obtained by the firewall:

        Firewall(config)# **dhcpd auto_config** [**outside**]

        You can use this command if your firewall is configured to obtain IP address information for its interface from an independent DHCP server. After the DNS and WINS server addresses and the domain name are learned from the DHCP server, the firewall can push those same values out to its own DHCP clients. In this scenario, the firewall usually acts as a DHCP client on its outside interface and as a DHCP server on its inside interface.

        or

    b. (Optional) Hand out DNS server addresses:

        Firewall(config)# **dhcpd dns** dns1 [dns2]

You can configure up to two DNS server addresses to hand out to DHCP clients. The server IP addresses are given as *dns1* and *dns2*.

   c. (Optional) Hand out WINS server addresses:

```
Firewall(config)# dhcpd wins wins1 [wins2]
```

WINS servers are used to resolve Microsoft NetBIOS names into IP addresses. You can configure up to two WINS server addresses to hand out to DHCP clients. The WINS IP addresses are given as *wins1* and *wins2*.

   d. (Optional) Hand out the domain name:

```
Firewall(config)# dhcpd domain domain_name
```

You can configure the domain name that the client will learn and use as *domain_name* (the fully qualified domain name, such as myexample.com).

3. Define the client lease time:

```
Firewall(config)# dhcpd lease lease_length
```

By default, the firewall supplies DHCP replies with lease times of 3600 seconds (1 hour). You can adjust the lease time to be *lease_length* seconds (300 to 2,147,483,647 seconds).

TIP   If your clients must compete for addresses in a relatively small pool, a shorter lease time is better. After a client is turned off, its lease runs out soon, and another client can be assigned that address.

If most of your clients are stable and stay in use most of the day, you can lengthen the lease time. A longer lease time reserves an address for a client, even if that client turns off and returns later.

Lease times also affect your ability to correlate workstations and their address assignments with Syslog entries from the firewall. Sometimes, you might need to track down which workstation was using a specific address on a certain day and time. The firewall logs only DHCP assignments, so if the lease times are long, the DHCP log entries are sparse and more difficult to find.

---

4. (Optional) Hand out options for Cisco IP Phones.

Cisco IP Phones must receive additional information about their environment through DHCP. This information is sent as DHCP options.

   a. Identify the IP phone TFTP server:

```
Firewall(config)# dhcpd option 66 {ascii server_name | ip server_ip}
Firewall(config)# dhcpd option 150 ip server_ip1 [server_ip2]
```

A Cisco IP Phone must find the TFTP server where it can download its configuration. This information is provided as either DHCP option 66 (a single TFTP server) or option 150 (up to two TFTP servers). You can define one or both of these options; the IP phone accepts and tries them both.

If you use **option 66**, you can use the **ascii** keyword to define the TFTP server's host name as *server_name* (a text string). Otherwise, you can use the **ip** keyword to define the server's IP address as *server_ip*.

If you use **option 150**, you can define one or two TFTP server addresses.

b. (Optional) Identify the IP phone default routers:

`Firewall(config)# dhcpd option 3 ip router_ip1 [router_ip2]`

By default, the firewall sends its own interface address as the client's default gateway. In some cases, there might be two potential gateways or routers for Cisco IP Phones to use. You can define these in DHCP option 3 as *router_ip1* and *router_ip2*.

c. (Optional) Provide a generic DHCP option:

`Firewall(config)# dhcpd option code {ascii string | ip ip_address | hex hex_string}`

If you need to provide an arbitrary DHCP option to clients, you can specify the option number as *code* (0 to 255). The option value can be an ASCII character string, an IP address, or a *string* of hexadecimal characters (pairs of hex digits with no white space and no leading 0x).

5. (Optional) Adjust the preassignment ping timer:

`Firewall(config)# dhcpd ping_timeout timeout`

When the firewall receives a DHCP request from a potential client, it looks up the next available IP address in the pool. Before a DHCP reply is returned, the firewall tests to make sure that the IP address is not already in use by some other host. (This could occur if another host had its IP address statically configured without the firewall's knowledge.)

The firewall sends an ICMP echo (ping) request and waits *timeout* milliseconds (100 to 10000 ms; the default is 750) for a reply. If no reply occurs in that time frame, it assumes that the IP address is indeed available and assigns it to the client. If an ICMP reply is received from that address, the firewall knows that the address is already taken.

6. Enable the DHCP server:

`Firewall(config)# dhcpd enable if_name`

The DHCP server starts listening for requests on the firewall interface named *if_name* (**inside**, for example). You can define and enable DHCP servers on more than one interface by repeating the sequence of DHCP configuration commands.

Section 3-3

TIP	You can display the current DHCP server parameters with the **show dhcpd** EXEC command. To see the current DHCP client-address bindings, use the **show dhcpd bindings** EXEC command. To see the number of different DHCP message types received, use the **show dhcpd statistics** EXEC command.
	You can also see information about DHCP activity by using the **debug dhcpd event** command. This can be useful if you think a client is requesting an address but is never receiving a reply.

DHCP Server Example

A PIX Firewall is configured as a DHCP server for clients on its inside interface. Clients are assigned an address from the pool 192.168.200.10 through 192.168.200.200. They also receive DNS addresses 192.168.100.5 and 192.168.100.6, WINS addresses 192.168.100.15 and 192.168.100.16, and a domain name of mywhatastrangeexample.com.

PIX 6.3	ASA or FWSM
Firewall(config)# **ip address inside 192.168.200.1 255.255.255.0** Firewall(config)# **dhcpd address 192.168.200.10-192.168.200.200 inside** Firewall(config)# **dhcpd dns 192.168.100.5 192.168.100.6** Firewall(config)# **dhcpd wins 192.168.100.15 192.168.100.16** Firewall(config)# **dhcpd domain mywhatastrangeexample.com** Firewall(config)# **dhcpd enable inside**	Firewall(config)# **interface gigabitethernet1** Firewall(config-if)# **description inside** Firewall(config-if)# **ip address 192.168.200.1 255.255.255.0** Firewall(config-if)# **exit** Firewall(config)# **dhcpd address 192.168.200.10-192.168.200.200 inside** Firewall(config)# **dhcpd dns 192.168.100.5 192.168.100.6** Firewall(config)# **dhcpd wins 192.168.100.15 192.168.100.16** Firewall(config)# **dhcpd domain mywhatastrangeexample.com** Firewall(config)# **dhcpd enable inside**

Updating Dynamic DNS from a DHCP Server

Traditionally, hostnames and IP addresses have been associated through the use of DNS, requiring static configurations. While this might be practical for servers, which rarely change their hostnames or addresses, it does not lend itself to timely updates for clients that frequently change IP addresses.

Dynamic DNS (DDNS) solves this problem by keeping the DNS function, but allowing records to be updated dynamically, as they change. DDNS is most useful when it is teamed with a DHCP server; as the DHCP server hands out IP addresses to clients, it can send a DDNS update immediately. This allows mobile or transient clients to keep a stable hostname and to always be found through a DNS lookup.

On the ASA platform, the DDNS database can be updated from the following sources:

- The ASA DHCP server, as it provides IP addresses to PC clients
- The ASA DHCP client, as it requests an address from an ISP
- PC clients, as they send a DHCP request; the ASA can relay the DNS information provided by the clients

On the ASA, DDNS uses the IETF standard method defined in RFC 2136. Through DDNS, the following DNS resource records can be updated for a host:

- *A* **resource record**—Contains the hostname-to-address mapping (for example, www.cisco.com resolves to 198.133.219.25)
- *PTR* **resource record**—Contains the address-to-hostname mapping (for example, 219.133.198.in-addr.arpa resolves to www.cisco.com)

To use DDNS, you must configure either a DHCP client, a DHCP server, or both on the ASA. The DHCP mechanism is always used to send updates to a DNS server that is DDNS-capable. You can use the following steps to configure DDNS support:

1. Identify DNS servers that support DDNS:

   ```
   asa(config)# dns server-group DefaultDNS
   asa(config-dns-server-group)# dns name-server ip_address
    [ip_address2]...[ip_address6]
   asa(config-dns-server-group)# exit
   ```

   You can enter up to six IP addresses of DDNS servers where the ASA can send dynamic updates.

2. Enable DNS use on an interface:

   ```
   asa(config)# dns domain-lookup if_name
   ```

   Identify the ASA interface that is closest to the DNS servers. The ASA sends DDNS updates on that interface.

3. Define an update method:

   ```
   asa(config)# ddns update method method_name
   ```

   The DDNS update method policy is known by the arbitrary *method_name* string.

4. Specify the update method:

   ```
   asa(DDNS-update-method)# ddns [both]
   ```

   By default, the ASA attempts to update only the A resource record. You can add the **both** keyword to make it update both the A and PTR resource records.

5. (Optional) Set the maximum update period:

```
asa(DDNS-update-method)# interval maximum days hours minutes seconds
```

By default, the ASA sends DDNS updates only as they occur, based on the activity of DHCP clients. You can also set a maximum update interval, so that the ASA does not wait more than a defined time before sending another update. The interval is defined as *days* (0 to 364), *hours* (0 to 23), *minutes* (0 to 59), and *seconds* (0 to 59) and should be chosen to match the requirements of the DDNS servers.

6. (Optional) Send DDNS updates from the ASA DHCP client:

```
asa(config)# interface if_name
asa(config-if)# ddns update method_name
asa(config-if)# ddns update hostname hostname
asa(config-if)# ip address dhcp [setroute]
```

The DDNS method named *method_name* (configured in Step 3) is used on the specified ASA interface. When the ASA DHCP client sends a DDNS update, it needs to know its own hostname. You can specify the hostname as *hostname*, as either a fully qualified domain name (FQDN) or as a hostname that is prepended to the ASA's domain name (configured with the **domain-name** command).

Finally, the **ip address dhcp** command starts the DHCP client and requests an IP address for the interface. As soon as an address is obtained, the DHCP client attempts to send its DDNS update to bind the IP address to the hostname.

You can also specify the DDNS policy for the ASA DHCP client with the following interface configuration command:

```
asa(config-if)# dhcp client update dns [server {both | none}]
```

By default, the ASA DHCP client does not update its DNS record on its own. Issuing this command enables the client to send DDNS updates through the ASA DHCP server, toward the DNS. The client instructs the server to send only PTR updates, unless the **server** keyword is added, along with either the **both** (send both A and PTR updates) or **none** (send no DDNS updates) keyword.

This command can also be given as a global configuration command, to provide a global policy for all interfaces. You can enter a global and an interface version of the same command; the interface command always overrides the global settings. Be aware that the global version of this command uses a hyphen (**dhcp-client**), while the interface version does not (**dhcp client**).

7. (Optional) Send DDNS updates from the ASA DHCP server:

A DHCP server can be configured on an ASA, usually facing the inside or secure side where client PCs are located. The ASA can send DDNS updates based on the requests made from the clients to the DHCP server. You can configure the ASA DHCP server to send DDNS updates with the following global configuration command:

```
asa(config)# dhcpd update dns [both] [override] [interface if_name]
```

As soon as this command is given, the ASA DHCP server sends updates for PTR resource records only. You can add the **both** keyword to send both A and PTR records. If you add the **override** keyword, the ASA DHCP server overrides the information contained in all DHCP client requests—including the ASA DHCP client configuration. For example, a DHCP client might try to send a PTR record, but the DHCP server can override that by sending both A and PTR records.

If you want to enable DDNS on only a single ASA interface, you can add the **interface** keyword. Otherwise, the ASA generates DDNS updates on any interface that has a DHCP server configured.

TIP   The ASA DHCP server generates DDNS updates on any interface that has a DHCP server configured. The ASA attempts a reverse DNS lookup on the DHCP client's IP address, to find the authoritative DNS for the client's domain. The Start of Authority (SOA) entry is requested for the client's IP address. If the DNS does not already have the client's domain configured, along with the SOA information, the ASA cannot register DDNS updates successfully.

In the case of private or RFC 1918 addresses inside the firewall boundary, the DNS does not return a valid SOA for the private subnet unless the DDNS-capable machines in your network are already preconfigured with definitions for your local subnets, along with a correct SOA entry.

Verifying DDNS Operation

Because you can configure both DHCP client and DHCP server on a single ASA, you might become confused about what is actually configured and running on which interfaces. You can use the **show dhcpd state** command to see where the client and server functions exist, as in the following example.

```
Firewall# show dhcpd state
Context  Configured as DHCP Server
Interface outside, Configured for DHCP CLIENT
Interface inside, Configured for DHCP SERVER
Interface dmz, Not Configured for DHCP
Interface management, Not Configured for DHCP
Firewall#
```

You can use the **show ddns update method** to see the configured method and the **show ddns update interface** command to see the DDNS method that is applied to each ASA interface. Finally, you can view debugging output by entering the **debug ddns** command.

As an example, suppose an ASA is to be configured to provide DDNS updates to a DNS server. The ASA should have a policy to allow updates to both the A and PTR resource records, using the update method called **myddns**. On the outside interface, the ASA uses its DHCP client to obtain an address. The DHCP client also is allowed to send DDNS updates with its hostname (asa.mycompany.com) and its newly obtained IP address.

On the inside interface, the ASA should be configured to run a DHCP server for inside clients. As inside clients send DHCP requests, their hostname and assigned IP addresses are sent on as DDNS updates. The following commands could be used to accomplish these example requirements.

```
Firewall(config)# hostname asa
Firewall(config)# domain-name mycompany.com
Firewall(config)# ddns update method myddns
Firewall(config)# ddns both
!
Firewall(config)# interface Ethernet0/0
Firewall(config-if)# nameif outside
Firewall(config-if)# security-level 0
Firewall(config-if)# ddns update hostname asa.mycompany.com
Firewall(config-if)# ddns update myddns
Firewall(config-if)# ip address dhcp setroute
!
Firewall(config-if)# interface Ethernet0/1
Firewall(config-if)# nameif inside
Firewall(config-if)# security-level 100
Firewall(config-if)# dhcp client update dns
Firewall(config-if)# ip address 192.168.100.1 255.255.255.0
Firewall(config-if)# exit
!
Firewall(config)# dns domain-lookup outside
Firewall(config)# dns server-group DefaultDNS
Firewall(config-dns-server-group)# name-server 128.163.111.7
Firewall(config-dns-server-group)# domain-name mycompany.com
Firewall(config-dns-server-group)# exit
Firewall(config)# dhcp-client update dns
Firewall(config)# dhcpd dns 128.163.97.5 128.163.3.10
Firewall(config)# dhcpd update dns both
!
Firewall(config)# dhcpd address 192.168.100.10-192.168.100.254 inside
Firewall(config)# dhcpd enable inside
```

Relaying DHCP Requests to a DHCP Server

Follow these steps to configure a firewall to act as a DHCP relay:

1. Define a real DHCP server:

   ```
   Firewall(config)# dhcprelay server dhcp_server_ip server_ifc
   ```

   A real DHCP server can be found at IP address *dhcp_server_ip* on the firewall interface named *server_ifc* (**inside**, for example). You can repeat this command to define up to four real DHCP servers.

   When DHCP requests (broadcasts) are received on one firewall interface, they are converted to UDP port 67 unicasts destined for the real DHCP servers on another interface. If multiple servers are defined, DHCP requests are relayed to all of them simultaneously.

2. (Optional) Adjust the DHCP reply timeout:

    `Firewall(config)#` **`dhcprelay timeout`** *`seconds`*

    By default, the firewall waits 60 seconds to receive a reply from a real DHCP server. If a reply is returned within that time, it is relayed back toward the client. If a reply is not returned within that time, nothing is relayed back to the client, and any overdue server reply is simply dropped. You can adjust the timeout to *seconds* (1 to 3600 seconds).

3. (Optional) Inject the firewall interface as the default gateway:

    `Firewall(config)#` **`dhcprelay setroute`** *`client_ifc`*

    When DHCP replies are returned by a real DHCP server, a default gateway could be specified in the reply packet. By default, this information is passed on through the firewall so that the client receives it.

    You can configure the firewall to replace any default gateway information with its own interface address. This causes the DHCP reply packet to list the firewall interface closest to the client, the interface named *client_ifc*, as the default gateway.

4. Enable the DHCP relay service:

    `Firewall(config)#` **`dhcprelay enable`** *`client_ifc`*

    The DHCP relay service is started only on the firewall interface named *client_ifc* (**inside**, for example). This is the interface where DHCP clients are located.

DHCP Relay Example

A DHCP relay is configured to accept DHCP requests from clients on the inside interface and relay them to the DHCP server at 192.168.1.1 on the DMZ interface. The firewall waits 120 seconds for a reply from the DHCP server. The firewall's inside interface address is given to the clients as a default gateway. You can use the following commands to accomplish this:

```
Firewall(config)# dhcprelay server 192.168.1.1 dmz
Firewall(config)# dhcprelay timeout 120
Firewall(config)# dhcprelay setroute inside
Firewall(config)# dhcprelay enable inside
```

TIP   You can monitor DHCP relay activity by looking at the output from the **show dhcprelay statistics** EXEC command. The output shows the counters of the various DHCP operations relayed to and from the real DHCP server, as in the following example:

```
Firewall# show dhcprelay statistics
Packets Relayed
BOOTREQUEST 0
DHCPDISCOVER 7
DHCPREQUEST 3
```

```
DHCPDECLINE 0
DHCPRELEASE 0
DHCPINFORM 0
BOOTREPLY 0
DHCPOFFER 7
DHCPACK 3
DHCPNAK 0
```

3-4: Multicast Support

To participate in forwarding and inspecting IP multicast traffic, a firewall can coexist with multicast routers running Protocol-Independent Multicast (PIM) sparse mode.

A firewall can operate as an *IGMP proxy agent*, also called a *stub router*. For all multicast-related operations, the firewall acts on behalf of the recipients. IGMP requests from recipient hosts on one firewall interface are intercepted, inspected, and relayed to multicast routers on another firewall interface.

Beginning with ASA 7.0 and FWSM 3.1(1), a firewall can also be configured to act as a PIM router so that it communicates with other PIM routers to build a complete multicast distribution tree.

After recipients join multicast groups, the firewall can intercept, inspect, and relay multicast traffic from the source on one interface to the recipients on another interface.

Multicast Overview

A network uses three basic types of IP traffic:

- **Unicast**—Packets that are sent from one source host address to a single destination host address. Unicast packets are forwarded by finding the destination IP address in routing tables.

- **Broadcast**—Packets that are sent from one source host address to a broadcast destination address. The destination can be all hosts (255.255.255.255), a directed broadcast to a subnet (that is, 192.168.10.255), or some portion of a subnet. A router or Layer 3 device does not forward these by default unless some method of relaying has been configured.

- **Multicast**—Packets that are sent from one source host address to a special group-based destination address. The destination represents only the hosts that are interested in receiving the packets, and no others. A router or Layer 3 device does not forward these packets by default unless some form of multicast routing is enabled.

Two extremes are covered here—a unicast, which travels from host to host, and a broadcast, which travels from one host to everyone on a segment. Multicast falls somewhere in the middle, where the intention is to send packets from one host to only the users who want to receive them—namely, those in the designated *multicast group*. Ideally, the recipients of multicast packets could be located anywhere, not just on the local segment.

Multicast traffic is generally unidirectional. Because many hosts receive the same data, it makes little sense to allow one of the hosts to send packets back toward the source over the multicast mechanism. Instead, a receiving host can send return traffic to the source as a unicast. Multicast traffic is also sent in a best-effort connectionless format. UDP (connectionless) is the commonly used format, whereas TCP (connection-oriented) is not.

Hosts that want to receive data from a multicast source can join or leave a multicast group dynamically. In addition, a host can decide to become a member of more than one multicast group at any time. The principal network task is then to figure out how to deliver multicast traffic to the group members without disturbing other uninterested hosts.

Multicast Addressing

Routers and switches must have a way to distinguish multicast traffic from unicasts or broadcasts. This is done through IP addressing by reserving the Class D IP address range, 224.0.0.0 through 239.255.255.255, for multicasting. Network devices can quickly pick out multicast IP addresses by looking at the four most-significant bits, which are always 1110.

How does a router or switch relate a multicast IP address to a MAC address? There is no ARP equivalent for multicast address mapping. Instead, a reserved Organizationally Unique Identifier (OUI) value is set aside so that multicast MAC addresses always begin with 0100.5e (plus the next-lower bit, which is 0). The lower 28 bits of the multicast IP address must also be mapped into the lower 23 bits of the MAC address by a simple algorithm.

Some of the IP multicast address space has been reserved for a particular use:

- **Complete multicast space (224.0.0.0 through 239.255.255.255)**—The entire range of IP addresses that can be used for multicast purposes.

- **Link-local addresses (224.0.0.0 through 224.0.0.255)**—Used by network protocols only on the local network segment. Routers do not forward these packets.

    This space includes the *all-hosts* address 224.0.0.1, *all-routers* 224.0.0.2, *OSPF-routers* 224.0.0.5, and so on. These are also known as *fixed-group addresses* because they are well-known and predefined.

- **Administratively scoped addresses (239.0.0.0 through 239.255.255.255)**—Used in private multicast domains, much like the private IP address ranges from RFC 1918. These addresses are not routed between domains, so they can be reused.

- **Globally scoped addresses (224.0.1.0 through 238.255.255.255)**—Used by any entity. These addresses can be routed across an organization or the Internet, so they must be unique and globally significant. (Think of this range as neither local nor private; it is the rest of the multicast range.)

Forwarding Multicast Traffic

IP multicast traffic must be forwarded from one network interface to another, just like any other Layer 3 packets are handled. The difference is in knowing where to forward the packets. For example, unicast IP packets have only one destination interface on a router or firewall (even if multiple paths exist). Multicast IP packets, however, can have many destination interfaces, depending on where the recipients are located.

Cisco firewalls running PIX 6.2 or 6.3 have a limited multicast capability. They can act only as a multicast forwarding proxy, also known as a *stub multicast router* (SMR), depending on other routers in the network to actually route the multicast packets. The firewalls can determine where the multicast recipients are located on their own interfaces. They must be statically configured to forward the multicast traffic between a source and the recipients.

Beginning with ASA 7.0 and FWSM 3.1(1), Cisco firewalls can participate in multicast routing by using the PIM routing protocol. This lets a firewall communicate with other PIM routers to distribute multicast traffic dynamically and along the best paths.

Multicast Trees

The routers in a network must determine a forwarding path to get multicast packets from the source (sender) to each of the recipients, regardless of where they are located. Think of the network as a tree structure. At the root of the tree is the source, blindly sending IP packets to a specific multicast address. Each router along the way sits at a branch or fork in the tree. If a router knows where all the multicast group recipients are located, it also knows which branches of the tree to replicate the multicast packets onto. Some routers have no downstream recipients, so they do not need to forward the multicast traffic. Other routers might have many downstream recipients.

This tree structure is somewhat similar to a spanning-tree topology because it has a root at one end and leaf nodes (the recipients) at the other end. The tree is also loop-free so that none of the multicast traffic gets fed back into the tree.

TIP   In multicast routing, the router nearest the multicast source is called the *first-hop router*. It is the first hop that multicast packets reach when they leave the source. Routers at the tree's leaf nodes, nearest the multicast receivers, are called *last-hop routers*. They are the last hop that multicast packets reach at the end of their journey.

Reverse Path Forwarding

Multicast routers usually have one test to perform on every multicast packet they receive. Reverse Path Forwarding (RPF) is a means to make sure packets are not being injected back into the tree at an unexpected location.

As a packet is received on a router interface, the source IP address is inspected. The idea is to verify that the packet arrived on the same interface where the source can be found. If this is true, the packet is actually proceeding out the tree's branches, away from the source. If this is not true, someone else has injected the packet on an unexpected interface, headed back down the tree's branches toward the source.

To perform the RPF test, a PIM router looks up the source address in its unicast routing table. If the next-hop interface used to reach the source address also matches the interface where the packet was received, the packet can be forwarded or replicated toward the multicast recipients. If not, the packet is quietly discarded.

IGMP: Finding Multicast Group Recipients

How does a router know of the recipients in a multicast group, much less their locations? To receive multicast traffic from a source, both the source and every recipient must first join a common multicast group, known by its multicast IP address.

A host can join a multicast group by sending a request to its local router. This is done through Internet Group Management Protocol (IGMP). IGMPv1 is defined in RFC 1112, and its successor, IGMPv2, is defined in RFC 2236. Think of IGMP as a means of maintaining group membership only on the local router.

When several hosts join a group by contacting their local routers, it is the multicast routing protocol (such as PIM) that "connects the dots" and forms the multicast tree between routers.

NOTE   Keep in mind that IGMP is always used on multicast routers and Cisco firewalls to interact with multicast hosts. In PIX 6.3 and earlier, Stub Multicast Routing offers IGMP for local group membership and IGMP forwarding so that multicast routers can use the IGMP information on a broader scale.

PIM is available only beginning with ASA 7.0 and FWSM 3.1(1). The firewall then becomes a true multicast router, running both PIM and IGMP.

IGMPv1

To join a multicast group, a host can dynamically send a *Membership Report* IGMP message to its local router (or firewall). This message tells the router what multicast address (group) the host is joining. The multicast address is used as the IGMP packet's destination IP address, as well as the group address requested in the message.

Every 60 seconds, one router on each network segment queries all the directly connected hosts to see if they are interested in receiving multicast traffic. This router is known as the *IGMPv1 Querier*. It functions simply to invite hosts to join a group.

Queries are sent to the 224.0.0.1 all-hosts multicast address for quick distribution. (By definition, every host must listen to the all-hosts address; no group membership is required.) If a host is interested in joining a group, or if it wants to continue receiving a group that it has already joined, it must respond to the router with a membership report.

Hosts can join multicast groups at any time. However, IGMPv1 does not have a mechanism to allow a host to leave a group if it is no longer interested in the group's content. Instead, routers age a multicast group out of an interface (network segment) if no membership reports are received for three consecutive query intervals. This means that, by default, multicast traffic is still sent onto a segment for up to 3 minutes after all the group members have stopped listening.

Notice that a router does not need to keep a complete host membership list for each multicast group that is active. Rather, it needs to record only which multicast groups are active on which interfaces.

IGMPv2

IGMP version 2 introduced several differences from the first version. Queries can be sent as *General Queries* to the all-hosts address (as in IGMPv1). They also can be sent as *Group-Specific Queries*, sent only to members of a specific group.

In addition, hosts are allowed to leave a group dynamically. When a host decides to leave a group it has joined, it sends a *Leave Group* message to the all-routers address (224.0.0.2). All routers on the local segment take note, and the Querier router decides to investigate further. It responds with a Group-Specific Query message, asking if anyone is still interested in receiving traffic for that group. Any other hosts must reply with a Membership Report. Otherwise, the Querier router safely assumes that there is no need to continue forwarding the group traffic on that segment.

NOTE   If any IGMPv1 routers are on a segment, *all* multicast routers on the segment must run IGMPv1. Otherwise, the IGMPv1 routers cannot understand the IGMPv2 messages.

IGMPv2 is enabled by default on Cisco router and firewall interfaces.

PIM: Building a Multicast Distribution Tree

PIM is a routing protocol that can be used to forward multicast traffic. PIM operates independently of any particular IP routing protocol. Therefore, PIM uses the IP unicast routing table and does not keep a separate multicast routing table. (The unicast routing table is itself routing protocol-independent because one or more routing protocols can be used to populate a single table.)

PIM can operate in two modes, depending on the density of the recipients in a multicast group. Cisco has developed a third hybrid mode as well. The PIM modes are as follows:

- **PIM dense mode (PIM-DM)**—Multicast routers assume that multicast recipients are located everywhere, on every router and every router interface. After a tree is built, its branches are pruned if a multicast group has no active recipients.

- **PIM sparse mode (PIM-SM)**—Multicast routers construct a distribution tree by adding branches only as recipients join a multicast group.

- **PIM sparse-dense mode**—Multicast routers operate in dense or sparse mode, depending on how the multicast group is configured.

In addition, two versions of the PIM protocol can be used in a network: PIM version 1 and PIM version 2.

Cisco firewalls running ASA 7.0 or later, as well as FWSM 3.1(1) or later, can operate only in PIM sparse mode, although they can coexist with other routers running PIM-SM or PIM sparse-dense mode.

PIM Sparse Mode

PIM sparse mode takes a "bottom-up" approach to constructing a multicast distribution tree. The tree is built by beginning with the recipients or group members at the end leaf nodes and extending back toward a central root point.

Sparse mode also works on the idea of a shared tree structure, where the root is not necessarily the multicast source. Instead, the root is a PIM-SM router that is centrally located in the network. This root router is called the *rendezvous point* (RP).

The tree from the RP to the group members is actually a subset of the tree that could be drawn from the source to the group members. If a multicast source anywhere in the network can register for group membership with the RP, the tree can be completed end-to-end. Because of this, the sparse mode tree is called a *shared tree*.

NOTE   Sparse mode multicast flows are designated by a (source,destination) pair. The letters S and G represent a specific source and group, respectively. An asterisk (*) can also be used to represent any source or destination. For example, multicast flows over the shared tree are described as (*,G) because the shared tree allows any source to send to a group G.

Section 3-4

In PIM-SM, the shared tree is built using the following basic sequence of steps:

1. A recipient host joins a multicast group by sending an IGMP Membership Report to the local router.

2. The router adds an (*,G) entry in its own multicast routing table, where G represents the group IP address. The router also maintains a list of outbound interfaces where group recipients are located.

3. The router sends a PIM Join request for (*,G) toward the RP at the tree's root.

4. The neighboring PIM router receives the Join request, adds a (*,G) entry in its own table, and adds the arriving interface to its list of outbound interfaces for the group. The neighboring PIM router then relays the Join request toward the RP.

5. When the RP finally receives the PIM Join request, it too adds a (*,G) entry and the arriving interface to its own table. The shared tree has now been built from a recipient host to the RP.

For example, consider the network shown in Figure 3-16. A firewall separates a public and private network and also acts as the RP for PIM multicast routing. Three receivers (end-user hosts) in the network join a single multicast group in preparation to receive traffic from a multicast source.

Figure 3-16   *A Sample Network with PIM Multicast Routers*

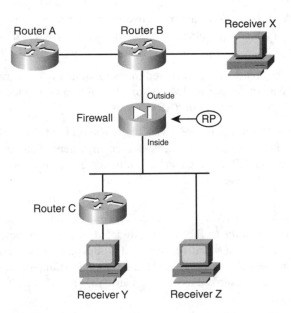

Figure 3-17 illustrates the group membership process. On the left side of the figure, the multicast receivers X, Y, and Z each send an IGMP membership request to join group address 239.0.0.1. Router B receives the request from Receiver X and also creates a multicast route entry (*,239.0.0.1)

that points back toward the receiver. Router B also sends a PIM Join message for (*,239.0.0.1) toward the RP, which adds the link between it and the firewall to the multicast tree.

Figure 3-17   *Building a Shared Multicast Tree with PIM*

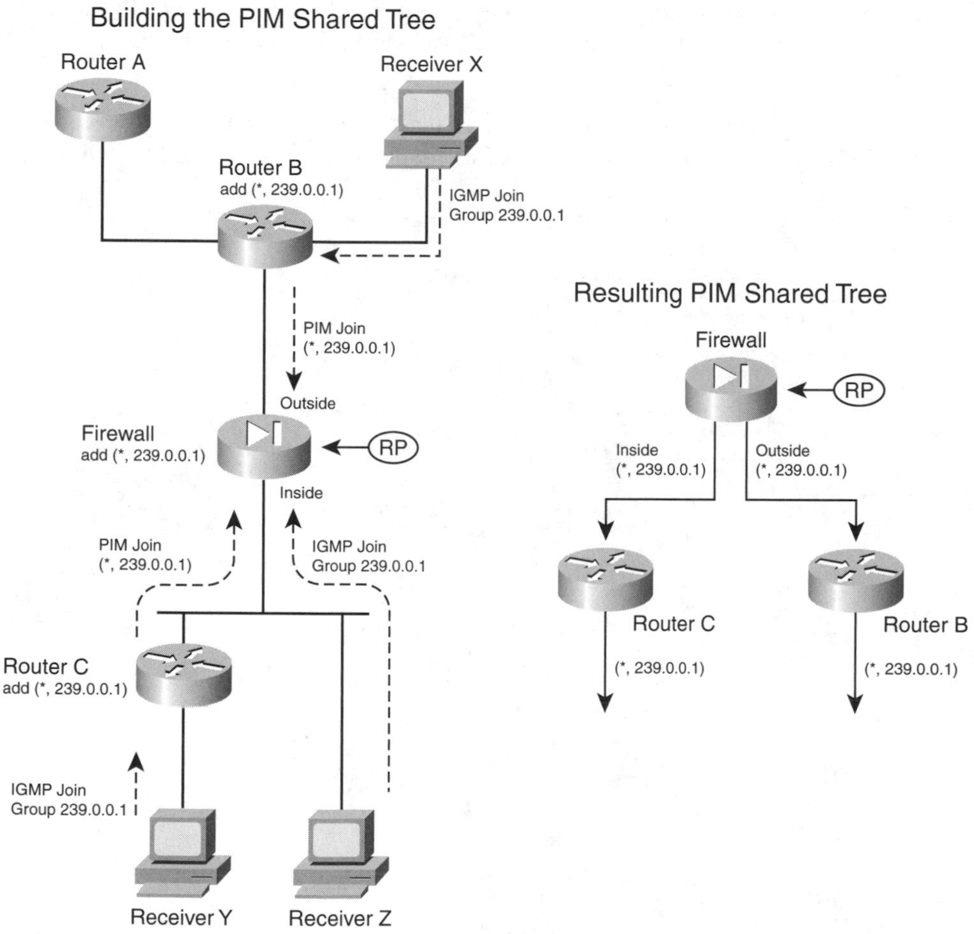

Router C takes similar steps for the IGMP request it receives from Receiver Y. Receiver Z is a slightly different case; the firewall receives its IGMP request directly because it is directly connected. The firewall adds a (*,239.0.0.1) multicast route entry to its table, pointing back toward the receiver on the inside interface.

Notice how all the IGMP membership reports terminate at the closest router (or firewall) while PIM Join messages travel from router to router. After the RP receives all the Join messages, the multicast tree is complete, as shown in the right portion of Figure 3-17. The network topology has been redrawn slightly to show how the RP (firewall) is at the root of the tree. This is called a *PIM shared tree* because it is used by all the devices participating in the multicast group. Routers that have no active multicast group receivers (Router A, for example) do not send a PIM Join message, so they do not become part of the tree.

A shared tree always begins with the RP at the root and progresses downward toward the leaf nodes, where the receivers are located. Only the PIM routers are shown, because they actually build and use the tree. PIM shared trees are always unidirectional. Multicast packets can only start at the RP and be sent toward the receivers.

Finally, a multicast source must also join the group so that traffic can flow toward the receivers. The left portion of Figure 3-18 illustrates this process, where the source is connected to Router C.

Figure 3-18 *Adding a Multicast Source to PIM Trees*

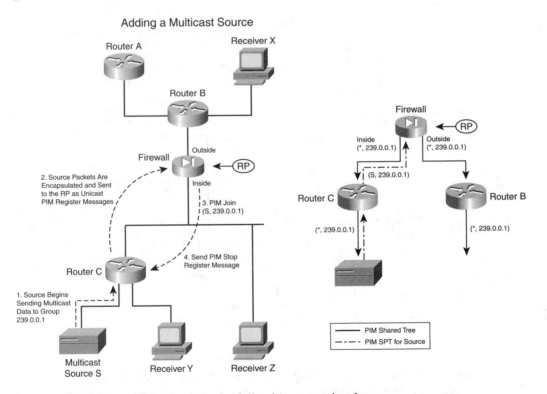

When a source joins a multicast group, the following steps take place:

1. A source S begins sending traffic to the multicast group address (239.0.0.1 in the example). Up to this point, the multicast tree has not been extended to the source. In fact, notice that the source is sending traffic *upstream* toward the RP! In the unidirectional shared tree, this is not allowed. This point is dealt with in the next few steps.

2. The nearest PIM router receives the traffic destined for the multicast group and realizes that it is coming from a source. The router must register the source with the RP so that it can become a part of the tree. The multicast packets are encapsulated in PIM Register messages that are sent to the RP as *unicasts*.

3. The RP unencapsulates the Register messages and sends the original multicast packets down the tree toward the receivers.

   The RP also sends an (S,G) PIM Join message downstream toward the source address so that a tree can be built from the source to the RP. In the example, this is a (S,239.0.0.1) multicast flow. The idea is to construct a path to carry multicast data from the source to the tree's root (the RP) so that it can flow downward toward the receivers.

NOTE   The tree built from the source to the RP is not a part of the PIM shared tree. Instead, it is called a shortest path tree (SPT) because it follows a path from a router (the RP in this case) directly to the source. Because the SPT is separate from the shared tree, multicast packets can travel upward toward the RP without interfering with packets traveling downward from the RP toward the receivers.

In effect, these are two unidirectional trees with the RP always serving as the root.

---

4. After the SPT has been built from the source to the RP, there is no need to keep encapsulating the source data as Register messages. The RP sends a PIM Register Stop message toward the source. When the leaf node router at the source receives this, it stops sending the Register messages and begins using the new SPT path.

The right portion of Figure 3-18 illustrates the resulting tree structures. The solid arrows show the PIM shared tree, from the RP down to the routers where receivers are located. The broken-line arrows represent the SPT that is built from the source up to the RP.

Although it is not shown in this example, last-hop PIM routers are allowed to perform an *SPT switchover* to attempt to build a more direct path to the multicast source. This process is very similar to the steps described previously, where specific (S,G) flows are added to the PIM routers along the path. After an SPT switchover occurs, the RP is no longer required to be at the root of the tree if a better path can be found.

To simplify the tree structure and improve efficiency, PIM can also support a bidirectional mode. If every PIM router supporting a multicast group is configured for bidirectional mode, a single multicast tree is formed to connect the multicast source to all its receivers.

Multicast packets can flow up or down the tree as necessary to disperse in the network. The PIM routers take on designated forwarder (DF) roles, deciding whether to forward multicast packets onto a network segment in the appropriate direction. Because a single bidirectional tree is used, the multicast source can join the group without the PIM source registration process.

Section 3-4

PIM RP Designation

In PIM sparse mode, every PIM router must know the RP's identity (IP address). After all, each router has to send PIM Join/Prune messages toward the RP by using its unicast routing table to find the correct interface.

The simplest method of identifying the RP is to manually configure its address in each PIM router. If there are not many PIM routers to configure, this method is very straightforward. However, if there are many PIM routers or if the RP address is likely to change in the future, manual configuration can be cumbersome.

NOTE   Beginning with ASA 7.0 and FWSM 3.1(1), static RP configuration is the only option available. Other more dynamic RP discovery methods are described in this section because they might be used on PIM routers in your network.

Cisco also provides a proprietary means to automatically inform PIM-SM routers of the appropriate RP for a group. This is known as *Auto-RP*. Routers that can potentially become an RP are configured as *candidate RPs*. These routers advertise their capability over the *Cisco-RP-Announce* multicast address 224.0.1.39.

These announcements are picked up by one or more centrally located and well-connected routers that have been configured to function as *mapping agents*. A mapping agent collects and sends RP-to-group mapping information to all PIM routers over the *Cisco-RP-Discovery* multicast address 224.0.1.40.

A mapping agent can limit the scope of its RP discovery information by setting the time-to-live (TTL) value in its messages. This limits how many router hops away the information will still be valid. Any PIM router within this space dynamically learns of the candidate RPs that are available to use.

The second version of PIM also includes a dynamic RP-to-group mapping advertisement mechanism. This is known as the *bootstrap router method* and is standards-based.

PIMv2 is similar to the Cisco Auto-RP method. First, a *bootstrap router* (BSR) is identified; this router learns about RP candidates for a group and advertises them to PIM routers. Only the BSR and candidate RPs have to be configured; all other PIM routers learn of the appropriate RP dynamically from the BSR.

These bootstrap messages permeate the entire PIM domain. The scope of the advertisements can be limited by defining PIMv2 border routers, which do not forward the bootstrap messages further.

NOTE If Auto-RP is being used in your network, be aware that an ASA or FWSM firewall cannot participate in the Auto-RP process. The firewall must have the PIM RP address statically configured.

However, the candidate RP announcements over 224.0.1.39 and the Router Discovery messages over 224.0.1.40 can pass *through* the firewall to reach PIM routers on the other side. Therefore, the Auto-RP mechanism can still work across the firewall, but the firewall cannot directly benefit from the dynamic RP discovery itself.

Configuring PIM

Use the following steps to configure PIM multicast routing on a firewall running ASA 7.0 or later, or a FWSM running 3.1(1) or later. Keep in mind that you have to configure explicit access list rules to permit multicast host access through a firewall.

All multicast traffic is subject to normal firewall inspection, with the exception of IGMP, PIM, OSPF, and RIPv2. You do not have to configure address translation for the multicast group addresses, however. The firewall automatically creates an internal identity NAT for addresses such as 239.0.0.1, 239.255.148.199, and so on.

1. Enable multicast routing:

PIX 6.3	—
ASA, FWSM	`Firewall(config)# multicast-routing`

Enabling multicast routing brings up PIM and IGMP on *every* firewall interface.

TIP You can verify the current PIM status on each interface by using the following command:

`Firewall# show pim interface {state-on | state-off}`
For example, a firewall with PIM enabled on its inside and outside interfaces produces the following output:

```
Firewall# show pim interface state-on
Address            Interface      PIM  Nbr   Hello DR    DR
                                       Count Intvl Prior
192.168.198.1      inside         on   1     30    1     192.168.198.4
192.168.93.135     outside        on   1     30    1     this system
Firewall# show pim interface state-off
Address            Interface      PIM  Nbr   Hello DR    DR
                                       Count Intvl Prior
192.168.77.1       dmz            off  0     30    1     not elected
Firewall#
```

---

2. Identify the RP:

PIX 6.3	—
ASA, FWSM	Firewall(config)# **pim rp-address** *ip_address* [*acl_name*] [**bidir**]

The RP is located at *ip_address*. By default, it is used for all 224.0.0.0/4 multicast group addresses. You can use the RP for specific multicast addresses by configuring a standard access list named *acl_name* and applying it in this command.

For example, the following commands can be used to define an RP for group addresses 239.0.0.0 through 239.0.0.15:

```
Firewall(config)# access-list MyGroups standard permit 239.0.0.0  255.255.255.240
Firewall(config)# pim rp-address 192.168.100.1 MyGroups
```

TIP   Because the firewall cannot participate in any dynamic RP discovery methods (Auto-RP or BSR), the RP address must be statically configured. If the firewall will act as the RP itself, use one of the firewall's own interface addresses as the RP address in this command. Then, for other routers, configure a static RP address using the address of the nearest firewall interface. Even though the firewall is configured with only one of its own interfaces as the RP address, it automatically supports the RP function for neighboring PIM routers on all other interfaces.

TIP   By default, the firewall operates in normal PIM sparse mode for the multicast groups and RP. You can add the **bidir** keyword if the RP and its associated PIM routers are operating in bidirectional mode. This allows multicast traffic to move toward and away from the RP in the sparse mode tree.

NOTE   If you configure bidirectional mode on one PIM router (or firewall) in your network, you must configure it on all of them. Otherwise, the bidirectional PIM routers introduce traffic.

3. (Optional) Adjust PIM parameters on a firewall interface.

    a. Specify an interface:

PIX 6.3	—
ASA, FWSM	Firewall(config)# **interface** *if_name*

The interface named *if_name* is selected.

b.   (Optional) Disable multicast support on an interface:

PIX 6.3	—
ASA, FWSM	`Firewall(config-if)#` **`no pim`**

If PIM is disabled on an interface and you need to reenable it, you can use the **pim** interface configuration command.

c.   (Optional) Set the PIM hello period:

PIX 6.3	—
ASA, FWSM	`Firewall(config-if)#` **`pim hello-interval`** *`seconds`*

A firewall periodically sends PIM hello messages on each interface where PIM is enabled. By default, hellos are sent every 30 seconds. You can set the interval to *seconds* (1 to 3600).

NOTE   The PIM hello interval does not have to be configured identically on neighboring routers. This is because each router advertises its own holdtime, or the amount of time a neighbor should wait to receive a hello message before expiring the neighbor relationship. This is usually set to 3 times the hello interval, or a default value of 90 seconds.

The hello interval affects how quickly a PIM neighbor can be discovered and how quickly it is declared unreachable if it becomes unresponsive.

---

d.   (Optional) Set the designated router (DR) priority:

PIX 6.3	—
ASA, FWSM	`Firewall(config-if)#` **`pim dr-priority`** *`priority`*

PIM advertises an interface priority so that connected PIM routers can elect a designated router. By default, a DR priority of 1 is used. You can set this to *priority* (0 to 4294967295). A higher priority is more likely to win the election; in the case of a tie, the router interface with the highest IP address wins.

e.   (Optional) Adjust the Join/Prune message interval:

PIX 6.3	—
ASA, FWSM	`Firewall(config-if)#` **`pim join-prune-interval`** *`seconds`*

Multicast routers must send periodic PIM Join/Prune messages to their upstream neighbors to maintain their position in the multicast tree. The idea is to maintain the forwarding state to a multicast router (or firewall) only if it still has active participants connected; otherwise, the state might be stale and should be flushed.

By default, Join/Prune messages are sent every 60 seconds. You can set this interval to *seconds* (10 to 600) if needed.

TIP   If you decide to change the time interval, be aware that it should be configured identically on all multicast routers participating in PIM. If three Join/Prune messages are missed (180 seconds with the default 60-second interval), the forwarding state is removed. Therefore, all routers should agree on the basic Join/Prune time interval.

---

4. (Optional) Filter PIM Register messages:

PIM Register messages are sent by first-hop DRs to the RP to inform it that a multicast source exists. The original multicast packets sent by the source are encapsulated and sent as unicast Register messages.

You can filter the PIM Register messages so that you have better control over where legitimate multicast sources or servers can be located and permitted to operate.

a.   Define a filter:

PIX 6.3	—
ASA, FWSM	`Firewall(config)# ` **`access-list`** ` acl_name ` **`extended {permit |`** **`deny}`** ` ip ` `src_ip src_mask dest_ip dest_mask` or `Firewall(config)# ` **`route-map`** ` map_name ` **`permit`** ` [sequence]` `Firewall(config-route-map)# ` **`match {interface`** ` if_name ` **`| ip`** **`address`** `   acl_name}`

You can filter Register messages based on any combination of the source address (first-hop DR address) and destination address (RP). Keep in mind that PIM Register messages are unicast to the RP and are not sent to the multicast group address.

You can define the filter using an extended access list or route map. Only Register messages that are permitted by the ACL or route map are allowed to reach their destination at the RP.

b.   Apply the filter to PIM:

PIX 6.3	—
ASA, FWSM	`Firewall(config)# ` **`pim accept-register {list`** ` acl_name ` **`| route-map`** `map_name}`

For example, you could use the following commands to allow the first-hop router 192.168.10.10 to register a directly connected multicast source with the RP located at 192.168.1.10:

```
Firewall(config)# access-list RegFilter extended permit ip host 192.168.10.10
   host 192.168.1.10
Firewall(config)# pim accept-register list RegFilter
```

5. (Optional) Prevent SPT switchover:

PIX 6.3	—
ASA, FWSM	Firewall(config)# pim spt-threshold infinity [group-list acl_name]

Multicast routers normally form a shared tree structure with the RP as the root. Multicast traffic must travel from the source through the RP and then on to the receivers.

By default, last-hop or leaf node routers with directly connected multicast receivers can (and do) join an SPT by sending a Join message directly to the multicast source. In effect, the resulting SPT has the fewest router hops from source to receiver and might not include the RP.

This can be useful if the RP is not located strategically or if the RP introduces latency with the multicast traffic passing through it. However, you might not want the tree structure to be altered for one or more multicast groups in your network. When the firewall is acting as a last-hop PIM router, you can prevent it from switching over to an SPT by using this command.

If you use the **infinity** keyword with no other arguments, the firewall must stay with the shared tree for all its groups. Otherwise, you can configure a standard access list that permits the specific multicast group addresses that should be kept on the shared tree. Apply the access list with the **group-list** *acl_name* keywords. The firewall is allowed to switch over to an SPT for all other groups.

6. (Optional) Define a static multicast route to a source:

In normal operation, a firewall running PIM dynamically builds a table of multicast "routes" based on the PIM and IGMP membership requests it receives. Multicast routes (mroutes) represent how multicast traffic is forwarded to group addresses—from a source address to a destination interface.

You can define static mroute entries to override or supplement the dynamic entries with the following command:

PIX 6.3	Firewall(config)# mroute src smask in_if_name dst dmask out_if_name
ASA, FWSM	Firewall(config)# mroute src mask in_if_name out_if_name [distance]

A static multicast route correlates a multicast source address with its Class D multicast group address. The firewall can then inspect and forward traffic from the source on one interface to recipients (and multicast routers) on another interface.

The multicast source is identified by its IP address *src*, subnet mask *smask* (usually 255.255.255.255), and the firewall interface named *in_if_name* where it connects. The multicast destination is the actual Class D group IP address *dst*, subnet mask *dmask*, and the firewall interface named *out_if_name* where recipients are located.

Section 3-4

Beginning with ASA 7.0 and FWSM 3.1(1), only the *out_if_name* is given. Notice that this form of the command resembles a reverse path rather than a traditional unicast static route. In other words, the mroute is defined by its source and not by a destination. Its only function is to define how a multicast source can be reached, independent of the normal unicast routing information.

On an ASA or FWSM, you can also specify an administrative *distance* (0 to 255; the default is 0) to influence how the firewall performs its RPF check. Normally, RPF involves checking the unicast routing table on the firewall, but a static mroute configuration overrides that. You can prefer other sources of routing information by adjusting the mroute distance, where a lower distance is more trusted or preferable.

Table 3-4 lists the default administrative distance assigned to routes on a firewall.

Table 3-4 *Default Administrative Distances by Route Type*

Source	Distance
mroute static route default	0
Directly connected interface	0
Static route entry	1
EIGRP summary route	5
EIGRP internal	90
OSPF	110
RIP	120
EIGRP external	170

For example, if the unicast routes learned through static **route** commands or directly connected interface addresses should be trusted more than the **mroute** entry for RPF, you could use the following command:

```
Firewall(config)# mroute 10.1.1.10 255.255.255.255 inside 10
```

Here, the multicast source is located on the inside interface at 10.1.1.10, and all multicast receivers are located on the outside interface. The administrative distance of 10 still makes this entry more preferable for RPF than unicast routes learned through RIP or OSPF.

Using a Multicast Boundary to Segregate Domains

IP Multicast address space is broken down into several ranges, each reserved for a different function. Some ranges, such as link-local addresses and administratively scoped addresses, are not meant to be routed across Layer 3 boundaries. Others, such as globally scoped addresses, are free to be routed anywhere—across organizational boundaries and across the Internet.

Administratively scoped addresses (239.0.0.0 through 239.255.255.255) are analogous to the private address ranges defined in RFC 1918. These addresses are locally significant, so it is not unusual to find the same addresses appearing in many different locations or organizations. What happens when

RP routers, each supporting its own administratively scope address range, become neighbors so that they begin sharing a multicast routing domain? Now multiple instances of the 239.0.0.0/8 multicast range exist, and the routing to that range becomes ambiguous.

If an ASA running 7.2(1) or later is located between multicast domains, you can configure it to act as a multicast boundary. In this role, the ASA matches multicast group addresses against an access list and blocks all multicast traffic in any direction except the addresses permitted by the access list. You can use the following steps to configure a multicast boundary.

1. Block multicast traffic in a standard access list:

   asa(config)# **access-list** *acl_name* **deny** *mcast_addr mask*

   The range of multicast group addresses to be stopped at the boundary is defined by *mcast_addr* and *mask*. The subnet mask should be given in the usual subnet mask format—not as an inverse mask used in Cisco IOS platforms. For example, you can identify the entire administratively scoped range by the following command:

   asa(config)# **access-list mcast_boundary deny 239.0.0.0 255.0.0.0**

2. Permit other multicast traffic in the standard access list:

   asa(config)# **access-list** *acl_name* **permit** *mcast_addr mask*

   As soon as the administratively scoped range has been identified and denied in step 1, you can identify any or all other multicast addresses to be permitted. For example, you can permit the full range of multicast address space (224.0.0.0 through 239.255.255.255) with the following command:

   asa(config)# **access-list mcast_boundary permit 224.0.0.0 240.0.0.0**

3. Apply the standard access list to the boundary interface:

   asa(config)# **interface** *if_name*
   asa(config-if)# **multicast boundary** *acl_name* [**filter-autorp**]

   You can add the **filter-autorp** keyword to have the ASA filter any Auto-RP discovery and announcement messages that attempt to cross the multicast boundary, too. This prevents a PIM router on one side of the boundary from becoming an RP on the other side for the denied multicast address range.

   As an example, an ASA's outside interface on ethernet0/0 could be made into a multicast boundary with the following command:

   asa(config)# **interface ethernet0/0**
   asa(config-if)# **multicast boundary mcast_boundary filter-autorp**

Filtering PIM Neighbors

An ASA can also be configured to prevent multicast routers on one interface from establishing a PIM neighbor relationship with multicast routers on other interfaces. In this role, the ASA filters PIM messages coming from source addresses identified by an access list. You might want to use this feature to prevent rogue or unauthorized routers from becoming PIM neighbors with your protected multicast routers.

You can use the following steps to configure PIM neighbor filtering:

1. Define an access list to filter PIM router source addresses:

```
asa(config)# access-list acl_name {permit | deny} ip_addr mask
```

Use the **permit** keyword to allow PIM messages to or from the IP addresses defined by *ip_addr mask*. The **deny** keyword can be used to filter or block PIM messages to or from specific addresses. For example, the following commands permit only outside multicast routers 10.10.1.10 and 10.10.1.20 to become PIM neighbors with inside routers. All other router addresses are filtered automatically because of the implicit **deny** at the end of the access list.

```
asa(config)# access-list pimneighbors permit 10.10.1.10 255.255.255.255
asa(config)# access-list pimneighbors permit 10.10.1.20 255.255.255.255
```

2. Apply the access list to a PIM neighbor filter on an ASA interface:

```
asa(config)# interface if_name
asa(config-if)# pim neighbor-filter acl_name
```

As an example, the access list from Step 1 could be applied to the outside interface (ethernet0/0) with the following commands:

```
asa(config)# interface ethernet0/0
asa(config-if)# pim neighbor-filter pimneighbors
```

Filtering Bidirectional PIM Neighbors

ASA 7.0 introduced the ability to enable PIM sparse mode neighbor relationships to form through an ASA. Beginning with ASA 7.2(1), bidirectional PIM relationships can also form through an ASA. In addition, you can configure an ASA to filter bidirectional neighbors so that you can control which multicast routers can participate in a bidirectional tree and a DF election.

You can use the following steps to configure a bidirectional PIM neighbor filter:

1. Define an access list to filter bidirectional PIM router source addresses:

```
asa(config)# access-list acl_name {permit | deny} ip_addr mask
```

Use the **permit** keyword to allow PIM messages to or from the IP addresses defined by *ip_addr mask*. The **deny** keyword can be used to filter or block PIM messages to or from specific addresses.

2. Apply the access list to a PIM bidirectional neighbor filter on an interface:

```
asa(config)# interface if_name
asa(config-if)# pim bidir-neighbor-filter acl_name
```

Configuring Stub Multicast Routing (SMR)

A firewall can be configured to participate as a stub multicast router. In this case, it acts as a proxy between fully functional PIM routers and multicast participants. Only IGMP messages are relayed between firewall interfaces; PIM routing is not used. In fact, as soon as SMR is configured, any existing **pim rp-address** commands for multicast routing are automatically removed from the configuration.

This is the only multicast function available in PIX release 6.3. It is optional in ASA releases if PIM is undesirable. The steps for configuring SMR are as follows:

1. Define the proxy agent (stub router).

   a. Enable multicast support toward multicast routers:

ASA, FWSM	—
PIX 6.x	Firewall(config)# **multicast interface** *if_name*

   The IGMP proxy agent becomes active on the firewall interface named *if_name*, where the multicast routers can be found. If a multicast source is on the outside, the outside interface should be used here. (This command is not necessary for IGMP proxy on an ASA platform.)

   b. (Optional) Add static multicast routes if the multicast source is on the inside:

ASA, FWSM	Firewall(config)# **mroute** *src mask in_if_name* **dense** *out_if_name* [*distance*]
PIX 6.3	Firewall(config-multicast)# **mroute** *src smask in_if_name dst dmask out_if_name*

   Use this command when a multicast source is on an internal firewall interface sending traffic to recipients on the outside. Because the firewall isolates any multicast routing between the recipients and the internal source, static routes must be configured.

   A static multicast route correlates a multicast source with its Class D multicast group address. The firewall can then inspect and forward traffic from the source on one interface to recipients (and multicast routers) on another interface.

   The multicast source is identified by its IP address *src*, subnet mask *smask* (usually 255.255.255.255), and the firewall interface named *in_if_name* where it connects. The multicast destination is the actual Class D group IP address *dst*, subnet mask *dmask*, and the firewall interface named *out_if_name* where recipients are located.

   Beginning with ASA 7.0(1), you must provide the *out_if_name* along with the **dense** keyword. Notice that this form of the command resembles a reverse path rather than a traditional unicast static route. In other words, the **mroute** is defined by its source and not by a destination. In fact, the multicast destination address is not specified.

With ASA releases, you can also specify an administrative *distance* (0 to 255; the default is 0) to influence how the firewall performs its RPF check. Normally, RPF involves checking the unicast routing table on the firewall, but a static **mroute** configuration overrides that. You can prefer other sources of routing information by adjusting the mroute distance, where a lower distance is more trusted or preferable.

Table 3-5 lists the default administrative distance assigned to routes on a firewall.

Table 3-5 *Administrative Distance by Route Type*

Source	Distance
mroute static route default	0
Directly connected interface	0
Static route entry	1
OSPF	110
RIP	120

For example, if the unicast routes learned through static **route** commands or directly connected interface addresses should be trusted more than the **mroute** entry for RPF, the following command could be used:

```
Firewall(config)# mroute 10.1.1.10 255.255.255.255 inside dense outside 10
```

Here, the multicast source is located on the inside interface at 10.1.1.10, and all multicast receivers are located on the outside interface. The administrative distance of 10 still makes this entry more preferable for RPF than unicast routes learned through RIP or OSPF.

2. (Optional) Configure multicast support for the recipients.

a. Enable multicast support on an interface where recipients are located:

ASA, FWSM	—
PIX 6.3	`Firewall(config)# multicast interface interface_name`

The IGMP proxy agent becomes active on the firewall interface named *interface_name*. This is usually the "inside" interface, closest to the multicast recipients. You can also use this command to configure multicast support on other firewall interfaces. (This command is not necessary for IGMP proxy on an ASA or FWSM platform.)

b. Enable the IGMP forwarding proxy:

ASA, FWSM	`Firewall(config)# interface in_if_name` `Firewall(config-if)# igmp forward interface if_name`
PIX 6.3	`Firewall(config-multicast)# igmp forward interface if_name`

The proxy agent listens for IGMP join and leave requests on the multicast interface and relays them to multicast routers on the interface named *if_name*. This is usually the outside interface, although you can repeat the command if recipients are located on other interfaces, too.

In ASA and FWSM releases, this command is used in interface configuration mode on the interface (*in_if_name*, such as GigabitEthernet1) that will forward IGMP traffic to recipients on interface *if_name* (**inside**, for example). For example, to forward IGMP from the inside interface (GigabitEthernet1) to recipients located on the outside interface (GigabitEthernet0), you would use the following commands:

```
Firewall(config)# interface GigabitEthernet1
Firewall(config-if)# description Inside
Firewall(config-if)# igmp forward interface outside
```

Configuring IGMP Operation

IGMP is used on firewall interfaces to handle multicast group membership for directly connected hosts. You can use the following configuration steps to tune or change the IGMP operation:

1. Select an interface to tune:

ASA, FWSM	`Firewall(config)# interface if_name`
PIX 6.3	`Firewall(config)# multicast interface if_name`

All subsequent IGMP configuration commands are applied to the interface you specify.

2. (Optional) Disable IGMP on the interface:

ASA, FWSM	`Firewall(config-if)# no igmp`
PIX 6.3	—

On ASA and FWSM platforms, IGMP is enabled on all firewall interfaces as soon as the **multicast-routing** command is used. You can use the **no igmp** command if you need to disable IGMP on the interface because no multicast hosts are present or allowed.

3. (Optional) Set the IGMP version:

ASA, FWSM	`Firewall(config-if)# igmp version {1	2}`
PIX 6.3	`Firewall(config-multicast)# igmp version {1	2}`

By default, a firewall communicates with hosts using IGMP version 2. You can change this to version 1 if needed. The IGMP version should match the capabilities of the recipient hosts.

4. (Optional) Tune IGMP query operation.

    a. (Optional) Set the IGMP query interval:

ASA, FWSM	Firewall(config-if)# **igmp query-interval** *seconds*
PIX 6.3	Firewall(config-multicast)# **igmp query-interval** *seconds*

This specifies how often, in seconds, the firewall sends IGMP query messages to the hosts to determine group memberships. The *seconds* value can be 1 to 3600; the PIX 6.3 default is 60 seconds, and the ASA and FWSM defaults are 125 seconds.

    b. (Optional) Set the maximum query response time:

ASA, FWSM	Firewall(config-if)# **igmp query-max-response-time** *seconds*
PIX 6.3	Firewall(config-multicast)# **igmp query-max-response-time** *seconds*

This command is used to determine how long the router waits for a response from a host about group membership. The default is 10 seconds. If a host does not respond quickly enough, you can lengthen this time value to *seconds* (1 to 25).

    c. (Optional) Set the querier response timer:

ASA, FWSM	Firewall(config-if)# **igmp query-timeout** *seconds*
PIX 6.3	—

By default, the firewall waits 255 seconds to hear from the current IGMP querier before it takes over that role. You can adjust the query timeout to *seconds* (60 to 300).

5. (Optional) Set limits on multicast group membership.

    a. (Optional) Limit the number of hosts per multicast group:

ASA, FWSM	Firewall(config-if)# **igmp limit** *number*
PIX 6.3	—

By default, a firewall maintains the forwarding state of up to 500 multicast recipients per interface. You can limit this further to *number* (1 to 500) hosts.

    b. (Optional) Limit the number of multicast groups supported:

ASA, FWSM	Firewall(config-if)# **igmp max-groups** *number*
PIX 6.3	Firewall(config-multicast)# **igmp max-groups** *number*

By default, up to 500 multicast groups can be supported on a firewall interface. You can change this limit to *number* (0 to 2000) groups if needed.

c. (Optional) Control the groups that hosts can join:

ASA, FWSM	Firewall(config-if)# **igmp access-group** *acl_name*
PIX 6.3	Firewall(config-multicast)# **igmp access-group** *acl_name*

When client hosts or multicast recipients attempt to join a multicast group, the firewall can filter the requests. If you place restrictions on groups, recipients can join only the group addresses that are permitted by the access list named *acl_name*.

TIP   You need to configure an access list before using this command. The access list should be of the following form:

ASA, FWSM	Firewall(config)# **access-list** *acl_name* **standard** {**permit** | **deny**} *group_address group_mask* or Firewall(config)# **access-list** *acl_name* **extended** {**permit** | **deny**} **ip any** *group_address group_mask*
PIX 6.3	Firewall(config)# **access-list** *acl_name* {**permit** | **deny**} **ip any** *group_address group_mask*

TIP   Multicast groups are identified by their Class D multicast addresses, which can be given as a network address and subnet mask. With ASA or FWSM, you can use either a standard or extended access list. In either case, the *group_address* and *group_mask* represent the multicast group.

For example, suppose multicast users on the inside interface should be allowed to join only group addresses 239.0.0.0 through 239.0.0.255. You would use the following commands:

ASA, FWSM	Firewall(config)# **access-list AllowedGroups standard permit ip 239.0.0.0 255.255.255.0** Firewall(config)# **interface GigabitEthernet1** Firewall(config)# **description Inside** Firewall(config-if)# **igmp access-group AllowedGroups**
PIX 6.3	Firewall(config)# **access-list AllowedGroups permit ip any 239.0.0.0 255.255.255.0** Firewall(config)# **multicast interface inside** Firewall(config-multicast)# **igmp access-group AllowedGroups**

Section 3-4

6. (Optional) Configure the firewall to become a member of a multicast group:

ASA, FWSM	`Firewall(config-if)# `**`igmp join-group`**` group-address`
	or
	`Firewall(config-if)# `**`igmp static-group`**` group-address`

PIX 6.3	`Firewall(config-multicast)# `**`igmp join-group`**` group-address`

The **igmp join-group** command allows you to specify a multicast *group-address* (a Class D multicast address) for the firewall interface to join. By joining a group, the firewall interface begins to accept packets sent to the multicast address. Therefore, it becomes a pingable member of the multicast group—something that can be a valuable testing tool.

As soon as the interface joins the group, the firewall also becomes a surrogate client so that multicast traffic can be forwarded to recipients that do not support IGMP. The interface group membership keeps the multicast path alive so that those hosts can continue to receive the traffic from the multicast source.

With ASA or FWSM, you can use the **igmp static-group** command to cause the firewall interface to join a group without actually accepting the multicast traffic itself. Instead, packets sent to the multicast *group-address* are forwarded to any recipients on the interface.

Stub Multicast Routing Example

A firewall separates a multicast source from its recipients. The source is located on the outside interface, and the recipients are on internal networks found on the inside interface. Recipients can join multicast groups only in the 224.3.1.0/24 and 225.1.1.0/24 ranges. The PIX 6.3 configuration commands needed are as follows:

```
Firewall(config)# access-list mcastallowed permit ip any 224.3.1.0 255.255.255.0
Firewall(config)# access-list mcastallowed permit ip any 225.1.1.0 255.255.255.0
Firewall(config)# multicast interface outside
Firewall(config-multicast)# exit
Firewall(config)# multicast interface inside
Firewall(config-multicast)# igmp forward interface outside
Firewall(config-multicast)# igmp access-group mcastallowed
```

Now, consider the same example, where the source and recipients trade places. If the multicast source (192.168.10.1) is located on the inside of the firewall, with recipients on the outside, the configuration could look like the following:

```
Firewall(config)# access-list mcastallowed permit ip any 224.3.1.0 255.255.255.0
Firewall(config)# access-list mcastallowed permit ip any 225.1.1.0 255.255.255.0

Firewall(config)# multicast interface inside
Firewall(config-multicast)# igmp forward interface outside
Firewall(config-multicast)# mroute 192.168.10.1 255.255.255.255 inside 224.3.1.0
  255.255.255.0 outside
Firewall(config-multicast)# mroute 192.168.10.1 255.255.255.255 inside 225.1.1.0
  255.255.255.0 outside
Firewall(config)# multicast interface outside
Firewall(config-multicast)# igmp access-group mcastallowed
```

PIM Multicast Routing Example

An ASA or FWSM is to be configured for PIM multicast routing between its inside and outside interfaces. The firewall acts as the RP for any multicast group address beginning with 239.

You could use the following configuration commands:

```
Firewall(config)# multicast-routing
Firewall(config)# interface GigabitEthernet1
Firewall(config-if)# nameif inside
Firewall(config-if)# security-level 100
Firewall(config-if)# ip address 192.168.198.1 255.255.255.0
Firewall(config-if)# exit
Firewall(config)# access-list PIMgroups standard permit 239.0.0.0 255.0.0.0
Firewall(config)# pim rp-address 192.168.198.1 PIMgroups
```

Verifying IGMP Multicast Operation

You can display the current multicast configuration on a firewall running PIX 6.3 with the **show multicast** command, as shown in the following example:

```
Firewall# show multicast
multicast interface outside
  igmp access-group mcastallowed
multicast interface inside
  igmp forward interface outside
  igmp access-group mcastallowed
Firewall#
```

As soon as multicast is configured and IGMP becomes active on some firewall interfaces, you can display IGMP activity with this EXEC command:

PIX 6.3	Firewall# **show igmp** [*group*] [**detail**]
ASA, FWSM	Firewall# **show igmp groups** [*group_address* | *if_name*] [**detail**]

If you do not use any arguments, the output displays all firewall interfaces configured for multicast. Otherwise, you can specify a multicast *group* or an interface.

In addition, the output displays any currently active multicast groups. For example, the following multicast group addresses are shown to be active with receivers on the inside and outside interfaces of an ASA or FWSM:

```
Firewall# show igmp groups
IGMP Connected Group Membership
Group Address       Interface     Uptime     Expires     Last Reporter
239.0.0.1           inside        1d01h      00:04:16    192.168.198.4
239.255.148.199     inside        1d01h      00:04:14    192.168.198.198
239.255.199.197     inside        1d01h      00:04:15    192.168.198.198
239.255.255.250     inside        1d01h      00:04:16    192.168.198.198
224.0.1.40          outside       1d01h      00:04:01    128.163.93.129
239.0.0.1           outside       1d01h      00:04:00    128.163.93.129
Firewall#
```

You can display the current IGMP settings on a specific firewall interface with this command:

PIX 6.3	Firewall# **show igmp interface** *interface_name* [**detail**]
ASA, FWSM	Firewall# **show igmp interface** *if_name*

The following example provides some sample output from this command:

```
Firewall# show igmp interface inside
inside is up, line protocol is up
  Internet address is 192.168.198.1/24
  IGMP is enabled on interface
  Current IGMP version is 2
  IGMP query interval is 125 seconds
  IGMP querier timeout is 255 seconds
  IGMP max query response time is 10 seconds
  Last member query response interval is 1 seconds
  Inbound IGMP access group is:
  IGMP limit is 500, currently active joins: 4
  Cumulative IGMP activity: 4 joins, 0 leaves
  IGMP querying router is 192.168.198.1 (this system)
Firewall#
```

Verifying PIM Multicast Routing Operation

After you enable multicast routing on an ASA or FWSM, you should verify that it is seeing hello messages from its PIM router neighbors. You can do this with the following command:

PIX 6.3	—
ASA, FWSM	Firewall# **show pim neighbor** [**count** │ **detail**] [*if_name*]

For example, the following output shows that a firewall is communicating with two PIM neighbors located on two different interfaces:

```
Firewall# show pim neighbor
Neighbor Address  Interface     Uptime      Expires DR pri Bidir
192.168.198.4     inside        1d02h       00:01:19 1 (DR)
10.1.93.1         outside       01:54:40    00:01:19 N/A
Firewall#
```

The **Uptime** column shows how long the firewall has been successfully receiving PIM hello messages from the peer router. The firewall must receive the next hello before the time shown in the **Expires** column reaches 0.

TIP   You can also verify that the firewall is sending its own PIM hellos by checking its neighbor status from a directly connected PIM router. For example, the router located on the firewall's outside interface shows the following information about the firewall as a PIM router:

```
Router# show ip pim neighbor
PIM Neighbor Table
Neighbor Address  Interface        Uptime    Expires   Ver  Mode
10.1.93.2    Vlan4                  01:59:15  00:01:34  v2   (DR)
Router#
```

You can display the current multicast routing table with the following command:

PIX 6.3	—
ASA, FWSM	Firewall# **show mroute** [{*group_address* | **active** | **count** | **pruned** | **reserved** | **summary**}]

Finally, a firewall maintains information about the PIM routing topology. This includes entries for each multicast flow that the firewall has received a PIM Join/Prune message about, as well as the flow uptime, RP for the group, firewall interfaces actively forwarding traffic for the flow, and various flags about the flow state.

As a quick summary of multicast flows in the topology table, you can use the following command:

```
Firewall# show pim topology route-count
PIM Topology Table Summary
  No. of group ranges = 6
  No. of (*,G) routes = 6
  No. of (S,G) routes = 2
  No. of (S,G)RPT routes = 2
Firewall#
```

The actual PIM topology information is displayed with the **show pim topology** command, as shown in the following example. Here, the firewall is the RP (192.168.198.1) for several of the multicast groups. A Cisco IP/TV multicast source is located at 192.168.198.198, using multicast group 239.255.199.197 for streaming video and 239.255.148.199 for streaming audio.

```
Firewall# show pim topology
IP PIM Multicast Topology Table
Entry state: (*/S,G)[RPT/SPT] Protocol Uptime Info
Entry flags: KAT - Keep Alive Timer, AA - Assume Alive, PA - Probe Alive,
    RA - Really Alive, LH - Last Hop, DSS - Don't Signal Sources,
    RR - Register Received, SR
(*,224.0.1.40) DM Up: 1d13h RP: 0.0.0.0
JP: Null(never) RPF: ,0.0.0.0 Flags: LH DSS
  outside            1d13h      off LI LH

(*,239.0.0.1) SM Up: 1d13h RP: 192.168.198.1*
JP: Join(never) RPF: Tunnel1,192.168.198.1* Flags: LH
  inside             1d13h      fwd Join(00:02:45) LI
  outside            1d13h      fwd LI LH
```

```
(*,239.255.148.199) SM Up: 1d13h RP: 192.168.198.1*
JP: Join(never) RPF: Tunnel1,192.168.198.1* Flags: LH
  outside             00:00:33  fwd LI LH
  inside              1d13h     fwd Join(00:03:14) LI

(192.168.198.198,239.255.148.199)RPT SM Up: 1d13h RP: 192.168.198.1*
JP: Prune(never) RPF: Tunnel1,192.168.198.1* Flags: KAT(00:02:59) RA RR
  inside              1d13h     off Prune(00:03:14)

(192.168.198.198,239.255.148.199)SPT SM Up: 00:04:00
JP: Join(never) RPF: inside,192.168.198.198* Flags: KAT(00:02:59) RA RR
  No interfaces in immediate olist

(*,239.255.199.197) SM Up: 1d13h RP: 192.168.198.1*
JP: Join(never) RPF: Tunnel1,192.168.198.1* Flags: LH
  outside             00:00:33  fwd LI LH
  inside              1d13h     fwd Join(00:03:20) LI

(192.168.198.198,239.255.199.197)RPT SM Up: 1d13h RP: 192.168.198.1*
JP: Prune(never) RPF: Tunnel1,192.168.198.1* Flags: KAT(00:02:56) RA RR
  inside              1d13h     off Prune(00:03:20)

(192.168.198.198,239.255.199.197)SPT SM Up: 00:04:08
JP: Join(never) RPF: inside,192.168.198.198* Flags: KAT(00:02:56) RA RR
  No interfaces in immediate olist

(*,239.255.255.250) SM Up: 1d13h RP: 192.168.198.1*
JP: Join(never) RPF: Tunnel1,192.168.198.1* Flags: LH
  outside             00:01:23  fwd LI LH
  inside              1d13h     fwd Join(00:02:59) LI
Firewall#
```

Each multicast flow is listed as (*,G), (S,G), or (S,G)RPT, where * means any source, **S** is a specific source address, and **G** is the multicast group address. In addition, the following values are shown:

- **Multicast protocol**—**SM** (sparse mode, used for most flows) or **DM** (dense mode).
- **Flow uptime**—The time elapsed since the flow was first created.
- **RP**—The address of the RP for the flow or group.
- **JP**—Join or Prune activity.
- **RPF**—Reverse path forwarding entry, or the interface where multicast data is expected to arrive.

In the example, the RPF is often shown as **Tunnel1,192.168.198.1**. In this case, the firewall acts as the RP, and bidirectional mode is not used. Therefore, the multicast data must pass from the source to the RP over an SPT to the RP before being forwarded down the shared PIM tree. The "tunnel" is a logical interface within the firewall that points back to the source.

- **Flags**—Various flags representing the flow's state.
- **Interface information**—A list of interfaces involved in the flow, their current forwarding state (**fwd** or **off**), and the most recent Join or Prune event with the elapsed time.

NOTE   The firewall automatically creates a multicast flow for (*,224.0.1.40), which is used for Cisco Auto-RP Discovery messages. The flow is listed as **DM** because it is a hop-by-hop announcement that does not depend on a sparse mode RP. To dynamically discover an RP, the discovery protocol cannot rely on an RP.

In the example, two multicast flows of interest are shaded. The first, (***,239.255.199.197**), represents the multicast flow from any source to group 239.255.199.197. This is the video stream of data being pushed down the shared multicast tree toward the receivers that have joined the group.

Note that the RPF or the source of the data is listed as **Tunnel1,192.168.198.1**, which is the firewall's inside interface. The firewall is acting as the RP, so it is receiving multicast data from the source over a special internal "tunnel" interface.

The second flow, (**192.168.198.198,239.255.199.197**)**SPT**, represents the multicast flow from the source (192.168.198.198) to the multicast group. This data is actually being fcd to the RP over an SPT built for this purpose—hence the **SPT** designation in the flow descriptor. The RPF points to the inside interface, where the source is located.

Refer to the following sections for information about these topics:

- **4-1: Using Security Contexts to Make Virtual Firewalls**—Presents the configuration steps needed to make one physical firewall platform emulate multiple virtual firewalls.

- **4-2: Managing the Flash File System**—Explains the types of images that are stored in nonvolatile firewall memory and how to work with them.

- **4-3: Managing Configuration Files**—Presents the methods you can use to configure firewalls and manage their configuration files.

- **4-4: Automatic Updates with an Auto Update Server**—Discusses a way to leverage a central server to update image and configuration files on multiple firewalls automatically.

- **4-5: Managing Administrative Sessions**—Presents the configuration steps necessary to permit administrative users to access a firewall for configuration, monitoring, or troubleshooting.

- **4-6: Firewall Reloads and Crashes**—Discusses how to perform a controlled firewall reload or reboot. After an unexpected firewall crash, you can also examine "post mortem" information about the cause of the crash.

- **4-7: Monitoring a Firewall with SNMP**—Explains Simple Network Management Protocol (SNMP) and how it can be used to obtain system information from a firewall.

CHAPTER 4

Firewall Management

Any firewall that is deployed in a network must also be managed. Firewall administrators need to be able to make configuration changes, define virtual firewall contexts for other entities, maintain the firewall operating system and configuration files, and monitor firewall operation.

This chapter presents the configuration steps and background information you need to perform these management functions.

4-1: Using Security Contexts to Make Virtual Firewalls

On Adaptive Security Applianace (ASA) and Firewall Services Module (FWSM) platforms, you can configure one physical firewall chassis to act as multiple virtual firewalls. Each virtual firewall is called a *context* because it is one partition or instance of a fully functional firewall.

Even though all the configured contexts are emulated by a single firewall CPU, the traffic inspection and security policies of each are kept separate, as if they were being handled by a dedicated physical firewall. Therefore, each context can be configured and managed by different administrators, or they can all be managed by one administrator who has access to them.

Traditionally, one physical firewall would be added to a network every time a new firewall function was needed. The cost of adding firewalls in this way is incremental. The ability to run multiple security contexts on a single firewall provides a way to limit the cost of firewall hardware. Firewall contexts can be added according to license limits. This capability does come with a trade-off, however, because all contexts must share the resources available on the hardware platform.

Security contexts can be useful in both service provider and enterprise environments. A service provider can partition one physical firewall into multiple security contexts that can be assigned to customers for a recurring cost. Each customer can configure and manage his or her respective context.

In an enterprise setting, multiple contexts could be assigned to individual departments or organizations where there is no overlap in security policies. Each department would operate its own firewall context independently of others. On the "public" side of each firewall, each context could connect to a shared or common Internet feed.

Security Context Organization

A Cisco firewall that can support security contexts can operate in only one of the following modes:

- **Single-context security mode**—One context is configured on one physical firewall platform. This is the traditional or default mode of operation.

- **Multiple-context security mode**—Two or more contexts can be configured on one physical firewall.

In multiple-context security mode, a firewall is organized into the following functions, each having its own user interface:

- **System execution space**—A special area where individual contexts are defined and physical firewall resources are mapped to them. Because the system execution space does not use security policies and cannot provide network connectivity, it cannot really function as a true firewall context.

- **Administrative context**—A fully functional virtual firewall that is used mainly to manage the physical firewall. You can configure security policies, network addressing and routing, and any other firewall function needed for administrative use. This context operates independently of any other context.

- **User contexts**—Fully functional virtual firewalls that can be configured and handed over to a third party if needed. Each user context can have its own security policies, network addressing, access control, and so on. Almost anything that can be configured on a single-firewall platform can be configured on a user context.

Figure 4-1 shows how a single physical firewall can be organized to provide multiple security contexts. Each context has its own set of virtual firewall interfaces that are mapped from the physical or VLAN firewall interfaces.

In practice, the physical firewall platform might not have enough interfaces to be able to map them one-to-one with context interfaces. In Figure 4-1, the firewall would need two unique physical interfaces for each context! Even if there were enough interfaces to go around, you might not want to use all of them in the first place when only a few could provide the necessary connectivity.

Sharing Context Interfaces

Multiple-context mode allows some flexibility in mapping interfaces. You can map one physical interface to one context interface when isolation from other firewalls is required.

You can also map one physical interface to several context interfaces so that the contexts share a single connection. This might be practical in an enterprise setting, where each context is designated for a different department. Most likely, an enterprise would have a single path toward the public Internet. Every department would share that path, provided by one physical firewall interface. As that interface is mapped to each context, the resulting logical or mapped interface would become the context's outside interface. Figure 4-2 illustrates this concept.

Physical interfaces can be shared in any configuration. For example, if two firewall contexts need to provide access to some authentication servers that they share, one physical interface could be mapped to those two contexts and no others.

Figure 4-1 *Single- and Multiple-Context Security Modes*

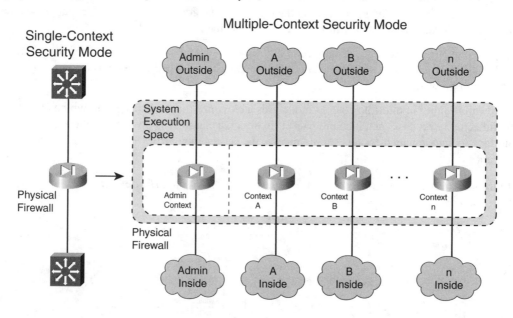

Figure 4-2 *Mapping Common Interfaces to Contexts*

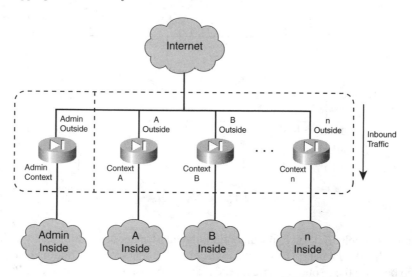

Finally, consider that all contexts are really emulated by one firewall platform. As packets enter a physical firewall interface, the firewall CPU must determine which context is the true destination.

If one physical interface is mapped to one context interface, the firewall CPU simply takes packets arriving on that interface and puts them in the queue for that context interface. The mapped context must be the virtual firewall that will inspect and handle the inbound traffic.

Suppose one physical interface is mapped to interfaces in several contexts. Now when packets arrive on that interface, the firewall CPU must decide which of the mapped contexts is the correct destination firewall.

A firewall running in multiple-context mode uses a *classifier* function to sort out which context should actually process each inbound packet. In effect, a classifier is positioned at each firewall interface to decide which context should receive packets as they arrive. Figure 4-3 illustrates this concept.

Figure 4-3 *Using a Packet Classifier to Match Inbound Traffic to a Security Context*

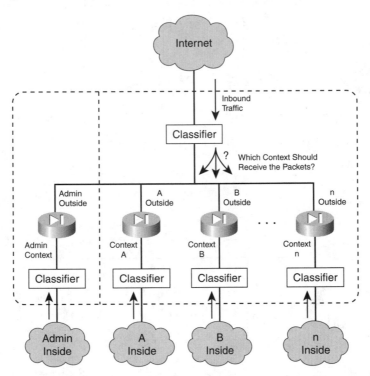

The classifier is simple; if it can find a unique source interface or destination address, it has enough information to hand off a packet to a context. The classifiers shown at the bottom of Figure 4-3 have an easy job because their source interfaces are mapped to a single unique context. Packets arriving on the inside interfaces are passed directly to the respective context inside interfaces to begin the normal firewall stateful inspection process.

However, if firewall interfaces are shared between contexts, as in the topmost interface shown in Figure 4-3, the problem becomes a bit more difficult. The classifier at the top of the figure is faced with the task of finding a unique destination context for each inbound packet.

A classifier does this by attempting to find the packet destination address defined in one of the connected contexts. The destination address must be uniquely identified in one of the following ways:

- A global address defined in a static NAT entry
- A global address used in an xlate entry
- A firewall interface address (used when packets are destined for the firewall itself)

A classifier also works in only one direction. Each packet that arrives on a shared interface is examined so that it can be sent to a specific context. Because of this, you should work through scenarios with a connection originating on each side of the firewall to make sure that the classifier process will work properly. The classifier must find the destination address as a global address entry in one (and only one) of the security contexts.

For example, Figure 4-4 shows a simple arrangement in which two security contexts are configured to share their outside interfaces toward the public network. The left side of the figure shows what happens when a connection is initiated from inside host 192.168.1.100 to outside host 198.133.219.25. Because the inside context interfaces are not shared, the classifier nearest to the inside host can simply send the packets to Context A, where the host is connected. At Context A, the inside address is translated to global address 207.246.96.47, because of a static NAT configuration.

For the return traffic from the outside host, the classifier examines arriving packets on the shared outside interfaces. The destination address is 207.246.96.47, which is found as a global address in the xlate table on Context A. Therefore, traffic originating on the inside network can make the round trip successfully.

On the right side of Figure 4-4, a connection originates from the outside host, located on the shared interfaces. Here, the destination address 207.246.96.47 is again found as a global address in a static NAT xlate entry on Context A. This traffic too can make the round trip.

What if a dynamic NAT or PAT were used instead of a static NAT? In that case, the dynamic NAT would be configured to use one or more global addresses during translation. In Figure 4-4, the global address is 207.246.96.46, which could be found in xlate entries for connections passing through Context A. The classifiers on either side of the firewall would have no problem finding the global address on Context A.

Issues with Sharing Context Interfaces

If you decide to share the inside context interfaces, you should be aware of a classifier limitation. Consider the arrangement shown in Figure 4-5, where Contexts A and B share their inside interfaces.

The classifier must examine packets entering from the inside networks to decide which context should receive them. A search is made to find the packet destination addresses in the context xlate tables. In particular, the classifier can find only global addresses in the tables. This means that there must already be a static NAT entry in place for the *outside* address to appear as a global address.

Figure 4-4   *Example of Sharing Outside Context Interfaces*

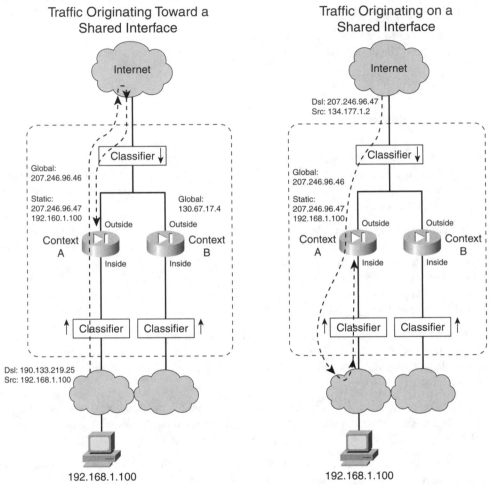

In practice, this is seldom successful. The outside context interface usually points toward a public network such as the Internet, where most or all of the addresses exist but are not configured into the context. Usually, a default route points the way toward the public network where a context can find every other host that is not explicitly configured. However, the classifier must use actual global addresses, not routes, so it cannot determine which context to use to reach outside hosts.

To remedy this situation, you would have to configure static NAT entries for each of the outside host addresses that might be involved in connections from the inside hosts! That might result in two extremes:

- The list of outside hosts would be too small to be practical for the inside users.

- The number of outside hosts would be much too great to try to configure.

Figure 4-5   *Example of Sharing Inside Context Interfaces*

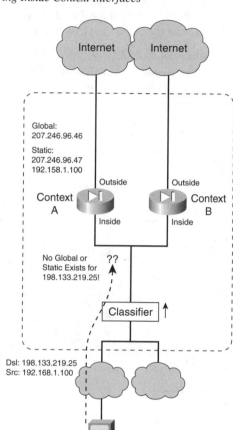

In most cases, the inside context interfaces are not shared because inside networks tend to be isolated and protected from every other network. However, another scenario deserves consideration. With multiple security contexts at your disposal, you might consider nesting or cascading contexts to provide layers or shells of security in an enterprise network.

Consider Figure 4-6, in which the left portion represents such a hierarchy of security contexts. The topmost context might be used at the boundary with the Internet to provide common security policies for the entire enterprise. Then other contexts might be nested below that to serve individual departments or buildings within the enterprise.

To test this scenario, the structure has been reduced on the right portion of the figure to show a cascade of just two security contexts. This turns out to be very similar to the previous example, in which the inside context interfaces were shared. However, it might not be obvious that the middle classifier is positioned where two context interfaces are shared. The Context A inside interface is shared with the Context B outside interface to build the cascading structure.

Again, when packets originating from the inside hosts reach this classifier, chances are that no static NAT or global address will be configured or found for outside Internet hosts. Therefore, that classifier cannot decide whether to send the packets to Context A or back to Context B.

As a result, you should plan on nesting or cascading security contexts only if you can provide static NAT entries for each outside host that inside hosts will be allowed to contact. Otherwise, you can build a nested arrangement from separate physical security appliance platforms, where classifiers are not needed between firewalls or contexts.

Figure 4-6 *Example of Nesting Security Contexts*

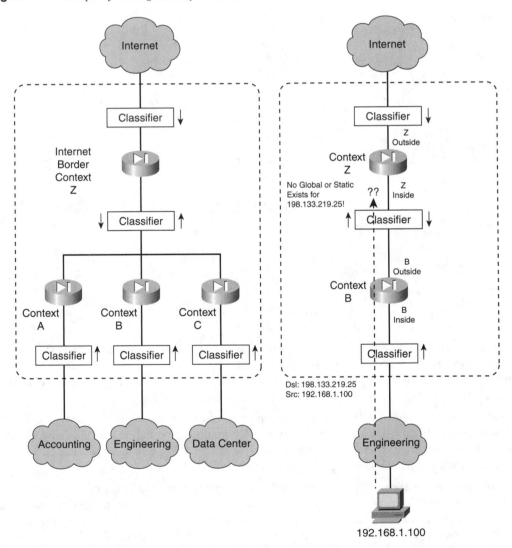

Solving Shared Context Interface Issues with Unique MAC Addresses

By default, every physical ASA interface uses its burned-in address (BIA) as its Media Access Control (MAC) address. Also, every subinterface of a physical interface uses the physical interface's MAC address. After the ASA is configured for multiple context mode, system context interfaces (both physical and subinterfaces) are allocated to other contexts. This means that the MAC address of a system context interface is reused on each of its associated context interfaces.

For example, consider an ASA that has the following system context configuration. Physical interface Ethernet0 is shared across all contexts as the single link to the outside world. Each context has a unique subinterface of Ethernet1 to use as its inside interface, as shown in the following system context configuration:

```
admin-context admin
context admin
  allocate-interface Ethernet0
  allocate-interface Ethernet1
  config-url flash:/admin.cfg
!
context ContextA
  allocate-interface Ethernet0
  allocate-interface Ethernet1.1
  config-url flash:/ContextA.cfg
!
context ContextB
  allocate-interface Ethernet0
  allocate-interface Ethernet1.2
  config-url flash:/ContextB.cfg
```

Next, it is useful to see how the ASA allocates its MAC addresses. In the following example, the system context interface MAC addresses are displayed with the **show interface** command. Notice that each physical interface (Ethernet0, Ethernet1, and so on) has a unique address. The MAC addresses for subinterfaces (Ethernet1.1 and Ethernet1.2) are not shown; they simply inherit the address of their parent physical interfaces.

```
asa-a# changeto system
asa-a# show interface | include (Interface | MAC)
Interface Ethernet0 "", is up, line protocol is up
        MAC address 000e.d7e6.af77, MTU not set
Interface Ethernet1 "", is up, line protocol is up
        MAC address 000e.d7e6.af78, MTU not set
Interface Ethernet1.1 "", is up, line protocol is up
Interface Ethernet1.2 "", is up, line protocol is up
Interface Ethernet2 "Failover", is up, line protocol is up
        MAC address 0005.5d19.019c, MTU 1500
Interface Ethernet3 "", is administratively down, line protocol is down
        MAC address 0005.5d19.019d, MTU not set
Interface Ethernet4 "", is administratively down, line protocol is down
        MAC address 0005.5d19.019e, MTU not set
Interface Ethernet5 "", is administratively down, line protocol is down
        MAC address 0005.5d19.019f, MTU not set
asa-a#
```

Finally, each context is visited to display the MAC addresses of its own interfaces. Because system context interface Ethernet0 is allocated to each of the other contexts as a shared outside interface (also called Ethernet0), notice that the highlighted MAC addresses are identical:

```
asa-a# changeto context admin
asa-a/admin# show interface | include (Interface | MAC)
Interface Ethernet0 "outside", is up, line protocol is up
        MAC address 000e.d7e6.af77, MTU 1500
Interface Ethernet1 "inside", is up, line protocol is up
        MAC address 000e.d7e6.af78, MTU 1500
asa-a/admin#
asa-a/admin# changeto context ContextA
asa-a/ContextA# show interface | include (Interface | MAC)
Interface Ethernet0 "outside", is up, line protocol is up
        MAC address 000e.d7e6.af77, MTU 1500
Interface Ethernet1.1 "inside", is up, line protocol is up
        MAC address 000e.d7e6.af78, MTU 1500
asa-a/ContextA#
asa-a/ContextA# changeto context ContextB
asa-a/ContextB# sh interface | include (Interface | MAC)
Interface Ethernet0 "outside", is up, line protocol is up
        MAC address 000e.d7e6.af77, MTU 1500
Interface Ethernet1.2 "inside", is up, line protocol is up
        MAC address 000e.d7e6.af78, MTU 1500
asa-a/ContextB#
```

Reusing the MAC addresses does not usually pose a problem because neighboring devices can still see a correspondence between a context interface's IP address and its MAC address. But what about the example case where the same physical or subinterface is allocated to several different firewall contexts? Each of the allocated context interfaces would have a unique IP address from the same shared subnet, but would reuse the same MAC address.

Neighboring devices might not be able to distinguish one context from another because of the shared MAC address. However, the ASA can usually accept traffic destined to the shared MAC address and figure out which context interface is the real recipient. The ASA uses a *classifier* function to examine incoming packets and pass them along to the correct context. The classifier works through the following sequence of conditions to map a packet's destination address to a context:

1. **A unique interface**—When one interface is allocated to only one context, the destination context is obvious.

2. **A unique MAC address**—The destination MAC address is found on only one context interface.

3. **A unique NAT entry**—A unique destination Internet Protocol (IP) address is needed, either through a global address configured in a static NAT entry or found in the xlate table.

Beginning with ASA 7.2(1), you can configure the ASA to use unique MAC addresses on *every* subinterface and context interface. Physical (system context) interfaces continue to use their burned-in addresses, whereas context interfaces receive MAC addresses that are automatically generated. You can use the following global configuration command to assign unique MAC addresses:

```
asa(config)# mac-address auto
```

This command can be used only in the system execution space because that is the source of all interface allocation. As soon as you enter the command, the interface MAC addresses is changed. You can revert back to the original interface MAC addresses by using the **no mac-address auto** command.

The MAC addresses are automatically generated according to the format spelled out in Table 4-1.

Table 4-1   *ASA-Generated MAC Address Format*

Failover Unit	MAC Address Format	Example
Active	12_*slot* . *port_subid* . *contextid*	1200.0000.0100
Standby	02_*slot* . *port_subid* . *contextid*	0200.0000.0100

The *slot* is the interface slot number, or 0 for platforms without slots. The *port* is the interface port number, and *subid* is the ASA's internal subinterface number. The *contextid* field is the context index, a number the ASA uses internally. You should not worry about what the internal numbering schemes mean—just know that you can easily distinguish the active and standby addresses by the leading 1 or 0 and that each context has a unique identifier.

Continuing the previous example, the **mac-address auto** command has been entered. The MAC addresses for each of the ASA's contexts are shown in the following output.

```
asa-a# changeto system
asa-a# show interface | include (Interface | MAC)
Interface Ethernet0 "", is up, line protocol is up
        MAC address 000e.d7e6.af77, MTU not set
Interface Ethernet1 "", is up, line protocol is up
        MAC address 000e.d7e6.af78, MTU not set
asa-a# changeto context admin
asa-a/admin# show interface | include (Interface | MAC)
Interface Ethernet0 "outside", is up, line protocol is up
        MAC address 1200.0000.0100, MTU 1500
Interface Ethernet1 "inside", is up, line protocol is up
        MAC address 1201.0000.0100, MTU 1500
asa-a/admin#
asa-a/admin# changeto context ContextA
asa-a/ContextA# show interface | include (Interface | MAC)
Interface Ethernet0 "outside", is up, line protocol is up
        MAC address 1200.0000.0200, MTU 1500
Interface Ethernet1.1 "inside", is up, line protocol is up
        MAC address 1201.0001.0200, MTU 1500
asa-a/ContextA#
```

```
asa-a/ContextA# changeto context ContextB
asa-a/ContextB# show interface | include (Interface 165168| MAC)
Interface Ethernet0 "outside", is up, line protocol is up
        MAC address 1200.0000.0300, MTU 1500
Interface Ethernet1.2 "inside", is up, line protocol is up
        MAC address 1201.0002.0300, MTU 1500
asa-a/ContextB#
```

The ASA automatically generates its MAC addresses using carefully selected parameters. The first six hex digits of the MAC address are referred to as the Organizational Unique Identifier (OUI) or the vendor code. Cisco uses 02xxxx and 12xxxx, neither of which is registered to another vendor. This should produce MAC addresses that are unique within your network, without duplicating the addresses used by other devices.

TIP	If you are running ASA 7.2(1) or later in multiple context mode, you should always enable unique interface MAC addresses with the **mac-address auto** command. You have no downside to using this command; after it has been configured, your firewall is always ready for any type of context arrangement, including shared interfaces and stacked or nested contexts.

In some rare cases, you could find that an automatically derived MAC address is conflicting with that of another device. How would you know if that happens? You might find that an ASA context is behaving erratically or you might see the following Syslog message in the ASA logs:

```
%ASA-4-405001: Received ARP request collision from 192.168.1.177/0201.0001.0200 on
interface inside
```

To remedy this situation, you can use the following interface configuration command to manually configure the ASA context interface MAC address to a different, unique value:

```
asa(config)# interface if_name
asa(config-if)# mac-address mac_address [standby mac_address]
```

The MAC address is entered in dotted triplet format (H.H.H), such as 0015.c557.f9bd. If your ASA is configured as part of a failover pair, remember to configure both the active and standby unit interface MAC addresses.

Configuration Files and Security Contexts

The firewall's flash memory file system is accessible only from the system execution space. This is because Flash is considered a controlled resource, available only to the physical firewall's administrators. If an individual user context is given over to be managed by a third party, it would not make sense to allow that third party to make changes to or allocate all of the firewall flash for his or her own use.

Where, then, are the firewall image and configuration files stored for a user context? None of the contexts runs its own firewall operating system image. Only one image is run in multiple-context mode, and that image is managed only by the system execution space. All other contexts appear to run the same image, as shown by the output generated by the **show version** command.

Configuration files, however, are used and maintained by each context. They have the following characteristics:

- The system execution space has both startup and running configuration files that are stored in the flash memory. The startup configuration file can be read, written, and copied, but it is kept in a hidden flash file system.

- Admin and user contexts have both startup and running configuration files. The startup configuration files can be stored in the flash file system or on an external TFTP, FTP, or HTTP server. When an external server is used, the user context administrators can have complete autonomy over the configuration and use of their firewall context.

- The system execution space configuration defines where each context's startup configuration file will be located.

Guidelines for Multiple-Context Configuration

You can configure and use several different types of contexts on a physical firewall or security appliance:

- **The *system execution space***—Although this is not a true context itself, it is the foundation for all other contexts.

- **The *admin* context**—A fully functional virtual firewall that can be used to administer the physical firewall platform.

- **One or more arbitrarily named user contexts**—Each context operates as an independent virtual firewall.

Each has a specific role within the firewall platform, making configuration somewhat confusing.

The system execution space handles context definition, overall firewall modes of operation, and the physical firewall resources. Therefore, it should be configured before resources and features become available to other contexts.

You can configure the following types of features in the system execution space:

- Physical firewall interfaces (speed, duplex, negotiation, descriptions, VLAN associations, and operational status)

- System images (firewall operating system and PIX Device Manager/Adaptive Security Device Manager [PDM/ASDM] management application)

- Firewall startup configuration file

- Context mode (single or multiple)

- Firewall mode (routing or transparent)
- Context definitions (configuration files, interface allocation, or mapping)
- Firewall failover
- Saving crash information
- Firewall system clock

You must enter firewall license activation keys from the system execution space. In addition, the system execution space provides all access to the firewall's flash file system.

However, the system execution space has no networking capability of its own. To access external network resources, such as a TFTP server containing the firewall image, the system execution space must work in conjunction with the admin context, where normal IP addressing and address translation are configured.

You should consider each nonsystem context to be a fully functional standalone firewall. Therefore, you can configure the admin and user contexts with all the firewall features presented in this book.

Initiating Multiple-Context Mode

Follow these steps to prepare a firewall for multiple-security context support:

1. Verify multiple-context licensing:

   ```
   Firewall# show activation-key
   ```

   A firewall can run in multiple-context mode only if it has been licensed to do so. As well, the maximum number of security contexts is set by the license. You can display the number of contexts supported by the current license, as shown in the following output:

   ```
   Firewall# show activation-key
   Serial Number:  401262144
   Running Activation Key: 0xcc05f166 0xd4c17b68 0x98501048 0x818cf190
     0x4133d195
   License Features for this Platform:
   Maximum Physical Interfaces : 10
   Maximum VLANs           : 100
   Inside Hosts            : Unlimited
   Failover                : Active/Active
   VPN-DES                 : Enabled
   VPN-3DES-AES            : Enabled
   Cut-through Proxy       : Enabled
   Guards                  : Enabled
   URL-filtering           : Enabled
   Security Contexts       : 5
   GTP/GPRS                : Enabled
   VPN Peers               : Unlimited
   This machine has an Unrestricted (UR) license.
   The flash activation key is the SAME as the running key.
   ```

2. (Optional) Install a new license activation key:

```
Firewall# activation-key key
```

You might need to install a new activation key if multiple-context mode is disabled or if you need to increase the number of supported contexts.

The *key* given here is a string of five groups of characters, each consisting of four pairs of hexadecimal digits. You can add a 0x prefix to each group of hex digits to denote the hex format, but this is not necessary. For example, you could use the following command:

```
Firewall# activation-key 59381b44 a46717cc a43114a8 8ce11438 862113ba
```

Refer to Section "2-2: Firewall Features and Licenses," in Chapter 2, "Configuration Fundamentals," for more information about configuring license activation keys.

3. Verify the security context mode:

```
Firewall# show mode
```

By default, a firewall operates in single-context mode. You can display the current mode with this command. If the firewall is currently running in single-context mode, you see the following output:

```
Firewall# show mode
Running Firewall mode: single
Firewall#
```

If the firewall is already running in multiple-context mode, you see the following output:

```
Firewall# show mode
Running Firewall mode: multiple
Firewall#
```

4. Initiate multiple-context mode:

```
Firewall(config)# mode [noconfirm] multiple
```

In single-context mode, all the firewall's configuration commands are contained in the startup configuration. Multiple-context mode changes this concept, because the initial startup configuration must contain commands that define the individual contexts. Each context has its own startup configuration file that configures features used only by that context.

If single-context mode already has some configuration when this command is used, an admin context is automatically created, and the appropriate commands are imported into it. Any interfaces that were configured and enabled are automatically mapped into the admin context, too. Otherwise, the admin context begins with no mapped interfaces.

The end result is that the firewall automatically generates the startup configuration for the system execution space, which is stored in a hidden flash file system. A startup configuration for the admin context is automatically generated and stored as the flash:/admin.cfg file.

Initiating multiple-context mode triggers the display of several prompts for you to confirm each action before it is carried out. You can use the **noconfirm** keyword to force the firewall to initiate multiple-context mode without any confirmation prompts.

NOTE After it is entered, the **mode** command does not appear in any firewall configuration. This is because it changes the firewall's behavior. The firewall still can remember which mode to use after booting up.

For example, a firewall running in single-context mode is configured to begin running in multiple-context mode. The **mode multiple** command produces the following output:

```
Firewall(config)# mode multiple
WARNING: This command will change the behavior of the device
WARNING: This command will initiate a Reboot
Proceed with change mode? [confirm]
Convert the system configuration? [confirm]
!
The old running configuration file will be written to flash
The admin context configuration will be written to flash
The new running configuration file was written
***
*** --- SHUTDOWN NOW ---
***
*** Message to all terminals:
***
***    change mode to flash
Flash Firewall mode: multiple
[output omitted]
Creating context 'system'... Done. (0)
Creating context 'null'... Done. (257)
Creating context 'admin'... Done. (1)
INFO: Context admin was created with URL flash:/admin.cfg
INFO: Admin context will take some time to come up .... please wait.
*** Output from config line 32, "  config-url flash:/admi..."
[output omitted]
Firewall# show mode
Running Firewall mode: multiple
Firewall#
```

Notice that several contexts are automatically created during this process: The system context is actually the system execution space, the null context serves as a placeholder or a system resource, and the admin context becomes the configuration for the administrative side of the firewall.

The number in parentheses after each context, such as (0), indicates the context number or index. The null context is always defined with the topmost index.

After you initiate multiple-context mode, the firewall also leaves hooks for a backout plan should you ever need to revert to single-context mode. The previous running configuration is automatically saved as the flash:/old_running.cfg file. If the **mode single** command is used in the future, the firewall attempts to use that file to re-create a single-context mode configuration. Therefore, you should consider leaving that file intact in the flash file system for future use.

Navigating Multiple Security Contexts

In multiple-context mode, it is possible to open an administrative session (console, Telnet, or Secure Shell [SSH]) to the firewall and then move around between security contexts. This allows you to configure and monitor any of the contexts as necessary without opening sessions to the individual virtual firewalls.

You can navigate between contexts only if you successfully connect and authenticate to the admin context or the system execution space first. At that point, you are considered an administrator of the physical firewall platform and any contexts that are configured.

If you connect to a user context first, the firewall limits your administrative session to only that context. This restricts the administrators of a user context from gaining access to any other context on the firewall. Each context is then independently managed from within that context.

Context Prompts

Moving between contexts can get confusing. During one administrative session, you might have to keep track of which physical firewall platform and which context (virtual firewall) you are connected to. Fortunately, the firewall gives you a landmark each time you move your session.

The firewall always updates its prompt to indicate which context you are currently accessing. The traditional prompt, *Firewall#*, represents the system context; *Firewall* represents the firewall's host name. Any other context is indicated by a prompt such as *Firewall/context#*, where *context* is the name of the context.

TIP   As you move into various contexts, keep in mind that each context has its own startup and running configuration. Therefore, the running configuration must be saved on each context independently.

Think of each context as an independent firewall. The admin context represents the firewall that is used by the platform administrators. The system execution space, although not a true context, provides the functions necessary to extend the physical firewall resources (interfaces, flash memory, context definitions, and so on) to any admin and user contexts.

Changing a Session to a Different Context

You can move your terminal session from one context to another, as long as you have the administrative rights to do so, by entering the following command:

```
Firewall# changeto {system | context name}
```

For example, suppose your firewall has the host name MyPix. It also has a system execution space (always created by default), an admin context, and a user context called CustomerA. You can use the following commands to navigate between contexts:

```
MyPix#
MyPix# changeto context admin
MyPix/admin#
MyPix/admin# changeto context CustomerA
MyPix/CustomerA#
MyPix/CustomerA# changeto system
MyPix#
```

Notice how the session prompt automatically changes to indicate the firewall and context name each time the session is moved. Keep in mind that the system execution space is always called **system** and not **context system**. Therefore, it does not really have a context name to be displayed in the prompt.

Configuring a New Context

All contexts must be defined from a firewall's system execution space. Make sure you position your session in the system space with the following command before continuing:

```
Firewall# changeto system
```

The firewall also needs an admin context to be able to communicate beyond itself. The admin context is usually built automatically when the firewall is configured for multiple-context mode. As well, each time the firewall boots up, you should see console messages indicating that the admin context has been rebuilt.

To see a list of the contexts that have been configured, you can use the following command:

```
Firewall# show context
```

In the following example, only the admin context has been built:

```
Firewall# show context
Context Name        Interfaces                     URL
*admin                                             flash:/admin.cfg
Total active Security Contexts: 1
Firewall#
```

To configure a new context, follow these steps:

 1. Name the context:

```
Firewall(config)# context name
```

Every context must have a name that is unique on the physical firewall platform. This name is used in the context definition, in commands used to change sessions over to the context, in the user interface prompt, and in some forms of logging messages.

TIP   You must add an admin context to every firewall so that it can communicate with the outside world. Therefore, the first context you should create is the admin context.

By default, the admin context is named "admin" and is created by using the **context admin** command. If you decide to give it some other arbitrary name, you will identify it as the admin context in a later configuration step.

---

2. (Optional) Label the context:

    Firewall(config-ctx)# **description** *text*

    You can define an arbitrary string of descriptive text (up to 200 characters) if you need to label a context with more information than just its name. For example, you might want to add a responsible person's name and contact information, or some specific information about the purpose of the context, such as the following:

    Firewall(config)# **context BuildingC_DataCenter**
    Firewall(config-ctx)# **description Contact John Doe, jdoe@mycompany.com,**
      (859)555-1234; schedule any context downtime one week ahead of time.

3. Map existing firewall interfaces into the context.

    Firewall interfaces (physical or logical) are always created and tuned from within the system execution space. All user contexts (including the admin context) begin with no interfaces when they are first defined. As well, no interfaces can be created from a user context.

    Instead, you must map specific interfaces from the system execution space into a user context. After an interface has been mapped, it can be configured with a name, a security level, and an IP address from that context's configuration mode.

    a. (ASA only) Map a physical interface:

        Firewall(config-ctx)# **allocate-interface** *physical-interface* [*map-name*]
          [**visible** | **invisible**]

        The physical firewall interface named *physical-interface* ("GigabitEthernet0," for example) is mapped into the current context.

        By default, the mapped interface appears with the same *physical-interface* hardware name in the context. If you would rather keep the interface hardware name hidden from the context users, you can specify an arbitrary interface name such as *map-name*. The context users then use that name to configure the interface.

By default, mapped interface hardware names are also kept invisible to context users who use the **show interface** command. This is identical to including the **invisible** keyword. If you want to provide a clue as to the context interface's position in the firewall platform, use the **visible** keyword. When a mapped interface is made visible, context users can see its "system name" in the **show interface** output, as in the following example:

```
Firewall(config)# context NewContext
Firewall(config-ctx)# allocate-interface ethernet1 test visible
Firewall(config-ctx)# exit
Firewall# changeto context NewContext
Firewall/NewContext# show interface test
Interface test "", is down, line protocol is down
        System name Ethernet1
        Available but not configured via nameif
Firewall/NewContext#
```

TIP   When you map an interface into a user context, you are actually creating a "hardware" name for that interface. You still have to configure the user context so that the new interface has a name, using the **nameif** interface configuration command. In the preceding example, context NewContext considers the new mapped interface name "test" to be the hardware device. Interface "test" does not have a name and a security level for firewall use until it is configured further. You could use the following commands to complete the interface configuration:

```
Firewall/NewContext# show running-config interface test
!
interface test
 no nameif
 no security-level
 no ip address
Firewall/NewContext# configure terminal
Firewall/NewContext(config)# interface test
Firewall/NewContext(config-if)# nameif outside
INFO: Security level for "outside" set to 0 by default.
Firewall/NewContext(config-if)# no shutdown
```

Now the **show interface** command shows the mapped interface "hardware" name (test), the logical name (outside), and the system platform name (Ethernet1), as shown in the following output:

```
Firewall/NewContext# show interface outside
Interface test "outside", is down, line protocol is down
        System name Ethernet1
        MAC address 00a0.c901.0201, MTU 1500
        IP address unassigned
            Received 0 packets, 0 bytes
            Transmitted 0 packets, 0 bytes
            Dropped 0 packets
Firewall/NewContext#
```

---

b.   Map a physical subinterface or VLAN interface.

In an ASA, a physical interface can operate as a trunk, transporting traffic over multiple VLANs, where each VLAN is mapped to a unique subinterface number. For example, in the system execution space, interface gigabitethernet1 operates as a trunk. VLAN 5 might be mapped to subinterface gigabitethernet1.5, and VLAN 7 might be mapped to gigabitethernet1.7. (The subinterface numbers are arbitrary and do not have to match the VLAN number.)

On an FWSM platform, only VLAN interfaces are supported as if they are physical interfaces.

You can map a subinterface or a VLAN interface from the system execution space to a user context, as if it were a physical interface. Use the following command to define a single mapping:

FWSM	Firewall(config-ctx)# **allocate-interface vlan***number* [*map_name*]
ASA	Firewall(config-ctx)# **allocate-interface** *physical-interface.subinterface* [*map_name*] [**visible** | **invisible**]

The physical subinterface named *physical-interface.subinterface* (ASA) or the Virtual LAN (VLAN) interface (FWSM) is mapped to the current context as an interface by the same name. You can include an arbitrary logical *map_name* if you want to keep the actual interface name hidden from the context users. In that case, the context users use *map_name* to further configure the interface.

You can also map a range of subinterfaces or VLAN interfaces, as long as their subinterface or VLAN numbers are contiguous. Use the following command to accomplish this mapping:

FWSM	Firewall(config-ctx)# **allocate-interface vlan***number***-vlan***number* [*map_name-map_name*]
ASA	Firewall(config-ctx)# **allocate-interface** *physical-interface.subinterface-physical.interface.subinterface* [*map_name-map_name*] [**visible** | **invisible**]

Specify the range of interfaces with the starting subinterface and the ending subinterface, separated by a hyphen. The physical interface name (*physical-interface*) must be identical in the range definition, with only the subinterface numbers changing. For example, the following command maps subinterface numbers 1 through 5:

```
Firewall(config-ctx)# allocate-interface
  gigabitethernet0.1-gigabitethernet0.5
```

For the FWSM platform, the range is given with the starting and ending VLAN interfaces, each beginning with the keyword **vlan** followed by the VLAN number. For example, the following command maps interfaces for VLANs 1 through 5:

```
Firewall(config-ctx)# allocate-interface vlan1-vlan5
```

Naturally, you can also map a range of subinterfaces or VLAN interfaces to a range of logical interface names. To do so, specify the range of map names from starting to ending, separated by a hyphen. The *map_name* is an arbitrary name ending with a number. Both the starting and ending *map_name* must be identical, except for the number. The starting and ending number must define a range of the same size as the physical or VLAN interface range.

For example, you can allocate a range of five physical subinterfaces to a range of five logical names with the following ASA command:

```
Firewall(config-ctx)# allocate-interface
  gigabitethernet0.1-gigabitethernet0.5 Int1-Int5
```

Similarly, you could use the following command on an FWSM platform:

```
Firewall(config-ctx)# allocate-interface vlan1-vlan5 Int1-Int5
```

NOTE   Although an interface can be mapped to other contexts, each context maintains its own interface state. For example, suppose physical interface GigabitEthernet0 has been mapped to interface0 in context admin. Context admin can shut down its interface0 while the physical interface GigabitEthernet0 is still up and functioning in the system execution space.

Naturally, the reverse is not true; the system execution space controls the interface state for all other contexts. If the system space has a physical interface administratively shut down (with the **shutdown** command), all other contexts with that interface mapped show it as simply "down" and not "administratively down."

Also notice that, in the system space, interfaces are strictly physical and do not have logical names or security levels. You can see this in the following example:

```
Firewall# show interface
Interface GigabitEthernet0 "", is up, line protocol is up
  Hardware is i82543 rev02, BW 1000 Mbps, Full-duplex
        Description: Outside public network (non-trunk)
        Available for allocation to a context
        MAC address 0003.479a.b395, MTU not set
        IP address unassigned
[output omitted]
Interface GigabitEthernet0.2 "", is up, line protocol is up
        VLAN identifier 2
        Description: VLAN 2 - inside private network
        Available for allocation to a context
Interface GigabitEthernet0.3 "", is up, line protocol is up
        VLAN identifier 3
        Description: VLAN 3 - stateful failover
        Available for allocation to a context
```

---

4. Define the context startup configuration location:

```
Firewall(config-ctx)# config-url url
```

The startup configuration can be located at a URL defined by *url* at any of the locations listed in Table 4-2.

Table 4-2 *Context Startup Configuration Locations*

Location	*url* Syntax
Flash memory (PIX)	**flash:**/[*path*/]*filename*
Flash memory (FWSM)	**disk:**/[*path*/]*filename*
TFTP server	**tftp://**[*user*[**:***password*]**@**]*server*[**:***port*]/[*path*/]*filename*[**;int=***if_name*]
FTP server	**ftp://**[*user*[**:***password*]**@**]*server*[**:***port*]/[*path*/]*filename*[**;type=***xy*] where *x* denotes ASCII mode (**a**) or binary mode (**i**) and *y* denotes passive mode (**p**) or normal mode (**n**)
HTTP server	**http**[**s**]**://**[*user*[**:***password*]**@**]*server*[**:***port*]/[*path*/]*filename*

CAUTION   As soon as you enter the **config-url** command, the system execution space attempts to load that configuration file *immediately*. This is done so that the new context can be built with a working configuration. If the URL points to a location external to the firewall, the IP connectivity configured on the admin context is used to reach the URL server.

However, be aware that if you reenter the **config-url** command to point to a new configuration file location, the configuration commands in that file are immediately merged with the context's running configuration. This could result in an undesirable configuration.

Within the new context, the URL pointing to the configuration file is used in place of a startup configuration file in flash memory. If the configuration file does not yet exist, the firewall creates the file with a minimal or blank context configuration.

Any commands that involve the startup configuration use the URL instead. For example, the **copy running-config startup-config** and **write memory** commands copy the current running configuration to a file defined by the URL.

In this fashion, the startup configuration can be uploaded to or downloaded from the URL location. The only exception is a URL that points to an HTTP or HTTPS server; then the file can only be downloaded to the firewall context.

For example, the following commands configure the CustomerA context to download its startup configuration from a TFTP server:

```
Firewall(config)# context CustomerA
Firewall(config-ctx)# config-url tftp://192.168.200.10/pixconfigs/
  CustomerA.cfg
```

TIP   You can name the configuration file with any arbitrary name, with or without a dotted suffix. Usually, it is a good idea to develop some sort of naming standard. For example, the filename might indicate the context name and a suffix of .cfg could be added to indicate that the file is a context configuration.

---

5. (Optional) Designate the admin context:

```
Firewall(config)# admin-context name
```

By default, the admin context is named "admin," and the following command is automatically added to the system execution space configuration:

```
Firewall(config)# admin-context admin
```

If you would rather use the context you have just created as the admin context, you can use the preceding command to assign its new role. The previous admin context still exists in the system execution space configuration and as a working context.

TIP   You must store the admin context startup configuration file in the internal flash memory so that it is always accessible. Make sure you have defined the configuration file location as such:

```
Firewall(config-ctx)# admin-context admin
Firewall(config-ctx)# config-url flash:/admin.cfg
```

If a context other than one called "admin" is configured as the admin context, the commands might appear as follows:

```
Firewall(config-ctx)# admin-context Main
Firewall(config-ctx)# config-url flash:/Main.cfg
```

Context Definition Example

Consider a physical firewall that is configured with three separate contexts for the enterprise:

- One for firewall administration
- One for Department A
- One for Department B

Figure 4-7 shows a network diagram of the multiple-context arrangement.

Figure 4-7   *Network Diagram of the Multiple-Context Example*

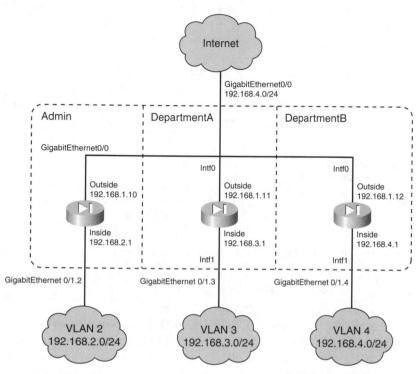

For the purposes of this example, each context is defined and configured with only basic interface parameters. The idea is to become familiar with context creation and configuration and interface allocation. You perform the configuration steps by connecting to the physical firewall console to gain access to the system execution space.

First, get a sampling of the physical interfaces that are available on the system execution space. These interfaces are available to be mapped into user contexts. The following command and output are used:

```
Firewall# show running-config
: Saved
:
ASA Version 8.0(1) <system>
!
interface GigabitEthernet0/0
 description Public interface
!
interface GigabitEthernet0/1
 description Trunk for private context interfaces
!
interface GigabitEthernet0/1.2
vlan 2
!
```

```
interface GigabitEthernet0/1.3
 vlan 3
!
interface GigabitEthernet0/1.4
 vlan 4
[output omitted]
```

Next, the admin context is used for firewall management, so it must be defined in the system execution space configuration. The admin startup configuration is stored in flash as the file admin.cfg. Two firewall interfaces are allocated to the context. Because it is the admin context, the interface names cannot be mapped to other arbitrary names. Use the following commands to configure the admin context:

```
Firewall# configure terminal
Firewall(config)# context admin
Firewall(config-ctx)# config-url flash:/admin.cfg
Cryptochecksum(unchanged): 352c788c 39cd2793 66c6ef98 c6bc632e
INFO: Context admin was created with URL flash:/admin.cfg
INFO: Admin context will take some time to come up .... please wait.
Firewall(config-ctx)#
Firewall(config-ctx)# allocate-interface GigabitEthernet0/0
Firewall(config-ctx)# allocate-interface GigabitEthernet0/1.2
Firewall(config-ctx)# exit
Firewall(config-ctx)# admin-context admin
Firewall(config)#
```

Now you can define a user context called DepartmentA. This is also done from the system execution space. Two firewall interfaces are allocated to the context, and the names are mapped to the generic values intf0 and intf1. For the present time, the context startup configuration is stored as a file named DepartmentA.cfg in flash memory. You can manage this file from the system execution space only, but context users can read or write to it using the **startup-config** command keyword. Later, the context users can arrange to store the file on an external server. When that happens, the following **config-url** command needs to be updated:

```
Firewall(config)# context DepartmentA
Firewall(config-ctx)# config-url flash:/DepartmentA.cfg
WARNING: Could not fetch the URL flash:/DepartmentA.cfg
INFO: Creating context with default config
Firewall(config-ctx)# description Virtual Firewall for Department A
Firewall(config-ctx)# allocate-interface GigabitEthernet0/0 intf0
Firewall(config-ctx)# allocate-interface GigabitEthernet0/1.3 intf1
Firewall(config-ctx)# exit
```

Define the user context DepartmentB with the following commands on the system execution space. This context is structured similarly to the DepartmentA context. The startup configuration also is stored on the firewall flash until it is moved later.

```
Firewall(config)# context DepartmentB
Firewall(config-ctx)# description Virtual firewall for Department B
Firewall(config-ctx)# config-url flash:/DepartmentB.cfg
WARNING: Could not fetch the URL flash:/DepartmentB.cfg
INFO: Creating context with default config
Firewall(config-ctx)# allocate-interface GigabitEthernet0/0 intf0
```

```
Firewall(config-ctx)# allocate-interface GigabitEthernet0/1.4 intf1
Firewall(config-ctx)# exit
Firewall(config)# exit
Firewall#
```

After all the contexts are defined, do not forget to save the system execution space configuration to flash memory using the following command:

```
Firewall# copy running-config startup-config
```

At this point, the firewall flash memory contains the startup configuration files for every user context. (The system execution space startup configuration file is always stored in a hidden flash file system.) The firewall flash memory looks something like this:

```
Firewall# dir flash:/
Directory of flash:/
3      -rw- 4958208    06:41:52 Nov 30 2004  image.bin
4      -rw- 8596996    10:12:38 Nov 12 2004  asdm.bin
10     -rw- 1591       16:45:18 Dec 03 2004  old_running.cfg
12     -rw- 1853       09:47:02 Dec 30 2004  admin.cfg
14     -rw- 2119       14:16:56 Dec 07 2004  CustomerA.cfg
16     -rw- 2002       14:19:44 Dec 07 2004  CustomerB.cfg
16128000 bytes total (2565231 bytes free)
Firewall#
```

NOTE   Notice that the system execution space contains an Adaptive Security Device Manager (ASDM) image file (asdm.bin). Users in other contexts cannot directly access the flash file system, so those contexts cannot use the image file. However, users in each context can run ASDM sessions to manage the context. The firewall coordinates all this from the system execution space from a single ASDM image. As expected, context users can see and manage only their own context.

Now, each user context can be configured as an independent firewall. Each one starts with an empty configuration, except for the mapped interface definitions, so the initial session must be opened from the system execution space. As soon as a context is configured with enough information to have network connectivity, users can connect through any other means (Telnet, SSH, ASDM, and so on).

First, change the session to the admin context and have a look at the available interfaces. Notice that each one is present but has no usable configuration.

```
Firewall# changeto context admin
Firewall/admin# show running-config
:
PIX Version 8.0(1) <context>
names
!
interface GigabitEthernet0/0
 no nameif
no security-level
```

```
 no ip address
!
interface GigabitEthernet0/1.2
 no nameif
 no security-level
 no ip address
[output omitted]
```

At a minimum, name the inside and outside interfaces, and configure them with IP addresses and security levels. You can do this with the following configuration commands (described in more detail in Chapter 3, "Building Connectivity"):

```
Firewall/admin# configure terminal
Firewall/admin(config)# interface GigabitEthernet0/0
Firewall/admin(config-if)# nameif outside
Firewall/admin(config-if)# security-level 0
Firewall/admin(config-if)# ip address 192.168.1.10 255.255.255.0
Firewall/admin(config-if)# no shutdown
Firewall/admin(config)# interface GigabitEthernet0/1.2
Firewall/admin(config-if)# nameif inside
Firewall/admin(config-if)# security-level 100
Firewall/admin(config-if)# ip address 192.168.2.1 255.255.255.0
Firewall/admin(config-if)# no shutdown
```

You can configure the DepartmentA and DepartmentB user contexts in a similar manner. Use the **changeto context DepartmentA** and **changeto context DepartmentB** commands to move the session to each context.

In this example, firewall interfaces are allocated to the user contexts with the mapped names intf0 and intf1. After you connect to a user context session, the only clue you have about a mapped interface is its generic or mapped name. After all, the idea behind mapping interfaces is to present context users with arbitrary interface names that do not represent physical hardware.

Therefore, you might have to return to the system execution space configuration to remember which physical firewall interface is mapped to which context interface and which context interface should be configured as inside and outside.

To continue the example, the DepartmentA user context is configured next. Notice the initial interface definitions:

```
Firewall/admin# changeto context DepartmentA
Firewall/DepartmentA# show running-config
: Saved
:
PIX Version 8.0(1) <context>
names
!
interface intf0
 no nameif
 no security-level
 no ip address
!
interface intf1
```

```
 no nameif
no security-level
 no ip address
[output omitted]
```

Now you can configure the context interfaces with the following commands:

```
Firewall/DepartmentA# configure terminal
Firewall/DepartmentA(config)# interface intf0
Firewall/DepartmentA(config-if)# nameif outside
Firewall/DepartmentA(config-if)# security-level 0
Firewall/DepartmentA(config-if)# ip address 192.168.1.11 255.255.255.0
Firewall/DepartmentA(config-if)# no shutdown
Firewall/DepartmentA(config)# interface intf1
Firewall/DepartmentA(config-if)# nameif inside
Firewall/DepartmentA(config-if)# security-level 100
Firewall/DepartmentA(config-if)# ip address 192.168.3.1 255.255.255.0
Firewall/DepartmentA(config-if)# no shutdown
```

TIP   After you move your session to a different user context, it might be tempting to use the **exit** command to return to the previously visited context or the system execution space. Entering **exit** only terminates your session with the current context, requiring you to authenticate with it again so that you can use the **changeto** command.

Think of each context as having its own virtual console connection. By using the **changeto** command, you move the console connection from one context to another.

Allocating Firewall Resources to Contexts

When a firewall platform is running in single-context security mode, you can configure and use only one operational firewall. Therefore, that firewall can use any or all of the available traffic inspection and session resources on that hardware platform. In other words, if the firewall uses most of its own resources while it does its job, its own performance is not affected.

In multiple-context security mode, however, all the configured contexts must share the available resources on their physical firewall platform. If one context becomes heavily loaded or highly utilized, it can use a majority of the traffic inspection resources. This can affect the other contexts by leaving them starved for the same resources.

Multiple-context mode can support resource allocation by imposing limits on how specific resources are used. You can configure resource limits in classes according to the resource type and assign memberships in the classes to contexts. Resource allocation has the following characteristics:

- Resource allocation is available on the FWSM, starting with release 2.2(1). Resource allocation is also available starting with ASA 7.2(1).

- Firewall resources that can be limited fall into several categories:

— **Stateful inspection**—The number of hosts, connections, address translations, and application inspections

— **MAC addresses**—The number of MAC addresses learned in transparent firewall mode

— **Syslog message generation rate**—The number of logging messages sent per second to Syslog servers

— **Administrative sessions**—The number of ASDM, Telnet, SSH, and IPSec connections to the firewall

- The default class permits unlimited use of most resources for all contexts by default. You can configure the default class and adjust specific resource limits in it, if needed.

- You can define and configure new classes with resource limits tailored for a certain level of service.

- You can impose specific limits on a context by assigning it membership in a class. Otherwise, every context that is not a class member belongs to the default class.

- Limits are set per class, not per context. Therefore, all contexts that are assigned to a class share various resources up to the limits of that class. To configure limits on a per-context basis, define one class per context and assign each context to its respective class.

- To exercise thorough control over system resources, you should define classes with specific limits. Then make sure every context is assigned to a class. After that is done, no context can inherit the unlimited resources of the default class.

You can use the following steps to define and apply classes of resource limits to security contexts:

1. Define a class of service.

   a. Identify the class:

       ```
       Firewall(config)# class name
       ```
       The class is named *name* (an arbitrary string up to 20 characters).

TIP   You can adjust the resource limits that are defined in the default class by using the class name *default* in this configuration step. The command syntax then becomes **class default**. By default, all the default class limits are set to unlimited (0), except for the following:

- ASDM sessions (the default is 5)

- Telnet sessions (the default is 5)

- SSH sessions (the default is 5)

- IPSec sessions (the default is 5)

- MAC addresses (the default is 65,535 entries)

---

   b. (Optional) Define a limit for all resources:

       ```
       Firewall(config-class)# limit-resource all number%
       ```

All resource types are limited to *number* (1 to 100) percent of the maximum available on the physical firewall platform. This limit overrides any resource types that are set in the class. After tnumber is set to 0, all resources are allowed to be unlimited. The value number must be followed by a percent character.

For example, to limit all resources to 50 percent of their possible values, you would use the following command:

```
Firewall(config-class)# limit-resource all 50%
```

c. (Optional) Define a limit for a single resource:

```
Firewall(config-class)# limit-resource [rate] resource_name number[%]
```

You can limit a specific firewall resource within the class. If you set a limit with this command, it overrides any limit set by the **limit-resource all** command or by the cific firewall.

You can limit the resource named resource_name to an actual value as number or to a percentage of the maximum possible value as number%. You can also add the rate keyword to indicate that number should be interpreted in units per second.

Use Table 4-3 to find resource names and their maximum values.

Table 4-3   *Resource Names and Maximum Values*

Resource_name	Resource Type	Platform Maximum
hosts	Number of concurrent hosts having connections	FWSM: 256,000 ASA: No limit
conns	Total UDP and TCP connections between any hosts	FWSM: 999,900 concurrent FWSM: 102,400 per second ASA: Limited by platform
xlates	Address translations	FWSM: 256,000 concurrent ASA: No limit
fixups (FWSM) **inspects** (ASA)	Application inspections	FWSM: 10,000 per second ASA: No limit
Mac-addresses	Transparent firewall MAC address table	65,535 concurrent
syslogs	Syslog messages generated	FWSM: 30,000 per second[1] ASA: No limit

1.   The FWSM can generate a sustained rate of 30,000 logging messages per second to a terminal session or the internal logging buffer. Sending messages to a Syslog server imposes additional packet overhead, reducing the actual rate to 25,000 messages per second.

Firewalls also support resource limits on various types of sessions that terminate on the firewall. Use Table 4-4 to find those resource names and maximum values.

Table 4-4 *Resource Names and Maximum Values for Terminating Session Types*

Resource_name	Resource Type	Platform Maximum
Asdm	Concurrent ASDM sessions	32 for ASA 80 for FWSM 3.1(1)
telnet	Concurrent Telnet sessions	100^1
ssh	Concurrent SSH sessions	100^1
ipsec	Concurrent IPSec connections	10^2

1. The FWSM can support up to 100 concurrent Telnet and SSH sessions over all contexts. It imposes a limit of five concurrent Telnet and five concurrent SSH sessions per context.

2. The FWSM can support up to ten concurrent IPSec connections over all contexts, or up to five concurrent connections per context.

You can repeat the **limit-resource** command to define other resource limits for the class. For example, a class called Silver is configured to limit all firewall resources to 25 percent of the maximum available resources. In addition, the number of xlates is limited to 50,000, and the number of conns is limited to 100,000. The number of Syslog messages is limited to 4000 per second. You can use the following commands to define these limits:

```
Firewall(config)# class Silver
Firewall(config-class)# limit-resource all 25%
Firewall(config-class)# limit-resource xlates 50000
Firewall(config-class)# limit-resource conns 100000
Firewall(config-class)# limit-resource rate syslogs 4000
```

  d. Exit the resource class submode:

```
Firewall(config-class)# exit
```

2. Assign a context to a class.

  a. Select a context:

```
Firewall(config)# context name
```

The context *name* should already be defined in the system execution space configuration.

  b. Assign it to a resource class:

```
Firewall(config-ctx)# member class
```

The context becomes a member of the resource allocation class named "class," as defined in Step 1. You can assign membership in only one user-defined class per context. Keep in mind that every context also belongs to the default class. Any resource limit that is not defined in "class" is then inherited from the default class.

3. Monitor resource allocation.

    a. Display class membership:

```
Firewall# show class
```

Each of the configured classes is shown with its member contexts. In the following example, all contexts are members of the "default" class, and only context 1 is a member of the "silver" class:

```
Firewall# show class
Class Name        Members    ID   Flags
default           All        1    0001
silver            1          2    0000
Firewall#
```

    b. Review resource allocation:

```
Firewall# show resource allocation [detail]
```

You can use this command to display the current breakdown of resource limits as percentages of the total available. Add the **detail** keyword to see a more detailed breakdown by resource and context, as in the following example:

```
Firewall# show resource allocation
Resource               Total          % of Avail
 Conns [rate]          85000            50.00%
 Fixups [rate]         50000            50.00%
 Syslogs [rate]        15000            50.00%
 Conns                 500000           50.05%
 Hosts                 131072           50.00%
 IPSec                 5                50.00%
 Mac-addresses         32767            49.99%
 ASDM                  5                 6.25%
 SSH                   50               50.00%
 Telnet                50               50.00%
 Xlates                131072           50.00%
Firewall# show resource allocation detail
Resource Origin:
        A       Value was derived from the resource %and
        C       Value set in the definition of this class
        D       Value set in default class
Resource        Class       Mmbrs  Origin    Limit      Total    Total %
Conns [rate]    default     all     CA    unlimited
                silver      1       CA       85000     85000    50.00%
                All Contexts:   1                      85000    50.00%
```

```
      Fixups [rate]    default       all    CA  unlimited
                       silver        1      CA     50000     50000   50.00%
                       All Contexts: 1                       50000   50.00%
      Syslogs [rate]   default       all    CA  unlimited
                       silver        1      CA     15000     15000   50.00%
                       All Contexts: 1                       15000   50.00%
      Conns            default       all    CA  unlimited
                       silver        1      CA    500000    500000   50.05%
                       All Contexts: 1                      500000   50.05%
   [output truncated]
```

c. Display the current resource usage:

```
Firewall# show resource usage [context context_name | top n | all |
    summary | system] [resource {[rate] resource_name | all} | detail]
    [counter counter_name [count_threshold]]
```

You can use this command to display the actual resources being used, as described in Table 4-5.

Table 4-5 *Options for Displaying Resources Being Used*

Keyword	Description
context *context_name*	Resources in use by the context named *context_name*
top *n* **resource** *resource_name*	Displays the *n* greatest users of a specific resource
all	Displays all resource usage information
summary	Displays a summary by resource type
system	Resources in use by the system execution space

You can also display the results for a specific resource by giving the **resource** keyword along with a *resource_name*.

Normally, each resource usage line is shown with the fields listed in Table 4-6.

Table 4-6 *Resource Usage Line Fields*

Label	Description
Current	The number of resources currently in use
Peak	The highest amount since counters were cleared
Limit	The limit imposed on a resource
Denied	How many times a resource use has been denied because of a limit
Context	The context using the resource

If you enter the **counter** keyword, you can display results based one of the following specific *counter_name* values: **current**, **peak**, **denied**, or **all**.

You can also get a feel for the complete variety and number of firewall resources used by a context. By adding the **detail** keyword, you can see all resources being used, whether or not the resources can be limited.

Verifying Multiple-Context Operation

To see the current admin context name and configuration URL, you can use the **show admin-context** command, as in the following example from an ASA platform:

```
Firewall# show admin-context
Admin: admin flash:/admin.cfg
Firewall#
```

To see information about the configured contexts, you can use the following command:

```
Firewall# show context [[detail] [name] | count]
```

You can specify a context *name* to see information about only that context. Otherwise, all the contexts are shown. Include the **detail** keyword to see a breakdown of each context resource, including the configuration URL and interface mappings.

The following example shows the output from an ASA that has three configured contexts: admin, CustomerA, and CustomerB.

```
Firewall# show context
Context Name      Interfaces              URL
*admin            GigabitEthernet0        flash:/admin.cfg
                  GigabitEthernet1.1
 CustomerA        GigabitEthernet0,       tftp://172.30.1.10/customerA.cfg
                  GigabitEthernet1.3
 CustomerB        GigabitEthernet1.2,3    tftp://172.16.0.20/customerB.cfg
Total active Security Contexts: 3
Firewall#
```

On an FWSM platform, the same command produces slightly different output:

```
Firewall# show context
Context Name    Class     Interfaces    URL
*admin          silver    Vlan10,100    disk:/admin.cfg
CustomerA       silver    Vlan20,100    tftp://172.30.1.10/customerA.cfg
CustomerB       default   Vlan30,100    tftp://172.16.0.20/customerB.cfg
```

You can add the **detail** keyword to see a breakdown of the context configuration. The following example shows the detailed configuration for a context named CustomerA:

```
Firewall# show context detail CustomerA
Context "CustomerA", has been created
  Desc: Virtual firewall for CustomerA's headquarters location
  Config URL: tftp://172.30.1.10/customerA.cfg
  Real Interfaces: GigabitEthernet0, GigabitEthernet1.3
```

```
    Mapped Interfaces: intf0, intf1
    Flags: 0x00000011, ID: 2
    Failover group: 1
Firewall#
```

Finally, although the firewall cannot limit CPU load as a resource that is shared across contexts, the firewall does keep CPU load statistics. You can see a breakdown of the CPU usage as it is distributed across all the configured contexts. Use the following command from the system execution space:

Firewall# **show cpu usage context** {*name* | **all**}

The following example shows CPU usage on a firewall configured with three contexts:

```
Firewall# show cpu usage context all
 5 sec  1 min  5 min  Context Name
 7.1%   8.0%   7.1%   system
12.0%  12.0%  10.0%   admin
27.7%  28.5%  27.0%   CustomerA
 4.0%   4.0%   4.0%   CustomerB
Firewall#
```

4-2: Managing the Flash File System

Every Cisco firewall has a flash (nonvolatile) memory file system. Files such as the firewall operating system image, a firewall management application image, and the firewall configuration can be stored for use. This section discusses the various types of files and how to navigate and use the flash file system. The flash file system can be characterized by the following features:

- The operating system for Cisco firewalls is stored in flash memory in a compressed format. In PIX 6.3 or earlier, only one image can be stored in flash at any time. FWSM allows one image to be stored in each of two flash memory partitions, although only one image can be run at any time.

  The ASA release loosens this restriction, allowing multiple images; however, only one of those images can run actively at any time.

- In ASA and FWSM multiple-context modes, only the system execution space can directly access and manage the flash file system. All other contexts have no knowledge of a flash file system and no means to manage one.

- When a firewall boots, it uncompresses and copies an executable image from flash to RAM. The image is actually run from RAM.

- While an image is being run, a different image can be copied or written into flash memory. In fact, the running image can be safely overwritten in flash, because it is run from RAM. The new image is not run until the next time the firewall reloads.

- The various Cisco firewall platforms have different flash memory organization and storage capabilities. Generally, flash memory is divided into partitions, each having its own restrictions on the types of files that can be stored there. Table 4-7 summarizes the flash memory differences:

Table 4-7   *Flash Memory Organization/Storage by Platform*

	PIX 6.3	ASA	FWSM
Flash partitions	1	2	6
File types allowed on partitions	One OS image One PDM image One crash dump	1: Open partition **flash:/**—OS images, ASDM images, configuration files, logging files, arbitrary files 2: Hidden partition—system startup configuration file, crash dump file	1: Maintenance image 2: Network configuration for maintenance image 3: Crash dump 4: **flash:/**—images (OS, ASDM, system startup configuration) 5: Alternative images 6: **disk:/**—security context configurations, RSA keys, arbitrary files

- The operating system and ASDM or PDM images must be compatible before ASDM/PDM can be used. An ASDM/PDM image can be loaded into flash at any time without requiring a firewall reload.

- An image (operating system or ASDM/PDM) can be transferred into a firewall by any of the following methods:

  — TFTP at the monitor prompt

  — TFTP from an administrative session (firewall console, Telnet, or SSH)

  — HTTP or HTTPS from a web server

  — The firewall polls an Auto Update Server (AUS) device periodically to see if a new image is available for it. If so, the image is downloaded using HTTPS (TCP port 443).

TIP   After an ASDM or PDM image is downloaded into the firewall flash memory, it can be used immediately. After an operating system image is downloaded, however, the firewall must be rebooted to run the new image. You have to manually force a reboot by using the **reload** EXEC command. Obviously, you can download a new OS image at any time—even while the firewall is in production. To run the new image, firewall service has to be interrupted during downtime or a maintenance window.

Navigating an ASA or FWSM Flash File System

ASA and FWSM platforms organize their flash file systems much like a traditional IOS file system, which must be formatted, and can contain a tree of directories, each containing arbitrary files. You can navigate the flash file system and manage any of its contents, as described in the following sections.

TIP   In ASA, you can use **flash:/** to reference the entire flash file system.

FWSM, however, uses **flash:/** to reference the flash partition that contains operating system and PDM images. You can use **disk:/** to reference the flash partition that contains configuration files and other arbitrary files.

Each administrative session maintains a current placeholder or current directory where the user is positioned within the firewall file system. This is very similar to navigating a file system from within a shell on a Windows or UNIX machine.

In an administrative session, you can take the following actions:

- List the files stored in a directory:

FWSM	Firewall# **dir** [**/all**] [**/recursive**] [**disk:**[*path*]]
ASA	Firewall# **dir** [**/all**] [**/recursive**] [**flash:**[*path*]]

By default, an administrative session begins in the flash:/ or disk:/ root directory, for ASA or FWSM, respectively. You can specify the **flash:** or **disk:** keyword and a *path* to view the contents of a different directory. The *path* also can contain regular expressions to match specific patterns within filenames.

For example, you can use the following command on an ASA to see a list of all configuration files (having a .cfg suffix) in flash:

```
Firewall# dir flash:*.cfg
Directory of flash:/*.cfg
10    -rw-  1575         23:05:09 Sep 30 2004  old_running.cfg
12    -rw-  3134         23:30:24 Nov 08 2004  admin.cfg
13    -rw-  1401         14:12:31 Oct 20 2004  CustomerA.cfg
14    -rw-  2515         23:29:28 Nov 08 2004  border.cfg
17    -rw-  1961         13:52:22 Oct 25 2004  datacenter.cfg
```

You can use the **/all** keyword to list all the files in the directory and the **/recursive** keyword to recursively look in all nested directories and list the files found.

- Display the current directory name:

FWSM	Firewall# **pwd**
ASA	Firewall# **pwd**

Because you can "move around" within the flash file system hierarchy, it is easy to forget where the current directory is pointed. In the following example, the user has moved into the Syslog directory in flash:

```
Firewall# pwd
flash:/syslog/
```

- Change to a different directory:

FWSM	Firewall# **cd** [**disk:**][*path*]
ASA	Firewall# **cd** [**flash:**][*path*]

You can specify a directory name as *path* relative to the file system's root. The keyword **flash:** or **disk:** is optional but is the default. If the **cd** command is used alone, the pointer is changed to the root directory in flash.

For example, the following commands move the user into the Syslog directory in flash:

```
Firewall# cd
Firewall# cd syslog
```

or

```
Firewall# cd flash:/syslog
```

- Display a file's contents:

FWSM	Firewall# **more** [**/ascii** | **/binary**] [**disk:**]*path*
ASA	Firewall# **more** [**/ascii** | **/binary**] [**flash:**]*path*

The file found at *filesystem:path* is displayed, one page at a time, in the current administrative session. By default, the **flash:** or **disk:** file system is assumed, and the file contents are shown as plain text. For example, the following command displays the flash:/mytest text file:

```
Firewall# more mytest
hello this is a test
the end
Firewall#
```

You can also display a file to see both the hex and ASCII representations of its contents. The file can contain either ASCII text or binary data. You can use either the **/binary** or **/ascii** keyword, because they produce identical results. The following example shows the same small text file in the dual format:

```
Firewall# more /ascii mytest
00000000:  68656c6c 6f207468 69732069 73206120    hell o th is i s a
00000010:  74657374 0d0a0d0a 74686520 656e64XX    test .... the  endX
Firewall#
```

TIP	Be careful when you use the **more** command. If you attempt to view the contents of a large binary file, such as by using **more image.bin** to view the PIX image file, you could be stuck waiting a very long time while every byte is shown as a literal (and often cryptic) character to your terminal session. If you want to look at the contents of a binary file, always use the **more /binary** or **more /ascii** forms of the command.

Administering an ASA or FWSM Flash File System

An ASA platform offers two file systems—a flash file system that is accessible to administrative users, and a hidden file system that contains system-related resources that are inaccessible. On an FWSM platform, both file systems are accessible. The flash file system can contain files and directories, each under user control.

In an administrative session, you can take the following management actions on the flash file system and its contents:

- Copy a file to or from flash.

  You can copy files according to the basic syntax **copy** *from to*, as in the following commands:

FWSM	Firewall# **copy disk:***path*/*filename url*
ASA	Firewall# **copy flash:***path*/*filename url*

or

FWSM	Firewall# **copy** *url* **disk:***path*/*filename*
ASA	Firewall# **copy** *url* **flash:***path*/*filename*

In the flash file system, files are identified by their *path*, relative to the flash root directory, and their *filename*. You can use regular expressions in the filename to select specific files if needed.

Files can be copied to or from a *URL*, which can be an FTP server, a TFTP server, or another location in flash. The respective URL formats are as follows:

```
ftp://[user[:password]@]server[:port]/[path/]filename[;type=xy]
tftp://[user[:password]@]server[:port]/[path/]filename
flash:path/filename
```

If a server requires user authentication, you can specify the user ID and password in the *user:password@* format.

TIP   Prior to ASA 7.2(1), the URL required an IP address; the firewall could not resolve fully qualified domain names (FQDN). If you are running ASA 7.2(1) or later, the firewall can use DNS to resolve the IP address in a URL.

Make sure you use the following commands to configure DNS resolution on a specific firewall interface, the firewall's default domain name, and one or more DNS addresses:

```
Firewall(config)# dns domain-lookup if_name
Firewall(config)# dns server-group name
Firewall(config-dns-server-group)# domain-name name
Firewall(config-dns-server-group)# name-server ip_addr [ip_addr2] [...]
  [ip_addr6]
Firewall(config-dns-server-group)# retries number
Firewall(config-dns-server-group)# timeout seconds
Firewall(config-dns-server-group)# exit
```

- Delete a file from flash:

FWSM	Firewall# **delete** [**/noconfirm**] [**/recursive**] [**disk:**][*/path*]*filename*
ASA	Firewall# **delete** [**/noconfirm**] [**/recursive**] [**flash:**][*/path*]*filename*

The file named *filename* is deleted from flash. You can specify the **flash:** or **disk:** keyword, as well as a *path*, if needed. If those are omitted, the flash file system is assumed, and the path is assumed to be the current working directory (as shown by the **pwd** command).

You can use the **/noconfirm** keyword to delete the file without being asked to confirm the action. Without this keyword, you must press the **Enter** key each time the firewall prompts you for confirmation. You can delete an entire directory and its contents recursively by using the **/recursive** keyword.

For example, suppose an old configuration file oldconfig.cfg exists in flash. First, a directory is shown to find the correct filename, and then the file is deleted using the following commands:

```
Firewall# dir flash:
Directory of flash:/
6      -rw-  4902912    17:11:35 Nov 22 2004  image.bin
10     -rw-  1575       23:05:09 Sep 30 2004  oldconfig.cfg
23     -rw-  8596996    10:12:38 Nov 12 2004  asdm.bin
Firewall# delete flash:oldconfig.cfg
Delete filename [oldconfig.cfg]
Delete flash:/oldconfig.cfg? [confirm]
Firewall#
```

- Rename a file:

FWSM	Firewall# **rename** [**/noconfirm**] [**disk:**] [*source-path*] [**disk:**] [*destination-path*]
ASA	Firewall# **rename** [**/noconfirm**] [**flash:**] [*source-path*] [**flash:**] [*destination-path*]

You can rename an existing file named source-path (a filename with an optional path) to destination-path. You can add the **flash:** or **disk:** file system keyword, but the flash memory is used by default. If you provide no other path information, the path is assumed to be the current working directory (as seen with the **pwd** command).

By default, the firewall prompts you for each argument as a confirmation. You can use the **/noconfirm** keyword to skip all the confirmation steps.

For example, the file flash:/capture1 is renamed flash:/capture2 using the following commands:

```
Firewall# rename flash:/capture1 flash:/capture2
Source filename [capture1]?
Destination filename [capture2]?
Firewall#
```

- Make a new directory:

FWSM	Firewall# **mkdir** [**/noconfirm**] [**disk:**]*path*
ASA	Firewall# **mkdir** [**/noconfirm**] [**flash:**]*path*

A new empty directory is created at *path*, which can contain a path and filename. You can add the **flash:** or **disk:** keyword, but it is assumed by default. The firewall prompts you for confirmation before creating the directory. You can use the **/noconfirm** keyword to skip the confirmation prompts.

For example, to create a new directory called MyStuff in the flash file system, you would use the following command sequence:

```
Firewall# mkdir flash:/MyStuff
Create directory filename [MyStuff]?
Created dir flash:/MyStuff
Firewall# dir flash:
Directory of flash:/
[output omitted]
64      drw-  0           16:02:57 Nov 23 2006  MyStuff
16128000 bytes total (2419712 bytes free)
Firewall#
```

- Remove a directory:

FWSM	Firewall# **rmdir** [**/noconfirm**] [**disk:**]*path*
ASA	Firewall# **rmdir** [**/noconfirm**] [**flash:**]*path*

A directory named path is removed or deleted from flash. The path can contain a directory path and filename if needed. The firewall prompts you for confirmation before removing the directory. You can use the **/noconfirm** keyword to skip the confirmation prompts.

A directory must be empty of files and other directories before it can be removed.

- Check the flash file system's integrity.

If you suspect that the flash file system might be corrupted, you can use the following command to check it:

FWSM	Firewall# **fsck disk:**
ASA	Firewall# **fsck flash:**

The ASA flash file system has been checked in the following example. The output shows the number of orphaned files and directories that are found. These files and directories have been created but can no longer be reached in the file system because the mechanism to index or point to them is corrupt.

```
Firewall# fsck flash:
Fsck operation may take a while. Continue? [confirm]
flashfs[7]: 32 files, 6 directories
flashfs[7]: 0 orphaned files, 0 orphaned directories
flashfs[7]: Total bytes: 16128000
flashfs[7]: Bytes used: 13607936
flashfs[7]: Bytes available: 2520064
flashfs[7]: flashfs fsck took 23 seconds.
Fsck of flash:: complete
Firewall#
```

- Destroy the entire flash file system:

FWSM	Firewall# **format disk:**
ASA	Firewall# **format flash:**

or

FWSM	—
ASA	Firewall# **erase flash:**

You should use the **format** and **erase** commands *only* in special cases, where the entire contents of flash memory (both accessible and hidden flash file systems) need to be erased. This might be desirable if a firewall is to be turned over or transferred to a different owner and the flash contents need to remain confidential.

Every file, including image files, configuration files, and licensing files, is overwritten with a 0xFF data pattern so that it is completely removed. A generic flash file system is then rebuilt.

Using the PIX 6.3 Flash File System

In PIX 6.3, the flash memory is organized as a "closed," flat file system. Only six different files can be stored in flash. These files are not directly accessible or readable, and there is no hierarchical structure (folders or directories) to navigate. In fact, the files do not even have filenames. Instead, the firewall displays only the file index numbers it assigns automatically:

- **0**—The operating system binary image.
- **1**—The startup configuration commands; these are copied into the running configuration (RAM) and are executed when the firewall boots.
- **2**—VPN and other keys and certificates.
- **3**—The PDM image (if present).
- **4**—A memory image saved after a firewall crash (if enabled).
- **5**—The file size of the compressed operating system image (file 0).

In PIX 6.3, you can display the flash files with the **show flashfs** command, as in the following example:

```
Firewall# show flashfs
flash file system:  version:3  magic:0x12345679
  file 0: origin:        0 length:1949752
  file 1: origin: 2097152 length:6080
  file 2: origin: 2228224 length:1504
  file 3: origin: 2359296 length:3126944
  file 4: origin:        0 length:0
  file 5: origin: 8257536 length:308
Firewall#
```

Identifying the Operating System Image

In PIX 6.3 and FWSM, only one operating system image file can be stored in flash at any time. The firewall automatically allocates storage for the image and handles its creation. In PIX 6.3, the image file is always indexed as file number 0 in the flash file system, as displayed by the **show flashfs** command. Therefore, when the firewall boots up, that image is always loaded into RAM and executed. In an FWSM, you can see a list of files in the image or application partition with the **dir flash:/** command.

The ASA code platform relaxes this restriction, allowing one or more operating system images to be stored in flash, as long as there is sufficient space to store them. Naturally, only one of the image files can run on the firewall at any time, so you must select one file for use. Use the following command to select the bootable image:

```
Firewall(config)# boot system flash:filename
```

Naturally, this command is stored in the running configuration after it is entered. It should also be written into the startup configuration so that the image can be identified during the next reload or bootup. The firewall searches for the specified file as soon as the command is entered. If the file cannot be found in flash, the command is accepted but a warning message is displayed.

You can also enter this command more than once to configure a list of image files that can be executed. The list of filenames is tried in sequence so that if one file is not found in flash, the next file is tried, and so on.

The firewall also maintains this value as an environment variable BOOT while it is running. If multiple **boot system** commands have been configured, the BOOT variable contains the entire sequence of values. You can display the current boot image setting with the following command:

```
Firewall# show bootvar
```

For example, two image files are stored in flash: flash:/image.bin and flash:/image-beta.bin. You can run either image on the firewall. For normal production use, image.bin is used, whereas image-beta.bin is occasionally run to test new firewall features. The following commands show the available images and then specify image.bin and image-beta.bin as the bootable image sequence:

```
Firewall# dir flash:
Directory of flash:/
4       -rw-  4976640      10:23:28 Apr 1 2007   image.bin
9       -rw-  5261204       4:10:17 May 6 2007   image-beta.bin
[output omitted]
Firewall# configure terminal
Firewall(config)# boot system flash:/image.bin
Firewall(config)# boot system flash:/image-beta.bin
Firewall(config)# exit
Firewall# copy running-config startup-config
Firewall#
Firewall# show bootvar
BOOT variable = flash:/image.bin
Current BOOT variable = flash:/image.bin;flash:/image-beta.bin
CONFIG_FILE variable =
Current CONFIG_FILE variable =
Firewall#
```

Notice that the BOOT variable has two different lines of output. The first, **BOOT variable**, shows the value obtained from the **boot system** commands at bootup time. The **Current BOOT variable** line shows the current value obtained by any additional **boot system** commands entered since bootup.

Upgrading an Image from the Monitor Prompt

If the firewall has no operating system image, you can still download one via TFTP from the monitor prompt. At this point, the firewall is not inspecting any traffic and has no running configuration. Follow these steps to download a firewall operating system image via TFTP:

1. Make sure a TFTP server is available.

    The TFTP server should have the firewall image available for downloading.

TIP   You can obtain TFTP server software from a variety of sources:

- Solarwinds.net TFTP server (http://www.solarwinds.net; free)
- Kiwi CatTools 2.x, Kiwi Enterprises (http://www.kiwisyslog.com; commercial package)
- Tftpd32 (http://tftpd32.jounin.net; free)
- tftpd, standard on UNIX systems (free)

At one time, Cisco offered a free TFTP server on Cisco.com. However, this was limited to Windows 95 installations, so it has since been dropped from support.

---

2. Boot the firewall to the monitor prompt.

    Just after booting the firewall, you can press the Esc or Break key to break the normal bootup sequence. Be sure to do this when the following output and prompt are displayed:

    ```
    Cisco Systems ROMMON Version (1.0(10)0) #0: Fri Mar 25 23:02:10 PST 2005

    Platform ASA5510

    Use BREAK or ESC to interrupt boot.
    Use SPACE to begin boot immediately.
    [The ESC key was pressed here]
    Boot interrupted.

    Management0/0
    Ethernet auto negotiation timed out.
    Interface-4 Link Not Established (check cable).

    Default Interface number-4 Not Up

    Use ? for help.
    rommon #0>
    ```

3. Identify the TFTP server.

NOTE   The parameters you assign here are used only temporarily until the firewall can download and run the new image. None of these commands is stored in a configuration; as soon as the firewall boots, they are lost.

---

a.   Identify the firewall interface where the TFTP server is located:

ASA	`monitor>` **`interface`** *`name`*
PIX 6.3	`monitor>` **`interface`** *`number`*

On an ASA platform, you identify the interface by its physical interface name. For example, you could use **ethernet0/0, ethernet0/1, ethernet0/2, ethernet0/3,** or **management0/ 0** on an ASA 5510.

TFTP on a PIX 6.3 platform uses the interface with index *number* (0 to $n - 1$, where n is the number of interfaces installed). During the bootup sequence, the firewall lists the physical interfaces that are installed. Some models also list their MAC addresses but do not number the interfaces. Therefore, it might not be clear how they correspond to the actual connections on the firewall. In any case, the first interface shown is always index 0.

TIP   On a PIX platform, when the installed interfaces are listed during bootup, only the interfaces that are *not* Gigabit Ethernet are shown. This is because you cannot use a Gigabit Ethernet interface to download a software image from the monitor prompt.

If you are stuck trying to figure out what interface names are available on an ASA, you can enter a bogus value for the interface name to get the valid names listed. For example, try something like **interface 0** to get the following list:

```
rommon #1> interface 0
Invalid interface name argument, Valid arguments are:
    Ethernet0/0
    Ethernet0/1
    Ethernet0/2
    Ethernet0/3
    Management0/0

interface <name>   ethernet interface port
rommon #1>
```

---

b.   Assign an IP address to the interface:

`monitor>` **`address`** *`ip-address`*

Here, the firewall needs just enough information to be able to contact the TFTP server. Only one physical interface can be used, so this IP address is applied to it. Because a subnet mask cannot be given, the firewall assumes a regular classful network mask (172.17.69.41 yields a Class B mask of 255.255.0.0, for example).

If your TFTP server is located on a different classful subnet, you can also specify a gateway address that can route between the firewall and the server. Use the following monitor command:

```
monitor> gateway ip-address
```

  c. Make sure that the firewall can reach the TFTP server.

   The firewall must be able to reach the server with a minimal amount of routing. You can use the following monitor command to test reachability:

```
monitor> ping ip-address
```

  d. Define the TFTP server's IP address:

```
monitor> server ip-address
```

  e. Define the image filename to fetch:

```
monitor> file filename
```

   The image file named *filename* is located in the TFTP server's root directory. This is often called the /tftpboot directory, but it depends on how your TFTP server is configured. As long as the file can be found in the TFTP server's root directory, you do not have to specify the directory name or path.

4. Copy the image from the TFTP server:

ASA	`monitor> tftpdnld`
PIX 6.3	`monitor> tftp`

On an ASA, you should see exclamation points as the TFTP download is progressing. A successful TFTP download should look something like the following:

```
Cisco Systems ROMMON Version (1.0(10)0) #0: Fri Mar 25 23:02:10 PST 2005

Platform ASA5510

Use BREAK or ESC to interrupt boot.
Use SPACE to begin boot immediately.
Boot interrupted.

Management0/0
Ethernet auto negotiation timed out.
Interface-4 Link Not Established (check cable).
Default Interface number-4 Not Up
```

```
Use ? for help.
rommon #0> interface etherenet0/0
Ethernet0/0
Link is UP
MAC Address: 0016.c789.c8a4
rommon #1> address 172.17.69.1
rommon #2> server 172.17.69.49
rommon #3> ping 172.17.69.49
Sending 20, 100-byte ICMP Echoes to 172.17.69.49, timeout is 4 seconds:
!!!!!!!!!!!!!!!!!!!!!
Success rate is 100 percent (20/20)
rommon #4> file image.bin
rommon #5> tftpdnld
ROMMON Variable Settings:
  ADDRESS=172.17.69.1
  SERVER=172.17.69.49
  GATEWAY=0.0.0.0
  PORT=Ethernet0/0
  VLAN=untagged
  IMAGE=image.bin
  CONFIG=
  LINKTIMEOUT=20
  PKTTIMEOUT=4
  RETRY=20

tftp image.bin@172.17.69.49 via 0.0.0.0
!!!!!!!!!!!!!!!!!!!!!!!!!!!!!!!!!!!!!!!!!!!!!!!!!!!!!
[output omitted]
!!!!!!!!!!!!!!!!!!!!
Received 14487552 bytes

Launching TFTP Image...

Cisco Security Appliance admin loader (3.0) #0: Thu Mar 29 01:42:31 MDT 2007
Loading...
```

A PIX 6.3 platform will show periods or dots as the TFTP download is progressing. After the download completes, the firewall needs confirmation before it actually writes the new image into its flash memory. You can also enter a new license activation key at the end of this process, if needed.

A successful TFTP download looks something like this:

```
Cisco Secure PIX Firewall BIOS (4.0) #39: Tue Nov 28 18:44:51 PST 2000
Platform PIX-525
System Flash=E28F128J3 @ 0xfff00000
Use BREAK or ESC to interrupt flash boot.
Use SPACE to begin flash boot immediately.
```

```
Flash boot in 8 seconds.
[ESC key pressed here]
Flash boot interrupted.
0: i8255X @ PCI(bus:0 dev:14 irq:10)
1: i8255X @ PCI(bus:0 dev:13 irq:11)
Use ? for help.
monitor>
monitor> interface 0
Using 0: i8255X @ PCI(bus:0 dev:14 irq:10), MAC: 0090.2744.5e66
monitor> address 172.17.69.1
monitor> ping 172.17.69.49
Sending 5, 100-byte 0x5b8d ICMP Echoes to 172.17.69.49, timeout is 4
  seconds:
!!!!!
Success rate is 100 percent (5/5)
monitor> server 172.17.69.41
monitor> file image.bin
monitor> tftp
tftp image.bin@172.17.69.41.................................................
.........................................................................
[output omitted]
...........................................................
Received 2064384 bytes.
Flash version 6.3(4), Install version 6.3(4)
Do you wish to copy the install image into flash? [n] y
Installing to flash
Serial Number: 807443449 (0x30209bf9)
Activation Key: c422440f 2eb1445a 46fb4413 74a344ee
Do you want to enter a new activation key? [n]
Writing 1941560 bytes image into flash...
```

5. Reload the firewall to run the new image:

```
monitor> reload
```

The firewall performs a reload immediately. You should see the usual bootup output on the console, followed by information about the new running image.

An ASA platform automatically reloads as soon as the code image TFTP download is finished.

Upgrading an Image from an Administrative Session

1. Make sure an image server is available.

The server should have the firewall image available for downloading, either by TFTP, FTP, HTTP, or HTTPS.

2. Make sure you have sufficient space on the flash file system.

   An ASA allows one or more image files as well as other files to be stored in flash, as long as you have sufficient space to contain them all. When a new image or file is downloaded, it is stored in flash with a specific filename. A file is overwritten only if an existing file in flash has an identical filename.

   You can use the following command to check the available (free) space in the flash memory:

   ```
   Firewall# dir flash:/
   ```

   For example, suppose a new firewall image is available on a server. The image file size is 4,995,512 bytes. First, the amount of free flash memory is checked, giving the following output:

   ```
   Firewall# dir flash:/
   Directory of flash:/
   6       -rw-  4976640      10:04:50 Nov 12 2004  image.bin
   10      -rw-  1575         23:05:09 Sep 30 2004  old_running.cfg
   12      -rw-  3134         23:30:24 Nov 08 2004  admin.cfg
   13      -rw-  1401         14:12:31 Oct 20 2004  CustomerA.cfg
   14      -rw-  2515         23:29:28 Nov 08 2004  border.cfg
   17      -rw-  1961         13:52:22 Oct 25 2004  datacenter.cfg
   23      -rw-  8596996      10:12:38 Nov 12 2004  asdm.bin
   21      drw-  704          15:06:09 Nov 22 2004  syslog
   32      -rw-  205          15:06:08 Nov 22 2004  stuff
   16128000 bytes total (2466816 bytes free)
   Firewall#
   ```

   Clearly, 2,466,816 bytes free is insufficient to store the new image unless the existing image (image.bin) is overwritten.

   On an FWSM or a PIX 6.3 platform, only one operating system image and one PDM image can be stored in the flash file system at any time. If a new image is downloaded, it automatically overwrites an existing image in flash.

3. Make sure the firewall can reach the server:

   ```
   Firewall# ping [interface] ip-address
   ```

   The server has IP address *ip-address*. The firewall should already have the necessary routing information to reach the server. You can specify the firewall interface where the server is located ("outside," for example) if the firewall cannot determine that directly. For example, this firewall can reach the server at 192.168.254.2:

   ```
   Firewall# ping 192.168.254.2
   Type escape sequence to abort.
   Sending 5, 100-byte ICMP Echos to 192.168.254.2, timeout is 2 seconds:
   !!!!!
   Success rate is 100 percent (5/5), round-trip min/avg/max = 1/1/1 ms
   Firewall#
   ```

4. (TFTP only) Identify a possible TFTP server:

```
Firewall(config)# tftp-server interface ip-address path
```

The TFTP server can be found at *ip-address* on the firewall interface named *interface* (**outside**), for example. As of FWSM 3.1(1) and ASA 7.0(1), the interface parameter is required. For prior releases, the firewall always assumes the inside interface is used for TFTP. The only way to override this assumption is by specifying a firewall interface in the **tftp-server** command. This interface is always used whenever files are copied to and from a TFTP server, even if the server address is different from the one configured with this command.

The image files are stored in the *path* directory on the TFTP server. This path is relative only to the TFTP process itself. For example, if the image files are stored in the topmost TFTP directory (/tftpboot within the server's file system, for example), the *path* would be /, or the root of the TFTP directory tree.

TIP   The **tftp-server** command is optional because most of the TFTP parameters can be given with the **copy** EXEC command when the image is downloaded.

---

5. Copy the image file from the server.

With any download method, the basic command syntax is:

```
Firewall# copy source  flash:[image | pdm | filename]
```

The image is downloaded and copied into flash memory as either an operating system **image** or a **pdm** image. Only one of either image type can be stored in the firewall flash, and their locations are automatically determined. In fact, PIX 6.3 restricts the image transfer to these two file types.

ASA and FWSM platforms make use of their more flexible flash file systems. From the system execution space, you can copy one or more image files into flash and then specify which image the firewall should use. You can give the destination filename as an arbitrary *filename*. You also can use the **image** or **asdm** keywords for backward compatibility. In that case, the firewall uses the image filename configured with the **boot system** or **asdm image** commands, respectively.

Also, you can choose TFTP, FTP, or HTTP as the copy method, as discussed in the following steps.

a. Use a TFTP server:

```
Firewall# copy tftp:[:[[//location][/pathname]] flash:[image | pdm |
  filename]
```

The image file is located on the TFTP server at *location*, which can be either a hostname (already defined with a **name** command) or an IP address. The image file is referenced by *pathname*, which can include any directory structure needed within TFTP, along with the filename. (If the actual path name of the TFTP directory contains spaces, you should first define the whole path name using the **tftp-server** command. Spaces are not allowed in the *pathname* here.)

If the *location* or *pathname* parameters are left out of this command, the firewall prompts you for those values.

If you add a colon after the **tftp** keyword, the firewall picks up the remaining parameters configured with the **tftp**-server command.

For example, suppose a new operating system image named newimage.bin is located on TFTP server 192.168.254.2. Recall that the firewall assumes that the TFTP server is located on the inside interface by default. In this case, it is located on the outside interface. You can download the new firewall image into flash memory using the following commands:

```
Firewall# configure terminal
Firewall(config)# tftp-server outside 192.168.254.2 /
Firewall(config)# exit
Firewall# copy tftp://192.168.254.2/newimage.bin flash:image
Address or name of remote host [192.168.254.2]?
Source filename [newimage.bin]?
Destination filename [image.bin]?
%Warning:There is a file already existing with this name
Do you want to over write? [confirm]
Accessing tftp://192.168.254.2/newimage.bin...!!!!!!!!!!!!!!!
[output omitted]
Writing file flash:/image.bin...
!!!!!!!!!!!!!!!!!!!!!!!!!!!!!!!!!!!!!!!!1
4976640 bytes copied in 143.380 secs (34801 bytes/sec)
Firewall#
```

b. Use an FTP server:

```
Firewall# copy ftp://[user[:password]@]server[:port]/[path/]filename
  [;type=xy] flash:[image | pdm | filename]
```

The FTP server is known as server by either an IP address or a hostname (the host name must be preconfigured with the **name** configuration command). If the server requires user authentication, the username and password are given as *user:password@*. By default, TCP port 21 is used; you can override this by specifying *port*.

The image file is found on the server with pathname *path* (relative to the user's home directory) and filename *filename*. By default, the firewall uses an FTP session in binary passive mode. You can use a different FTP mode by appending the **;type=**xy keyword, where x is a single letter **a** (ASCII) or **i** (image or binary) and y is a single letter **p** (passive) or **n** (normal). For example, **;type=ip** is the default binary passive mode.

As an example, suppose an image named *newimage.bin* is located on an FTP server at 192.168.254.2. The server requires authentication using username *myuserid* and password *mypassword*, and the image is stored in the *Images* directory. You can download the new firewall image into flash memory using the following command:

```
Firewall# copy ftp://myuserid:mypassword@192.168.254.2/Images/
  newimage.bin flash:image
Address or name of remote host [192.168.254.2]?
Source filename [newimage.bin]?
Destination filename [image.bin]?
%Warning:There is a file already existing with this name
Do you want to over write? [confirm]
Accessing ftp://myuserid:mypassword@192.168.254.2/Images/newimage.bin...
!!!!!!!!!!!!!!
[output omitted]
Writing file flash:/image.bin...
!!!!!!!!!!!!!!!!!!!!!!!!!!!!!!!!!!!!!!!!1
4976640 bytes copied in 149.110 secs (33375 bytes/sec)
Firewall#
```

c. Use an HTTP or HTTPS server:

```
Firewall# copy http[s]://[user:password@]location[:port ]/
  http_pathname flash[:[image | pdm | filename]
```

You can use either **http** (HTTP, port 80) or **https** (HTTPS or SSL, port 443), depending on how the web server is configured.

If user authentication is required, it can be given as *user:password@*. The web server has a name or IP address given by location. (If a host name is used, it must also be defined in the firewall with the **name** command.) By default, the port number is either TCP 80 or TCP 443, according to the **http** or **https** keyword. You can override the TCP port number by giving it as *port*.

The image file can be found on the server at the path *http_pathname*. The directory hierarchy is relative to the web server's file structure.

For example, a PIX operating system image named *newimage.bin* is stored on the web server at http://192.168.254.2 in the default directory. The server requires authentication using username *myuserid* and password *mypassword*. You can download the new firewall image into flash memory using the following command:

```
Firewall# copy http://myuserid:mypassword@192.168.254.2/newimage.bin flash:image.bin
Address or name of remote host [192.168.254.2]?
Source filename [newimage.bin]?
Destination filename [image.bin]?
%Warning:There is a file already existing with this name
Do you want to over write? [confirm]
Accessing http://192.168.254.2/newimage.bin...!!!!!!!!!!!!!!!!!!!
```

```
[output omitted]
Writing file flash:/image.bin...
!!!!!!!!!!!!!!!!!!!!!!!!!!!!!!!!!!!!!!!
[output omitted]
4902912 bytes copied in 137.730 secs (35787 bytes/sec)
Firewall#
```

Upgrading an Image Automatically

You can also configure a firewall to automatically poll a central server to see if a new image file exists. If a newer image is available, the firewall downloads it without any intervention on your part. This functionality is available with an Auto Update Server (AUS) and is discussed in detail in Section "4-4: Automatic Updates with an Auto Update Server."

4-3: Managing Configuration Files

A firewall keeps a "startup" configuration file in flash memory. These configuration commands are not lost after a reload or power failure.

As soon as a firewall boots up, the startup configuration commands are copied to the "running" configuration file in RAM (volatile) memory. Any command that is entered or copied into the running configuration is also executed at that time.

As you enter configuration commands, be aware that they are present only in the temporary running configuration. After you have verified the operation of the new configuration commands, you should be sure to save the running configuration into flash memory. This preserves the configuration in case the firewall reloads later.

You can enter configuration commands into the firewall using the following methods:

- Command-line interface (CLI), where commands are entered through a console, Telnet, or SSH session on the firewall. The **configure terminal** command is used for this.
- A management application such as PDM or Firewall Management Center (within VMS).
- Imported by a TFTP file transfer.
- Imported by a web server.
- An automated or forced update from an AUS.

Managing the Startup Configuration

In PIX releases 6.3 and earlier, as well as FWSM releases, a firewall has one startup configuration that is stored in flash memory. This configuration file is read upon bootup and is copied into the running configuration.

ASA platforms running 7.0 or later have the capability to maintain one or more startup configuration files in flash, provided that you have sufficient space to store them. Only one of these can be used at boot time.

This section discusses the tasks that can be used to maintain and display the startup configuration file.

Selecting a Startup Configuration File

In ASA platforms, having multiple startup configurations makes configuration rollback easy. The startup configuration contents can be saved in one file during the time that the firewall configuration is stable. If major configuration changes need to be made, the new updated running configuration can be saved to a new startup configuration file. The next time the firewall is booted, it can use this new file.

If you encounter problems with the new configuration, you can make one configuration change to force the firewall to roll back or use a previous version of the startup configuration.

By default, a firewall stores its startup configuration in a hidden partition of flash memory. That file has no usable name and can be viewed only through the **show startup-configuration** command.

To force the firewall to use a different startup configuration filename, you can use the following command:

```
Firewall(config)# boot config url
```

url represents the location of the startup configuration file. It can be **flash:**/*path*, **disk0:**/*path*, or **disk1:**/*path*, depending on which flash file systems the firewall platform supports. PIX models have only a **flash:/** file system, whereas the ASA platforms can support flash or disk flash file systems.

Be aware that the **boot config** *url* command effectively changes an environment variable used only by the running configuration. When you use this command, be sure to save the running configuration with the **copy running-config startup-config** or **write memory** command.

At this point, the firewall uses the new *url* and saves the startup configuration in that file, not in the default location. If the file does not exist, a new file is created; if it does exist, the running configuration is merged with that file's contents. The environment variable is also updated and is used during the next boot cycle to find the new startup configuration file.

You can see the startup configuration environment variable with the **show bootvar** command. The following example begins with the default location, signified by the empty *Current CONFIG FILE variable* value. When the **boot config** command is used, the current value is updated to show the new file location.

However, until the running configuration is saved to the new startup configuration location, the new file is not present in flash. As well, the startup configuration file used at boot time is still the default (shown by an empty *CONFIG FILE variable* line). After the configuration is saved, the new file is used during the next firewall boot.

```
Firewall# show bootvar
BOOT variable = flash:/image.bin
Current BOOT variable = flash:/image.bin
CONFIG_FILE variable =
Current CONFIG_FILE variable =
Firewall# configure terminal
Firewall(config)# boot config flash:/startup-1.cfg
INFO: Converting myconfig.cfg to flash:/startup-1.cfg
```

```
Firewall(config)# exit
Firewall# show bootvar
BOOT variable = flash:/image.bin
Current BOOT variable = flash:/image.bin
CONFIG_FILE variable =
Current CONFIG_FILE variable = flash:/startup-1.cfg
Firewall# dir flash:/
Directory of flash:/
6       -rw-  5031936     10:21:11 Dec 21 2006  image.bin
23      -rw-  8596996     10:12:38 Nov 12 2006  asdm.bin
16128000 bytes total (2450944 bytes free)
Firewall#
Firewall# copy running-config startup-config
Source filename [running-config]?
Cryptochecksum: a8885ca7 9782e279 c6794487 6480e76a
3861 bytes copied in 0.900 secs
Firewall# show bootvar
BOOT variable = flash:/image.bin
Current BOOT variable = flash:/image.bin
CONFIG_FILE variable = flash:/startup-1.cfg
Current CONFIG_FILE variable = flash:/startup-1.cfg
Firewall# dir flash:/
Directory of flash:/
6       -rw-  5031936     10:21:11 Dec 21 2006  image.bin
23      -rw-  8596996     10:12:38 Nov 12 2006  asdm.bin
20      -rw-  3861        23:12:20 Dec 30 2006  startup-1.cfg
```

Finally, notice that even though a new location and a new filename are used for the startup configuration, you do not have to specify those when you save the running configuration later. The firewall continues to work with the **startup-config** keyword, but it uses the new *url* to reference the actual file. In other words, **copy running-config startup-config** always uses the current and correct location.

Displaying the Startup Configuration

You can display the contents of the startup configuration with either of these commands:

```
Firewall# show startup-config
```

or

```
Firewall# show configuration
```

In PIX 6.3, the latter command is actually **show configure**.

In the first line of the startup configuration, you can find its time stamp. This shows when the running configuration was saved to flash the last time and who saved it. For example, the generic user enable_15 (someone in privileged EXEC or enable mode) saved this configuration:

```
Firewall# show startup-config
: Saved
: Written by enable_15 at 17:41:51.013 EST Mon Nov 22 2006
PIX Version 8.0(1)
```

```
names
!
interface Ethernet0
 shutdown
[output omitted]
```

Saving a Running Configuration

You can view or save a firewall's running configuration with one of the methods described in the following sections.

Viewing the Running Configuration

You can use the following commands to display the current running configuration:

Firewall# **write terminal**

or

Firewall# **show running-config**

The running configuration is displayed to the current terminal session. If the configuration is longer than your current session page length (24 lines by default), you have to press the spacebar to page through it.

However, in ASA, FWSM, and PIX 6.3 platforms, you can filter the output by using one of the following keywords at the end of the command:

Firewall# **show running-config** | {**begin** | **include** | **exclude** | **grep** [**-v**]} *reg-exp*

You can start the first line of output at the line where the regular expression *reg-exp* appears in the configuration with the **begin** keyword.

If you are looking for lines that contain only the regular expression *reg-exp*, use the **include** or **grep** keyword. You can also display only the lines that do not contain the *reg-exp* with the **exclude** or **grep** **-v** keyword.

The regular expression can be a simple text fragment or a more complex form containing wildcard and pattern-matching characters. For example, **include int** finds any line that contains "int" (including words such as "interface") located anywhere in the text.

These options are very handy if you have a firewall with a large configuration. Rather than paging through large amounts of configuration output, you can instantly find what you are looking for.

Saving the Running Configuration to Flash Memory

After you make configuration changes to a firewall and they are satisfactory, you should make them permanent by saving the running configuration to flash memory. You can use the following command to accomplish this:

Firewall# **write memory**

All the current configuration commands are stored in the startup configuration area in flash memory. You should always run this command after making configuration changes. Otherwise, you might forget to save them later when the firewall is reloaded.

In ASA and FWSM, the **write memory** command is supported for backward compatibility. A new form of the **copy** command is also provided, using the following syntax:

```
Firewall# copy running-config startup-config
```

> **TIP** In multiple context mode, each context's running configuration must be saved individually. This usually means you have to move into each context with the **changeto** command and then use the **write memory** or **copy running-config startup-config** command.
>
> Beginning with ASA 7.2(1) and FWSM 3.1(1), you can save all context configurations with a single command. In the system execution space, use the following command:
>
> ```
> Firewall# write memory all
> ```
> The **copy** command does not have the same capability.

When the configuration is saved or displayed, the firewall also displays a *cryptochecksum*, or a message digest 5 (MD5) hash of the configuration file contents. This value serves as a type of fingerprint that can be used to evaluate the configuration file's integrity. The configuration file's size is also shown, as in the following example:

```
Firewall# copy running-config startup-config
Source filename [running-config]?
Cryptochecksum: 71a4cecb 97baf374 10757e38 a320cc43
2909 bytes copied in 0.520 secs
Firewall#
```

> **TIP** You can use the MD5 cryptochecksum value as a quick check to see if a firewall's configuration has changed since it booted. First, find the MD5 hash that was saved with the startup configuration by looking at the last line of the **show startup-config** or **show config** command. Then compare that to the MD5 hash of the current running configuration, shown in the last line of the **show running-config** command or with the output of the **show checksum** command. If the two hash values differ, the configuration has changed.
>
> Comparing the two cryptochecksum values in the following example shows that the configuration has been changed:
>
> ```
> Firewall# show startup-config | include checksum
> Cryptochecksum:3750a83d00922b80ffef78e92865b09a
> ```

```
Firewall# show running-config | include checksum
Cryptochecksum:a5bdac82909dc8717e494cfabc2d363d
Firewall#
```

Saving the Running Configuration to a TFTP Server

You can use the following steps to save the current running configuration to an external file server:

1. (Optional) Identify the TFTP server:

   ```
   Firewall(config)# tftp-server [interface] ip-address path
   ```

   The TFTP server can be found on the firewall's *interface* at IP address *ip-address*. By default, the inside interface is assumed. The running configuration file is stored in the *path* directory on the TFTP server. This path is relative only to the TFTP process itself. For example, if the file is stored in the topmost TFTP directory (/tftpboot, for example), the *path* would be /, or the root of the TFTP directory tree.

   TIP   The **tftp-server** command is not necessary, because all the TFTP parameters can be given with the **write net** or **copy** EXEC command when the configuration is saved. However, the firewall always assumes the *inside* interface will be used for TFTP. The only way to override this assumption is by specifying a firewall *interface* (**inside** or **outside**, for example) in the **tftp-server** command. This interface is always used whenever files are copied to and from a TFTP server, even if the server address is different.

   ---

2. Save the configuration:

   ```
   Firewall# write net [[server-ip-address]:[filename]]
   ```

   The TFTP server can be identified by giving its IP address here as *server-ip-address*. The configuration is saved in a file named *filename* in the TFTP root directory on the server.

   If the server is not specified here, the values configured by the **tftp-server** command are used. You can also override the server address configured with the **tftp-server** command by specifying an address here.

   ASA and FWSM platforms also offer the **copy** command, which can be used to copy the running configuration to a TFTP server. You can use the following command:

   ```
   Firewall# copy running-config
     tftp://[user[:password]@]server[:port]/[path/]filename
   ```

   Here, the running configuration is copied as a file with the filename *filename*. You can provide a path to specify where the file should be stored on the server. The path is relative to the TFTP server's root directory. If the server requires user authentication, the user ID and password can be given in the form *user:password@*.

For example, the running configuration is to be saved as the file *firewall.confg* on the TFTP server at 192.168.208.40, located on the firewall's dmz interface. The following commands can be used to accomplish this:

```
Firewall(config)# tftp-server dmz 192.168.208.40 /
Firewall(config)# exit
Firewall# write net 192.168.208.40:firewall.confg
```

or

```
Firewall# copy running-config tftp://192.168.208.40/firewall.confg
```

Forcing the Running Configuration to Be Copied Across a Failover Pair

During the bootup sequence, the active firewall copies its complete running configuration to the standby firewall. The active unit also copies any configuration commands to the standby unit as they are entered and executed.

Under normal conditions, the standby unit can keep its running configuration up to date and synchronized with the active unit. Sometimes it is possible for the two units to become unsynchronized. This can occur when configuration changes are made while the failover cable is disconnected, while the LAN-based failover connection is broken, or while the two units are running different OS releases. In these cases, you might see some of the logging messages in Table 4-8 generated when stateful failover cannot synchronize the two firewall units.

Table 4-8 *Logging Messages Resulting from Stateful Failover Synchronization Errors*

Message ID	Description
%ASA-1-105020	(Primary) Incomplete/slow configuration replication.
%ASA-3-210006	Stateful failover is unable to locate a NAT group for the IP address on the standby unit.
%ASA-3-210008	Unable to find a translation slot (xlate) record for a stateful failover connection.
%ASA-3-210020	Stateful failover is unable to allocate a specific PAT address that is in use.
%ASA-3-210021	Stateful failover is unable to create a translation slot (xlate).

If you make configuration changes on the standby firewall unit, those changes are not replicated back toward the active unit. Instead, you see the following message:

```
*** WARNING ***
    Configuration Replication is NOT performed from Standby unit to Active unit.
    Configurations are no longer synchronized.
```

If you find that the running configurations are no longer identical and synchronized between the active and standby units, you can use the following command on the active unit to force a complete copy to be sent to the standby unit:

```
Firewall# write standby
```

Forcing the Startup (Nonvolatile) Configuration to Be Cleared

Sometimes you might need to begin with an empty configuration on a firewall. This might happen if you reuse an existing firewall in a different scenario or if you inherit a firewall from someone else.

The following command erases all configuration commands from the startup configuration in flash memory:

```
Firewall# write erase
```

This command does not disturb or erase the current running configuration. After the startup configuration is erased, you can use the **reload** EXEC command to reboot the firewall with the new, empty startup configuration.

Importing a Configuration

You can copy configuration commands into a firewall's running configuration with one of the methods documented in the following sections.

Entering Configuration Commands Manually

You can begin entering configuration commands in a terminal session (console, Telnet, or SSH) after you use the following command:

```
Firewall# configure terminal
```

Commands are entered into the running configuration in RAM and are executed as they are entered. To end configuration mode, press **Ctrl-z** or enter **exit**.

TIP In a failover pair of firewalls, configuration commands should be entered only on the active unit. As you enter configuration commands into the active unit, they are copied to the standby unit. Therefore, the failover configurations are automatically synchronized.

If you enter configuration commands on the standby unit, they are not replicated to the active unit. Therefore, the firewall configurations become different and are unsynchronized.

Merging Configuration Commands from Flash Memory

The commands stored in the startup configuration in flash memory can be copied over and merged into the running configuration after you issue the following command:

```
Firewall# configure memory
```

This is useful when the running configuration has been mistakenly cleared or the wrong configuration has been imported.

In ASA and FWSM platforms, you can achieve the same results with the following command:

```
Firewall# copy startup-config running-config
```

TIP   Remember that configuration commands are *merged* from flash into RAM. This means that commands in the running configuration are preserved, and the commands stored in flash are copied into the running configuration in RAM.

If similar commands are stored in both the startup and running configurations, the startup commands overwrite the others. In effect, this can result in a running configuration that is a mixture of startup and running configurations. It is a common misconception that the running configuration is erased before the startup configuration is copied onto it.

To erase the running configuration before the merge, use the **clear configure all** configuration command first. However, be aware that any existing configuration commands that provide IP addressing, routing, and administrative access are removed immediately. Unless you are connected to the firewall console, you could find that you become cut off from the newly cleared firewall.

Merging Configuration Commands from a TFTP Server

You can use the following steps to merge configuration commands from a file contained on an external TFTP server:

1. (Optional) Identify the TFTP server:

```
Firewall(config)# tftp-server [interface] ip-address path
```

The TFTP server can be found on the firewall's *interface* at IP address *ip-address*. By default, the **inside** interface is assumed. The configuration file is copied from the *path* directory on the TFTP server. This path is relative only to the TFTP process itself. For example, if the file is stored in the topmost TFTP directory (/tftpboot, for example), the path would be simply a forward slash, as /, denoting the root of the TFTP directory tree.

2. Fetch and merge the configuration:

```
Firewall(config)# configure net [[server-ip-address]:[filename]]
```

The TFTP server can be identified by giving its IP address here as *server-ip-address*. The configuration is retrieved from the file named *filename* in the TFTP root directory on the server.

If the server is not specified here, the values configured by the **tftp-server** command are used. You can also override the server address configured with the **tftp-server** command by specifying an address here.

Although the ASA and FWSM support the legacy **configure net** command, they also offer the following new form of the **copy** command to achieve similar results:

```
Firewall# copy tftp://[user[:password]@]server[:port]/[path/]filename
  running-config
```

Here, the file named *filename* is found at *path* on the TFTP server at IP address *server*. If the server requires user authentication, you can give the user ID and password using the *user:password@* format.

Merging Configuration Commands from a Web Server

If you have a configuration file stored on an external web server, you can use the following command to merge its contents with the running configuration:

```
Firewall(config)# configure http[s]://[user:password@]location[:port]/
  http-pathname
```

You can use either the **http** (HTTP, port 80) or **https** (HTTPS or SSL, port 443) protocol to transfer the configuration file, depending on how the web server is configured.

If user authentication is required, it can be given as *user:password@*. The web server has a name or IP address given by *location*. (If a host name is used, it must also be defined in the firewall with the **name** command.) By default, the port number is either 80 or 443, according to the **http** or **https** keyword. You can override the port number by giving it as *port*.

The configuration file can be found on the server at the path *http-pathname*. The directory hierarchy is relative to the web server's file structure.

ASA and FWSM platforms also offer the following form of the **copy** command that achieves similar results:

```
Firewall# copy http[s]://[user[:password]@]server[:port]/[path/]filename
  running-config
```

For example, suppose a configuration file named fwtemplate.cfg is stored on the web server at 172.30.22.17. User authentication is required, using user ID fwadmin and password myadminpw. You can use the following commands to merge the file with the running configuration:

```
Firewall# configure https://pixadmin/myadminpw@172.30.22.17/pixtemplate.cfg
```

or

```
Firewall# copy https://fwadmin/myadminpw@172.30.22.17/fwtemplate.cfg
  running-config
```

Merging Configuration Commands from an Auto Update Server

You can use an Auto Update Server (AUS) as a platform to automatically merge a stored configuration file with the running configuration. Having the firewall pick up a new configuration file update is easier than a manual method if you have many firewalls to maintain.

The AUS feature is discussed in detail in the next section of this chapter.

4-4: Automatic Updates with an Auto Update Server

With an AUS, you can use one central location as a distribution point for the firewall image and configuration updates. This can be handy if you have many firewalls to maintain.

Ordinarily, you would have to manually transfer a new image or configuration file to each firewall individually. With AUS, each firewall can poll periodically to see if a new file is available. If a newer file is found, the firewall automatically downloads it without any further intervention.

A firewall can be configured to act as an Auto Update client, where it polls a central Auto Update Server for updates. ASA and PIX platforms can poll an AUS beginning with release 7.0(1); FWSM can poll an AUS beginning with release 3.1(1).

Traditionally, only specialized network management applications could operate as Auto Update Servers. These include Cisco Security Manager (CSM), Cisco VPN/Security Management Solution (VMS), and Resource Manager Essentials (RME, a part of CiscoWorks). Beginning with ASA 7.2(1), you can also configure an ASA platform to act as an AUS.

Configuring a Firewall as an Auto Update Client

Use the following steps to configure a firewall as an Auto Update client, so that it can periodically poll an AUS for new image and configuration files.

1. Make sure an AUS is available.

    The firewall should be defined in the AUS, and the new image or configuration file should be assigned to or associated with it.

    As soon as you load an image or configuration file into the AUS and associate it to a firewall, the firewall client can download and begin using the file the very next time it polls AUS. The client firewall checks to see if the file is newer than the one it is currently running. If so, it automatically downloads that file.

    Be aware that when a client firewall downloads an updated operating system image file from an AUS, it automatically reloads itself so that it can begin running the new image. The reload happens immediately, with little or no warning!

    In some circumstances, the AUS administrator can force AUS to send the firewall a request to download the configuration immediately—regardless of the AUS polling schedule.

2. Make sure the AUS can be reached:

```
Firewall# ping [interface] ip-address
```

Here, the AUS has IP address *ip-address*. The firewall should already have the necessary routing information to reach the AUS device. You can specify a firewall interface ("outside," for example) where the AUS can be found if the firewall cannot determine that directly.

3. Identify the image and ASDM files to update.

If the firewall polls an AUS and finds a newer file to download, it has to know where it should store the files. For a configuration file, the firewall simply merges the newer configuration file into its running configuration.

However, operating system and ASDM image files must be stored in the firewall's flash memory with specific filenames. You should define the image file locations and names with the following configuration commands:

```
Firewall(config)# boot system device:/filename
Firewall(config)# asdm image device:/filename
```

For example, if your firewall is running an image called *image.bin* and an ASDM image called *asdm.bin*, located in the flash filesystem, you could use the following commands:

```
Firewall(config)# boot system flash:/image.bin
Firewall(config)# asdm image flash:/asdm.bin
```

If the file locations are not configured at all, the firewall does not attempt to download new files from the AUS. Instead, it aborts the update and creates log message 612002, "Auto Update failed: Flash open failed."

TIP   You should keep your operating system and ASDM image filenames as generic as possible. In other words, do not include the release number in the filename. The Auto Update process downloads new files right onto the location of existing files, reusing the original filenames.

If you keep the names generic, then a file called *flash:/image.bin* will always contain the up-to-date image. However, if you use a filename like *flash:/asa801.bin*, it might contain ASA release 8.0(1) today, but it might also contain ASA release 8.0(2) tomorrow. The filename is completely arbitrary, but it can become confusing to you if you use the name as an indicator of the release level.

---

4. Give the firewall an identity:

ASA	Firewall(config)# **auto-update device-id {hardware-serial** I **hostname** I **ipaddress** [*if_name*] I **mac-address** [*if_name*] I **string** *text*}
FWSM	Firewall(config)# **auto-update device-id {hardware-serial** I **hostname** I **ipaddress** [*if_name*] I **mac-address** [*if_name*] I **string** *text*}
PIX 6.3	Firewall(config)# **auto-update device-id {hardware-serial** I **hostname** I **ipaddress** [*if_name*] I **mac-address** [*if_name*] I **string** *text*}

When an Auto Update client firewall polls the AUS, the AUS must be able to determine which files are associated with that firewall. After all, the AUS might be managing image and configuration files for many different firewalls in your organization.

You can choose how the firewall is identified to AUS with one of the following device ID methods:

- Host name (**hostname**)—The name set by the **hostname** configuration command is used. This is the default device ID.

- Firewall serial number (**hardware-serial**)—The number shown in the **show version** EXEC command is used.

- Interface IP address (**ipaddress**)—The address of the interface named *if_name* is used.

- Interface MAC address (**mac-address**)—The address of the interface named *if_name* is used.

- Text string (**string**)—The arbitrary alphanumeric string *text* is used. This can be useful when none of the other device ID options is relevant in your environment.

When a firewall device is configured in the AUS, it must also be uniquely identified with one of these methods. Make sure that the device ID configured in the **auto-update device-id** command matches the device ID configured in the AUS; otherwise, no files will be automatically updated between the AUS and the firewall.

TIP	Even though the client firewall is configured with a device ID, it also sends other information about itself. For example, the hardware platform family (ASA, PIX, or FWSM) and the specific model number are sent to the AUS.

With this information, the AUS can offer the files that are appropriate for the device family, the hostname, serial number, MAC address, and so on. |

5. (Optional) Set the polling schedule.

   Choose one of the methods described in Steps 5a and 5b to set the schedule when the firewall polls the AUS. You can set a regular polling interval with **auto-update poll-period** or a specific time schedule with **auto-update poll-at** command. However, you cannot configure both methods.

CAUTION	As you configure the polling schedule, keep in mind that the client firewall automatically reloads itself after a new operating system image is downloaded. Make sure you choose polling times where a reload and loss of traffic is acceptable—perhaps during a regular maintenance window or during regular periods of low traffic volume or impact.

    a. Define the AUS polling period:

ASA	Firewall(config)# **auto-update poll-period** *poll-period* [*retry-count* [*retry-period*]]
FWSM	Firewall(config)# **auto-update poll-period** *poll-period* [*retry-count* [*retry-period*]]
PIX 6.3	Firewall(config)# **auto-update poll-period** *poll-period* [*retry-count* [*retry-period*]]

The firewall polls the AUS every *poll-period* minutes (the default is 720 minutes, or 12 hours). If an AUS connection fails, the firewall can retry the connection *retry-count* times (the default is 0—no retries). If the *retry-count* is nonzero, the AUS connections are retried every *retry-period* minutes (1 to 35791 minutes; the default is 5 minutes).

The first poll does not begin until *poll-period* minutes after the command is entered.

    b. Poll at a specific day and time:

ASA	Firewall(config)# **auto-update poll-at** *days hh:mm* [**randomize** *minutes*] [*retry-count* [*retry-period*]]
FWSM	-
PIX 6.3	-

Beginning with ASA 7.2(1), you can configure specific days and times to poll the AUS. Specify the days as a list of one or more day names separated by spaces. You can use any of the following: **monday**, **tuesday**, **wednesday**, **thursday**, **friday**, **saturday**, **sunday**, **daily** (every day of the week), **weekdays** (Monday through Friday), or **weekend** (Saturday and Sunday). The day names are not case sensitive.

Define the time to poll on each of the days as *hh:mm*, in 24-hour format. Make sure the firewall clock is configured accurately. For more information, see Section "10-1: Managing the Firewall Clock" in Chapter 10, "Firewall Logging."

You can also use the **randomize** keyword to specify the number of minutes past the *hh:mm* time that the firewall can poll the AUS. The firewall attempts to choose a random value within the time range so that it does not always poll at the same exact time each day. This is useful if you have a large number of firewalls polling a single AUS so that they do not all try to download files simultaneously.

If an AUS connection fails, the firewall can retry the connection *retry-count* times (the default is 0—no retries). If the *retry-count* is nonzero, the AUS connections are retried every *retry-period* minutes (1 to 35,791 minutes; the default is 5 minutes).

6. (Optional) Make Auto Update polling mandatory:

ASA	Firewall(config)# **auto-update timeout** *period*
FWSM	Firewall(config)# **auto-update timeout** *period*
PIX 6.3	-

If your security policies dictate that your firewalls must be updated with the most recent code images at all times, you can configure ASA and FWSM platforms to require Auto Update service.

In this case, the firewall must successfully contact the AUS at each scheduled interval. If the AUS is not reachable for a period of time, defined as *period* seconds (0 to 35,791 seconds), the firewall stops passing any traffic through itself. This can be considered a brute force security method, where the firewall does not operate unless it is sure it has the latest code image.

CAUTION   Use caution if you decide to enable mandatory Auto Update polling, because an unreachable AUS might cause the firewall to abruptly stop forwarding traffic when you least expect it. By default, the *period* is set to 0 seconds, disabling the feature.

---

7. Identify the AUS URL:

ASA	Firewall(config)# **auto-update server** *url* [**source** *interface*] [**verify-certificate**]
FWSM	Firewall(config)# **auto-update server** *url* [**verify-certificate**]
PIX 6.3	Firewall(config)# **auto-update server** *url* [**verify-certificate**]

The firewall locates the AUS by its URL, given as the text string *url*. You can specify the URL in one of the following formats, depending on which AUS platform is being used:

AUS in a network management application	**http[s]**://[*username:password*@]*AUSserver-IP-address*[:*port*]/**autoupdate/AutoUpdateServlet**
AUS on an ASA	**https://** *username:password*@*AUSserver-IP-address*/**admin/auto-update**

The URL can use **http** (HTTP, port 80) or **https** (HTTPS or SSL, port 443) to communicate with the AUS. If you are using an ASA platform as the AUS, you must use the **https** keyword here.

The firewall can authenticate itself using a valid AUS *username* and *password*. If your AUS is embedded in a network management application, then authentication is optional. Usually this type of AUS identifies the firewall by the device ID that is configured in Step 3.

On an ASA AUS platform, however, authentication is required. The username can be any valid username that is accepted by ASDM. If no usernames are configured on the ASA AUS, then the *username* value should be left blank and *password* should be the enable password of the ASA.

TIP   AUS uses the same web server and authentication methods that are used by ASDM. If you can successfully authenticate to an ASDM session, you can use the same username and password for AUS. You can use the **aaa authentication http console** command to enable specific username authentication; if you use the **no** form of the command, the username must be blank and the enable password used.

The IP address of the AUS is given as *AUSserver-IP-address*. The port used can be determined by the **http** or **https** keyword (80 or 443, respectively) or by an explicit *port* value. If you choose an arbitrary port number, make sure the AUS is configured to operate over the same port. With an ASA AUS, only the **http** keyword (TCP port 443) can be used.

The path name shown as **/autoupdate/AutoUpdateServlet** is the standard value for AUS in a Cisco network management system. If you are using an ASA platform as an AUS, the path must be given as **/admin/auto-update**.

You can optionally make the firewall verify the SSL certificate from the AUS as an added security feature. This prevents the firewall from downloading files from a rogue AUS machine. The client firewall must have its own certificate issued by the same certificate authority (CA) as the AUS.

Finally, you can repeat the **auto-update server** *url* command to define multiple AUS. The client firewall begins with the first AUS configured. If it is unreachable or unresponsive, the client moves on to the next AUS in the list, and so on, in a round robin fashion.

As an example, an ASA is configured as an Auto Update client. The AUS is a network management application located at 10.10.10.1. The client ASA should poll the AUS each Saturday and Sunday at 11:30 p.m., but also at a random time up to 30 minutes later. If the AUS is not responsive, the client should retry three more times at 5-minute intervals.

The following configuration commands could be used to accomplish this:

```
Firewall(config)# auto-update device-id hostname
Firewall(config)# auto-update poll-at saturday sunday 23:30 randomize 30 3 5
Firewall(config)# auto-update server https://10.10.10.1/autoupdate/AutoUpdateServlet
```

Suppose the same ASA client is configured to use another ASA as the AUS, located at 10.10.10.10. The ASA AUS is configured to use its default authentication, with no username and the enable password ausenablepass. The following configuration commands could be used instead:

```
Firewall(config)# auto-update device-id hostname
Firewall(config)# auto-update poll-at saturday sunday 23:30 randomize 30 3 5
Firewall(config)# auto-update server https://:ausenablepass@10.10.10.10/admin/auto-update
```

Notice that when the username is left blank, the colon must still be given as a separator just before the password. If the ASA AUS is configured to use actual usernames, such as a user named ausclient, the last command would appear as follows:

```
Firewall(config)# auto-update server
https://ausclient:password123@10.10.10.10/admin/auto-update
```

Verifying Auto Update Client Operation

After an Auto Update client has been configured, the polling operation becomes rather silent. You can verify the AUS operation or monitor its progress in several ways.

On the client firewall, you can use the following EXEC command to see the current AUS poll status:

```
Firewall# show auto-update
```

For example, the following output from a client firewall shows the server URL (an ASA acting as an AUS, in this case), the polling schedule, and the device ID. The date and time of the next poll cycle is shown, along with the date and time of the last poll. During the last poll, the ASDM image was updated with a new image file from the AUS.

```
Firewall# show auto-update
Server: https://10.10.10.10/admin/auto-update
Poll weekend randomly between 23:30 and 0:00, retry count: 3, retry period: 5 minutes
Timeout: none
Device ID: host name [Firewall]
Next poll in 2148.23 minutes at 23:37:22 UTC Sat Apr 14 2007
Last poll: 23:32:10 UTC Sat Apr 7 2007
Last ASDM update: 23:32:10 UTC Sat Apr 7 2007
Firewall#
```

You should also know what to expect when a client firewall successfully polls an AUS and downloads a new file.

As soon as a new configuration file is retrieved from AUS, the firewall executes a **clear xlate** command automatically. This clears the translation table in preparation for a changed configuration, but might temporarily disrupt active connections through the firewall.

As soon as a new operating system image file is retrieved from the AUS, the client firewall writes the file to its flash memory and then reloads itself *immediately and without prior warning*. The reload disrupts active connections and traffic passing through the firewall until the updated image is booted and operational.

If an ASDM image is retrieved from the AUS, the new file is written into flash memory and is available for new ASDM sessions. No other firewall operations are disrupted.

TIP   Sometimes you might configure a polling schedule, only to realize that it should be cancelled or changed. To change the polling schedule, locate the **poll-period** or **poll-at** command in the running configuration, then reenter the command with the new polling schedule. The new schedule takes effect immediately and can be confirmed by using the **show auto-update** command.

Configuring a Firewall as an Auto Update Server

You can configure an ASA to act as an AUS, if the ASA is running release 7.2(1) or later. This can be useful if you do not have an enterprise network management platform with an embedded AUS. The ASA AUS can be used to offer operating system and ASDM image files to other ASA and PIX firewall platforms—as long as they are running release 7.2(1) or later already.

The image file can be stored on an external web server or on the ASA AUS itself. The most scalable solution is to store firewall image files on a web server. There you have more space for large image files and CPU resources dedicated to serving up files via HTTPS or SSL. The web server does not have to keep track of which image file should go to which firewall platform—the ASA AUS manages the file associations and simply directs the Auto Update clients toward the correct file on the web server.

If you choose to store image files on the ASA, you are limited by the size of the ASA's flash memory. In addition, the ASA's CPU can be impacted when Auto Update clients begin downloading new images from it. This can affect the ASA's performance as a security appliance, so use caution as you configure new Auto Update client firewalls. At the least, the clients should be configured to poll the ASA AUS during scheduled maintenance windows or during times of low traffic impact.

You can use the following steps to configure an ASA as an AUS:

1. Associate client firewalls with an image file.

   For each image file the AUS offers, you need to define the potential client firewalls that can receive the file. For example, maybe you might want all ASA platforms, regardless of model, to receive the same image file. Or an ASA 5510 might receive one file, whereas an ASA 5550 might receive another file. PIX platforms running a PIX version of ASA code could receive still other files.

   Choose one of the methods described in 1a, 1b, 1c, or 1d to identify potential clients and their image. In each of the methods, the configuration command ends with the following syntax:

   `component {image | asdm} url url-string rev-nums rev-nums`

   The **component** keyword is used to define the image file as either an operating system image (**image**) or an ASDM image (**asdm**).

   The file is located by its URL, given as *url_string*. The URL is returned to the Auto Update client, which in turn attempts to download the file directly.

If the file is actually stored on an external web server, the *url_string* is simply the URL where the file can be accessed. For example, if the file *asa801.bin* is stored on the web server at 10.10.10.1 in the /firewall-images directory, the *url_string* would be:

```
http://10.10.10.1/firewall-images/asa801.bin
```

If the file is stored on an ASA AUS, the *url_string* is slightly different. The ASA AUS always requires HTTPS with client authentication, so a username and password must be given. The *url_string* format would be:

```
https://username:password@10.10.10.1/admin/flash/asa801.bin
```

Finally, the AUS must identify an image release number with the image file. The **rev-nums** keyword specifies a release or revision number string, *rev_nums*. Although the *rev_nums* string is completely arbitrary, you should specify the exact release number of the software image.

For example, ASA release 7.2(1) would be defined as **rev-nums 7.2(1)**, release 8.0(1) would be **rev-nums 8.0(1)**, and release 8.0(3)32 would be **rev-nums 8.0(3)32**.

TIP   The **rev-nums** value is returned to an Auto Update client so that the client can decide if the server's image is newer than the image it is already running. In other words, the client's version (displayed by the **show version** command) is compared against the **rev-nums** *rev_nums* string from the AUS.

If the server's image is newer (a greater release number), the client attempts to download the file at the URL it received. If the release number is not greater, the client waits until the next polling cycle and checks again.

When the client polls the AUS, it checks both the operating system image and the ASDM image *rev_nums* values. The client downloads either file (or both) if it has a higher revision number.

---

a.   Offer a file to a family of client firewalls:

```
Firewall(config)# client-update family {asa | pix | family_name} component {image
| asdm} url url-string rev-nums rev-nums
```

With the **family** keyword, a family of firewalls is defined as a common platform, such as ASA or PIX, which includes all of the specific models. For example, using the **asa** keyword would associate ASA 5505, ASA 5510, ASA 5520, ASA 5540, and ASA 5550 clients with a single image file.

If, for some reason, you find that your client firewalls do not fit into one of the predefined family names, you can enter an arbitrary text string as the *family_name*.

b.   Offer a file to a specific model of client firewalls:

```
Firewall(config)# client-update type type component {image | asdm} url url-string
rev-nums rev-nums
```

With the **type** keyword, a type of firewall platform is defined as a specific model. You can use one of the following predefined ASA model types: **asa5505**, **asa5510**, **asa5520**, **asa5540**, or **asa5550**. For a PIX client, you can use one of the following: **pix-515**, **pix-515e**, **pix-525**, or **pix-535**.

For models that do not match any of the predefined **type** keywords, you can enter *type* as an arbitrary text string.

TIP   Before you choose a **type** keyword, you should verify that your client firewall actually matches the type that is configured on the AUS. If the client reports a hardware type that is different from that configured on the AUS, the client does not download any files.

For example, some ASA 5510 devices identify themselves as "asa5510", whereas other ASA 5510 devices report "asa5510-k8" instead. How can you verify the hardware or model type? Look at the output of the **show version** command on the client firewall. The client reports its hardware type as the string right after "Hardware:". For example, the following output shows that an ASA 5510 identifies itself as an "ASA5510-K8" hardware type:

```
Firewall# show version
Cisco Adaptive Security Appliance Software Version 8.0(1)
Device Manager Version 6.0(1)
Compiled on Thu 29-Mar-07 01:37 by builders
System image file is "disk0:/image.bin"
Config file at boot was "startup-config"

Firewall up 6 hours 54 mins

Hardware:   ASA5510-K8, 256 MB RAM, CPU Pentium 4 Celeron 1600 MHz
Internal ATA Compact Flash, 256MB
BIOS Flash M50FW080 @ 0xffe00000, 1024KB
[output truncated]
```

Therefore, the following command would associate this client with the appropriate image file:

```
Firewall(config)# client-update type asa5510-k8 component image ...
```

---

c.   Offer a file to a specific client firewall:

```
Firewall(config)# client-update device-id dev_string component {image | asdm} url
url_string rev-nums rev_nums
```

With the **device-id** keyword, a single, specific client firewall is targeted for the image file. When the client polls the AUS, it presents its own device ID—either its hostname, serial number, IP address, MAC address, or an arbitrary text string. You should define *dev_string* to match the device ID that the client is configured to send.

d. Offer a file to any client firewall:

```
Firewall(config)# client-update component {image | asdm} url url_string rev-nums
rev_nums
```

With the **component** keyword alone, no other means of identifying client firewalls is used. The AUS matches any polling client to the image file. This method should be used only if all of your client firewalls are of the same platform or family. Otherwise, an ASA might receive a PIX iamge, or vice versa.

2. Enable the AUS feature:

```
Firewall(config)# client-update enable
```

After the AUS feature is configured and enabled, it goes about its business rather silently. You can use two debugging methods to monitor the AUS activity:

a. Debug HTTP server activity:

```
Firewall# debug http
```

The ASA AUS uses its own HTTP server to communicate with firewall clients. If image files are stored on the ASA's flash file system, the same HTTP server delivers the image files to the client.

You can enable debug output for the HTTP server with this command. The debug output is sent to your CLI session while the session remains active. The HTTP debug output shows each request from the client, the username sent by the client to authenticate with the AUS, and files sent to the client.

b. Debug the AUS activity:

```
Firewall# debug auto-update server
```

You can enable debug output for the AUS with this command. The debug output shows the device attributes and identity sent with each client poll. You can use this information to verify the device ID, family, and hardware type being sent by the client so that your AUS is configured to match. The debug output also shows the image file URL and revision number that are returned to the client after an appropriate image file is found for the client.

In the following example, an ASA 5510 client (10.10.10.99) polls the AUS (10.10.10.10). The client authenticates itself with the username "ausclient". As soon as it is authenticated with the ASA AUS HTTP server, the client sends its device ID, platform family, and platform type. The ASA AUS uses that information to find an appropriate image file.

First, the client firewall is configured with the following **auto-update** commands:

```
Firewall-client(config)# auto-update device-id hostname
Firewall-client(config)# auto-update poll-at weekend 23:30 randomize 30 3
Firewall-client(config)# auto-update server https://*@10.10.10.10/admin/auto-update
```

The ASA AUS is configured with the following **client-update** commands:

```
Firewall-aus(config)# username ausclient password password123
Firewall-aus(config)# aaa authentication http console LOCAL
Firewall-aus(config)# client-update type asa5510-k8 component image url http://
10.10.10.200/asa801-k8.bin rev-nums 8.0(1)
Firewall-aus(config)# client-update type asa5510-k8 component asdm url https://
ausclient:password123@10.10.10.10/flash/asdm-601.bin rev-nums 6.0(1)
Firewall-aus(config)# client-update enable
```

Both HTTP and AUS debug output are shown in the following example:

```
HTTP: processing POST URL '/admin/auto-update' from host 10.10.10.99
HTTP: Authentication username = 'ausclient'
Auto-update server: Processing DeviceDetails from host 10.10.10.99
   DeviceID: Firewall
   PlatformFamily: ASA
   PlatformType: ASA5510-K8
Auto-update server: Sent UpdateInfo to host 10.10.10.99
   Component: asdm, URL: https://ausclient:password123@10.10.10.10/flash/asdm.bin,
Version: 6.0(1)
   Component: image, URL: http://10.10.10.200/asa801-k8.bin, Version: 8.0(1)
HTTP: processing GET URL '/flash/asdm-601.bin' from host 10.10.10.10
HTTP: Authentication username = 'ausclient'
HTTP: sending file: flash:/asdm-601.bin, length: 6727152
```

Notice that the AUS informs the client of two image files: one ASDM image and one operating system image.

The URLs of each are also sent, so the client can locate the files if it decides that it needs to download them. The ASDM image file is located on the AUS's own flash file system, whereas the operating system image is located on an external web server.

4-5: Managing Administrative Sessions

Administrators and firewall users can open interactive sessions with a firewall using any of the following methods:

- A terminal emulator connected to the console port
- Telnet
- SSH
- Web-based management applications such as ASDM or PDM

The following sections provide information about the configuration and use of these methods.

Console Connection

Most Cisco firewall and security appliances have a physical console connection that can be used to access a user interface. The console port is an asynchronous serial interface operating at 9600 baud.

Because of its relatively slow speed, the console should be used only to initially configure the firewall or to access it over an out-of-band connection as a last resort.

Because the FWSM is integrated into a Catalyst 6500 or 7600 switch chassis, it does not have a readily accessible console port. It does have an emulated console connection you can reach from the switch user interface by specifying the FWSM module number in the following command:

```
Switch# session slot module processor 1
```

The **session slot** command is actually a special Telnet session to the FWSM over the Catalyst 6500 backplane. Normally, the emulated console session provides reliable access to the FWSM, even if none of its interfaces are operational.

TIP   The FWSM also has a physical console port, like any other firewall platform. However, the console is not easy to access—it is an RJ-45 jack labeled "P0", located on the FWSM's printed circuit board.

If you decide to use this console port, you should connect a cable while the FWSM is pulled out of the switch chassis. Then, slide the FWSM in and carefully thread the cable out through an adjacent slot.

Even if you do not connect to the onboard console port, the FWSM keeps a running 1 KB buffer that captures all of the console's output. You can view the console buffer with the **show console-output** EXEC command. You can also clear the console buffer with the **clear console-output** EXEC command. The console buffer can be useful when you need to see the actual bootup messages from the last FWSM boot sequence.

The console port is always active and cannot be disabled. When a user connects to the console port with a terminal emulator, the firewall immediately begins at the unprivileged or user EXEC level. To use any type of administrative or configuration commands, the console user must move into privileged EXEC or enable mode.

Best practice dictates having the firewall close any user session that has been idle for a period of time. By default, console connections never idle out. You can change this behavior with the following configuration command:

```
Firewall(config)# console timeout minutes
```

Here, *minutes* is the idle time value from 0 (no idle timeout; the default) to 60 minutes.

TIP   Even though the FWSM does not have an easily accessible console port, the **console timeout** command can still be used to close an idle console session. Evidently, this command is meant for environments where the embedded console port is permanently connected to a PC or an out-of-band terminal server.

Section 4-5

You can also configure various methods to authenticate users who connect to the console port. Chapter 5, "Managing Firewall Users," covers these methods in greater detail.

Telnet Sessions

Remote administrators can connect to the firewall using Telnet. Telnet sessions use TCP port 23 and provide the standard firewall command-line interface. Accessing the firewall through Telnet has the following characteristics:

- Up to five different Telnet sessions can be open to the firewall concurrently.

- Telnet access is much more efficient than the firewall's console port. Large amounts of output can be displayed without imposing a heavy load on the firewall CPU.

- Information sent over a Telnet connection is not secure. No data encryption or authentication is used. (SSH is a more secure alternative.)

- Telnet access is permitted on "internal" firewall interfaces if the firewall is configured to do so. The firewall does not permit inbound Telnet connections on its outside interface unless IPSec is configured on that interface for a secure VPN connection.

To configure Telnet operation, use the following configuration steps:

1. Allow incoming Telnet connections on an interface:

| ASA, FWSM | `Firewall(config)# telnet ip_address netmask if_name` |
| PIX 6.3 | `Firewall(config)# telnet ip_address [netmask] [if_name]` |

By default, no Telnet connections are permitted. This command permits inbound Telnet connections from the source addresses defined by *ip_address* and *netmask*. The inbound firewall interface is specified as *if_name* (**inside** or **dmz**, for example). You can repeat this command to define multiple Telnet sources.

PIX 6.3 allows these parameters to be optional. If no interface name is given, the firewall allows Telnet connections from the source address on all its interfaces except the outside. ASA and FWSM platforms, however, are more specific and require all the options to be given with the command.

For example, the following command permits inbound Telnet from a host at 192.168.4.13 and the subnet 192.168.177.0/24 on the inside interface:

```
Firewall(config)# telnet 192.168.4.13 255.255.255.255 inside
Firewall(config)# telnet 192.168.177.0 255.255.255.0 inside
```

2. (Optional) Set the Telnet idle timeout:

```
Firewall(config)# telnet timeout minutes
```

By default, Telnet sessions are automatically closed if they have been idle for 5 minutes. You can change the idle timeout period to *minutes* (ASA and FWSM: 1 to 1440 minutes, or 24 hours; PIX 6.3: 1 to 60 minutes).

SSH Sessions

Remote administrators can also connect to the firewall using SSH. SSH sessions use TCP port 22 and provide the standard firewall CLI. Accessing the firewall through SSH has the following characteristics:

- Up to five different SSH sessions can be open to the firewall concurrently.

- An SSH session offers a Telnet look and feel while offering a high level of security.

- SSH can be permitted on any firewall interface, including the outside.

- A firewall can support two versions of SSH: SSHv1 (beginning with PIX 6.3, ASA 7.0[1], and FWSM) and SSHv2 (beginning with ASA 7.0[1] and FWSM 3.1[1]).

- SSHv2 offers data integrity and encryption that is superior to SSHv1.

TIP   SSH sessions always require a username and password for authentication. If no specific authentication method is configured other than a basic password, or if the configured AAA authentication servers are unreachable, you can use username **pix** and the normal EXEC-level password set with the **passwd** command.

Although you might not expect it, the **pix** username works on a PIX, ASA, or FWSM platform.

To configure SSH operation, use the following configuration steps:

1. Generate an RSA key pair.

   An RSA key pair is needed as a part of the SSH security mechanisms. By default, no RSA keys exist in a firewall, so they must be created and saved.

   a. Define a domain name for the firewall:

ASA, FWSM	Firewall(config)# **domain-name** *name*
PIX 6.3	Firewall(config)# **domain-name** *name*

   The domain name is given as *name* (a text string up to 63 characters). This is usually the domain name of the organization or enterprise where the firewall is located, although you can use any arbitrary name. Because the domain name is included in the RSA key pair computation, you should try to use a name that will be stable over time. Otherwise, the RSA keys must be rebuilt with any new domain name configured later.

b. Compute the RSA key pair:

ASA, FWSM	Firewall(config)# **crypto key generate rsa general-keys** [**modulus** *modulus*]
PIX 6.3	Firewall(config)# **ca generate rsa key** [*modulus*]

A general-purpose RSA key pair is computed with a modulus or length of *modulus* bits (**512**, **768**, **1024**, or **2048**; the default is 768). Generally, a greater modulus provides more security because it makes reversing the key operations more difficult. Longer keys also take longer to generate, requiring more firewall CPU resources. This is not a critical issue, however, because RSA keys are generated only once or only after long periods of time.

As a compromise, the current industry best practice recommends a modulus of 1024 bits.

If you do not define a domain name before using this command, a default domain name (ciscofwsm.com on an FWSM or ciscopix.com on a PIX or ASA) is used.

c. Save the RSA key information:

ASA, FWSM	–
PIX 6.3	Firewall(config)# **ca save all**

The contents of the RSA key pair are not saved as a part of the firewall configuration. Instead, they must be saved into a private flash memory area. In an ASA or FWSM 3.1+, the RSA keys are automatically saved each time they are generated.

TIP   You can display the public portion of an RSA key pair with the following commands:

ASA, FWSM	Firewall# **show crypto key mypubkey rsa**
PIX 6.3	Firewall# **show ca mypubkey rsa**

If the firewall's domain name ever changes, the RSA key pair must be cleared and rebuilt. You can use the following commands to clear the stored key pair:

ASA, FWSM	Firewall# **crypto key zeroize rsa default**
PIX 6.3	Firewall# **ca zeroize rsa**

Repeat Steps 1a through 1c to regenerate a new key pair based on the new domain name.

---

2. Allow incoming SSH connections on an interface:

ASA, FWSM	Firewall(config)# **ssh** *ip_address netmask if_name*
PIX 6.3	Firewall(config)# **ssh** *ip_address* [*netmask*] [*if_name*]

By default, no SSH connections are permitted. This command permits inbound SSH connections from the source address given by *ip_address* and *netmask* on the firewall interface named *if_name* (**inside** or **outside**, for example).

In PIX 6.3, if the *netmask* is omitted, a host mask of 255.255.255.255 is assumed. If the *if_name* is omitted, the firewall automatically duplicates this command for each of its active interfaces.

You can repeat this command to define multiple SSH sources and source interfaces.

3. (Optional) Specify the supported SSH versions:

ASA, FWSM	`Firewall(config)# [no] ssh version {1	2}`
PIX 6.3	—

In releases before ASA 7.0(1) and FWSM 3.1(1), SSHv1 is the only version that is supported. Beginning with ASA 7.0(1) and FWSM 3.1(1), both versions 1 and 2 are supported by default.

This command can be used to restrict SSH support to only a single version, either version **1** or **2**. To return to the default where both versions are allowed, use the **no ssh version** command with no other arguments.

You can see what SSH versions are currently allowed by using the **show ssh** command. In the following example, SSH support starts with only version 1. The firewall is configured back to the default for versions 1 and 2. Then only version 2 is configured.

```
Firewall# show ssh
Timeout: 30 minutes
Versions allowed: 1
172.21.4.0 255.255.255.0 outside
172.21.6.0 255.255.255.0 outside
Firewall# configure terminal
Firewall(config)# no ssh version
Firewall(config)#
Firewall# show ssh
Timeout: 30 minutes
Versions allowed: 1 and 2
172.21.4.0 255.255.255.0 outside
172.21.6.0 255.255.255.0 outside
Firewall# configure terminal
Firewall(config)# ssh version 2
Firewall(config)#
Firewall# show ssh
Timeout: 30 minutes
Version allowed: 2
172.21.4.0 255.255.255.0 outside
172.21.6.0 255.255.255.0 outside
Firewall#
```

4. (Optional) Set the SSH idle timeout:

```
Firewall(config)# ssh timeout minutes
```

SSH sessions idle out after 5 minutes by default. You can change the idle timeout to *minutes* (1 to 60).

ASDM/PDM Sessions

You can also manage, configure, and monitor a firewall through a web-based application. ASDM and PDM are two of the supported applications. Each one runs from an image stored on the firewall itself, which was made available through an embedded web server.

The web-based management application is named differently for the various firewall platforms:

- PDM 3 (PIX 500 series running PIX 6.3)
- PDM 4 (FWSM)
- ASDM 5.0 (ASA and PIX running 7.0), ASDM 6.0 (ASA and PIX running 8.0).

You can use the following steps to configure and prepare a firewall for PDM or ASDM use:

1. Identify the PDM/ASDM image to use:

ASA	`Firewall(config)# asdm image device:/path`
PIX 6.3, FWSM	—

In releases before ASA 7.0(1), the ASDM image is always stored in a fixed location in flash memory. For example, PIX 6.3 uses flash file 3. Beginning with ASA 7.0 (1), you can specify the flash *device* (**flash:/**, **disk0:/**, or **disk1:/**) and *path* to the ASDM image file. If the firewall is in multiple-context security mode, you can use this command only from the system execution space.

In the following example, the ASDM image file is stored as flash:/asdm.bin (flash:/ is also disk0:/ on this platform):

```
Firewall# dir flash:/
Directory of disk0:/
10    -rw- 8688476    06:25:20 Dec 21 2006  asdm.bin
11    -rw- 5031936    06:12:14 Dec 21 2006  image.bin
62881792 bytes total (44142592 bytes free)
Firewall# configure terminal
Firewall(config)# asdm image disk0:/asdm.bin
```

2. Install the ASDM/PDM image file.

You can copy an ASDM or PDM image file into a firewall's flash memory with the following commands:

ASA	`Firewall# copy url device:/path`
PIX 6.3, FWSM	`Firewall# copy tftp[:[[//location][/pathname]]] flash:pdm`

Before ASA 7.0, the PDM image file was automatically stored in the correct location. Therefore, only the **flash:pdm** destination was needed.

Beginning with ASA 7.0(1), the ASDM image file can be stored anywhere in flash memory and can have an arbitrary filename. You can have one or more ASDM image files stored in flash at any time, provided that you have sufficient storage space, but only one of them can be used to run the application.

The source *url* can be one of the following:

```
ftp://[user[:password]@]server[:port]/[path/]filename[;type=xy]
tftp://[user[:password]@]server[:port]/[path/]filename
http[s]://[user[:password]@]server[:port]/[path/]filename
```

If the server requires user authentication, you can specify the user ID and password in the *user:password@* format. Section "4-2: Managing the Flash File System," provides more details about copying files into flash memory.

On an ASA, the destination must be a local flash device, such as **flash:/, disk0:/,** or **disk1:/,** in a specific path name, given by */path*. On FWSM or PIX platforms, the ASDM image file is always written to a fixed location; it overwrites an existing file if one is present.

3. Permit incoming access.

   ASDM and PDM are web-based applications. Therefore, clients must connect to an HTTP server that is embedded in the firewall.

   a. Identify client locations:

ASA, FWSM	Firewall# **http** *ip_address subnet_mask if_name*
PIX 6.3	Firewall# **http** *ip_address* [*subnet_mask*] [*if_name*]

   Only source or client addresses that fall within the address range given by *ip_address* and *subnet_mask* and are located on the firewall interface named *if_name* (**outside**, for example) are allowed to connect to the firewall's HTTP server.

   On ASA and FWSM platforms, all the arguments are required and must be given in the command. Prior releases allow optional arguments. For example, if the subnet mask is omitted, a host mask of 255.255.255.255 is assumed. If the interface name *if_name* (**outside**, for example) is omitted, the **inside** interface is assumed.

NOTE After you have configured access to the HTTP server, you do not also have to add anything to any of the firewall's access lists. Inbound HTTP access to the firewall itself is permitted on the configured interface(s) automatically.

---

   b. Enable the embedded HTTP server:

   ```
   Firewall# http server enable
   ```

Starting the ASDM or PDM Application from a Web Browser

To run ASDM or PDM from a web browser, point your web browser to the following URL:

`https://`*`ip_address`*`[/admin]`

The *ip_address* is the address (or host name) of the firewall interface that is configured to allow HTTP server connections.

The **/admin** portion of the URL is applicable only to ASA platforms. If the SSL VPN feature is also enabled, the security appliance's default web page (**https://***ip_address*) is devoted to SSL VPN services rather than ASDM. In this case, you can differentiate between the services by using a more specific URL:

* ASDM—**https://***ip_address***/admin**
* SSL VPN—**https://***ip_address***/access**

NOTE   Your browser must allow popups from the firewall's address, because ASDM/PDM is automatically started in a new browser window. As well, ASDM/PDM runs as a Java applet that is downloaded from the firewall. Your browser must support Java so that the applet can be run.

As ASDM or PDM begins, you need to authenticate as an administrative user. The firewall can have an authentication method that is specific to HTTP connections, configured with the **aaa authentication http console** command. Depending on the configuration, you need to use one of the following credentials:

* **Default authentication**—No usernames are defined or used. Therefore, leave the username field blank and enter the enable password.

* **Local authentication**—Usernames are used and are defined locally on the firewall with the **username** command. Enter a valid username that can use privilege level 15 (enable or privileged EXEC mode) and the appropriate password.

* **AAA authentication**—Usernames are used and are defined on external AAA servers. Enter a valid username that can use privilege level 15 (enable or privileged EXEC mode) and the appropriate password.

TIP   When the ASDM or PDM application connection is initiated, the firewall sends its self-signed SSL certificate to your web browser. Sometimes a browser cannot verify the certificate because the firewall is not known as a trusted certificate authority. If this happens, you likely will see a message from the web browser.

You can choose to accept the certificate temporarily or permanently if you are comfortable that you are connecting to the correct firewall. You can check the firewall's identity by viewing the certificate; the Common Name (CN) attribute is made up of the firewall's host name and domain name.

You might also see an error regarding a domain name mismatch. If the firewall's interface IP address is not registered in a DNS, the browser cannot confirm that its IP address and certificate CN (fully qualified domain name) correlate. If you are comfortable with the mismatch, you can choose to continue.

Starting ASDM from a Local Application

Beginning with ASA 7.0(1), you can run ASDM from a web browser or from a "launcher" application that has been downloaded directly to your PC. The first time you use ASDM, you should point your web browser to the following URL:

`https://ip-address/admin`

This brings up a web page where you can choose the ASDM access method. Figure 4-8 shows an example of this opening page.

Figure 4-8 *Initial ASDM Launch Page*

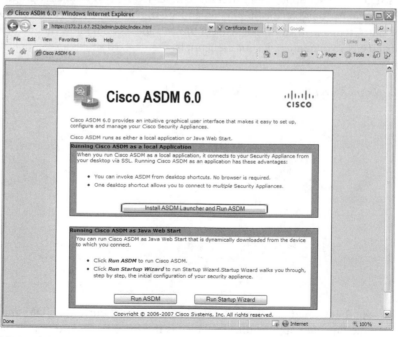

Running ASDM as a local application is usually better because you can use one common program on your PC to access one or more ASA devices. The application also maintains a drop-down list of firewall addresses where you have connected in the past, making it easy to select a target firewall without having to use browser bookmarks or enter URLs.

When the local application is installed, an installer file is downloaded, as shown in Figure 4-9. The installer runs automatically.

Figure 4-9 *Local ASDM Application Installation*

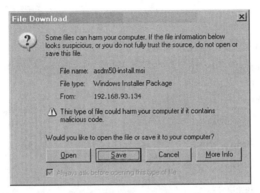

To run the ASDM launcher application, start the local Cisco ASDM Launcher program. On a Windows PC, it can be found on the Start menu under **Programs > Cisco ASDM Launcher**. When the launcher starts, it displays a drop-down list of firewall addresses it knows about. Select an address from the list and enter your authentication credentials. Figure 4-10 shows an example of the launcher application.

Figure 4-10 *Local ASDM Launcher Application*

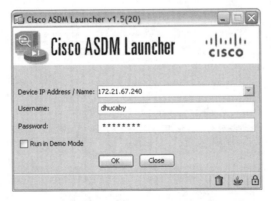

After you have authenticated, the firewall downloads the most current ASDM application code to your PC via the launcher application. This means the local application rarely needs to be updated. Instead, the PC is always kept current with the actual ASDM software that is contained in the firewall's ASDM image. As soon as ASDM launches, it looks like the window shown in Figure 4-11.

Figure 4-11 *Sample ASDM Session*

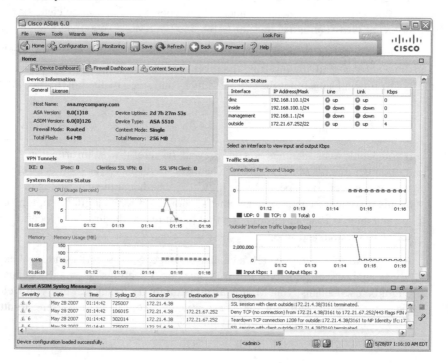

User Session Banners

You can configure a banner of text that the firewall will display to any administrative users. You can use the following three types of banners:

- **Message of the Day (MOTD)**—An informational message that is shown before the login prompt in a Telnet, SSH, or console session. This might include network news, access policy information, or legal warnings to be presented to potential users.

- **Login**—A message that is shown after the MOTD prompt and just before the firewall login prompt. This might be useful to show a name, location, or other access parameters.

- **Exec**—A message that is shown just after a user successfully logs in and reaches EXEC mode. This might be useful if you need to present some final words of caution or a warning to the user who has just logged in and is about to view or change something on the firewall.

To configure one of these banners, use the following configuration command:

```
Firewall(config)# banner {exec | login | motd} text
```

Here, the banner is created one line of text at a time. Do not enclose the *text* in quotation marks; the text begins after the banner type keyword and ends at the end of the line. Repeat this command for subsequent lines of the banner.

You cannot edit a banner; you have to delete the entire banner with the **no banner** {**exec** | **login** | **motd**} command and re-enter it. To delete banners of all types, you can use the **clear banner** (PIX 6.x and FWSM 2.x) or **clear configure banner** (ASA and FWSM 3.x) command.

You can also customize the banner's appearance by including the firewall's host name or domain name. This is done automatically by inserting the token strings **$(***hostname***)** and **$(***domain***)** within the banner text. The firewall substitutes the current values configured by the **hostname** and **domain-name** commands.

TIP   If you decide to use banners on your firewall, be careful what information you include. Remember that the MOTD and login banners are displayed as soon as a Telnet or SSH session connection is opened to the firewall—whether someone can log in or not. That means if someone can initiate a Telnet session and see the login prompt, he can also see any detailed banner information that might reveal the firewall's location, model, software version, and so on.

Also be careful when you craft a banner message. Most security and legal experts advise against using any type of "Welcome" or "Greetings" message, because this might be used against you. Malicious users might try to suggest that you welcomed them into your firewall! For some best-practice recommendations, refer to http://www.cisco.com/warp/public/707/21.html#warnin.

Monitoring Administrative Sessions

Having a console interface and network access, a firewall can allow several people to be connected at any time.

You can monitor all the active Telnet sessions on a firewall with the EXEC command **who**, which provides a list of Telnet session numbers along with the originating IP address, as in the following example:

```
Firewall# who
        1: 172.21.4.16
Firewall#
```

If you need to close a Telnet session that is either hung or unwanted, use the **who** command to find the session's index number. Then use the **kill** *telnet_id* privileged EXEC command, where *telnet_id* is the session index, to terminate that session immediately and without warning. For example, the following commands could be used to end the Telnet session coming from IP address 10.6.6.6:

```
Firewall# who
0: From 10.10.10.71
1: From 192.168.199.4
2: From 10.6.6.6
Firewall# kill 2
```

You can also monitor active SSH sessions with this EXEC command:

```
Firewall# show ssh sessions
```

For example, a generic user ("pix") has several SSH sessions open. Notice that SSH version 1 is actually shown as version 1.5. Version 1.5 is commonly used with Cisco IOS Software and has several security fixes beyond that of version 1.0.

```
Firewall# show ssh sessions
SID Client IP       Version Mode Encryption Hmac     State            Username
0   172.21.4.14     1.5     -    3DES       -        SessionStarted   pix
1   172.21.4.14     2.0     IN   aes256-cbc sha1     SessionStarted   pix
                            OUT  aes256-cbc sha1     SessionStarted   pix
2   172.21.4.14     1.5     -    3DES       -        SessionStarted   pix
3   172.21.4.14     1.5     -    3DES       -        SessionStarted   pix
4   172.21.4.14     1.5     -    3DES       -        SessionStarted   pix
```

You can disconnect an active or hung SSH session with the following command:

```
Firewall# ssh disconnect session-id
```

To display the active ASDM or PDM management application sessions, you can use the following command:

ASA, FWSM	Firewall# **show asdm sessions**
PIX 6.3	Firewall# **show pdm sessions**

You can disconnect an active PDM session with the following command:

ASA, FWSM	Firewall# **asdm disconnect** *session-id*
PIX 6.3	Firewall# **pdm disconnect** *session-id*

TIP   A firewall can also generate an audit trail that shows user activity. To do this, logging must be enabled on the firewall. See Chapter 10 for logging configuration details.

- User authentication messages are generated at Syslog severity 6 (Informational). This also includes SSH and ASDM/PDM sessions.

- User privilege level event messages are generated at Syslog severity 5 (Notification).

- Firewall commands executed by users are logged at Syslog severity 5 (Notification), and **show** commands executed are logged at Syslog severity 7 (Debugging).

4-6: Firewall Reloads and Crashes

During a firewall's normal operation, you might find an occasion to manually reboot or reload it. As well, the firewall might crash on its own, because of some unexpected software or hardware problem, and possibly reload itself. The following sections discuss the methods you can use to make a firewall reload and diagnose the cause of a crash.

Reloading a Firewall

To manually trigger a firewall reload, choose one of the options discussed in the following sections. You can initiate a firewall reload only from privileged EXEC (enable) mode. On an ASA or FWSM firewall platform running in multiple-context security mode, you can initiate a reload only from the system execution space.

Reloading a Firewall Immediately

You can use the following command to initiate an immediate reload. Be aware that as soon as the reload begins, all existing connections through the firewall are dropped, and traffic cannot pass through for a minute or more. Reloads should be initiated only during a network maintenance window.

ASA, FWSM	`Firewall# reload [noconfirm] [max-hold-time {minutes	hhh:mm}] [quick] [save-config] [reason text]`
PIX 6.3	`Firewall# reload [noconfirm]`

With PIX 6.3, a manual reload occurs immediately. The firewall prompts you for a confirmation of the reload and to save the running configuration if it differs from the startup configuration. To answer the confirmations, you can enter **y** or just press the Enter key. You can avoid all the confirmation prompts by using the **noconfirm** keyword.

ASA and FWSM platforms add more flexibility to the reload process. By default, the firewall informs all the administrative users with active sessions (console, Telnet, and SSH) of the impending reload. It also attempts to shut down each of its software modules (IPSec VPN remote access, for example) before the reload. This allows every reload to happen gracefully, without catching users and functions off-guard.

You can use one or more of these keywords with the **reload** command to change the reload behavior:

- **max-hold-time**—You can limit how long the firewall waits to inform users and shut down security functions. Specify the number of *minutes* to wait (1 to 33960) or as hours and minutes *hhh:mm* (up to 566 hours 0 minutes). After that maximum hold time expires, the firewall is free to abruptly perform the reload.

- **quick**—Perform an abrupt reload without informing users or shutting down processes.

- **save-config**—Force the firewall to save the running configuration to the nonvolatile startup configuration—even if it has already been previously saved.

- **reason**—Provides a descriptive reason for the reload as *text* (an arbitrary string of up to 255 characters). The reason text is displayed to any active administrative users connected with console, Telnet, or SSH sessions.

Reloading a Firewall at a Specific Time and Date

Beginning with ASA 7.0(1) and FWSM 3.1(1), you can schedule a firewall reload at some specific time in the future. This might be handy if reloads are permitted only during a predetermined maintenance window. The command for reloading a firewall at a specific time and date is as follows:

ASA, FWSM	Firewall# **reload at** *hh:mm* [*month day* | *day month*] [**max-hold-time** {*minutes* | *hhh:mm*}] [**noconfirm**] [**quick**] [**save-config**] [**reason** *text*]
PIX 6.3	—

A firewall can schedule a reload at a specific hour and minute, given as *hh:mm*. You can also specify a *month* and *day* (1 to 31). The month can be abbreviated as long as it denotes a unique month name. If no date is given, the reload time is assumed to be within the next 24 hours. Also, the date and time must be within 576 hours 0 minutes (or 24 days) from the time the command is issued.

The remaining **reload** keywords are optional and are discussed in the preceding section.

Before using this command, be certain that the firewall clock is set and is accurate. You should also confirm that the reload time is based on the same time zone information that the firewall is using. Otherwise, your concept of the reload schedule might be quite different from the firewall's concept! You can view the current firewall date and time with the **show clock** command.

If needed, you can set the date and time with the following command:

Firewall# **clock set** *hh:mm:ss* {*month day* \| *day month*} *year*

Refer to Section "10-1: Managing the Firewall Clock," in Chapter 10 for complete information about setting and maintaining the clock.

Reloading a Firewall After a Time Interval

You can schedule a firewall reload after a specified amount of time has elapsed. This might be useful if the reload should be delayed from the present time, to allow users a "grace period" to complete their work. The command for reloading a firewall after a time interval is as follows:

ASA, FWSM	Firewall# **reload in** {*minutes* | *hh:mm*} [**max-hold-time** {*minutes* | *hhh:mm*}] [**noconfirm**] [**quick**] [**save-config**] [**reason** *text*]
PIX 6.3	—

You can schedule a reload at some specific delay after the current time. The delay is given as *minutes* (1 to 34560) or as hours and minutes as *hhh:mm*. In either case, the delay limit is 576 hours 0 minutes from the current time.

The remaining **reload** keywords are optional and are discussed in the section "Reloading a Firewall Immediately" earlier in the chapter.

TIP   On ASA and FWSM platforms, you can display a scheduled reload that is pending with the **show reload** command. If you need to cancel the reload ahead of time, use the **reload cancel** command. Obviously, as soon as the actual reload has begun, there is no way to cancel it.

The following example shows how a reload is scheduled at a certain date and time and how that reload is later canceled.

```
Firewall# show clock
16:10:01.743 EST Sun May 6 2007
Firewall# reload at 23:50 may 9 save-config reason Firewall is being
  reloaded for an OS Image upgrade
Cryptochecksum: f96855f6 676cf300 d7f31ae8 bd4cbdcf
3250 bytes copied in 0.530 secs
Proceed with reload? [confirm]
Firewall#
***
*** --- SHUTDOWN in 79:38:41 ---
***
*** Message to all terminals:
***
***    Firewall is being reloaded for an OS Image upgrade
Firewall#
Firewall# show reload
Reload scheduled for 23:50:00 EST Wed May 9 2007 (in 79 hours and 38
  minutes) by enable_15 from ssh (remote 172.21.6.1)
Reload reason: Firewall is being reloaded for an OS Image upgrade
Firewall#
Firewall# reload cancel
Firewall#
***
*** --- SHUTDOWN ABORTED ---
Firewall#
Firewall# show reload
No reload is scheduled.
Firewall#
```

When a reload has been successfully scheduled, the firewall also generates Syslog message ID 199007. If a reload is canceled, a Syslog message 199008 is generated. Both messages are default severity level 5.

Obtaining Crash Information

If a firewall crashes for some reason, you might be left with few clues other than it reloaded or was left at the monitor prompt. You can configure the firewall to save a crashinfo image of its RAM memory as a file in flash memory. The image also includes the output of many commands that show the status of the firewall and its resources. A firewall stores only one crashinfo file; subsequent crashes overwrite it. Therefore, only information from the most recent crash is available.

After a crash, you can examine the crashinfo file to determine the cause of the crash—even after a power cycle or reload. This information is useful to the engineers at the Cisco Technical Assistance Center (TAC) as they track down the source of a firewall problem.

The following sections discuss preparing for and examining a crashinfo image.

Controlling Crashinfo Creation

You can use the following configuration command to automatically save a crashinfo file during a firewall crash:

ASA, FWSM	Firewall(config)# **no crashinfo save disable**
PIX 6.3	Firewall(config)# **crashinfo save enable**

By default, crashinfo collection is enabled on all firewall and security appliance platforms. If you decide to disable crashinfo collection, you can use the following command:

ASA, FWSM	Firewall(config)# **crashinfo save disable**
PIX 6.3	Firewall(config)# **crashinfo save disable**

In ASA, PIX, and FWSM releases, you can see the current status of crashinfo creation by using the **show crashinfo save** command.

When a PIX 6.3 platform crashes, an image of the firewall RAM is saved in flash memory as file number 4. The size of the image equals the amount of RAM in the firewall.

On ASA and FWSM platforms, the crashinfo file is created and saved in a hidden flash file system. The actual file cannot be seen in a directory listing, nor can its location be specified or changed.

Generating a Test Crashinfo Image

To create a test version of a crashinfo file and store it in flash memory, enter the following command:

FWSM	Firewall(config)# **crashinfo test**
PIX 6.3	Firewall(config)# **crashinfo test**
ASA	Firewall# **crashinfo test**

The firewall operation is not hindered or interrupted by entering this command. This command can be used if you just want to get a feel for the crashinfo process and the crashinfo file contents. (Notice that this is a configuration command for PIX 6.3 and FWSM, and a privileged EXEC command for ASA.)

Forcing an Actual Firewall Crash

You can make the firewall produce an error that actually causes itself to crash and to save a legitimate crashinfo image file by entering the following command:

ASA, FWSM	Firewall# **crashinfo force {page-fault| watchdog}**
PIX 6.3	Firewall(config)# **crashinfo force {page-fault| watchdog}**

Either a page fault or a watchdog fatal error can be used to cause the crash. A **page-fault** crash occurs when a firewall process tries to access memory that is outside its own use. A **watchdog** crash occurs because a firewall process has become unresponsive or hung. In practice, the type of crash does not really matter. The goal is to confirm the process of saving a crashinfo file when the firewall actually crashes.

Notice that this is a configuration command for PIX 6.3, and is a privileged EXEC command for ASA and FWSM.

CAUTION   The **crashinfo force** command is useful only for testing the crashinfo procedure. Because it actually crashes the firewall when it is used, you should use this command only under controlled circumstances. As soon as the firewall crashes, no traffic is inspected or passes through it.

In the following example, a watchdog timeout error is used to trigger an actual firewall crash:

```
Firewall# config terminal
Firewall# crashinfo force watchdog
WARNING: This command will force the PIX to crash and reboot. Do you wish to
  proceed? [confirm]:
Watchdog timeout failure! Please contact customer support.
    PC         SP        STATE      Runtime     SBASE       Stack Process
Hrd 001eaa09 0090edc4 00555848          0 0090de3c 3628/4096 arp_timer
Lsi 001effad 009d1fec 00555860          0 009d1074 3928/4096 FragDBGC
Lwe 00119abf 00a5555c 00558fc0          0 00a546f4 3688/4096 dbgtrace
Lwe 003e3f55 00a576ec 0054e188          0 00a557a4 7788/8192 Logger
Hwe 003e80d0 00a5a7e4 0054e438          0 00a5886c 8024/8192 tcp_fast
Hwe 003e8049 00a5c894 0054e438          0 00a5a91c 8024/8192 tcp_slow
Lsi 003006f9 0293c984 00555860          0 0293b9fc 3944/4096 xlate clean
Lsi 00300607 0293da24 00555860          0 0293caac 3888/4096 uxlate clean
[output omitted]
Rebooting....
```

Viewing the Crashinfo Information

After the crashinfo file is written, it cannot be uploaded from the firewall. Instead, you can view its contents when you enter the following command:

ASA, PIX, FWSM	Firewall# **show crashinfo**

The **show crashinfo** command displays all the relevant process and stack trace information that was active during the crash. You should capture all this text output with a terminal emulator so that it can be saved to a file and sent to Cisco TAC.

The first line of output also tells what triggered the crashinfo image. If the line is ":Saved Test Crash," the image was saved by the **crashinfo test** command. Otherwise, ":Saved Crash" indicates that the file is the result of an actual firewall crash, as in the following example:

```
Firewall# show crashinfo
: Saved_Crash
Thread Name: ci/console (Old pc 0x0011f217 ebp 0x02fb2d50)
Traceback:
0: 00104bf8
1: 00102155
2: 0010014a
3: 00338b55
4: 00338c1b
[output omitted]
```

Deleting the Previous Crashinfo File Contents

Each time a crashinfo file is created, its contents replace the previous file contents. Therefore, only one crashinfo file is stored at any given time, and flash memory is not used up after multiple crashes.

You can, however, clear the contents of the current crashinfo file with the following command:

ASA, FWSM	`Firewall# clear crashinfo`
PIX 6.3	`Firewall(config)# clear crashinfo`

This might be useful if your firewall has experienced a crash in the past and you have already resolved the cause of that crash. In that case, you might want an empty crashinfo file to signify that no further crashes have occurred.

4-7: Monitoring a Firewall with SNMP

Simple Network Management Protocol (SNMP) is a protocol that allows the exchange of information about managing a network device. Cisco firewalls can participate in SNMP as follows:

- A Management Information Base (MIB) is a collection of variables stored on a network device. The device can update the variables, or they can be queried from an external source.

- MIBs are structured according to the SNMP MIB module language, which is based on the Abstract Syntax Notation 1 (ASN.1) language.

- An SNMP agent runs on a firewall and maintains various MIB variables. Any query of the variables must be handled through the agent.

Section 4-7

- The SNMP agent can also send unsolicited messages, or *traps*, to an SNMP manager. Traps are used to alert the manager of changing conditions on the firewall.

- An SNMP manager is usually a network management system that queries MIB variables, can set MIB variables, and receives traps from a collection of network devices.

- Cisco firewalls can use SNMP version 1 (SNMPv1), the original version. SNMPv1, based on RFC 1157, has only basic cleartext community strings for security. Access is limited to read-only requests from the IP addresses of one or more SNMP managers.

- Beginning with ASA 7.0(1) or FWSM 1.1(1), firewalls can also support SNMP version 2c (SNMPv2c), an enhanced version based on RFCs 1901, 1905, and 1906. SNMPv2c improves on bulk information retrieval and error reporting but still uses only basic cleartext community strings and IP addresses to provide security. (SNMP security is available only in SNMPv3, which currently is not supported on any Cisco firewall platform.)

TIP   SNMP requests and responses are sent using UDP port 161. Notifications or traps are sent using UDP port 162. The SNMP management station can be located on any interface of a firewall, provided that the firewall has sufficient routing information to reach it.

Overview of Firewall SNMP Support

Firewalls can participate in SNMP by maintaining several MIBs. The MIB values are constantly updated with the current values that are in use. For example, one MIB parameter records the average firewall CPU load over a 5-second period. This is based on the CPU usage measurements that can also be shown from the firewall CLI.

SNMP MIBs represent data as a hierarchical tree structure; each MIB variable is referenced by its object identifier (OID). OIDs are formed by concatenating the name or number of a tree branch as the tree is followed from the root to the object's location in dotted notation.

Figure 4-12 shows the top layers of the standard MIB tree, along with the lower layers that apply to firewalls. The root layer is unnamed. All MIB variables that are useful for network management are located under the internet subtree. Following the tree structure downward, internet is referenced as OID iso.org.dod.internet or 1.3.6.1.

TIP   Your SNMP management station needs to have several firewall-specific MIBs compiled into its database. Make sure you find these MIBS: IF-MIB, RFC1213-MIB, CISCO-MEMORY-POOL-MIB, CISCO-PROCESS-MIB, ENTITY-MIB, CISCO-SMI, and CISCO-FIREWALL-MIB.

ASA also adds CISCO-IPSEC-FLOW-MONITOR-MIB, CISCO-FIPS-STAT-MIB, and ALTIGA-SSL-STATS-MIB.

These can all be obtained for free from Cisco.com at http://www.cisco.com/public/sw-center/netmgmt/cmtk/mibs.shtml.

Firewall MIBs

A firewall uses the mgmt subtree (iso.org.dod.internet.mgmt or 1.3.6.1.2) to contain several useful objects, all organized under the mib-2 subtree (1.3.6.1.2.1). These objects are defined in the RFC1213-MIB file (1.3.6.1.2.1.11). They fall into these categories:

- **system**—Descriptions of the firewall, uptime, and network services
- **interfaces**—Parameters and counters for each interface
- **ip**—IP addresses, subnet masks, and broadcast addresses assigned to each interface

Many of the values maintained in the mib-2 subtree can also be seen with the **show snmp-server** (PIX 6.x), **show running-config snmp-server** (ASA), **show version**, and **show interface** EXEC commands.

The EntityMIB subtree (1.3.6.1.2.1.47) is also included. It is defined by the ENTITY-MIB file, which is based on RFC 1212. This was added to ASA 7.0(1) to support the firewall chassis and field-replaceable units (FRU) available on the ASA platforms.

The private (1.3.6.1.4) subtree contains one subtree, enterprise (1.3.6.1.4.1), where all network vendor-specific objects are located. The Cisco private MIB structure is contained in the cisco subtree (1.3.6.1.4.1.9). The set of specific MIBs that are included under the cisco MIB tree varies according to the hardware platform (router, switch, firewall, and so on).

A firewall maintains several subtrees under iso.org.dod.internet.private.enterprise.cisco.mgmt, as follows:

- The ciscoMemoryPool subtree (1.3.6.1.4.1.9.9.48) has objects that are defined in the CISCO-MEMORY-POOL-MIB file. These describe the current status of firewall memory. It can also be seen with the **show blocks** EXEC command.

- The ciscoProcess subtree (1.3.6.1.4.1.9.9.109) is defined by the CISCO-PROCESS-MIB file. These values describe the firewall's CPU usage over 5-second, 1-minute, and 5-minute periods. The same values can be seen with the **show cpu usage** EXEC command.

- The ciscoFirewall subtree (1.3.6.1.4.1.9.9.147) is defined by the CISCO-FIREWALL-MIB file. A number of values are maintained that describe the current memory buffer usage (cfwBuffer-Stat) and the connection usage (cfwConnectionStat) in the firewall. These correspond to the output of the **show memory** and **show conn count** EXEC commands, respectively.

- The ciscoIpSecFlowMonitorMIB subtree (1.3.6.1.4.1.9.9.171) is defined by the CISCO-IPSEC-FLOW-MONITOR-MIB file. This was added to ASA and FWSM platforms to support IPSec VPN functionality to report on tunnel statistics.

Figure 4-12 *SNMP MIB Structure*

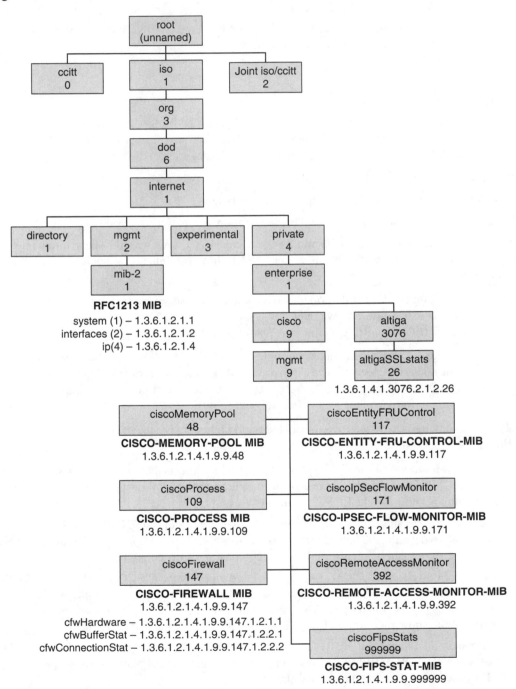

- The ciscoRemoteAccessMonitorMIB subtree (1.3.6.1.4.1.9.9.392) is defined by the CISCO-REMOTE-ACCESS-MONITOR-MIB file. This was added to ASA 7.0(1) to support VPN client session statistics, but removed in ASA 8.0.

- The ciscoFipsStatsMIB subtree (1.3.6.1.4.1.9.9.999999) is defined by the CISCO-FIPS-STAT-MIB file. This was added to ASA 7.0(1) to support reporting on IPSec cryptographic engine operations, but removed in ASA 8.0.

- The altigaSSLstats subtree (1.3.6.1.4.1.3076.2.1.2.26) is defined by the ALTIGA-SSL-STATS-MIB file. This was added to ASA 7.0(1) to support reporting on SSL VPN session statistics.

Firewall SNMP Traps

A firewall can send notification or trap messages to SNMP management stations when certain events occur. This allows the management station to receive alerts in real time and relay them to the appropriate networking personnel.

Generic traps are sent when firewall links (interfaces) go up or down, when the firewall is reloaded (a "warm start") or booted up (a "cold start" after power is applied) for some reason, and when an SNMP poll has been received with an incorrect community string. Syslog messages can also be sent as SNMP traps if the firewall is configured to do so.

When SNMP traps are sent, the firewall's OID is included. This allows the SNMP management station to determine what type of device has sent the trap. Cisco firewall models use the unique OIDs shown in Table 4-9. Notice that the OIDs use most of the same tree hierarchy as SNMP MIBs. For example, 1.3.6.1.4.1.9. would lead to the private.enterprise.cisco. subtree. This is followed by .1., which points to the Cisco products subtree, which is followed by a number that uniquely identifies the firewall model.

The only exception is when Syslog messages are sent as SNMP traps with the **logging history** command. The OID used is always 1.3.6.1.4.1.9.9.41.2, regardless of the sending firewall platform.

TIP   You can find the entire list of Cisco product OIDs in the CISCO-PRODUCT-MIB file at ftp://ftp.cisco.com/pub/mibs/oid/CISCO-PRODUCTS-MIB.oid.

Table 4-9 *Firewall OID Values Used in SNMP Traps*

Firewall Model	OID
PIX 501	1.3.6.1.4.1.9.1.417
PIX 506	1.3.6.1.4.1.9.1.389
PIX 506E	1.3.6.1.4.1.9.1.450

continues

Section 4-7

Table 4-9 *Firewall OID Values Used in SNMP Traps (Continued)*

PIX 515 single context mode PIX 515 security context PIX 515 system context	1.3.6.1.4.1.9.1.390 1.3.6.1.4.1.9.1.678 1.3.6.1.4.1.9.1.768
PIX 515E single context mode PIX 515E security context PIX 515E system context	1.3.6.1.4.1.9.1.451 1.3.6.1.4.1.9.1.677 1.3.6.1.4.1.9.1.769
PIX 520	1.3.6.1.4.1.9.1.391
PIX 525 single context mode PIX 525 security context PIX 525 system context	1.3.6.1.4.1.9.1.392 1.3.6.1.4.1.9.1.676 1.3.6.1.4.1.9.1.770
PIX 535 single context mode PIX 535 security context PIX 535 system context	1.3.6.1.4.1.9.1.393 1.3.6.1.4.1.9.1.675 1.3.6.1.4.1.9.1.771
FWSM single context mode FWSM security context	1.3.6.1.4.1.9.1.522 1.3.6.1.4.1.9.1.674
ASA 5505	1.3.6.1.4.1.9.1.745
ASA 5510	1.3.6.1.4.1.9.1.669
ASA 5520 single context mode ASA 5520 security context ASA 5520 system context	1.3.6.1.4.1.9.1.670 1.3.6.1.4.1.9.1.671 1.3.6.1.4.1.9.1.764
ASA 5540 single context mode ASA 5540 security context ASA 5540 system context	1.3.6.1.4.1.9.1.672 1.3.6.1.4.1.9.1.673 1.3.6.1.4.1.9.1.765
ASA 5550 single context ASA 5550 security context ASA 5550 system context	1.3.6.1.4.1.9.1.753 1.3.6.1.4.1.9.1.763 1.3.6.1.4.1.9.1.766
Other (original PIX models)	1.3.6.1.4.1.9.1.227

SNMP Configuration

You can use the following steps to configure SNMP operation so that a firewall or security appliance platform can be remotely monitored:

1. Define the SNMP identity.

   a. Identify the firewall location:

ASA, FWSM	Firewall(config)# **snmp-server location** *string*
PIX 6.3	Firewall(config)# **snmp-server location** *string*

   Someone at a management station can learn of the firewall's location by querying the location. This is given by *string* (a text string of up to 127 characters, including spaces).

   b. Identify the firewall administrator:

ASA, FWSM	Firewall(config)# **snmp-server contact** *string*
PIX 6.3	Firewall(config)# **snmp-server contact** *string*

   Querying this string tells someone who to contact in case of firewall problems or issues. The contact information is given by *string* (a text string of up to 127 characters).

2. Allow SNMP access.

   a. Permit access for a specific management station:

ASA, FWSM	Firewall(config)# **snmp-server host** *if_name ip_addr* [**poll** | **trap**] [**community** *commstr*] [**version** *version*] [**udp-port** *udp_port*]
PIX 6.3	Firewall(config)# **snmp-server host** *if_name ip_addr* [**poll** | **trap**]

   The management station can be found on the firewall interface named *if_name* (**inside** or **outside**, for example) at IP address *ip_addr*. This command can be repeated to define up to five different stations for PIX 6.3 or up to 32 stations for ASA and FWSM.

   The type of access opened to the management station is given by the **poll** or **trap** keywords. With **poll**, the station is allowed to poll the firewall with SNMP queries. The **trap** keyword allows the firewall to send SNMP traps to the management station. By default, only the cold start, link up/down, and SNMP authentication failure traps are sent. On an FWSM platform, you can add the udp-port keyword to specify the **UDP port** that is used when sending SNMP traps.

   If neither keyword is given, both poll and trap actions are permitted. Specifying **poll** causes traps to be denied, and specifying **trap** causes polls to be denied.

   ASA and FWSM platforms allow additional SNMP parameters to be set on a per-server basis. You can use the **community** keyword to specify a community string *commstr* (up to 32 characters, without spaces) that is used as a weak authentication for the server. If a community string is not defined with this command, a global community string (defined in Step 2b) is automatically configured for the server. If no global string has been defined, the server entry is marked as "pending" until a valid community string is defined.

By default, SNMP version 1 is used. You can use the **version** keyword to specify the SNMP version that the server uses as *version* (1 for SNMPv1 or 2c for SNMPv2c). If the server uses something other than the default UDP port 161, you can set the *UDP port* to udp_port (0 to 65535).

b.   Define an SNMP community string:

ASA, FWSM	Firewall(config)# **snmp-server community** *key*
PIX 6.3	Firewall(config)# **snmp-server community** *key*

A community string acts as a shared secret password that authenticates any management station's SNMP polls. If the string key (up to 32 characters, without spaces; the default is **public**) matches between the incoming polls and the firewall itself, the polls are answered. If this command is not entered, default community string **public** is used.

ASA and FWSM use this command to define one "global" community string that can be used for any SNMP server that is configured without one. If this command is not entered, there is no default community string. Instead, community strings can be configured on a per-host basis as part of the **snmp-server host** command.

TIP   Even though the SNMP community string is sent as cleartext within SNMP packets, it should still be viewed as a rudimentary password security method. Therefore, you should always change its value to something other than the default "public."

---

c.   (Optional) Define the SNMP poll UDP port:

ASA, FWSM	Firewall(config)# **snmp-server listen-port** *port*
PIX 6.3	—

ASA and FWSM platforms use this command to define a "global" UDP port that can be used to listen for SNMP polls. By default, UDP port 161 is used. This can be overridden on a per-host basis with the **snmp-server host** command.

d.   (Optional) Send specific trap types:

ASA, FWSM	Firewall(config)# **snmp-server enable traps** {**all** | *type*}
PIX 6.3	Firewall(config)# **snmp-server enable traps**

In PIX platforms, only generic SNMP traps are sent to any management station configured for traps. This includes cold start, link up/down, and SNMP authentication failure traps.

You can also send Syslog messages as SNMP traps with this command. You can set the severity level threshold of the messages to be sent with the **logging history** *level* command.

ASA and FWSM offer more types of traps to be identified and sent. The **all** keyword allows all types of traps. You can specify a trap *type* as one of the following sets of keywords:

— **firewall** [**security**]

Traps are sent for any type of firewall inspection, content inspection, attack detection, and so on, as defined in the CISCO-FIREWALL-MIB file. The security traps are assumed, whether or not the **security** keyword is given.

— **snmp** [**authentication**] [**coldstart**] [**linkdown**] [**linkup**]

Generic SNMP traps are sent for SNMP authentication failures, firewall cold starts (power cycles), and interface state changes. These are defined in the SNMPv2-MIB file. If only the **snmp** keyword is given, all the optional keywords are assumed.

— **syslog**

Syslog messages are sent as SNMP traps. You should also set the severity level threshold of the messages to be sent with the **logging history** *level* command.

The following trap *type* and keywords can be used on ASA and FWSM platforms only:

— **entity** [**config-change**] [**fru-insert**] [**fru-remove**]

Traps are sent if the firewall configuration is changed or if an FRU is installed or removed (ASA platforms only). These are defined in the CISCO-ENTITY-FRU-CONTROL-MIB file. If only the **entity** keyword is given, all the optional keywords are assumed.

— **ipsec** [**start**] [**stop**]

Traps are sent based on IPSec tunnel creation and deletion, as defined in the CISCO-IPSEC-FLOW-MONITOR-MIB file. If only the **ipsec** keyword is given, the other options are assumed.

— **remote-access** [**session-threshold-exceeded**]

Traps are sent as VPN clients connect and disconnect, as defined in the CISCO-REMOTE-ACCESS-MONITOR-MIB file. Optionally, traps can be sent if the number of VPN client sessions exceeds a threshold.

Refer to the following sections for information about these topics:

- **5-1: Managing Generic Users**—Covers how default "generic" or ambiguous users can be allowed to connect to a firewall and execute commands or make configuration changes.

- **5-2: Managing Users with a Local Database**—Presents methods to configure unique usernames locally on the firewall. You can then manage these users' privileges and monitor their activity.

- **5-3: Defining AAA Servers for User Management**—Discusses external servers that can be used to authenticate, authorize, and keep accounting records about user activity on and through a firewall.

- **5-4: Configuring AAA to Manage Administrative Users**—Explains the configuration steps needed to offload user management functions when administrative users connect to a firewall.

- **5-5: Configuring AAA for End-User Cut-Through Proxy**—Covers the methods that can be used to authenticate users initiating connections through a firewall and to authorize their ability to do so.

- **5-6: Firewall Password Recovery**—Discusses procedures that can be used to recover or bypass a firewall's privileged user password when it is lost or forgotten.

Managing Firewall Users

Although its primary function is to provide and enforce security policies at the boundaries of networks, a Cisco firewall also supports several methods to manage users who interact with it. Firewall users fall into the following general categories:

- **Administrative users**—Users who can open administrative sessions *with* the firewall to make configuration changes or to monitor activity. These users can connect to the firewall through the console, Telnet, Secure Shell (SSH), or the PIX Device Manager (PDM)/Adaptive Security Device Manager (ASDM) application.

- **End users**—These are users who need to open connections *through* the firewall. These connections can use various protocols, which are all ultimately inspected by the firewall. When the user first initiates a connection, the firewall intervenes with an authentication challenge. If the user successfully authenticates, that connection is opened. Through the *cut-through* proxy feature, the firewall opens future connections for that user without any intervention.

- **VPN users**—Remote-access users who need to open VPN client connections to the firewall. The firewall can use extended authentication (xauth) to authenticate the users before the VPN connections are completed.

Firewalls can perform three basic operations to manage any user's access:

- **Authentication**—A user's identity is verified against known credentials.

- **Authorization**—A user's privileges are predefined and approved by a third party.

- **Accounting**—A user's activity is recorded for auditing or billing purposes.

Finally, a Cisco firewall can support several levels of user management, based on the amount of control and security that is required. For example, a firewall can authenticate a user based on a generic password only, against a local or internal user database, or against databases maintained on external servers.

When users log in to a firewall, they are assigned a privilege level from 1 to 15 (0 is available, but is not used). User authentication and privilege levels are used for all management interfaces:

- The command-line interface
- Adaptive Security Device Manager (ASDM)
- Cisco Security Manager (CSM) or VPN/Security Management Solution (VMS)

By default, users begin at level 1 and move to level 15 only when they successfully enter privileged EXEC or *enable* mode.

Firewall commands are also given various privilege levels, so users can run only commands that are at the same level as or at a lower level than their own. By default, all firewall commands (both EXEC and configuration) are given privilege level 0 (the lowest) or 15 (the highest). Additional levels between 0 and 15 can be defined if the user community needs to be segmented further.

5-1: Managing Generic Users

By default, administrative users can authenticate with a firewall by using only a password. After they are authenticated, these users are known by the generic username enable_1.

The firewall prompts you for the password in Telnet and SSH sessions, but not in console sessions. On the console, a user is immediately placed at the unprivileged level.

With SSH sessions, users are prompted for a username and password. You can use the username **pix** as the generic username.

TIP	Even though you might be using an ASA or FWSM platform, you can still use **pix** as a username. The generic username began with the PIX family and has been retained since.

The following sections present the configuration steps needed to authenticate administrative users based only on a password or on a username and password pair, and to authenticate end users initiating traffic through the firewall.

Authenticating and Authorizing Generic Users

Generic user authentication is performed using only passwords. Users are authorized to perform certain actions based on the privilege level that they are permitted to use. Passwords can be defined for the two default privilege levels 0 and 15, as well as other arbitrary levels, using the following configuration steps:

1. Set the unprivileged mode password:

ASA, FWSM   Firewall(config)# {**password** | **passwd**} *password* [**encrypted**]

PIX 6.3   Firewall(config)# {**password** | **passwd**} *password* [**encrypted**]

The generic user at privilege level 0 can be authenticated by entering the password string *password*. After the command is entered, the password string is encrypted whenever the configuration is displayed. This is denoted by the **encrypted** keyword.

You can also transfer this command to another firewall by copying and pasting. As long as the **encrypted** keyword is retained, the new firewall can use the same encrypted password.

TIP   You can use the following commands to reset the level 0 password to the default value **cisco**:

| ASA, FWSM | Firewall(config)# **clear {password** I **passwd}** |
| PIX 6.3 | Firewall(config)# **clear {password** I **passwd}** |

---

2. Set a privileged-mode password:

| ASA, FWSM | Firewall(config)# **enable password** [*pw*] [**level** *priv_level*] [**encrypted**] |
| PIX 6.3 | Firewall(config)# **enable password** [*pw*] [**level** *priv_level*] [**encrypted**] |

The password for privilege level *priv_level* is set to the string *pw*. If the **level** keyword is omitted, the password for enable mode or privilege level 15 is assumed.

You can use this command to define a new unique privilege level to support a subset of administrative users. Specify the *priv_level* as a level between 0 and 15.

If you need to reset the privilege level password to its default value (no password), use the **enable password** configuration command with no *pw* string given.

TIP   Administrative users can gain access to a specific privilege level by using the **enable** *level* command, where *level* is 0 to 15 (the default is 15).

Accounting of Generic Users

When a firewall is configured to authenticate administrative users with only a password, you can perform user accounting only through the logging function. You should make sure the following Syslog message IDs are enabled to use them as an audit trail of user activity. The default severity levels are shown in parentheses:

- **611101 (6)**—Successful user authentication
- **611102 (6)**—Failed user authentication
- **111008 (5)**—User executed the command text

- **111009 (6)**—User executed the command show text
- **611103 (5)**—User logged out
- **502103 (5)**—User changed privilege levels

It might seem odd that users connecting through the firewall console are not logged with a 611101 authentication message. This is because the console remains logged in to the generic privilege level 1 user at all times.

For example, the following output shows the Syslog audit trail for a user who moved into privilege level 15 (enable mode) and made a configuration change. Later, you might need to trace back and see which user made a specific change to the firewall.

```
single_vf : %PIX-7-111009: User 'enable_1' executed cmd: show clock
single_vf : %PIX-5-502103: User priv level changed: Uname: enable_15 From: 1 To:
  15
single_vf : %PIX-5-111008: User 'enable_1' executed the 'enable' command.
single_vf : %PIX-5-111008: User 'enable_15' executed the 'configure terminal'
  command.
single_vf : %PIX-5-111008: User 'enable_15' executed the 'access-list acl_outside
  permit ip any any' command.
single_vf : %PIX-5-611103: User logged out: Uname: enable_1
```

> **TIP**   Although the default generic user authentication is flexible and convenient, it offers little security benefit. For example, users log in by entering the level 1 password only. This means that every user must know and use the same password; there will never be an audit trail showing exactly who logged in. All level 1 users are simply shown as enable_1.
>
> The level 15 enable access is similar—users must enter one enable password that is common to all administrators. Those users are simply shown as enable_15. Again, no accurate audit trail shows what user made what configuration change to the firewall.
>
> Best practice dictates authenticating users with usernames that uniquely identify them. Each user also has a unique password and can be assigned to a specific privilege level if needed. This can be done in a local (internal) user database or on an external user database server.

5-2: Managing Users with a Local Database

You can configure a firewall to control user access by defining users in its local database. This approach assigns usernames and passwords to each end user, allowing access rights and accounting trails to be granular and specific.

Each user must use a unique username when accessing or passing through the firewall. For administrative users, privilege levels can be defined to authorize their ability to access firewall commands. User activity can also be tracked and identified by the unique usernames.

You can define usernames locally on the firewall if external user management servers (RADIUS, TACACS+, and so on) are unavailable or impractical. However, local user management does have some limitations. For example, each user's password must be configured and updated on the firewall. Usernames must be added or deleted as users come and go from the enterprise. If a consistent user management framework must be used across the network, each user's credentials and access rights must be maintained at *every* location.

Without a central point of management, local user databases do not scale very well and can become difficult to administer. Best practice is to use external user management servers first and then fall back on a local user database as a last resort.

Authenticating with Local Usernames

You can use the following configuration steps to define usernames locally on the firewall.

1. Define each firewall user:

   ```
   Firewall(config)# username username [{nopassword | password password}
      [encrypted]] privilege level
   ```

   The user identified as *username* (a text string of up to 15 characters) can have a password configured with the **password** keyword. After *password* is entered, it is encrypted automatically so that the cleartext string is never displayed in the configuration. If this command is copied and pasted from one firewall to another, the **encrypted** keyword specifies that the password string is already encrypted before the command is executed.

   If you choose to configure the user with no password, using the **nopassword** option, the blank password is still displayed as an encrypted string. However, you should carefully consider this, because anyone will be able to log in to the firewall (and potentially make configuration changes) by knowing only the username.

   A privilege level must be given as *level* (1 to 15), where 15 is the highest level the user is allowed to reach. This limit applies only when enable authentication is configured. (See Step 3.)

   Privilege level 1 is the lowest and offers the user the least capability. At level 15, the user can access and use any command on the firewall platform. All users begin at level 1 when they successfully authenticate. To move to a higher privilege level, users must issue the **enable** command.

2. Enable local user authentication:

   ```
   Firewall(config)# aaa authentication {serial | telnet | ssh | http} console LOCAL
   ```

You can enable user authentication locally on the firewall for any of the following access methods:

- **serial** (console connection)
- **telnet** (Telnet)
- **ssh** (SSH sessions)
- **http** (Web-based management with PDM or ASDM)

You can repeat this command to define local authentication for more than one connection type.

You must always use the **console** keyword, indicating that firewall management sessions are being authenticated. The **LOCAL** keyword causes the firewall's local username database to be used for authentication.

TIP   It might seem odd to use the **aaa** command here, even though external AAA servers are not used for the local user database. The firewall processes all user management functions involving usernames as AAA functions. A predefined AAA server group called *LOCAL* uses the *LOCAL* "protocol," as if the following command were used:

```
Firewall(config)# aaa-server LOCAL protocol local
```

Requests that would go out to an external AAA server are intercepted and handled internally according to the local username database.

---

3. (Optional) Authenticate users for enable mode:

```
Firewall(config)# aaa authentication enable console LOCAL
```

By default, privilege level 15 is defined with the **enable password** configuration command. Any user who can successfully authenticate with the firewall can also use the **enable** command to move to level 15—*regardless of the privilege level set for the username*. As well, all users share the same password for privilege level 15.

You can configure enable authentication so that each user must enter an independent enable password to reach a higher privilege level. With local authentication, the enable password is the same as the username password for each user.

After a user is authenticated with his or her enable password, the privilege level is changed to the level configured for the username. In other words, the privileged EXEC level is set on a per-user basis; not every user automatically arrives at level 15.

For example, suppose the username **userjoe** is created with a privilege level limit of 15. A second user, **userbob**, has a privilege level limit of 5. Local authentication is used for SSH sessions. Enable authentication is configured locally so that each user can enter his or her password to move into the respective privilege level, as demonstrated with the following commands:

```
Firewall(config)# username userjoe password joespasswd privilege 15
Firewall(config)# username userbob password bobspasswd privilege 5
```

```
Firewall(config)# aaa authentication ssh console LOCAL
Firewall(config)# aaa authentication enable console LOCAL
```

User userjoe logs in to the firewall and moves into his privileged EXEC level (15). Each time, userjoe's username password is used for authentication. The **show curpriv** command verifies the user's current identity and privilege level, as shown in the following output:

```
login as: userjoe
userjoe@192.168.77.14's password:
Type help or '?' for a list of available commands.
Firewall> show curpriv
Username : userjoe
Current privilege level : 1
Current Mode/s : P_UNPR
Firewall> enable
Password: ********
Firewall# show curpriv
Username : userjoe
Current privilege level : 15
Current Mode/s : P_PRIV
Firewall#
```

Authorizing Users to Access Firewall Commands

Users are authorized to execute firewall commands based on a comparison of their current privilege level and each command's privilege level. If the user's level is greater than or equal to the command's level, the user is allowed to use the command. If not, an error is returned.

By default, only a simple authorization test is used. Users at privilege level 1 can use only commands that are set at level 1. If a user can move to any level greater than 1, he or she can access any other command—even commands set for level 15.

You can use local command authorization to achieve more granularity. When it is enabled, strict privilege level comparisons are done for each command that is entered. Users who have privilege levels lower than the commands they try to use are rejected.

Each firewall command has a privilege level associated with it. Some command keywords can be used in several different modes, such as **show** (as in **show pager**), **clear** (as in **clear pager**), and **configure** (as in **pager 24** in configuration mode). Each of these is considered a separate command, having a unique privilege level. Therefore, the privilege levels are assigned according to the command keyword and the mode in which it is used. EXEC mode commands that can be run without the **show** or **clear** keywords are referenced in **configure** mode. An example is the **help** command.

By default, the commands shown in Table 5-1 are accessed with privilege level 0; all other commands default to level 15.

Table 5-1   *Commands Accessed with Privilege Level 0*

Command	PIX 6.3	ASA	FWSM
`Firewall> enable`	Yes	Yes	Yes
`Firewall> exit`	Yes	Yes	Yes
`Firewall> quit`	Yes	Yes	Yes
`Firewall> help`	Yes	Yes	Yes
`Firewall> login`	Yes	Yes	Yes
`Firewall> logout`	Yes	Yes	Yes

`Firewall> pager`
`Firewall> clear pager`
`Firewall> show pager`
	Yes	No	No

`Firewall> ping`	No	Yes	Yes
`Firewall> traceroute`	No	Yes	No
`Firewall> show checksum`	Yes	Yes	Yes
`Firewall> show curpriv`	Yes	Yes	Yes
`Firewall> show history`	Yes	Yes	Yes
`Firewall> show version`	Yes	Yes	Yes
`Firewall> show flash:`	No	Yes	No
`Firewall> show debug`	No	Yes	No

Local user authorization is configured using the following steps:

1. (Optional) Display the current privilege levels for commands:

   ASA,   `Firewall# show privilege {all | command` *command* `| level` *level*`}`
   FWSM

   PIX 6.3   `Firewall# show privilege {all | command` *command* `| level` *level*`}`

   You can see the current privilege level configured for **all** possible firewall commands, or for only a single **command** *command* (only the first keyword). You can also see all the commands available to a user at a given privilege **level** *level* (0 to 15). (The default privilege levels are not shown in the configuration file. On an ASA or FWSM platform, you can see default settings for any command with the **show run all** command.)

2. Set a command's privilege level:

ASA, Firewall(config)# **privilege** [**show** | **clear** | **cmd**] **level** *level* [**mode**
FWSM *mode*] **command** *command*

PIX 6.3 Firewall(config)# **privilege** {**show** | **clear** | **configure**} **level** *level*
[**mode** {**enable** | **configure**}] **command** *command*

For the mode (**show**, **clear**, or **configure**) of the command keyword *command*, a new privilege *level* (0 to 15) is assigned. In ASA and FWSM, the **configure** mode is known only as **cmd** mode.

Some commands can also be used in several submodes within a single mode. In PIX 6.3, for example, the **clear logging** command can be run from **enable** mode or **configure** mode. In either case, the contents of the logging buffer are cleared, but you might want to restrict that command when a user is in one mode versus another.

In ASA and FWSM, you can set command privilege levels with a greater granularity. You can use the **mode** keyword to identify a specific mode or submode where the **command** keyword is used. The *mode* parameter can be given as any one of the keywords shown in Table 5-2, usually shown in the firewall configuration mode prompt.

Table 5-2 *ASA Privileged Command Mode Values*

mode Keyword	Mode Description
aaa-server-group	AAA server group configuration mode
aaa-server-host	AAA server host configuration mode
cache	WebVPN cache configuration mode
class	Resource class configuration mode
config-dap-webvpn	Dynamic access policy WebVPN configuration mode
config-group-webvpn	Group policy WebVPN configuration mode
config-mount-cifs	CIFS mount configuration mode
config-mount-ftp	FTP mount configuration mode
config-mount-nfs	NFS mount configuration mode
config-username-webvpn	Username WebVPN configuration mode
config-webvpn-customization	WebVPN customization configuration mode
config-webvpn-sso-saml	WebVPN SAML SSO server configuration mode
config-webvpn-sso-siteminder	WebVPN SiteMinder SSO server configuration mode
config-zonelabs-integrity	Zonelabs Firewall Server configuration mode
configure	Global configuration mode

continues

Section 5-2

Table 5-2 *ASA Privileged Command Mode Values (Continued)*

mode Keyword	Mode Description
context	Context configuration mode
crypto-ca-cert-chain	Crypto certificate entry mode
crypto-ca-cert-map	Certificate map entry mode
crypto-ca-crl	Certificate authority trustpoint CRL entry mode
crypto-ca-server	Certificate Server entry mode
crypto-ca-trustpoint	Certificate authority trustpoint entry mode
crypto-isakmp-policy	Crypto ISAKMP policy configuration mode
crypto-pubkey	Crypto subsystem public key entry mode
ctl-provider	CTL Provider configuration mode
dns-server-group	DNS server group configuration mode
dual-service-object-group	Dual Service object group configuration
dynamic-access-policy-record	Dynamic access policy record attribute configuration mode
dynupd-method	Dynamic DNS update method configuration mode
enable	EXEC mode (the keyword is converted to **exec**)
exec	EXEC mode
fover-group	Failover user group configuration mode
ftp-map	ftp-map configuration mode
group-policy	group-policy attribute configuration mode
gtpmap	GTP class map configuration mode
h225-map	h225-map configuration mode
hsi-group	hsi-group configuration mode
http-map	http-map configuration mode
icmp-object-group	ICMPtype object group configuration mode
imap4s	imap4s configuration mode
interface	Interface configuration mode
ldap	LDAP configuration mode
mgcp-map	mgcp-map configuration mode
mpf-class-map	MPF Class Map configuration mode
mpf-policy-map	MPF Policy Map configuration mode
mpf-policy-map-class	MPF Policy Map class configuration mode

Table 5-2   *ASA Privileged Command Mode Values (Continued)*

mode Keyword	Mode Description
mpf-policy-map-param	MPF policy map parameter configuration mode
nac-policy	NAC policy nac-framework configuration mode
network-object-group	Network object group configuration mode
pop3s	pop3s configuration mode
priority-queue	priority-queue configuration mode
protocol-object-group	Protocol object group configuration mode
qosclassmap	QoS class map configuration mode
qospolicymap	QoS policy map configuration mode
qospolicymapclass	QoS policy map class configuration mode
route-map	Route map configuration mode
router	Router configuration mode
routing	Routing configuration mode
service-object-group	Service object group configuration mode
sla-monitor	IP SLA Monitor entry configuration
sla-monitor-echo	IP SLA Monitor echo configuration
smtps	smtps configuration mode
snmp-map	snmp-map configuration mode
subinterface	Subinterface configuration mode
tcp-map	tcp-map configuration mode
test-dynamic-access-policy	Test dynamic access policy configuration
tls-proxy	TLS proxy configuration mode
trange	time-range configuration mode
tunnel-group-general	tunnel-group general attribute configuration mode
tunnel-group-ipsec	tunnel-group IPSec attribute configuration mode
tunnel-group-ppp	tunnel-group PPP attribute configuration mode
tunnel-group-webvpn	tunnel-group WebVPN attribute configuration mode
username	username attribute configuration mode
vpn-load-balancing	Configure VPN load balancing
webvpn	WebVPN configuration mode

For example, users at or above level 8 can be allowed to show the connection table entries:

```
Firewall(config)# privilege show level 8 command conn
```

ASA and FWSM can also accept this command as

```
Firewall(config)# privilege show level 8 mode exec command conn
```

3. Enable local command authorization:

```
Firewall(config)# aaa authorization command LOCAL
```

Each time a user attempts to use a firewall command, the firewall authorizes the user based on the local **privilege** configuration commands.

Accounting of Local User Activity

With local user authentication and authorization, user accounting can be performed only through the logging function. You should make sure that the following Syslog message IDs are enabled to use them as an audit trail of user activity. The default severity levels are shown in parentheses:

- **611101 (6)**—Successful user authentication
- **611102 (6)**—Failed user authentication
- **502103 (5)**—User changed privilege levels
- **111008 (5)**—User executed the command text
- **111009 (7)**—User executed the command show text
- **611103 (5)**—User logged out

For example, suppose someone managed to log in to a firewall, clear its configuration, and reload it. If Syslog were configured on the firewall, you might be able to find an audit trail with clues as to who took those actions. In the following output, a user named **userjane** has authenticated, used the **enable** command to move into privilege level 15, cleared the configuration, and reloaded the firewall:

```
%ASA-6-109005: Authentication succeeded for user 'userjane' from 172.28.4.41/0 to
   10.1.1.10/24 on interface outside
%ASA-6-611101: User authentication succeeded: Uname: userjane
%ASA-5-502103: User priv level changed: Uname: userjane From: 1 To: 15
%ASA-5-111008: User 'userjane' executed the 'enable' command.
%ASA-7-111009: User 'userjane' executed cmd: show clock
%ASA-5-111008: User 'userjane' executed the 'write erase' command.
%ASA-5-111008: User 'userjane' executed the 'reload' command.
```

5-3: Defining AAA Servers for User Management

A firewall can interface with external user management servers to offload any authentication, authorization, or accounting (AAA) functions. This provides a very scalable solution, because all user identities, privileges, and activity logs can be centralized.

You can use the following steps to configure AAA servers and server groups for all AAA-related firewall functions:

1. Define the AAA server group and protocol:

   ASA,   `Firewall(config)# `**`aaa-server`**` server_tag `**`protocol {tacacs+ | radius}`**
   FWSM

   PIX 6.3   `Firewall(config)# `**`aaa-server`**` server_tag `**`protocol {tacacs+ | radius}`**

   A group of servers is named *server_tag* (an arbitrary string without white space) using a common AAA protocol. All firewall platforms support the **tacacs+** or **radius** protocol. In fact, PIX 6.3 has the following three predefined server groups:

   ```
   aaa-server TACACS+ protocol tacacs+
   aaa-server RADIUS protocol radius
   aaa-server LOCAL protocol local
   ```

   With ASA and FWSM, only the LOCAL group is predefined. You can also use other AAA protocols if they exist in your network. Specific protocol parameters are configured on a per-server basis in Step 2.

   TIP   You can define multiple AAA servers in a single group. Table 5-3 lists the maximum number of server groups and servers per group.

Table 5-3   *AAA Server Limits by Security Platform*

Platform	Server Groups	Servers per Group
PIX 6.3	14	14
ASA single context	18	16
ASA multiple contexts	7	4
FWSM single context	15	16
FWSM multiple contexts	4	4

The firewall sends requests to the first server configured in the group. If that server does not answer within a configurable time, the other servers in the group are tried in succession.

a. (Optional) Set the server failure threshold:

ASA,   `Firewall(config-aaa-server-group)# ` **`max-failed-attempts`** `number`
FWSM

PIX 6.3   `Firewall(config)# ` **`aaa-server`** `server_tag` **`max-failed-attempts`**
          `number`

If a AAA server is unreachable, the firewall retries its request. After *number* (1 to 5; the default is 3) failed attempts, the firewall declares that server dead and moves on to the next server in the group.

b. (Optional) Define a server reactivation policy:

ASA,   `Firewall(config-aaa-server-group)# ` **`reactivation-mode {depletion`**
FWSM   **`[deactivation`** `minutes`**`] | timed}`**

PIX 6.3   `Firewall(config)# ` **`aaa-server`** `server_tag` **`deadtime`** `minutes`

By default, any server that is considered deactivated remains deactivated until no more usable servers remain in the group. This is called **depletion** mode.

If only one server group is configured for a AAA function, all servers are immediately reactivated after depletion so that they can be tried again.

If multiple server groups are configured for a AAA function, a depleted group is skipped so that the next server group can be used. The depleted group is declared dead for the duration of the **deadtime** timer, configured as *minutes* (1 to 1440; the default is 10 minutes). After that time, the failed servers are reactivated in the group, and that group is eligible for new AAA requests.

In ASA and FWSM, you can use an alternative policy called *timed* reactivation. Here, any failed or deactivated server is automatically reactivated after 30 seconds.

c. (Optional) Define an accounting policy:

ASA,   `Firewall(config-aaa-server-group)# ` **`accounting-mode {single |`**
FWSM   **`simultaneous}`**

PIX 6.3   -

If you are using AAA accounting, you can specify how the accounting information will be sent. With the **single** keyword, accounting messages are sent to only the active server. The firewall can also send the accounting messages to every server in the group if the **simultaneous** keyword is used.

2. Add a server to the group.

a. Identify the server:

ASA, FWSM	`Firewall(config)# `**`aaa-server`**` server_tag [(if_name)] `**`host`**` server_ip [key] [`**`timeout`**` seconds]`
PIX 6.3	`Firewall(config)# `**`aaa-server`**` server_tag [(if_name)] `**`host`**` server_ip [key] [`**`timeout`**` seconds]`

The server located on the firewall interface named (*if_name*) (be sure to include the parentheses) at IP address *server_ip* is added to the *server_tag* group. If you do not specify the interface, the outside interface is assumed. The firewall can use the string *key* (a text string of up to 127 characters without spaces) for all exchanges with the server. Therefore, you must configure the same key on the server and the firewall.

If a response is not received from the server within a timeout period of *seconds* (the default is 5 seconds), the firewall sends the same request to the next server in the group.

b. (Optional) Set the server deactivation timer:

ASA, FWSM	`Firewall(config-aaa-server-host)# `**`timeout`**` seconds`
PIX 6.3	-

The firewall continues to retry requests for a timeout period of *seconds* (1 to 60; the default is 10 seconds) before it declares the server dead. After that point, the next server in a server group is tried.

c. (Optional) Use one common port for all server protocols:

ASA, FWSM	`Firewall(config-aaa-server-host)# `**`server-port`**` port`
PIX 6.3	-

Each AAA protocol uses a different default port for its services. For example, TACACS uses port 49, Kerberos uses 88, Lightweight Directory Access Protocol (LDAP) uses 389, NT uses 139, and Security Dynamics Incorporated (SDI) uses 5500. You can configure the firewall to use one *port* (1 to 65535) for any protocol used on the server, as long as the server is also configured to use the same port.

Although it is not necessary, using one common port for any AAA protocol can simplify the types of traffic passing between the firewall and the server. This in turn might simplify any firewall or router access lists that need to permit the AAA traffic.

Section 5-3

3. (Optional) Adjust RADIUS server parameters.

    a. (Optional) Adjust the RADIUS port numbers:

ASA, FWSM	`Firewall(config-aaa-server-host)#` **`authentication-port`** `port`
	`Firewall(config-aaa-server-host)#` **`accounting-port`** `port`
PIX 6.3	`Firewall(config)#` **`aaa-server`** `{`**`radius-authport`** `|` **`radius-acctport`**`}` `[port]`

By default, a firewall uses UDP/TCP port 1645 for RADIUS authentication and port 1646 for accounting.

TIP   You should confirm that your RADIUS server uses matching port numbers. If it does not, you can configure the authentication port (**radius-authport**) or the accounting port (**radius-acctport**) to *port*. Some RADIUS servers use legacy values of 1812 for authentication and 1813 for accounting.

---

    b. Set the RADIUS key:

ASA, FWSM	`Firewall(config-aaa-server-host)#` **`key`** `key`
PIX 6.3	-

In ASA and FWSM, the RADIUS *key* (a text string of up to 127 characters without spaces) should be configured as a host parameter. You must configure the same key on the firewall and the RADIUS server.

    c. (Optional) Set the retry interval:

ASA, FWSM	`Firewall(config-aaa-server-host)#` **`retry-interval`** `seconds`
PIX 6.3	-

If the server does not answer a RADIUS request, the firewall retries it after *seconds* (1 to 10; the default is 10 seconds) has elapsed.

    d. (Optional) Use one common password for server requests:

ASA, FWSM	`Firewall(config-aaa-server-host)#` **`radius-common-pw`** `string`
PIX 6.3	-

You can configure a common password that the firewall will use for all RADIUS authorization requests. The password is given as *string* (up to 127 characters).

4. (Optional) Adjust Kerberos server parameters.

   a. Define the Kerberos realm name:

ASA, FWSM	`Firewall(config-aaa-server-host)# ` **`kerberos-realm`** ` string`
PIX 6.3	

   The Kerberos realm name defined on the server is *string* (up to 64 characters with no spaces).

   b. (Optional) Set the retry interval:

ASA, FWSM	`Firewall(config-aaa-server-host)# ` **`retry-interval`** ` seconds`
PIX 6.3	-

   If the server does not answer a RADIUS request, the firewall retries it after *seconds* (1 to 10; the default is 10 seconds) has elapsed.

5. (Optional) Adjust LDAP server parameters.

   a. (Optional) Use SASL authentication:

ASA, FWSM	`Firewall(config-aaa-server-host)# ` **`sasl-mechanism`** ` {`**`digest-md5`** ` |` **`kerberos`** ` server_group_name}`
PIX 6.3	-

   The firewall authenticates with an LDAP server on behalf of the actual clients by using Simple Authentication and Security Layer (SASL). With the **digest-md5** keyword, an MD5 hash of the username and password is sent to the LDAP server. Kerberos can be used instead, with the **kerberos** keyword. The *server_group_name* is the name of the AAA server group used for Kerberos.

   b. (Optional) Secure the LDAP communication:

ASA, FWSM	`Firewall(config-aaa-server-host)# ` **`ldap-over-ssl enable`**
PIX 6.3	-

Normally, traffic between the firewall and the LDAP server is sent in the clear. With the **ldap-over-ssl** command, an SSL connection is brought up so that the LDAP traffic is secured.

c. (Optional) Set the LDAP server type:

ASA, FWSM	`Firewall(config-aaa-server-host)#` **server-type {auto-detect | microsoft | sun | generic}**
PIX 6.3	-

By default, the firewall attempts to automatically detect the type of LDAP server it is communicating with. You can use this command to define the server type if auto-detection is not giving the results you expect. The server type can be **auto-detect** (the default), **microsoft** (Microsoft LDAP), **sun** (Sun LDAP), or **generic** (generic LDAPv3).

d. Set the starting point in the LDAP hierarchy:

ASA, FWSM	`Firewall(config-aaa-server-host)#` **ldap-base-dn** *string*
PIX 6.3	-

To process a AAA request, the LDAP server should begin its search at the distinguished name (DN) given by string (up to 128 characters). A DN has the form *XX=xxxx,YY=yyyy,...* where *XX* and *YY* are abbreviations for parameters within the hierarchy, and *xxxx* and *yyyy* are strings. For example, a DN string can be o=MyCompany.com or o=MyCompany.com,ou=Engineering.

e. Limit the scope of an LDAP search:

ASA, FWSM	`Firewall(config-aaa-server-host)#` **ldap-scope {onelevel | subtree}**
PIX 6.3	-

By default, the LDAP server is asked to search only one tree level (**onelevel**) below the base DN. If your LDAP hierarchy is structured such that there are many levels below the base, you can use the **subtree** keyword to force a search of the entire subtree.

f. Define the relative DN attributes to search:

ASA, FWSM	`Firewall(config-aaa-server-host)#` **ldap-naming-attribute** *string*
PIX 6.3	-

When a user is authenticated or authorized, the firewall can pass only the username and password to the LDAP server. The firewall must also inform the LDAP server which DN attributes are necessary to uniquely identify a user during a search. These are given as *string* (up to 128 characters).

For example, if usernames are referenced in the Common Name attribute (the CN field of a DN), the following command would be used:

```
Firewall(config-aaa-server-host)# ldap-naming-att cn
```

g.   Authenticate the firewall:

ASA,	`Firewall(config-aaa-server-host)# ldap-login-dn` *string*
FWSM	`Firewall(config-aaa-server-host)# ldap-login-password` *string*
PIX 6.3	-

The firewall must authenticate itself with the LDAP server when AAA requests are sent. This is done with a DN and a password, which are strings of up to 128 and 64 characters, respectively.

For example, a firewall might authenticate itself with the following DN and password commands:

```
Firewall(config-aaa-server-host)# ldap-login-dn cn=firewall,
  o=mycompany.com,ou=networking
Firewall(config-aaa-server-host)# ldap-login-password mysecretpassword
```

h.   (Optional) Map user-defined LDAP attributes to Cisco LDAP attributes:

If you are adding a firewall to an existing LDAP environment, you might need to map existing, user-defined attributes to Cisco LDAP attributes. The mapping is defined as an attribute map with the **ldap-attribute-map** global configuration command. You can map attribute names and attribute values as needed, using the **map-name** and **map-value** commands, respectively:

ASA,	`Firewall(config-aaa-server-host)# ldap-attribute-map` *map_name*
FWSM	`Firewall(config-aaa-server-host)# exit`
	`Firewall(config)# ldap-attribute-map` *map_name* `{auto-detect | microsoft | sun | generic}`
	`Firewall(config-ldap-attribute-map)# map-name` *user_attribute_name cisco_attribute_name*
	`Firewall(config-ldap-attribute-map)# map-value` *user_attribute_name user_value_string cisco_value_string*
PIX 6.3	-

6. (Optional) Identify the NT domain controller:

ASA, FWSM	`Firewall(config-aaa-server-host)# `**`nt-auth-domain-controller`** *`string`*
PIX 6.3	-

The name of the Windows NT Primary Domain Controller (PDC) is defined as *string* (up to 16 characters).

7. (Optional) Adjust SDI SecureID server parameters.

   a. Define the SDI protocol version:

ASA, FWSM	`Firewall(config-aaa-server-host)# `**`sdi-version`** `{`**`sdi-pre-5`** `|` **`sdi-5`**`}`
PIX 6.3	-

The SDI version should be set to reflect the version used on the server: **sdi-pre-5** (releases before 5.0) or **sdi-5** (release 5.0 or later).

   b. (Optional) Set the retry interval:

ASA, FWSM	`Firewall(config-aaa-server-host)# `**`retry-interval`** *`seconds`*
PIX 6.3	-

If the server does not answer an SDI request, the firewall retries it after *seconds* (1 to 10; the default is 10 seconds) has elapsed.

5-4: Configuring AAA to Manage Administrative Users

You can use external AAA servers to manage users who connect to the firewall for administrative purposes. Usernames and passwords are created or deleted on one or more centralized AAA servers. The firewall can query the servers when users connect and need to be authenticated. Firewall command authorization can also be used when various users must be limited to specific privilege levels and sets of commands. A firewall can also generate user accounting information that is collected by the external servers.

You can use the configuration steps covered in the following sections to set up AAA for administrative user management.

Enabling AAA User Authentication

Follow these steps to configure administrative user authentication with AAA servers:

1. Authenticate with a AAA server group:

   Firewall(config)# **aaa authentication {serial | telnet | ssh | http} console**
      server_tag [**LOCAL**]

   The AAA server group named *server_tag* is used to handle authentication requests. The server group must be configured as a separate step, as described in section 5-3, "Defining AAA Servers for User Management." Each server defined in the group is tried in succession in case some are unreachable or unavailable.

   If all the servers in the group are down or the firewall cannot reach any of them because of networking issues, the user authentication fails. This means that you can effectively be locked out of the firewall, unable to make any configuration changes or execute any commands.

   As a fallback measure, you can add the **LOCAL** keyword to make the firewall use local authentication after trying the AAA server group. Even if the network is down, the local user database always is available as a way to authenticate with and connect to the firewall. You should define some administrative users on the firewall with the **username** command. You do not need to duplicate the entire set of users defined on the AAA servers. Just define enough usernames to allow you and your staff to connect.

2. (Optional) Authenticate users for enable mode:

   Firewall(config)# **aaa authentication enable console** *server_tag* [**LOCAL**]

   By default, privilege level 15 is defined with the **enable password** configuration command. Any user who can successfully authenticate with the firewall can also use the **enable** command to move to level 15, *regardless of the privilege level set for the username.* As well, all users share the same password for privilege level 15.

   You can configure enable authentication so that each user must enter an independent enable password to reach a higher privilege level. With an AAA server group, you can define a unique enable password for each user.

   After a user is authenticated with his or her enable password, the privilege level is changed to the level configured for the username. In other words, the privileged EXEC level is set on a per-user basis; not every user automatically arrives at level 15.

TIP   Enable authentication is fully functional with TACACS+ servers, because they support per-user enable passwords and enable privilege level settings. You can also use RADIUS servers for this, but each user's enable password is always identical to his or her RADIUS password. As well, RADIUS does not directly support enable privilege levels for users.

Figure 5-1 shows an example of the User Setup configuration for a user in CiscoACS. Under **Advanced TACACS+ Settings**, the user's maximum privilege level is set to 15 for any AAA client accessible to the user. The per-user enable password has also been configured in the **TACACS+ Enable Password** section as a separate password maintained in the CiscoACS database.

Figure 5-1 *Enabling Authentication Configuration on a CiscoACS Server*

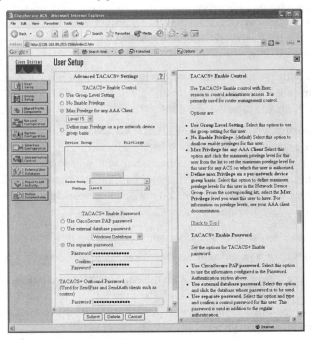

With CiscoACS, make sure the enable authentication options are made available in the user or group setup screens. In the **Interface Configuration**, go to **Advanced Options** and make sure the **Per-User TACACS+/RADIUS Attributes** option is checked. You should also go to **Interface Configuration** and select **TACACS+(Cisco IOS)**; make sure the **Advanced TACACS+ Features** option is checked.

For example, suppose a firewall needs to be configured to use a farm of five RADIUS servers for administrative user authentication. The server has IP addresses 192.168.100.10 through 14, all located on the inside firewall interface. These servers authenticate users connecting to the console port, Telnet, SSH, and web-based management applications. As a fallback, local authentication is used to support a single user ID, *admin*, in case none of the RADIUS servers can be reached.

The following configuration commands can be used to complete the scenario:

```
Firewall(config)# aaa-server RADIUS_FARM protocol radius
Firewall(config)# aaa-server RADIUS_FARM (inside) host 192.168.100.10 key
  Server1Key
```

```
Firewall(config)# aaa-server RADIUS_FARM (inside) host 192.168.100.11 key
   Server2Key
Firewall(config)# aaa-server RADIUS_FARM (inside) host 192.168.100.12 key
   Server3Key
Firewall(config)# aaa-server RADIUS_FARM (inside) host 192.168.100.13 key
   Server4Key
Firewall(config)# aaa-server RADIUS_FARM (inside) host 192.168.100.14 key
   Server5Key
Firewall(config)# aaa authentication serial console RADIUS_FARM LOCAL
Firewall(config)# aaa authentication telnet console RADIUS_FARM LOCAL
Firewall(config)# aaa authentication ssh console RADIUS_FARM LOCAL
Firewall(config)# aaa authentication http console RADIUS_FARM LOCAL
Firewall(config)# aaa authentication enable console RADIUS_FARM LOCAL
Firewall(config)# username admin password AdminPW privilege 15
```

Enabling AAA Command Authorization

If you are using external TACACS+ servers, you can configure command authorization with the following configuration command:

```
Firewall(config)# aaa authorization command server_tag [LOCAL]
```

In ASA or FWSM, you can add the **LOCAL** keyword to allow a fallback method of local command authorization in case none of the TACACS+ servers can be reached.

On a CiscoACS server, you can follow these steps to configure command authorization:

1. In **Interface Configuration**, go to **TACACS+(Cisco IOS)**. Under **TACACS+ Services**, check the **Shell(exec)** boxes for User or Group. This displays command authorization options in the user and/or group configuration pages.

2. Select **User Setup** or **Group Setup**, depending on whether command authorization will be configured per user or per group. Select the appropriate user or group from the list.

3. Under **TACACS+ Settings**, look for the **Shell Command Authorization Set** section. Select **Per User** (or **Per Group**) **Command Authorization**. You can configure specific commands to permit or deny for the user or group. For all other "unmatched" or unspecified Cisco IOS commands, choose whether the CiscoACS server will **Permit** or **Deny** them.

4. To authorize a specific command, check the **Command** box and enter the first command keyword in the text box. You can also specify command arguments or keywords in the **Arguments** box. Under **Unlisted arguments** (arguments or keywords that you do not explicitly list for the command), select whether to **Permit** or **Deny** them.

   The ACS page can display space for more than one command to be configured. You can enter an additional command in each section that begins with a "Command" checkbox. Click the **Submit** button at the bottom of the page when all the command arguments have been entered. You can add more commands to the list by selecting the user or group again. Each time you configure a command, it is appended to the list of commands and arguments on the configuration page.

Section 5-4

Figure 5-2 shows an example of how a CiscoACS group has been configured so that **enable** and **exit** are permitted commands. All other commands are denied for the group.

Figure 5-2 *CiscoACS TACACS+ Command Authorization*

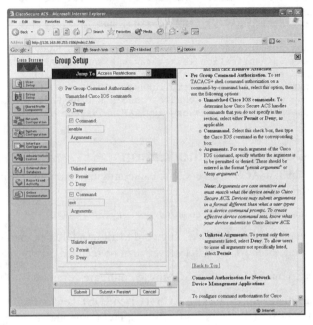

5. You can also define lists of permitted firewall commands, which can be applied to users or groups in CiscoACS.

a. Go to Shared Profile Components, and select **Shell Command Authorization Set**.

Enter one command (only the first keyword) at a time in the text box, and click **Add Command**. If you need to specify keywords that can appear after the command keyword, enter those in the rightmost text box. Be sure to begin each line with **permit** or **deny**, followed by the command arguments and keywords.

Choose whether unmatched (unlisted) commands will be permitted or denied. Then click **Submit**.

In Figure 5-3, a shell command authorization set has been configured to allow a subset of users to display various firewall resources. With the **show** command, only specific keywords are permitted. Any other command that is not listed is denied.

Figure 5-3 *CiscoACS Command Authorization Set Configuration*

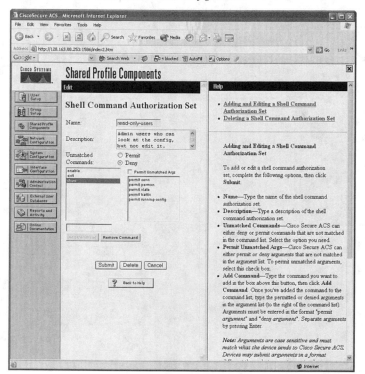

b. After a command authorization set is configured, you can apply it in **User Setup** or **Group Setup**. Under the **Shell Command Authorization Set** section, you can select the set in the drop-down list. Figure 5-4 shows how the read-only-users command authorization set can be applied to any network device that CiscoACS makes available to a group.

TIP   If you decide to enable command authorization, you should make sure you define an administrative user who can always access all firewall commands. In other words, disable command authorization for at least one administrative user so that you have a fallback plan. Otherwise, it is possible to misconfigure command authorization for users or groups such that you are effectively denied from making configuration changes on the firewall.

Figure 5-4 *Applying a CiscoACS Command Authorization Set*

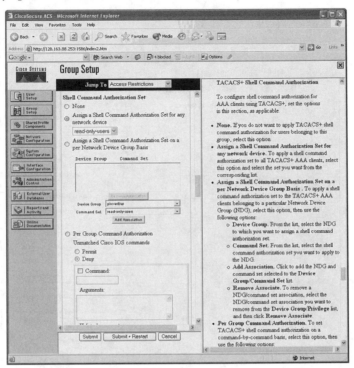

Enabling AAA Command Accounting

In PIX 6.3 or FWSM prior to 3.1(1), AAA command accounting can be performed only through the logging function. In that case, you should make sure the following Syslog message IDs are enabled to use them as an audit trail of user activity. The default severity levels are shown in parentheses:

- **611101 (6)**—Successful user authentication
- **611102 (6)**—Failed user authentication
- **502103 (5)**—User changed privilege levels
- **111008 (5)**—User executed the command *text*
- **111009 (7)**—User executed the command **show** *text*
- **611103 (5)**—User logged out

Beginning with ASA 7.0(1) and FWSM 3.1(1), accounting records can be generated each time an administrative user executes a firewall command. These accounting records can be sent to one or more AAA RADIUS or TACACS+ accounting servers.

To enable command accounting, you can use the following configuration command:

```
Firewall(config)# aaa accounting command [privilege level] server_tag
```

Accounting records are generated only when users execute commands at or above the privilege level *level* (0 to 15; the default is 0). The accounting records are sent to the current active server in the server group configured as *server_tag*.

With CiscoACS, you can view accounting records by clicking the **Reports and Activity** button. Then click **TACACS+ Accounting** or **RADIUS Accounting**. All accounting reports are in comma-separated value (CSV) format and can be displayed in a web browser.

5-5: Configuring AAA for End-User Cut-Through Proxy

A firewall can be configured to require users to authenticate before connections are permitted. As soon as an authentication is successful, it is cached and used to permit subsequent connections from the same user.

The firewall functions as an authentication proxy, because cached authentication information is used in place of repeated authentication credentials entered by the user. Connections simply "cut through" the firewall in a very efficient fashion.

Devices that initiate connections but cannot participate in authentication (Cisco IP phones, for example) can be exempted from AAA and allowed to pass through the firewall.

Authenticating Users Passing Through

You can use the following steps to configure AAA authentication for cut-through proxy users:

1. (Optional) List protocols that trigger authentication:

   ```
   Firewall(config)# aaa authentication {include | exclude} service if_name
       local_ip local_mask [foreign_ip foreign_mask] server_tag
   ```

   To trigger user authentication, use the **include** keyword and identify the triggering protocol as *service*. This usually is a protocol that can support native authentication, where a username and password exchange is possible. These are **telnet**, **ssh**, **ftp**, **http**, and **https**, which can also be written as **tcp/23**, **tcp/22**, **tcp/21**, **tcp/80**, and **tcp/443**, respectively.

   You can also specify other types of traffic as **udp/***port*, **tcp/***port*, **icmp/***type*, or *protocol/port* (the IP protocol number and port number). You can use 0 for a *port* or *type* to indicate a wildcard for any value, as in **tcp/0** for any TCP port. Notice that these values always pertain to the destination port and never the source port.

> **NOTE** Be aware that the cut-through proxy authentication process can be triggered only with Telnet, SSH, FTP, HTTP, or HTTPS traffic. If you specify other types of traffic, those packets are dropped unless the user has already authenticated and has a cut-through proxy session already initiated.

Authentication is triggered for connections initiated from the firewall interface named *if_name* ("inside," for example) from local addresses defined by *local_ip* and *local_mask*. You can define specific destination addresses by *foreign_ip* and *foreign_mask* if needed. To indicate a wildcard local or foreign address, you can use 0s or the **any** keyword for the address and mask values.

Authentication is performed by contacting the server group name *server_tag*. This can be a TACACS+ group name, a RADIUS group name, or the firewall itself with the **LOCAL** keyword.

> **TIP** With the **include** keyword, no traffic is allowed to pass from a given user (source address) until that user has successfully authenticated using Telnet, FTP, HTTP, or HTTPS. You can define protocols that are allowed to pass without authentication by using the **exclude** keyword.

2. (Optional) Use an access list to trigger authentication:

    Firewall(config)# **aaa authentication match** *acl_name if_name server_tag*

Here, an access list named *acl_name* is used to match connections that are initiated from hosts on the firewall interface named *if_name*. Protocols that can be authenticated are defined in **permit** statements in the access list.

Because this is the most specific method of traffic authentication, it is also the preferred method. You can make the matching conditions very specific by giving the local (source) and foreign (destination) addresses. Remember that the matching protocol is always specified as the destination port in the access list entry.

The authentication server group named *server_tag* is used to handle the actual authentication. This can be a TACACS+ server group name, a RADIUS server group name, or the firewall itself as **LOCAL**.

For example, all IP traffic coming from source addresses 172.16.0.0/24 should be authenticated before being passed through the firewall. In addition, all HTTP and HTTPS connections initiated from the inside interface should be authenticated. Authentication is handled by servers assigned to the default TACACS+ server group. The following commands can be used to accomplish this:

```
Firewall(config)# access-list AuthList1 permit ip 172.16.0.0 255.255.255.0
  any
Firewall(config)# access-list AuthList1 permit tcp any any eq http
Firewall(config)# access-list AuthList1 permit tcp any any eq https
Firewall(config)# aaa authentication match AuthList1 inside TACACS+
```

3. (Optional) Use SSL for all web-related authentication:

```
Firewall(config)# aaa authentication secure-http-client
```

By default, if a user initiates authentication with Telnet, FTP, or HTTP traffic, his or her username and password credentials are collected as cleartext through a popup browser window. You can use this command to force the firewall to use SSL to collect this information securely with encryption.

NOTE   A firewall supports only 16 simultaneous SSL sessions for the initial user authentication. Any connections that require additional SSL sessions are dropped until a new session can be started.

---

4. (Optional) Exempt devices from authentication.

   a. Define a list of exempt MAC addresses:

   ```
   Firewall(config)# mac-list id {deny | permit} mac macmask
   ```

   The device list is named *id* (an arbitrary text name). You can **permit** the device to pass without authentication or **deny** it from doing so. The device is identified by its Media Access Control (MAC) address *mac* (in dotted-triplet form, as in 1111.2222.3333) and a MAC address mask *macmask* (in dotted-triplet format, where a 1 bit matches and a 0 bit ignores). To match a single-device MAC address, the *macmask* is given as **ffff.ffff.ffff**.

   You can repeat this command to define multiple MAC addresses in a single list. For example, the following MAC list allows the host using MAC address 0006.5b02.a841 or 0040.9646.6cf6 to initiate connections without authentication:

   ```
   Firewall(config)# mac-list Exemptions permit 0006.5b02.a841 ffff.ffff.ffff
   Firewall(config)# mac-list Exemptions permit 0040.9646.6cf6 ffff.ffff.ffff
   ```

NOTE If you decide to list device MAC addresses here, those devices must be located on the firewall interface's IP subnet. In other words, they cannot lie beyond a router, or their MAC addresses will become obscured by the router.

Any devices not explicitly permitted or denied in a MAC address control list are subject to any other authentication methods that are configured on the firewall interface.

---

  b. Apply the list to authentication:

```
Firewall(config)# aaa mac-exempt match id
```

The MAC address control list named *id* is used to permit or deny specific hosts from passing without authentication.

5. (Optional) Limit per-user proxy connections:

```
Firewall(config)# aaa proxy-limit {proxy_limit | disable}
```

By default, a firewall supports cut-through proxy for up to 16 concurrent active connections per user. You can change this limit to *proxy_limit* (1 to 128 concurrent connections per user) or **disable** the limit completely.

6. (Optional) Adjust the cut-through proxy session timer.

The firewall keeps two timers for each user's connection activity after a successful authentication: an absolute timer and an inactivity timer.

  a. Adjust the absolute timer:

```
Firewall(config)# timeout uauth hh[:mm[:ss]] absolute
```

By default, the absolute timer is used to require a user to reauthenticate if a new connection is initiated at least 5 minutes after the previous authentication. This timer runs for each user who authenticates with the cut-through proxy feature. The user must authenticate again if a new connection begins after the timer has expired, even if other connections are active or still initiating.

You can set the absolute timer by giving the hours, minutes, and seconds duration. Notice that minutes and seconds are both optional. It might seem intuitive that giving two digits (**60**, for example) would mean seconds, but in fact it means hours.

  b. Adjust the inactivity timer:

```
Firewall(config)# timeout uauth hh[:mm[:ss]] inactivity
```

By default, the inactivity timer is set to 0, which disables it for each user. You can use this timer to require a user to reauthenticate only after all his or her connections become idle or inactive (no data passed) for a period of time. Opening a new connection also resets the counter.

You can set the inactivity timer by giving the hours, minutes, and seconds duration. Notice that minutes and seconds are both optional. It might seem intuitive that giving two digits (**60**, for example) would mean seconds, but in fact it means hours.

TIP   Setting and using the user authentication (uauth) timers is a bit of a trade-off. The absolute timer forces a strict authentication policy, making users reauthenticate again and again at regular intervals. This can be beneficial to protect access to sensitive data, but it also can be a nuisance to the end users.

The inactivity timer is less secure but more user-friendly. As long as a connection is kept alive, the user is not asked to authenticate again.

You can use both timers to gain some benefits from each. Always make sure that the inactivity timer is set to a value less than the absolute timer. In addition, the absolute timer must be set to a value less than the xlate timer. The idea is to require an absolute timer authentication only after all sessions become inactive. Any existing xlate entries for the user's connections should also stay alive until both types of timers have expired and the user has been given a chance to reauthenticate.

You can use the **show timeout** command to see the current values of all connection timers. For example, this firewall is configured to reauthenticate users after their connections have been idle for 15 minutes and at regular 30-minute intervals:

```
Firewall# show timeout
timeout xlate 3:00:00
timeout conn 1:00:00 half-closed 0:10:00 udp 0:02:00 rpc 0:10:00 h225 1:00:00
timeout h323 0:05:00 mgcp 0:05:00 sip 0:30:00 sip_media 0:02:00
timeout uauth 0:30:00 absolute uauth 0:15:00 inactivity
Firewall#
```

Authorizing User Activity with TACACS+ Servers

You can follow these steps to configure traffic authorization using AAA and TACACS+ servers:

1. List protocols that require authorization:

   ```
   Firewall(config)# aaa authorization {include | exclude} service if_name
       local_ip local_mask foreign_ip foreign_mask server_tag
   ```

   The protocol that must be authorized for a user is identified as *service* with the **include** keyword. The protocol can be **telnet**, **ftp**, **http**, **any**, or *protocol/port* (decimal IP protocol number and decimal port number).

Connections using this protocol are initiated on the firewall interface named *if_name* from local addresses defined by *local_ip* and *local_mask*. You can define specific destination addresses by *foreign_ip* and *foreign_mask* if needed. To indicate a wildcard local or foreign address, use 0s for the address and mask values. This is similar to the **any** keyword in Cisco router IOS software.

Authorization is performed by contacting the TACACS+ server group name *server_tag*. For example, the following commands cause the firewall to generate requests to see if the users are authorized to initiate FTP and Telnet connections. All other connection types are authorized without explicit AAA authorization requests.

```
Firewall(config)# aaa authorization include ftp inside 0 0 0 0 TACACS_Farm
Firewall(config)# aaa authorization include telnet inside 0 0 0 0 TACACS_Farm
```

2. (Optional) Use an access list to trigger authorization:

```
Firewall(config)# aaa authorization match acl_name if_name server_tag
```

Here, an access list named *acl_name* is used to match connections that are initiated from the firewall interface named *if_name*. Protocols that are checked for authorization are defined in **permit** statements in the access list. You can make the matching conditions very specific by giving the local (source) and foreign (destination) addresses.

This is the preferred method of defining authorization, because the access list is the most scalable and easiest to administer. Remember that the matching protocol is always specified as the destination port in the access list entry.

The TACACS+ server group named *server_tag* is used to handle the actual authorization.

3. Configure a user's TACACS+ profile.

To authorize a user to use a protocol, you must configure the user's profile on the TACACS+ server. TACACS+ has a facility to authorize only commands to be executed; therefore, the protocol is considered a "command" even though it is not.

You should configure the command by using any of the valid keywords or *protocol/port* definitions that are supported by the **aaa authorization** {**include** ׀ **exclude**} command. For example, you can use the **telnet**, **ssh**, **ftp**, **http**, or **https** keyword along with an optional permitted destination address. You can give the permitted address as **any** or **.*** if no granularity is required.

For example, suppose a CiscoACS server is configured with a command authorization set called *guests* that allows HTTP, ICMP, SMTP, and DNS traffic from any host. Figure 5-5 shows the **Shell Command Authorization Set** configuration page. Each of the protocols is listed as a "command" by using a keyword or the *protocol/port*.

Figure 5-5   *Sample Configuration of CiscoACS Traffic Authorization*

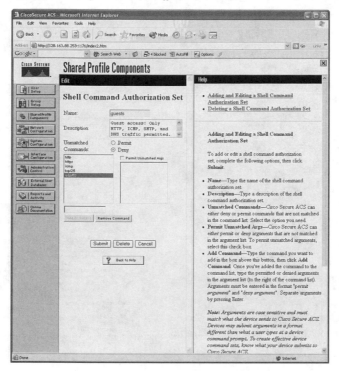

You then apply the shell command authorization set to a **User Setup** or **Group Setup** in CiscoACS by selecting it from the drop-down list. Figure 5-6 shows how the guests set is configured for a group of users.

Figure 5-6 *Applying Traffic Authorization to a User Group in CiscoACS*

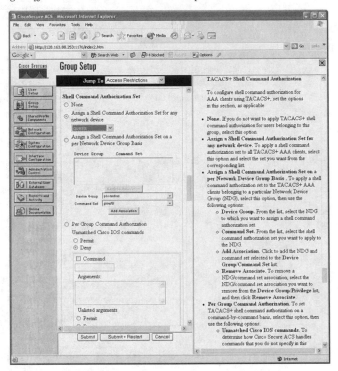

Authorizing User Activity with RADIUS Servers

User authorization is not available as a part of the RADIUS protocol. However, if you have only RADIUS servers available and you need to set up authorization for user traffic, you can use access lists to emulate authorization.

The RADIUS server can be configured to return a reference to an access list that is based on a user's authorization. The firewall can use the access list information to permit or deny the user's connections as they are initiated. You have two ways to approach RADIUS authorization:

- The RADIUS server returns the name of an access control list (ACL) that is defined locally on the firewall.

- The RADIUS server returns the contents of an ACL that is downloaded and used by the firewall. The ACL is actually defined on the RADIUS server, not on the firewall.

You can use the following steps to configure RADIUS user authorization:

1. (Optional) Reference an ACL from the AAA server.

   a. Configure access lists to permit specific traffic:

   ```
   Firewall(config)# access-list acl_name permit protocol any foreign_ip
     foreign_mask operator port
   ```

   Add a **permit** access list entry for a protocol and destination address that should be
   allowed for a user. Normally, the access list entries are configured for groups of users so
   that one policy can be applied to multiple users.

   Remember that the access list has an implicit **deny any any** at the end, so any traffic not
   specifically permitted in the list is rejected.

   b. Add the access list name to the RADIUS user profiles.

   The RADIUS server simply returns a text value for attribute 11 from the user's profile.
   This is returned when the user *authenticates*, so RADIUS authentication must also be configured on the firewall. Attribute 11 is called filter-id. When the firewall receives this
   attribute value, it uses it to reference an access list by the same name.

   On a CiscoACS server, begin by making the filter-id parameter available to user or group
   configurations. Go to **Interface Configuration**, select **RADIUS(IETF)**, and make sure
   that attribute **[011]Filter-Id** is checked for **User** and/or **Group**.

   Next, go to **User Setup** or **Group Setup**, select a user or group, and click **Edit Settings**.
   In the **IETF RADIUS Attributes** section, look for attribute **[011]Filter-Id**. Check that
   box and enter the name of the ACL in the text box.

   For example, suppose an ACL named *acl_http_only* is used to "authorize" or control a
   user's access through a firewall. Only HTTP and HTTPS connections are allowed. First,
   the access list must be configured on the firewall with the following commands:

   ```
   Firewall(config)# access-list acl_http_only permit tcp any any eq www
   Firewall(config)# access-list acl_http_only permit tcp any any eq https
   ```

   Next, the user (or group) profile in CiscoACS must be configured with the ACL name as
   RADIUS attribute 11, as shown in Figure 5-7.

Figure 5-7 *Defining the Filter-Id Attribute in CiscoACS*

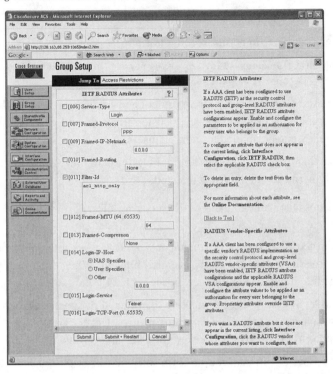

TIP   If attribute 11 (shown as [011]Filter-Id in CiscoACS) is not defined for a user, the AAA
server does not return that attribute. In this case, traffic is assumed to be authorized.

If attribute 11 is defined for a user on the AAA server but the corresponding ACL is not
configured on the firewall, all traffic for that user is denied. This is because a
nonexistent ACL is being referenced.

Instead of attribute 11, you can also use a vendor-specific attribute-value pair. Use
vendor 9 attribute 1, with the value text acl=*acl_id*.

2. (Optional) Download an ACL from the RADIUS server.

Rather than preconfiguring ACLs on the firewall to authorize user traffic, you can use a RADIUS
server to download the actual ACL content to the firewall. ACLs can be downloaded per user or
per group. In either case, the ACL is actually downloaded during user authentication so that it
is available when the users begin initiating connections. ACLs can be created on the RADIUS
server at the same time a new user is added, making the administration a bit easier.

When the RADIUS profile is being edited, you can choose a "downloadable ACL" and enter the ACL contents exactly as you would in a firewall session.

If the firewall is configured for RADIUS authentication, it also begins accepting any downloadable ACLs that are returned in a RADIUS exchange. The firewall requests an ACL download only if the specified ACL is not already configured on the firewall. No other authorization commands are necessary.

a.   Create the downloadable ACL on the RADIUS server.

In CiscoACS, go to **Shared Profile Components** and select **Downloadable IP ACLs**. Click the **Add** button to create a new ACL. Give the ACL a name and an optional description.

To configure the ACL contents, click the **Add** button. You must enter the ACL name again, along with the actual ACL **permit** or **deny** statements in the **ACL Definitions** text box. As soon as the ACL contents are in place, click the **Submit** button.

Figure 5-8 shows an example in which a downloadable ACL called http_only has been created.

Figure 5-8   *An Example of a Downloadable ACL in CiscoACS*

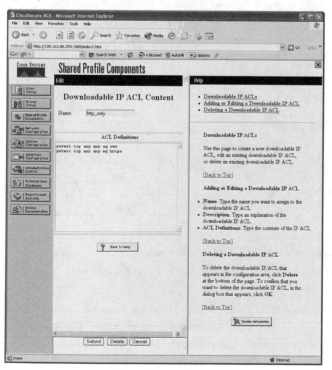

You should see a list of downloadable ACLs that includes the new ACL as well as the CiscoACS default called **permit_anything**.

b. Assign the downloadable ACL to a user or group.

In CiscoACS, go to **User Setup** or **Group Setup**. In the **Downloadable ACSs** section, check the **Assign IP ACL** box and select the appropriate ACL from the drop-down list. In Figure 5-9, the http_only ACL has been selected and will be downloaded when the user authenticates with the CiscoACS server.

Figure 5-9 *Assigning a Downloadable ACL in CiscoACS*

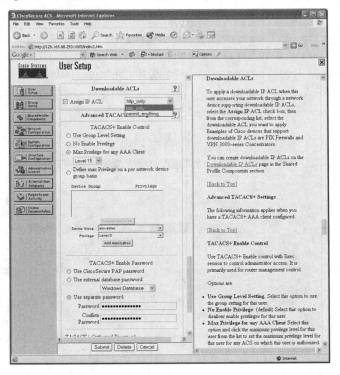

c. Enable downloadable ACLs on the firewall:

```
Firewall(config)# access-group access-list {in | out} interface if_name
  per-user-override
```

After downloadable ACLs are accepted from a AAA server, they must be treated like any other access list—they must be applied to an interface. Therefore, you can use the **per-user-override** keyword when you apply an access list to an interface with the **access-group** command.

Any downloadable ACLs simply override the contents of the existing access list for a given end user. The access list statements are not replaced, however; the per-user ACL is evaluated first, ahead of the regular access list.

TIP   Downloadable ACLs are active only as long as the user is authenticated on the firewall. As soon as the uauth timer expires for a user, the corresponding downloadable ACL is removed. When the user initiates a new connection and authenticates again, the downloadable ACL is retrieved and put into service once more.

You can verify downloadable ACLs on a firewall as they are being used. First, use the **show uauth** *username* and look for the access list that has been downloaded from the RADIUS server. This is indicated by a line beginning with **access-list** followed by the ACL name that was dynamically created. Next, use the **show access-list** command to see the current contents and counters for the ACL entries. The following example demonstrates this downloadable ACL verification process:

```
Firewall# show uauth dhucaby
user 'dhucaby' at 192.168.199.4, authenticated
access-list #ACSACL#-ASA-dhucaby_access_list-1cff1dd1
absolute timeout: 0:05:00
inactivity timeout: 0:00:00
Firewall#
Firewall# show access-list #ACSACL#-ASA-dhucaby_access_list-1cff1dd1
access-list #ACSACL#-ASA-dhucaby_access_list-1cff1dd1; 3 elements
access-list #ACSACL#-ASA-dhucaby_access_list-1cff1dd1
  permit tcp any any eq http (hitcnt=17)
access-list #ACSACL#-ASA-dhucaby_access_list-1cff1dd1
  permit tcp any 172.17.3.0 255.255.255.0 eq telnet (hitcnt=5)
access-list #ACSACL#-ASA-dhucaby_access_list-1cff1dd1
  deny ip any any (hitcnt=201)
Firewall#
```

Downloaded ACLs always have this naming format:

```
#ACSACL#-acl_name-versionID
```

where *acl_name* is the name of the access list (ASA-dhucaby_access_list in the preceding example) and *versionID* is a string of digits that uniquely identifies the current ACL (1cff1dd1 in the example). If the ACL is updated on the RADIUS server, the *versionID* is changed.

Keeping Accounting Records of User Activity

You can use the following steps to configure user activity accounting using AAA servers:

1. (Optional) List protocols that will be tracked:

```
Firewall(config)# aaa accounting {include | exclude} service if_name
  local_ip local_mask foreign_ip foreign_mask server_tag
```

Section 5-5

The firewall sends accounting records when a user initiates a connection on the firewall interface named *if_name* with protocol *service* (**telnet**, **ftp**, **http**, **any**, or *protocol/port*), as long as you use the **include** keyword. You can further specify the user traffic by giving the local and foreign IP addresses and masks. You can also use a wildcard for any of the address and mask values by giving a 0 value.

Usually, you can enter this command with the same arguments as the **aaa authentication** command. In this way, the firewall tracks the same connection activity for which it acts as a cut-through proxy. Accounting records are sent only to the active AAA server in the server group named *server_tag*. The active server is determined by the firewall's AAA authentication feature.

TIP   If you plan to generate accounting information for all user traffic involving a specific protocol, you can use this alternative form of the command:

```
Firewall(config)# aaa accounting {include | exclude} service if_name
    server_tag
```

---

2. (Optional) Use an access list to trigger accounting:

```
Firewall(config)# aaa accounting match acl_name if_name server_tag
```

Here, an access list named *acl_name* is used to match connections that are initiated from the firewall interface named *if_name*. Protocols that are recorded are defined in **permit** statements in the access list.

This method of traffic accounting is preferred, because it is more scalable and easier to maintain. You can make the matching conditions very specific by giving the local (source) and foreign (destination) addresses. The AAA server group named *server_tag* is used to receive accounting information.

AAA Cut-Through Proxy Configuration Examples

In a sample network, user authentication is used on a firewall to require users on the inside to authenticate before initiating outbound connections. Users located on the 192.168.128.0/27 subnet should have all traffic except outbound DNS requests subject to authentication. The DNS traffic should be allowed without authentication so that users can resolve host names.

Three TACACS+ servers are available on the inside network:

- 192.168.4.10
- 192.168.4.11
- 192.168.4.12

These are tried in succession until a responsive server is found. User authentication should be performed over an HTTPS session so that username and password credentials are encrypted from the client to the firewall. (The TACACS+ exchanges between the firewall and the servers are encrypted as part of the TACACS+ protocol.)

After a user is authenticated, the firewall performs cut-through proxy service until the user's sessions have been idle for one hour. After two hours, each user is required to reauthenticate.

You can use the following configuration commands to satisfy the cut-through proxy requirements:

```
aaa-server tacacs-servers protocol tacacs+
aaa-server tacacs-servers (inside) host 192.168.4.10 SpecialKey99
aaa-server tacacs-servers (inside) host 192.168.4.11 SpecialKey99
aaa-server tacacs-servers (inside) host 192.168.4.12 SpecialKey99
aaa authentication include any inside 192.168.128.0 255.255.128.0 0 0 tacacs-servers
aaa authentication exclude udp/53 inside 192.168.128.0 255.255.128.0 0 0 tacacs-servers
aaa authentication secure-http-client
timeout uauth 1:00:00 inactivity
timeout uauth 2:00:00 absolute
```

Remember that only Telnet, SSH, FTP, HTTP, and HTTPS traffic can actually trigger a prompt for user authentication. What, then, is the point of excluding DNS for this example? Until a user authenticates, *all* traffic is dropped. By excluding DNS from authentication, those requests are allowed to pass on through, so the inside users might be able to resolve addresses and then initiate connections like HTTP that can trigger the actual authentication.

You can also use an access list to trigger the authentication process. An access list might be preferable if you need fine granularity over combinations of source and destination addresses and protocols. The ACL and AAA commands required for the same example are as follows:

```
access-list acl_aaa_trigger permit ip 192.168.128.0 255.255.128.0 any
access-list acl_aaa_trigger deny udp 192.168.128.0 255.255.128.0 any eq domain
aaa authentication match acl_aaa_trigger inside tacacs-servers
aaa authentication secure-http-client
```

You can also apply AAA to authorize end-user connections through the firewall. The following command makes all outbound connections from the inside users subject to authorization:

```
aaa authorization include any inside 192.168.128.0 255.255.128.0 0 0 tacacs-servers
```

Each new connection is presented to the active TACACS+_server in the *tacacs-servers* server group. The users or user groups must be configured in the TACACS+ servers to authorize the appropriate protocols.

Finally, the AAA servers are used to collect accounting information about end-user activity through the firewall. Only HTTP, HTTPS, and FTP connections are recorded. You can use the following firewall configuration commands to implement this accounting action:

```
aaa accounting include http inside 192.168.128.0 255.255.128.0 0 0 tacacs-servers
aaa accounting include tcp/443 inside 192.168.128.0 255.255.128.0 0 0 tacacs-servers
aaa accounting include ftp inside 192.168.128.0 255.255.128.0 0 0 tacacs-servers
```

Section 5-5

5-6: Firewall Password Recovery

If the first-level (Telnet) and privileged user (enable) passwords on a functioning Cisco firewall are unknown or have been forgotten, it is possible to recover control of the device. The password recovery procedure varies according to the firewall platform and is explained in the sections that follow.

Recovering an ASA Password

On an ASA, the configuration register is changed to allow booting without the startup configuration file. The ASA can boot its normal operating system image. Without the startup configuration, you can move directly into the privileged EXEC mode without having to use an enable password.

Follow these steps to recover from an unknown password:

1. Connect to the ASA console.

2. Power cycle the ASA.

   The ASA must be reloaded so that you have a chance to break out of the normal boot sequence and change the configuration register.

   If the ASA is already running and you do not have the enable password, you will not be able to reload it unless you turn its power off and then back on.

3. Press the **Escape** key when you are prompted.

   When you see "Use BREAK or ESC to interrupt boot.", you have 10 seconds to press the **Escape (Esc)** key. The ASA should end up at a **rommon** prompt, as in the following example.

   ```
   Rebooting....
   Booting system, please wait...
   CISCO SYSTEMS
   Embedded BIOS Version 1.0(10)0 03/25/05 22:42:05.25

   Low Memory: 631 KB
   High Memory: 256 MB
   PCI Device Table.
   Bus Dev Func VendID DevID Class              Irq
    00  00  00   8086  2578  Host Bridge
    00  01  00   8086  2579  PCI-to-PCI Bridge
   [device list output omitted]

   Evaluating BIOS Options ...
   Launch BIOS Extension to setup ROMMON

   Cisco Systems ROMMON Version (1.0(10)0) #0: Fri Mar 25 23:02:10 PST 2005

   Platform ASA5510
   ```

```
Use BREAK or ESC to interrupt boot.
[ESC pressed here]
Use SPACE to begin boot immediately.
Boot interrupted.

Management0/0
Ethernet auto negotiation timed out.
Interface-4 Link Not Established (check cable).
Default Interface number-4 Not Up
Use ? for help.
rommon #0>
```

4. Edit the configuration register:

```
rommon #0> confreg
```

The **confreg** command displays the current configuration register contents and allows you to enter a new value. Be sure to write down the value that is shown so that you can restore it later.

When you are prompted to change the configuration, enter **y** and press **Enter**. Then answer each of the questions by pressing the **Enter** key to accept the default value. The only exception is the "disable system configuration?" question; answer **y** and press the **Enter** key, as in the following example:

```
rommon #0> confreg
Current Configuration Register: 0x00000001
Configuration Summary:
  boot default image from Flash

Do you wish to change this configuration? y/n [n]: y
enable boot to ROMMON prompt? y/n [n]:
enable TFTP netboot? y/n [n]:
enable Flash boot? y/n [n]:
select specific Flash image index? y/n [n]:
disable system configuration? y/n [n]: y
go to ROMMON prompt if netboot fails? y/n [n]:
enable passing NVRAM file specs in auto-boot mode? y/n [n]:
disable display of BREAK or ESC key prompt during auto-boot? y/n [n]:

Current Configuration Register: 0x00000040
Configuration Summary:
  boot ROMMON
  ignore system configuration
Update Config Register (0x40) in NVRAM...
rommon #1>
```

In the example, notice that the configuration register has gone from 0x00000001 to 0x00000040.

5. Reload the ASA:

```
rommon #1> boot
```

In the following example, the **boot** command is used to reload the ASA. At the end of the boot sequence, the console is left at the EXEC level prompt.

```
Launching BootLoader...
Boot configuration file contains 2 entries.


Loading disk0:/asa800-248-k8.bin... Booting...
Loading...

Processor memory 180940800, Reserved memory: 20971520 (DSOs: 0 + kernel: 20971520)
[output omitted]
Copyright  1996-2007 by Cisco Systems, Inc.

                 Restricted Rights Legend

Use, duplication, or disclosure by the Government is
subject to restrictions as set forth in subparagraph
(c) of the Commercial Computer Software - Restricted
Rights clause at FAR sec. 52.227-19 and subparagraph
(c) (1) (ii) of the Rights in Technical Data and Computer
Software clause at DFARS sec. 252.227-7013.

              Cisco Systems, Inc.
              170 West Tasman Drive
              San Jose, California 95134-1706


Ignoring startup configuration as instructed by configuration register.
INFO: Converting  to disk0:/
Type help or '?' for a list of available commands.
ciscoasa>
```

6. Enter privileged EXEC mode.

Because the startup configuration file was ignored, the enable password is unset. Therefore, you can just press the **Enter** key with a blank password:

```
ciscoasa> enable
Password:
ciscoasa#
```

7. Restore the running configuration:

```
ciscoasa# copy startup-config running-config
Destination filename [running-config]?
Cryptochecksum (unchanged): e4cd72c3 e3a210b0 cafaccc4 eb376c85
7028 bytes copied in 2.440 secs (3514 bytes/sec)
Firewall#
```

8. Reset the passwords.

Now that you are in privileged EXEC mode, you can edit the passwords that were previously stored in the configuration. Use the **password** and **enable password** commands to set the passwords to new, known values:

```
Firewall# configure terminal
Firewall(config)# password password
Firewall(config)# enable password enablepass
```

9. Restore the configuration register:

```
Firewall(config)# config-register hex-value
```

Enter the original configuration value you recorded in step 4, as in the following example:

```
Firewall(config)# config-register ?
configure mode commands/options:
  <0x0-0xffffffff>  Configuration register value
Firewall(config)# config-register 0x00000001
Firewall(config)#
```

10. Save the running configuration:

```
Firewall# copy running-config startup-config
```

As soon as the running configuration is saved into the startup configuration file, the firewall uses the new passwords the next time it is reloaded.

TIP   You can use the **show version** command to see the configuration register settings at any time. The register contents are shown toward the end of the output, as in the following example:

```
Firewall# show version
Cisco Adaptive Security Appliance Software Version 8.0(0)248
Device Manager Version 6.0(0)120
[output omitted]
Serial Number: JKX1014K074
Running Activation Key: 0x70192e4e 0x507e3e04 0xa8f2f16c 0x85c40864
0x4907ef91
Configuration register is 0x40 (will be 0x1 at next reload)
Configuration last modified by enable_15 at 12:25:07.492 EDT Fri Apr 20 2007
Firewall#
```

Recovering a PIX Password

On a PIX platform, a password recovery utility must be downloaded to the firewall from a TFTP server. This procedure is very similar to upgrading the OS image from the PIX monitor prompt.

Follow these steps to reload and erase the PIX passwords:

1. Make sure a TFTP server is available.

   The TFTP server should have a copy of the correct PIX Password Lockout Utility software. You can find this utility on Cisco.com at

   http://www.cisco.com/warp/customer/110/np*XX*.bin

   where *XX* is the PIX OS software release. For example, the utility for PIX OS 6.3 is called np63.bin.

2. Boot the firewall to the monitor prompt.

   Just after booting the firewall, press the **Esc** key to break the normal bootup sequence.

3. Identify the TFTP server.

   a. Identify the firewall interface where the TFTP server is located:

   ```
   monitor> interface number
   ```

   TFTP uses the interface with index *number* (0 to $n - 1$, where n is the number of interfaces installed). During the bootup sequence, the firewall lists the physical interfaces and their MAC addresses.

   b. Assign an IP address to that interface:

   ```
   monitor> address ip-address
   ```

   Here, the firewall needs just enough information to be able to contact the TFTP server. Only one physical interface can be used, so this IP address is applied to it. Because a subnet mask cannot be given, the firewall assumes a regular classful network mask (172.17.69.41 yields a Class B mask of 255.255.0.0, for example).

   If your TFTP server is located on a different classful subnet, you can also specify a gateway address that can route between the firewall and the server. Use the following monitor command:

   ```
   monitor> gateway ip-address
   ```

   c. Make sure the firewall can reach the TFTP server.

   The firewall must be able to reach the server with a minimal amount of routing. You can use the following monitor command to test reachability:

   ```
   monitor> ping ip-address
   ```

   d. Define the TFTP server's IP address:

```
monitor> server ip-address
```

   e. Define the utility filename to fetch:

```
monitor> file npXX.bin
```

The utility file named np*XX*.bin (replace *XX* with the release number) is located in the TFTP server's root directory. This is often called the /tftpboot directory, but it depends on how your TFTP server is configured.

4. Copy the utility from the TFTP server:

```
monitor> tftp
```

When the download is complete, the utility runs and prompts you to clear the PIX passwords. If you answer **y** to the prompt, the firewall reloads, and the passwords are reset to their default values (enable_1 is **cisco**; enable_15 is blank).

Recovering an FWSM Password

Follow these steps to reload and erase the FWSM passwords:

1. Boot the FWSM into the maintenance partition:

```
Router# hw-module module slot-number reset cf:1

Router# session slot slot-number processor 1
```

From the Catalyst 6500 Supervisor IOS EXEC prompt, the FWSM in slot *slot-number* can be reset so that it reboots into its maintenance partition. Log in as the user **root**. The default root password is **cisco**.

2. Reset the passwords in the compact Flash configuration file:

```
root@localhost# clear passwd cf:partition_number
root@localhost# exit
```

The FWSM compact Flash is organized into the five partitions listed in Table 5-4.

Table 5-4 *FWSM Compact Flash Partitions*

Partition	Function	Description
cf:1	Maintenance	Used for module file maintenance and upgrades
cf:2	Network configuration	Maintenance image network configuration
cf:3	Crash dump	Crashinfo contents
cf:4	Application	Firewall image and configuration
cf:5	Application	Alternative image and configuration

Section 5-6

To clear the passwords in the application partition, where the normal firewall image is executed, use *partition-number* **4** or **5**, depending on which one contains the bootable image. For example, the **clear passwd cf:4** command clears the passwords in the application partition 4 configuration file.

You are prompted to delete the password configuration commands (enable_1 becomes **cisco**; enable_15 becomes blank) and any AAA commands.

3. Reload the FWSM into the application partition:

```
Router# hw-module module slot-number reset cf:partition-number
```

Specify the partition number that contains the bootable firewall image.

The application partition image is booted. You can log in to the FWSM using the default passwords.

TIP   The FWSM contains two types of partitions you can boot: the maintenance partition and the application partition. You can reset the passwords in either partition by first booting into the opposite partition. For example, as the preceding sequence of steps illustrates, you can reset the application partition passwords by booting into the maintenance partition. You also can reset the maintenance partition passwords by booting into the application partition.

You cannot clear the passwords in the configuration of the partition that is booted, however. You can clear them only in a partition that is not currently in use.

Refer to the following sections for configuration information about these topics:

- **6-1: Routed and Transparent Firewall Modes**—Discusses the two modes of firewall operation. Routed mode (the default) operates at Layer 3, while transparent mode operates at Layer 2. This section also covers the steps needed to configure transparent mode.

- **6-2: Address Translation**—Presents the underlying Layer 3 address translation methods that occur during traffic inspection. This section covers the configuration steps needed to translate IP addresses from one firewall interface to another. Several different methods of address translation are possible, each of which is covered.

- **6-3: Controlling Access with Access Lists**—Provides the steps you can use to configure object groups and access lists to define firewall policies.

- **6-4: Shunning Traffic**—Presents a method that can be used to manually stop traffic to and from hosts immediately. This is particularly useful when a host is attacking others and needs to be stopped.

CHAPTER 6

Controlling Access Through the Firewall

A firewall's main function is to provide effective security between pairs of its interfaces. To do this, all of the traffic destined to pass through it must undergo a variety of operations, inspections, translations, filters, and special handling. You must configure each aspect of these actions in order to thoroughly enforce the security policies that apply to your network.

All of the features related to controlling user access *through* the firewall have been collected in this chapter. The size of the chapter is a testament to the broad range of security policy tools available to you, as a firewall administrator.

6-1: Routed and Transparent Firewall Modes

Traditionally, Cisco firewalls have operated by performing Layer 3 (IP address) operations. Naturally, the stateful inspection process can look at higher layers within the IP packets being examined. But the firewall itself has maintained its own interface IP addresses and acted as a router or gateway to the networks that connect to it. As well, all of the traffic inspection and forwarding decisions are based on Layer 3 (IP address) parameters. This is known as the *routed firewall mode*. Each firewall interface must be connected to a different IP subnet, and be assigned an IP address on that subnet. When a routed firewall is installed or inserted into a network for the first time, the network must become segmented across the firewall's interfaces. For example, where a single IP subnet used to be, the inside and outside interfaces now form the boundary of two separate subnets.

This can make the installation difficult, as some readdressing must take place. The easiest approach is to keep the original IP addressing on the firewall's inside interface, where the majority of protected hosts reside. The outside interface can take on an address from a new subnet that is shared between the firewall and the next-hop router. In other words, the outside of the firewall usually has a lesser number of directly connected hosts to readdress to a new subnet.

Routed firewalls can also participate in IP routing by using a dynamic routing protocol such as RIP or OSPF. The firewall can coexist with other routers in the network and maintain a dynamic routing table.

By default, the Adaptive Security Appliance (ASA) and Firewall Services Module (FWSM) platforms are configured for routed mode. You can configure IP addresses on the firewall interfaces, IP routing, and other Layer 3 features by following the guidelines found in Chapter 3, "Building Connectivity."

TIP   You can see the current firewall mode by using the following command:

Firewall# **show firewall**

The result is either "Firewall mode: Router" or "Firewall mode: Transparent". If you
need to configure a firewall back to routed mode, use the following command:

Firewall(config)# **firewall router**

A Cisco firewall can also be configured to operate in *transparent firewall mode*. The firewall appears
to operate as a Layer 2 device, without becoming a router hop or a gateway to the connected
networks. This is also known as a *Layer 2 firewall* or a *stealth firewall*, because its interfaces have
no IP addresses and cannot be detected or manipulated. Only a single management address can be
configured on the firewall.

As a Layer 2 device, a transparent mode firewall can be dropped or wedged into an existing network,
separating the inside and outside without changing any existing IP addresses. This is commonly
called *bump-in-the-wire* because the firewall does not break or segment the IP subnet along a wire—
it more or less becomes part of the wire. This makes a new installation very straightforward.

TIP   Cisco firewalls running PIX release 6.3 or earlier operate solely in the routed firewall
mode. Beginning with FWSM 2.2(1) and PIX 7.0, you can configure a firewall to
operate in either the routed or transparent firewall mode, but not both.

You can think of a transparent mode firewall as a type of transparent bridge, where packets are
bridged from one interface to another based only on their MAC addresses. The firewall maintains a
MAC address table from received packets, containing the source MAC address and the source
interface. The firewall is able to forward a packet by knowing the location or the egress interface of
the destination MAC address.

Figure 6-1 illustrates the transparent firewall process. Host A sends a packet to Host B. Notice that
Hosts A and B are located on the same IP subnet. Their *local-ip* and *foreign-ip* addresses only
designate that "local" is on the inside of the firewall and "foreign" is on the outside. When the
firewall builds a conn table entry, the host addresses are shown in this fashion.

TIP   In transparent mode, a firewall can support only two interfaces—the *inside* and the
outside. If your firewall supports more than two interfaces from a physical and
licensing standpoint, you can assign the inside and outside to two interfaces arbitrarily.
As soon as those interfaces are configured, the firewall does not permit a third interface
to be configured.

Some platforms also support a dedicated management interface, which can be used for all firewall management traffic. However, the management interface cannot be involved in accepting or inspecting user traffic.

In multiple context mode, each context also has two interfaces (inside and outside). However, each context must use a pair of interfaces that is different than any other context. In other words, contexts cannot share inside and outside interfaces because of the bridging operation.

Figure 6-1 *Transparent Firewall Operation*

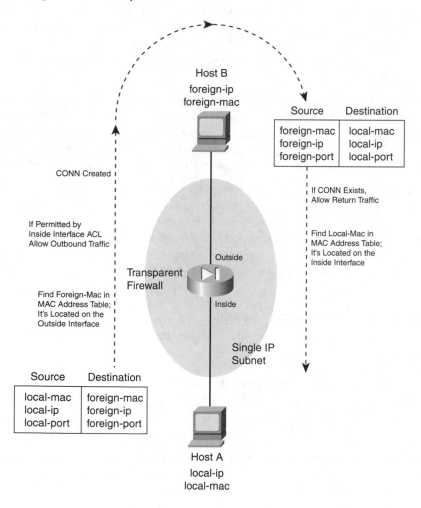

When a firewall enters transparent mode, it no longer supports or has a need for address translation. After all, that is a function based on having different IP subnets on different firewall interfaces. In transparent mode, both interfaces must share the same IP subnet. However, IP packets are still inspected without the Layer 2 limitation. Full extended access lists (IP protocol and port numbers) are used to evaluate traffic policies, and the firewall's application inspection engines are able to interpret IP activity at any layer.

If a transparent firewall acts as a Layer 2 device, is it limited to only IP traffic? From a traffic inspection standpoint, it is; only IP traffic can be inspected and policies enforced. However, from a bridging perspective, the firewall can transparently bridge non-IP packets from one interface to another. This is done by configuring the permitted EtherTypes explicitly in a special interface access list.

A transparent firewall can also maintain an Address Resolution Protocol (ARP) table, where Media Access Control (MAC) and Internet Protocol (IP) addresses are associated as a pair. These are learned from ARP replies that are overheard on an interface. Normally, the ARP table is used only for management traffic to and from the transparent firewall, when the firewall itself needs to send packets to a destination.

You can configure the firewall to support ARP inspection, which can detect and prevent ARP spoofing. ARP requests and replies are forwarded through the firewall by default, as if the two firewall interfaces were bridged. This creates the potential for a malicious host to send spoofed ARP replies with its own MAC address. By doing so, the malicious host can advertise itself as a router's IP address, causing other hosts to send their traffic to it instead of the router.

ARP inspection uses static ARP entries as the basis for its inspection process. The firewall examines each ARP reply packet it overhears and compares the source IP and MAC addresses, as well as the source interface, to known static entries in its own ARP table. If the ARP reply matches an existing entry, it is allowed to pass through the firewall. If any of its information conflicts with an existing entry, the firewall assumes the ARP reply contains spoofed addresses and drops the packet. If an existing ARP entry cannot be found, the firewall can be configured to transmit or drop the ARP reply packet.

Configuring a Transparent Firewall

Use the following steps to configure a firewall for transparent mode.

1. Enter transparent firewall mode:

   ```
   Firewall(config)# firewall transparent
   ```

   By default, a firewall operates in the routed mode. You can use this command to initiate the transparent firewall mode. Transparent mode begins immediately and does not require a firewall reload.

   Because transparent and routed modes use different approaches to network security, the running configuration is cleared as soon as transparent mode begins. The idea is to enter transparent mode and build an appropriate configuration from scratch.

   For that reason, you should save the routed mode running configuration to Flash memory or to an external server. That way, you have a copy in case you need to revert back to routed mode or you need to refer to some portion of that configuration.

You can always display the current firewall mode with the **show firewall** command. As an example, a firewall is configured for transparent mode in the following command sequence:

```
Firewall# show firewall
Firewall mode: Router
Firewall# configure terminal

Firewall(config)# firewall transparent
Switched to transparent mode
Firewall(config)# exit
Firewall#

Firewall# show firewall
Firewall mode: Transparent
Firewall#
```

2. Configure an interface

   In transparent mode, none of the firewall interfaces can support an IP address. You still have to configure the necessary interface media parameters (speed and duplex), any virtual LAN (VLAN) information, a logical name, and a security level. These parameters are configured in the following steps:

   a. Define a physical interface.

FWSM	N/A

ASA	`Firewall(config)# interface hardware-id`
	`Firewall(config-if)# speed {auto I 10 I 100 I nonegotiate}`
	`Firewall(config-if)# duplex {auto I full I half}`
	`Firewall(config-if)# [no] shutdown`

   The interface is referenced by its *hardware-id*, such as **GigabitEthernet0** or **Ethernet0**. (The actual name is not case sensitive when you enter it.)

   You can set the interface speed with one of the **auto** (negotiate the speed; the default), **10** (10 Mbps only), **100** (100 Mbps only), or **nonegotiate** (fiber optic interfaces only) keywords. The duplex mode can be set using one of the following keywords: **auto** (auto-negotiate; the default)**, full** (full-duplex only), or **half** (half-duplex only).

   By default, interfaces are administratively shut down with the **shutdown** command. You can enable an interface by using the **no shutdown** interface configuration command.

   b. Define a VLAN interface.

FWSM	`Firewall(config)# interface vlan vlan_id`
ASA	`Firewall(config)# interface hardware_id[.subinterface]` `Firewall(config-subif)# vlan vlan_id`

On a FWSM platform, VLAN interfaces are inherent, as it has no physical interfaces at all. Only the VLAN number *vlan_id* needs to be provided.

On an ASA, logical VLAN interfaces must be carried over a physical trunk interface, identified as *hardware-id* (**GigabitEthernet0**, for example). A *subinterface* number is added to the physical interface name to create the logical interface. This is an arbitrary number that must be unique for each logical interface. The VLAN number is specified as *vlan-id* in a separate **vlan** subinterface configuration command.

Packets being sent out a logical VLAN interface are tagged with the VLAN number as they enter the physical trunk link. The VLAN number tag is stripped off at the far end of the trunk, and the packets are placed onto the corresponding VLAN. The same process occurs when packets are sent toward the firewall on a VLAN.

The trunk encapsulation used is always IEEE 802.1Q, and the tagging encapsulation and unencapsulation are automatically handled at each end of the trunk. Make sure the far end switch is configured to trunk unconditionally.

c. Name the interface and assign a security level.

FWSM	Firewall(config)# **nameif** *vlan-id if_name* **security***level*
ASA	Firewall(config-if)# **nameif** *if_name* Firewall(config-if)# **security-level** *level*

On a FWSM platform, the interface is identified by its *vlan-id* (**vlan5** for example; the word **vlan** is always present). If multiple security context mode is being used, the *vlan-id* could be an arbitrary name that has been mapped to the context by the **allocate-interface** command in the system execution space.

The interface is given the arbitrary name *if_name* (1 to 48 characters) that other firewall commands can use to refer to it. For example, you could name an interface as "inside", "outside", or something completely different.

A security level is also assigned to the interface as a *level* (a number 0 to 100, from lowest to highest). On a FWSM, the level must be given immediately following the **security** keyword, as in **security** *level*. Security levels 0 and 100 are reserved for the "outside" and "inside" interfaces, respectively. Other perimeter interfaces should have levels between 1 and 99.

As an example, the outside interface could be configured as follows:

FWSM	Firewall(config)# **nameif vlan10 outside security0**
ASA	Firewall(config)# **interface gigabitethernet0** Firewall(config-if)# **nameif outside** Firewall(config-if)# **security-level 0**

TIP   Security levels are only used to determine how the firewall inspects and handles traffic. For example, traffic passing from a higher security interface toward a lower one is assumed to be going toward a less secure area. Therefore, it is forwarded with less stringent policies and traffic coming in toward a higher security area.

In addition, firewall interfaces must have different security levels, unless the **same-security-traffic permit inter-interface** global configuration command has been used.

3. Configure a management address:

    Firewall(config)# **ip address** *ip_address subnet_mask*

    The firewall can support only a single IP address for management purposes. The address is not bound to an interface, as in routed mode. Rather, it is assigned to the firewall itself, accessible from either of the bridged interfaces.

    The management address is used for all types of firewall management traffic, such as Telnet, SSH, HTTP, SNMP, Syslog, TFTP, FTP, and so on.

TIP   A transparent firewall can also support multiple security contexts. In that case, interface IP addresses must be configured from the respective context. The system execution space uses the admin context interfaces and IP addresses for its management traffic.

4. (Optional) Configure routing information for management purposes:

    Firewall(config)# **route** *if_name foreign_network foreign_mask gateway* [*metric*]

    You can configure a static route to allow the firewall to send management traffic to addresses that are not on the local IP subnet. Dynamic routing protocols are not supported in the transparent firewall mode.

    The remote network can be found on the firewall interface named *if_name* (**outside**, for example), and has network address *foreign_network* and subnet mask *foreign_mask*. The next-hop router address is given as *gateway*. You can also specify a distance *metric*, which is the number of router hops until the gateway is reached. If you omit the *metric*, it defaults to one hop.

    You can repeat this command to define other stable, static routes.

    You do not have to configure a static route for the subnet directly connected to the firewall interfaces. However, you should define one static route as a default route toward the outside public network. For that, use **0** for the *foreign_network* and *foreign_mask* values. If you have other IP subnets active on the inside of the firewall, you need to define static routes for each of them.

As an example, a firewall is located on the network 10.1.0.0 255.255.0.0. Its next-hop router on the outside interface is 10.1.1.1. A router exists at 10.1.1.2 on the inside of the firewall, where subnets 192.168.1.0/24 and 192.168.100.0/24 can be found. The following commands can be used to configure this routing information on a transparent firewall:

```
Firewall(config)# route outside 0 0 10.1.1.1 1
Firewall(config)# route inside 192.168.1.0 255.255.255.0 10.1.1.2 1
Firewall(config)# route inside 192.168.100.0 255.255.255.0 10.1.1.2 1
```

5. (Optional) Manipulate the MAC address learning process:

    By default, a firewall learns MAC addresses as they are received on any interface. You can use the following commands to display the current MAC address learning state and the current MAC address table entries, respectively:

    ```
    Firewall# show mac-learn
    Firewall# show mac-address-table [count] [static] [if_name]
    ```

    You can specify a single interface as *if_name* on an ASA or as **interface** *if_name* on a FWSM platform.

    As an example, the following output indicates that MAC address learning is enabled on both firewall interfaces, and the MAC address table has been populated with a few entries:

    ```
    Firewall# show mac-learn
    interface                         mac learn
    -----------------------------------------
     outside                          enabled
     inside                           enabled
    Firewall#
    Firewall# show mac-address-table
    interface     mac   address       type        Age(min)
    -------------------------------------------------------
    outside       00a0.c900.0201      dynamic     5
    inside        0050.e2c6.f680      dynamic     4
    outside       0008.20f7.fbfc      dynamic     4
    Firewall#
    ```

    You can use any of the following steps to modify the MAC address learning process:

    a. (Optional) Set the MAC address table aging time:

        ```
        Firewall(config)# mac-address-table aging-time minutes
        ```

        As new addresses are learned, they are placed in the MAC address table. If no traffic is seen to include a MAC address that is already in the table, that entry is aged out and removed after *minutes* (5 to 720 minutes, default 5).

b. (Optional) Define a static MAC address table entry:

Firewall(config)# **mac-address-table static** *if_name mac_address*

You might define a static entry for a MAC address that can never be learned. This might occur if a host or server always listens to traffic using one MAC address and transmits using another. In that case, the transmit address can be learned, while the receiver address cannot.

After a static entry is configured, the firewall always expects that MAC address to be found on the specified interface. If the same MAC address appears on a different firewall interface, the firewall drops those packets.

As an example, the following commands configure two static entries in the MAC address table:

Firewall(config)# **mac-address-table static inside 0006.5b02.a841**
Firewall(config)# **mac-address-table static outside 0040.9646.6cf6**

c. (Optional) Disable MAC address learning on an interface:

Firewall(config)# **mac-learn** *if_name* **disable**

By default, MAC address learning is enabled on every firewall interface. You can disable it on a firewall interface named *if_name* (**outside**, for example) so that only static MAC address table entries are used during a packet forwarding operation.

This might be handy in a scenario where you want to keep tight control over the MAC addresses that can be learned dynamically. However, static entries would need to be added for each new host, increasing the amount of firewall administration needed.

6. (Optional) Use ARP inspection

a. Add a static ARP entry:

Firewall(config)# **arp** *if_name ip_address mac_address*

The IP address will be associated with the MAC address (dotted triplet *nnnn.nnnn.nnnn* format). These are expected to be found on the firewall interface named *if_name* (**outside**, for example).

Static ARP entries never age out. To clear a static ARP entry, repeat the command by beginning with the **no** keyword.

TIP The **arp** command syntax also includes an optional **alias** keyword. In routed firewall mode, this makes the firewall use proxy ARP when it gets an ARP request for that address, rather than forward the request on through to the actual target.

In transparent mode, this keyword has no effect. The firewall will not interact with other hosts using Layer 3 mechanisms, so proxy ARP is not possible.

As an example, the following commands configure static ARP entries in preparation for ARP inspection:

```
Firewall(config)# arp inside 192.168.198.199 0006.5b02.a841
Firewall(config)# arp outside 172.21.4.9 0040.9646.6cf6
```

b. Enable ARP inspection on an interface:

```
Firewall(config)# arp-inspection if_name enable [flood | no-flood]
```

By default, ARP inspection is disabled on all firewall interfaces. When enabled, ARP replies received on the interface named *if_name* (**outside** for example) are inspected and matched against known static ARP entries. One of the following actions is taken:

— If the MAC address and the IP address are both found in the ARP table in a single entry, the ARP reply must be valid and is allowed to pass through the firewall.

— If either the MAC address or the IP address is found in the ARP table, but not both in a single entry, the ARP reply contains invalid or spoofed information. Therefore, it is dropped and not forwarded through the firewall.

— If neither MAC nor IP address is found in the ARP table, you can select the action as one of: **flood** (forward or flood the ARP packet out the other firewall interface so it can reach its destination) or **no-flood** (drop the ARP packet without forwarding it). By default, the **flood** action is assumed.

TIP   ARP inspection is only effective in handling ARP packets that need to traverse the firewall. In other words, the ARP requester and responder are located on different firewall interfaces. If both hosts are located on the same firewall interface, the ARP reply can be answered directly without having to pass through the firewall.

You can display the ARP inspection status on each interface with the following command:

```
Firewall# show arp-inspection
```

For example, the firewall in the following output has ARP inspection enabled on both interfaces, but only the inside interface is configured to flood unknown ARP replies:

```
Firewall# show arp-inspection
interface              arp-inspection       miss
------------------------------------------------
outside                enabled              no-flood
inside                 enabled              flood
Firewall#
```

TIP	If you are having trouble getting ARP inspection to work properly, make sure that all of the addresses involved in ARP requests and replies are configured as static ARP entries. If the firewall receives an ARP packet and finds a corresponding entry in its ARP table that was learned dynamically, the ARP packet is dropped. Only static ARP entries are used with ARP inspection.

For example, ARP inspection has been enabled on the outside interface of a firewall. The firewall has already learned the MAC and IP addresses for a router on the outside, and has created a dynamic ARP entry for it. When the router sends an ARP reply toward the outside firewall interface, ARP inspection rejects it. The following syslog output is generated when this happens:

```
%ASA-3-322002: ARP inspection check failed for arp response received from host
0008.20f7.fbfc on interface outside. This host is advertising MAC Address
0008.20f7.fbfc for IP Address 192.168.93.129, which is dynamically bound to
MAC Address 0008.20f7.fbfc
Firewall# show arp
        outside 192.168.93.129 0008.20f7.fbfc
        outside 192.168.93.130 0008.20f7.fb00
        inside 192.168.93.134 0050.e2c6.f680
Firewall#
```

Although it looks like everything matches up with the outside host's addresses, the problem is that the ARP entry was dynamically learned and created.

---

7. Configure interface access lists.

   Before traffic can be forwarded through the firewall, make sure to configure the appropriate security policies by applying an access list to each interface. Access lists are covered in detail in Section 6-3, "Controlling Access with Access Lists."

8. Configure a forwarding policy for non-IP protocols.

   a. Define an access list:

FWSM	Firewall(config)# **access-list** acl_id **ethertype** {**permit** | **deny**} {**unicast** | **multicast** | **broadcast** | ethertype}
ASA	Firewall(config)# **access-list** acl_id **ethertype** {**permit** | **deny**} {**any** | **bpdu** | **ipx** | **mpls-unicast** | **mpls-multicast** | ethertype}

By default, only IP packets are allowed to pass through a firewall (providing the packets are permitted by the various inspection processes). You can create an access list that defines a policy on whether non-IP protocols can be forwarded through the firewall.

This command defines an Access Control Entry (ACE) for the access list named acl_id. You can **permit** or **deny** the EtherType that is specified. There is always an implicit **deny**

all ACE at the end of every access list. Therefore, all non-IP EtherTypes are dropped unless they are explicitly permitted in an access list.

The EtherType value can be one of the following: **any** (any non-IP packet), **bpdu** (bridge protocol data units, used for Spanning Tree Protocol operation), **ipx** (Novell IPX, 0x8137 and 0x8138), **mpls-unicast** (MPLS unicast, 0x8847), or **mpls-multicast** (MPLS multicast, 0x8848). You can also specify a numeric *ethertype* value, which is a 16-bit hex number greater than 0x600.

TIP　Well-known EtherType values are assigned and maintained by the IEEE. You can search or download the most current list of values at standards.ieee.org/regauth/ethertype/index.shtml. Many other values are not publicly registered, and are not shown in that listing.

You can repeat the **access-list** *acl_id* **ethertype** command to add more EtherTypes to be permitted or denied.

b. Apply the EtherType access list to an interface:

```
Firewall(config)# access-group acl_id {in | out} interface if_name
```

The EtherType access list named *acl_id* is applied to the firewall interface named *if_name* (**outside**, for example). Generally this should be done in the **in** (inbound) direction, as the EtherType should be evaluated as packets are received, before being inspected.

You can apply one EtherType access list and one extended IP access list to the same interface.

TIP　A Cisco firewall can inspect only IP packets; no inspection is possible for non-IP EtherTypes. This means you have to explicitly permit those EtherTypes in an access list and apply the list to both the inbound and outbound interfaces in the inbound direction.

For example, the following commands configure a firewall to permit IEEE 802.1d Spanning Tree BPDU and Novell IPX traffic, while denying all other non-IP packets. The access list is applied to the inbound direction on both sides of the firewall, allowing bidirectional forwarding.

```
Firewall(config)# access-list MyEthertypes ethertype permit bpdu
Firewall(config)# access-list MyEthertypes ethertype permit ipx
Firewall(config)# access-group MyEthertypes interface in outside
Firewall(config)# access-group MyEthertypes interface in inside
```

6-2: Address Translation

Cisco firewalls provide security policies and traffic inspection using two basic principles:

- **Address translation**—When a host on one firewall interface initiates a connection to a host on a different interface, the firewall must provide a way to translate the IP addresses across itself appropriately. Even if the IP addresses should appear identically on both sides of the firewall, a translation must still occur.

  One exception to this is when the **same-security-traffic** command is used to allow traffic to pass between interfaces with an identical security level. In that case, address translation can still be configured if it is needed, but it is not required. The other exception is when the **no nat-control** command is used. This is the default beginning with ASA 7.0 and FWSM 3.1(1), which allows hosts to initiate connections through the firewall without requiring address translation.

- **Access control**—After an address translation is established, traffic is inspected and allowed only if the appropriate interface access lists permit it.

This section covers the address translation process, which forms the basis for the routed firewall mode, as relationships between inside and outside IP addresses are built as needed.

TIP   Address translation is inherent when a firewall is configured for routed mode. Beginning with ASA 8.0, address translation can be used in transparent mode as well.

Defining Access Directions

A firewall differentiates its interfaces by providing more security to some and less security to others. Therefore, it is important to understand how the interfaces relate to each other and how access is provided as traffic moves through a firewall.

TIP   By default, all firewall interfaces must be assigned a unique security level value, causing some interfaces to have more security while others have less. Beginning with ASA 7.2(1) and FWSM 2.2(1), you can use the **same-security-traffic permit inter-interface** to configure a firewall such that its interfaces have the same relative level of security. This command is discussed in the "Same-Security Access" section in this chapter.

Outbound Access

Outbound access is defined as connections that are initiated from a higher security interface toward a lower security interface. In other words, users on a more secure network want to connect to something on a less secure network.

Examples of outbound access are connections from the inside (higher security) to the outside (lower security).

The firewall can limit the number of simultaneous connections that are used by an address translation, as well as how many embryonic (not fully initialized) connections can be formed.

You must configure two firewall mechanisms to allow outbound connections:

- **Address translation**—Local (more secure) addresses must be mapped to global (less secure) addresses across two firewall interfaces.

- **Outbound access**—The firewall only builds outbound connections that meet security policy requirements configured as an access list. (ASA and PIX platforms allow outbound connections to be initiated without an access list, by default. The FWSM requires an access list to permit outbound connections.)

Inbound Access

Inbound access is defined as connections that are initiated from a lower security interface toward a higher security interface. In other words, users on a less secure network want to connect to something on a more secure network.

Examples of inbound access are connections from the outside to the inside.

The firewall can limit the number of simultaneous connections that are used by an address translation, as well as how many embryonic (not fully initialized) connections can be formed.

You must configure two firewall mechanisms to allow inbound connections:

- **Address translation**—Local (more secure) addresses must be mapped to global (less secure) addresses across two firewall interfaces.

- **Inbound access**—The firewall allows only inbound connections that meet security policy requirements configured as an access list. You must apply an access list to the lower security interface to permit only the specific inbound connections that are to be allowed.

Same-Security Access

ASA 7.0 and FWSM 2.2(1) introduced the capability to configure multiple interfaces with the same level of security. In this case, it is not easy to classify the traffic passing between same-security interfaces as inbound or outbound.

Why would you ever want to define two or more interfaces as having the same level of security? Perhaps the interfaces support groups of users or resources that should be allowed to freely exchange information. In other words, the user communities are equally trusted and are under the same administrative control.

In addition, Cisco firewalls have a finite number of unique security levels that you can assign to interfaces. Security levels 0 to 100 can be used, representing the lowest to the highest security, respectively. On some firewall platforms, you can arbitrarily define logical firewall interfaces. If your environment needs to support more than 100 different firewall interfaces, you will not be able to assign more than 100 unique security levels. Some of the interfaces will have to be configured with identical security levels.

Same-security access has the following characteristics:

- **Address translation**—You can choose to use or not use address translation between same-security interfaces.

- **Access**—Where many of the firewall inspection features normally limit, filter, or inspect traffic in one direction (inbound or outbound), the same operations can occur in both directions between same-security interfaces.

As well, traffic between same-security interfaces is inherently permitted without any requirement for access lists. To enable traffic to pass between interfaces that have the same security level, use the following global configuration command:

```
Firewall(config)# same-security-traffic permit inter-interface
```

Sometimes you might want to allow traffic to enter and exit the same firewall interface. This can be handy for VPN peers that have tunnels built to the firewall, but need traffic to pass back out to other VPN peers or other networks connected to the same interface.

Firewalls do not normally allow traffic to "hairpin" or come back out the same interface. Beginning with ASA 7.2(1) and FWSM 2.3(1), you can use the following global configuration command to permit hairpin traffic:

```
Firewall(config)# same-security-traffic permit intra-interface
```

In this case, the interface itself is considered to have the same security level in both directions, hence the **intra-interface** keyword.

Types of Address Translation

A firewall can translate the IP addresses of hosts on one interface to identical or different addresses on another interface. This translation does not have to occur in the same fashion for all hosts on all interfaces. In fact, the firewall can be very flexible with address translation, depending on the needs of the hosts, their applications, or the security policies required.

As the firewall builds address translations, it maintains entries in a translation database. These are known as *xlate* entries, and can be displayed by the **show xlate** command. (This command is more fully explained in Chapter 11, Section "11-3: Verifying Firewall Connectivity.") An xlate entry must exist before inbound connections will be permitted to reach an inside host through an outside address.

For example, in the following output, the firewall is performing two different types of address translation. In the two lines that begin with **Global**, static NAT is being used. The local or inside address is always translated to the same global or outside address, regardless of what protocol or port number is being used.

In the lines that begin with **PAT**, Port Address Translation (PAT) is being used to allow multiple local or inside hosts to be translated to one or more global or outside addresses. The translation is performed dynamically, on a per-connection basis. Each local address and port number used in a connection is translated to the global address, but with a unique global port number. The port numbers are shown in parentheses.

```
Firewall# show xlate
22499 in use, 24492 most used
Global 10.1.1.17 Local 192.168.1.11
Global 10.1.1.16 Local 192.168.1.10
PAT Global 10.1.2.1(10476) Local 192.168.40.251(4705)
PAT Global 10.1.2.1(10382) Local 192.168.48.11(3134)
PAT Global 10.1.2.1(10372) Local 192.168.236.69(1716)
[output omitted]
```

Fully initialized connections are also kept in a connection database. These are known as *conn* entries, shown by the **show conn** command. Before two hosts can communicate through a firewall, an xlate entry must be created, a connection must be permitted by an access list (if one is required on an interface), and a conn entry must be created.

To continue the previous example, the following output from the **show conn** command displays any active connections currently being inspected by the firewall. (This command is more fully explained in Chapter 11, Section "11-3: Verifying Firewall Connectivity.")

```
Firewall# show conn
UDP out 195.242.2.2:53 in 192.168.48.11:3134 idle 0:00:10 flags d
TCP out 207.46.245.60:80 in 192.168.236.69:1716 idle 0:06:18 Bytes 937 flags UIO
[output omitted]
```

The **in** addresses shown in these two lines correspond to the **Local** addresses of the last two lines in the xlate table of the previous example. Inside host 192.168.48.11 is using its UDP port 3134 to open a DNS request with outside host 195.242.2.2 on UDP port 53.

In the second line, inside host 192.168.236.69 has opened a connection to TCP port 80 on outside host 207.46.245.60. Notice that each entry in the conn table also has an idle timer and connection flags. The TCP conn entry also has a byte count, showing the total amount of data that has been sent or received over that connection.

Table 6-1 lists the types of address translation supported by Cisco firewalls, along with the respective configuration commands that can be used. Each translation type inherently allows connections to be initiated in the inbound, outbound, or both directions, as shown in the rightmost column.

Table 6-1 *Address Translation Types Supported by Cisco Firewalls*

Translation Type	Application	Basic Command	Direction Connections Can Be Initiated
Static NAT	Real source addresses (and ports) are translated to mapped addresses (and ports)	**static**	Inbound or outbound
Policy NAT	Conditionally translates real source address (and port) to a mapped address	**static access-list**	Inbound or outbound
Identity NAT	No translation of real source addresses	**nat 0**	Outbound only
NAT Exemption	No translation of real source addresses matched by access list	**nat 0 access-list**	Inbound or outbound
Dynamic NAT	Translates real source addresses to a pool of mapped addresses	**nat** *id* **global** *id address-range*	Outbound only
PAT	Translates real source addresses to a single mapped address with dynamic port numbers	**nat** *id* **global** *id address*	Outbound only

The **static** command creates a persistent translation between a real and a mapped address. This sets the stage to allow both outbound and inbound connections to be initiated. The actual xlate entries are created when the **static** command is entered.

In each of the **nat** command forms shown, the translation is used for *outbound* connections only, initiated by an inside host. Inbound traffic is then permitted only if it is return traffic from an outbound connection or if it is explicitly permitted by an inbound access list applied to the outside interface. One exception is NAT exemption, which allows connections to be initiated in the outbound *and* inbound directions.

Sometimes you might need to use a form of the **nat** command to translate the source addresses of outside hosts that are allowed to initiate connections. You can apply each of the **nat** translation processes in reverse, by adding the **outside** keyword.

TIP   In all forms of inside address translation (without the **outside** keyword), only the pertinent addresses on the higher security interface are subject to translation. In other words, the inside source address is translated in the outbound direction, while the inside destination address is translated in the inbound direction.

The **outside** keyword reverses this—only the addresses on the lower security interface are subject to translation. This is often called *Outside NAT* or *Bidirectional NAT*.

You can also configure a firewall to allow two or more firewall interfaces to have an equal security level. In this case, no higher or lower security boundary exists between the two interfaces. Therefore, address translation does not apply between them.

If you configure several address translation operations, you might have some overlap between them. For example, the same local address might appear in more than one NAT definition. To resolve any ambiguity, the firewall evaluates the various types of NAT in the following order before creating an xlate entry:

1. NAT exemptions (**nat 0 access-list** commands)

2. Policy NAT (**static access-list** commands)

3. Static NAT (**static** commands without port numbers)

4. Static PAT (**static** commands with port numbers)

5. Policy NAT (**nat** *nat_id* **access-list** commands)

6. Dynamic NAT and PAT (**nat** *nat_id* commands)

If multiple commands of the same translation type are configured, they are evaluated in sequential order until the first match occurs.

Each type of address translation is described in more detail in the sections that follow.

TIP Be aware that the interface names, address, and port designations have changed in the firewall command syntax related to address translation. In legacy PIX 6.x commands, the terms *local* and *global* are relative to inside and outside interfaces, respectively.

Beginning with FWSM 2.2 and ASA 7.0, address translation is configured using the terms *real* and *mapped*, referring to parameters before and after translation, respectively. Although *real* and *mapped* are shown in this chapter, they can be used interchangeably with *local* and *global*.

Handling Connections Through an Address Translation

Once an address translation is set up across two firewall interfaces, hosts have the potential to open connections through the firewall. Hopefully, hosts that are permitted to traverse the firewall will be on their good behavior and attempt to open only the legitimate connections they need. But if one connection can be initiated, multitudes more might follow, especially if some malicious intent is involved. Fortunately, Cisco firewalls have the capability to enforce connection limits on hosts passing through.

Both the **static** and **nat** commands have parameters that can be configured to define connection limits. You can use the following parameter syntax, which can be found in each form of the **static** and **nat** commands presented in this chapter:

ASA, FWSM	... [**norandomseq**] [[**tcp**] *max_conns* [*emb_limit*]] [**udp** *udp_max_conns*]

UDP and TCP Connection Limits

By default, a firewall allows an unlimited number of outbound connections to be opened across an address translation. If this situation is abused, it is possible to open so many connections that cause firewall resources and destination host resources to become exhausted.

On all firewall platforms, you can limit this to *max_conns* (1 to 65535 simultaneous connections, default 0 or unlimited). This becomes the combined total of UDP and TCP connections that are initiated from the inside hosts using the address translation.

You can also define separate UDP and TCP connection limits for each host using the address translation. You can specify the maximum number of TCP connections with the **tcp** keyword followed by *max_conns* (1 to 65535 simultaneous connections, 0 for unlimited). The maximum number of UDP "connections" can be set with the **udp** keyword followed by *udp_max_conns* (1 to 65535, 0 for unlimited). Because UDP is a connectionless protocol, the firewall views each unique pair of host addresses and unique UDP port numbers as a separate connection that is using a conn table entry.

TIP   As soon as the connection limit is reached for a host, any subsequent connection attempt is dropped. However, any connections that have already been built are subject to a connection idle timeout. If the firewall does not see any data passing over a connection for a specified time period, that connection is automatically closed.

Separate idle timers are maintained for UDP and TCP connections. You can display the idle timer thresholds with the **show running-config timeout** command, as in the following example. The TCP idle timer is shown as *conn*, while the UDP idle timer is *udp*:

```
Firewall# show running-config timeout
timeout xlate 0:06:00
timeout conn 1:00:00 half-closed 0:10:00 udp 0:02:00 icmp 0:00:02 sunrpc
0:10:00 h323
0:05:00 h225 1:00:00 mgcp 0:05:00 mgcp-pat 0:05:00 sip 0:30:00 sip_media
0:02:00
timeout uauth 0:05:00 absolute
Firewall#
```

You can set the idle timers with the following global configuration command:

```
Firewall(config)# timeout [conn hh:mm:ss] [udp hh:mm:ss]
```

You can set the TCP **conn** timer from 00:05:00 (5 minutes) to 1192:59:59, or 0:00:00 for an unlimited time. The UDP **udp** timer can be set from 00:01:00 (1 minute) to 1192:59:59, or 0:00:00 for an unlimited time. The TCP and UDP timers default to 1 hour and 2 minutes, respectively.

Limiting Embryonic Connections

By default, a firewall allows an unlimited number of TCP connections to be initiated to a target host across an address translation. Recall that a TCP connection has a three-way handshake (SYN-SYN/ACK-ACK) that must be completed between two hosts before the connection can be established. If the handshake sequence is not yet completed, the connection is called an *embryonic* (initialized but not yet formed) connection.

An embryonic connection can result from a handshake that is delayed or lost. Therefore, under normal conditions, hosts maintain the initiated connection while they wait for the handshake completion. A malicious user can also abuse this by attempting to initiate multitudes of embryonic connections to a target host, as a denial-of-service attack. None of the SYN packets used to initiate the connections are ever answered by the malicious user; rather, the idea is to overwhelm the target with too many potential connections while it waits for the originator to answer with the handshake.

A firewall can limit the number of embryonic TCP connections initiated to a host across a translated address. This only applies to *inbound* connections, where outside hosts are initiating TCP connections to inside hosts.

Until this limit is reached, the firewall inspects each SYN packet, adds a new conn table entry (marked as embryonic), and forwards the SYN on to the destination host. If the inside host replies with a SYN/ACK, followed by an ACK from the outside host to complete the TCP connection handshake, then the firewall updates its conn table entry (marked as open connections) and allows the connection to form. If the three-way handshake is not completed within 30 seconds, the firewall deletes the connection entry because of the "SYN timeout".

However, while the limit is reached or exceeded, the firewall begins to intercept each new SYN packet and answers on behalf of the target inside host. This is not added as an entry in the firewall's conn table. Instead, an "empty" SYN/ACK packet is returned to the outside host, as if the inside host had sent it. If the originating host actually replies with an ACK, the handshake is completed between the firewall and the inside host and the connection is built.

The firewall keeps track of the initial SYN packets and the SYN/ACK replies it sends by keeping a table of *SYN cookies*, or unique identifiers. In this fashion, the firewall acts as a connection proxy, absorbing the effects of an excessive amount of TCP connection requests.

For address translation with the **static** command, this applies only to *inbound* connections aimed at higher security interfaces. The limit, *emb_limit* (0 to 65535), defaults to 0 (unlimited number of embryonic connections) and is ignored for outbound connections.

The opposite is true for the same embryonic connection limit *emb_limit* parameter in the **nat** command, which is applied to *outbound* connections aimed toward lower security interfaces. Here, you can limit the potential for denial-of-service attacks initiated by inside hosts.

TCP Initial Sequence Numbers

By default, when the firewall creates new *outbound* TCP connections, it assigns a randomized TCP initial sequence number (ISN). This is useful to prevent outside users from being able to predict or guess the sequence number and hijack a connection.

Normally, hosts provide their own random ISNs when they initiate new TCP connections. However, the TCP/IP protocol stack in some operating systems has a weak implementation of this, allowing the ISN to be predicted. The firewall maintains the original ISN for use with the originating host and overwrites this value for use with the destination host. Therefore, neither the originating nor target host is aware that the ISN has been altered or further randomized.

Sometimes this additional ISN operation interferes with a protocol that is passing through a firewall. For example, some protocols such as BGP use a packet authentication method such as MD5 to preserve the integrity of a message. The originating host computes a hash value over the whole TCP packet, including the original ISN, and includes this within the packet payload. To authenticate the message, the receiving host should be able to recompute the hash and get the same value.

However, if the ISN has been randomized after the original hash value was computed, a different hash value will result and the packet authentication will fail. You can use the **norandomseq** keyword to keep the local firewall from changing the ISN, so that only one firewall is randomizing it.

TIP   You should always depend on the additional security provided by a firewall's ISN randomization, unless you notice that it is creating problems with a protocol or application. Only then, consider using the nondefault **norandomseq** setting to disable the randomization.

Static NAT

Static NAT can be used when an internal or real host needs to have the same mapped address for every outbound connection that is initiated. As well, inbound connections can also be initiated to the internal host, if they are permitted by security policies.

Address translation occurs on a one-to-one persistent basis. Each static translation that is configured causes a static xlate entry to be created. Figure 6-2 illustrates static NAT operation during an outbound connection. Inside Host A is initiating a connection to outside Host B. Notice that only the real (local) IP address is being translated, as the source address in the outbound direction, and as the destination address in the inbound direction for return traffic.

Figure 6-2 *Static NAT Operation Across a Firewall*

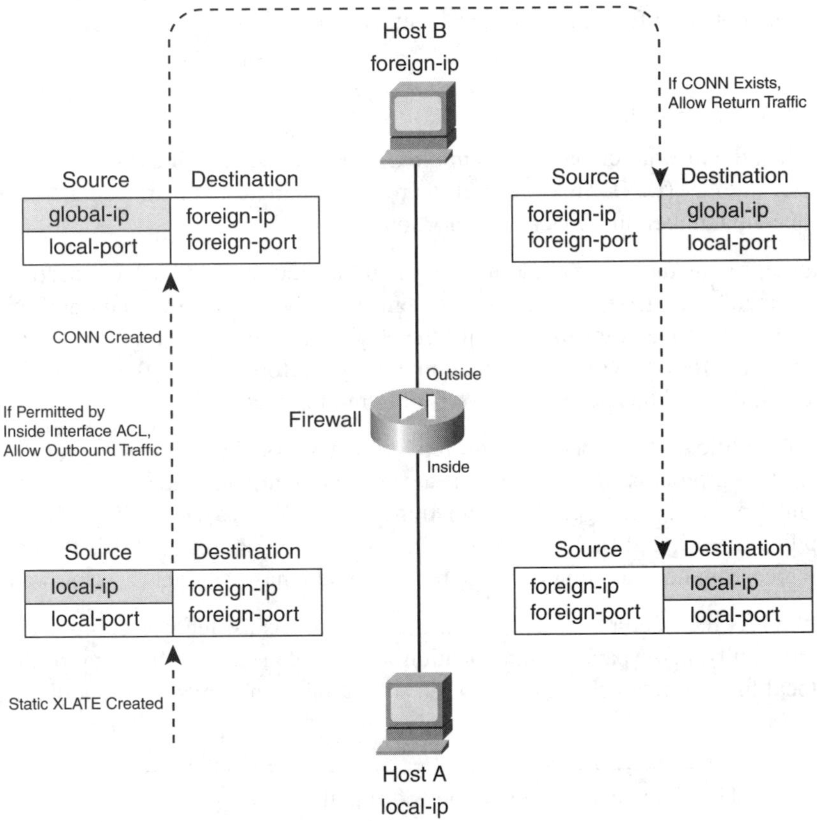

You can use the following command to configure a static NAT entry:

ASA, FWSM	Firewall(config)# **static** (*real_ifc*,*mapped_ifc*) {*mapped_ip* | **interface**} {*real_ip* [**netmask** *mask*]} [**dns**] [**norandomseq**] [[**tcp**] *max_conns* [*emb_limit*]] [**udp** *udp_max_conns*]
PIX 6.3	Firewall(config)# **static** (*real_ifc*,*mapped_ifc*) {*mapped_ip* | **interface**} {*real_ip* [**netmask** *mask*]} [**dns**] [**norandomseq**] [*max_conns* [*emb_limit*]]

A static NAT entry is created across the firewall interfaces named *real_ifc* (**inside** for example) and *mapped_ifc* (**outside** for example). The real IP address *real_ip* is translated to the mapped IP address *mapped_ip* only when the firewall needs to forward a packet between the *real_ifc* and *mapped_ifc* interfaces. The addresses can be a single IP address (use **netmask 255.255.255.255**) or an entire

IP subnet address (use **netmask** with the correct subnet mask). By default, if the **netmask** keyword is omitted, a host mask is assumed.

This command causes the address translation to be carried out regardless of the IP protocol or port number being used. If you need a static translation only for a specific UDP or TCP port number, you can define a static PAT entry with the following command:

ASA, FWSM	Firewall(config)# **static** (*real_ifc*,*mapped_ifc*) {**tcp** | **udp**} {*mapped_ip* | **interface**} *mapped_port* {*real_ip real_port* [**netmask** *mask*]} [**dns**] [**norandomseq**] [[**tcp**] *max_conns* [*emb_limit*]] [**udp** *udp_max_conns*]
PIX 6.3	Firewall(config)# **static** (*real_ifc*,*mapped_ifc*) {**tcp** | **udp**} {*mapped_ip* | **interface**} *mapped_port* {*real_ip real_port* [**netmask** *mask*]} [**dns**] [**norandomseq**] [*max_conns* [*emb_limit*]]

Now the firewall translates the *real_ip* and *real_port* to the *mapped_ip* and *mapped_port* values.

The firewall can inspect and alter DNS packets if the **dns** keyword is added. If the real address is found in the packet, it is rewritten with the mapped address.

As an example, consider two hosts that reside on the inside of a firewall, using private IP addresses 192.168.100.100 and 192.168.100.170. Outbound connections from these hosts should appear as 169.65.41.100 and 169.65.41.170, respectively. Because the hosts must always receive the same mapped addresses, static NAT should be used. Figure 6-3 shows a network diagram for this scenario.

Figure 6-3   *Network Diagram for the Static NAT Example*

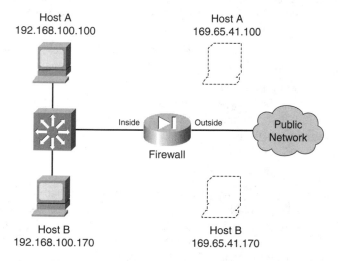

The static NAT entries could be configured with the following commands:

```
Firewall(config)# static (inside,outside) 169.65.41.100 192.168.100.100 netmask
255.255.255.255 0 0
Firewall(config)# static (inside,outside) 169.65.41.170 192.168.100.170 netmask
255.255.255.255 0 0
```

The netmask is given as a host mask (255.255.255.255), because each translation is applied to a single host address.

To extend this example further, suppose inbound SMTP and HTTP connections to 169.65.41.100 could be sent to two separate inside hosts, each handling one of the two types of connections. Static PAT is a good solution for this scenario. With the following commands, SMTP connections are translated to inside host 192.168.100.100, while HTTP connections are translated to 192.168.100.200. An access list is also applied to the outside interface, to permit inbound SMTP and HTTP connections.

```
Firewall(config)# static (inside,outside) tcp 169.65.41.100 smtp 192.168.100.100 smtp
netmask 255.255.255.255 0 0
Firewall(config)# static (inside,outside) tcp 169.65.41.100 www 192.168.100.200 www
netmask 255.255.255.255 0 0
Firewall(config)# access-list acl_outside permit tcp any host 169.65.41.100 eq smtp
Firewall(config)# access-list acl_outside permit tcp any host 169.65.41.100 eq www
Firewall(config)# access-group acl_outside in interface outside
```

TIP   Notice that the order of the two addresses is reversed from the order of the two interfaces, implying that the IP addresses should be different. If an inside host has an IP address that can appear on the outside without being translated, you can enter *real_ip* and *mapped_ip* as the same address.

However, you should do that only if you intend to permit inbound connections to that address. A static NAT defined with identical addresses creates an xlate entry that can allow hosts on the outside to access the inside host.

If no address translation is needed, a better solution is to use identity NAT (the **nat 0** command) or NAT exemption (the **nat 0 access-list** command).

If inbound connections are not needed, you should define an identity NAT. Xlate entries are only created when connections are initiated from the inside, offering a more secure solution. If inbound and outbound connections should be allowed to initiate, NAT exemption is the better choice.

You can also configure a static NAT entry based on the mapped (global) firewall interface, even if its address is not known ahead of time. In that case, you can use the **interface** keyword to translate the address it pulled from a DHCP server. For example, the following command translates the outside interface address to the inside host address 192.168.100.100. No matter what IP address the outside interface has, the translation takes place with the correct value.

```
Firewall(config)# static (inside,outside) interface 192.168.100.100 netmask
255.255.255.255
```

Policy NAT

You can use policy NAT when real addresses need to be translated to several different mapped addresses, depending on a policy decision. An access list is used to trigger the address translation only when a match is permitted. Policy NAT can be configured in two ways:

- A conditional **static** command, where inside real addresses are translated to predictable mapped addresses, depending on the outcome of an access list. This form of translation can be used if inbound connections are expected and permitted to the inside hosts.

- A conditional **nat** command, where inside real addresses are translated to different mapped addresses defined in **global** commands, depending on the outcome of an access list. Use this form if the inside hosts are only expected to initiate outbound connections; inbound connections to those hosts will not be allowed.

You can use the following steps to configure a policy NAT:

1. Identify the translation policy:

    ```
    Firewall(config)# access-list acl_name permit ip real-ip real_mask  foreign_ip
    foreign_mask
    ```

    An access list named *acl_name* is used to identify traffic by source (*real_ip real_mask)* and destination (*foreign_ip foreign_mask*). When an outbound packet triggers the **permit** statement, a matching policy NAT **static** or **nat** command is also triggered. The *real_ip* address given here is the address that is ultimately translated. You can substitute the **host** *real_ip* keyword pair if the source is a single host.

    You use *foreign_ip* and *foreign_mask* to define a destination host or a whole subnet on the public network. You can also substitute the **host** *foreign_ip* keyword pair if the destination is a single host.

    You can repeat this **access-list** command to define other source/destination combinations that trigger a matching **static** command.

2. (**static** Only) Define the **static** command translation:

ASA, FWSM	Firewall(config)# **static** (*real_ifc,mapped_ifc*) *mapped_ip* **access-list** *acl_name* [**dns**] [**norandomseq**] [[**tcp**] *max_conns* [*emb_limit*]] [**udp** *udp_max_conns*]
PIX 6.3	Firewall(config)# **static** (*real_ifc,mapped_ifc*) *mapped_ip* **access-list** *acl_name* [**dns**] [**norandomseq**] [*max_conns* [*emb_limit*]]

    A conditional static NAT or policy NAT translation is defined across the firewall interfaces named *real_ifc* and *mapped_ifc*. Here, the *mapped_ip* address replaces the *real_ip* address matched in the access list named *acl_name*.

    You can repeat this command to define multiple NAT policies. Each **static** command should reference a different access list.

3. (**nat** Only) Define the **nat** command translation.

   a. Configure a global address:

   ```
   Firewall(config)# global (mapped_ifc) nat_id {global_ip [-global_ip] [netmask
   global_mask]} | interface
   ```

   Global IP addresses are used as mapped or translated addresses, and are defined as a single address (*global_ip*) or a range of addresses (*global_ip-global_ip*). The global definition must be identified with a NAT ID *nat_id* (1 to 2,147,483,647), which is linked to **nat** commands with the same value.

   The destination or mapped interface is given as *mapped_ifc* (**outside**, for example), complete with surrounding parentheses. Therefore, NAT occurs for traffic that matches a policy and also exits this interface.

   You can specify a subnet mask as *global_mask*, so that the firewall automatically excludes the network and broadcast addresses from the range of global addresses given. You can also use the **interface** keyword to use the mapped interface's IP address as the global address. In this case, the translation is performed using PAT, as many real IP addresses could become translated to the single interface address.

   b. Configure a NAT translation:

ASA, FWSM	`Firewall(config)# nat (real_ifc) nat_id access-list acl_name [dns] [outside] [[tcp] max_conns [emb_limit]] [norandomseq] [udp udp_max_conns]`
PIX 6.3	`Firewall(config)# nat (real_ifc) nat_id access-list acl_name [dns] [outside] [norandomseq] [max_conns [emb_limit]]`

   Define the NAT translation to occur at the local or real interface named *real_ifc* (**inside**, for example). The address translation will use mapped addresses defined in **global** commands using the same NAT ID *nat_id* as is given here.

   The translation only occurs if the extended access list *acl_name* matches a permit statement. You can match against source and destination addresses and port numbers.

   As an example, suppose two hosts reside on the inside of a firewall, using private IP addresses 192.168.100.100 and 192.168.100.170. Outbound connections from Host A should appear as different global addresses, depending on the destination of the connection. The inside network interfaces with several different external business partners, each expecting Host A to reside in a different address space. This is a good application for *policy NAT*, also called *conditional NAT*.

   If Host A opens a connection to the 10.10.0.0/16 network, it should appear as global address 192.168.254.10. If Host A opens a connection to the 10.50.0.0/16 network, it should appear as 192.168.254.50. Lastly, if Host A opens a connection to any other destination, it should appear as global address 192.168.254.100. Figure 6-4 shows a network diagram for this scenario.

Figure 6-4   *Network Diagram for the Policy NAT Example*

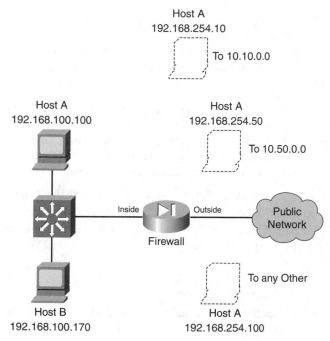

First, policy NAT using **static** commands is considered. The policy NAT entries could be configured with the following commands:

```
Firewall(config)# access-list hostApolicy10 permit ip host 192.168.100.100
10.10.0.0 255.255.0.0
Firewall(config)# static (inside,outside) 192.168.254.10 access-list
hostApolicy10 0 0
Firewall(config)# access-list hostApolicy50 permit ip host 192.168.100.100
10.50.0.0 255.255.0.0
Firewall(config)# static (inside,outside) 192.168.254.50 access-list
hostApolicy50 0 0
Firewall(config)# static (inside,outside) 192.168.254.100 192.168.100.100 netmask
255.255.255.255 0 0
```

If ACL **hostApolicy10** matches and permits traffic, Host A is translated to 192.168.254.10. If ACL **hostApolicy50** matches and permits traffic, Host A is translated to 192.168.254.50.

You might be inclined to define a third policy access list that denies the other two conditions, and then permits everything else. However, policy NAT will not accept an access list that contains **deny** statements; the idea is to permit the traffic where you need a translation. Instead, you can use a regular static NAT (without an access list) to define the third condition. Now the inside address 192.168.100.100 has been defined in three different address translation commands. This works because the more specific static translations (policy NAT) are evaluated first, followed by regular static NAT.

Finally, policy NAT with **nat** commands is used. You could use the following configuration commands:

```
Firewall(config)# access-list hostApolicy10 permit ip host 192.168.100.100
10.10.0.0 255.255.0.0
Firewall(config)# global (outside) 1 192.168.254.10 255.255.255.255
Firewall(config)# nat (inside) 1 access-list hostApolicy10
Firewall(config)# access-list hostApolicy50 permit ip host 192.168.100.100
10.50.0.0 255.255.0.0
Firewall(config)# global (outside) 2 192.168.254.50 255.255.255.255
Firewall(config)# nat (inside) 2 access-list hostApolicy50
Firewall(config)# access-list hostApolicy100 permit ip host 192.168.100.100 any
Firewall(config)# global (outside) 3 192.168.254.100 255.255.255.255
Firewall(config)# nat (inside) 3 access-list hostApolicy100
```

Traffic passing from host 192.168.100.100 to the 10.10.0.0/16 subnet, for example, matches the permit statement in access list *hostApolicy10*, which triggers the **nat** command with ID 1. This causes the inside host address to be translated to the address defined in global ID 1, 192.168.254.10.

Identity NAT

Identity NAT can be used when the real host and the mapped address are identical. In other words, the same IP subnet appears on both sides of the firewall. This is useful if you have registered IP addresses on the inside, and you have no need to translate them on the outside.

You can use the following command to configure an identity NAT:

ASA, FWSM	Firewall(config)# **nat** (*real_ifc*) **0** *real_ip real_mask* [**dns**] [**norandomseq**] [[**tcp**] *max_conns* [*emb_limit*]] [**udp** *udp_max_conns*]
PIX 6.3	Firewall(config)# **nat** (*real_ifc*) **0** *real_ip real_mask* [**dns**] [**norandomseq**] [*max_conns* [*emb_limit*]]

Notice that the *nat_id* here is always zero. This is a special case of the translation policy, one that does not require a corresponding **global** command.

Recall that the **static** command can also set up an identity NAT, where the real address appears unchanged on the mapped side. In other words, no real NAT is taking place.

What is the difference between using **static** and using **nat 0**, if both prevent NAT from occurring? When the **static** command defines an identity NAT, connections involving the real address can be initiated in *both* directions through the firewall (assuming the connections are permitted by access lists).

As soon as the **static** command is entered, the firewall creates static **xlate** entries when the real hosts attempt outbound connections that are permitted through the firewall. Likewise, it is also possible for outside hosts to reach the real hosts in the inbound direction, because the xlate entries will still be created.

If you define the same real host with a **nat 0** command, that host can only initiate *outbound* connections. No inbound connections are allowed. Therefore, the **nat 0** command sets up a one-way path without translating the real address.

As a last note, you should avoid configuring both **static** and **nat 0** commands for the same real addresses. It might seem logical to define both to prevent NAT from occurring, but the two methods are really mutually exclusive.

As an example, consider two hosts that reside on the inside of a firewall. The inside network uses a publicly registered IP subnet of 128.163.89.0/24. For this reason, no address translation is necessary, as the inside hosts can appear on the outside with publicly routable addresses.

An identity NAT can be used in this case. For example, Host A at 128.163.89.199 on the inside will also appear as 128.163.89.199 on the outside. In fact, the whole subnet will be defined in a similar manner. Figure 6-5 shows a network diagram for this scenario.

Figure 6-5 *Network Diagram for the Static Identity NAT Example*

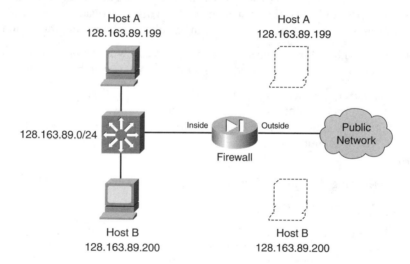

If both outbound *and* inbound connections should be possible, you should consider using the **nat 0 access-list** command to define a NAT exemption. This is discussed fully in the next section "NAT Exemption." The NAT exemption entries for the whole subnet could be configured as follows:

```
Firewall(config)# access-list ExemptList permit ip 128.163.89.0 255.255.255.0 any
Firewall(config)# nat (outside) 0 access-list ExemptList
```

You should also configure the appropriate access lists to permit the inbound and outbound connections for this subnet.

TIP	Legacy PIX 6.3 platforms create xlate entries for each individual host contained in the identity NAT subnet. For large subnets, the number of static xlate entries can grow quite large. Beginning with ASA 7.0, the firewall builds a single xlate entry representing an entire subnet.

To configure the identity NAT for outbound use only, you could use the following command:

```
Firewall(config)# nat (inside) 0 128.163.89.0 255.255.255.0
```

The subnet mask, given as 255.255.255.0, defines the extent of the addresses that have identity translation entries. It also allows the firewall to prevent translations from being built for the network (128.163.89.0) and broadcast (128.163.89.255) addresses.

NAT Exemption

Sometimes you might have specific real (local) IP addresses that need to bypass NAT and appear untranslated. This might be needed only for individual IP addresses or for unique traffic flows. NAT exemption is similar to an Identity NAT, where the real and mapped IP addresses are identical. However, NAT exemption uses an access list to define a policy for bypassing translation.

Unlike identity NAT, which allows connections to be initiated only in the *outbound* direction, NAT exemption allows connections to be initiated in *either* the inbound or outbound direction.

NAT exemption is most often used in conjunction with VPN connections. Inside addresses might normally be translated for all outbound connections through a firewall. If a remote network is reachable through a VPN tunnel, the inside hosts might need to reach remote VPN hosts without being translated. NAT exemption provides the policy mechanism to conditionally prevent the address translation.

You can use the following steps to configure NAT exemption:

1. Define the policy with an access list:

ASA, FWSM	`Firewall(config)# access-list acl_name [extended] permit ip local_ip local_mask foreign_ip foreign_mask`
PIX 6.3	`Firewall(config)# access-list acl_name permit ip local_ip local_mask foreign_ip foreign_mask`

Local addresses that are permitted by an entry in the access list are exempted from translation. Normally, you should only configure **permit** statements as a part of the NAT exemption access list. (Although **deny** statements are allowed, you would really be defining conditions to deny when NAT should be denied!)

In addition, only the **ip** protocol is allowed in the access list. NAT exemption is evaluated based on source and destination addresses—not on IP protocols or port numbers.

2. Add the access list to the policy:

ASA, FWSM	`Firewall(config)# nat (`*`real_ifc`*`) 0 access-list` *`acl_name`* `[dns] [outside]` `[[tcp]` *`max_conns`* `[`*`emb_limit`*`] [norandomseq]] [udp` *`udp_max_conns`*`]`
PIX 6.3	`Firewall(config)# nat (`*`real_ifc`*`) 0 access-list` *`acl_name`* `[dns] [outside]` `[`*`max_conns`* `[`*`emb_limit`*`] [norandomseq]]`

Packets permitted by the access list named *acl_name* are exempted from translation. In other words, those packets are passed on out a different firewall interface with the original real address unchanged.

Notice that the *nat_id* here is always zero. This is a special case of the translation policy, one that does not require a corresponding **global** command.

As a last note, you should avoid configuring both **static** and **nat 0** commands for the same real addresses. It might seem logical to define both to prevent NAT from occurring, but the two methods are really mutually exclusive.

As an example, a firewall is configured to use PAT on all outbound traffic. However, inside addresses in the 192.168.1.0/24 subnet should not be translated when connections are initiated to the 192.168.77.0/24 and 192.168.100.0/24 subnets. The following commands can be used to configure both PAT and NAT exemption:

```
Firewall(config)# nat (inside) 1 0 0
Firewall(config)# global (outside) 1 interface
Firewall(config)# access-list exempt1 permit ip 192.168.1.0 255.255.255.0
192.168.77.0 255.255.255.0
Firewall(config)# access-list exempt1 permit ip 192.168.1.0 255.255.255.0
192.168.100.0 255.255.255.0
Firewall(config)# nat (inside) 0 access-list exempt1
```

Although two different address translation methods are configured, no conflict exists between them regarding the translation of 192.168.1.0/24 hosts. This is because of the order that NAT operations are performed. NAT exemption is always evaluated before any other translation type.

Dynamic Address Translation (NAT or PAT)

Dynamic address translation can be used to allow hosts with real addresses to share or "hide behind" one or more common mapped addresses. Address translation occurs on a many-to-one basis, in a dynamic fashion. This can be accomplished in two ways:

- **Dynamic NAT**—Inside host addresses are translated to values pulled from a pool of mapped addresses. Each inside address gets exclusive use of the mapped address it is assigned, for the duration of any active connections. As soon as all of a host's connections are closed, that mapped address is returned to the pool.

  This means that all inside hosts must compete for the use of the mapped addresses. If the mapped address pool is too small, some hosts could be denied because their translations could not be set up.

- **Dynamic PAT**—Inside host addresses are translated to a single mapped address. This is possible because the inside port numbers can be translated to a dynamically assigned port number used with the mapped address.

  Because port numbers are used as part of the translation, each dynamic PAT entry can support only a single connection (protocol and port number) from a single inside host. In other words, if one inside host initiates two outbound connections, two PAT entries are created—each using a unique port number with the mapped address.

  When a connection is closed, its dynamic PAT entry is deleted after 30 seconds. The mapped port number becomes available for use again.

  Each mapped address has the potential to provide up to 65,535 dynamic PAT entries for a single IP protocol (UDP or TCP, for example), because that many unique port numbers are available. Additional mapped addresses can be used, adding 65,535 more port numbers to the pool. As soon as the port numbers from one mapped address have been exhausted, the next configured mapped address will be used.

Figure 6-6 illustrates dynamic NAT, where Host A is initiating a connection to Host B. Notice that the *real-ip* is translated to *mapped-ip-n,* which is one of a possible pool of mapped addresses. The real-port is not translated, however, because it is still unique to the mapped address. For return traffic, the firewall must translate the destination address back to the original *real-ip.*

Figure 6-7 illustrates dynamic PAT. Notice the procedure is almost identical to that of dynamic NAT in Figure 6-6. The difference is that a dynamic *mapped-port* value is used, rather than a dynamic *mapped-ip.* The combination of mapped IP and port numbers keep the connection unique so that it can be translated back to the real address and port for return traffic.

For dynamic translation (either NAT or PAT), you configure the mapped addresses that can be used, along with the translation policy that will trigger the translation.

Mapped addresses are defined in groups, where *nat_id* (1 to 2,147,483,647) is a group index that corresponds to a matching translation policy. You can repeat the **global** commands that follow with the same *nat_id* to define more mapped addresses to use for the translation policy.

1. Define mapped addresses for NAT:

   ```
   Firewall(config)# global (mapped_ifc) nat_id global_ip[-global_ip] [netmask
   global_mask]
   ```

   You can use mapped addresses that are located on the firewall interface named *mapped_ifc* (**outside**, for example) for address translation. You can define a single *global_ip* address or a range of addresses as the starting and ending addresses *global_ip-global_ip.* A subnet mask can be given with the **netmask** keyword, where *global_mask* matches the mask in use on the global IP subnet. If the mask is given, it is used to determine and reserve the network and broadcast addresses so that they are not used for translation.

Figure 6-6   *Dynamic PAT Operation Across a Firewall*

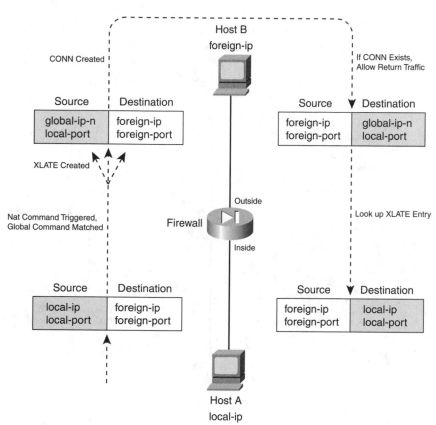

As an example, the following command can be used to configure 10.1.2.1 through 10.1.2.254 as global (mapped) addresses on the outside interface for NAT ID 1. These addresses will be used for translation triggered by the corresponding NAT policy for NAT ID 1, with the **nat 1** command.

```
Firewall(config)# global (outside) 1 10.1.2.1-10.1.2.254 netmask 255.255.255.0
```

> **TIP**   The global addresses can be located on the IP subnet assigned to the firewall interface, although it is not required. You can also use other addresses, as long as devices on the outside network can route those addresses back to the firewall interface.

2. Define one or more mapped addresses for PAT:

```
Firewall(config)# global (mapped_ifc) nat_id {global_ip | interface}
```

Figure 6-7 *Dynamic PAT Operation Across a Firewall*

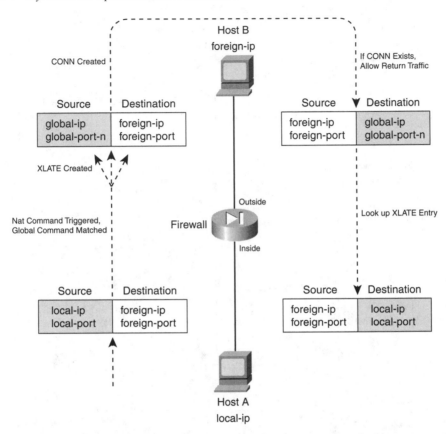

You can also specify single mapped addresses for PAT, where many real addresses are translated to or "hide behind" a single mapped address. To do this, use the **global** command with a single *global_ip* address. You can repeat the command to define other single mapped addresses to use for PAT. As soon as one mapped address is exhausted of its port numbers, the next mapped PAT address is used.

For example, the following commands set aside three mapped addresses for dynamic PAT usage in NAT group 2:

```
Firewall(config)# global (outside) 2 130.65.77.24
Firewall(config)# global (outside) 2 130.65.77.25
Firewall(config)# global (outside) 2 130.65.77.26
```

You can also use the **interface** keyword to use the IP address of the interface itself as a PAT address. This is handy when the firewall requests a dynamic IP address from a service provider and the address is not known ahead of time. The following command shows an example, where the outside interface address is added to the list of mapped PAT addresses in NAT group 2:

```
Firewall(config)# global (outside) 2 interface
```

TIP	If a range of mapped addresses is defined, the firewall uses these addresses first to create new address translations. These are used only for dynamic NAT, where a single local address is translated to a single mapped address. As soon as the connections belonging to a translation close or time out, that mapped address is released back into the pool of available addresses.
	If all of the dynamic NAT mapped addresses are in use, the firewall begins creating translations based on any single dynamic PAT mapped addresses that are defined.

3. Define a translation policy.

Outbound address translation occurs when a packet is sent from a real interface that has a **nat** policy to a mapped interface that has a **global** definition. The **nat** and **global** definitions must match by having the same *nat_id* index.

In the translation policy **nat** commands, the real firewall interface is named *real_ifc*. Do not forget the parentheses, as in **(inside)**.

The firewall can inspect and alter DNS packets if the **dns** keyword is added. If the real address is found in the packet, it is rewritten with the translated or mapped address.

The following command syntax defines a translation policy:

ASA, FWSM	Firewall(config)# **nat** (*real_ifc*) *nat_id real_ip* [*mask* [**dns**] [**outside**][[**tcp**] *max_conns* [*emb_limit*] [**norandomseq**]] [**udp** *udp_max_conns*]
PIX 6.3	Firewall(config)# **nat** (*real_ifc*) *nat_id real_ip* [*mask* [**dns**] [**outside**] [[**norandomseq**] [*max_conns* [*emb_limit*]]]]

The real address is defined as *real_ip*, which can be a single IP address or a subnet address with a subnet *mask*.

As an example, the following command can be used to trigger dynamic NAT or PAT when inside addresses in the 192.168.100.0/24 subnet initiate outbound connections. This NAT policy uses NAT ID 1; the corresponding **global** command must also use NAT ID 1.

Firewall(config)# **nat (inside) 1 192.168.100.0 255.255.255.0**

You can also use an access list to trigger the dynamic NAT or PAT translation. This allows the translation to be conditional as well as dynamic. First, define an access list with the following command:

ASA, FWSM	Firewall(config)# **access-list** *acl_name* [**extended**] **permit** *protocol real_ip real_mask* [*operator port*] *foreign_ip foreign_mask* [*operator port*]
PIX 6.3	Firewall(config)# **access-list** *acl_name* **permit** *protocol real_ip real_mask* [*operator port*] *foreign_ip foreign_mask* [*operator port*]

The real source addresses will be candidates for dynamic NAT or PAT if they are matched by a **permit** statement in the access list. You can only use **permit** statements when you configure the access list.

However, you can be specific in the access list by specifying an IP *protocol* (**tcp** or **udp**, for example) and source and destination operators (**eq**, for example) and *port* numbers. These values are not used in the actual dynamic NAT or PAT operation; they are only used to define the traffic that triggers the translation.

As soon as the access list is configured, add it to the translation policy with the following command syntax:

ASA, FWSM	Firewall(config)# **nat** (*real_ifc*) *nat_id* **access-list** *acl_name* [**dns**] [**outside**][[**tcp**] *max_conns* [*emb_limit*] [**norandomseq**]] [**udp** *udp_max_conns*]
PIX 6.3	Firewall(config)# **nat** [(*local_interface*)] *nat_id* **access-list** *acl_name* [**dns**] [**norandomseq**] [*max_conns* [*emb_limit*]]]

The access list named *acl_name* is used by the translation policy to identify packets to be translated. For example, the following commands cause dynamic translation with NAT ID 1 to be used when inside hosts in 192.168.1.0/24 initiate connections to the 10.1.0.0/16 network, as matched by access list FlowA. When the same inside hosts initiate connections to the 10.2.0.0/16 network, matched by access list FlowB, NAT ID 2 is used.

```
Firewall(config)# access-list FlowA permit ip 192.168.1.0 255.255.255.0 10.1.0.0
255.255.0.0
Firewall(config)# access-list FlowB permit ip 192.168.1.0 255.255.255.0 10.2.0.0
255.255.0.0
Firewall(config)# global (outside) 1 interface
Firewall(config)# global (outside) 2 interface
Firewall(config)# nat (inside) 1 access-list FlowA
Firewall(config)# nat (inside) 2 access-list FlowB
```

Dynamic NAT and PAT Example

A firewall connects to the outside network using IP address 169.54.122.1 255.255.255.128. The rest of that subnet is available for the firewall to use as dynamic NAT and/or PAT addresses. Several different IP subnets are on the inside of the firewall: 172.16.0.0/16, 172.17.0.0/16, and various others. (The firewall must have **route** commands defined or dynamic routing information to reach these inside networks, because they are not directly connected to it. Those commands are not shown here.)

Several different NAT and PAT definitions are needed in this scenario, as shown in Figure 6-8. Hosts on the inside network 172.16.0.0 255.255.0.0 are allowed to make outbound connections and will be translated using the global address pool 169.54.122.10 through 169.54.122.60. As long as these addresses are available, they will be assigned as dynamic NAT. If all of the addresses in the pool are in use, the next translation will use global address 169.54.122.61 for dynamic PAT. These are configured as nat/global group ID 1.

Figure 6-8 *Network Diagram for the Dynamic NAT and PAT Example*

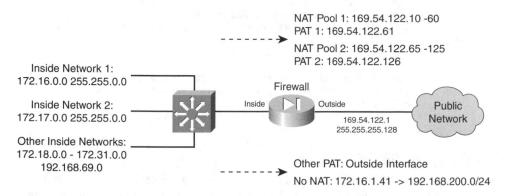

A similar translation arrangement is needed for inside network 172.17.0.0 255.255.0.0. These use global pool 169.54.122.65 through 169.54.122.125 for NAT and global address 169.54.122.126 for PAT. These are configured as nat/global group ID 2.

For other inside networks, a default translation arrangement uses the firewall's outside interface address for dynamic PAT. The nat/global group ID 3 performs this function.

One other exception must be made to the address translation mechanism: When inside host 172.16.1.41 opens outbound connections to the 192.168.200.0/24 network, its address should not be translated at all. This is configured using nat group 0, as a NAT exemption identified by access list **acl_no_nat**.

Finally, an access list is applied to the inside interface, controlling the outbound traffic. By default, the firewall will allow outbound traffic from that interface even if no access list exists. The decision is made to use an access list, only to prevent hosts on the inside from spoofing source IP addresses that are different than the inside subnets. Access list **acl_inside** is used for this purpose.

TIP   You can also use the **ip verify reverse-path interface inside** command to enable reverse path forwarding lookups. This feature verifies that each packet's source address did indeed come from a subnet that the firewall expects to be located on the source interface. In effect, spoofed addresses are detected. This command is covered in more detail in Chapter 3, "Building Connectivity."

You can configure the firewall for this scenario with the following commands:

```
Firewall(config)# global (outside) 1 169.54.122.10-169.54.122.60 netmask 255.255.255.128
Firewall(config)# global (outside) 1 169.54.122.61
Firewall(config)# nat (inside) 1 172.16.0.0 255.255.0.0 0 0
Firewall(config)# global (outside) 2 169.54.122.65-169.54.122.125 netmask 255.255.255.128
Firewall(config)# global (outside) 2 169.54.122.126
```

```
Firewall(config)# nat (inside) 2 172.17.0.0 255.255.0.0 0 0
Firewall(config)# global (outside) 3 interface
Firewall(config)# nat (inside) 3 access-list nat_0 0 0 0
Firewall(config)# access-list acl_no_nat permit ip host 172.16.1.41 192.168.200.0
255.255.255.0
Firewall(config)# nat (inside) 0 access-list acl_no_nat

Firewall(config)# access-list acl_inside permit ip 172.16.0.0 255.240.0.0 any
Firewall(config)# access-list acl_inside permit ip 192.168.69.0 255.255.255.0 any
Firewall(config)# access-list acl_inside deny ip any any
Firewall(config)# access-group acl_inside in interface inside
```

Controlling Traffic

A host on one firewall interface is allowed to create any type of connection to a host on a different firewall interface as long as an address translation can be made (if required) and any relevant interface access lists permit it.

As soon as address translation methods have been configured between pairs of firewall interfaces, you must also configure and apply access lists to the appropriate interfaces.

You can configure and use an access list to limit the types of traffic in a specific direction. When the ACL permits traffic, connections are allowed to pass; when it denies traffic, those packets are dropped at the firewall.

In addition, when an xlate entry is created for a new connection and the interface access lists permit the initial traffic, the return traffic specific to that connection is also permitted—only because the firewall has built the proper xlate and conn entries for it.

You can use the following sequence of steps to configure an access list:

1. Use an access list to permit allowed traffic:

ASA, FWSM	Firewall(config)# **access-list** *acl_id* [**line** *line-num*] [**extended**] {**permit** | **deny**} {*protocol* | **object-group** *protocol_obj_group*} {*source_addr* *source_mask* | **object-group** *network_obj_group*} [*operator sport* | **object-group** *service_obj_group*] {*destination_addr destination_mask* | **object-group** *network_obj_group*} [*operator dport* | **object-group** *service_obj_group*] [**log** [[**disable** | **default**] | [*level*]]] [**interval** *secs*]] [**time-range** *name*] [**inactive**]
PIX 6.3	Firewall(config)# **access-list** *acl_id* [**line** *line-num*] {**permit** | **deny**} {*protocol* | **object-group** *protocol_obj_group*} {*source_addr* *source_mask* | **object-group** *network_obj_group*} [*operator sport* | **object-group** *service_obj_group*] {*destination_addr destination_mask* | **object-group** *network_obj_group*} [*operator dport* | **object-group** *service_obj_group*] [**log** [[**disable** | **default**] | [*level*]]] [**interval** *secs*]]

Be aware that any source and destination addresses you specify are relative to any address translation that occurs on the interface where the access list is applied.

For example, suppose inside address 192.168.1.1 will be translated to outside address 204.152.16.1. If the access list will be applied to the outside interface to permit inbound connections, then you should use destination address 204.152.16.1 because the host is known by that address on the outside.

Likewise, if the access list will be applied to the inside interface to limit outbound traffic, you should use source address 192.168.1.1.

To configure the access list named **acl_id**, you should refer to Section 6-3, "Controlling Access with Access Lists," which covers ACLs in much greater detail.

If you are creating several access lists, you might consider assigning them meaningful names. For example, an ACL that will control access on the outside interface could be named **acl_outside**. Although it is not necessary to begin the name with **acl_**, that does provide a handy clue that an ACL is being referenced when you look through a large firewall configuration.

2. Apply the access list to a firewall interface:

ASA, FWSM	Firewall(config)# **access-group** acl_id {**in** | **out**} **interface** interface_name [**per-user-override**]
PIX 6.3	Firewall(config)# **access-group** acl_id **in interface** interface_name [**per-user-override**]

The access list named acl_id is applied to the interface named interface_name (**inside**, for example). The access list evaluates or filters traffic only in the direction specified: **in** (traffic arriving on the interface) or **out** (traffic leaving the interface).

If you use downloadable access lists from a RADIUS server, you can add the **per-user-override** keyword. This allows any downloaded ACLs to override the ACL applied to the interface. In other words, the per-user downloaded ACLs will be evaluated first, before the interface ACL.

Controlling Access with Medium Security Interfaces

So far, inbound and outbound access has been discussed in relation to two firewall interfaces—the inside and the outside. If your firewall has other "medium security" interfaces (security levels between 0 and 100), you face some additional considerations. These interfaces are usually used as demilitarized zone (DMZ) networks, where services are made available to the public networks while offering a certain level of security. DMZ networks are then isolated from the highest security inside networks, although their services can be accessed from the inside.

Outbound access from a medium security interface to a lower one is really no different than from the inside interface. You still need to configure the following:

- Address translation with the **static** command or with the **global** and **nat** commands. This allows hosts on the DMZ to appear on the outside with a valid address.

- An access list applied to the medium security interface. This allows hosts on the DMZ to be permitted to initiate inbound connections toward the inside interface. The same access list also controls outbound connections from the DMZ.

Figure 6-9 shows how outbound access can be configured on a firewall with three interfaces. Basically, you need to consider each interface separately and decide which other lower security interfaces will be involved in the outbound connections. For those interface pairs, configure address translation (if required) and make sure any interface access lists allow the outbound connections.

You should also consider inbound connections, made from a lower security interface toward a higher security DMZ interface. This could include connections from the outside interface toward a DMZ interface, or from a DMZ toward the inside interface.

Inbound access into a medium security interface is really no different than into the inside interface. You still need to configure address translation (if required) so that hosts on the higher security interface appear as a mapped address on the lower security interface.

An access list should also be applied to the interface with the lowest security level of the connection. For example, if an outside host is allowed to connect to a DMZ host, an ACL applied to the outside interface must permit the inbound connection.

Figure 6-9 *Outbound Access on a Firewall with Three Interfaces*

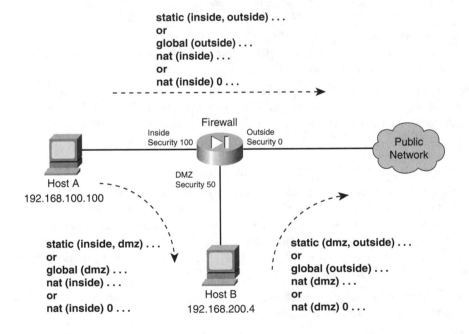

Similarly, if a DMZ host is allowed to connect to an inside host, an ACL must be applied to the DMZ interface that permits the inbound connection. The ACL must be applied to the interface closest to the source of inbound connections.

Figure 6-10 shows how inbound access can be configured on a firewall with three interfaces. Basically, you need to consider each interface separately and decide which other higher security interfaces will accept inbound connections from it. For those interface pairs, configure address translation (if required) and make sure any interface access lists allow only specific inbound connections.

Figure 6-10 *Inbound Access on a Firewall with Three Interfaces*

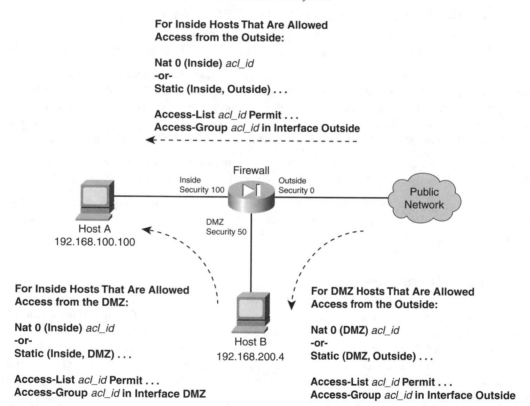

An access list must be applied to each lower security interface so that specific inbound connections are permitted. This sounds straightforward, but some interesting implications must be considered.

In Figure 6-10, for example, the outside interface can accept inbound connections that are destined for the DMZ network, as well as for the inside network. Therefore, the access list applied to the outside interface should be configured to permit the necessary connections to the global addresses of the DMZ hosts as well as the inside hosts.

Now consider the DMZ interface. Hosts on the DMZ network might initiate inbound connections to the inside interface. Therefore, the access list applied to the DMZ interface should be configured to permit inbound traffic to the global addresses of the inside hosts.

Suppose DMZ hosts are also allowed to initiate outbound connections toward the outside network. The access list applied to the DMZ interface must also be configured to permit these outbound connections, in addition to any inbound traffic toward the inside. It is easy to forget that access lists applied to medium security interfaces should permit traffic destined for several locations.

6-3: Controlling Access with Access Lists

On a Cisco firewall, you can use access lists to filter traffic coming into or out of a firewall interface. Access lists that are applied to interfaces become an integral part of the traffic inspection mechanism.

Access lists can be defined using the familiar Cisco IOS Software ACL format. However, one important difference exists between the firewall and IOS ACL formats: Firewalls use real subnet masks (a 1-bit matches, a 0-bit ignores), while IOS platforms use a wildcard mask (a 0-bit matches, a 1-bit ignores). For example, the subnet 192.168.199.0/24 would be configured as **192.168.199.0 255.255.255.0** on an ASA or FWSM, and as **192.168.199.0 0.0.0.255** on an IOS platform.

Access lists are configured one line at a time; every line that makes up a single access list must have an identical ACL name. Each line of an access list is called an *Access Control Entry (ACE)*.

Cisco firewalls also offer an ACL configuration feature not found in the IOS Software. Access lists can be configured in a modular fashion, using defined *object groups* as a type of macro. Object groups are discussed in detail in the "Defining Object Groups" section.

Compiling Access Lists

Access lists are normally evaluated in sequential order, as they appear in the firewall configuration. As access lists grow in length, the amount of time needed to evaluate the ACEs in sequence can also grow. Fortunately, the ASA and FWSM platforms compile access lists into a more efficient *Turbo ACL* format. On a PIX platform, you can compile ACLs beginning with release 6.2. Once compiled, access lists can be evaluated in a deterministic fashion, without the need to work through each ACE in sequence. In other words, the time required to find and evaluate any specific ACE within the entire access list is more or less constant.

In PIX releases 6.2 and 6.3, access lists must have at least 19 ACEs before they can be compiled into the Turbo ACL format. If they have less than 19 entries, it becomes more efficient for the firewall to evaluate them sequentially. As well, compiled ACLs are stored in Flash memory so that they can be retrieved in their native compiled format even after a reboot.

On a PIX platform, TurboACLs can be compiled when they are first configured, and at most every time when they are edited thereafter. ASAs running 7.0 or later automatically compile access lists immediately after they are edited or configured—usually after every ACE is entered. This is important because any configuration changes you make to ACLs take effect right away. This process is completely hidden, so that you are never aware that an ACL is compiled or not. It simply exists in human-readable form in the firewall configuration.

A FWSM automatically compiles and applies ACLs in real-time by default too. However, you can configure it to use manual compilation instead.

Recompiling an ACL is a silent process, but can burden an already loaded firewall CPU. For this reason, you might choose to manually compile and apply ACL changes so that the only occur at predetermined times. For example, you might plan on making changes to large ACLs during a time of low traffic through the firewall or during a scheduled maintenance window.

On a FWSM, you can use the following command to see whether ACLs are compiled automatically or manually:

```
Firewall# show access-list mode
```

You can use the following command to configure whether access lists will be compiled automatically (the default) or manually:

```
Firewall(config)# access-list mode {auto-commit | manual-commit}
```

In the manual-commit mode, you have to manually compile and commit ACLs to FWSM memory after they are edited, in order for them to be updated and used. If you forget to commit the ACL changes, the FWSM keeps using the previously compiled ACL contents it already has in memory. The following configuration command can be used to commit *all* access lists configured on the FWSM:

```
Firewall(config)# access-list commit
```

Configuring an Access List

You can use the steps presented in this section to configure a firewall access list. The access list exists in the firewall configuration, but does not actively do anything until you apply it to a firewall interface or to some other firewall function.

Access lists are defined simply by entering ACE commands in global configuration mode. There is no need to define the access list name first; just the action of entering an ACE with an ACL ID *acl_id* (an arbitrary text name) is enough to make it a part of that access list. However, as soon as an access list is defined with at least one ACE, the order the ACEs are entered becomes important.

When you enter a new ACE into the configuration, it is always appended to the end or bottom of the access list. Therefore, the order that ACEs appear in an access list is important. This is because access lists are evaluated line-by-line, in sequential order. To designate an ACE's exact position within a whole access list, you can specify a line number as part of the ACE configuration.

In addition, every access list ends with an implicit, hidden **deny ip any any** ACE. Even though a newly configured ACE is appended to the bottom of the access list, the implicit deny ACE always comes after that. In effect, anything that is not explicitly permitted by an ACE somewhere in the access list will be denied by this final implicit ACE.

Section 6-3

Adding an ACE to an Access List

You can define an access list entry with the following configuration command:

```
Firewall(config)# access-list acl_id [line line-num] [extended] {permit | deny} protocol
source_addr  source_mask [operator sport] destination_addr destination_mask  [operator
dport] [log [[disable | default] | [level]]] [interval secs]] [time-range name] [inactive]
```

Although the command syntax looks complex, the concept is simple: Either **permit** or **deny** traffic from a source (using an optional source port) to a destination (using an optional destination port). An access list can be built from many different keywords and parameters. You might find Figure 6-11 helpful, as it shows the basic ACE syntax and how each portion can be configured.

Figure 6-11 *Cisco Firewall ACE Structure and Composition*

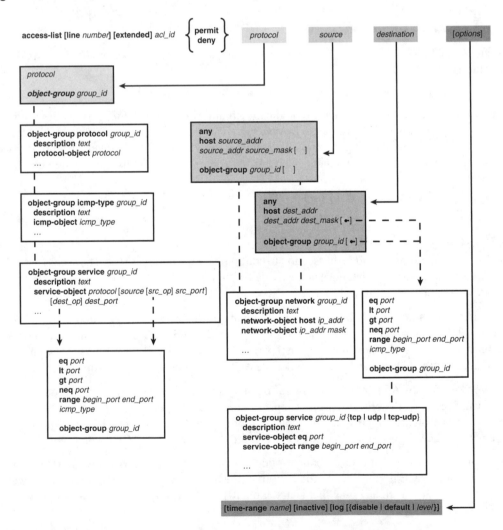

To simplify complex traffic definitions, you can also define groups of parameters as object groups; the object groups are then referenced in the ACE configurations. (Object groups are covered in the "Defining Object Groups" section in this chapter.)

TIP   You can use a similar ACE command syntax to create an access list for IPv6 traffic. Use the following guidelines when you adapt the syntax for IPv6:

- Use the **ipv6 access-list** command keywords instead of **access-list**.
- Whenever an IP subnet is given with *source_addr source_mask* or *destination_addr destination_mask*, substitute the IPv6 address prefix as *source_ipv6_prefix/prefix_length* or *destination_ipv6_prefix/prefix_length*.
- Whenever specific host addresses are needed, substitute **host** *ip_address* with **host** *ipv6_address*.

First, begin by identifying the protocol of interest. The matched *protocol* can be **ip** (any IP protocol), **icmp** (1), **tcp** (6), **udp** (17), **ah** (51), **eigrp** (88), **esp** or **ipsec** (50), **gre** or **pptp** (47), **igmp** (2), **igrp** (9), **ipinip** (4), **nos** (94), **ospf** (89), **pim** (103), **pcp** (108), or **snp** (109). You can also specify the *protocol* as a decimal number (0-255) to identify a protocol that does not have a predefined keyword.

Source and destination addresses can be explicit IP addresses or subnets, and the masks are regular subnet masks.

TIP   Cisco firewalls do not use the "inverted" masks required by routers running Cisco IOS Software. Instead, think of a firewall mask as a normal IP subnet mask, where a 1 bit matches a bit value and a 0 bit ignores it.

If you need to identify a specific host in an access list, you can give its IP address and a host mask (255.255.255.255). You can also specify the same thing by using the **host** keyword followed by the IP address.

To specify a wildcard or "any" IP address, you can use IP address 0.0.0.0 and mask 0.0.0.0 (0 bits in the mask ignore the value). You can also do the same thing by using the **any** keyword in place of an address and mask.

TIP   For inbound firewall rules, ACEs are usually concerned with the destination address and destination port values. This would be useful to allow outside hosts to connect to inside web or email servers, for example. You should always define an ACE with as specific source and destination information as possible. The goal is to define the most strict security policy while allowing users to connect to necessary resources.

As well, you should always include access list rules that filter out attempts to spoof legitimate IP addresses (RFC2827) or use IP addresses set aside for private network use (RFC1918). For example, the following ACEs can be used to deny RFC1918 source addresses:

```
Firewall(config)# access-list anti_spoof deny ip 10.0.0.0 255.0.0.0 any
Firewall(config)# access-list anti_spoof deny ip 172.16.0.0 255.240.0.0 any
Firewall(config)# access-list anti_spoof deny ip 192.168.0.0 255.255.0.0 any
```

If you need to match against a source or destination port number, you can add one of the following keywords as an optional operator:

Less Than	**lt** *port*
Greater Than	**gt** *port*
Equal To	**eq** *port*
Not Equal To	**neq** *port*
Range	**range** *lower upper*

The operator compares the port number to the value given by *port* (a single decimal number; for a range, give two numbers for lower and upper limits). Port numbers can be given as predefined keywords or as decimal numbers. The keywords supported by Cisco firewalls are listed in Appendix A: "Well-Known Protocol and Port Numbers."

In the case of an ICMP (protocol **icmp**) ACE, no operator keyword is used. Instead, the ICMP message type is given alone, in place of the port number.

By default, each ACE is enabled and actively used when it is configured. However, individual ACEs can be disabled without removing them from the configuration. This might be handy if you need to troubleshoot or temporarily deactivate a firewall rule. To do this, reenter the ACE configuration command along with the **inactive** keyword. To reenable an ACE, reenter it without the **inactive** keyword.

You can also configure individual ACEs so that they are active and evaluated only during a predefined time range. Time-based ACEs can be useful if you have security policies that change, based on the time of day, day of the week, and so on. After an access list is configured, you can always remove an ACE or insert an ACE at a specific location within the access list. These tasks are covered in the next section.

TIP ASA and FWSM access lists are always assumed to use the "extended" format, where both source and destination addresses and ports can be specified. This is very similar to extended IP access lists on IOS router and switch platforms. However, the ASA and

FWSM firewalls can support both "standard" and "extended" forms, although standard ACLs are reserved for use with routing protocols.

You might be wise to get into the habit of using the **extended** keyword when you configure, edit, or delete ACE commands. Even if you do not specify the keyword when an ACE is entered, it is automatically inserted into the configuration. The **extended** keyword becomes important when you need to remove an ACE, as it must be given from the command line.

Remember that even though an access list is properly configured, it will not be used until it is applied to a firewall function. Access lists are most often used by applying them to firewall interfaces. Access lists can be applied to interfaces in the inbound and outbound directions independently.

Manipulating Access Lists

Every access list contains statements that are internally numbered. If you type in a new ACE without using a line number, it is simply added to the end of the list (just prior to the implicit **deny ip any any** ACE). If you do include a line number, the new ACE is inserted into the list just prior to the current ACE at that position. The current ACE is not replaced; rather, it and all ACEs below it are moved down one line to make room for the new ACE.

TIP   Prior to FWSM 2.3, line numbers were not used at all. In that case, you would have to edit an ACL simply by adding new ACEs or deleting existing ones.

Typically, a firewall numbers ACEs in an ACL with incremental values: the first ACE is line 1, the second ACE is line 2, and so on. However, the ACL line numbers are not shown in the configuration. To see them, you can use the **show access-list** [*acl_id*] command. For example, suppose the following ACL has been configured in a firewall:

```
Firewall(config)# access-list test permit tcp any host 192.168.10.1 eq www
Firewall(config)# access-list test permit udp any host 192.168.10.2 eq domain
Firewall(config)# access-list test permit tcp any host 192.168.10.3 eq smtp
```

When the running-configuration is displayed, the access list is shown just as it was entered. Notice that the final implicit **deny any any** is not shown, although it is actually present.

```
Firewall# show running-config
[output omitted]
access-list test extended permit tcp any host 192.168.10.1 eq www
access-list test extended permit udp any host 192.168.10.2 cq domain
access-list test extended permit tcp any host 192.168.10.3 eq smtp
```

No line numbers are shown, though the **extended** keyword has been added even though the ACE lines were not manually entered that way. To see the ACL line numbers, use the **show access-list** command, as follows:

```
Firewall# show access-list test
access-list test line 1 extended permit tcp any host 192.168.10.1 eq www (hitcnt=1784)
access-list test line 2 extended permit udp any host 192.168.10.2 eq domain (hitcnt=37465)
access-list test line 3 extended permit tcp any host 192.168.10.3 eq smtp (hitcnt=43544)
```

If a new ACE is entered without specifying a line number, it simply goes to the end of the ACL:

```
Firewall(config)# access-list test permit udp any host 192.168.10.4 eq tftp
Firewall(config)# exit
Firewall# show access-list test
access-list test line 1 extended permit tcp any host 192.168.10.1 eq www
(hitcnt=1784)
access-list test line 2 extended permit udp any host 192.168.10.2 eq domain
(hitcnt=37465)
access-list test line 3 extended permit tcp any host 192.168.10.3 eq smtp (hitcnt=43544)
access-list test line 4 extended permit udp any host 192.168.10.4 eq tftp (hitcnt=0)
```

Finally, suppose another new ACE is configured so that it appears at ACL line 2. Notice how the ACEs that were previously at lines 2 and 3 are moved down in the following output, to make room for the new ACE at line 2:

```
Firewall(config)# access-list test line 2 deny udp 192.168.200.0 255.255.255.0 host
192.168.10.2 eq domain
Firewall(config)# exit
Firewall# show access-list test
access-list test line 1 extended permit tcp any host 192.168.10.1 eq www (hitcnt=1784)
access-list test line 2 extended deny udp 192.168.200.0 255.255.255.0 host 192.168.10.2
eq domain (hitcnt=0)
access-list test line 3 extended permit udp any host 192.168.10.2 eq domain (hitcnt=37465)
access-list test line 4 extended permit tcp any host 192.168.10.3 eq smtp (hitcnt=43544)
access-list test line 5 extended permit udp any host 192.168.10.4 eq tftp (hitcnt=0)
```

Beginning with ASA 7.0 and FWSM 2.2, you can make an existing ACE inactive without removing it from the ACL configuration. To do this, enter the complete ACE command again, followed by the **inactive** keyword. The ACE will still be included in the running configuration, but will not be evaluated in the ACL as long as it is inactive. To make the ACE active again, reenter the whole ACE command without the **inactive** keyword.

To remove an existing ACE, use the **no** keyword followed by the complete ACE command line. For example, suppose the following access list has been configured on a firewall (notice the **extended** keyword present in the output):

```
Firewall# show run access-list acl_outside
access-list acl_outside extended permit ip any any
access-list acl_outside extended permit tcp any host 10.3.3.3 eq www
access-list acl_outside extended permit tcp any host 10.3.3.4 eq smtp
```

Obviously, the first ACE could pose a security risk because it might allow all types of traffic to pass. Therefore, you could delete that ACE by using the following command:

```
Firewall# configure terminal
Firewall(config)# no access-list acl_outside extended permit ip any any
```

Remember to include the **extended** keyword, so that the entire ACE syntax is matched. No ACL line numbers can be specified when you delete an ACE.

You can also remove an entire access list, including each of its ACE lines, from the running configuration. However, it is a good idea to first make sure the access list is no longer referenced in any other firewall feature or applied to any firewall interface. This prevents a feature from trying to reference an access list that no longer exists.

Then you can use the following command syntax to remove the access list:

ASA, FWSM 2.3+	`Firewall(config)# clear configure access-list acl_name`

FWSM 2.2-, PIX 6.3	`Firewall(config)# no access-list acl_name`
	or
	`Firewall(config)# clear access-list acl_name`

Notice how the **clear configure access-list** command is quite different from the **no access-list** *acl_name* that you might have expected—the difference in syntax might just prevent you from accidentally deleting a very large or important access list someday!

Suppose you configure an ACL with a name, and you decide that you need to change its name at a later date. Normally, this would be a cumbersome process. You would have to create a new ACL by reentering each of the ACE lines along with the new ACL name and then delete the old ACL.

Beginning with ASA 8.0, you can easily rename an ACL with just one configuration command. Use the following command syntax to change the ACL name from *old_acl_name* to *new_acl_name*:

```
asa(config)# access-list old_acl_name rename new_acl_name
```

Adding Descriptions to an Access List

Access lists can become very large, especially if your network has many security policies, many hosts, and many types of traffic to protect with a firewall. Large access lists can be difficult to read (for a human) because it might not be clear what a particular ACE is doing or what its original purpose was.

You can add access list entries that contain text descriptions or remarks to provide some readable clues. Remark ACEs can be added anywhere within an access list, provided you can supply a line number when you configure them. As well, you can configure as many remark ACEs as necessary in an access list.

To add a remark ACE to an access list, use the following command:

```
Firewall(config)# access-list acl_id [line line-num] remark text
```

A new ACE is added to the access list named *acl_id* and contains only the word **remark** followed by the description *text* (arbitrary text string, 1 to 100 characters). If the **line** keyword is used, the remark is added just prior to the current ACE at line *line-num*.

TIP   Remark ACEs are useful as descriptions or reminders of the purpose for the ACE or group of ACEs that follow them. Keep in mind that the remark lines are not tied to actual ACEs; they only occupy space in the ACL. If you remove or relocate an ACE, a remark line might be left behind in its original position. In other words, unless you remove or relocate remark lines and their associated ACEs, the remarks might become confusing or meaningless.

Defining a Time Range to Activate an ACE

Once configured, access list entries are active all the time. Beginning with ASA 7.0 and FWSM 3.1(1), you can use two mechanisms to control whether an ACE is actively being evaluated or not:

- Adding the **inactive** keyword to an ACE configuration disables it until the keyword is removed.

- Adding a defined time range to an ACE configuration, during which the ACE will be actively used. Outside the time range, the ACE will be inactive.

To control an ACE with a time range, you must configure the time range itself first. You can use the steps that follow to configure a time range. Once configured, the time range must also be applied to specific ACEs, as discussed in the section, "Adding an ACE to an Access List."

TIP   Because a time range controls the state of access list entries, you should make sure the firewall's internal clock is set to the correct date and time. Otherwise, the firewall might not provide the proper security policies at the expected times.

To learn more about setting the firewall clock and synchronizing it with an accurate, external source, refer to Section "10-1: Managing the Firewall Clock," in Chapter 10, "Firewall Logging."

---

1.   Create the time range definition:

ASA, FWSM	Firewall(config)# **time-range** *name*
PIX 6.3	N/A

The time range is referenced by its *name* (arbitrary text string, up to 64 characters).

2. (Optional) Define a recurring time period:

ASA, FWSM	Firewall(config-time-range)# **periodic** *start-day hh:mm* **to** *end-day hh:mm* or Firewall(config-time-range)# **periodic** *days-of-the-week hh:mm* **to** *hh:mm*
PIX 6.3	N/A

You can define the time period in two ways. In the first form of the command, a continuous time period is defined. This begins on *start-day* at time *hh:mm* (24-hour format) and ends on *end-day* at time *hh:mm* (24-hour format). The day parameters can be one of the following: **Sunday**, **Monday**, **Tuesday**, **Wednesday**, **Thursday**, **Friday**, or **Saturday**. These are not case sensitive and can be abbreviated, as long as they are not ambiguous.

In the second form, the period lasts from *hh:mm* to *hh:mm* (24-hour format, both within the same day), only on the days listed in *days-of-the-week*. This is one of the following keywords: **daily** (Monday-Sunday), **weekdays** (Monday-Friday), or **weekends** (Saturday-Sunday). You can also use a list of one or more of the following day keywords separated by spaces: **Sunday**, **Monday**, **Tuesday**, **Wednesday**, **Thursday**, **Friday**, or **Saturday**.

You can repeat either of these commands in the same time range definition to add more time periods.

As an example, a time range is configured to define "after hours". For the weekday (Monday through Friday) period between 5:00pm until 8:00am the following morning, two separate **periodic** commands must be used. This is because the time between the start and end times cannot cross midnight and into the following day. A third periodic range is given for weekends, from midnight Saturday until 11:59pm Sunday using the following commands:

```
Firewall(config)# time-range after_hours
Firewall(config-time-range)# periodic weekdays 17:00 to 23:59
Firewall(config-time-range)# periodic weekdays 00:00 to 08:00
Firewall(config-time-range)# periodic saturday 00:00 to sunday 23:59
Firewall(config-time-range)# exit
```

3. (Optional) Define an absolute time period:

ASA, FWSM	Firewall(config-time-range)# **absolute** [**start** *hh:mm day month year*] [**end** *hh:mm day month year*]
PIX 6.3	N/A

The time period has an absolute starting time and date and an ending time and date. The times are given as *hh:mm* (24-hour format), and dates as *day* (1-31), *month* name, and *year* (1993-2035).

If you omit the start limit, the time range begins immediately and runs until the end limit. If you provide a start limit, but omit the end limit, the time range runs indefinitely as soon as the start limit occurs.

As an example, in the configuration that follows, one time range named *Dec2010* is configured to define the entire month of December, 2010. A second time range named *End_2010* is configured to start immediately and end at the very end of December, 2010.

```
Firewall(config)# time-range Dec2010
Firewall(config-time-range)# absolute start 00:00 1 december 2010 end 23:59 30
december 2010
Firewall(config-time-range)# exit
Firewall(config)# time-range End_2010
Firewall(config-time-range)# absolute end 23:59 31 december 2010
Firewall(config-time-range)# exit
```

4. Reference the time range in an ACE.

    In the ACE configuration, add the **time-range** *name* keyword and argument to the **access-list** ACE command.

Access List Examples

A firewall connects an inside network (192.168.17.0/24) to an outside network. Inside hosts include a DNS server, a mail server, and two other servers that support extranet services. Assume that the inside hosts have a NAT exemption to the outside, such that they maintain their same IP addresses. The outside hosts include two extranet servers on the 172.22.10.0/24 network.

The following rules should be configured on the firewall, as shown by the actual configuration commands:

*   ICMP traffic from the outside should be limited to only ICMP echo (ping) requests, ICMP time-exceeded replies (needed for traceroute support), and ICMP unreachables (needed for path MTU discovery).

    ```
    Firewall(config)# access-list acl_outside permit icmp any 192.168.17.0 255.255.255.0
    echo
    Firewall(config)# access-list acl_outside permit icmp any 192.168.17.0 255.255.255.0
    time-exceeded
    Firewall(config)# access-list acl_outside permit icmp any 192.168.17.0 255.255.255.0
    unreachable
    ```

*   Only DNS traffic from the outside is permitted to inside host 192.168.17.21.

    ```
    Firewall(config)# access-list acl_outside permit udp any host 192.168.17.21 eq domain
    ```

*   Only SMTP, POP3, and NNTP traffic from the outside is permitted to inside host 192.168.17.22.

    ```
    Firewall(config)# access-list acl_outside permit tcp any host 192.168.17.22 eq smtp
    Firewall(config)# access-list acl_outside permit tcp any host 192.168.17.22 eq pop3
    Firewall(config)# access-list acl_outside permit tcp any host 192.168.17.22 eq nntp
    ```

*   Outside hosts 172.22.10.41 and 172.22.10.53 are allowed to send SQLnet and FTP packets toward the two inside hosts 192.168.17.100 and 192.168.17.114.

    ```
    Firewall(config)# access-list acl_outside permit tcp host 172.22.10.41 host
    192.168.17.100 eq sqlnet
    Firewall(config)# access-list acl_outside permit tcp host 172.22.10.41 host
    192.168.17.100 eq ftp
    ```

```
Firewall(config)# access-list acl_outside permit tcp host 172.22.10.53 host
192.168.17.100 eq sqlnet
Firewall(config)# access-list acl_outside permit tcp host 172.22.10.53 host
192.168.17.100 eq ftp
Firewall(config)# access-list acl_outside permit tcp host 172.22.10.41 host
192.168.17.114 eq sqlnet
Firewall(config)# access-list acl_outside permit tcp host 172.22.10.41 host
192.168.17.114 eq ftp
Firewall(config)# access-list acl_outside permit tcp host 172.22.10.53 host
192.168.17.114 eq sqlnet
Firewall(config)# access-list acl_outside permit tcp host 172.22.10.53 host
192.168.17.114 eq ftp
```

TIP   Notice that only the FTP control port (TCP 21) is specified in the access list, even though a separate FTP data connection is opened on a different port. As long as FTP inspection is enabled with the **inspect ftp** command, you do not have to explicitly configure the data port in the access list. Instead, the firewall automatically permits the additional inbound FTP data connection when it is negotiated dynamically.

Finally, the access list must be applied to the outside interface, in the inward direction:

```
Firewall(config)# access-group acl_outside in interface outside
```

Most of the security policies or rules in this example can be easily configured. The final rule, however, requires a bit more work defining a one-to-one relationship between outside and inside hosts, along with a combination of TCP ports that will be permitted. The more hosts and services you have on each side, the more complicated and lengthy the access list gets. ACL complexity can be greatly reduced by using object groups, as discussed in the following section.

Defining Object Groups

Object groups can be thought of as a type of macro used within access lists. Object groups can contain lists of IP addresses, ICMP types, IP protocols, or ports. You can define several different types of object groups, each containing a list of similar values, as follows:

- **Network object group**—Contains one or more IP addresses.
- **Protocol object group**—Contains one or more IP protocols.
- **ICMP object group**—Contains one or more ICMP types.
- **Basic service object group**—Contains one or more UDP or TCP port numbers.
- **Enhanced service object group**—Beginning with ASA 8.0, service object groups can contain any mix of protocols, ICMP types, UDP ports, and TCP ports. Enhanced service object groups can be used for either source or destination services, or both, in the access list configuration.

Section 6-3

Object groups can also be nested; that is, one object group can contain members that are themselves object groups of the same type.

TIP   When object groups are configured, it is possible to use the same name for object groups of different types. For example, a network object group might be called "Engineering" and contain IP addresses of hosts in the engineering department. A service (application port) object group could also be called "Engineering", and contain a set of TCP ports needed in the engineering department.

While the firewall might be able to sort out the object groups into the correct types, name duplication can be confusing for human users. It is usually a good idea to add a little tag into each object group's name to help differentiate their purposes. For example, you could use "Engineering_hosts" and "Engineering_ports". In fact, beginning with ASA 7.0, all object groups are required to have unique names.

The steps needed to configure each type of object group are presented in the sections that follow. The command syntax is identical on the ASA and FWSM firewall platforms. As soon as an object group is defined or configured, it can be referenced within one or more access lists.

Defining Network Object Groups

You can use the following steps to configure a network object group containing a list of IP addresses.

1. Name the object group:

   ```
   Firewall(config)# object-group network group_id
   ```

   The group is named *group_id* (arbitrary text string, 1 to 64 characters).

2. (Optional) Add a description:

   ```
   Firewall(config-network)# description text
   ```

   You can add a descriptive string *text* (up to 200 characters) to help explain the purpose of the object group.

3. Add an IP address to the list:

   ```
   Firewall(config-network)# network-object host ip_addr
   ```
   or
   ```
   Firewall(config-network)# network-object ip_addr mask
   ```

   The IP address can be given as the **host** keyword with a single address *ip_addr*. If you have preconfigured a hostname with the **host** command, the hostname can be used here. You can also define an IP subnet with a subnet mask, if needed.

   You can repeat this command to define more IP addresses in the object group.

4. (Optional) Reference another network object group:

```
Firewall(config-network)# group-object group_id
```

Sometimes you might define a network object group for one purpose and need to include it in a larger object group. You can include another object group by referencing its group name *group_id*. This group must be configured before including it here.

As an example, suppose you need to configure the same access list statement for a list of three IP addresses (192.168.1.10, 192.168.1.20, and 192.168.1.30) and one IP subnet (192.168.2.0/ 24), all assigned to hosts in the Accounting department. The following network object group could be configured with the list of addresses, prior to applying it within an access list.

```
Firewall(config)# object-group network Accounting_addrs
Firewall(config-network)# description List of Accounting Dept IP addresses
Firewall(config-network)# network-object host 192.168.1.10
Firewall(config-network)# network-object host 192.168.1.20
Firewall(config-network)# network-object host 192.168.1.30
Firewall(config-network)# network-object 192.168.2.0 255.255.255.0
Firewall(config-network)# exit
```

Now suppose that list of addresses is also a part of a larger list containing the hosts of a remote site. A new object group could be configured for the remote site, containing other object groups defined for various departments. You could use the following commands:

```
Firewall(config)# object-group network RemoteSite_addrs
Firewall(config-network)# description List of IP addresses used in the Remote Site
Firewall(config-network)# group-object Accounting_addrs
```

Defining Protocol Object Groups

You can use the following steps to configure a protocol object group, containing a list of IP protocols.

1. Name the object group:

```
Firewall(config)# object-group protocol group_id
```

The group is named *group_id* (arbitrary text string, 1 to 64 characters).

2. (Optional) Add a description:

```
Firewall(config-protocol)# description text
```

You can add a descriptive string *text* (up to 200 characters) to help explain the purpose of the object group.

3. Add an IP protocol to the list:

```
Firewall(config-protocol)# protocol-object protocol
```

Section 6-3

The IP protocol can be given as *protocol*, a decimal number (1 to 255), or one of the names listed in Table 6-2. To match any IP protocol, use the value **ip.**

Table 6-2 *IP Protocol Names/Numbers*

Protocol Name	Protocol Number
icmp	1
igmp	2
ipinip	4
tcp	6
igrp	9
udp	17
gre or pptp	47
esp or ipsec	50
ah	51
icmp6	58
eigrp	88
ospf	89
nos	94
pim	103
pcp	108
snp	109

You can repeat this command to define more IP protocols in the group.

4. (Optional) Reference another protocol object group:

```
Firewall(config-protocol)# group-object group_id
```

Sometimes you might define a protocol object group for one purpose and need to include it in a larger protocol object group. You can include another object group by referencing its group name *group_id*. You must configure this group prior to referencing it.

As an example, a protocol object group named Tunnels_proto is configured to contain a list of tunneling protocols (GRE, IP-in-IP, ESP, and AH). A second group named Routing_proto contains a list of routing protocols (IGRP, EIGRP, and OSPF). These object groups can then become a part of a larger list called Group1_proto, using the following commands:

```
Firewall(config)# object-group protocol Tunnels_proto
Firewall(config-protocol)# description Tunneling Protocols
Firewall(config-protocol)# protocol-object gre
```

```
Firewall(config-protocol)# protocol-object ipinip
Firewall(config-protocol)# protocol-object esp
Firewall(config-protocol)# protocol-object ah
Firewall(config-protocol)# exit
!
Firewall(config)# object-group protocol Routing_proto
Firewall(config-protocol)# description Routing Protocols
Firewall(config-protocol)# protocol-object igrp
Firewall(config-protocol)# protocol-object eigrp
Firewall(config-protocol)# protocol-object ospf
Firewall(config-protocol)# exit
!
Firewall(config)# object-group protocol Group1_proto
Firewall(config-protocol)# description Group1 list of protocols
Firewall(config-protocol)# group-object Tunnels_proto
Firewall(config-protocol)# group-object Routing_proto
```

Defining ICMP Type Object Groups

You can use the following steps to configure an ICMP type object group, containing a list of ICMP type values.

1. Name the object group:

   ```
   Firewall(config)# object-group icmp-type group_id
   ```

   The group is named *group_id* (arbitrary text string, 1 to 64 characters).

2. (Optional) Add a description:

   ```
   Firewall(config-icmp-type)# description text
   ```

   You can add a descriptive string *text* (up to 200 characters) to help explain the purpose of the object group.

3. Add an ICMP type to the list:

   ```
   Firewall(config-icmp-type)# icmp-object icmp_type
   ```

   The ICMP type can be given as *icmp_type*, a number from 0 to 255, or one of the decimal numbers or names listed in Table 6-3.

Table 6-3 *ICMP Type Names/Numbers*

ICMP Type Name	Number
echo-reply	0
unreachable	3
source-quench	4
redirect	5

continues

Table 6-3 *ICMP Type Names/Numbers (Continued)*

ICMP Type Name	Number
alternate-address	6
echo	8
router-advertisement	9
router-solicitation	10
time-exceeded	11
parameter-problem	12
timestamp-request	13
timestamp-reply	14
information-request	15
information-reply	16
mask-request	17
mask-reply	18
traceroute	30
conversion-error	31
mobile-redirect	32

You can repeat the **icmp-object** *icmp_type* command to define more ICMP types in the group.

4. (Optional) Reference another ICMP object group:

```
Firewall(config-icmp-type)# group-object group_id
```

Sometimes you might define an icmp-type object group for one purpose and need to include it in a larger object group. You can include another object group by referencing its group name *group_id*. You must configure this group before referencing it with the preceding command.

As an example, an icmp-type object group named "Ping" is configured to contain ICMP types echo and echo-reply. Then that object group is included as a part of a more encompassing icmp-type object group that also contains the unreachable, redirect, and time-exceeded types. You can use the following commands to accomplish this:

```
Firewall(config)# object-group icmp-type Ping_icmp
Firewall(config-icmp)# icmp-object echo
Firewall(config-icmp)# icmp-object echo-reply
Firewall(config-icmp)# exit
!
Firewall(config)# object-group icmp-type BiggerList_icmp
Firewall(config-icmp)# group-object Ping_icmp
Firewall(config-icmp)# icmp-object unreachable
```

```
Firewall(config-icmp)# icmp-object redirect
Firewall(config-icmp)# icmp-object time-exceeded
```

Defining Basic Service Object Groups

You can use the following steps to configure a service object group, containing a list of port numbers.

1. Name the object group:

```
Firewall(config)# object-group service group_id {tcp | udp | tcp-udp}
```

The group is named *group_id* (arbitrary text string, 1 to 64 characters). Ports defined in the group can be used in access list statements that match TCP ports (**tcp**), UDP ports (**udp**), or either TCP or UDP port numbers (**tcp-udp**).

TIP   Object groups configured for **tcp** can be used only in access list statements that match TCP port numbers. Likewise, **udp** object groups can match only UDP port numbers. If you need to match an application that uses the same port number over both TCP and UDP, you can use the **tcp-udp** object group. You still need to have separate TCP and UDP access list statements, but they can both reference the same object group.

---

2. (Optional) Add a description:

```
Firewall(config-service)# description text
```

You can add a descriptive string *text* (up to 200 characters) to help explain the purpose of the object group.

3. Add a port number to the list:

```
Firewall(config-service)# port-object eq port
```
or
```
Firewall(config-service)# port-object range begin_port end_port
```

A specific port number can be given with the **eq** keyword as *port*, a decimal number or name. With the **range** keyword, you can also specify a range of port values from *begin_port* to *end_port*. Refer to Appendix A for a complete list of well-known protocol and port number keywords supported by Cisco firewalls.

You can repeat this command to define more IP addresses in the group.

4. (Optional) Reference another basic service object group:

```
Firewall(config-service)# group-object group_id
```

Sometimes you might define a service object group for one purpose and need to include it in a larger object group. You can include another object group by referencing its group name *group_id*. You must configure this group prior to referencing it.

As an example, one object group is defined to contain the HTTP and HTTPS TCP ports for web services. A second group is defined to contain the SMTP, POP3, and IMAP4 TCP ports for e-mail services. A third object group is defined to contain both of the other groups, in addition to the TCP port range 2000 through 2002. You can use the following commands to accomplish this:

```
Firewall(config)# object-group service Web_ports tcp
Firewall(config-service)# description TCP ports used by web browsers
Firewall(config-service)# port-object eq www
Firewall(config-service)# port-object eq https
Firewall(config-service)# exit
!
Firewall(config)# object-group service Mail_ports tcp
Firewall(config-service)# description TCP ports used for email
Firewall(config-service)# port-object eq smtp
Firewall(config-service)# port-object eq pop3
Firewall(config-service)# port-object eq imap4
Firewall(config-service)# exit
!
Firewall(config)# object-group service Example_ports tcp
Firewall(config-service)# description A bunch of TCP ports
Firewall(config-service)# group-object Web_ports
Firewall(config-service)# group-object Mail_ports
Firewall(config-service)# port-object range 2000 2002
```

Defining an Enhanced Service Object Group

Beginning with ASA 8.0, you can define a single enhanced service object group that can contain any combination of protocols, ICMP types, UDP ports, and TCP ports. This is important because it greatly simplifies object group configuration and use.

Use the following steps to configure an enhanced service object group:

1. Name the object group:

   ```
   Firewall(config)# object-group service group_id
   ```

   The group is named *group_id* (an arbitrary string of 1 to 64 characters). Notice that no other keywords are used to identify the group as a specific type.

2. (Optional) Add a description:

   ```
   Firewall(config-service)# description text
   ```

You can add a descriptive string *text* (up to 200 characters) to help explain the purpose of the object group.

3. Add a service object to the list:

```
Firewall(config-service)# service-object  protocol [source [src_op] src_port]
[dest_op] dest_port
```

In one service object definition, you can identify the protocol, source port, and destination port. The source port information is optional; if you do not provide the **source** keyword, only the destination port is assumed. If you do provide the **source** keyword, you need to also supply the source *and* destination parameters.

You can use the keywords listed in Table 6-4 when you configure the protocol and port parameters:

Table 6-4   protocol/port/type *Parameter Keywords for Enhanced Service Objects*

protocol Keyword	*port* or *type* Keyword
ah	
eigrp	
esp (same as **ipsec**)	
gre	
icmp *type*	**0–255** **alternate-address, conversion-error, echo, echo-reply, information-reply, information-request, mask-reply, mask-request, mobile-redirect, parameter-problem, redirect, router-advertisement, router-solicitation, source-quench, time-exceeded, timestamp-reply, timestamp-request, traceroute, unreachable**
icmp6 *type*	**0–255** **echo, echo-reply, membership-query, membership-reduction, membership-report, neighbor-advertisement, neighbor-redirect, neighbor-solicitation, packet-too-big, parameter-problem, router-advertisement, router-renumbering, router-solicitation, time-exceeded, unreachable**
igmp	
igrp	
ip	
ipinip	
ipsec (same as **esp**)	
nos	
ospf	

continues

Section 6-3

Table 6-4   protocol/port/type *Parameter Keywords for Enhanced Service Objects (Continued)*

protocol Keyword	*port* or *type* Keyword
pcp	
pim	
pptp	
snp	
udp *port*	0–65535 biff, bootpc, bootps, cifs, discard, dnsix, domain, echo, http, isakmp, kerberos, mobile-ip, nameserver, netbios-dgm, netbios-ns, nfs, ntp, pcanywhere-status, pim-auto-rp, radius, radius-acct, rip, secureid-udp, sip, snmp, snmptrap, sunrpc, syslog, tacacs, talk, tftp, time, who, www, xdmcp
tcp *port*	0–65535 aol, bgp, chargen, cifs, citrix-ica, cmd, ctiqbe, daytime, discard, domain, echo, exec, finger, ftp, ftp-data, gopher, h323, hostname, http, https, ident, imap4, irc, kerberos, klogin, kshell, ldap, ldaps, login, lotusnotes, lpd, netbios-ssn, nfs, nntp, pcanywhere-data, pim-auto-rp, pop2, pop3, pptp, rsh, rtsp, sip, smtp, sqlnet, ssh, sunrpc, tacacs, talk, telnet, uucp, whois, www
tcp-udp *port*	0–65535 cifs, discard, domain, echo, http, kerberos, nfs, pim-auto-rp, sip, sunrpc, tacacs, talk, www

The source and destination operators, *src_op* and *dest_op*, can be given as one of the following keywords:

- Less Than: **lt** *port*
- Greater Than: **gt** *port*
- Equal To: **eq** *port*
- Not Equal To: **neq** *port*
- Range: **range** *lower upper*

4. (Optional) Reference another service object group:

```
Firewall(config-service)# group-object group_id
```

Sometimes you might define a service object group for one purpose and need to include it in a larger object group. You can include another object group by referencing its group name *group_id*. You must configure this group prior to referencing it.

As an example of an enhanced service object group, suppose you would like to identify packets containing ICMP echo and echo-reply, IPsec ESP (IP protocol 50), ISAKMP (UDP port 500), UDP port 10000, and HTTP. With object groups on a FWSM or an ASA prior to ASA 8.0, you would have to configure individual object groups for each type of traffic, as shown in the following example:

```
Firewall(config)# object-group icmp test-icmp
Firewall(config-icmp)# description ICMP types to identify
Firewall(config-icmp)# icmp-object echo
Firewall(config-icmp)# icmp-object echo-reply
Firewall(config-icmp)# exit
Firewall(config)# object-group protocol test-protocol
Firewall(config-protocol)# description Protocols to identify
Firewall(config-protocol)# protocol-object esp
Firewall(config-protocol)# exit
Firewall(config)# object-group service test-service1 udp
Firewall(config-service)# description UDP ISAKMP
Firewall(config-service)# port-object eq isakmp
Firewall(config-service)# exit
Firewall(config)# object-group service test-service2 udp
Firewall(config-service)# description UDP 10000
Firewall(config-service)# port-object eq 10000
Firewall(config-service)# exit
Firewall(config)# object-group service test-service3 tcp
Firewall(config-service)# description TCP 80
Firewall(config-service)# port-object eq www
Firewall(config-service)# exit
```

In contrast, with ASA 8.0, all of the traffic types can be identified using a *single* enhanced service object group as demonstrated in the configuration that follows. Notice how the configuration is smaller and that only a single object group needs to be referenced.

```
Firewall(config)# object-group service test
Firewall(config-service)# description Enhanced Service Obj Group
Firewall(config-service)# service-object icmp echo
Firewall(config-service)# service-object icmp echo-reply
Firewall(config-service)# service-object esp
Firewall(config-service)# service-object udp eq isakmp
Firewall(config-service)# service-object udp source 10000
Firewall(config-service)# service-object tcp eq www
Firewall(config-service)# exit
```

Using Object Groups in an Access List

After you have defined an object group, it must be referenced in an access list before it can be used. You can substitute the object group in place of the appropriate protocol, address, or port parameters within the **access-list** command syntax. In the complete command syntax that follows, notice the location of each of the regular object group keywords:

```
Firewall(config)# access-list acl_id [line line-num] [extended] {permit | deny}
    {protocol | object-group protocol_obj_group}
    {source_addr  source_mask | object-group network_obj_group}
    [operator sport | object-group service_obj_group]
    {destination_addr destination_mask | object-group network_obj_group}
    [operator dport | object-group service_obj_group]
    [log [[disable | default] | [level]]] [interval secs]]
    [time-range name] [inactive]
```

You can substitute the following regular ACE parameters with the object group syntax shown:

Regular ACE Parameters	Substitute This Object Group Syntax
protocol	**object-group** *protocol_grp_id*
icmp *icmp-type*	**object-group** *icmp_grp_id*
address mask	**object-group** *network_grp_id*
operator port	**object-group** *service_grp_id*

As you begin to use object groups, think of the common things in security policies that can be grouped together: ICMP packet types, inside and/or outside host addresses, protocols, and port numbers. Consider the following example, which is identical to the scenario presented in the "Access List Examples" section.

```
Firewall(config)# object-group icmp-type allowed-icmp
Firewall(config-icmp)# description ICMP traffic allowed inside
Firewall(config-icmp)# icmp-object echo
Firewall(config-icmp)# icmp-object time-exceeded
Firewall(config-icmp)# icmp-object unreachable
Firewall(config-icmp)# exit
Firewall(config)# object-group service mail-services tcp
Firewall(config-service)# description Email and News services to 192.168.17.22
Firewall(config-service)# port-object eq smtp
Firewall(config-service)# port-object eq pop3
Firewall(config-service)# port-object eq nntp
Firewall(config-service)# exit
Firewall(config)# object-group network extranet-hosts
Firewall(config-network)# description Extranet hosts allowed in for backend services
Firewall(config-network)# network-object host 172.22.10.41
Firewall(config-network)# network-object host 172.22.10.53
Firewall(config-network)# exit
Firewall(config)# object-group network extranet-targets
Firewall(config-network)# description Inside servers supporting extranet servers
Firewall(config-network)# network-object host 192.168.17.110
Firewall(config-network)# network-object host 192.168.17.114
Firewall(config-network)# exit
Firewall(config)# object-group service extranet-services tcp
Firewall(config-service)# description Extranet backend services allowed
Firewall(config-service)# port-object eq sqlnet
Firewall(config-service)# port-object eq ftp
Firewall(config-service)# exit
```

Now the actual access list is configured, including any references to the object groups that have been configured:

```
Firewall(config)# access-list acl_outside permit icmp any 192.168.17.0 255.255.255.0
object-group allowed-icmp
Firewall(config)# access-list acl_outside permit udp any host 192.168.17.21 eq domain
Firewall(config)# access-list acl_outside permit tcp any host 192.168.17.22 object-group
mail-services
Firewall(config)# access-list acl_outside permit tcp object-group extranet-hosts object-
group extranet-targets object-group extranet-services
```

This time, the number of object group commands seems to be lengthy but the access list is rather short. The idea is to make the ACL as short as possible to become more abstract and readable. If you have defined your object groups with meaningful names, you begin to see the access list defined with abstract functions or quantities.

You can always make adjustments to the security policies by adding or deleting lines from object groups. Even if the object group definitions become very lengthy, it does not really impact the firewall's performance—the overall access list is compiled so that it can match traffic in a consistent amount of time, regardless of the actual ACL length.

Although the access list is much shorter in the running-configuration when it includes object group references, this is primarily for a firewall administrator's benefit.

Internally, the firewall expands the object groups (even nested ones) out into the full access list configuration. If the firewall is configured to compile ACLs, then the expanded result is compiled and used. You can display the full access list with the **show access-list** command, as in the following example:

```
Firewall# show access-list acl_outside
access-list acl_outside; 15 elements

access-list acl_outside line 1 extended permit icmp any 192.168.17.0 255.255.255.0 object-
group allowed-icmp

access-list acl_outside line 1 extended permit icmp any 192.168.17.0 255.255.255.0 echo
(hitcnt=0)

access-list acl_outside line 1 extended permit icmp any 192.168.17.0 255.255.255.0 time-
exceeded (hitcnt=0)

access-list acl_outside line 1 extended permit icmp any 192.168.17.0 255.255.255.0
unreachable (hitcnt=0)

access-list acl_outside line 2 extended permit udp any host 192.168.17.21 eq domain
(hitcnt=0)
access-list acl_outside line 3 extended permit tcp any host 192.168.17.22 object-group
mail-services
access-list acl_outside line 3 extended permit tcp any host 192.168.17.22 eq smtp
(hitcnt=0)
access-list acl_outside line 3 extended permit tcp any host 192.168.17.22 eq pop3
(hitcnt=0)
access-list acl_outside line 3 extended permit tcp any host 192.168.17.22 eq nntp
(hitcnt=0)
access-list acl_outside line 4 extended permit tcp object-group extranet-hosts object-
group extranet-targets object-group extranet-services
access-list acl_outside line 4 extended permit tcp host 172.22.10.41 host 192.168.17.110
eq sqlnet (hitcnt=0)
access-list acl_outside line 4 extended permit tcp host 172.22.10.41 host 192.168.17.110
eq ftp (hitcnt=0)
access-list acl_outside line 4 extended permit tcp host 172.22.10.41 host 192.168.17.114
eq sqlnet (hitcnt=0)
access-list acl_outside line 4 extended permit tcp host 172.22.10.41 host 192.168.17.114
eq ftp (hitcnt=0)
access-list acl_outside line 4 extended permit tcp host 172.22.10.53 host 192.168.17.110
eq sqlnet (hitcnt=0)
```

Section 6-3

```
access-list acl_outside line 4 extended permit tcp host 172.22.10.53 host 192.168.17.110
eq ftp (hitcnt=0)
access-list acl_outside line 4 extended permit tcp host 172.22.10.53 host 192.168.17.114
eq sqlnet (hitcnt=0)
access-list acl_outside line 4 extended permit tcp host 172.22.10.53 host 192.168.17.114
eq ftp (hitcnt=0)
Firewall#
```

Even though this access list was reported to have 15 elements (ACEs), notice what has happened with the line numbers. The line numbers follow the ACL in the running configuration, where the object groups have not been expanded. However, in this output, the line numbers do not increment as long as the ACEs are part of the same object-group expansion. This is shown by the shaded text, where "line 1" represents all of the ACEs from the object-group *allowed-icmp*.

The real beauty of object groups can be seen when you need to make changes to existing firewall rules. For example, suppose you have a host on the DMZ (10.1.1.1) that needs to communicate with another host on the inside (192.168.10.30). With an access list, you might configure these ACEs:

```
Firewall(config)# access-list acl_dmz extended permit tcp host 10.1.1.1 host
192.168.10.30 eq https
Firewall(config)# access-list acl_dmz extended permit tcp host 10.1.1.1 host
192.168.10.30 eq www
Firewall(config)# access-list acl_dmz extended permit tcp host 10.1.1.1 host
192.168.10.30 eq sqlnet
Firewall(config)# access-list acl_dmz extended permit tcp host 10.1.1.1 host
192.168.10.30 eq 5003
```

That seems straightforward enough, until you need to add a second DMZ host at a later date. You could replicate the four ACE command lines to permit traffic from the new DMZ server, as follows:

```
Firewall(config)# access-list acl_dmz extended permit tcp host 10.1.1.1 host
192.168.10.30 eq https
Firewall(config)# access-list acl_dmz extended permit tcp host 10.1.1.1 host
192.168.10.30 eq www
Firewall(config)# access-list acl_dmz extended permit tcp host 10.1.1.1 host
192.168.10.30 eq sqlnet
Firewall(config)# access-list acl_dmz extended permit tcp host 10.1.1.1 host
192.168.10.30 eq 5003
Firewall(config)# access-list acl_dmz extended permit tcp host 10.1.1.2 host
192.168.10.30 eq https
Firewall(config)# access-list acl_dmz extended permit tcp host 10.1.1.2 host
192.168.10.30 eq www
Firewall(config)# access-list acl_dmz extended permit tcp host 10.1.1.2 host
192.168.10.30 eq sqlnet
Firewall(config)# access-list acl_dmz extended permit tcp host 10.1.1.2 host
192.168.10.30 eq 5003
```

Replicating ACEs might become cumbersome if you continue to add even more DMZ hosts that need the same rules. Even worse, what if you begin adding hosts on the inside that need to receive the same types of traffic from the DMZ hosts?

Instead, you can use object groups to work smarter. Define one network object group for the DMZ hosts and another for the inside hosts:

```
Firewall(config)# object-group network dmz_hosts
Firewall(config-network)# network-object host 10.1.1.1
Firewall(config-network)# network-object host 10.1.1.2
Firewall(config-network)# exit
Firewall(config)# object-group network inside_hosts
Firewall(config-network)# network-object host 192.168.10.30
Firewall(config-network)# exit
Firewall(config)# access-list acl_dmz extended permit tcp object-group dmz_hosts object-group inside_hosts eq https
Firewall(config)# access-list acl_dmz extended permit tcp object-group dmz_hosts object-group inside_hosts eq www
Firewall(config)# access-list acl_dmz extended permit tcp object-group dmz_hosts object-group inside_hosts eq sqlnet
Firewall(config)# access-list acl_dmz extended permit tcp object-group dmz_hosts object-group inside_hosts eq 5003
```

Now when you need to add a new DMZ host, you simply make one addition to the *dmz_hosts* object group:

```
Firewall(config)# object-group network dmz_hosts
Firewall(config-network)# network-object host 10.1.1.3
Firewall(config-network)# exit
```

The firewall automatically expands the object group within the ACL, and the necessary rules are replicated with the new DMZ host address! You can easily add new addresses to the list of inside hosts as well.

You could also carry this idea one step further by creating a service object group that contains all of the TCP ports that are common to the groups of hosts. To do this, you could enter the following configuration commands:

```
Firewall(config)# object-group service dmz_inside tcp
Firewall(config-service)# port-object eq https
Firewall(config-service)# port-object eq www
Firewall(config-service)# port-object eq sqlnet
Firewall(config-service)# port-object eq 5003
Firewall(config-network)# exit
Firewall(config)# access-list acl_dmz extended permit tcp object-group dmz_hosts object-group inside_hosts object-group dmz_inside
```

The basic service object group must be referenced in the place of source or destination ports in the ACE.

Beginning with ASA 8.0, you have the advantage of defining an enhanced service object group that can contain any combination of protocol, source port, and destination port parameters. After you configure an enhanced service object group, you need reference it only once in the **access-list** command. The firewall takes care of expanding the object group into all of the appropriate parameter locations in the ACE.

This makes the **access-list** command syntax a little simpler:

```
Firewall(config)# access-list acl_id [line line-num] [extended] {permit | deny}
   object-group enh_service_obj_group
   {source_addr  source_mask | object-group network_obj_group}
   {destination_addr destination_mask | object-group network_obj_group}
   [log [[disable | default] | [level]]] [interval secs]]
   [time-range name] [inactive]
```

Notice that the enhanced service object group completely takes the place of the protocol, source port, and destination port parameters.

The following example shows the configuration of an enhanced service object group to identify the ESP protocol; ISAKMP (UDP destination port 500); UDP destination ports 10000 through 10001; TCP destination port 10000; ICMP echo, echo-reply, and time-exceeded types; and connections from TCP source port 5000 to destination port 6970. Then the object group is applied to access list **acl_outside** from any source address to destination host 10.10.10.10.

```
Firewall(config)# object-group service group1
Firewall(config-service)# service-object esp
Firewall(config-service)# service-object udp eq isakmp
Firewall(config-service)# service-object udp range 10000 10001
Firewall(config-service)# service-object tcp eq 10000
Firewall(config-service)# service-object icmp echo
Firewall(config-service)# service-object icmp echo-reply
Firewall(config-service)# service-object icmp time-exceeded
Firewall(config-service)# service-object tcp source 5000 6970
Firewall(config-service)# exit
Firewall(config)# access-list acl_outside extended permit object-group group1 any host
10.10.10.10
```

Because an enhanced service object group is referenced only once in an ACE, it might be confusing how it actually expands within the access list. You can see the final results with the **show access-list** command:

```
asa-a/admin# show access-list acl_outside
access-list acl_outside; 8 elements
access-list acl_outside line 1 extended permit object-group group1 any host 10.10.10.10
0x1a469c46
access-list acl_outside line 1 extended permit esp any host 10.10.10.10 (hitcnt=0)
0x6b6ae91e
access-list acl_outside line 1 extended permit udp any host 10.10.10.10 eq isakmp
(hitcnt=0) 0x2b45ae69
access-list acl_outside line 1 extended permit udp any host 10.10.10.10 range 10000 10001
(hitcnt=0) 0x25eb4d7a
access-list acl_outside line 1 extended permit tcp any host 10.10.10.10 eq 10000
(hitcnt=0) 0x1dda7d99
access-list acl_outside line 1 extended permit icmp any host 10.10.10.10 echo (hitcnt=0)
0xa2294c03
access-list acl_outside line 1 extended permit icmp any host 10.10.10.10 echo-reply
(hitcnt=0) 0xb1c482a3
access-list acl_outside line 1 extended permit icmp any host 10.10.10.10 time-exceeded
(hitcnt=0) 0xd8647b13
```

```
access-list acl_outside line 1 extended permit tcp any eq 5000 host 10.10.10.10 eq 6970
(hitcnt=0) 0xcc3269c
asa-a/admin#
```

Logging ACE Activity

By default, no syslog messages are generated for **permit** ACEs, but each traffic flow that matches a **deny** ACE triggers a syslog 106023 message (default severity level 4, warnings). If you want to disable syslog completely for an individual ACE, add the **log disable** keywords. For example, by adding **log disable** to the following command, the firewall will not generate a syslog message:

```
Firewall(config)# access-list acl_outside deny icmp any any log disable
```

TIP   You can also change the severity level of the 106023 message, if the default level 4 is not appropriate. Use the following command:

```
Firewall(config)# logging message 106023 level level
```

The new *level* is one of the following keywords or numbers: **emergencies (0)**, **alerts (1)**, **critical (2)**, **errors (3)**, **warnings (4)**, **notifications (5)**, **informational (6)**, or **debugging (7)**.

You can also enable syslog activity for both permit and deny conditions. When the **log** keyword is added to an **access-list** command, it will enable syslog 106100 messages (default severity 6, informational) for each connection that is permitted or denied by the ACE. Subsequent flows or connections cause the ACE hit count to be incremented.

After a time interval, another syslog 106100 message is generated for the connection, showing the updated hit count. You can use the **interval** keyword to alter this syslog hold interval to *secs* (1 to 600 seconds, default 300).

You can also change the syslog severity level for message 106100 by adding the *level* value (0 to 7, default 6 or "informational").

TIP   Syslog usage on a Cisco firewall is covered in more detail in Chapter 10.

If the ACE with the **log** keyword is denying packets, the firewall caches the denied flow so that it can be tracked. Because of this, there must be a limit to the number of cached denied flows to keep the firewall's memory from becoming exhausted.

After the limit is reached, syslog message 106101 is generated. You can limit the number of cached denied flows with the following command:

```
Firewall(config)# access-list deny-flow-max n
```

This sets the maximum number of flows denied by an ACE to *n* flows. The maximum limit is dependent upon the amount of firewall RAM: 4096 flows (more than 64 MB RAM), 1024 flows (16 MB to 64 MB RAM), or 256 flows (less than 16 MB RAM). On a firewall running PIX 7.0 or later, you can use the **access-list deny-flow-max ?** command to display the maximum limit value for that platform.

You can also set the cache limit syslog interval with the following command:

```
Firewall(config)# access-list alert-interval secs
```

Syslog message 106101 is generated each time the cache limit is reached, but only at an interval of *secs* (1 to 3600 seconds, default 300).

Monitoring Access Lists

You can review an access list definition by displaying the firewall configuration with this EXEC command:

```
Firewall# show running-config
```

or

```
Firewall# write term
```

To jump right to the access-list in the configuration, you can use this variation:

```
Firewall# show running-config | begin access-list [acl_id]
```

Or to display only the lines of the access-list configuration and nothing else, you can use a further variation:

```
Firewall# show running-config | include access-list [acl_id]
```

Beginning with ASA 7.0, you can display an access-list configuration with this command:

```
Firewall# show running-config access-list [acl_id]
```

Object groups and access list contents are shown exactly as they were configured. In fact, only the object group references are shown in the ACL configuration; the actual object group definitions are shown in a different point in the configuration. This makes it difficult to review a large access list because you have to refer back and forth between the ACL and any object groups.

After an access list has been configured and applied to an interface, you can monitor its use. Use this EXEC command to see a breakdown of ACL contents and activity counters:

```
Firewall# show access-list [acl_id]
```

Each line of the ACL is shown, along with a hit counter indicating how many connections or flows (or packets for ICMP) have been matched by that line. This is shown as "(hitcnt=n)" at the end of each ACE. For example, an access list configured to permit inbound HTTP connections to several web servers is shown to have the following contents and hit counters:

```
Firewall# show access-list acl_outside
access-list acl_outside line 1 permit tcp any host 192.168.3.16 eq www (hitcnt=97)
access-list acl_outside line 2 permit tcp any host 192.168.3.19 eq www (hitcnt=69513)
access-list acl_outside line 3 permit tcp any host 192.168.3.23 eq www (hitcnt=12)
access-list acl_outside line 4 permit tcp any host 192.168.3.231 eq www (hitcnt=82)
access-list acl_outside line 5 permit tcp any host 192.168.3.242 eq www (hitcnt=27)
```

From this information, it is clear that host 192.168.3.19 (line 2) is receiving the greatest volume of inbound HTTP connections.

TIP   Beginning with ASA 7.3(1) and FWSM 3.1, each line of the **show access-list** command output ends with a unique string of hex numbers. For example, see how the following line ends with *0xa2294c03*:

```
access-list acl_outside line 5 extended permit tcp any host 192.168.3.242 eq
www (hitcnt=27) 0xa2294c03
```

The hex string listed is the same string that is generated in syslog messages 106023 (deny packet by ACL, default warnings level) and 106100 (deny/permit packet by ACL, default informational level). This does not mean much for human readers, but it gives Adaptive Security Device Manager (ASDM) an easy way to reference syslog messages it collects with the actual ACL lines that generated the messages.

Now suppose that an object group has been configured to list the web servers with the following commands:

```
Firewall(config)# object-group network web-servers
Firewall(config-network)# network-object host 192.168.3.16
Firewall(config-network)# network-object host 192.168.3.19
Firewall(config-network)# network-object host 192.168.3.23
Firewall(config-network)# network-object host 192.168.3.231
Firewall(config-network)# network-object host 192.168.3.242
Firewall(config-network)# exit
Firewall(config)# access-list acl_outside permit tcp any object-group web-servers eq www
```

Using the **show access-list** command also expands any object groups that are referenced in an ACL. This allows you to see the actual ACEs that the firewall is evaluating. In this example, the ACL would be expanded as follows:

```
Firewall# show access-list acl_outside
access-list acl_outside line 1 permit tcp any object-group web-servers eq www
access-list acl_outside line 1 permit tcp any host 192.168.3.16 eq www (hitcnt=97)
access-list acl_outside line 1 permit tcp any host 192.168.3.19 eq www (hitcnt=69513)
access-list acl_outside line 1 permit tcp any host 192.168.3.23 eq www (hitcnt=12)
access-list acl_outside line 1 permit tcp any host 192.168.3.231 eq www (hitcnt=82)
access-list acl_outside line 1 permit tcp any host 192.168.3.242 eq www (hitcnt=27)
```

Section 6-4

Notice that each line of the output is shown as line 1 of the ACL. Although the object group is expanded and evaluated as sequential ACEs, it appears as the one ACE that referenced it.

TIP   You can reset the hit counters of an ACL by using this command:

```
Firewall# clear access-list acl_id counters
```

In releases prior to ASA 7.0, be careful when you use this command—if you omit the **counters** keyword, the entire ACL named *acl_id* is removed from the firewall configuration! ASA 7.0 and later, as well as all releases of FWSM, do not allow this command to be executed unless the **counters** keyword is included, so you are in no danger of deleting any configuration.

6-4: Shunning Traffic

Sometimes it might be possible for malicious hosts to open connections into the protected network. This could occur if the inbound access list policies are not configured correctly or tightly. As soon as these connections are noticed (after they are built), you might want to react by blocking connections coming from the malicious source address.

To do this, you could edit the access list each time the source of an attack is discovered. This would deny any future connections; xlate entries would also need to be cleared to drop existing connections. This would also quickly become an administrative burden.

A more efficient alternative is the **shun** command. When a shun is activated, all current connections from a malicious host can be dropped and all future connections blocked.

Connections are shunned regardless of the firewall interface being traversed. The firewall examines the connection table and the connection building process to identify and shun the specified connections.

Shuns can be configured through the firewall command-line interface (CLI) or through an automatic action from a Cisco Intrusion Protection System or an integrated feature such as Threat Detection. After shuns are configured, they remain in place until they are removed.

Shuns are dynamic in nature, and are *not* stored as a part of the firewall configuration. If the firewall loses power or reloads, any active shuns are lost. As well, shuns are *not* maintained in a failover firewall pair. If the units failover, any active shuns are lost.

You can use the following steps to configure a shun:

1. Manually shun connections:

ASA, FWSM	`Firewall# shun src_ip [dst_ip sport dport [protocol]] [vlan_id]`
PIX 6.3	`Firewall# shun src_ip [dst_ip sport dport [protocol]]`

You can shun any new connections (any IP protocol) passing through the firewall originating from source address *src_ip*. This is most useful to stop an attack that is in progress from the source address to many destinations. Any existing connections stay up, however. Those must idle out of the xlate and conn tables normally, or you can clear any related xlate entries to manually kill the connections.

For more granular shunning, you can also identify the destination address *dst_ip*, the source and destination ports *sport* and *dport*, and the *protocol*. You can only define one shun entry per source and destination address pair. When a shun is defined, all existing and future connections are blocked until the shun is later removed.

2. Display active shuns:

```
Firewall# show shun [src_ip]
```

All active shuns are listed. If a specific source address *src_ip* is given, only shuns involving that address are shown.

As an example, the following output displays the four shuns that are currently active. The source interface is automatically determined and shown in parentheses.

```
Firewall# show shun
shun (outside) 172.21.104.93 0.0.0.0 0 0
shun (outside) 172.21.196.50 0.0.0.0 0 0
shun (inside) 192.168.198.24 0.0.0.0 0 0 0
shun (outside) 10.10.1.1 172.21.4.19 0 80 6
Firewall#
```

Notice in the shaded output line that an inside host has been the target of a shun. Shuns can be used on any host located on any interface. In this case, the inside host was playing the role of the malicious user, attacking hosts on the outside of the firewall.

You can monitor the activity of each active shun with the **show shun statistics** command. Each of the firewall interfaces are shown, along with the current shun activity. The firewall looks at its routing information to determine the interfaces where shun source addresses can be found. These interfaces are shown as "ON". A cumulative count of shunned connections is also shown.

Each configured shun is listed with its source address, a cumulative count of shunned connections, and the total elapsed time since the shun was enabled.

For example, a firewall is configured with a long list of shun commands. Notice that the outside interface, where malicious hosts on the public Internet were discovered, has had 17,184,951 shunned connections. The inside interface has had even more! In this case, a number of inside hosts have been discovered to be compromised and participating in malicious activity toward the outside network. Until these hosts can be cleaned, they have been "quarantined" through the use of firewall shuns.

```
Firewall# show shun statistics
stateful=OFF, cnt=0
dmz2=OFF, cnt=0
outside=ON, cnt=17184951
```

```
inside=ON, cnt=255823449
```

```
Shun 172.21.96.89 cnt=32502918, time=(112:04:34)
Shun 172.21.61.83 cnt=0, time=(112:04:32)
Shun 172.21.24.79 cnt=0, time=(112:04:35)
Shun 172.21.108.68 cnt=0, time=(112:04:35)
Shun 192.168.93.16 cnt=0, time=(112:04:34)
Shun 172.21.184.106 cnt=21277328, time=(112:04:33)
Shun 192.168.97.9 cnt=0, time=(112:04:34)
Shun 172.21.184.107 cnt=21264263, time=(112:04:33)
Shun 192.168.228.11 cnt=0, time=(243:35:21)
Shun 192.168.228.12 cnt=0, time=(243:35:18)
Shun 192.168.228.13 cnt=0, time=(243:35:16)
Shun 172.21.184.108 cnt=21311395, time=(112:04:33)
Shun 192.168.228.14 cnt=0, time=(243:35:12)
Shun 192.168.228.15 cnt=0, time=(243:35:10)
Shun 172.21.72.99 cnt=334699, time=(112:04:34)
[output omitted]
```

TIP To avoid sifting through long lists of shun statistics to find a single source address, you can filter the output through the **include** or **grep** commands. In this example, only the shun for source address 172.21.72.99 is needed. It is shown to have blocked 334,699 packets, and has been active for 112 hours, 13 minutes, and 19 seconds:

```
Firewall# show shun statistics | include 172.21.72.99
Shun 172.21.72.99 cnt=334699, time=(112:13:19)
Firewall#
```

You can remove an existing shun for a specific source address with the following global configuration command:

```
Firewall(config)# no shun src_ip
```

Shun Example

A host at 172.21.4.8 is discovered to be involved in malicious activity. (In this example, only a Telnet connection is shown for simplicity.) A shun will be configured on the firewall to stop any current or future connections involving that host.

First, look at an active connection involving 172.21.4.8:

```
Firewall# show conn
1 in use, 3 most used
TCP out 172.21.4.8:4334 in 192.168.199.100:23 idle 0:00:04 Bytes 138 flags UIOB
Firewall#
```

It does have at least one active connection, so a shun is put into place:

```
Firewall# shun 172.21.4.8
```

```
Shun 172.21.4.8 successful
Firewall# show conn
1 in use, 3 most used
TCP out 172.21.4.8:4334 in 192.168.199.100:23 idle 0:04:25 Bytes 138 flags UIOB
Firewall#
```

Indeed, the current connection has become unresponsive from 172.21.4.8 (as shown by the increasing idle time), and it is also unable to start new sessions through the firewall. But why is the connection still shown in the firewall's connection table?

First, look at the buffered syslog information on the firewall. Hopefully it will show something interesting:

```
Firewall# show logging
Syslog logging: enabled
    Facility: 20
    Timestamp logging: enabled
    Standby logging: disabled
    Console logging: disabled
    Monitor logging: disabled
    Buffer logging: level informational, 3523423 messages logged
    Trap logging: level informational, 3523423 messages logged
        Logging to outside 192.168.199.10 (EMBLEM format)
    History logging: disabled
    Device ID: hostname "Firewall"
401002: Shun added: 172.21.4.8 0.0.0.0 0 0
111008: User 'enable_15' executed the 'shun 172.21.4.8' command.
401004: Shunned packet: 172.21.4.8 ==> 169.54.89.249 on interface outside
401004: Shunned packet: 172.21.4.8 ==> 169.54.89.249 on interface outside
401004: Shunned packet: 172.21.4.8 ==> 169.54.89.249 on interface outside
401004: Shunned packet: 172.21.4.8 ==> 169.54.89.249 on interface outside
```

The syslog record shows that the shun was put into place and that it is actively shunning new packets. Why didn't the active connection drop immediately? The answer is this: After the shun became active, the firewall began dropping packets involving 172.21.4.8. The TCP connection shown in the connection table was already established, after a three-way handshake. As soon as packets started being dropped, the TCP connection became isolated; each host in the connection was no longer able to hear from the other end.

As a result, the TCP connection becomes a "half-open" or "half-closed" connection until it either times out or both endpoints handshake with a FIN flag. The firewall will keep the shunned connection in its table until its own half-closed timer expires. This can be seen by verifying the timer value and the shun statistics:

```
Firewall# show conn
1 in use, 3 most used
TCP out 172.21.4.8:4334 in 192.168.199.100:23 idle 0:06:48 Bytes 138 flags UIOB
pix-f# sh timeout
timeout xlate 3:00:00
timeout conn 1:00:00 half-closed 0:10:00 udp 0:02:00 rpc 0:10:00 h225 1:00:00
timeout h323 0:05:00 mgcp 0:05:00 sip 0:30:00 sip_media 0:02:00
timeout uauth 0:05:00 absolute
```

Section 6-4

```
Firewall# show shun statistics
outside=ON, cnt=13
inside=ON, cnt=0
dmz=OFF, cnt=0

Shun 10.1.1.1 cnt=0, time=(121:03:07)
Shun 192.168.200.199 cnt=0, time=(119:52:22)
Shun 172.21.4.8 cnt=13, time=(0:03:58)
Firewall#
```

Indeed, the half-closed timer is 10 minutes and the active connection has only been shunned for 3 minutes and 58 seconds. As soon as 10 minutes have elapsed, the TCP connection is deleted from the firewall's table.

Refer to the following sections for information about these topics:

- **7-1: Filtering Content**—Covers third-party web content-filtering applications you can use to control outbound access through a firewall.

- **7-2: Defining Security Policies in a Modular Policy Framework**—Explains the modular approach to configuring and enforcing security policies. Traffic can be matched with one type of policy module and acted on within another policy module. The whole hierarchy of policies is then applied to firewall interfaces and traffic inspection.

- **7-3: Application Inspection**—Provides an overview of the mechanisms a Cisco firewall uses to inspect specific application traffic. Some applications embed information about their connections within normal UDP or TCP traffic, requiring additional inspection by the firewall.

CHAPTER 7

Inspecting Traffic

A firewall maintains the state of connections passing through it to provide effective security. Connection state involves parameters such as address translation, connection direction and flow, and limits on the connection itself. In addition, a firewall must be able to inspect various protocols as they pass through, so that the protocols themselves meet criteria defined in the security policies.

This chapter covers the tools and features you can use to gain a more thorough inspection of traffic content. Your firewall can filter traffic based on its content, inspect traffic based on a hierarchical policy definition, and inspect many application layer protocols.

7-1: Filtering Content

A firewall normally allows outbound HTTP or HTTPS connections to any URL, provided that the outbound access list permits the connection. An audit trail of URL activity is available only through the firewall Syslog records, using Syslog message 304001 at the default severity level, 5 (notifications).

Cisco firewalls can use third-party web content-filtering applications to enforce URL policies. These content filters run on a local server but download periodic updates of web content databases. Web content is categorized, and content rules can be applied to corporate users or groups of users.

When a user sends a URL request, the firewall relays the request to the content-filtering server. If the server determines that the user is allowed to view the URL and its content, the firewall permits the connection to proceed.

If the content-filtering server denies the URL request, the firewall redirects the user's browser to a "block" page, indicating that the server blocked or denied the request.

The content-filtering server can apply its policies on a per-user basis if necessary. It obtains the user's credentials (username, IP address, destination URL, and address) directly from the user's host PC. This also provides an accounting log of user activity.

The following commercial content-filtering applications are compatible with Cisco firewalls:

- N2H2 (http://www.n2h2.com)
- Websense (http://www.websense.com)

Configuring Content Filters

You can use the following steps to configure content filtering on a Cisco firewall. The command syntax is basically the same across the FWSM, PIX, and ASA platforms, so only a single syntax form is shown for each command.

TIP   Content filtering is triggered by the HTTP inspection engine, which must be enabled before any content servers can be contacted. If you are about to configure content filtering, make sure you have the **fixup protocol http** (PIX 6.x) or **inspect http** (ASA and FWSM) command in the running configuration.

Likewise, if this command is disabled, Websense and N2H2 content filtering is disabled too.

---

1. Identify the filter servers:

   ```
   Firewall(config)# url-server [(if_name)] vendor n2h2 host local_ip
     [port number] [timeout seconds] [protocol {tcp | udp}]
   ```

   or

   ```
   Firewall(config)# url-server [(if_name)] vendor websense host local_ip
     [timeout seconds] [protocol {tcp | udp} version]
   ```

   The filtering server is located on the firewall interface named (*if_name*) (the parentheses must be included) at the IP address *local_ip*. By default, the inside interface is assumed. For security best practice, the server should not be located on the outside or a public interface.

   By default, N2H2 uses TCP/UDP port 4005 to filter information exchanges. You can specify a nondefault port number with the **port** keyword.

   You can repeat this command to define up to 16 servers using the same filtering software. The firewall waits until a timeout period of *seconds* expires (the default is 5 seconds) if a filtering server does not respond. In that case, the same request is sent to the next server configured.

   TCP connections are used by default for both N2H2 and Websense servers. You can use either **tcp** or **udp**, depending on your requirements. Websense also allows a software *version* to be specified: **1** (using TCP or UDP) or **4** (using UDP only).

   In ASA and FWSM, you can add **connections** *num_conns* after the **tcp** keyword. This limits the number of simultaneous TCP connections the firewall can open to the content filter server to *num_conns* (1 to 100; the default is 5).

2. Define a filtering policy:

   ```
   Firewall(config)# filter url [http | port[-port]] local_ip local_mask
     foreign_ip foreign_mask [allow] [proxy-block] [longurl-truncate |
     longurl-deny] [cgi-truncate]
   ```

You can define one or more broad filtering policies with this command and then make specific exceptions in the next step. Web traffic is defined as **http** (port 80), *port* (a single port number), or *port-port*, a range of ports.

You can provide the local (source) and foreign (destination) IP addresses and subnet masks. When web clients using local addresses send HTTP requests to web servers with foreign addresses, those requests are subject to filtering. In most cases, you can define the policy to use any local address and any foreign address. To do this, specify the local and foreign values as 0s (0 0 0 0).

For example, you could use the following command to filter the content of HTTP connections from inside hosts on the 192.168.100.0/24 subnet destined for any outside address. Here, the "any" destination address is given as **0 0**:

```
Firewall(config)# filter url http 192.168.100.0 255.255.255.0 0 0
```

By default, if none of the filtering servers is available, the HTTP requests are dropped. This assumes that the filtering policies must be strictly enforced, requiring filtering servers to make decisions at all times. If this is too restrictive for your environment, you can add the **allow** keyword so that HTTP requests are allowed by the firewall if no filtering servers respond.

To prevent web clients from using an HTTP proxy server to relay HTTP requests, add the **proxy-block** keyword.

You can also define how the firewall reacts when very long URLs (longer than the URL buffer defined in Step 7) are used in HTTP requests. The **longurl-truncate** keyword sends only the source address or host name to the filtering server. The **longurl-deny** keyword causes the firewall to reject the HTTP request directly, without consulting the filtering server. In the case of CGI scripts, the **cgi-truncate** keyword causes CGI scripts to be sent to the filtering server as regular URLs. In other words, the CGI portion of the original URL is removed from the filtering server's decision process.

3. (Websense only) Define a filtering policy for HTTPS:

```
Firewall(config)# filter https dest-port local_ip local_mask foreign_ip
  foreign_mask [allow]
```

You can also allow HTTPS traffic to be filtered by a Websense server. Identify the HTTPS port as *dest-port* (usually port 443). Connections that are subject to filtering have clients using local (source) addresses defined by *local_ip* and *local_mask* and web servers using foreign (destination) addresses defined by *foreign_ip* and *foreign_mask*.

Add the **allow** keyword if you want the firewall to go ahead and allow connections when all the Websense servers are unresponsive. Otherwise, HTTPS connections are dropped if they are not explicitly allowed by a filtering server.

4. (Websense only) Define a filtering policy for FTP:

```
Firewall(config)# filter ftp dest-port local_ip local_mask foreign_ip
  foreign_mask [allow] [interact-block]
```

If you have a Websense server, you can filter FTP connections based on **GET** commands. The FTP port is given as *dest-port* (usually port 21).

Add the **allow** keyword if you want the firewall to allow FTP connections when all the Websense servers are unresponsive.

The **interact-block** keyword causes connections coming from interactive FTP clients to be rejected. In an interactive FTP client, a user can initiate the connection and then change directories at will. When files are requested from the FTP server, the full path name is not sent in the request. The filenames are relative to the current directory path, so the filtering server cannot correctly determine if the user is requesting something that should be denied.

For example, you could use the following command to require Websense approval for all FTP **GET** commands initiated through the firewall. Interactive FTP clients are blocked:

```
Firewall(config)# filter ftp 21 0 0 0 0 allow interact-block
```

5. Make exceptions to the filtering policy:

```
Firewall(config)# filter {url | https | ftp} except local_ip local_mask
  foreign_ip foreign_mask
```

You might have some web clients, users, or automated processes that need to send different types of requests without a filtering server's inspection or intervention. You can define exceptions to the overall filtering policy by giving the protocol (**url**, **https**, or **ftp**), as well as the local (source) and foreign (destination) addresses and subnet masks.

Clients using a matching local address are allowed to complete a transaction with a server using a matching foreign address. You can use 0 to indicate an "any" or wildcard-matching condition for any of the address and mask values.

For example, inside host 10.10.1.100 and hosts on the entire 10.10.2.0/24 subnet should be exempt from HTTP (URL) filtering. Inside host 10.10.3.14 also should be exempt from FTP filtering. You could use the following commands to accomplish this:

```
Firewall(config)# filter url except 10.10.1.100 255.255.255.255 0 0
Firewall(config)# filter url except 10.10.2.0 255.255.255.0 0 0
Firewall(config)# filter ftp except 10.10.3.14 255.255.255.255 0 0
```

6. (Optional) Use an HTTP response buffer to return web content faster:

```
Firewall(config)# url-block block block_buffer_limit
```

When a web client requests web content from a foreign site, the firewall relays the request toward the website and sends a request to the filtering server—all in parallel. By default, if the web server responds before the filtering server, the content is dropped at the firewall. If the filtering server responds first with its permission data, the web content is allowed through when it arrives.

You can use an HTTP response buffer in the firewall to store web content until the filtering server has time to respond. As soon as the server approves the URL for the web client, the buffered contents are read and relayed to the client.

The HTTP response buffer can be enabled to store up to *block_buffer_limit* (0 to 128) 1550-byte blocks in memory.

7. (Optional; Websense only) Adjust the maximum acceptable URL length.

   a. Buffer URLs before sending Websense requests:

   Firewall(config)# **url-block url-mempool** *memory_pool_size*

   By default, a firewall accepts URLs that are up to 1159 bytes long before sending a request to either Websense or N2H2. You can adjust the URL buffer so that several large URLs can be gathered and sent to a Websense server. The URL buffer limit can be set to *memory_pool_size* (2 to 10240 kilobytes).

   b. Set the maximum acceptable URL length:

   Firewall(config)# **url-block url-size** *long_url_size*

   To allow URLs longer than 1159 bytes to be sent to a Websense server, set the URL length to *long_url_size* (2, 3, or 4 kilobytes). You need to adjust this limit only if you have cases in which very long URLs (greater than 1159 bytes) are being rejected.

8. (Optional) Use a cache to store filtering permissions:

   Firewall(config)# **url-cache {dst | src_dst}** *kbytes*

   As a firewall sends requests to a filtering server, it can also cache the results that are returned. For subsequent requests for the same web client and target website, the firewall can quickly retrieve the cached permissions rather than waiting for the filtering server to respond again.

   By default, the URL cache is disabled. The firewall sends each request to the filtering server and waits for each response before passing the return web content.

   You can use the **dst** keyword to cache permission results based on the URL destination address only. If every web client behind the firewall shares the same policy on the filtering server, there is no need to cache the source information too. If web clients have different policies on the filtering server, you should use the **src_dst** keyword to gather source and destination information in the cache.

   You can also set the size of the URL cache to *kbytes* (1 to 128 kilobytes).

TIP   During normal requests to the filtering server, the server keeps a record of user activity in its accounting logs. When a URL cache is used (except with Websense version 1), these logs can still be collected, because the firewall still sends each request to the server, even though it might have a matching entry in its cache. The filtering requests and cache lookups happen in parallel so that a cache hit produces a quick permission result. In this case, any reply from the server is simply dropped. If an entry is not in the cache, no time is wasted, because the filtering server will have already sent a reply.

You can monitor the status of the URL cache with the **show url-cache statistics** command. If the cache is performing efficiently, you should see a large percentage of hits in relation to the number of lookups.

For example, the following output shows that 432 URL lookups occurred; 396 of those resulted in a cache hit, where the result was already in the cache. This represents a high hit percentage, indicating that the cache is doing its job.

```
Firewall# show url-cache statistics
URL Filter Cache Stats
----------------------
    Size :      128KB
 Entries :      219
  In Use :      105
 Lookups :      432
    Hits :      396
Firewall#
```

9. (Optional) Filter ActiveX content:

```
Firewall(config)# filter activex {port[-port] | except}local_ip local_mask
  foreign_ip foreign_mask
```

ActiveX objects that are found on connections using destination port number *port* (or a range of ports *port-port*) are subject to being blocked by the firewall. The connections must be initiated by clients using matching local (source) addresses toward servers using matching foreign (destination) addresses. You can substitute 0s as a wildcard "any" for any address or mask field.

The firewall blocks ActiveX objects by looking for the HTML <object> and </object> tags. The tags are commented out before the content is forwarded to the client. The client cannot interpret the result as a valid ActiveX object. Nested objects are also blocked, because the first-level objects are commented out.

You can also use the **except** keyword to define address pairs where ActiveX filtering should not be performed.

10. (Optional) Filter Java content:

```
Firewall(config)# filter java {port[-port] | except} local_ip mask
  foreign_ip mask
```

Java applets that are found on connections using destination port number *port* (or a range of ports *port-port*) are subject to being blocked by the firewall. The connections must be initiated by clients using matching local (source) addresses toward servers using matching foreign (destination) addresses. You can substitute 0s as a wildcard "any" for any address or mask field.

The firewall blocks Java objects by looking for the HTML <applet> and </applet> tags. The tags are commented out before the content is forwarded to the client.

You can also use the **except** keyword to define address pairs where Java filtering should not be performed.

TIP You can monitor the performance of the URL buffer with the **show url-block block stats** command, as in the following example:

```
Firewall# show url-block block stats
URL Pending Packet Buffer Stats with max block  0
-----------------------------------------------------
Cumulative number of packets held:              0
Maximum number of packets held (per URL):       0
Current number of packets held (global):        0
Packets dropped due to
        exceeding url-block buffer limit:       0
        HTTP server retransmission:             0
Number of packets released back to client:      0
Firewall#
```

If you are using content-filtering servers, you can monitor their activity with the **show url-server stats** (PIX 6.3) or **show url-server statistics** (ASA and FWSM) command. In the following example, two Websense servers are used. A total of 447,869 URL requests have been sent to the servers, 394,410 of those were permitted, and 53,459 of them were denied because of the local content policies configured on the servers. Notice that one server is up, but the other is unresponsive.

```
Firewall# show url-server stats
URL Server Statistics:
----------------------
Vendor                          websense
URLs total/allowed/denied       447869/394410/53459
URL Server Status:
------------------
172.16.10.50            UP
172.16.10.55            DOWN
```

You can also get an idea about the rate at which the firewall is sending URL requests to the content-filtering servers. Use the **show perfmon** command, and look for the **URL Access** row to see how many new URLs are being requested per second.
The **URL Server Req** row shows the rate at which the requests are being sent to the content-filtering servers.

```
Firewall# show perfmon
PERFMON STATS:     Current      Average
Xlates             39/s         0/s
Connections        110/s        1/s
TCP Conns          80/s         0/s
UDP Conns          29/s         0/s
URL Access         57/s         0/s
URL Server Req     50/s         0/s
TCP Fixup          5033/s       0/s
TCPIntercept       0/s          0/s
HTTP Fixup         2293/s       0/s
FTP Fixup          4/s          0/s
AAA Authen         0/s          0/s
```

```
AAA Author            0/s          0/s
AAA Account           0/s          0/s
pix#
```

Content-Filtering Examples

A corporation has two Websense servers located on the firewall's DMZ interface at 192.168.199.10 and 192.168.199.11. The firewall intercepts every HTTP request and relays them to the Websense servers. If neither server responds within the default 5-second period (for each server), the firewall allows the request.

The only exceptions to this policy are with all hosts on the 192.168.4.0/24 subnet, which are allowed to request any URL with no Websense intervention. Inside host 192.168.7.33 is allowed to request any URL as well. Inside host 192.168.7.40 is allowed to request URLs from outside server 172.24.1.10 without Websense intervention. If the inside host requests URLs from any other address, Websense is consulted.

All HTTPS and FTP requests are subject to the local Websense server policies.

To improve filtering server response, 128 blocks of memory are dedicated to buffering web content that arrives before the filtering server can respond. A cache is also configured so that repeated URL requests can be serviced immediately without waiting for further filtering server replies. This cache uses 128 KB of memory and is based on the source and destination address combinations.

The configuration for this example is as follows:

```
Firewall(config)# url-server (dmz) vendor websense host 192.168.199.10 protocol TCP
version 4
Firewall(config)# url-server (dmz) vendor websense host 192.168.199.11 protocol TCP
version 4
Firewall(config)# filter url http 0 0 0 0 allow proxy-block
Firewall(config)# filter url except 192.168.4.0 255.255.255.0 0 0
Firewall(config)# filter url except 192.168.7.33 255.255.255.255 0 0
Firewall(config)# filter url except 192.168.7.40 255.255.255.255 172.24.1.10
255.255.255.255
Firewall(config)# filter https 443 0 0 0 0 allow
Firewall(config)# filter ftp 21 0 0 0 0 allow
Firewall(config)# url-block block 128
Firewall(config)# url-cache src_dst 128
```

Using a Web Cache for Better HTTP Performance

Beginning with ASA 7.2(1), an ASA platform can redirect inbound HTTP connections to an external web cache server if the web page has been accessed before. The Web Cache Communication Protocol version 2 (WCCPv2) is used to identify a request for a previously viewed web page and to redirect the client to the web cache server.

If a connection is redirected to the cache server, it bypasses some of the normal inspection processes such as URL filtering, TCP intercept, Intrusion Prevention System (IPS), and so on.

The client and the web cache server must be located on the same firewall interface for the WCCP redirect feature to work. As soon as the firewall redirects the client from the requested destination to the web cache server, the client can then communicate with the web cache server directly.

You can use the following steps to configure WCCP redirect:

1. Enable WCCP:

```
Firewall(config)# wccp {web-cache | service_number} [redirect-list access-list]
[group-list access-list] [password password]
```

WCCP can participate in the web cache service or in service group number *service_number* (0 to 255). You can repeat this command to identify more than one service number. To control the traffic that is redirected to the service group, configure an access list that permits traffic to be redirected. Then apply the access list here with the **redirect-list** keyword.

You can limit the web caches that can participate in the service group with the **group-list** keyword. The access list should permit cache IP addresses that are allowed to participate.

If your service group uses MD5 authentication, you can use the **password** keyword to define a password string of up to seven characters.

2. Enable WCCP redirection on an interface:

```
Firewall(config)# wccp interface interface_name service redirect in
```

7-2: Defining Security Policies in a Modular Policy Framework

Traditionally, Cisco firewalls have supported security policies that are applied to *all* traffic passing through them. Although that does offer a common level of security to all the protected networks and hosts, it does not offer a way to fine-tune or vary the policies according to differing requirements.

Beginning with ASA 7.0(1) and FWSM 3.1(1), a Cisco firewall can be configured to provide security policies that are tailored for various traffic types, quality of service (QoS), or inspection requirements. This is known as the *modular policy framework* (MPF).

With the MPF feature, you can define policies to identify a specific set of traffic and take any of the following actions on it:

- **Apply application inspection engines**—You can tailor the stateful inspection process that is performed on a very specific type of traffic. Different sets of traffic can be inspected differently.

- **Set connection limits**—The firewall can control the volume of UDP and TCP connections that are initiated for matched traffic.

- **Adjust TCP parameters**—Values carried in the TCP header can be inspected, changed, or normalized in very specific ways. This can be done differently for each set of traffic identified.

- **Limit management traffic**—Connections that terminate on the firewall itself can be limited, just like other types of connections that pass through the firewall. Configuring limits on management traffic can help prevent unnecessary strain on the firewall CPU.

- **Send traffic to a Security Services Module (SSM)**—The ASA platform can divert specific traffic to an embedded Advanced Inspection and Prevention (AIP) module or an embedded Content Security and Control (CSC) module.

- **Limit the bandwidth used**—You can tailor traffic policers to limit the bandwidth used by predefined sets of traffic. For example, mission-critical applications might be allowed to use any available bandwidth, whereas peer-to-peer file-sharing applications are limited to a small portion of interface bandwidth.

- **Provide priority handling**—Specific types of traffic can be given priority over other types as packets are sent out a firewall interface. This allows time-critical applications to receive premium service as those packets are inspected and passed through the firewall.

As shown in Figure 7-1, you can configure security policies in a modular fashion. Traffic is classified according to an arbitrary type, and a policy can take some arbitrary action on it. The policy is actually carried out on a firewall interface or globally on all interfaces. This whole process is configured in scalable pieces, according to the following model:

- **Class map**—A template that uses a **match** command to classify or identify types of traffic.

- **Policy map**—A list of policies, each referencing a class map to match or identify traffic and an action to take on that traffic.

- **Service policy**—A policy map is applied to one or all firewall interfaces, defining an entire set of match/action policies.

The Modular Policy Framework is a bit of a double-edged sword. On one hand, it is a very versatile means of defining robust security policies. On the other hand, it is so versatile that it can be confusing to configure.

As you begin to configure your security policies, you should outline the structure of the policy map as a list of the individual policies. Each policy needs a class map to identify the traffic and an action to perform on the traffic.

In a sense, you have to work backward first, because you need to configure class maps to identify traffic before the policy map can reference those class maps.

Classifying Layers 3 and 4 Traffic

As traffic moves through the firewall, it can be identified or classified according to the matching conditions defined in a class map. You can configure multiple class maps to identify several different classes of traffic, if needed. Then a different policy can be applied to each traffic class.

The following sections discuss how you can configure a class map for identifying a specific type of traffic according to parameters found in Layers 3 and 4, or the IP and UDP or TCP packet headers, respectively.

Figure 7-1   *The Modular Policy Framework for Applying Security Policies*

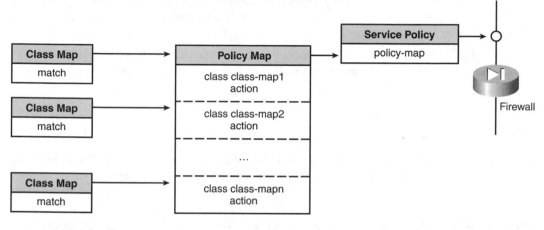

Match Conditions:
- Match Port Number
- Match Through an Access List
- Match Traffic Flow
- Match IP Precedence
- Match DSCP
- Match RTP Port Range
- Match VPN Tunnel Group

- Match Anything
- Match default-inspection-traffic

Actions:
- Inspect Traffic
- Set Connection Options
- Send to AIP or CSC SSM
- Police Traffic
- Send to Priority Queue

TIP   A class map can also match against other conditions that are based on parameters further inside an IP, UDP, or TCP packet. This type of class map is used in conjunction with application layer inspection policies and is discussed in Section "7-3: Application Inspection."

The class map is defined and described by the following configuration commands. In addition, you add more commands to identify specific traffic, as described in the sections beginning with "Match Against..." that follow. Finally, the class map is used to identify traffic as part of the policy map configuration in the section titled "Defining a Layer 3/4 Policy."

1. Define the class map:

```
Firewall(config)# class-map class_map_name
```

The class map is named *class_map_name* (an arbitrary string of up to 40 characters).

You can define only one matching condition in a class map. The only exceptions are **match tunnel-group** and **match default-inspection-traffic**, which are described in further detail in the "Match Against a VPN Tunnel Group" and "Match Default Traffic" sections, respectively.

After creating a class map, you can change its name without deleting it and reconfiguring it. To do this, use the following command while in class map configuration mode:

```
Firewall(config-cmap)# rename name
```

2. (Optional) Add a description to the class map:

```
Firewall(config-cmap)# description text
```

You can add a string of descriptive *text* (up to 200 characters) to a class map. This description can help firewall administrators identify or understand the class map's purpose.

Match Against a Destination Port Number

You can set up a class map to examine the destination TCP or UDP port in IP packets moving into or out of a firewall interface. Use the following command to set up the matching condition:

```
Firewall(config-cmap)# match port {tcp | udp} {eq port | range start end}
```

The matching protocol is either **tcp** or **udp**. You can define an exact match with the **eq** keyword as *port*, either a supported keyword or a decimal number 1 through 65535. Otherwise, you can use the **range** keyword to define a match against a range of port values, from *start* to *end*.

For example, the following commands define class maps that match HTTP and SIP traffic, respectively:

```
Firewall(config)# class-map class_http
Firewall(config-cmap)# match port tcp eq http
Firewall(config-cmap)# exit
Firewall(config)# class-map class_sip
Firewall(config-cmap)# match port udp eq sip
Firewall(config-cmap)# exit
```

Match Against an Access List

You can use the access list to match several different protocols, ports, or address pairs. This is a convenient way to classify disparate types of traffic into a single class that ultimately has an action applied. The following steps show how to configure and then apply an access list in a class map.

1. Define the access list:

```
Firewall(config)# access-list acl_id [line line-num] [extended]
    {permit | deny} {protocol | object-group protocol_obj_group}
    {source_addr source_mask | object-group network_obj_group}
    [operator sport | object-group service_obj_group]
```

```
{destination_addr destination_mask | object-group network_obj_group}
[operator dport | object-group service_obj_group]
[time-range name]
```

Any traffic that matches a **permit** statement in the access list becomes matched traffic in the class map. You can have **deny** statements in the access list, but they never result in a match for the class map.

Section "6-3: Controlling Access with Access Lists" in Chapter 6, "Controlling Access Through the Firewall," covers access list configuration in detail.

TIP   If you need to match against source and/or destination addresses in the access list, you need to consider any address translations that are occurring. Specify IP addresses with the values they will have *after* address translation. In other words, the match operation in a class map is handled after any relevant address translations.

For example, suppose a static NAT entry is configured so that inside host 192.168.198.17 appears as 128.163.93.134 on the outside. If an access list is used to match inbound traffic to that host, the inside or local address (after translation) should be specified, as demonstrated here:

```
Firewall(config)# static (inside,outside) 128.163.93.134 192.
168.198.17 netmask 255.255.255.255 0 0
Firewall(config)# access-list test extended permit tcp any host
  192.168.198.17 eq http
Firewall(config)# class-map test_class
Firewall(config-cmap)# match access-list test
```

---

2.   Apply the access list as the matching condition:

```
Firewall(config-cmap)# match access-list acl_name
```

The access list named *acl_name* is used as a template to match traffic. Only one access list can be defined for matching in a class map.

For example, the following commands enable a single class map and **match** command to match several different types of traffic:

```
Firewall(config)# access-list MyTraffic extended permit tcp any
  any eq http
Firewall(config)# access-list MyTraffic extended permit tcp any
  any eq https
Firewall(config)# access-list MyTraffic extended permit tcp any
  any eq 8080
```

```
Firewall(config)# class-map MyClass
Firewall(config-cmap)# match access-list MyTraffic
```

Match Against QoS Parameters

Quality of service (QoS) is a device's capability to forward packets in an efficient, predictable, and reliable manner. Some types of traffic, such as voice and video applications, require data to be delivered without delay and without jitter (variations in delay).

In releases before ASA 7.0(1), a firewall could handle traffic only on a "best-effort" basis, in which packets were inspected and forwarded in the order in which they were received. Beginning with ASA 7.0(1), a firewall can classify packets and place them in a priority queue. This interface queue is serviced ahead of any other queue so that any priority packets are sent first.

You can use class maps to match against two types of QoS parameters: IP Precedence and Differentiated Services Code Point (DSCP). These values are included in every IP packet header. They indicate the QoS level that is needed for each packet's delivery. IP Precedence is included in the type of service (ToS) byte.

ToS and DSCP are two different interpretations of the same 1-byte field in the IP header, as shown in Figure 7-2. Specifically, IP Precedence is a 3-bit value (P2 to P0), and DSCP is a 6-bit value (DS5 to DS0).

Figure 7-2 *ToS and DSCP Byte Formats*

ToS Byte:	P2	P1	P0	T3	T2	T1	T0	Zero
DS Byte:	DS5	DS4	DS3	DS2	DS1	DS0	ECN1	ECN0
	(Class Selector)			(Drop Precedence)				

The DSCP value is broken down into the following components:

- **Class selector (3 bits)**—Classifies packets into eight classes: class 0 (best effort, the default), classes 1 through 4 (assured forwarding [AF]), class 5 (expedited forwarding [EF]), and classes 6 and 7 (used for network control traffic).

- **Drop precedence (3 bits)**—Within a class, packets are marked according to the tolerance for being dropped: High (3), Medium (2), and Low (1). Packets with a lower drop precedence need better service.

When DSCP values are written as a codepoint name, the format is class (AF or EF), followed by the class level (1 to 4), followed by the drop precedence. For example, DSCP AF21 is assured forwarding class 2, drop precedence 1. The best-service value is EF, which has no class or drop precedence.

Table 7-1 compares the IP Precedence and DSCP fields with their possible values. You can use this table as a quick reference when defining or interpreting values from either field.

Table 7-1   *Mapping of IP Precedence and DSCP Values*

IP Precedence (3 Bits)			DSCP (6 Bits)				
Name	Value	Bits	Per-Hop Behavior	Class Selector	Drop Precedence	Codepoint Name	DSCP Bits (Decimal)
Routine	0	000	Default	—	—	Default	000 000 (0)
Priority	1	001	AF	1	1: Low 2: Medium 3: High	AF11 AF12 AF13	001 010 (10) 001 100 (12) 001 110 (14)
Immediate	2	010	AF	2	1: Low 2: Medium 3: High	AF21 AF22 AF23	010 010 (18) 010 100 (20) 010 110 (22)
Flash	3	011	AF	3	1: Low 2: Medium 3: High	AF31 AF32 AF33	011 010 (26) 011 100 (28) 011 110 (30)
Flash Override	4	100	AF	4	1: Low 2: Medium 3: High	AF41 AF42 AF43	100 010 (34) 100 100 (36) 100 110 (46)[1]
Critical[1]	5	101	EF	—	—	EF	101 110 (46)[1]
Internetwork Control	6	110	—	—	—	—	(48 to 55)
Network Control	7	111	—	—	—	—	(56 to 63)

Section 7-2

1. IP Precedence value 5 (DSCP EF) corresponds to the range of DSCP bits 101000 through 101111, or 40 through 47. However, only the value 101110 or 46 is commonly used and is given the EF designation.

You can use the following steps to configure a QoS parameter to match against. You can use either IP Precedence or DSCP values.

1. (Optional) Match against the IP Precedence value:

```
Firewall(config-cmap)# match precedence value1 [value2 [value3
  [value4]]]
```

The IP precedence field in the ToS byte of the IP header is examined in each packet going into or out of a firewall interface. You can specify up to four different precedence values to match against. These can be given as any of the following decimal numbers or keywords: **routine (0)**, **priority (1)**, **immediate (2)**, **flash (3)**, **flash-override (4)**, **critical (5)**, **internet (6)**, or **network (7)**.

As a rule of thumb, a higher precedence means a better QoS should be used. IP precedence is usually set by the originating host, or it can be set or overridden by a router along the traffic path. In other words, before you can depend on matching an IP precedence value, you should be confident that some other device is setting the values properly.

For example, the following commands configure a class map that matches against the **critical** and **flash-override** values:

```
Firewall(config)# class-map high_precedence
Firewall(config-cmap)# match precedence 4 5
Firewall(config-cmap)# exit
```

2. (Optional) Match against the DSCP value:

```
Firewall(config-cmap)# match dscp value1 [value2 ...[value8]]
```

The DSCP value in the IP header is examined in each packet going into or out of a firewall interface. You can specify up to eight different DSCP values to match against. These can be given as a decimal number (0 to 63) or as one of the following keywords: **default (0)**, **cs1 (8)**, **af11 (10)**, **af12 (12)**, **af13 (14)**, **cs2 (16)**, **af21 (18)**, **af22 (20)**, **af23 (22)**, **cs3 (24)**, **af31 (26)**, **af32 (28)**, **af33 (30)**, **cs4 (32)**, **af41 (34)**, **af42 (36)**, **af43 (38)**, **cs5 (40)**, **ef (46)**, **cs6 (48)**, or **cs7 (56)**.

DSCP is usually set by the originating host, or it can be set or overridden by a router along the traffic path. In other words, before you can depend on matching a certain DSCP value, you should be confident that some other device is setting the values properly.

For example, the following commands define class maps that match against the EF DSCP value and all AF4 values:

```
Firewall(config)# class-map dscp_ef
Firewall(config-cmap)# match dscp ef
Firewall(config-cmap)# exit
Firewall(config)# class-map dscp_af4
Firewall(config-cmap)# match dscp af41 af42 af43
Firewall(config-cmap)# exit
```

Match Against a Range of Real-Time Transport Protocol (RTP) Port Numbers

RTP is most often used for audio or video streams, where data is sent in one direction using a range of UDP port numbers. You can match RTP by defining the port range beginning at *starting_port*

(2000 to 65535) and continuing for *range* (0 to 16383) ports with the following configuration command:

```
Firewall(config-cmap)# match rtp starting_port range
```

For example, to match against RTP ports 2000 through 2100, you could use the following commands:

```
Firewall(config)# class-map rtp
Firewall(config-cmap)# match rtp 2000 100
Firewall(config-cmap)# exit
```

Match Against a VPN Tunnel Group

If the firewall is configured to support and terminate Virtual Private Network (VPN) tunnels, you can match the traffic passing through a tunnel belonging to a specific tunnel group *name*. In this way, firewall service policies can be applied on a per-tunnel group basis:

```
Firewall(config-cmap)# match tunnel-group name
```

You can also add a second **match** condition to classify each traffic flow (connections using a common destination address) within a tunnel group:

```
Firewall(config-cmap)# match flow ip destination-address
```

This is most often used in conjunction with the **police** action in a policy map so that traffic flows to unique destination addresses within a tunnel group can be policed to a certain data rate.

Match All Traffic

All packets passing into or out of a firewall interface can be matched and identified with a class map. This is a handy way to subject all types of traffic to an action in a policy map. Use the following configuration command to match any traffic:

```
Firewall(config-cmap)# match any
```

Match Default Traffic

To perform the default application inspections, a firewall must first match the various traffic types. This command sets up this default arrangement by matching against predefined protocols and port numbers for the respective applications:

```
Firewall(config-cmap)# match default-inspection-traffic
```

This command is configured in the *inspection_default* class map as part of the default firewall configuration. See the section "Default Policy Definitions" for more details.

Classifying Management Traffic

Beginning with ASA 8.0(1), you can define a special "mananagement" class map type to match specific traffic that terminates on the firewall itself. For example, you might want to match against HTTP traffic so that you can limit the number of ASDM connections users can attempt to start.

By classifying management traffic as a special case, you can configure specific policies to help prevent denial-of-service attacks on the firewall itself. Otherwise, once you enable the firewall's HTTP server to offer the ASDM management interface, malicious users might also make use of the HTTP service and perhaps cripple the firewall's CPU.

You can define a management class map with the following configuration command:

```
Firewall(config)# class-map type management mgmt_cmap_name
```

Then define matching conditions that will identify the specific management traffic. You can match against an access list with the following commands:

```
Firewall(config-cmap)# match access-list acl_name
```

A previously configured access list will permit the management traffic so that it is matched here. The access list does not actually permit or deny the management traffic from reaching or being interpreted by the firewall—it is only used to match the management traffic for further handling.

You can also match against the TCP or UDP port numbers used in the management traffic with the following command:

```
Firewall(config-cmap)# match port {tcp | udp} {eq port_number | range low high}
```

The protocol is identified as **tcp** or **udp**. Use the **eq** keyword to give a specific port number, or the **range** keyword to give a range of port numbers (*low* to *high*). Port numbers can be any number 1-65535. You cannot use any other keywords that represent port numbers, such as **www**, **ssh**, and so on. Also, the port numbers represent the destination port for the management service that is running on the firewall.

You can repeat the **match** commands to define other management traffic that should be classified.

Once the management class map has been configured, you can reference it with the **class** command, as you would a normal Layer 3/4 class map. The only difference is that management traffic terminating on the firewall itself will be classified and handled as a unique policy, separate from any other regular traffic policy.

Defining a Layer 3/4 Policy

After Layer 3 or 4 traffic has been identified or classified, the firewall can take some action on it. You can define a policy map that contains one or more class maps, followed by an action for each. The entire policy map is then applied to one or all firewall interfaces, where the classifications and actions are carried out.

You can follow these steps to configure a policy map and apply it to a firewall interface:

1. Define a policy map:

    ```
    Firewall(config)# policy-map policy_map_name
    ```

    The policy map is named *policy_map_name* (an arbitrary string of up to 40 characters).

    As soon as you create a policy map, you can change its name without deleting it and reconfiguring it. To do this, use the following command while in policy map configuration mode:

    ```
    Firewall(config-pmap)# rename name
    ```

2. (Optional) Add a description to the policy map:

    ```
    Firewall(config-pmap)# description text
    ```

    You can add a string of descriptive *text* (up to 200 characters) to a policy map that can help firewall administrators identify or understand the policy map's purpose.

3. Match traffic with a class map:

    ```
    Firewall(config-pmap)# class {class_map_name | class-default}
    ```

    You can specify the class map named *class_map_name* to identify a specific type of traffic. This can be a Layer 3/4 class map configured with the **class-map** *cmap_name* command, or a management class map configured with the **class-map type management** *cmap_name* command.

    You also can use the **class-default** keyword to use the default class map. This is a handy way to identify all the traffic that has not been classified in any other class map. The **class-default** class map is automatically configured in a firewall by default, and it contains only the **match any** command. Therefore, this class map should be the last one defined in a policy.

    For example, a class map named MyClass is configured and used in a policy map in the following commands:

    ```
    Firewall(config)# class-map MyClass
    Firewall(config-cmap)# match any
    Firewall(config-cmap)# exit
    Firewall(config)# policy-map MyPolicy
    Firewall(config-pmap)# class MyClass
    ```

4. Take an action on the matched traffic.

    After class maps are defined in a policy map, the policy map is applied to a firewall interface as a service policy, independent of traffic direction. In other words, traffic can be matched and acted on in a bidirectional manner, whether it is inbound or outbound. Some restrictions do apply, however.

Section 7-2

Table 7-2 lists each policy map action according to its supported traffic direction. Policing and Low-Latency Queuing (LLQ) are typically techniques performed on packets that are leaving the firewall on an interface. Therefore, those two actions are unidirectional, in the outbound direction only.

Table 7-2 *Policy Map Actions per Supported Traffic Direction*

Bidirectional Action	Unidirectional Action
Application inspection (**inspect**)	Policers (**police**)
Connection options (**set connection**)	Low-Latency Queuing (**priority**)
Intrusion Prevention System module (**ips**)	—
Content Security and Control module (**csc**)	—

You can configure one or more of the following actions to take on the matched traffic:

- Inspect the traffic with an application inspection engine
- Set connection limits
- Adjust TCP options
- Inspect the traffic with an Intrusion Prevention System (IPS) module (ASA platform only)
- Inspect the traffic with a Content Security and Control (CSC) module (ASA platform only)
- Police the traffic to a rate limit
- Use LLQ for priority handling

These policy actions are discussed in the following sections.

5. Repeat Steps 3 and 4 to define other policies.

6. Apply the policy map as a service policy:

```
Firewall(config)# service-policy policy_map_name {global | interface if_name}
```

After you have finished adding **class** commands and their corresponding actions, you can apply the completed policy map so that it can be used.

The policy map named *policy_map_name* is applied as a service policy to one or more firewall interfaces. You can specify a single interface with the **interface** keyword and the interface name *if_name* (**outside**, for example). Only one policy map can be applied to a service policy, and only one service policy can be applied to an interface.

You can also use the **global** keyword to apply the service policy to all firewall interfaces simultaneously. You can configure only one global service policy. By default, only the *global_policy* policy map is applied globally.

Set Connection Limits on the Matched Traffic

You can configure one or more actions within a policy map to limit various aspects of TCP connections, as discussed in the following tasks:

* Set TCP connection timeouts:

FWSM	Firewall(config-pmap-c)# **set connection timeout** [**embryonic** {*hh:mm:ss* | **0**}] [**half-closed** {*hh:mm:ss* | **0**}] [**tcp** {*hh:mm:ss* | **0**}
ASA	Firewall(config-pmap-c)# **set connection timeout** [**embryonic** {*hh:mm:ss* | **0**}] [**half-closed** {*hh:mm:ss* | **0**}] [**tcp** {*hh:mm:ss* | **0**} [**dcd** [*retry_interval* [*max_retries*]]

For matched packets, you can adjust the TCP connection timeout limits and set them as the appropriate conn entries are dynamically created.

Refer to Table 7-3 for each type of connection timeout and its associated keyword.

Table 7-3 *TCP Connection Timeout Limit Options*

Description	Keyword for set connection timeout command	Timeout values
Automatically close embryonic (not completely opened) connections after a timeout	**embryonic** {*hh:mm:ss* | **0**}	Default: 30 seconds Minimum: 5 seconds
Automatically close half-closed (partially closed, or incomplete FIN-FIN handshake) connections after a timeout	**half-closed** {*hh:mm:ss* | **0**}	Default: 10 minutes Minimum: 5 minutes
Automatically close TCP connections that have been idle after a timeout	**tcp** {*hh:mm:ss* | **0**}	Default: 1 hour Minimum: 5 minutes
Use Dead Connection Detection (DCD) to probe for defunct idle connections	**dcd** [*retry_interval* [*max_retries*]]	*retry_interval* = 15 seconds *max_retries* = 5

In each case, the timeout value is set to *hh:mm:ss* (24-hour format) or **0** for unlimited time.

With the **tcp** keyword, the firewall identifies any TCP connection that has been idle for longer than the timeout value and automatically closes it. While this is a handy housekeeping function, it closes *any* TCP connection that has been idle more than a fixed amount of time.

Some TCP connections can remain idle for an extended period of time, but still be valid. For example, suppose the TCP idle timeout is set to 5 minutes. A Telnet session through the firewall to a host could very easily stay idle for more than 5 minutes, while the user answered a telephone call or got up to do something else. Closing idle, but valid, connections would become a nuisance to the end users.

Beginning with ASA 7.2(1), you can add the **dcd** keyword in conjunction with the **tcp** timeout function. After a TCP connection has been idle for the **tcp** timeout duration, the firewall begins to send probes to the client and server. The probes stimulate the hosts to answer; if they both answer, the connection must still be valid and should not be closed for being idle.

DCD probes are sent at *retry_interval* seconds. If no response is received, the probes are resent for *max_retries* times. If there still is no response at that point, the connection is presumed to be idle and is automatically closed.

TIP   What sort of probes does a firewall send for DCD? It sends a minimum size packet with the ACK bit set, using the same IP addresses and TCP ports that the actual TCP connection uses. In this way, the client and server each think it is simply answering a TCP ACK sent by its peer. No data changes hands, other than basic acknowledgments.

• Set connection volume limits:

FWSM	Firewall(config-pmap-c)# **set connection** [**conn-max** *n*] [**random-sequence-number** {**enable** | **disable**}]
ASA	Firewall(config-pmap-c)# **set connection** [**conn-max** *n*] [**embryonic-conn-max** *n*] [**per-client-embryonic-max** *n*] [**per-client-max** *n*] [**random-sequence-number** {**enable** | **disable**}]

By default, an unlimited number of simultaneous UDP and TCP connections are allowed across an address translation. The **set connection** command can be used in a policy map to set connection limits on traffic to and from specific hosts.

The connection limits configured with **set connection** are very similar to the limits set in address translation commands such as **static** and **nat**. See "Handling Connections Through an Address Translation" in Section "6-2: Routed Firewall Mode and Address Translation," for more information.

TIP   If connection limits are configured in a policy map (**set connection**) and an address translation (**static** or **nat**), and a traffic flow applies to both conditions, the lower connection limit is enforced.

Refer to Table 7-4 for each type of connection limit and its associated keyword:

Table 7-4 *Connection Limiting Options*

Description	Keyword for set connection command	Values
Limit the total simultaneous connections in use by all traffic matching the policy	`conn-max` *n*	Default: 0 (unlimited) Maximum: 65535
Limit the total number of embryonic connections opened for all traffic matching the policy	`embryonic-conn-max` *n*	Default: 0 (unlimited) Maximum: 65535
Limit the total number of embryonic connections opened on a per-client or host basis	`per-client-embryonic-max` *n*	Default: 0 (unlimited) Maximum: 65535
Limit the total number of simultaneous connections in use on a per-client or host basis	`per-client-max` *n*	Default: 0 (unlimited) Maximum: 65535
Assign a random initial sequence number (ISN) for each new TCP connection	`random-sequence-generator {enable	disable}`	Default: **enable**

When the maximum number of connections is reached, the firewall begins dropping any new connections. As soon as one of the embryonic connection limits is reached, the firewall begins intercepting new connections and acting as a proxy for the connection target.

You can also use the **random-sequence-generator** keyword to **enable** or **disable** randomization of the initial sequence number (ISN) when TCP connections are established.

TIP   You can monitor the activity of **set connection** policy actions with the following command:

Firewall# **show service-policy set connection**

The following example shows the connection volume limits and timeout values that have been configured in a service policy named **policy-outbound**:

```
Firewall# show service-policy set connection
Global policy:
  Service-policy: global_default
Interface outside:
  Service-policy: policy-outbound
    Class-map: outbound
      Set connection policy: conn-max 100 embryonic-conn-max 10
        current embryonic conns 0, current conns 0, drop 0
```

```
                Set connection timeout policy:
                  tcp 0:30:00
                  DCD: enabled, retry-interval 0:01:0, max-retries 5
                  DCD: client-probe 5, server-probe 5, conn-expiration 0
        Firewall#
```

Adjust TCP Options for the Matched Traffic

You can define a TCP map that acts as a template for modifying various options in the TCP header of matched packets. Use the following configuration steps to create and use a TCP map:

1. Define the TCP map:

   Firewall(config)# **tcp-map** *tcp_map_name*

   The TCP map is given an arbitrary name *tcp_map_name*.

2. Use one or more of the commands listed in Table 7-5 to specify actions to take on the TCP header.

Table 7-5 *TCP Header Actions*

Action Description	Command Syntax
Verifies that TCP retransmissions are consistent with the originals. Packets must arrive in sequential order.	Firewall(config-tcp-map)# **check-retransmission**
Verifies the TCP checksum and drops the packet if it fails.	Firewall(config-tcp-map)# **checksum-verification**
Takes action (the default is **drop**) if a packet's maximum segment size (MSS) exceeds the value set when the TCP connection began.	Firewall(config-tcp-map)# **exceed-mss {allow | drop}**
Takes action (the default is **allow**) on the reserved bits in the TCP header. This is a 3-bit field after the Data Offset field, which should always be cleared to 0.	Firewall(config-tcp-map)# **reserved-bits {allow | clear | drop}**
SYN packets are permitted to contain payload data, according to the TCP definition. By default, the firewall **allow**s them. If end hosts cannot handle this properly, the firewall can **drop** those packets.	Firewall(config-tcp-map)# **syn-data {allow | drop}**
Drops packets that masquerade as retransmissions of prior packets that passed inspection but were dropped because of time-to-live (TTL) expiration. (This is enabled by default.)	Firewall(config-tcp-map)# **ttl-evasion-protection**

Table 7-5 *TCP Header Actions (Continued)*

Action Description	Command Syntax
Takes action (the default is **clear**) on the contents of the TCP URG (urgent) flag and pointer. URG can be used to request priority handling of a packet, but this is not well-defined.	`Firewall(config-tcp-map)#` **urgent-flag {allow | clear}**
Takes action (the default is **allow-connection**) when the TCP window size is advertised as greatly disparate values for no apparent reason.	`Firewall(config-tcp-map)#` **window-variation {allow-connection | drop-connection}**
Takes action (the default is **allow**) if Selective ACK (SACK, TCP option 4) is set.	`Firewall(config-tcp-map)#` **tcp-options selective-ack {allow | clear}**
Takes action (the default is **allow**) if the time stamp (TCP option 8) is used. If **clear** is used, the Round-Trip Time Measurement (RTTM) and Protection Against Wrapped Sequences (PAWS) mechanisms are broken.	`Firewall(config-tcp-map)#` **tcp-options timestamp {allow | clear}**
Takes action (the default is **allow**) if the window scale (TCP option 3) flag is set to expand the TCP window field from 16 to 32 bits.	`Firewall(config-tcp-map)#` **tcp-options window-scale {allow | clear}**
Takes action on packets that use TCP option numbers within the range *lower* to *upper*. The lower and upper limit values can be 6, 7, or 9 to 255. TCP option 2 (MSS), option 3 (window scale), options 4 and 5 (SACK), and option 8 (time stamp) are not valid in this range because they are addressed with other **tcp-options** commands.	`Firewall(config-tcp-map)#` **tcp-options range** *lower upper* **{allow | clear | drop}**

If you have experimented with a command or its settings, you can use **default** *command* to set it back to its default configuration. For example, suppose you have entered the **check-retransmission** command but have decided to return the feature to its default state. Is the default on or off? No worries—just enter the following command to automatically choose the default:

```
Firewall(config-tcp-map)# default check-retransmission
```

3. End the TCP map configuration with the **exit** command.

4. Apply the TCP map as a template action with the following policy map configuration command:

```
Firewall(config-pmap-c)# set connection advanced-options tcp_map_name
```

| TIP | You will not be able to move directly from the TCP map configuration mode into the policy map configuration mode. After you exit the TCP map configuration mode in Step 3, get back into the policy map configuration mode with the following commands:

```
Firewall(config)# policy-map policy_map_name
Firewall(config-pmap)# class class_map_name
Firewall(config-pmap-c)#
```

For example, a TCP map named *conform_tcp* is defined to drop TCP connections that try to use a nonzero value in the reserved bits field. As well, if TCP options 6, 7, or 9 through 255 are present, the connection is dropped.

You can use the following commands to accomplish this. Notice that to use the **set connection advanced-options** command in a policy map, you still have to configure a class map to match the relevant traffic. In this case, all TCP packets should be matched—something that can be done only by using an access list.

```
Firewall(config)# tcp-map conform_tcp
Firewall(config-tcp-map)# reserved-bits drop
Firewall(config-tcp-map)# tcp-options range 6 7 drop
Firewall(config-tcp-map)# tcp-options range 9 255 drop
Firewall(config-tcp-map)# exit
Firewall(config)# access-list acl_tcp permit tcp any any
Firewall(config)# class-map MyClass
Firewall(config-cmap)# match access-list acl_tcp
Firewall(config-cmap)# exit
Firewall(config)# policy-map MyPolicy
Firewall(config-pmap)# class MyClass
Firewall(config-pmap-c)# set connection advanced-options conform_tcp
Firewall(config-pmap-c)# exit
Firewall(config-pmap)# exit
Firewall(config)# service-policy MyPolicy interface outside
```

You can monitor the activity of any configured **tcp-options** policy commands with the following command:

```
Firewall# show service-policy set connection
```

In the following example, a TCP map named **conform_tcp** has been applied as a policy action in the **policy-outbound** service policy. Counters are displayed for each type of packet drop that can be configured regarding the TCP options field:

```
Firewall# show service-policy set connection
Global policy:
  Service-policy: asa_global_fw_policy
Interface outside:
  Service-policy: policy-outbound
    Class-map: outbound
      Set connection policy: conn-max 100 embryonic-conn-max 10
        current embryonic conns 0, current conns 0, drop 0
      Set connection timeout policy:
        tcp 0:30:00
```

```
Set connection advanced-options: conform_tcp
   Retransmission drops: 0          TCP checksum drops : 0
   Exceeded MSS drops  : 0          SYN with data drops: 0
   Out-of-order packets: 0          No buffer drops    : 0
   Reserved bit cleared: 0          Reserved bit drops : 0
   IP TTL modified     : 0          Urgent flag cleared: 0
   Window varied resets: 0
   TCP-options:
      Selective ACK cleared: 0      Timestamp cleared  : 0
      Window scale cleared : 0
      Other options cleared:
      Other options drops:
Firewall#
```

Send the Matched Traffic to an IPS Module

The Cisco ASA platform has a Security Services Module (SSM) slot that can be populated with a hardware module to handle Intrusion Prevention System (IPS) functions. This module is called the Advanced Inspection and Prevention (AIP) SSM. The ASA firewall must first match packets that are candidates for IPS inspection. Those packets are then offloaded to the AIP for IPS analysis.

NOTE   With an AIP SSM installed, an ASA platform can take advantage of the more than 1000 available IPS signatures. However, if an AIP is not installed (ASA or PIX platforms), only the basic IPS feature configured with the **ip audit** command can be used.

You can configure two different methods of handing off packets to the AIP:

- **inline**—The AIP operates inline with the firewall so that matched packets flow from the firewall to the AIP, are inspected and acted upon by the AIP, and then flow back to the firewall.

- **promiscuous**—Matched packets are duplicated and sent to the AIP for IPS inspection. However, the original packets are still handled normally by the ASA firewall.

You can configure a method by using one of the following commands:

Firewall(config-pmap-c)# **ips inline {fail-open | fail-close}**

or

Firewall(config-pmap-c)# **ips promiscuous {fail-open | fail-close}**

With either method, you can configure the firewall's action if the IPS hardware has failed. Use the **fail-open** keyword to allow matched packets to move through the firewall normally.

Otherwise, you can use the **fail-close** keyword to have tighter control over IPS policy enforcement. The firewall drops the matched packets if the IPS hardware has failed, preventing a potential vulnerability from being propagated into the protected network.

For example, the following commands are used to configure a firewall to match any IP traffic and send it to the AIP module. The IPS process is to be inline with the firewall, and connections should be closed if the IPS module has failed. The whole policy is applied to the outside interface.

```
Firewall(config)# class-map IPS_Class
Firewall(config-cmap)# match any
Firewall(config-cmap)# exit
Firewall(config)# policy-map MyPolicy
Firewall(config-pmap)# class IPS_Class
Firewall(config-pmap-c)# ips inline fail-close
Firewall(config-pmap-c)# exit
Firewall(config-pmap)# exit
Firewall(config)# service-policy MyPolicy interface outside
```

You can monitor the activity of a service policy that sends matched packets to an AIP module with the following command:

```
Firewall# show service-policy ips
```

TIP   Chapter 12, "ASA Modules," covers the AIP SSM configuration in greater detail.

Send the Matched Traffic to a CSC Module

You can populate the SSM slot in an ASA platform with a Content Security and Control (CSC) module. The CSC can perform anti-virus, anti-spam, anti-spyware, and anti-phishing functions on packets that are sent to it.

The CSC operates in an inline mode as follows:

1. The traffic matching a policy is sent to the CSC.

2. The CSC inspects and acts on malicious content.

3. The CSC sends the traffic back to the firewall.

You can configure the policy map action to send matching traffic to the CSC with the following command:

```
Firewall(config-pmap-c)# csc {fail-open | fail-close}
```

You can configure the firewall's action if the CSC hardware has failed and cannot be reached. Use the **fail-open** keyword to allow matched packets to move through the firewall normally, without the CSC's inspection.

Otherwise, use the **fail-close** keyword to have tighter control over the CSC's policy enforcement. The firewall drops the matched packets if the CSC hardware has failed.

TIP   Chapter 12 covers the CSC SSM configuration in greater detail.

Use a Policer to Limit the Matched Traffic Bandwidth

Beginning with ASA 7.0(1), you can define traffic policers in a policy map to control the amount of interface bandwidth given to specific traffic. Packets that are identified with a **match** command in a class map can be applied to a policer.

You can configure a policer as an action within a policy map with the following command:

```
Firewall(config-pmap-c)# police {output | input} conform_rate [burst_bytes]
  [conform-action {drop | transmit}] [exceed-action {drop | transmit}]
```

Matched packets are held to a strict bandwidth policy. They can use up to *conform_rate* bits per second, given as 8000 (8 kbps) to 2,000,000,000 (2 Gbps). While the *conform_rate* bandwidth is not being exceeded, the firewall takes the **conform-action** and either **drop**s the conforming packets or **transmit**s them (the default).

You can also specify an "instantaneous" amount of burst traffic that is allowed when the *conform_rate* is exceeded. This is given as *burst_bytes*, 1000 (1 KB) to 512,000,000 (512 MB); this is 1500 bytes by default. If the conform rate is exceeded by more than the burst size, the traffic is considered nonconforming, and the **exceed-action** is taken. The firewall can either **drop** (the default) or **transmit** the nonconforming packets.

NOTE   It might seem odd that the *conform_rate* is specified in bits per second while the burst is given in bytes. This is because of how the policer operates. A 10-millisecond (ms) clock interval is used to measure policed traffic. The byte counts of matching packets are added to a "bucket" whose "high water mark" is set to the amount of traffic that can be transmitted in one clock tick. In addition, the bucket is emptied at every interval of the policer clock (10 ms).

While the *conform_rate* is not exceeded, the bucket should never fill. If a burst size is configured, it is added to the bucket's high water mark. Therefore, in one clock tick (10 ms), the amount of matching traffic can exceed the conforming amount by the burst size in bytes.

In releases prior to ASA 7.2(1), policers can examine and limit traffic rates in the *outbound* direction only. You can use the **output** keyword to police traffic being output on an interface, but this is not really necessary, because that is the default and the only direction possible.

Beginning with ASA 7.2(1), policers can be used to control the rates of incoming traffic as well. When you configure a policer, you have to select whether it operates in the **input** or **output** direction after it is applied to an interface.

For example, suppose a policer has been configured to limit outbound HTTP traffic to an aggregate rate of 8 kbps. Conforming traffic is transmitted, but traffic that exceeds the conform rate is dropped. The HTTP servers are located on the inside of the firewall, and all relevant clients are located outside. The following commands show this configuration:

```
Firewall(config)# access-list outbound_http extended permit tcp any eq http any
Firewall(config)# class-map class_http
Firewall(config-cmap)# match access-list outbound_http
Firewall(config-cmap)# exit
Firewall(config)# policy-map mypolicy
Firewall(config-pmap)# class class_http
Firewall(config-pmap-c)# police output 8000 conform-action transmit exceed-action drop
Firewall(config-pmap-c)# exit
Firewall(config-pmap)# exit
Firewall(config)# service-policy mypolicy interface outside
```

You could also add a policer to control the rate of inbound FTP traffic to an aggregate rate of 128 kbps. You could use the following commands to configure the FTP policer:

```
Firewall(config)# class-map class_ftp
Firewall(config-cmap)# match port tcp eq 20
Firewall(config-cmap)# exit
Firewall(config)# policy-map mypolicy
Firewall(config-pmap)# class class_ftp
Firewall(config-pmap-c)# police input 128000 conform-action transmit exceed-action drop
Firewall(config-pmap-c)# exit
Firewall(config-pmap)# exit
```

In effect, you just have to edit the policy map to add in a new policy for the inbound traffic. The policy map was already applied to the outside interface in the first part of the example.

You can monitor policer activity with the following command:

```
Firewall# show service-policy [interface ifc_name]
```

For example, the following output corresponds to the previous sample configuration:

```
Firewall# show service-policy interface outside
Interface outside:
  Service-policy: policy-outbound
    Class-map: class_http
      Output police Interface outside:
        cir 8000 bps, bc 1500 bytes
        conformed 223 packets, 16502 bytes; actions:  transmit
        exceeded 377 packets, 27898 bytes; actions:  drop
        conformed 6320 bps, exceed 11744 bps
    Class-map: class_ftp
      Input police Interface outside:
        cir 128000 bps, bc 4000 bytes
        conformed 67 packets, 9120 bytes; actions:  transmit
```

```
        exceeded 34 packets, 3942 bytes; actions:  drop
        conformed 1298 bps, exceed 3114 bps
Firewall#
```

Notice that the command output includes current estimates of the bits per second for the "conformed" and "exceed" traffic based on the policer's actions. For the policer in the output direction, the committed information rate (**cir**) is shown to be 8000 bps, and the committed burst (**bc**) is the default 1500 bytes (one packet).

As an extra step, a burst size of 12,000 bytes (eight 1500-byte packets) is then configured for the same output policer using the following command:

```
Firewall(config-pmap-c)# police output 8000 12800 conform-action transmit exceed-action
drop
```

The idea is to add the capability for periodic bursts of traffic over the conform rate to get through unaltered, as long as the traffic rate stays below the conform rate. If the traffic rate is sustained at a high rate, where the policer must keep it rate-limited, only a single burst of excessive traffic is permitted.

Monitoring the policer from the command line shows the updated burst size and the estimated conformed and exceeded rates. However, notice that the following output does not really give an indication of the burst activity:

```
Firewall# show service-policy interface outside
Interface outside:
  Service-policy: policy-outbound
    Class-map: outbound
      police Interface outside:
        cir 8000 bps, bc 12800 bytes
        conformed 2294 packets, 169756 bytes; actions:  transmit
        exceeded 3986 packets, 294964 bytes; actions:  drop
        conformed 5376 bps, exceed 11176 bps
    Class-map: class_ftp
      Input police Interface outside:
        cir 128000 bps, bc 4000 bytes
        conformed 67 packets, 9120 bytes; actions:  transmit
        exceeded 34 packets, 3942 bytes; actions:  drop
        conformed 1298 bps, exceed 3114 bps
Firewall#
```

To see the effects of the policer at work, you can use the ASDM application to display a graph of interface bit rates. Figure 7-3 shows this graph during the time that the example output policer was configured. On the left, where the bit rate averages around 20,000 bps, no policer was configured. This represents the true data rate through the outside firewall interface.

When the data rate falls off abruptly to about 7000 bps, the policer has just been configured, with a *conform-rate* of 8000 bps. No burst size has been configured other than the default. Notice a spike toward the right side of the graph. At that point, the policer was reconfigured with the addition of the

12,800-byte burst size. Because the traffic rate was already at a sustained level above the *conform-rate*, the policer allowed only a single burst of traffic to get through before throttling the rate back to the *conform-rate* value.

Figure 7-3 *The Effects of a Policer on Interface Traffic*

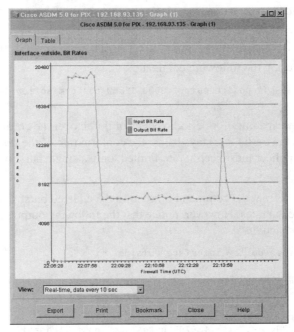

Give Priority Service (LLQ) to Matched Traffic

Ordinarily, packets are placed on the "normal" queue of a firewall interface after they are inspected. The contents of this queue are transmitted in the order that they were placed in the queue, with no regard for the packet contents or QoS requirements. In other words, packets exit a firewall in a best-effort fashion.

Beginning with ASA 7.0(1), a firewall also supports a strict priority queue that can be enabled on each interface. Packets in the priority queue are serviced and sent out before any packets from the normal queue. Therefore, the priority queue is not affected by the volume or types of traffic contained in the normal queue. The priority queue can be used to provide premium service to delay- and jitter-intolerant applications such as streaming video and voice.

You can use the following command to place the matched traffic in the priority queue on the egress interface:

```
Firewall(config-pmap-c)# priority
```

Refer to Chapter 3, "Building Connectivity," Section "3-1: Configuring Interfaces," for more information about priority queue operation.

For example, suppose a firewall is configured to place various types of voice-related packets in its priority interface queues. Class maps are configured to match control packets used for Cisco Skinny and Session Initiation Protocol (SIP). Another class map matches the RTP audio bearer packets. A final class map matches any packet that has its IP DSCP value set to EF (46), indicating the need for priority service. The following configuration commands are used to implement these requirements:

```
Firewall(config)# class-map Class_Skinny
Firewall(config-cmap)# match port tcp range 2000 2002
Firewall(config-cmap)# exit
Firewall(config)# class-map Class_RTP
Firewall(config-cmap)# match rtp 16384 16383
Firewall(config-cmap)# exit
Firewall(config)# class-map Class_SIP
Firewall(config-cmap)# match port udp eq sip
Firewall(config-cmap)# exit
Firewall(config)# class-map Class_DSCP
Firewall(config-cmap)# match dscp ef
Firewall(config-cmap)# exit
!
Firewall(config)# policy-map MyPolicy
Firewall(config-pmap)# class Class_Skinny
Firewall(config-pmap-c)# priority
Firewall(config-pmap-c)# exit
Firewall(config-pmap)# class Class_RTP
Firewall(config-pmap-c)# priority
Firewall(config-pmap-c)# exit
Firewall(config-pmap)# class Class_SIP
Firewall(config-pmap-c)# priority
Firewall(config-pmap-c)# exit
Firewall(config-pmap)# class Class_DSCP
Firewall(config-pmap-c)# priority
Firewall(config-pmap-c)# exit
Firewall(config)# service-policy MyPolicy interface outside
Firewall(config)# service-policy MyPolicy interface inside
```

Default Policy Definitions

An ASA running release 7.0(1) or later, or a FWSM running 3.1(1) or later, automatically configures a default class map and a default policy map. The default policy map is referenced by a service policy that is applied globally to all firewall interfaces. Figure 7-4 shows the default modular policies.

Figure 7-4 *Default Modular Policy Definitions*

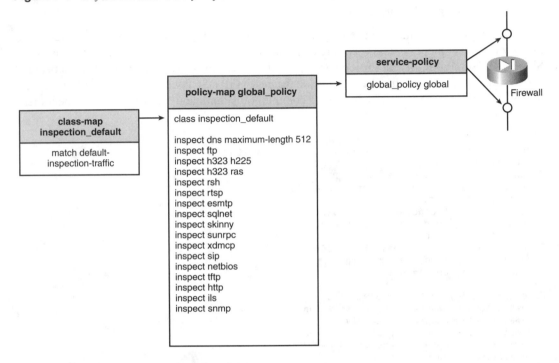

The default class map is named **inspection_default**. It matches against a predefined set of protocols and port numbers called **default-inspection-traffic**. This is a "catchall" case that matches against the default primary ports for every possible inspection engine.

TIP   The **default-inspection-traffic** definition does not appear in the firewall configuration. To see how it is defined, use the context-based help within a class-map configuration, as in the following example:

```
Firewall(config)# class-map test
Firewall(config-cmap)# match ?
mpf-class-map mode commands/options:
  access-list              Match an Access List
  any                      Match any packet
  default-inspection-traffic Match default inspection traffic:
                  ctiqbe----tcp--2748    dns-------udp--53
                  ftp-------tcp--21      gtp-------udp--2123,3386
                  h323-h225-tcp--1720    h323-ras--udp--1718-1719
                  http------tcp--80      icmp------icmp
                  ils-------tcp--389     mgcp------udp--2427,2727
                  netbios---udp--137-138 radius-acct---udp--1646
                  rpc-------udp--111     rsh-------tcp--514
```

rtsp------tcp--554	sip-------tcp--5060
sip-------udp--5060	skinny----tcp--2000
smtp------tcp--25	sqlnet----tcp--1521
tftp------udp--69	xdmcp-----udp--177

The default policy map is named **global_policy**. It references only the **inspection_default** class map. It also has a set of predefined actions, which invoke the inspection engines as shown in Figure 7-4.

The default service policy references policy map **global_policy** and applies it to "global," or to every active firewall interface. The net effect of the default configuration is as follows:

- All traffic is matched against the default inspection engine settings.

- Only the 22 predefined inspection engines are active. Only traffic matching the default protocols and ports of these are inspected. All other traffic is denied unless other nondefault policies are configured.

- Traffic matching the default inspection engines is inspected, regardless of the firewall interface.

You can add your own modular policies to the default policies in two ways:

- You can configure the existing default class map and policy map to add additional matches and actions.

  Although this simplifies the configuration because you do not have to configure new class maps and policy maps, any changes you make to the default policies are applied to all the firewall interfaces. In other words, you lose some ability to fully customize the security policies, because the **global_policy** policy map is applied globally by default.

- You can configure new class maps and new policy maps and apply those to one or more interfaces with a service policy. This approach offers the most scalability and granularity.

  You can apply only one policy map to an interface with a service policy. However, you can apply your own policy map to an interface, even if the default policy map is already applied in the default service policy. One service policy can overlay the default service policy on any interface because the default is used globally.

7-3: Application Inspection

A stateful firewall can easily examine the source and destination parameters of packets passing through it. Many applications use protocols that also embed address or port information *inside* the packet, requiring special handling for examination.

Application inspection allows a firewall to dig inside the packets used by certain applications. The firewall can find and use the embedded information in its stateful application layer inspection engines.

Embedded address information can also become confusing when you use NAT. If the packet addresses are being translated, the firewall must also perform the same translation on any corresponding embedded addresses.

Application inspection also monitors any secondary channels or "buddy ports" that are opened as a part of an application connection. Only the primary or well-known port needs to be configured for the application inspection. In addition, only the primary port needs to be permitted in an access list applied to a firewall interface.

This becomes important for inbound connections, where permitted ports must be explicitly configured in the access list. Any secondary connections that are negotiated are tracked, and the appropriate access (additional xlate and conn entries) is added automatically.

To illustrate how this works, consider a simple example with the passive FTP application protocol, as shown in Figure 7-5. An FTP client is located on the outside of a firewall, and the FTP server is inside. The access list applied to the outside interface only permits inbound connections to TCP port 21, the FTP control channel. As soon as the client opens a connection to port 21, the server responds with the port number of the data channel the client should use next.

Figure 7-5 *An Example of FTP Application Inspection*

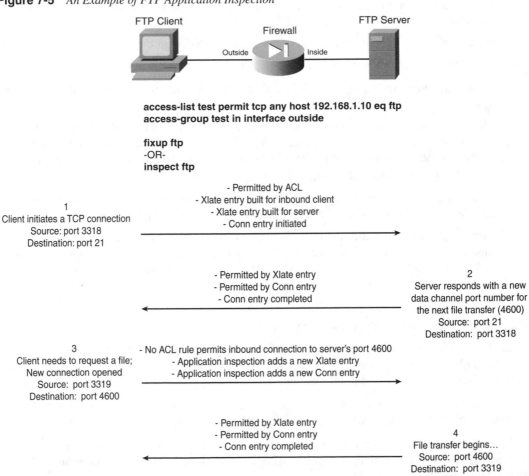

When the client initiates the inbound data connection to the server's negotiated port number, the firewall does not have an explicit access list statement to permit it. In fact, because the new connection port is negotiated within a previous FTP exchange over the control channel, the port number cannot be known ahead of time. However, the FTP application inspection understands the FTP protocol and listens to the packet exchange between the client and server. The firewall overhears the data channel port negotiation and can automatically create xlate and conn entries for it dynamically.

In releases before ASA 7.0(1), application inspection is called a *fixup*. If a fixup is enabled, it is used to examine *all* traffic passing through the firewall. Beginning with ASA 7.0(1) and FWSM 3.1(1), application inspection is much more flexible. Inspection engines can be used to examine specific types of traffic.

Table 7-6 lists the applications and well-known ports supported for application inspection on Cisco firewall platforms running PIX software.

Table 7-6 *Application Inspection: Applications and Ports Supported*

Application Protocol	Keyword	PIX 6.3	ASA, FWSM
CTIQBE	ctiqbe	TCP 2748 (disabled)	TCP 2748 (disabled)
CU-SeeMe	—	UDP 7648 (always enabled)	—
DNS	dns	UDP 53	UDP 53
ESMTP	esmtp	—	TCP 25
ESP-IKE	esp-ike	— (disabled)	—
FTP	ftp	TCP 21	TCP 21
GTP version 1	gtp	—	UDP 2123, 3386 (disabled)
H.323: H225 H.323: RAS	h323 h225 h323 ras	TCP 1720 UDP 1718 to 1719	TCP 1720 UDP 1718 to 1719
HTTP	http	TCP 80	TCP 80 (disabled)
ICMP	icmp	—	(no port; disabled)
ICMP Error Messages	icmp error	(no port)	(no port; disabled)
ILS/LDAP	ils	TCP 389	TCP 389
MGCP	mgcp	UDP 2427, 2727 (disabled)	UDP 2427, 2727 (disabled)
NBDS	netbios	UDP 138 (always enabled)	UDP 138
NBNS	netbios	UDP 137 (always enabled)	UDP 137

continues

Section 7-3

Table 7-6 *Application Inspection: Applications and Ports Supported (Continued)*

Application Protocol	Keyword	PIX 6.3	ASA, FWSM
PPTP	pptp	TCP 1723 (disabled)	TCP 1723 (disabled)
RSH	rsh	TCP 514	TCP 514
RTSP	rtsp	TCP 554	TCP 554
SIP	sip	UDP/TCP 5060	UDP/TCP 5060
Skinny/SCCP	skinny	TCP 2000	TCP 2000
SMTP	smtp	TCP 25	TCP 25 (disabled)
SNMP	snmp	UDP 161, 162 (disabled)	UDP 161, 162
SQL*Net	sqlnet	TCP 1521	TCP 1521
SunRPC	sunrpc	TCP/UDP 111 (always enabled)	TCP/UDP 111
TFTP	tftp	UDP 69	UDP 69
VDOLive	—	TCP 7000 (always enabled)	—
Windows Media (Netshow)	—	TCP 1755 (always enabled)	—
XDMCP	xdmcp	UDP 177 (always enabled)	UDP 177

Configuring Application Inspection

By default, PIX 6.3 enables only the CU-SeeMe, DNS, FTP, H.323, HTTP, ILS/LDAP, NetBIOS, RSH, RTSP, SIP, SKINNY/SCCP, SMTP, SQL*Net, SunRPC, TFTP, VDO Live, Windows Media, and XDMCP fixups. If the **fixup** command is configured for an application protocol, then the firewall inspects that traffic with an inspection engine.

On an ASA or FWSM platform, application inspection occurs only on traffic that has been classified and applied to a policy. When you use the **inspect** command, as in the following command syntax, only the inspection engine that you specify examines traffic identified by the class map:

```
Firewall(config-pmap-c)# inspect inspect_name [options]
```

As you might imagine, application layer inspection depends heavily on the MPF structure that is described in Section "7-2: Defining Security Policies in a Modular Policy Framework." Within a single policy map, you can configure Layer 3/4 traffic policies, as well as application layer inspection engine definitions.

As soon as an inspection policy is configured, you can monitor its activity with the following command:

```
Firewall# show service-policy
```

This command displays each active service policy, along with the class map and action breakdown. If **inspect** commands are configured as part of a service policy, each one is listed, along with counters for packets inspected and dropped and connections reset. The inspection engines configured in the default global policy **global_policy** are shown in the following example:

```
Firewall# show service-policy
Global policy:
  Service-policy: global_policy
    Class-map: inspection_default
      Inspect: dns maximum-length 512, packet 10, drop 0, reset-drop 0
      Inspect: ftp, packet 39, drop 0, reset-drop 0
      Inspect: h323 h225, packet 0, drop 0, reset-drop 0
      Inspect: h323 ras, packet 0, drop 0, reset-drop 0
      Inspect: rsh, packet 0, drop 0, reset-drop 0
      Inspect: rtsp, packet 0, drop 0, reset-drop 0
      Inspect: esmtp, packet 28, drop 0, reset-drop 0
      Inspect: sqlnet, packet 0, drop 0, reset-drop 0
      Inspect: skinny, packet 0, drop 0, reset-drop 0
      Inspect: sunrpc, packet 0, drop 0, reset-drop 0
      Inspect: xdmcp, packet 0, drop 0, reset-drop 0
      Inspect: sip, packet 0, drop 0, reset-drop 0
      Inspect: netbios, packet 27, drop 0, reset-drop 0
      Inspect: tftp, packet 0, drop 0, reset-drop 0
      Inspect: icmp error, packet 0, drop 0, reset-drop 0
      Inspect: icmp, packet 76800, drop 13628, reset-drop 0
```

You can configure any of the supported application layer inspection engines by using the configuration command syntax listed in Table 7-7.

FWSM and ASA (releases 7.0[1] or later) use the **inspect** command. In releases prior to ASA 7.0(1), the **fixup** command configures application inspection and default port numbers.

Table 7-7 lists the command syntax to configure each type of inspection engine for ASA, FWSM, and PIX 6.3 platforms. For application inspection engines that are more advanced, refer to the section of this chapter referenced in the table.

Table 7-7 *Configuring Application Layer Inspection Engines*

Application for Inspection	Command	
CTIQBE	ASA	`Firewall(config-pmap-c)#` **inspect ctiqbe**
	FWSM	`Firewall(config-pmap-c)#` **inspect ctiqbe**
	PIX	`Firewall(config)#` **fixup protocol ctiqbe 2748**
CU-SeeMe	ASA	—
	FWSM	—
	PIX	Always enabled. Supported by the H.323 fixup.

continues

Table 7-7 *Configuring Application Layer Inspection Engines (Continued)*

Application for Inspection	Command	
DCERPC	ASA	Firewall(config-pmap-c)# **inspect dcerpc** [*dcerpc_pmap_name*] See the section "Configuring DCERPC Inspection" later in the chapter.
	FWSM	—
	PIX	—
DNS	ASA	Firewall(config-pmap-c)# **inspect dns** [*dns_pmap_name*] See the section "Configuring DNS Inspection" later in the chapter.
	FWSM	Firewall(config-pmap-c)# **inspect dns** [**maximum-length** *max_pkt_length*]
	PIX	Firewall(config)# **fixup protocol dns** [**maximum-length** *max_pkt_length*]
ESMTP	ASA	Firewall(config-pmap-c)# **inspect esmtp** [*esmtp_pmap_name*] See the section "Configuring ESMTP Inspection" later in the chapter.
	FWSM	—
	PIX	—
ESP with PAT (IPSec)	ASA	—
	FWSM	—
	PIX	Firewall(config)# **fixup protocol esp-ike**
FTP	ASA	Firewall(config-pmap-c)# **inspect ftp** [*ftp_pmap_name*] See the sections "Configuring FTP Inspection—ASA 7.2(1) or Later" and "Configuring FTP Inspection—FWSM and ASA 7.0-7.1" later in the chapter.
	FWSM	Firewall(config-pmap-c)# **inspect ftp** [**strict** [*ftp_map_name*]]
	PIX	Firewall(config)# **fixup protocol ftp** [**strict**] [*port*]
GTP	ASA	Firewall(config-pmap-c)# **inspect gtp** [*gtp_pmap_name*] See the sections "Configuring GTP Inspection—ASA 7.2(1) and Later" and "Configuring GTP Inspection—FWSM and ASA 7.0-7.1" later in the chapter.

Table 7-7   *Configuring Application Layer Inspection Engines (Continued)*

Application for Inspection	Command	
	FWSM	`Firewall(config-pmap-c)#` **inspect gtp**[*gtp_map_name*]
	PIX	—
H.323	ASA	`Firewall(config-pmap-c)#` **inspect h323** [*h323_pmap_name*] See the section "Configuring H.323 Inspection" later in the chapter.
	FWSM	`Firewall(config-pmap-c)#` **inspect h323 {h225** [*h225_map*] | **ras}**
	PIX	`Firewall(config)#` **fixup protocol h323 {h225 | ras}** *port*[*-port*]
HTTP	ASA	`Firewall(config-pmap-c)#` **inspect http** [*http_pmap_name*] See the sections "Configuring HTTP Inspection—ASA 7.2(1) and Later" and "Configuring HTTP Inspection—FWSM and ASA 7.0-7.1" later in the chapter.
	FWSM	`Firewall(config-pmap-c)#` **inspect http** [*http_map_name*]
	PIX	`Firewall(config)#` **fixup protocol http** [*port*[*-port*]]
ICMP	ASA	`Firewall(config-pmap-c)#` **inspect icmp** [**error**] See the section "Configuring ICMP Inspection" later in the chapter.
	FWSM	`Firewall(config-pmap-c)#` **inspect icmp** [**error**]
	PIX	`Firewall(config)#` **fixup protocol icmp error**
Internet Locator Service (ILS)/ LDAP	FWSM 2.x	`Firewall(config)#` **fixup protocol ils** [*port*[*-port*]]
	6.x	`Firewall(config)#` **fixup protocol ils** [*port*[*-port*]]
	7.x	`Firewall(config-pmap-c)#` **inspect ils**
Instant Messaging	ASA	`Firewall(config-pmap-c)#` **inspect im** [*im_pmap_name*] See the section "Configuring Instant Messaging (IM) Inspection" later in the chapter.
	FWSM	—
	PIX	—

continues

Table 7-7 *Configuring Application Layer Inspection Engines (Continued)*

Application for Inspection	Command	
IPSec Passthru	ASA	Firewall(config-pmap-c)# **inspect ipsec-pass-thru** [*ipsec_pmap_name*] See the section "Configuring IPSec Passthru Inspection" later in the chapter.
	FWSM	—
	PIX	—
MGCP	ASA	Firewall(config-pmap-c)# **inspect mgcp** [*mgcp_pmap_name*] See the section "Configuring MGCP Inspection—ASA 7.2(1) and Later" later in the chapter.
	FWSM	Firewall(config-pmap-c)# **inspect mgcp** [*mgcp_map_name*]
	PIX	Firewall(config)# **fixup protocol mgcp** [*port*[-*port*]]
NetBIOS	ASA	Firewall(config-pmap-c)# **inspect netbios** [*netbios_pmap_name*] See the section "Configuring NetBIOS Inspection" later in the chapter.
	FWSM	Firewall(config-pmap-c)# **inspect netbios**
	PIX	Always enabled.
PPTP	ASA	Firewall(config-pmap-c)# **inspect pptp**
	FWSM	Firewall(config-pmap-c)# **inspect pptp**
	PIX	Firewall(config)# **fixup protocol pptp** *port*
RADIUS Accounting	ASA	Firewall(config-pmap-c)# **inspect radius-accounting** [*radius_pmap_name*] See the section "Configuring RADIUS Accounting Inspection" later in the chapter.
	FWSM	—
	PIX	—
RSH	ASA	Firewall(config-pmap-c)# **inspect rsh**
	FWSM	Firewall(config-pmap-c)# **inspect rsh**
	PIX	Firewall(config)# **fixup protocol rsh** [*port*]
RTSP	ASA	Firewall(config-pmap-c)# **inspect rtsp**
	FWSM	Firewall(config-pmap-c)# **inspect rtsp**

Table 7-7 *Configuring Application Layer Inspection Engines (Continued)*

Application for Inspection	Command	
	PIX	`Firewall(config)# ` **`fixup protocol rtsp`** `[port]`
SIP	ASA	`Firewall(config-pmap-c)# ` **`inspect sip`**
	FWSM	`Firewall(config-pmap-c)# ` **`inspect sip`**

	PIX	`Firewall(config)# ` **`[no] fixup protocol sip udp`** **`5060`**
		`Firewall(config)# ` **`fixup protocol sip`** `[port[-`
		`port]`

Skinny (SCCP)	ASA	`Firewall(config-pmap-c)# ` **`inspect skinny`**
	FWSM	`Firewall(config-pmap-c)# ` **`inspect skinny`**
	PIX	`Firewall(config)# ` **`fixup protocol skinny`** `[port[-` `port]`
SMTP	ASA	Handled as ESMTP; see the section "Configuring ESMTP Inspection" later in the chapter.
	FWSM	`Firewall(config-pmap-c)# ` **`inspect esmtp`**
	PIX	`Firewall(config)# ` **`fixup protocol smtp`** `[port[-` `port]]`
SNMP	ASA	See the section "Configuring SNMP Inspection" later in the chapter.
	FWSM	`Firewall(config-pmap-c)# ` **`inspect snmp`** `[snmp_map_name]`
	PIX	`Firewall(config)# ` **`fixup protocol snmp 161-162`**
SQL*Net	ASA	`Firewall(config-pmap-c)# ` **`inspect sqlnet`**
	FWSM	`Firewall(config-pmap-c)# ` **`inspect sqlnet`**
	PIX	`Firewall(config)# ` **`fixup protocol sqlnet`** `[port[-` `port]]`
SunRPC	ASA	`Firewall(config-pmap-c)# ` **`inspect sunrpc`**

continues

Table 7-7 *Configuring Application Layer Inspection Engines (Continued)*

Application for Inspection	Command	
	FWSM	`Firewall(config-pmap-c)# inspect sunrpc`
	PIX	Always enabled
TFTP	ASA	`Firewall(config-pmap-c)# inspect tftp`
	FWSM	`Firewall(config-pmap-c)# inspect tftp`
	PIX	`Firewall(config)# fixup protocol tftp [port[-port]]`
XDMCP	ASA	`Firewall(config-pmap-c)# inspect xdmcp`
	FWSM	`Firewall(config-pmap-c)# inspect xdmcp`
	PIX	Always enabled

Notice that none of the ASA or FWSM inspection engine configuration commands accepts a port number. These firewall platforms have a default concept of application port numbers, so you don't have to define them. Any traffic that is matched by a class map will be processed through the appropriate inspection engine, using the default port number.

If a nondefault port is needed, traffic must be matched against the nondefault port in a class map and then sent to an inspection engine specified in a policy map.

In Table 7-7, notice that the **inspect** command does not accept any port numbers for the case in which the default application port needs to be changed. The default port numbers are defined by the **match default-inspection-traffic** command, which is configured by default.

You can change the default port by matching traffic based on the new port number and then using a policy to subject that traffic to the inspection engine.

For example, the **inspect http** command uses default TCP port 80 for its inspection. If you need to use TCP 8080 instead, use the following commands:

```
Firewall(config)# class-map http_8080
Firewall(config-cmap)# match port tcp eq 8080
Firewall(config-cmap)# exit
Firewall(config)# policy-map MyPolicies
Firewall(config-pmap)# class http_8080
Firewall(config-pmap-c)# inspect http
Firewall(config-pmap-c)# exit
Firewall(config-pmap)# exit
Firewall(config)# service-policy MyPolicies interface inside
```

That isn't to say that once you choose a different port for an inspection engine, the original port cannot still be used. Because the structure of policy maps and class maps is modular, you can add another class-map to match another port. The following example shows a policy-map configuration that uses the HTTP inspection engine to use TCP port 80, as well as TCP port 8080.

```
Firewall(config)# class-map http_8080
Firewall(config-cmap)# match port tcp eq 8080
Firewall(config-cmap)# exit
Firewall(config)# class-map http_80
Firewall(config-cmap)# match port tcp eq 80
Firewall(config-cmap)# exit
Firewall(config)# policy-map MyPolicies
Firewall(config-pmap)# class http_8080
Firewall(config-pmap-c)# inspect http
Firewall(config-pmap-c)# exit
Firewall(config-pmap)# class http_80
Firewall(config-pmap-c)# inspect http
Firewall(config-pmap)# exit
Firewall(config)# service-policy MyPolicies interface inside
```

As the ASA software releases progress, the MPF continues to get more flexible and versatile. There are now so many pieces to the MPF puzzle that you can become overwhelmed on where to start and how to approach the configuration.

Figure 7-6 shows the entire range of things you can configure as a part of the MPF structure. As well, dotted lines show how one piece of the MPF is configured and then referenced in another piece. Refer to this figure to keep your bearings as you configure various class maps and policy maps in the remainder of this chapter.

Matching Text with Regular Expressions

Beginning with ASA 7.2(1), you can define a regular expression to use when matching text fields in many of the application layer inspection engines. Regular expressions can be defined in two ways:

- A single regular expression configured with the following command:

  ```
  Firewall(config)# regex regex_name regular_expression
  ```

- A group of regular expressions configured as a class map with the following commands:

  ```
  Firewall(config)# class-map type regex match-any regex_cmap_name
  ```

  ```
  Firewall(config-cmap)# match regex regex_name
  ```

  The class map consists of one or more **match regex** commands, each referencing a single regular expression configured with the **regex** command.

Within a **regex** command, you have to define the actual regular expression as a string of up to 100 characters. You can use regular characters in the *regular_expression* string to match text literally, and you can include special metacharacters to match text in a more abstract way.

Table 7-8 lists the metacharacters and their functions.

Figure 7-6 *The Entire MPF Structure and Interrelationships*

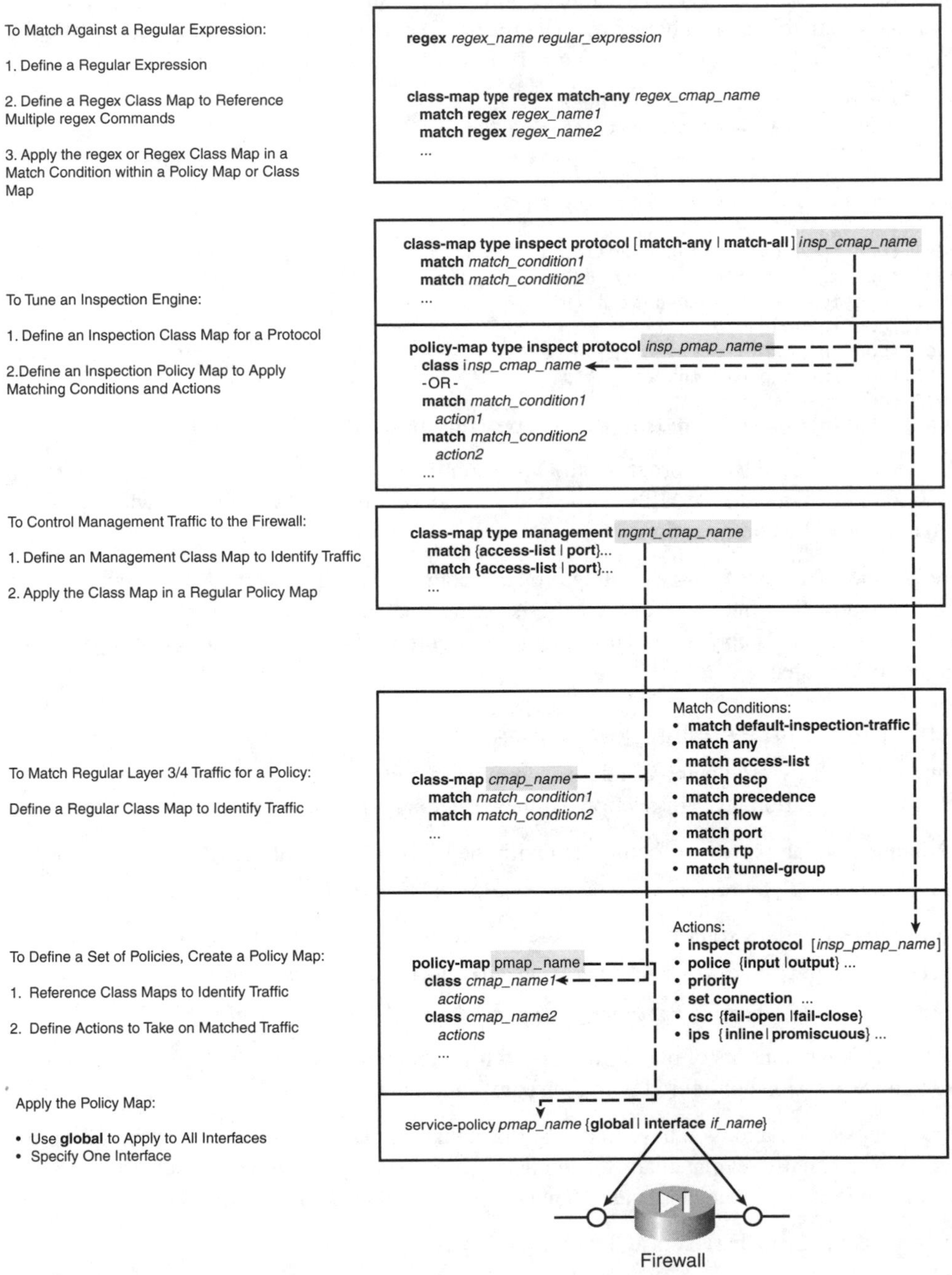

To Match Against a Regular Expression:

1. Define a Regular Expression

2. Define a Regex Class Map to Reference Multiple regex Commands

3. Apply the regex or Regex Class Map in a Match Condition within a Policy Map or Class Map

```
regex regex_name regular_expression


class-map type regex match-any regex_cmap_name
    match regex regex_name1
    match regex regex_name2
    ...
```

```
class-map type inspect protocol [ match-any | match-all ] insp_cmap_name
    match match_condition1
    match match_condition2
    ...
```

To Tune an Inspection Engine:

1. Define an Inspection Class Map for a Protocol

2. Define an Inspection Policy Map to Apply Matching Conditions and Actions

```
policy-map type inspect protocol insp_pmap_name
    class insp_cmap_name
    - OR -
    match match_condition1
        action1
    match match_condition2
        action2
    ...
```

To Control Management Traffic to the Firewall:

1. Define an Management Class Map to Identify Traffic

2. Apply the Class Map in a Regular Policy Map

```
class-map type management mgmt_cmap_name
    match {access-list | port}...
    match {access-list | port}...
    ...
```

To Match Regular Layer 3/4 Traffic for a Policy:

Define a Regular Class Map to Identify Traffic

```
class-map cmap_name
    match match_condition1
    match match_condition2
    ...
```

Match Conditions:
- **match default-inspection-traffic**
- **match any**
- **match access-list**
- **match dscp**
- **match precedence**
- **match flow**
- **match port**
- **match rtp**
- **match tunnel-group**

To Define a Set of Policies, Create a Policy Map:

1. Reference Class Maps to Identify Traffic

2. Define Actions to Take on Matched Traffic

```
policy-map pmap_name
    class cmap_name1
        actions
    class cmap_name2
        actions
    ...
```

Actions:
- **inspect protocol** [insp_pmap_name]
- **police** {**input** | **output**} ...
- **priority**
- **set connection** ...
- **csc** {**fail-open** | **fail-close**}
- **ips** {**inline** | **promiscuous**} ...

Apply the Policy Map:

- Use **global** to Apply to All Interfaces
- Specify One Interface

```
service-policy pmap_name {global | interface if_name}
```

Firewall

Table 7-8 *Regular Expression Metacharacters*

Metacharacter	Name	Function
.	Dot	Matches any single character Example: **b.d** matches bad, bbd, bcd, bdd, bed, and so on
( )	Subexpression	Groups the characters inside the parentheses as a single expression for matching with other metacharacters.
|	Or	Matches either expression that | separates Example: **com|net** matches whatever.com or whatever.net Example: **Ma(r|y)** matches Mar or May
?	Question mark	Matches 0 or 1 of the expression just before the ? Example: **e?smtp** matches smtp (zero e's) or esmtp (1 e) Example: **(12)?** matches 4444, 12444, 1212444, and so on
*	Asterisk	Matches 0, 1, or any number of the expression just before the * Example: **w*** matches cisco.com and www.cisco.com
+	Plus	Matches at least 1 of the expression just before the + Example: **w+** matches www.cisco.com, but not cisco.com
{*n*}	Repeat	Matches if the expression just before {*n*} is repeated exactly n times Example: **(test){2}** matches testtest but not testtesttest
{*n*,}	Minimum repeat	Matches if the expression just before {*n*,} is repeated at least n times Example: **(test){2}** matches testtest and also testtesttest
[*abc*]	Character class	Matches any of the characters listed between the square brackets Example: **[dfhl]og** matches dog, fog, hog, and log, but not frog
[^*abc*]	Not character class	Matches any character that is not listed between the brackets Example: **[^dfhl]og** matches cog, but not dog, fog, hog, or log.
[*a-c*]	Character range class	Matches any character in the range from *a* to *c* Example: **[a-z]** matches any lower case letter, **[A-Z]** matches any upper case letter, **[0-9]** matches any digit.
^	Caret	The caret matches the beginning of a line; any expression following the caret will be matched only if it appears at the beginning of a line. Example: **^Dear** matches "Dear John", but not "John Dear"

continues

Table 7-8 *Regular Expression Metacharacters (Continued)*

Metacharacter	Name	Function
\	Escape	The metacharacter following \ will be treated as a literal character; this is useful when you need to match against something that is normally interpreted as a metacharacter. Example: ***Test** matches *Test*
\r	Carriage return	Matches a carriage return character (ASCII 13 or 0x0d)
\n	Newline	Matches a newline character (ASCII 10 or 0x0a)
\t	Tab	Matches a tab character (ASCII 9 or 0x09)
\f	Form feed	Matches a form feed character (ASCII 12 or 0x0c)
\x*NN*	Escaped hex number	Matches an ASCII character that has the two-digit hex code NN Example: **\x20** matches a space (ASCII 32)
NN	Escaped octal number	Matches an ASCII character that has the three-digit octal code NNN Example: **\040** matches a space (ASCII 32)

As an example of a regular expression configuration, two standalone **regex** commands are used to match against "cisco.com" and "mysite0.com", "mysite1.com", and so on.

```
Firewall(config)# regex Group1 cisco\.com
Firewall(config)# regex Group2 mysite[0-9]\.com
```

Suppose you want to apply both of these regular expressions to a policy. You can group them together into a single regex class map with the following commands:

```
Firewall(config)# class-map type regex match-any my_regex_groups
Firewall(config-cmap)# match regex Group1
Firewall(config-cmap)# match regex Group2
Firewall(config-cmap)# exit
```

Regular expressions can be difficult to formulate, especially when metacharacters are used. You can experiment with a regular expression from the regular EXEC level prompt—without having to make any configuration changes first. Use the following command to test a regular expression:

```
Firewall# test regex input_text  regular_expression
```

Enter some sample *input_text*, as if the firewall is searching through a URL or some other text field. Enter the regular expression you want to test. If the input text or regular expression contains any spaces, be sure to surround the text string with quotation marks.

The firewall will return the result of the regular expression match. In the following examples, the firewall has announced if the regular expression match has succeeded or failed. Remember that a failed match does not necessarily indicate that your regular expression is incorrect or poorly formed—your regular expression needs correcting only if it produces results that do not match your expectations.

```
Firewall# test regex "see the dog run" "dog | cat"
INFO: Regular expression match succeeded.
Firewall# test regex "see the pig run" "dog | cat"
INFO: Regular expression match failed.
Firewall# test regex "the frog is big" "[dfhl]og"
INFO: Regular expression match failed.
```

Configuring DCERPC Inspection

Distributed Computing Environment Remote Procedure Call (DCERPC) is a Microsoft protocol used by client machines to run software remotely from a server. The clients communicate with an Endpoint Mapper, which sets up secondary connections for the clients to use when they begin remote program execution.

Beginning with ASA 7.2(1), you can enable DCERPC inspection with an optional inspection policy map. Use the following steps to configure DCERPC inspection:

1. (Optional) Define a DCERPC inspection policy map:

   ```
   Firewall(config)# policy-map type inspect dcerpc dcerrpc_pmap_name
   ```

2. Set DCERPC parameters:

   ```
   Firewall(config-pmap)# parameters
   ```

   First, enter the **parameters** mode, then configure one or more parameters with the commands shown in the following table:

Parameter Command Syntax	Description
`Firewall(config-pmap-p)# timeout pinhole hh:mm:ss`	Adjust the pinhole timer; by default, DCERPC pinholes are closed after 2 minutes.
`Firewall(config-pmap-p)# endpoint-mapper [epm-service-only] [lookup-operation [timeout hh:mm:ss]]`	Tune the endpoint mapper service: Use **epm-service-only** to enforce the use of the endpoint mapper service during binding, **lookup-operation** to enable the lookup function, and **timeout** to set the timeout value for pinholes created during lookup.

3. Enable DCERPC inspection:

   ```
   Firewall(config-pmap-c)# inspect dcerpc [dcerpc_pmap_name]
   ```

   The **inspect dcerpc** command must be entered as an action in a policy map. If you have configured a DCERPC inspection class map, you can identify it here as *dcerpc_pmap_name*.

As an example, DCERPC inspection is enabled with a pinhole timeout of 5 minutes. You could use the following commands to accomplish this purpose:

```
Firewall(config)# policy-map type inspect dcerpc_policy
Firewall(config-pmap)# parameters
Firewall(config-pmap-p)# timeout pinhole 0:5:0
```

```
!
Firewall(config)# class-map MyClass
Firewall(config-cmap)# match any
Firewall(config-cmap)# exit
Firewall(config)# policy-map MyPolicy
Firewall(config-pmap)# class MyClass
Firewall(config-pmap-c)# inspect dcerpc dcerpc_policy
Firewall(config-pmap-c)# exit
Firewall(config-pmap)# exit
Firewall(config)# service-policy MyPolicy interface outside
```

Configuring DNS Inspection

If DNS inspection is enabled, a firewall will tear down the DNS connection after the first reply from a DNS server is seen. The DNS record is also examined, and the A-record is rewritten according to any address translation stemming from the **alias**, **static**, and **nat** commands. By default, the DNS message length is held to 512 bytes.

Beginning with ASA 7.2(1), DNS inspection parameters can be defined in an inspection policy map, which is applied to the DNS inspection engine. You can use the following steps to configure DNS inspection:

1. (Optional) Define a DNS inspection policy map:

   Firewall(config)# **policy-map type inspect dns** [**match-any** | **match-all**] *pmap_name*

   By default, the policy map matches the first condition found, if multiple **match** commands are configured. This is the same as giving the **match-any** keyword. You can use the **match-all** keyword instead, to require that every **match** command is met.

2. Define matching conditions and their actions:

Match and Action Command Syntax	Description
Firewall(config-pmap)# **match** [**not**] **dns-class** {**eq** *value* | **IN**} | {**range** *min max*}} Firewall(config-pmap-c)# {**drop** | **drop-connection** | **enforce-tsig**} [**log**]	Match: DNS class as a value (0–65535) or **IN** or a range. Action: Drop the packet, drop or reset the connection, enforce a TSIG resource record; log optional.
Firewall(config-pmap)# **match** [**not**] **dns-type** {**eq** *value*} | {**range** *min max*}} Firewall(config-pmap-c)# {**drop** | **drop-connection** | **enforce-tsig**} [**log**]	Match: DNS query or resource record type. Type value can be 0–65535 or one of the following keywords: **A** (IPv4 address record), **AXFR** (zone transfer), **CNAME** (canonical name), **IXFR** (incremental transfer), **NS** (authoritative name server), **SOA** (start of authority), **TSIG** (transaction signature). Type can also be a range of values. Action: Drop the packet, drop or reset the connection, enforce a TSIG resource record; log optional.

`Firewall(config-pmap)# ` **`match`** `[` **`not`** `]` **`domain-name regex`** `{` *`regex`* ` | ` **`class`** *`regex_class_name`* `}`
 	
`Firewall(config-pmap-c)# {` **`drop`** ` | ` **`drop-connection`** ` | ` **`enforce-tsig`** `}` `[` **`log`** `]`
	Match: Domain name, as a regular expression.
	
	Action: Drop the packet, drop or reset the connection, enforce a TSIG resource record; log optional.

`Firewall(config-pmap)# ` **`match`** `[` **`not`** `]` **`header-flag`** *`value`* `Firewall(config-pmap-c)# {` **`drop`** ` | ` **`drop-connection`** ` | ` **`mask`** ` | ` **`enforce-tsig`** `}` `[` **`log`** `]`	Match: Header flag, a hex value 0x0-0xffff or one of the following keywords: **AA** (authoritative answer), **QR** (query), **RA** (recursion available), **RD** (recursion desired), or **TC** (truncation). Action: Drop the packet, drop or reset the connection, mask the header flag, or enforce a TSIG resource record; log optional.
`Firewall(config-pmap)# ` **`match`** `[` **`not`** `]` **`question`** `Firewall(config-pmap-c)# {` **`drop`** ` | ` **`drop-connection`** ` | ` **`enforce-tsig`** `}` `[` **`log`** `]`	Match: DNS question field. Action: Drop the packet, drop or reset the connection, or enforce a TSIG resource record; log optional.

`Firewall(config-pmap)# ` **`match`** `[` **`not`** `]` **`resource-record`** `{` **`additional`** ` | ` **`answer`** ` | ` **`authority`** `}`
 	
`Firewall(config-pmap-c)# {` **`drop`** ` | ` **`drop-connection`** ` | ` **`enforce-tsig`** `}` `[` **`log`** `]`
	Match: DNS resource record type.
	
	Action: Drop the packet, drop or reset the connection, or enforce a TSIG resource record; log optional.

As well, you can configure a DNS inspection class map with the **class-map type inspection dns** *dns_cmap_name* command. That inspection class map can contain any of the **match** commands listed here, along with their associated action commands. The idea is to group match and action commands that might be needed in multiple DNS inspection policies.

Then you can reference the inspection class map in the inspection policy map with the following command:

`Firewall(config-pmap)# ` **`class`** *`dns_cmap_name`*

By referencing the inspection class map in several places, you save yourself the trouble of configuring the same **match** and action commands again and again.

3. Set DNS parameters:

`Firewall(config-pmap)# ` **`parameters`**

First, enter the **parameters** mode and then configure one or more parameters with the commands shown in the following table:

Parameter Command Syntax	Description
Firewall(config-pmap-p)# **dns-guard**	Enable the DNS Guard feature (enabled by default).
Firewall(config-pmap-p)# **id-mismatch** {**count** *number seconds*} **action log**	Log when ID mismatches occur over a threshold of *number* in *seconds* (default 30 in 3 seconds).
Firewall(config-pmap-p)# **id-randomization**	Randomize the DNS identifier to help prevent DNS poisoning attacks; by default, the DNS identifier field is passed through the firewall unchanged.
Firewall(config-pmap-p)# **message-length maximum** {*max_length* | {**client** *max_length* [**auto**]} | {**server** *max_length* [**auto**]}}	Set the maximum DNS message size globally as *max_length* (512-65535 bytes) or for the **client** or the **server**.
Firewall(config-pmap-p)# **nat-rewrite**	Rewrite the A record according to NAT (the default)
Firewall(config-pmap-p)# **protocol-enforcement**	Examine DNS messages for strict protocol checks (the default)
Firewall(config-pmap-p)# **tsig enforced action** [**drop**] **log**	Require TSIG resource records; if they are not found in DNS messages, a log message is generated. Add **drop** to drop the messages, too.

4. Enable DNS inspection:

```
Firewall(config-pmap-c)# inspect dns [dns_pmap_name]
```

The **inspect dns** command must be entered as an action in a policy map. You can also apply a DNS inspection policy map by giving its name *pmap_name*.

As an example, a DNS inspection policy map is configured to match zone transfer requests and to drop and log them. The inspection engine is also configured to randomize the ID field. The following commands can be used to configure DNS inspection:

```
Firewall(config)# policy-map type inspect dns match-any MyDNSPolicy
Firewall(config-pmap)# match dns-type eq AXFR
Firewall(config-pmap-c)# drop log
Firewall(config-pmap-c)# exit
Firewall(config-pmap)# parameters
Firewall(config-pmap-p)# id-randomization
Firewall(config-pmap-p)# exit
Firewall(config-pmap)# exit
Firewall(config)# policy-map MyPolicy
Firewall(config-pmap)# class class-default
Firewall(config-pmap-c)# inspect dns MyDNSPolicy
Firewall(config-pmap-c)# exit
Firewall(config-pmap)# exit
Firewall(config)# service-policy MyPolicy interface outside
```

Configuring ESMTP Inspection

ESMTP inspection can be used to detect a variety of suspicious email activity. As well, it can block specific senders, receivers, and attempts at mail relay.

Beginning with ASA 7.2(1), ESMTP inspection parameters can be defined in an inspection policy map, which is applied to the ESMTP inspection engine. You can use the following steps to configure ESMTP inspection:

1. (Optional) Define an ESMTP inspection policy map:

   ```
   Firewall(config)# policy-map type inspect esmtp esmtp_pmap_name
   ```

2. Define any matching conditions and their actions:

Match and Action Command Syntax	Description
`Firewall(config-pmap)# match [not] body {length gt length}	{line gt length}}`	Match: Mail message body length (**length**) or line length (**line**, 1–998 characters).
`Firewall(config-pmap-c)# {drop-connection	reset} [log]`	Action: Drop or reset the connection; log optional.
`Firewall(config-pmap)# match [not] cmd {{RCPT count gt number}	{line length gt length}	{verb verb}}`	Match: ESMTP command; RCPT *number* is number of recipients (1–10,000), line *length* (1–998 characters), *verb* is one of the following ESMTP verbs: **AUTH, DATA, EHLO, ETRN, HELO, HELP, MAIL, NOOP, QUIT, RCPT, RSET, SAML, SOML,** or **VRFY.**
`Firewall(config-pmap-c)# {drop-connection	reset	rate-limit rate	mask} [log]`	Action: Drop or reset the connection, rate limit the messages to *rate* messages per second, mask the message; log optional.
`Firewall(config-pmap)# match [not] ehlo-reply-parameter {8bitmime	auth	binarymime	checkpoint	dsn	ecode	etrn	others	pipelining	size	vrfy}`	Match: EHLO reply parameter.
`Firewall(config-pmap-c)# {drop-connection	reset	mask} [log]`	Action: Drop or reset the connection or mask the message; log optional.
`Firewall(config-pmap)# match [not] header {{length gt length}	{line length gt length}	{to-fields count count}}`	Match: Mail message header length, line count (1–998 characters), or the number of To: fields (1–10,000).
`Firewall(config-pmap-c)# {drop-connection	reset} [log]`	Action: Drop or reset the connection; log optional.
`Firewall(config-pmap)# match [not] invalid-recipients count gt count`	Match: Maximum number of 5xx error messages from invalid recipients; *count* (1–1000 recipients).
`Firewall(config-pmap-c)# {drop-connection	reset} [log]`	Action: Drop or reset the connection; log optional.

Match and Action Command Syntax	Description
`Firewall(config-pmap)# match [not] mime {encoding {7bit	8bit	base64	binary	others	quoted-printable}}	{filename length gt `*`length`*`}	{filetype regex {`*`regex`*`	class `*`regex_cmap_name`*`}}`  `Firewall(config-pmap-c)# {drop-connection	reset} [log]`	Match: MIME encoding type, filename length (1–1000 characters), or filetype (regular expression). Action: Drop or reset the connection; log optional.
`Firewall(config-pmap)# match [not] sender-address {{length gt `*`length`*`}	{regex {`*`regex`*`	class `*`regex_cmap_name`*`}}`  `Firewall(config-pmap-c)# {drop-connection	reset} [log]`	Match: Sender address *length* (1–1000 characters) or content (regular expression). Action: Drop or reset the connection; log optional.

3. Set ESMTP parameters:

   `Firewall(config-pmap)# parameters`

   First, enter the **parameters** mode, then configure one or more parameters with the commands shown in the following table:

Parameter Command Syntax	Description
`Firewall(config-pmap-p)# mail-relay `*`domain_name`*` action [drop-connection] log`	For a mail relay using the domain name, either drop the connection and/or log.
`Firewall(config-pmap-p)# mask-banner`	Mask or obfuscate the mail server banner.
`Firewall(config-pmap-p)# special-character action [drop-connection] log`	If special characters pipe (|), back quote (`` ` ``), or NUL are present in the sender or receiver address, drop the connection and/or log.

4. Enable ESMTP inspection:

   `Firewall(config-pmap-c)# inspect esmtp [`*`esmtp_pmap_name`*`]`

   The **inspect esmtp** command must be entered as an action in a policy map. You can also apply an ESMTP inspection policy map by giving its name *esmtp_pmap_name*.

As an example, an ESMTP application inspection policy map is configured to reset and log connections when more than 100 email recipients are given in a message.

As well, the security policies prevent anyone from sending email using an address that is outside the domain name "mycompany.com." A regular expression **PermittedSenders** is configured to match against email addresses containing "@mycompany.com". The policy map matches against any sender address that does not contain the regular expression. Connections attempting to send to those addresses are simply reset and logged.

Finally, any connections attempting to use a mail relay in the domain "mycompany.com" will be dropped and logged.

The following configuration commands can be used to configure these ESMTP inspection policies:

```
Firewall(config)# regex PermittedSenders "@mycompany.com"
Firewall(config)# policy-map type inspect esmtp MyESMTPPolicy
Firewall(config-pmap)# match cmd RCPT count gt 100
Firewall(config-pmap-c)# reset log
Firewall(config-pmap-c)# exit
Firewall(config-pmap)# match not sender-address regex PermittedSenders
Firewall(config-pmap-c)# reset log
Firewall(config-pmap-c)# exit
Firewall(config-pmap)# parameters
Firewall(config-pmap-p)# mail-relay mycompany.com action drop-connection log
Firewall(config-pmap-p)# exit
Firewall(config-pmap)# exit
Firewall(config)# policy-map MyPolicy
Firewall(config-pmap)# class class-default
Firewall(config-pmap-c)# inspect esmtp MyESMTPPolicy
Firewall(config-pmap-c)# exit
Firewall(config-pmap)# exit
Firewall(config)# service-policy MyPolicy interface outside
```

Configuring FTP Inspection—ASA 7.2(1) or Later

FTP can be used to exchange files between a client and a server. FTP is defined in RFC 959. By default, the regular FTP inspection engine maintains any secondary connections negotiated by FTP clients and servers. FTP commands and responses are also tracked.

You can use the following steps to configure FTP inspection in ASA 7.2(1) or later:

1. (Optional) Define an FTP inspection policy map:

    ```
    Firewall(config)# policy-map type inspect ftp ftp_pmap_name
    ```

2. (Optional) Define any matching conditions and their actions:

Match and Action Command Syntax	Description

`Firewall(config-pmap)# match [not] filename regex {regex | class regex_cmap_name}`
 	
`Firewall(config-pmap-c)# reset`
	Match: Filename with regular expression
	
	Action: Reset the connection

`Firewall(config-pmap)# match [not] filetype regex {regex | class regex_cmap_name}`
 	
`Firewall(config-pmap-c)# reset`
	Match: File type with a regular expression
	
	Action: Reset the connection

`Firewall(config-pmap)# match [not] server regex {regex | class regex_cmap_name}`
 	
`Firewall(config-pmap-c)# reset`
	Match: Server banner information with a regular expression
	
	Action: Reset the connection

Match and Action Command Syntax	Description
`Firewall(config-pmap)# match [not]` `username regex {regex	class` `regex_cmap_name}`  `Firewall(config-pmap-c)# reset`	Match: Username with a regular expression Action: Reset the connection

`Firewall(config-pmap)# match [not]`
`request-command command1 [command2]`
`...[commandn]`
 	
`Firewall(config-pmap-c)# reset`
	Match: One or more FTP commands, from the following list: **appe** (append to a file), **cdup** (change to the parent directory), **dele** (delete a file on the server), **get** (get a file), **help** (get server help), **mkd** (create a directory), **put** (put a file), **rmd** (remove a directory), **rnfr** (rename from), **rnto** (rename to), **site** (server specific command), or **stou** (store a file with a unique name). Specify multiple commands by separating them with spaces.
	
	Action: Reset the connection

As well, you can configure an FTP inspection class map with the **class-map type inspection ftp** *ftp_cmap_name* command. That inspection class map can contain any of the **match** commands listed here, along with their associated action commands. The idea is to group match and action commands that might be needed in multiple FTP inspection policies.

Then you can reference the inspection class map in the inspection policy map with the following command:

`Firewall(config-pmap)# class ftp_cmap_name`

By referencing the inspection class map in several places, you save yourself the trouble of configuring the same **match** and action commands again and again.

3. Set FTP parameters:

`Firewall(config-pmap)# parameters`

First, enter the **parameters** mode and then configure one or more parameters with the following commands:

Parameter Command Syntax	Description
`Firewall(config-pmap-p)# mask-banner`	Mask or obfuscate the server banner
`Firewall(config-pmap-p)# mask-syst-reply`	Hide the server response from the clients

4. Enable FTP inspection:

`Firewall(config-pmap-c)# inspect ftp [ftp_pmap_name]`

The **inspect ftp** command must be entered as an action in a policy map. You can also apply an FTP inspection policy map by giving its name as *ftp_pmap_name*.

As an example, an FTP inspection policy map is configured to reset any connection where the client attempts to use any FTP command other than the read-only CDUP, GET, and HELP commands. As well, the inspection engine will mask any FTP server's banner so that clients cannot glean any details about the server from it. The following commands can be used to configure the FTP inspection policies:

```
Firewall(config)# policy-map type inspect ftp MyFTPPolicy
Firewall(config-pmap)# match not request-command cdup get help
Firewall(config-pmap-c)# reset
Firewall(config-pmap-c)# exit
Firewall(config-pmap)# parameters
Firewall(config-pmap-p)# mask-banner
Firewall(config-pmap-p)# exit
Firewall(config-pmap)# exit
Firewall(config)# policy-map MyPolicy
Firewall(config-pmap)# class class-default
Firewall(config-pmap-c)# inspect ftp MyFTPPolicy
Firewall(config-pmap-c)# exit
Firewall(config-pmap)# exit
Firewall(config)# service-policy MyPolicy interface outside
```

Configuring FTP Inspection—FWSM and ASA 7.0-7.1

For ASA releases prior to 7.2(1) and FWSM, you can use the following commands to configure FTP inspection and an FTP map:

1. Define the FTP map name:

   ```
   Firewall(config)# ftp-map ftp_map_name
   ```

   The FTP map is named *ftp_map_name* (up to 64 characters).

2. (Optional) Deny specific FTP request commands:

   ```
   Firewall(config-ftp-map)# deny-request-cmd request_list
   ```

   The firewall drops FTP commands listed in *request_list* before they reach the server. You can list one or more of the following FTP command keywords, separated by spaces: **appe** (append to a file), **cdup** (change to the parent directory), **dele** (delete a file), **get** (retrieve a file), **help** (get help from the FTP server), **mkd** (make a new directory), **put** (store a file), **rmd** (remove a directory), **rnfr** (rename a file from), **rnto** (rename a file to), **site** (a server-specific command), or **stou** (store a file with a unique name).

3. (Optional) Mask the reply to a **syst** command:

   ```
   Firewall(config-ftp-map)# mask-syst-reply
   ```

   An FTP client can send the **syst** command to find out which operating system the FTP server uses. When the **mask-syst-reply** command is used, the firewall masks the server's reply with Xs so that the information remains hidden.

4. Enable the FTP inspection engine

   ```
   Firewall(config-pmap-c)# inspect ftp [strict [ftp_map_name]]
   ```

With the **strict** keyword, FTP connections will be inspected for compliance with the RFC. If you defined an FTP map, it can be applied here as *ftp_map_name*.

As an example, suppose FTP inspection is configured to deny any FTP command operation that would alter files or directories on the FTP server. You could use the following commands to accomplish this purpose:

```
Firewall(config)# ftp-map MyFTPfilter
Firewall(config-ftp-map)# deny-request-cmd appe dele mkd put rmd rnfr rnto stou
Firewall(config-ftp-map)# exit
!
Firewall(config)# class-map _MyClass
Firewall(config-cmap)# match any
Firewall(config-cmap)# exit
Firewall(config)# policy-map MyPolicy
Firewall(config-pmap)# class MyClass
Firewall(config-pmap-c)# inspect ftp strict MyFTPfilter
Firewall(config-pmap-c)# exit
Firewall(config-pmap)# exit
Firewall(config)# service-policy MyPolicy interface outside
```

Configuring GTP Inspection—ASA 7.2(1) and Later

GPRS Tunneling Protocol (GTP) is used to tunnel multiprotocol packets through a General Packet Radio Service (GPRS) network between different GPRS Support Nodes (GSN).

Beginning with ASA 7.2(1), you can enable GTP inspection with an optional inspection policy map. Use the following steps to configure GTP inspection:

1. (Optional) Define a GTP inspection policy map:

```
Firewall(config)# policy-map type inspect gtp gtp_pmap_name
```

2. Define matching conditions and their actions:

Match and Action Command Syntax	Description
Firewall(config-pmap)# **match** [**not**] **apn regex** {*regex* I **class** *regex_cmap_name*} Firewall(config-pmap-c)# {**drop** I **drop-connection** I **reset**} [**log**]	Match: Access point name using regular expression. Action: Drop the packet, drop or reset the connection; log optional.
Firewall(config-pmap)# **match** [**not**]**message id** {*message_id* I **range** *low high*} Firewall(config-pmap-c)# {**drop** I **drop-connection** I **reset**} [**log**]	Match: GTP message ID as a value or range of values 1–255. Action: Drop the packet, drop or reset the connection; log optional.

Match and Action Command Syntax	Description
`Firewall(config-pmap)#` **match** `[not]` **message length min** `min_length` **max** `max_length`	Match: GTP message length within a range; *min_length* and *max_length* are 1–65535; length is GTP header plus body.
`Firewall(config-pmap-c)#` `{`**drop** `|` **drop-connection** `|` **reset**`}}` `[`**log**`]`	Action: Drop the packet, drop or reset the connection; log optional.
`Firewall(config-pmap)#` **match** `[not]` **version** `{`*version_id* `|` *low high*`}`	Match: GTP message version as a value (0–255) or range.
`Firewall(config-pmap-c)#` `{`**drop** `|` **drop-connection** `|` **reset**`}}` `[`**log**`]`	Action: Drop the packet, drop or reset the connection; log optional.

3. Set GTP parameters:

`Firewall(config-pmap)#` **parameters**

First, enter the **parameters** mode and then configure one or more parameters with the commands shown in the following table:

Parameter Command Syntax	Description
`Firewall(config-pmap-p)#` **permit errors**	Allow invalid GTP packets.
`Firewall(config-pmap-p)#` **permit response to-object-group** `to_obj_group_id` **from-object-group** `from_obj_group_id`	Allow GTP responses from GSNs other than the original target, if GSNs are operating as a pool. A pool is defined in a network object group (**object-group network** *obj_group_id*).
`Firewall(config-pmap-p)#` **request-queue** `max_requests`	Set the maximum number (default 200) of GTP requests that will be queued while waiting for a response.
`Firewall(config-pmap-p)#` **timeout** `{`**gsn** `|` **pdp-context** `|` **request** `|` **signaling** `|` **t3-response** `|` **tunnel**`}` `hh:mm:ss`	Set the inactivity timers as **gsn** (inactivity time before a GSN is removed), **pdp-context** (maximum time to begin receiving PDP context), **request** (maximum time to begin receiving a GTP message), **signaling** (inactivity time before GTP signaling is removed), **t3-response** (maximum wait time for a response before GTP connection is removed), or **tunnel** (inactivity time before GTP tunnel is torn down).
`Firewall(config-pmap-p)#` **tunnel-limit** `max_tunnels`	Set the maximum number of active GTP tunnels.

4. Enable GTP inspection:

`Firewall(config-pmap-c)#` **inspect gtp** `[gtp_pmap_name]`

The **inspect gtp** command must be entered as an action in a policy map. If you have configured a GTP inspection class map, you can identify it here as *gtp_pmap_name*.

As an example, a GTP inspection policy map is configured to drop connections that have GTP messages other than a minimum length of 1 and maximum length of 2048. A GTP tunnel limit of 100 is also enforced. The following commands can be used to configure the GTP policies:

```
Firewall(config)# policy-map type inspect gtp MyGTPPolicy
Firewall(config-pmap)# match not message length min 1 max 2048
Firewall(config-pmap-c)# drop-connection
Firewall(config-pmap-c)# exit
Firewall(config-pmap)# parameters
Firewall(config-pmap-p)# tunnel-limit 100
Firewall(config-pmap-p)# exit
Firewall(config-pmap)# exit
!
Firewall(config)# policy-map MyPolicy
Firewall(config-pmap)# class class-default
Firewall(config-pmap-c)# inspect gtp MyGTPPolicy
Firewall(config-pmap-c)# exit
Firewall(config-pmap)# exit
Firewall(config)# service-policy MyPolicy interface outside
```

Configuring GTP Inspection—FWSM and ASA 7.0-7.1

GPRS Tunneling Protocol (GTP) is used to tunnel multiprotocol packets through a General Packet Radio Service (GPRS) network between different GPRS Support Nodes (GSN).

Follow these steps to configure a GTP map for use with the **inspect gtp** command:

1. Define the GTP map name:

    ```
    Firewall(config)# gtp-map gtp_map_name
    ```

    The GTP map is named *gtp_map_name* (up to 64 characters). You must apply the GTP map in a policy map with the following command before it can be used:

    ```
    inspect gtp gtp_map_name
    ```

2. (Optional) Add a GTP map description:

    ```
    Firewall(config-gtpmap)# description string
    ```

    You can add an arbitrary text *string* (up to 200 characters) as a description of the GTP map.

3. Customize GTP options.

    You can use any of the commands listed in Table 7-9 to set a specific GTP inspection parameter in GTP map configuration mode.

Table 7-9   *Setting GTP Inspection Parameters*

Parameter Description	Command Syntax
Allows only international mobile system identifier (IMSI) prefixes: Mobile Country Code (*mcc_code*, three digits) and Mobile Network Code (*mnc_code*, three digits).	Firewall(config-gtp-map)# **mcc** *mcc_code* **mnc** *mnc_code*

Table 7-9 *Setting GTP Inspection Parameters (Continued)*

Parameter Description	Command Syntax
Allows packets with errors.	Firewall(config-gtp-map)# **permit errors**
Drops an access point.	Firewall(config-gtp-map)# **drop apn** *access_point_name*
Drops a message ID (1 to 256).	Firewall(config-gtp-map)# **drop message** *message_id*
Drops the GTP version (0 to 255).	Firewall(config-gtp-map)# **drop version** *version*
Sets the maximum number of requests to be queued waiting for a response (1 to 4294967295; the default is 200).	Firewall(config-gtp-map)# **request-queue** *max_requests*
Permits messages within *min* (1 to 65536) and *max* (1 to 65536) bytes.	Firewall(config-gtp-map)# **message-length min** *min* **max** *max*
Permits no more than *max* tunnels (1 to 4294967295; the default is 500).	Firewall(config-gtp-map)# **tunnel-limit** *max*

For example, the following commands configure a GTP map that allows GTP packets only from Mobile Country Code 310, Mobile Network Codes 001 and 002. All others are dropped. In addition, GTP messages must be between 1 and 2048 bytes in length. Up to 100 GTP tunnels are allowed to pass through the firewall. The GTP map is then applied to the **inspect gtp** command as part of a policy map.

```
Firewall(config)# gtp-map Secure_gtp
Firewall(config-gtp-map)# mcc 310 mnc 001
Firewall(config-gtp-map)# mcc 310 mnc 002
Firewall(config-gtp-map)# message-length min 1 max 2048
Firewall(config-gtp-map)# tunnel-limit 100
Firewall(config-gtp-map)# exit
!
Firewall(config)# policy-map MyPolicy
Firewall(config-pmap)# class class-default
Firewall(config-pmap-c)# inspect gtp Secure_gtp
Firewall(config-pmap-c)# exit
Firewall(config-pmap)# exit
Firewall(config)# service-policy MyPolicy interface outside
```

Configuring H.323 Inspection

Beginning in ASA 7.2(1), you can configure an H.323 application layer inspection engine. This feature tracks H.323 connections, as well as the subsequent H.245 and RTP port numbers and traffic flows.

You can use the following steps to configure H.323 inspection:

1. (Optional) Define an H.323 inspection policy map:

    ```
    Firewall(config)# policy-map type inspect h323 h323_pmap_name
    ```

2. (Optional) Define any matching conditions and their actions:

Match and Action Command Syntax	Description

`Firewall(config-pmap)# match [not] called-party regex {regex | class regex_cmap_name}`
 	
`Firewall(config-pmap-c)# {drop | drop-connection | reset}`
	Match: Called party
	
	Action: Drop the packet, drop the connection, or reset the connection

`Firewall(config-pmap)# match [not] calling-party regex {regex | class regex_cmap_name}`
 	
`Firewall(config-pmap-c)# {drop | drop-connection | reset}`
	Match: Calling party
	
	Action: Drop the packet, drop the connection, or reset the connection

`Firewall(config-pmap)# match media-type {audio | video | data}`
 	
`Firewall(config-pmap-c)# drop`
	Match: Media type
	
	Action: Drop the packet

As well, you can configure an H.323 inspection class map with the **class-map type inspection h323** *h323_cmap_name* command. That inspection class map can contain any of the **match** commands listed here, along with their associated action commands. The idea is to group match and action commands that might be needed in multiple H.323 inspection policies.

Then you can reference the inspection class map in the inspection policy map with the following command:

`Firewall(config-pmap)# class h323_cmap_name`

By referencing the inspection class map in several places, you save yourself the trouble of configuring the same **match** and action commands again and again.

3. Set H.323 parameters:

`Firewall(config-pmap)# parameters`

First, enter the **parameters** mode and then configure one or more parameters with the following commands:

Parameter Command Syntax	Description
`Firewall(config-pmap-p)# call-duration-limit {hh:mm:ss | 0}`	Set the call duration time limit or **0** for no limit
`Firewall(config-pmap-p)# call-party-numbers`	Enforce sending call party numbers during the call setup
`Firewall(config-pmap-p)# h245-tunnel-block action {drop-connection |log}`	When an H.245 tunnel is detected, either drop the connection or generate a log
`Firewall(config-pmap-p)# hsi-group group`	Set the HSI group number

Parameter Command Syntax	Description
`Firewall(config-pmap-p)# `**`rtp-conformance`** **`[enforce-payloadtype]`**	Make sure pinhole RTP packets conform to the RFC; use **enforce-payloadtype** to enforce audio or video, according to signaling
`Firewall(config-pmap-p)# `**`state-checking`**	Check the state of H.323 connections

4. Enable H.323 inspection:

```
Firewall(config-pmap-c)# inspect h323 [h323_pmap_name]
```

The **inspect h323** command must be entered as an action in a policy map. You can also apply an FTP inspection policy map by giving its name as *h323_pmap_name*.

As an example, an H.323 inspection policy map is configured to permit only calls from calling parties beginning with the "859555" prefix (4 digits to follow) and to called parties beginning with the "502555" prefix (4 digits to follow). The inspection engine will also require call party numbers to be included during call setup. It will also enforce RFC conformance for the RTP traffic and will track the state of the H.323 connection. The following commands can be used to configure the H.323 inspection engine policies:

```
Firewall(config)# regex Party1 "859555...."
Firewall(config)# regex Party2 "502555...."
Firewall(config)# policy-map type inspect h323 MyH323Policy
Firewall(config-pmap)# match not calling-party regex Party1
Firewall(config-pmap-c)# drop-connection
Firewall(config-pmap-c)# exit
Firewall(config-pmap)# match not called-party regex Party2
Firewall(config-pmap-c)# drop-connection
Firewall(config-pmap-c)# exit
Firewall(config-pmap)# parameters
Firewall(config-pmap-p)# call-party-numbers
Firewall(config-pmap-p)# rtp-conformance
Firewall(config-pmap-p)# state-checking
Firewall(config-pmap-p)# exit
Firewall(config-pmap)# exit
!
Firewall(config)# policy-map MyPolicy
Firewall(config-pmap)# class class-default
Firewall(config-pmap-c)# inspect h323 MyH323Policy
Firewall(config-pmap-c)# exit
Firewall(config-pmap)# exit
Firewall(config)# service-policy MyPolicy interface outside
```

Configuring HTTP Inspection—ASA 7.2(1) and Later

You can use the following steps to configure the HTTP application layer inspection engine in ASA 7.2(1) or later:

1. (Optional) Define an HTTP inspection policy map:

```
Firewall(config)# policy-map type inspect http http_pmap_name
```

Section 7-3

2. (Optional) Define any matching conditions and their actions:

Match and Action Command Syntax	Description
Firewall(config-pmap)# **match** [**not**] **req-resp content-type mismatch** Firewall(config-pmap-c)# {**drop-connection** | **reset**} [**log**]	Match: HTTP content type mismatch Action: Drop or reset the connection; log optional
Firewall(config-pmap)# **match** [**not**] **request args** {*regex* | **class** *regex_cmap_name*} Firewall(config-pmap-c)# {**drop-connection** | **reset**} [**log**]	Match: HTTP request arguments with a regular expression Action: Drop or reset the connection; log optional
Firewall(config-pmap)# **match** [**not**] **request body** {**length gt** *length* | **regex** {*regex* | **class** *regex_cmap_name*}} Firewall(config-pmap-c)# {**drop-connection** | **reset**} [**log**]	Match: HTTP request body length (in bytes) or content (with a regular expression) Action: Drop or reset the connection; log optional
Firewall(config-pmap)# **match** [**not**] **request header** *field* {**count gt** *count* | **length gt** *length* | **regex** {*regex* | **class** *regex_cmap_name*}} Firewall(config-pmap-c)# {**drop-connection** | **reset**} [**log**]	Match: HTTP request header field as a keyword from the list shown in Table 7-10 **count** tallies the number of instances (0-127) of the header field, **length** measures the length (1-32767 characters) of the header field, **regex** matches against a regular expression. Action: Drop or reset the connection; log optional
Firewall(config-pmap)# **match** [**not**] **request method** *method* Firewall(config-pmap-c)# {**drop-connection** | **reset**} [**log**]	Match: HTTP request method type as a keyword from the list shown in Table 7-10 Action: Drop or reset the connection; log optional
Firewall(config-pmap)# **match** [**not**] **request uri** {**length gt** *length* | **regex** {*regex* | **class** *regex_cmap_name*} Firewall(config-pmap-c)# {**drop-connection** | **reset**} [**log**]	Match: HTTP request URI field length (1-65535 characters) or context (regular expression) Action: Drop or reset the connection; log optional
Firewall(config-pmap)# **match** [**not**] **response body** {**active-x** | **java-applet** | **length** *length* | **regex** {*regex* | **class** *regex_cmap_name*}} Firewall(config-pmap-c)# {**drop-connection** | **reset**} [**log**]	Match: HTTP response body content (ActiveX or Java), body length, or body content (regular expression) Action: Drop or reset the connection; log optional

Match and Action Command Syntax	Description
`Firewall(config-pmap)# match [not] response header field {count gt count	length gt length	regex {regex	class regex_cmap_name}}`  `Firewall(config-pmap-c)# {drop-connection	reset} [log]`	Match: HTTP response header *field* as a keyword from the list shown in Table 7-10 **count** tallies the number of instances (0-127) of the header field, **length** measures the length (1-32767 characters) of the header field, **regex** matches against a regular expression. Action: Drop or reset the connection; log optional
`Firewall(config-pmap)# match [not] response status-line regex {regex	class regex_cmap_name}`  `Firewall(config-pmap-c)# {drop-connection	reset} [log]`	Match: HTTP response status line content (regular expression) Action: Drop or reset the connection; log optional

As well, you can configure an HTTP inspection class map with the **class-map type inspection http** *http_cmap_name* command. That inspection class map can contain any of the **match** commands listed here, along with their associated action commands. The idea is to group match and action commands that might be needed in multiple HTTP inspection policies.

Then you can reference the inspection class map in the inspection policy map with the following command:

`Firewall(config-pmap)# class http_cmap_name`

Table 7-10   *Keywords for HTTP Match Request/Response Header and Method Commands*

Command	Acceptable Keywords
match request header *field*	**accept, accept-charset, accept-encoding, accept-language, allow, authorization, cache-control, connection, content-encoding, content-language, content-length, content-location, content-md5, content-range, content-type, cookie, count, date, expect, expires, from, host, if-match, if-modified-since, if-none-match, if-range, if-unmodified-since, last-modified, length, max-forwards, non-ascii, pragma, proxy-authorization, range, referer, te, trailer, transfer-encoding, upgrade, user-agent, via, warning**
match request method *method*	**bcopy, bdelete, bmove, bpropfind, bproppatch, connect, copy, delete, edit, get, getattribute, getattributenames, getproperties, head, index, lock, mkcol, mkdir, move, notify, options, poll, post, propfind, proppatch, put, revadd, revlabel, revlog, revnum, save, search, setattribute, startrev, stoprev, subscribe, trace, unedit, unlock, unsubscribe**

continues

Table 7-10   *Keywords for HTTP Match Request/Response Header and Method Commands (Continued)*

Command	Acceptable Keywords
match response header *field*	**accept-ranges, age, allow, cache-control, connection, content-encoding, content-language, content-length, content-location, content-md5, content-range, content-type, count, date, eTag, expires, last-modified, length, location, non-ascii, pragma, proxy-authenticate, retry-after, server, set-cookie, trailer, transfer-encoding, upgrade, vary, via, warning, www-authenticate**

By referencing the inspection class map in several places, you save yourself the trouble of configuring the same **match** and action commands again and again.

3. Set HTTP parameters:

```
Firewall(config-pmap)# parameters
```

First, enter the **parameters** mode and then configure one or more parameters with the following commands:

Parameter Command Syntax	Description
`Firewall(config-pmap-p)# body-match-maximum [size]`	Set the maximum number of characters to search in the body content.
`Firewall(config-pmap-p)# protocol-violation [{drop-connection I reset} [log]]`	Check for HTTP protocol violations; if any are found, drop or reset the connection; log optional
`Firewall(config-pmap-p)# spoof-server text`	Set the spoof server field to the string *text*.

4. Enable HTTP inspection:

```
Firewall(config-pmap-c)# inspect http [http_pmap_name]
```

The **inspect http** command must be entered as an action in a policy map. You can also apply an HTTP inspection policy map by giving its name as *http_pmap_name*.

As an example, an HTTP inspection policy map **MyHTTPPolicy** is used to enforce two policies:

- Drop connections that have a content type mismatch or a URI length of more than 1024 characters

- Log but permit connections that return ActiveX or Java applet content

The policies are configured as two HTTP inspection class maps. The following commands can be used to configure the HTTP inspection policies:

```
Firewall(config)# class-map type inspect http match-any MyHTTPClass_drop
Firewall(config-cmap)# match req-resp-content-type mismatch
Firewall(config-cmap)# match request uri length gt 1024
Firewall(config-cmap)# exit
Firewall(config)# class-map type inspect http match-any MyHTTPClass_log
Firewall(config-cmap)# match response body active-x
Firewall(config-cmap)# match response body java-applet
Firewall(config-cmap)# exit
```

```
!
Firewall(config)# policy-map type inspect http MyHTTPPolicy
Firewall(config-pmap)# class MyHTTPClass_drop
Firewall(config-pmap-c)# drop-connection
Firewall(config-pmap-c)# exit
Firewall(config-pmap)# class MyHTTPClass_log
Firewall(config-pmap-c)# log
Firewall(config-pmap-c)# exit
Firewall(config-pmap)# exit
!
Firewall(config)# policy-map MyPolicy
Firewall(config-pmap)# class class-default
Firewall(config-pmap-c)# inspect http MyHTTPPolicy
Firewall(config-pmap-c)# exit
Firewall(config-pmap)# exit
Firewall(config)# service-policy MyPolicy interface outside
```

Configuring HTTP Inspection—FWSM and ASA 7.0-7.1

HTTP is used to exchange data between a client and a server. Most often, this is used between a client's web browser and a web server. HTTP is defined in RFC 1945 (HTTP v1.0) and RFC 2616 (HTTP v1.1). The basic HTTP inspection engine (beginning with PIX 6.3 **fixup http**) performs URL logging and Java and ActiveX filtering and enables the use of Websense or N2H2 for URL filtering.

Beginning with ASA 7.0(1) and FWSM 3.1(1), HTTP application inspection can be enhanced with any of the following criteria:

- HTTP traffic must conform to RFC 2616 (HTTP 1.1)
- Allowed message body or content length size
- Message content type matches the HTTP header
- Allowed request and response header size
- Allowed URI length
- Allowed use of port 80 for non-HTTP applications
- Allowed request methods

To configure enhanced HTTP inspection, you can follow these steps to configure an HTTP map for use with the **inspect http** command:

1. Define the HTTP map name:

    ```
    Firewall(config)# http-map http_map_name
    ```

    The HTTP map is named *http_map_name* (up to 64 characters). The HTTP map must be applied with the following command in a policy map before it can be used:

    ```
    inspect http http_map_name
    ```

2. (Optional) Check the message content length:

    ```
    Firewall(config-http-map)# content-length {[min minimum] [max maximum]}
      action {allow | drop | reset} [log]
    ```

If the HTTP message content is larger than *minimum* (1 to 65535 bytes) and smaller than *maximum* (1 to 50,000,000 bytes), it is allowed to pass. If it fails this test, one of the following actions is taken: **allow** the packet to pass, **drop** the packet, or **reset** the HTTP connection.

If the **min** keyword is omitted, the content length must be less than *maximum*. If **max** is omitted, the length must be greater than *minimum*. You can also use the **log** keyword to generate Syslog messages based on the action taken.

You can configure only one **content-length** command in an HTTP map.

For example, the following commands allow message lengths greater than 256 bytes to pass. Packets smaller than 256 bytes fail the test, triggering the action to reset the TCP connection and generate a Syslog message:

```
Firewall(config)# http-map Filter_http
Firewall(config-http-map)# content-length min 256 action reset log
Firewall(config-http-map)# exit
```

3. (Optional) Verify the message content type:

```
Firewall(config-http-map)# content-type-verification [match-req-rsp] action
   {allow | drop | reset} [log]
```

Each HTTP message is examined to make sure the content type stated in the HTTP header matches the message's actual content and that the content is an acceptable type. You can add the **match-req-rsp** keyword to verify that the content type in each HTTP request header matches the content type returned in the corresponding HTTP response header.

Table 7-11 lists the acceptable content types.

Table 7-11 *Acceptable HTTP Message Content Types*

Content	Type
application/	msword, octet-stream, pdf, postscript, vnd.ms-excel, vnd.ms-powerpoint, x-gzip, x-java-arching, x-java-xm, zip
audio/	*, basic, midi, mpeg, x-adpcm, x-aiff, x-ogg, x-wav
image/	*, cgf, gif, jpeg, png, tiff, x-3ds, x-bitmap, x-niff, x-portable-bitmap, x-portable-greymap, x-xpm
text/	*, css, html, plain, richtext, sgml, xmcd, xml
video/	*, -flc, mpeg, quicktime, sgi, x-avi, x-fli, x-mng, x-msvideo

If all these tests pass, the packet is allowed to pass. If a packet fails the tests, one of the following actions is taken: **allow** the packet to pass, **drop** the packet, or **reset** the HTTP connection.

For example, the following commands allow verified messages to pass. If the verification fails, those packets are also allowed (**action allow**), but a Syslog message is generated:

```
Firewall(config)# http-map Filter_http
Firewall(config-http-map)# content-type-verification match-req-rsp action
   allow log
Firewall(config-http-map)# exit
```

4. (Optional) Check the header length:

```
Firewall(config-http-map)# max-header-length {[request length] [response
   length]} action {allow | drop | reset} [log]
```

If you use the **request** keyword, the HTTP request header length must be less than *length* (0 to 65535 bytes). If you use the **response** keyword, the corresponding HTTP response header must be less than *length* (0 to 65535 bytes).

If a packet fails this test, one of the following actions is taken: **allow** the packet to pass, **drop** the packet, or **reset** the HTTP connection.

For example, the following commands allow HTTP request messages with header lengths of less than 200 bytes. The corresponding HTTP response headers must also be less than 200 bytes. Otherwise, the HTTP connection is reset.

```
Firewall(config)# http-map Filter_http
Firewall(config-http-map)# max-header-length request 200 response 200
   action reset log
Firewall(config-http-map)# exit
```

5. (Optional) Check the Uniform Resource Identifier URI length:

```
Firewall(config-http-map)# max-uri-length length action {allow | drop |
   reset} [log]
```

The length of the URI in an HTTP request message must be less than *length* (1 to 65535) bytes. If its length is greater, one of the following actions is taken: **allow** the packet to pass, **drop** the packet, or **reset** the HTTP connection.

For example, the following commands allow HTTP requests with URIs shorter than 256 bytes to pass. If the URIs are longer, the HTTP connection is reset:

```
Firewall(config)# http-map Filter_http
Firewall(config-http-map)# max-uri-length 256 action reset log
Firewall(config-http-map)# exit
```

6. (Optional) Test for HTTP port cloaking:

```
Firewall(config-http-map)# port-misuse {default | im | p2p | tunnelling}
   action {allow | drop | reset} [log]
```

HTTP port cloaking is used to transport traffic from a non-HTTP application over the standard HTTP port. These applications appear to use regular HTTP, as if they were web-based applications. The firewall can detect some misuses of the HTTP port by examining the entire contents of each HTTP packet.

You can use one of the following keywords to detect a specific tunneling application:

- **im**—Instant messaging applications. In PIX 7.0, only Yahoo Messenger is detected.

- **p2p**—Peer-to-peer applications. In PIX 7.0, Kazaa and Gnutella can be detected.

- **tunnelling**—Data from arbitrary applications is tunneled inside HTTP request messages to bypass normal firewalls. In PIX 7.0, the following tunneling applications can be detected:

  — **HTTPort/HTTHost**—http://www.htthost.com

  — **GNU Httptunnel**—http://www.nocrew.org/software/httptunnel.html

  — **GotoMyPC**—http://www.gotomypc.com

  — **Firethru Fire Extinguisher**—http://www.firethru.com

  — **Http-tunnel.com Client**—http://www.http-tunnel.com

If the application is detected, the corresponding **action** is taken: **allow** the packet to pass, **drop** the packet, or **reset** the HTTP connection.

You can also use the **default** keyword to define an action to be taken for any HTTP port misuse application that is not one of the keywords listed.

You can repeat this command to define multiple applications to detect.

For example, the following commands reset connections if a peer-to-peer application, a tunneling application, or any other unrecognized port-cloaking application is detected. Only instant messaging applications are allowed to pass through.

```
Firewall(config)# http-map Filter_http
Firewall(config-http-map)# port-misuse im action allow
Firewall(config-http-map)# port-misuse default action reset log
Firewall(config-http-map)# exit
```

7. (Optional) Check the HTTP request method:

```
Firewall(config-http-map)# request-method {rfc | ext} {method | default}
  action {allow | drop | reset} [log]
```

By default, all HTTP request methods are allowed. You can define a policy for a specific request method based on whether it is a request method defined in RFC 2616 (**rfc**) or an HTTP extension method (**ext**).

For **rfc**, you can use one of the following *method* keywords: **connect**, **delete**, **get**, **head**, **options**, **post**, **put**, or **trace**.

For **ext**, you can use one of the following *method* keywords: **copy**, **edit**, **getattribute**, **getattributenames**, **getproperties**, **index**, **lock**, **mkdir**, **move**, **revadd**, **revlabel**, **revlog**, **revnum**, **save**, **setattribute**, **startrev**, **stoprev**, **unedit**, or **unlock**.

You can also use the **default** keyword to define an action to be taken for any request method not explicitly configured.

If the specified method is detected, the corresponding action is taken: **allow** the packet to pass, **drop** the packet, or **reset** the HTTP connection.

You can repeat this command to define multiple request method policies.

For example, the following commands allow any of the RFC 2616 request methods to pass. If any of the extension's request methods is detected, the HTTP connection is reset:

```
Firewall(config)# http-map Filter_http
Firewall(config-http-map)# request-method rfc default action allow
Firewall(config-http-map)# request-method ext default action reset log
Firewall(config-http-map)# exit
```

8. (Optional) Check for RFC 2616 compliance:

```
Firewall(config-http-map)# strict-http action {allow | drop | reset}
  [log]
```

By default, HTTP packets that are not compliant with RFC 2616 are dropped. You can specify a different action to take when noncompliant traffic is detected: **allow** the packet to pass, **drop** the packet, or **reset** the HTTP connection.

You can add the **log** keyword to generate Syslog messages when the action is taken.

For example, the following commands allow noncompliant HTTP messages to be forwarded. As an audit trail, Syslog messages are sent when this occurs:

```
Firewall(config)# http-map Filter_http
Firewall(config-http-map)# strict-http action allow log
Firewall(config-http-map)# exit
```

9. (Optional) Check the transfer encoding type:

```
Firewall(config-http-map)# transfer-encoding type {type | default}
  action {allow | drop | reset} [log]
```

Transfer encoding is used to convert a document into a form that can be transported over HTTP. You can specify a transfer encoding *type* as one of the keywords listed in Table 7-12.

Table 7-12 *Transfer Encoding Types for HTTP*

Transfer Encoding *type*	Description
chunked	The message is sent as a series of "chunks"
compress	UNIX file compression
deflate	zlib format (RFC 1950) and deflate compression (RFC 1951)
gzip	GNU zip (RFC 1952)
identity	No transfer encoding is used

You can also use the **default** keyword to match all transfer encoding types other than the ones you explicitly configure.

When this transfer encoding type is detected in an HTTP message, the specified action is taken: **allow** the packet to pass, **drop** the packet, or **reset** the HTTP connection.

For example, the following commands allow the **identity** and **gzip** encodings, and all other types cause the HTTP connection to be reset:

```
Firewall(config)# http-map Filter_http
Firewall(config-http-map)# transfer-encoding type identity action  allow
Firewall(config-http-map)# transfer-encoding type gzip action allow
Firewall(config-http-map)# transfer-encoding type default action reset  log
Firewall(config-http-map)# exit
!
Firewall(config)# class-map _MyClass
Firewall(config-cmap)# match port tcp eq 80
Firewall(config-cmap)# exit
Firewall(config)# policy-map MyPolicy
Firewall(config-pmap)# class MyClass
Firewall(config-pmap-c)# inspect http Filter_http
Firewall(config-pmap-c)# exit
Firewall(config-pmap)# exit
Firewall(config)# service-policy MyPolicy interface outside
```

Configuring ICMP Inspection

Internet Control Message Protocol (ICMP) is used in a variety of ways to test and exchange network parameters between devices. For example, the ping "application" can be used to send echo requests from one host to another; the target host is expected to return echo replies. This tests the hosts' livelihood and the network's connectivity.

In platform releases prior to ASA 7.0(1) and FWSM 3.1(1), a firewall can allow ICMP traffic to pass through, but only if interface access lists are configured to explicitly permit it. As ICMP packets cross from one firewall interface to another, a special ICMP xlate entry is created. However, this xlate is used only to provide the translation—not to provide ICMP inspection. ICMP xlate entries have a fixed idle time of about 30 seconds.

Outbound pings might be allowed, but the return traffic is blocked at the outside interface unless that access list permits it to enter. It becomes difficult to know which outside addresses will return legitimate ICMP traffic, so a **permit icmp any any** is often added to the outside access list. Obviously, such a broad rule leaves the door open for malicious users to abuse inbound ICMP into a network.

Beginning with FWSM 3.1(1) and ASA 7.0(1), an ICMP inspection engine is available. Rather than explicitly configuring access list rules to permit inbound ICMP traffic, the firewall can selectively (and automatically) permit return traffic based on the original outbound requests.

For example, as an inside host sends an ICMP echo packet toward an outside host, the firewall builds the ICMP xlate entry. The source and destination addresses are examined, along with the ICMP message type and code, the ICMP identifier, and the ICMP sequence number fields. This forms a five-tuple of information that can be inspected and matched.

For example, the following output represents the ICMP xlate entry that was created when inside host 192.168.198.199 (translated to global address 10.10.1.1) sent one ICMP echo request packet to outside host 10.10.10.10:

```
%ASA-6-305011: Built dynamic ICMP translation from inside:192.168.198.199/512 to
   outside:10.10.1.1/1
Firewall# show xlate
5 in use, 12 most used
PAT Global 10.10.1.1(1) Local 192.168.198.199 ICMP id 512
[output omitted]
```

Here, **/512** and **ICMP id 512** represent the inside host's ICMP identifier field value. During the dynamic address translation, the firewall creates a dynamic ICMP identifier for the outside target. This is shown as **/1** and **(1)** after the 10.10.1.1 address lines.

The ICMP inspection engine examines return ICMP traffic, looking for packets that are expected in response to a prior request. ICMP is IP protocol 1. It does not include any mechanisms for establishing a connection or tracking the state of a message exchange. The ICMP inspection engine must use the five-tuple of ICMP information gathered from request and response packets to approximate a connection state.

In fact, after an ICMP xlate is created and a request packet goes out, the firewall creates a special ICMP connection entry apart from the normal conn table entries. The following Syslog message was generated when the special connection was created:

```
%ASA-6-302020: Built ICMP connection for faddr 10.10.10.10/0 gaddr 10.10.1.1/1
   laddr 192.168.198.199/512
```

Finally, the ICMP inspection engine permits only one response to return for every request that is sent out. The ICMP sequence numbers must also match between a request and a reply packet. With "stateful" ICMP inspection, the ICMP connections and xlate entries can be quickly torn down as soon as the appropriate reply is received.

You can see this in the following Syslog output, which resulted from one ICMP echo request packet being sent from inside host 192.168.198.199 (translated to global address 10.10.1.1) to outside host 10.10.10.10. (Message ID 711001 was produced because the **debug icmp trace** command was also used.)

```
%ASA-6-609001: Built local-host outside:10.10.10.10
%ASA-6-305011: Built dynamic ICMP translation from inside:192.168.198.199/512 to
   outside:10.10.1.1/2
%ASA-6-302020: Built ICMP connection for faddr 10.10.10.10/0 gaddr 10.10.1.1/2
   laddr 192.168.198.199/512
%ASA-7-711001: ICMP echo request (len 32 id 512 seq 25344) 192.168.198.199 >
   10.10.10.10
%ASA-7-711001: ICMP echo reply (len 32 id 2 seq 25344) 10.10.10.10 > 10.10.1.1
%ASA-6-302021: Teardown ICMP connection for faddr 10.10.10.10/0 gaddr 10.10.1.1/2
   laddr 192.168.198.199/512
%ASA-6-609002: Teardown local-host outside:10.10.10.10 duration 0:00:00
```

The time from when the xlate entries were first created until the ICMP connection entry was deleted and the xlates torn down is shown to be 0:00:00 (less than 1 second)! The ICMP inspection engine allows the connectionless and stateless ICMP protocol to be used through a firewall while maintaining a high level of security.

By default, ICMP inspection is not enabled. To enable it, you can add the following command to a policy map as an action:

```
Firewall(config-pmap-c)# inspect icmp
```

For example, you might want to add ICMP inspection to the default service policy that is applied to all firewall interfaces. To do so, you only need to add the **inspect icmp** command to the default **global_policy** policy map that is already defined. This policy map is already applied as a global service policy, so you do not need to define it separately. You can use the following commands to add the inspection to the default policy map:

```
Firewall(config)# policy-map global_policy
Firewall(config-pmap)# class inspection_default
Firewall(config-pmap-c)# inspect icmp
Firewall(config-pmap-c)# exit
Firewall(config-pmap)# exit
Firewall(config)#
```

By default, ICMP inspection does not permit any ICMP error packets to return through an address translation. This is because an ICMP error message can be sent from an address other than the original ICMP target. For example, if the IP time-to-live (TTL) value expires on an ICMP echo request that was sent to an outside host, an intervening router sends an ICMP error message back to the inside host. That packet uses the *router's* own IP address as the source address—not the ICMP echo target host's address.

When a router replies with an ICMP error packet, it must also include the first 64 bytes of the original IP packet as the error message payload. When a host receives the error packet, it can look inside the payload to see the original source and destination addresses, protocol, port numbers, and so on.

You can use the following command to enable ICMP error processing as part of the ICMP inspection:

```
Firewall(config-pmap-c)# inspect icmp error
```

Now the firewall examines ICMP error packet payloads to find the original packet details. If it can match those to known ICMP "connections" and xlate entries, it can work out the address translation and permits the ICMP error packet to reach the original sender.

Configuring Instant Messaging (IM) Inspection

Beginning in ASA 7.2(1), you can configure an application layer inspection engine that enforces policies related to instant messaging applications. Use the following steps to configure and tune the IM inspection engine:

1. (Optional) Define an IM inspection policy map:

    ```
    Firewall(config)# policy-map type inspect im im_pmap_name
    ```

2. (Optional) Define any matching conditions and their actions:

Match and Action Command Syntax	Description
`Firewall(config-pmap)# match [not] filename regex {regex	class regex_cmap_name}`  `Firewall(config-pmap-c)# {drop-connection	reset}`	Match: Filename in file transfer (except MSN Messenger) Action: Drop or reset the connection
`Firewall(config-pmap)# match [not] ip-address ip_address subnet_mask` `Firewall(config-pmap-c)# {drop-connection	reset}`	Match: Client IP address Action: Drop or reset the connection
`Firewall(config-pmap)# match [not] login-name regex {regex	class regex_cmap_name}`  `Firewall(config-pmap-c)# {drop-connection	reset}`	Match: Client's IM login name Action: Drop or reset the connection
`Firewall(config-pmap)# match [not] peer-ip-address ip_address subnet_mask` `Firewall(config-pmap-c)# {drop-connection	reset}`	Match: Peer IP address (client or server) Action: Drop or reset the connection
`Firewall(config-pmap)# match [not] peer-login-name regex {regex	class regex_cmap_name}`  `Firewall(config-pmap-c)# {drop-connection	reset}`	Match: Peer's IM login name (client only) Action: Drop or reset the connection
`Firewall(config-pmap)# match [not] protocol [msn-im] [yahoo-im]` `Firewall(config-pmap-c)# {drop-connection	reset}`	Match: IM protocol Action: Drop or reset the connection
`Firewall(config-pmap)# match [not] service {chat	conference	file-transfer	games	voice-chat	webcam}`  `Firewall(config-pmap-c)# {drop-connection	reset}`	Match: IM service Action: Drop or reset the connection
`Firewall(config-pmap)# match [not] version regex {regex	class regex_cmap_name}`  `Firewall(config-pmap-c)# {drop-connection	reset}`	Match: IM file transfer service version Action: Drop or reset the connection

Section 7-3

As well, you can configure an IM inspection class map with the **class-map type inspection im** *im_cmap_name* command. That inspection class map can contain any of the **match** commands listed here, along with their associated action commands. The idea is to group match and action commands that might be needed in multiple IM inspection policies.

Then you can reference the inspection class map in the inspection policy map with the following command:

```
Firewall(config-pmap)# class im_cmap_name
```

By referencing the inspection class map in several places, you save yourself the trouble of configuring the same **match** and action commands again and again.

There are no parameters to set for the IM inspection policy map.

3. Enable IM inspection:

```
Firewall(config-pmap-c)# inspect im [im_pmap_name]
```

The **inspect im** command must be entered as an action in a policy map. You can also apply an FTP inspection policy map by giving its name as *pmap_name*.

As an example, an IM inspection engine policy is configured to reset connections when clients attempt to transfer files with ".exe" in their names. As well, webcam services are prevented by resetting the connections. The following commands can be used to configure the IM inspection policies:

```
Firewall(config)# regex IMblock1 ".*\.exe"
Firewall(config)# policy-map type inspect im MyIMPolicy
Firewall(config-pmap)# match filename regex IMblock1
Firewall(config-pmap-c)# reset
Firewall(config-pmap-c)# exit
Firewall(config-pmap)# match service webcam
Firewall(config-pmap-c)# reset
Firewall(config-pmap-c)# exit
Firewall(config-pmap)# exit
!
Firewall(config)# policy-map MyPolicy
Firewall(config-pmap)# class class-default
Firewall(config-pmap-c)# inspect im MyIMPolicy
Firewall(config-pmap-c)# exit
Firewall(config-pmap)# exit
Firewall(config)# service-policy MyPolicy interface outside
```

Configuring IPSec Passthru Inspection

Beginning with ASA 7.2(1), a firewall can be configured to inspect IPSec tunnels that pass through it. Because the IPSec tunnels do not terminate on the firewall directly, the firewall is not able to inspect the traffic in any detail.

Instead, the tunneled traffic is likely encrypted and secured; the firewall can only monitor the number of tunnels passing through to individual client IP addresses and the amount of time the tunnels have been idle.

You can use the following steps to configure IPSec Passthru inspection in ASA 7.2(1) or later:

1. (Optional) Define an IPSec Passthru inspection policy map:

   ```
   Firewall(config)# policy-map type inspect ipsec-pass-thru ipsec_pmap_name
   ```

   No matching conditions need to be configured for this inspection engine.

2. Set IPSec Passthru parameters:

   ```
   Firewall(config-pmap)# parameters
   ```

   First, enter the **parameters** mode and then configure one or more parameters with the following commands:

Parameter Command Syntax	Description
`Firewall(config-pmap-p)# ah [per-` `client-max number] [timeout hh:mm:ss]`	Set the maximum number of AH mode tunnels allowed from any one client (**per-client-max**, 0–65,535) or the tunnel idle timeout (**timeout**).
`Firewall(config-pmap-p)# esp [per-` `client-max number] [timeout hh:mm:ss]`	Set the maximum number of ESP mode tunnels allowed from any one client (**per-client-max**, 0–65,535) or the tunnel idle timeout (**timeout**).

3. Enable IPSec Passthru inspection:

   ```
   Firewall(config-pmap-c)# inspect ipsec-pass-thru [ipsec_pmap_name]
   ```

   The **inspect ipsec-pass-thru** command must be entered as an action in a policy map. You can also apply an IPSec Passthru inspection policy map by giving its name as *ipsec_pmap_name*.

As an example, an IPSec Passthru policy map is configured to enforce an idle timeout of 12 hours on client ESP tunnels passing through the firewall. The following commands can be used to configure the IPSec Passthru policy and inspection engine:

```
Firewall(config)# policy-map type inspect ipsec-pass-thru MyIPsecPolicy
Firewall(config-pmap)# parameters
Firewall(config-pmap-p)# esp timeout 12:00:00
Firewall(config-pmap-p)# exit
Firewall(config-pmap)# exit
Firewall(config)# policy-map MyPolicy
Firewall(config-pmap)# class class-default
Firewall(config-pmap-c)# inspect ipsec-pass-thru MyIPsecPolicy
Firewall(config-pmap-c)# exit
Firewall(config-pmap)# exit
Firewall(config)# service-policy MyPolicy interface outside
```

Configuring MGCP Inspection—ASA 7.2(1) and Later

Media Gateway Control Protocol (MGCP) is used by call agents to control media gateways (devices that convert telephone circuit audio to data packets). A firewall's MGCP inspection engine can monitor the "pinholes" or connections that are built as call agents and gateways communicate.

You can use the following steps to configure MGCP inspection in ASA 7.2(1) or later:

1. (Optional) Define an MGCP inspection policy map:

   ```
   Firewall(config)# policy-map type inspect mgcp mgcp_pmap_name
   ```

   No matching conditions need to be configured for the MGCP inspection engine.

2. Set MGCP parameters:

   ```
   Firewall(config-pmap)# parameters
   ```

   First, enter the **parameters** mode and then configure one or more parameters with the commands shown in the following table:

Parameter Command Syntax	Description
`Firewall(config-pmap-p)# call-agent ip_address group_id`	Set the IP address and call group ID of the call agents that can manage gateways in the same group.
`Firewall(config-pmap-p)# gateway ip_address group_id`	Set the IP address and call group ID of a gateway that can be controlled by a call agent in the same group.
`Firewall(config-pmap-p)# command-queue limit`	Set the maximum number of queued MGCP messages until a response is received.

3. Enable MGCP inspection:

   ```
   Firewall(config-pmap-c)# inspect mgcp [mgcp_pmap_name]
   ```

   The **inspect mgcp** command must be entered as an action in a policy map. You can also apply an FTP inspection policy map by giving its name as *pmap_name*.

As an example, an MGCP inspection policy map is configured to control which call agents can manage which gateways. Call agents 10.5.5.1 and 10.5.5.2 can manage gateways 10.1.1.100 and 10.1.1.101. Call agents 10.5.5.3 and 10.5.5.4 can manage gateways 10.1.1.200 and 10.1.1.201. The following commands can be used to configure the MGCP inspection engine policies:

```
Firewall(config)# policy-map type inspect mgcp MyMGCPPolicy
Firewall(config-pmap)# parameters
Firewall(config-pmap-p)# call-agent 10.5.5.1 10
Firewall(config-pmap-p)# call-agent 10.5.5.2 10
Firewall(config-pmap-p)# call-agent 10.5.5.3 20
Firewall(config-pmap-p)# call-agent 10.5.5.4 20
Firewall(config-pmap-p)# gateway 10.1.1.100 10
Firewall(config-pmap-p)# gateway 10.1.1.101 10
Firewall(config-pmap-p)# gateway 10.1.1.200 20
Firewall(config-pmap-p)# gateway 10.1.1.201 20
Firewall(config-pmap-p)# exit
Firewall(config-pmap)# exit
!
Firewall(config)# policy-map MyPolicy
Firewall(config-pmap)# class class-default
```

```
Firewall(config-pmap-c)# inspect mgcp MyMGCPPolicy
Firewall(config-pmap-c)# exit
Firewall(config-pmap)# exit
Firewall(config)# service-policy MyPolicy interface outside
```

Configuring an MGCP Map—FWSM and ASA 7.0-7.1

Media Gateway Control Protocol (MGCP) is used by call agents to control media gateways (devices that convert telephone circuit audio to data packets).

You can follow these steps to configure an MGCP map for use with the **inspect mgcp** command:

1. Define the MGCP map name:

   ```
   Firewall(config)# mgcp-map mgcp_map_name
   ```

   The MGCP map is named *mgcp_map_name* (up to 64 characters). You must apply the MGCP map in a policy map with the following command map before it can be used:

   ```
   inspect mgcp mgcp_map_name
   ```

2. Customize MGCP options:

   You can use any of the commands listed in Table 7-13 to set a specific MGCP inspection parameter in MGCP map configuration mode.

Table 7-13   *Setting MGCP Inspection Parameters*

Parameter Description	Command Syntax
Defines a call agent (*ip_address*) as part of a group (*group_id*, 0 to 4294967295).	`Firewall(config-mgcp-map)# call-agent ip_address group_id`
Permits call agents in a group (*group_id*, 0 to 4294967295) to manage the gateway at *ip_address*.	`Firewall(config-mgcp-map)# gateway ip_address group_id`
Sets the maximum number of requests to be queued waiting for a response (1 to 4294967295; the default is 200).	`Firewall(config-mgcp-map)# command-queue limit`

For example, suppose an MGCP map is configured to allow call agents at 192.168.77.10 and 192.168.77.11 to control the gateway at 192.168.100.1. Those call agents are defined as group 1. The call agents at 192.168.77.12 and 192.168.77.13 are defined as group 2 and are allowed to control a different gateway at 192.168.100.2. The MGCP map is then applied to the **inspect mgcp** command in a policy map. The following commands are used:

```
Firewall(config)# mgcp-map MyMGCPMap
Firewall(config-mgcp-map)# call-agent 192.168.77.10 1
Firewall(config-mgcp-map)# call-agent 192.168.77.11 1
Firewall(config-mgcp-map)# gateway 192.168.100.1 1
Firewall(config-mgcp-map)# call-agent 192.168.77.12 2
```

```
Firewall(config-mgcp-map)# call-agent 192.168.77.13 2
Firewall(config-mgcp-map)# gateway 192.168.100.2 2
Firewall(config-mgcp-map)# exit
!
Firewall(config)# policy-map MyPolicy
Firewall(config-pmap)# class class-default
Firewall(config-pmap-c)# inspect mgcp MyMGCPMap
Firewall(config-pmap-c)# exit
Firewall(config-pmap)# exit
Firewall(config)# service-policy MyPolicy interface outside
```

Configuring NetBIOS Inspection

The NetBIOS Name Service (NBNS) is a protocol that is used to resolve NetBIOS names to IP addresses. A firewall can inspect NBNS traffic to update embedded IP addresses according to any active address translations. The inspection engine can also monitor the NetBIOS exchanges, to make sure everything follows the RFC that defines NetBIOS.

You can use the following steps to configure NetBIOS inspection in ASA 7.2(1) or later:

1. (Optional) Define an NetBIOS inspection policy map:

   Firewall(config)# **policy-map type inspect netbios** *netbios_pmap_name*

   No matching conditions need to be configured for the NetBIOS inspection engine.

2. Set NetBIOS parameters:

   Firewall(config-pmap)# **parameters**

   First, enter the **parameters** mode and then configure one or more parameters with the commands shown in the following table:

Parameter Command Syntax	Description
Firewall(config-pmap-p)# **protocol-violation action** [**drop**] **log**	If NetBIOS packets are found to be violating the RFC, drop the connection and/or log it.

3. Enable NetBIOS inspection:

   Firewall(config-pmap-c)# **inspect netbios** [*netbios_pmap_name*]

   The **inspect netbios** command must be entered as an action in a policy map. You can also apply a NetBIOS inspection policy map by giving its name as *pmap_name*.

Configuring RADIUS Accounting Inspection

RADIUS is a protocol that can be used for user authentication, authorization, and to keep an audit trail of user accounting information. Beginning in ASA 7.2(1), the ASA platform has an application layer inspection engine for RADIUS accounting traffic.

It is important to maintain the integrity of RADIUS accounting because it usually contains a record of customer activity for billing purposes.

You can use the following steps to configure RADIUS accounting inspection in ASA 7.2(1) or later:

1. (Optional) Define a RADIUS accounting inspection policy map:

   Firewall(config)# **policy-map type inspect radius-accounting** *radius_pmap_name*

   No matching conditions need to be configured for the RADIUS accounting inspection engine.

2. Set RADIUS accounting parameters:

   Firewall(config-pmap)# **parameters**

   First, enter the **parameters** mode and then configure one or more parameters with the following commands:

Parameter Command Syntax	Description
Firewall(config-pmap-p)# **host** *hostname* [**key** *key_string*]	Identify a RADIUS host that will be inspected; *hostname* can be IP address or a hostname string; *key_string* can be up to 128 characters long.
Firewall(config-pmap-p)# **send response**	Send a RADIUS Accounting-Response Start and Stop messages to the sender of the respective request messages.
Firewall(config-pmap-p)# **timeout users** *hh:mm:ss*	Set an inactivity timer for RADIUS accounting users; a timeout of 0:0:0 will tear down the RADIUS accounting connection immediately.
Firewall(config-pmap-p)# **validate-attribute** *attribute_number*	Validate the RADIUS accounting attribute number (1–191) when it appears in messages. Vendor Specific Attributes (VSA) are not supported.

3. Enable RADIUS accounting inspection:

   Firewall(config-pmap-c)# **inspect radius-accounting** [*radius_pmap_name*]

   The **inspect radius-accounting** command must be entered as an action in a policy map. You can also apply a RADIUS accounting inspection policy map by giving its name as *pmap_name*.

As an example, a RADIUS accounting inspection policy is configured to identify the RADIUS host at 192.168.10.10 using the secret key "BigSecretKey". The inspection engine will always send a Start and Stop message back to the requester, ensuring that the accounting records are not spoofed to exploit spoofing of billing records.

```
Firewall(config)# policy-map type inspect radius-accounting MyRADIUSPolicy
Firewall(config-pmap)# parameters
Firewall(config-pmap-p)# host 192.168.10.10 key BigSecretKey
Firewall(config-pmap-p)# send response
```

```
Firewall(config-pmap-p)# exit
Firewall(config-pmap)# exit
!
Firewall(config)# policy-map MyPolicy
Firewall(config-pmap)# class class-default
Firewall(config-pmap-c)# inspect radius-accounting MyRADIUSPolicy
Firewall(config-pmap-c)# exit
Firewall(config-pmap)# exit
Firewall(config)# service-policy MyPolicy interface outside
```

Configuring SNMP Inspection

Simple Network Management Protocol (SNMP) is used to monitor and manage devices with an SNMP agent from a management station. By default, all versions of SNMP are allowed to pass through a firewall, as long as SNMP itself (UDP port 161) is permitted.

You can use the following steps to configure enhanced SNMP inspection, which allows specific versions of SNMP to be denied. For example, SNMPv1 has no mechanisms for security, so your network security policies might not allow that type of traffic to be used.

An SNMP map is used with the **inspect snmp** command to define additional parameters for inspection.

TIP   Beginning with ASA 7.2(1), most of the application layer inspection engines switched to an MPF-based configuration, using the **policy-map type inspect** command to configure inspection options. The SNMP inspection engine did not follow that model; instead, it is configured using the **snmp-map** command.

---

1. Define the SNMP map name:

   `Firewall(config)# snmp-map snmp_map_name`

   The SNMP map is named *snmp_map_name* (up to 64 characters).

2. Deny a specific SNMP version:

   `Firewall(config-snmp-map)# deny version {1 | 2 | 2c | 3}`

   You can repeat this command to deny more than one SNMP version.

3. Enable SNMP inspection:

   `Firewall(config-pmap-c)# inspect snmp snmp_map_name`

   The **inspect snmp** command must be entered as an action in a policy map. You can also apply an SNMP inspection map by giving its name as *snmp_map_name*.

For example, the following commands define an snmp-map that denies packets using SNMP versions 1 and 2 during SNMP inspection. The SNMP map is then applied to the **inspect snmp** command in a policy map.

```
Firewall(config)# snmp-map Filter_snmp
Firewall(config-snmp-map)# deny version 1
Firewall(config-snmp-map)# deny version 2
Firewall(config-snmp-map)# exit
!
Firewall(config)# class-map _MyClass
Firewall(config-cmap)# match any
Firewall(config-cmap)# exit
Firewall(config)# policy-map MyPolicy
Firewall(config-pmap)# class MyClass
Firewall(config-pmap-c)# inspect snmp Filter_snmp
Firewall(config-pmap-c)# exit
Firewall(config-pmap)# exit
Firewall(config)# service-policy MyPolicy interface outside
```

Refer to the following sections for information about these topics:

- **8-1: Firewall Failover Overview**—Provides a concise reference of information about how Cisco firewall failover works.

- **8-2: Configuring Firewall Failover**—Covers the steps needed to configure and use firewalls as a failover pair.

- **8-3: Firewall Failover Configuration Examples**—Presents several complete examples of different types of failover configurations.

- **8-4: Managing Firewall Failover**—Explains the commands you can use to verify failover operation and to manually intervene in the failover process.

- **8-5: Upgrading Firewalls in Failover Mode**—Discusses a strategy for upgrading the operating system image on a failover pair of firewalls.

CHAPTER 8

Increasing Firewall Availability with Failover

The previous chapters in this book explain how to configure a single Cisco firewall to inspect traffic and provide the necessary security policies in a network. As long as that firewall continues to run properly, has a continuous source of power, and has consistent network connectivity, it can offer reliable service. What happens when those conditions are less than perfect?

Cisco firewalls can be configured as failover pairs, allowing two physical firewall platforms to operate in tandem. The result is greater reliability, because one or both firewalls are always available for use. Firewall failover is possible in two forms:

- **Active-standby**—One firewall takes on the *active* role, handling all the normal security functions. The other firewall stays in *standby* mode, ready to take over the active role in the event of a failure.

- **Active-active**—Both firewalls can operate with one or more separate security contexts. For each context, one firewall can take on the active role, handling all the normal firewall functions for that context. The other firewall can take on the standby role for the context, waiting to take over the active role from its peer.

The active and standby roles can be arbitrarily assigned across the whole set of security contexts. In this way, one firewall is active for one group of contexts, and the other firewall is active for another group.

8-1: Firewall Failover Overview

When a single firewall is used in a network, the security it provides generally has the following attributes:

- **Lower cost**—Only one hardware platform and a software license are needed.

- **Single point of failure**—If the firewall hardware or software fails, no traffic can be forwarded from one side to the other.

- **Performance is limited**—The total throughput of the stateful inspection process is limited to the firewall's maximum performance.

If one firewall is potentially a single point of failure, it is logical to think that two firewalls would be better. Cisco firewalls can be made more available when they are configured to work as a failover pair. Firewall failover can operate in two different fashions: active-standby and active-active. The characteristics of each can be described as follows:

- Two firewalls can act as an active-standby failover pair, having the following characteristics:

  — Total cost is increased, because two firewalls must be used.

  — The firewall pair can be physically separated, allowing no single point of failure.

  — Performance is the same as that of a single firewall, because only one of the pair can actively inspect traffic at any time.

  — If the active firewall fails, the standby firewall can take over traffic inspection.

  — Active-standby failover is available on all Adaptive Security Appliance (ASA), PIX, and Firewall Services Module (FWSM) platforms and software releases, as long as a *single* security context is configured.

- Two firewalls can act as an active-active failover pair, which requires two firewalls configured for multiple-security context mode. The characteristics of this functionality are as follows:

  — Cost is doubled over that of a single firewall, because two fully functional firewalls must be used.

  — The firewall pair can be physically separated.

  — For each security context, one firewall takes on an active role, and the other is in standby mode.

  — Performance can be doubled over that of a single firewall. The failover roles can be alternated across multiple contexts, allowing both firewalls to actively inspect traffic for different contexts simultaneously.

  — If the active firewall for a context fails, the standby firewall for that context can take over traffic inspection.

  — Active-active failover is available on ASA platforms running release 7.0(1) or greater, PIX (515E, 525, and 535), and on FWSM platforms running release 3.1(1) or greater.

TIP   Beginning with ASA 8.0(1), firewall interfaces can be configured into a logical group for redundancy. Redundant interfaces are not a replacement for failover operation; rather they can offer some additional benefits to a failover pair.

If an interface within a redundant group fails, another interface on the same firewall unit can instantly take over—without losing connectivity and without triggering a firewall failover. To recover from other failures outside of a redundant interface group, firewall failover comes into play.

How Failover Works

Firewall failover is currently available on the ASA platforms, PIX 515E, 525, and 535 models, and on the Catalyst 6500 FWSM.

Failover can be configured only if the firewall licensing enables it.

For active-standby failover, one firewall must have an "unrestricted" license, and the other has an "unrestricted" or "failover-only" license. The FWSM has active-standby failover enabled by default.

For active-active failover, both firewalls must have an "unrestricted" license. This is because both can actively inspect traffic at the same time.

Two identical firewall units can coexist as a failover or redundant pair by having their roles coordinated. In active-standby failover, one unit functions as the *active* unit and the other as the *standby* unit for all traffic inspection at any given time. One of the two firewalls always sits idle, waiting to take over the active role. Figure 8-1 illustrates this arrangement. The firewall on the left is active, and the one on the right is in standby mode.

Figure 8-1 *Active-Standby Firewall Failover Concept*

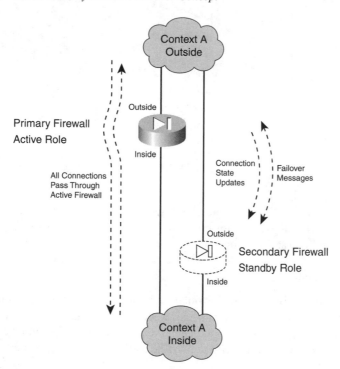

The two firewalls are in regular communication with each other over either a serial failover cable or a LAN-based connection. The firewalls can be configured for stateful failover so that the active unit keeps the standby unit synchronized with information about connections that are built or torn down.

Each interface of the active unit must connect to the respective interface of the standby unit so that each firewall can monitor the health of the interfaces.

If a failure is detected on the active unit, the two firewalls effectively swap roles. Figure 8-2 shows this concept. The firewall on the right has moved from the standby role into the active role.

Figure 8-2 *Active-Standby Failover After a Failure*

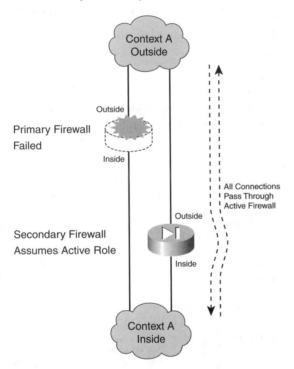

In active-active failover, the firewalls still alternate their roles so that one unit is active and one is in standby. The difference is that the active-standby combination is carried out on a *per-context* basis, with each firewall running multiple security contexts. If the active-standby roles are alternated across different security contexts, both units can actively inspect traffic at the same time—hence the term *active-active* failover, where neither unit is required to sit idle.

Figure 8-3 illustrates the active-active concept, in which each firewall is configured to run two separate security contexts, Context A and Context B. Now each context in one firewall can take on either the active or standby role, and the corresponding context in the other firewall takes on the alternate role. In the figure, the top firewall has the active role for Context A, and the bottom firewall is active for Context B.

If the active roles are divided appropriately across the firewalls, it becomes possible for both firewalls to be active on at least one context at any time. In other words, one whole firewall is not required to sit idle.

Figure 8-3   *Active-Active Firewall Failover Concept*

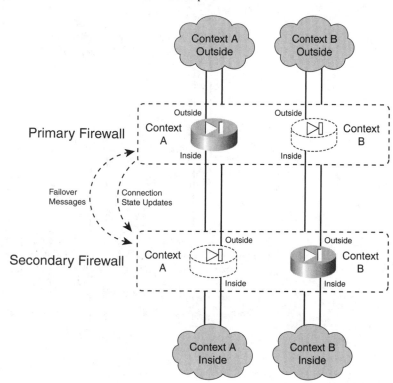

During a failure in active-active failover, the two firewalls effectively swap roles, but only for contexts in which a failure is detected. In Figure 8-4, the entire top firewall has failed, rendering both of its contexts useless. The bottom firewall then takes on the active role for Context A and Context B, although it was already active for Context B.

Firewall Failover Roles

A failover pair of firewalls can be located together if needed. A pair of Catalyst 6500 FWSMs can even be located in a single switch chassis. However, if the firewalls are geographically separated, they are less vulnerable to power or network outages or other disasters. Cisco firewalls can be separated and still function as a failover pair. Two FWSMs can also be split across a pair of switches.

The active unit performs all the firewall functions, whereas the standby only waits for the active unit to fail. At that time, the two units exchange roles until the next failure. In an active-active pair, the two exchange roles within each security context during a failure.

Figure 8-4 *Active-Active Failover After a Failure*

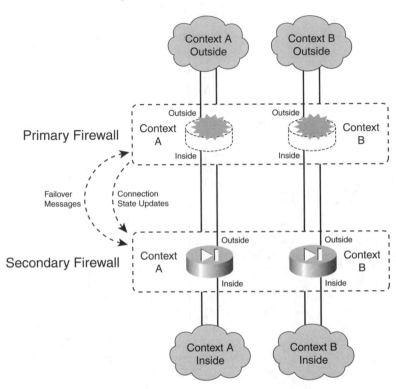

Configuration changes should always be made on the active unit. The firewall configurations are always coordinated between the two failover units using any of the following methods:

- The active unit automatically updates the running configuration of the standby unit as commands are entered, so the two are always synchronized.

- The **copy running-config startup-config** and **write mem** commands save the running configuration to Flash memory on the active unit and then to the Flash on the standby unit.

- The **write standby** command can be used to force the running configuration to be replicated from the active unit to the standby unit.

NOTE Only the running configuration is kept automatically synchronized between failover peers. The startup configuration is not affected until you manually synchronize the two units by using the **write memory** or **copy running-config startup-config** command on the active unit.

Also, each firewall maintains its own Flash file system. Files are not replicated across Flash file systems as a part of failover. This means that each firewall must maintain its own operating system and Cisco Adaptive Security Device Manager (ASDM) images. To upgrade a software image, you must upgrade each of the failover peers independently.

From a physical standpoint, one firewall is configured to be the *primary* unit, and the other becomes the *secondary* unit. These roles are used only to determine the IP and MAC addresses of the active and standby units, not the active and standby roles. The following actions are taken based on the primary and secondary designations:

- The active unit takes on the MAC and IP addresses of the primary physical firewall on each interface.

- The standby unit takes on the MAC and IP addresses of the secondary physical firewall on each interface.

- The units toggle or swap these addresses after a failover occurs so that the addresses of the active unit interfaces are always consistent and predictable.

The primary and secondary roles can be determined by one of the following configurations:

- **LAN-based failover**—The two units communicate across a LAN connection. The firewalls can be separated up to the distance limitation of the LAN media. Primary and secondary roles are manually configured. Configuration changes are replicated across the LAN at a high speed.

- **Failover cable**—A 6-foot serial cable connects the two firewalls. The "primary" end of the cable connects to the primary firewall (the firewall with an "unrestricted" license) and the "secondary" end to the secondary firewall. Configuration changes are replicated over the cable at 115.2 kbps. (The failover cable is unavailable on the ASA or FWSM platforms.)

NOTE   The failover pair of firewalls must be exactly the same model and have at least the minimum amount of RAM, the same amount of Flash memory, identical operating system releases, and compatible failover licensing.

Beginning with FWSM release 2.2 and ASA release 7.0(1), each of the firewalls can run different operating system maintenance releases during an image upgrade. The "hitless upgrade" or "zero downtime upgrade" feature allows failover operation to continue as long as the pair of firewalls is running the same software major and minor release. For example, failover can continue to work even if one unit runs PIX 8.0(1) while the other runs 8.0(3). However, the two firewalls cannot run in failover mode if one runs 8.0(1) and the other runs 7.2(1).

Detecting a Firewall Failure

Each interface of one firewall must connect to the same network as the corresponding interface of the other firewall. Each firewall can then monitor every active interface of its failover peer.

The active and standby firewalls determine a failure by sending hello messages to each other at regular intervals (every 15 seconds by default). These messages are sent over the failover cable (if present) or the LAN-based failover interface to detect failures of an entire firewall. The hellos are also sent on all interfaces configured for failover so that the firewall peer can determine the health of each interface. These messages are sent as short packets using IP protocol 105.

If a hello message is not received on the failover LAN or the failover cable for three polling intervals (the default), the firewall declares the other unit "failed" and attempts to become the active unit.

The firewalls can also use a configurable hold timer that must expire before declaring the other unit failed. You can shorten the hello and hold timers so that a failure is detected sooner, if desired.

With a failover cable, a power failure or a reload on one firewall unit can be sensed on the other unit. Firewalls linked by a LAN-based failover connection can sense a peer's health only via the regular hello messages. If one firewall is powered off, its peer can detect the failure only by noticing the absence of several consecutive hellos.

Sometimes, a firewall interface (or the network providing its connectivity) might fail while the firewall stays operational. Failover peers can detect interface failures according to the following conditions:

- If the two firewall units have changed failover roles or one of them has just powered up, the switch ports connected to the interfaces might move through the Spanning Tree Protocol states before forwarding traffic again. While a switch port is in the Listening and Learning states, regular data packets are not forwarded. This can cause failover hello messages to be dropped, causing the firewalls to begin testing their interfaces.

  To prevent this from happening, a firewall interface enters the Waiting state for two hello message periods. If more hello messages are missed after that, the interface is tested. Otherwise, failover just monitors the interface normally. With the default hello interval (15 seconds), interface testing does not begin until 30 seconds after the interface changes state. This coordinates well with the default Spanning Tree Protocol timers, which can block traffic for two periods of the Forward Delay timer (15 seconds).

- If a failover message is not seen on an interface within three polling intervals (the default), that interface is moved into a "testing" mode to determine if a failover is necessary. The other firewall is notified of the test via the failover cable or the LAN-based interface.

- Interfaces in the "testing" mode are moved through the following sequence of tests:

  — **Interface status**—The interface is failed if the link status is down.

  — **Network activity**—If no packets are received over a 5-second interval, testing continues; otherwise, the interface can still be used.

— **ARP**—The interface stimulates received traffic by sending Address Resolution Protocol (ARP) requests for the ten newest entries in the firewall's ARP table. If no traffic is received in 5 seconds, testing continues.

— **Ping**—Traffic is stimulated by sending an Internet Control Message Protocol (ICMP) echo request to the broadcast address on the interface. If no replies are received over a 5-second interval, both the interface and the testing firewall unit are marked in a "failed" state.

- At the conclusion of the tests, the two firewalls attempt to compare their status. If the standby firewall has more operational interfaces than the active unit, a failover occurs. However, if both units have similar failures, no failover occurs.

Failover Communication

Firewall pairs can support several different types of failover, depending on how they are configured. Each type allows the firewalls to communicate with each other in a slightly different manner:

- **Stateless failover**—The state of UDP and TCP connections is not kept when the standby firewall becomes active. All active connections are dropped and must be reestablished.

- **Stateful failover**—The state of UDP and TCP connections, as well as address translations (xlates), H.323, Serial Interface Protocol (SIP), and Multiple Gateway Control Point (MGCP) connections, are sent to the standby firewall over the stateful LAN interface. This stateful data is updated in real time as a stream of packets using IP protocol 8.

- **LAN-based failover**—Failover communication between the firewalls is carried over a LAN rather than the serial failover cable. Only failover hello messages and configuration replication updates are carried over the LAN-based connection.

  LAN-based failover requires one physical interface to be set aside for failover traffic. If stateful failover is being used, too, it should have its own interface. However, it can be configured to share the same interface with LAN-based failover. The LAN-based failover interface cannot be a subinterface or a virtual LAN (VLAN) on a trunk interface.

Figure 8-5 illustrates the basic connections for a failover pair. One of the firewalls is always active and takes on the active IP addresses for all its interfaces. The other firewall is standby and takes on the standby addresses.

Each firewall interface must connect to the same network IP subnet as the corresponding interface on the failover peer. For example, if the active unit's outside interface uses 192.168.177.1, the standby unit's outside interface must use an address in that same subnet. Obviously, each pair of peer interfaces must be connected on a common VLAN or Layer 2 network. In other words, the two firewalls must be able to send hello messages on an interface and reach the peer's corresponding interface without using a router or default gateway.

Figure 8-5 *Basic Firewall Failover Pair Connections*

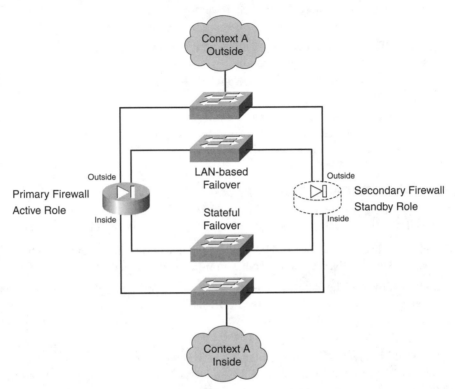

The failover PIX pair can have a serial failover cable connecting them if they are in close proximity and do not need a high-speed link for configuration updates. The failover pair can also connect by a LAN-based failover link that uses a physical LAN interface on each firewall. LAN-based failover is available on PIX, ASA, and FWSM platforms and allows the failover pair to be separated by long distances, if necessary.

Stateful failover also requires a LAN-based link between the firewalls. This link can share the LAN-based failover interface, or it can be an interface set aside for stateful updates. A higher-speed interface is preferable, to support a high rate of connection state updates. In fact, you should choose the fastest interface that is present on the firewall platform so that state information can be replicated as fast as connections are formed.

Active-Active Failover Requirements

In active-active failover, the two firewalls are assigned the customary primary and secondary roles. You can give the primary or secondary unit priority for becoming the active unit on a per-context basis. This applies to the admin and any user contexts.

Because only two firewalls are permitted in a failover pair, there can be only two combinations of primary and secondary:

- A—primary, B—secondary
- A—secondary, B—primary

Each of these combinations is called a *failover group*. Therefore, the contexts are assigned membership in one of the two failover groups.

Figure 8-6 shows the basic arrangement of the failover pair of firewalls, along with security contexts, failover groups, and firewall states (active or standby).

Within a failover group, either the primary or secondary firewall is given preference for becoming the active unit. One firewall can even preempt or usurp the active role if it does not already have it. This means that on a given firewall unit, all contexts in a failover group take on the same active or standby state. The same contexts on the other firewall take on the alternate state.

Figure 8-6 *Active-Active Failover with Multiple Security Contexts*

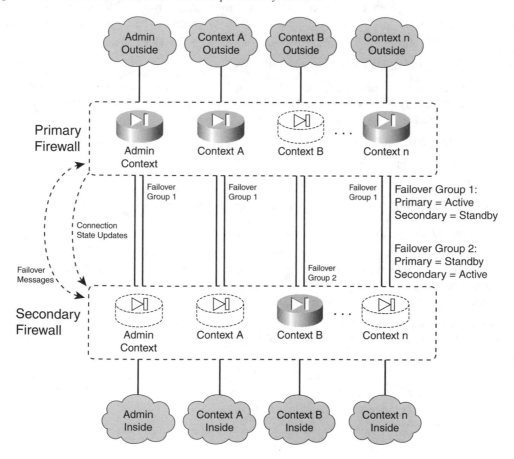

Because you configure each context's membership in a failover group, you can control the distribution of active contexts between the two physical firewalls. Some contexts might be heavily loaded, while others are not. Therefore, simply dividing the contexts evenly between the firewalls does not always result in an even distribution of firewall CPU, memory, and performance. You might have to experiment with context membership to maximize the use of each firewall.

8-2: Configuring Firewall Failover

To configure failover on a pair of Cisco firewalls, you can use the configuration steps listed in this section. Before failover is configured and enabled, you need to enter the configuration commands on each firewall. After failover is enabled, all configuration commands should be entered only on the active firewall. This is because the active unit replicates the configuration commands to the standby unit automatically. The only exception is any command related to failover itself.

For active-active failover, all failover configuration commands must be entered on the system execution space of the firewall that is currently active for failover group 1. This is because the failover for the system space is always handled by failover group 1. The failover IP addresses and interface monitoring must be configured in the individual security contexts.

1. Identify the primary and secondary firewall units.

   Failover communication depends on each firewall having a distinct role. The primary unit must have an "Unrestricted" license, and the secondary unit can have an "Unrestricted," "Failover Only," or "Active-Active Failover Only" license.

   If both units have an "Unrestricted" license, the roles can be chosen arbitrarily.

   You need to assign the primary and secondary roles in one of two ways:

   — By connecting labeled ends of a failover cable (see Step 2)

   — By configuring the roles in LAN-based failover (see Step 3a)

2. (Optional) Connect the firewalls with the serial failover cable.

   By default, the serial failover cable is expected to connect two PIX firewalls before failover can be used. If you intend to use this method of failover communication, connect the cable connector labeled "Primary" to the nine-pin failover connector on the primary unit. Then connect the "Secondary" end to the secondary unit.

   From this point on, the two units communicate failover "hello," configuration changes, and stateful update messages over the serial cable.

TIP   To bring up failover mode, you must use either the serial failover cable described here or LAN-based failover, configured in the next step.

---

3. (Optional) Connect the firewalls over a LAN for LAN-based failover.

A LAN connection can be used to carry failover communication much more efficiently than the serial failover cable. It can also be used if the two firewalls must be geographically separated.

You should use a Fast Ethernet or Gigabit Ethernet connection that is dedicated to failover traffic. The connection between firewalls should be on an isolated virtual LAN (VLAN), configured for full duplex and fast convergence so that the connection is highly available.

TIP   Do not use a crossover Ethernet cable or a fiber-optic patch cable to directly connect the two failover LAN interfaces if the firewalls are located close to each other. Instead, each interface should connect to a switch port so that the link status is always up to one firewall interface if the other firewall interface fails. Otherwise, both units sense a link-down condition and assume that their own interfaces have a failure.

You should also prepare the switch ports where the LAN-based failover interfaces connect so that failover communication can begin almost immediately. You should enable Spanning Tree Protocol PortFast and disable trunking and EtherChannel negotiation. You can use the following IOS Software commands to configure the switch ports:

```
Switch# configure terminal
Switch(config)# interface type mod/num
! Enable PortFast for immediate traffic forwarding
Switch(config-if)# spanning-tree portfast
! Disable trunking by making it an access switch port
Switch(config-if)# switchport mode access
! Disable EtherChannel negotiation
Switch(config-if)# no channel-group
```

Configuration Steps 3a through 3e should be used to configure the primary unit. Be sure to use the **failover lan unit primary** command described in Step 3a.

Then, connect to the secondary unit and repeat the same commands to configure LAN-based failover on it. The commands should be identical, except for the **failover lan unit secondary** command described in Step 3a. Otherwise, do not try to exchange the IP addresses between primary and secondary units in the other commands. The failover pair sorts out the IP addresses according to their roles.

a.   Identify the primary and secondary units:

FWSM	Firewall(config)# **failover lan unit** {**primary** | **secondary**}
PIX 6.3	Firewall(config)# **failover lan unit** {**primary** | **secondary**}
ASA	Firewall(config)# **failover lan unit** {**primary** | **secondary**}

Each unit must be configured with its own failover identity, because no physical failover cable connection exists to differentiate them.

NOTE   Normally, you make configuration changes to only one firewall unit (the active one), and the changes are replicated automatically. In this step, each firewall must have a different keyword (**primary** or **secondary**) in its configuration to differentiate its firewall identity. Therefore, you must add this command to the primary and secondary firewalls independently.

---

b.   (FWSM only) Allow the primary FWSM to preempt the secondary:

```
Firewall(config)# failover preempt [delay]
```

Normally, the firewall that has the active role keeps it until it fails or until you manually intervene. Beginning with FWSM 3.2(1), you can configure the primary FWSM to pre-empt its peer for control over the active role. With the **failover preempt** command, as soon as the primary FWSM boots up, it can preempt the secondary unit and take over the active role. By default, the primary unit preempts immediately. You can set a *delay* (1 to 1200 seconds) to force the primary unit to wait before assuming the active role.

c.   Configure the LAN interface to be used:

FWSM	`Firewall(config)# failover interface ip if_name ip_address mask` `standby ip_address`

PIX 6.3	`Firewall(config)# interface phy_if phy_speed`
	`Firewall(config)# nameif phy_if if_name security level`
	`Firewall(config)# ip address if_name ip_address netmask`
	`Firewall(config)# failover ip address if_name ip_address`

ASA	`Firewall(config)# interface phy_if`
	`Firewall(config-if)# speed speed`
	`Firewall(config-if)# duplex duplex`
	`Firewall(config-if)# no shutdown`
	`Firewall(config-if)# exit`
	`Firewall(config)# failover interface ip if_name ip_address mask`
	`standby ip_address`

You need to configure the LAN interface for its name, speed, duplex, and security level on PIX 6.3 and ASA platforms. On any platform, you need to provide an IP address for the active unit and the standby unit.

On an ASA, the physical interface *phy_if* (**ethernet***n* or **gigabitethernet***n*) can be configured for only speed and duplex, which are both optional. The **failover interface ip** command assigns an IP address for the active and standby units according to an arbitrary interface name *if_name*. At this point, the interface name is not bound to a physical interface for LAN-based failover.

NOTE   Failover interfaces on FWSM and ASA platforms are not assigned IP addresses as part
of interface configuration mode. This is because the active-active failover commands
must be configured in the system execution space, which does not participate in IP
communication.

In PIX 6.3, interface *phy_if* is of the form **ethernet***n* (10/100) or **gb-ethernet***n* (Gigabit Ethernet). The *hardware_speed* can be one of the following: **10baset** (10 Mbps half duplex), **10full**
(10 Mbps full duplex), **100basetx** (100 Mbps half duplex), **100full** (100 Mbps full duplex),
1000auto (Gigabit autonegotiation), **1000full** (Gigabit autonegotiation to use full duplex
only), or **1000full nonegotiate** (Gigabit full duplex). Assign an arbitrary interface named
if_name ("lan-fo" or "failover," for example) and a security level as **security** *level* (0 to 100).

d.   Identify the LAN interface used for failover communication:

FWSM	Firewall(config)# **failover lan interface** *if_name* **vlan** *vlan*
PIX 6.3	Firewall(config)# **failover lan interface** *if_name*
ASA	Firewall(config)# **failover lan interface** *if_name phy_if*

All failover communication is sent and received over the interface named *if_name*. On an
ASA, you must also bind the failover LAN interface name to a physical interface *phy_if*
(**ethernet***n* or **gigabitethernet***n*). On an FWSM, you must bind the failover LAN interface
name to a VLAN number *vlan*.

TIP   With two FWSMs, the failover LAN interface is also a specific VLAN. If the two
FWSMs are located in a single Catalyst 6500 chassis, the VLAN is used only internally
within the chassis. If the two FWSMs are located in two separate switches, you must
define this VLAN on and pass it between both switches. You can do this with a single-
VLAN link or over a trunk link.

Before you can use the failover LAN interface VLAN, you must define it on the switch
supervisor and then make it available to the FWSM by including it in the **firewall vlan-
group** *group-name vlan-list* and **firewall module** *module* **vlan-group** *group-name*
commands.

e.   (Optional) Encrypt failover messages:

FWSM	Firewall(config)# **failover key** {*key-string*	**hex** *key*}
PIX 6.3	Firewall(config)# **failover lan key** *key-string*
ASA	Firewall(config)# **failover key** {*key-string*	**hex** *key*}

Because other stations might intercept or overhear traffic on the failover LAN, you can define a preshared key to make the failover traffic more secure. The key is used to authenticate the failover pair of firewalls, as well as to encrypt the failover information. You can define the key as *key-string* (an arbitrary text string up to 63 characters) or as a hexadecimal *key* (an arbitrary string of exactly 32 hex digits).

The *key-string* is not displayed in the firewall configuration after it is configured.

Obviously, the same *key-string* must be configured on both primary and secondary firewalls so that the failover traffic can be encrypted and unencrypted correctly between them. If the keys are not identical, you will see the following message on the firewall console:

```
WARNING: Failover message decryption failure. Please make sure both  units have
the same failover shared key and crypto license
```

f. Enable LAN-based failover:

FWSM	—
PIX 6.3	`Firewall(config)# failover lan enable`
ASA	—

By default, a PIX failover pair expects to use the serial failover cable. You must start LAN-based failover explicitly with this command. From that point on, a connected serial cable is no longer used and can be removed.

On an ASA or FWSM, LAN-based failover is the only method for failover communication. Therefore, it is enabled by default.

4. (Active-active only) Define failover groups.

Failover groups must be configured from the system execution space on the primary firewall only.

a. Choose a failover group:

```
Firewall(config)# failover group {1 | 2}
```

Only two failover groups are supported. Because the failover mechanism in each group is independent, each group has its own active and standby roles. Contexts are assigned membership in one of the two groups listed in Step 9.

b. Prefer a firewall unit to have the active role:

```
Firewall(config-fover-group)# {primary | secondary}
```

In an initial condition, where the firewalls have booted up or failover has just been enabled, and both firewalls are functioning properly, one of them must be "elected" to take on the active failover role. By default, the primary unit has a higher priority to become active in each failover group.

You can designate a higher priority for the **primary** or **secondary** firewall unit with this command for the failover group being configured. Naturally, if that unit fails, the other unit still can take over the active role.

c. (Optional) Allow the higher-priority unit to assume immediate control:

```
Firewall(config-fover-group)# preempt
```

Normally, if an active unit fails, the standby unit assumes the active role indefinitely. The firewall units do not automatically revert to their original roles after a failure is resolved. Instead, they keep their roles until another failure occurs or there is manual intervention.

You can use the **preempt** command to allow the higher-priority unit in a failover group to always preempt the other unit for active control.

For example, suppose you have configured failover group 1 to give higher priority for the active role to the secondary unit. Normally, if the secondary unit fails, the primary unit assumes the active role and keeps it even after the secondary unit is restored. With **preempt**, the secondary unit can take over the active role as soon as it is restored to service. You would use the following commands to accomplish this:

```
Firewall(config)# failover group 1
Firewall(config-fover-group)# secondary
Firewall(config-fover-group)# preempt
```

5. (Optional) Use virtual MAC addresses for an interface:

FWSM	—
PIX 6.3	`Firewall(config)# failover mac address` *if_name active_mac* `standby_mac`
ASA single context	`Firewall(config)# failover mac address` *phy_if active_mac* `standby_mac`
ASA multiple context	`Firewall(config)# failover group {1	2}` `Firewall(config-fover-group)# mac address` *phy_if active* `mac standby_mac`

Normally, the active and standby units exchange information about their MAC addresses as a part of the regular failover messages. If the active unit goes down, the standby can replace the MAC addresses on all its interfaces with the previous active unit's addresses. In the rare case where both units fail and the standby unit is rebooted alone, the standby unit has no knowledge of what the active MAC addresses should be. This is because the MAC address information was not exchanged between the units because of the failure.

This command allows both units to have stable information about what the active (*active_mac*) and standby (*standby_mac*) MAC addresses should be on an interface. In PIX 6.3, the interface name *interface-name* (**outside**, for example) is used, whereas an ASA uses the physical interface name (**gigabit0**, for example). Both addresses are given in dotted-triplet format, such as 0006.5b02.a841.

In ASA, the MAC addresses are defined as global values in single-context mode, where only active-standby failover applies. If the firewalls are operating in multiple-context mode, where active-active failover is used, the MAC addresses are configured within the failover group on the system execution space because two different failover groups of contexts are maintained.

TIP   To use the **failover mac address** command, you must be able to give *unique* MAC addresses to both the active and standby unit interfaces. Finding unique values is not always straightforward. An easy method is to display the burned-in addresses (BIAs) of all interfaces on the primary and secondary firewall units with the **show interface** command.

The addresses of the primary unit can always be assigned to the active firewall, and those of the secondary unit can be assigned to the standby firewall. After all, that is how the IP addresses are handled. Then, for each interface, use the command **failover mac address** *interface primary_mac secondary_mac*. At that point, it is usually a good idea to save the configurations and reboot both firewall units to make sure that the new MAC addresses are being used correctly.

If you are using LAN-based failover, the MAC addresses of that interface cannot be changed or defined using this command. Instead, the default BIAs of that interface are used. This is because even though the active and standby roles change during a failover, the primary and secondary roles do not. Therefore, the primary and secondary units must have consistent identities and interface addresses.

---

6. (Optional) Define a health monitoring policy.

    a. Evaluate the health of the failover peer:

FWSM	Firewall(config)# **failover polltime [unit] [msec]** *time* **[holdtime** *holdtime*]
PIX 6.3	Firewall(config)# **failover poll** *time*
ASA	Firewall(config)# **failover polltime [unit] [msec]** *time* **[holdtime [msec]** *holdtime*]

    Each failover unit sends periodic hello messages to its peer over the serial failover cable or the LAN-based failover interface. This is offered as evidence that the unit is still alive.

    In FWSM or PIX 6.3, you can adjust the hello message interval to time (3 to 15 seconds; the default is 15). On an ASA, you can use *time* (1 to 15 seconds; the default is 1) to give the interval in whole-second increments. You can also use **msec** *time* (500 to 999 milliseconds; the default is 500) to set the interval more granularly. Beginning with ASA 7.2(1), the minimum poll time is reduced to 200 milliseconds, making sub-second failover times possible.

The **unit** keyword can be used to denote hello timing between *units* or failover peers, rather than between individual interfaces. However, if *unit* is not given, it is assumed anyway; the keyword exists only to make the command easier for administrators to interpret.

One unit expects to receive hellos from its peer at regular intervals, although it does not know what that interval should be. If no hello messages are received before a holdtime timer expires, the other peer is considered to have failed. In ASA and FWSM, you can set that timer by adding **holdtime** *holdtime* (3 to 45 seconds; FWSM default is 45, ASA default is 15). PIX 6.3 uses a fixed holdtime that is always 3 times the hello interval. (The default is 3 times 15, or 45 seconds.) Beginning with ASA 7.2(1), you can add the **msec** keyword to set the holdtime in milliseconds (800 to 999 milliseconds).

The holdtime timer must always be set to a minimum of 3 times the unit hello interval. This is because the firewalls always check for the loss of at least three consecutive hellos from a peer before taking action. If the **holdtime** keyword is not given, the firewall adjusts the holdtime automatically. The only exception to this behavior is if the unit hello interval is set to 5 seconds or less, where the default holdtime is automatically set to 15 seconds. This is done to prevent very aggressive failure detection with very short hello intervals.

TIP   In ASA, the most aggressive peer monitoring policy has a unit interval of 200 milliseconds and a minimum holdtime of 800 milliseconds. This allows a standby unit to detect a failure with the active unit and take over its role within 800 milliseconds. In comparison, PIX 6.3 allows a minimum hello interval of 3 seconds, but with a minimum holdtime of 15 seconds.

Be careful if you decide to tighten up the unit and holdtime intervals for a more aggressive failure detection policy. Delayed or lost hellos on a congested LAN-based failover interface could be misinterpreted as a failure. If your LAN-based failover traffic is carried over switches that separate the two firewall units, make sure the switches are configured to use the most efficient spanning-tree and link-negotiation features possible. Otherwise, a Layer 2 topology change (a link or switch failure) could block the failover messages for up to 50 seconds!

---

b. Evaluate the health of interfaces:

PIX 6.3	N/A
ASA, FWSM single context	Firewall(config)# **failover polltime interface** [**msec**] *time* [**holdtime** *holdtime*]
ASA, FWSM multiple context	Firewall(config)# **failover group** {**1** | **2**} Firewall(config-fover-group)# **polltime interface** [**msec**] *time* [**holdtime** *holdtime*]

Failover hello messages are sent out firewall interfaces at *time* (3 to 15 seconds; FWSM default is 15, ASA default is 5) intervals. A corresponding holdtime timer exists. On an ASA, the *holdtime* can range from 5 to 75 seconds (default 5), while a FWSM uses 3 to 15 seconds (default 15) for interface monitoring.

In ASA, the interface polltime is a global value in single-context mode, where only active-standby failover applies. If the firewalls are operating in multiple-context mode, where active-active failover is used, polltime is configured within the failover group on the system execution space because two different failover groups of contexts are maintained.

With PIX 6.3, hello messages are sent out *all* connected interfaces at the same interval as failover unit hello messages. This interval is set with the **failover poll** command.

c. Define an interface failure policy:

PIX 6.3	N/A
ASA, FWSM single context	`Firewall(config)# `**`failover interface-policy`** *`num`*`[%]`
ASA, FWSM multiple context	`Firewall/context(config)# `**`failover interface-policy`** *`num`*`[%]`

By default, if a firewall tests and finds that at least one of its monitored interfaces has failed, it declares itself failed. In that case, if the firewall was in active mode, the other unit takes over the active role.

To set the self-declared failure threshold, you can specify the number of failed interfaces as *num* (1 to the maximum number of interfaces; the default is 1) or a percentage of failed interfaces as *num*% (1 percent to 100 percent).

Notice that the interface failure policy is set on a *per-context* basis. On a single-context firewall, this is configured in global configuration mode. If multiple-context mode is running, you must connect to the appropriate security context and enter the command there.

7. (Optional) Use stateful failover for maximum availability.

Stateful failover can be used to synchronize the standby failover unit with connection information from the active unit. In this way, as connections are built or torn down, the standby unit can always keep its inspection tables up to date. If a failover occurs, the standby unit can take over the active role and maintain all the open connections without interruption.

Stateful failover requires a LAN connection between firewalls. This is to support the high bandwidth needed to carry updates about connections that are being inspected. Be aware that no stateful information is carried over the serial failover cable if one is being used to connect the firewalls.

a. Configure an interface to use for stateful update traffic:

FWSM	`Firewall(config)# ` **`failover interface ip`** ` if_name ip_address` ` mask ` **`standby`** ` ip_address`

PIX 6.3	`Firewall(config)# ` **`interface`** ` phy_if phy_speed`
	 `Firewall(config)# ` **`nameif`** ` phy_if  if_name ` **`security`** `level`
	 `Firewall(config)# ` **`ip address`** ` if_name ip_address netmask`
	 `Firewall(config)# ` **`failover ip address`** ` if_name ip_address`

ASA	`Firewall(config)# ` **`interface`** ` phy_if`
	 `Firewall(config-if)# ` **`speed`** ` speed`
	 `Firewall(config-if)# ` **`duplex`** ` duplex`
	 `Firewall(config-if)# ` **`no shutdown`**
	 `Firewall(config-if)# ` **`exit`**
	 `Firewall(config)# ` **`failover interface ip`** ` if_name ip_address`
	 ` mask ` **`standby`** ` ip_address`

The stateful interface needs to be configured for its name, speed, duplex, and security level. It also needs an IP address for the active unit and the standby unit.

In ASA, the physical interface *phy_if* (**ethernet***n* or **gigabitethernet***n*) can be configured only for speed and duplex, which are both optional. The **failover interface ip** command assigns an IP address for the active and standby units according to an arbitrary interface name *if_name*. At this point, the interface name is not bound to a physical interface for stateful failover. This is done in Step 7c.

In PIX 6.3, interface *phy_if* is of the form **ethernet***n* (10/100) or **gb-ethernet***n* (Gigabit Ethernet). The *hardware_speed* can be one of the following: **10baset** (10 Mbps half duplex), **10full** (10 Mbps full duplex), **100basetx** (100 Mbps half duplex), **100full** (100 Mbps full duplex), **1000auto** (Gigabit autonegotiation), **1000full** (Gigabit autonegotiation to use full duplex only), or **1000full nonegotiate** (Gigabit full duplex). Assign an arbitrary interface name *if_name* ("stateful," for example) and a security level as **security***level* (0 to 100).

The two firewalls should have a dedicated link for this purpose, because stateful updates occur in real time as connections form or go away.

TIP   You can use one dedicated LAN interface (10/100 or Gigabit Ethernet) to carry both LAN-based failover and stateful failover information. The interface bandwidth must be large enough to carry the aggregate failover load.

However, it is always best to keep the LAN-based failover and stateful failover data streams on *separate* interfaces. The stateful failover data stream is usually much larger than the LAN-based failover because of the usually large number of connections that come and go. Therefore, you should set aside the fastest firewall interface that is available for stateful failover.

Section 8-2

In addition, LAN-based failover messages must be able to travel between the two units without being lost or delayed. Otherwise, the loss of LAN-based failover messages indicates that one or both units have failed.

You can link the two stateful failover interfaces directly with a fiber-optic or crossover patch cord without connecting them to intermediate switches. However, neither firewall unit can determine which unit has had an interface failure, because the link status is lost on both units simultaneously.

The best-practice recommendations stress the need for an active device such as a switch to connect the stateful failover interfaces. If one unit loses an interface, a switch would keep the link status up for the other firewall unit.

In the case of FWSMs, they each have a 6-Gbps internal trunk link to the switch backplane. With their high performance, stateful failover information can easily burst up to the link bandwidth. Therefore, if two FWSMs are located in separate chassis, you should provide a stateful failover VLAN link of at least 6 Gbps. You can do this by aggregating Gigabit Ethernet links into a Gigabit EtherChannel.

b. Identify the interface used for stateful failover communication:

FWSM	`Firewall(config)#` **`failover link`** *`if_name`* [**`vlan`** *`vlan`*]
PIX 6.3	`Firewall(config)#` **`failover link`** *`if_name`*
ASA	`Firewall(config)#` **`failover link`** *`if_name`* [*`phy_if`*]

All stateful failover updates are sent and received over the interface named *if_name* (**stateful**, for example). Stateful failover can share the same interface as LAN-based failover if needed. However, you should always try to keep stateful and LAN-based failover isolated on two separate interfaces set aside for these purposes.

In ASA, you must also bind the interface name *if_name* (**stateful**, for example) to the physical interface name *phy_if* (**gigabit0**, for example). On a FWSM, you must bind the interface name *if_name* to a VLAN number *vlan*. If LAN-based and stateful failover share the same interface, the LAN-based **failover lan interface** command already configures this binding. In that case, the physical interface *phy_if* or VLAN *vlan* can be omitted from this command.

j. Keep stateful information about HTTP sessions:

PIX 6.3	`Firewall(config)#` **`failover replicate http`**
ASA, FWSM single context	`Firewall(config)#` **`failover replication http`**
ASA, FWSM multiple context	`Firewall(config)#` **`failover group {1	2}`** `Firewall(config-fover-group)#` **`replication http`**

By default, connection state information is replicated to the standby unit for all TCP protocols except HTTP. The HTTP connections are unique because they are short-lived, usually lasting only as long as it takes to load a web page. If a firewall failover occurs, chances are that any active HTTP requests will be retried or new ones will be generated without any connection state information. However, if it is important that all HTTP connections be preserved across an actual firewall failover, use this command.

In ASA and FWSM, HTTP state replication is a global value in single-context mode, where only active-standby failover applies. If the firewalls are operating in multiple-context mode, where active-active failover is used, HTTP state replication is configured within the failover group on the system execution space because two different failover groups of contexts are maintained.

TIP   Beginning in ASA 8.0(1), session initiation protocol (SIP) signaling is also replicated between firewalls operating as a failover pair. FWSM 3.2 adds authentication, authorization, and accounting (AAA) state replication between a failover pair. These state replications are always enabled and cannot be configured.

---

8. Enable the failover process:

FWSM	`Firewall(config)# failover`
PIX 6.3	`Firewall(config)# failover`
ASA	`Firewall(config)# failover`

By default, failover is disabled even though you can configure the failover features. You must use the **failover** command to enable failover on the primary unit. Then, connect to the secondary unit and enter the command there too. After both units have failover enabled, they should discover each other and begin cooperating as a failover pair. At that time, the primary unit should begin replicating its configuration to the secondary unit.

As well, each of the configuration commands entered from this point on is automatically replicated from the active unit to the standby unit.

9. (Active-active only) Assign contexts to failover groups.

By default, all configured contexts belong to failover group 1. To assign the admin or a user context to a failover group, use the following commands in the system execution space:

PIX 6.3	—
ASA, FWSM single context	—
ASA, FWSM multiple context	`Firewall(config)# context name` `Firewall(config-ctx)# join-failover-group {1	2}`

A context can be a member of only one failover group. You can repeat these commands to assign other contexts to a failover group.

10. Give each firewall interface an active and a standby IP address:

FWSM single context	```Firewall(config)# nameif if_device if_name security_level```
	```Firewall(config)# ip address if_name ip_address [mask]```
	``` [standby```
	``` ip_address]```

FWSM multiple context	```Firewall/context(config)# nameif if_device if_name```
	```security_level```
	```Firewall/context(config)# ip address if_name ip_address```
	```[mask]```
	``` [standby ip_address]```

PIX 6.3	```Firewall(config)# nameif if_device if_name security_level```
	```Firewall(config)# ip address if_name ip_address [mask]```
	```Firewall(config)# failover ip address if_name ip_address```

ASA single context	```Firewall(config)# interface type[mod/]num```
	```Firewall(config-if)# ip address ip_address [mask] [standby```
	``` ip_address]```

ASA multiple context	```Firewall/context(config)# interface type[mod/]num```
	```Firewall/context(config-if)# ip address ip_address [mask]```
	``` [standby ip_address]```

On the interface *if_name*, the active unit uses an IP address given by the **ip address** command. The standby unit uses a different address given by the **failover ip address** command or the **standby** keyword. After a failover occurs, the two units swap IP addresses so that the active unit always uses a consistent address. Although the standby interface is not active, it can respond to pings from other hosts to show that the unit is alive.

In ASA or FWSM multiple-context mode, most of the failover configuration must be done in the system execution space. However, to assign IP addresses to the various context interfaces, you need to connect to each context and configure them there. This applies to the admin context as well as any configured user contexts.

NOTE Identical interfaces on the active and standby firewalls or contexts must have IP addresses that belong to the same network subnet. For example, if interface gigabit0 on the active unit is given 192.168.1.1 255.255.255.0 as its address, the standby unit's gigabit0 interface must also belong to the 192.168.1.0/24 subnet.

---

11. (Optional) Identify interfaces to be monitored:

PIX 6.3	N/A
ASA, FWSM single context	```Firewall(config)# monitor-interface if_name```
ASA, FWSM multiple context	```Firewall/context(config)# monitor-interface if_name```

Before a firewall can measure a threshold of its own failed interfaces, you must identify each interface to be monitored. By default, all physical interfaces are monitored, but no logical interfaces (VLANs) are monitored. A firewall can monitor up to 250 interfaces.

You can enable monitoring on an interface by giving its name as *if_name* (**outside**, for example). If you want to disable monitoring on an interface, begin this command with the **no** keyword. This command can be repeated to identify more than one interface.

For active-active failover, interfaces are marked for monitoring in each of the configured admin and user contexts.

TIP   You can display a list of interfaces and their monitoring status with the **show failover** command. For example, the following output shows that the outside interface of the admin context and the inside and outside interfaces of the CustomerA context are being monitored. The interfaces of the CustomerB context are not:

```
Firewall# show failover
Failover On
Cable status: N/A - LAN-based failover enabled
Failover unit Primary
Failover LAN Interface: Failover Ethernet0 (up)
Unit Poll frequency 3 seconds, holdtime 9 seconds
Interface Poll frequency 15 seconds
Interface Policy 1
Monitored Interfaces 4 of 250 maximum
Group 1 last failover at: 15:33:52 EST Dec 1 2004
Group 2 last failover at: 12:33:40 EST Nov 30 2004

    This host:    Primary
    Group 1       State:          Standby Ready
                  Active time:    233703 (sec)
    Group 2       State:          Active
                  Active time:    168885 (sec)
admin Interface outside (192.168.93.141): Normal
CustomerA Interface outside (192.168.93.142): Normal
CustomerA Interface inside (192.168.200.11): Normal
CustomerB Interface inside (192.168.220.10): Normal (Not-Monitored)
CustomerB Interface outside (192.168.200.12): Normal (Not-Monitored)

    Other host:   Secondary
    Group 1       State:          Active
                  Active time:    71814 (sec)
    Group 2       State:          Standby Ready
                  Active time:    136665 (sec)
admin Interface outside (192.168.93.138): Normal
CustomerA Interface outside (192.168.93.139): Normal
CustomerA Interface inside (192.168.200.10): Normal
CustomerB Interface inside (192.168.220.11): Normal (Not-Monitored)
CustomerB Interface outside (192.168.200.13): Normal (Not-Monitored)
```

Section 8-2

8-3: Firewall Failover Configuration Examples

This section presents several examples of firewall failover configuration, each with a different set of platforms or failover modes. In each example, two firewalls are configured as a failover pair. Each interface from the failover pair connects to a separate switch or VLAN so that the failover feature can exchange hello messages and detect failures.

Active-Standby Failover Example with PIX Firewalls

Figure 8-7 shows the IP addresses of each interface. The addresses of the standby unit interfaces are also given. Stateful failover is used so that connection state information is passed to the standby unit in real time. An example of failover using the serial failover cable is shown first, followed by a LAN-based failover scenario. Following the failover guidelines, a separate VLAN or switch is used for stateful failover (the "stateful" interface) and for LAN-based failover (the "lanfo" interface) information exchange.

Figure 8-7   *Network Diagram for the Active-Standby Example*

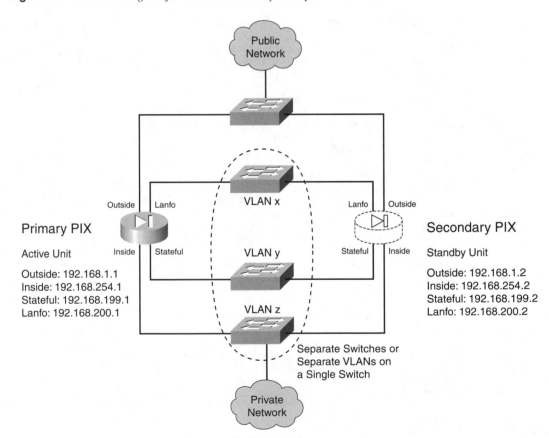

The failover pair is configured to use the most aggressive peer monitoring policy possible, using a peer hello interval of 3 seconds on PIX 6.3 and 200 milliseconds on ASA.

Preliminary configuration for stateful failover using is as follows:

PIX 6.3 Configuration	ASA Configuration

`Firewall(config)# nameif gb-`
`  ethernet0 outside security0`
`Firewall(config)# ip address outside`
`  192.168.1.1 255.255.255.0`
`Firewall(config)# failover ip`
`  address outside 192.168.1.2`
 	
`Firewall(config)# nameif gb-`
`  ethernet1 inside security100`
`Firewall(config)# ip address inside`
`  192.168.254.1 255.255.255.0`
`Firewall(config)# failover ip`
`  address inside 192.168.254.2`
 	
`Firewall(config)# nameif gb-`
`  ethernet2 stateful security20`
`Firewall(config)# ip address`
`  stateful 192.168.199.1`
`    255.255.255.0`
`Firewall(config)# failover ip`
`  address stateful 192.168.199.2`
 	
`Firewall(config)# failover link`
`  stateful`
`Firewall(config)# failover replicate`
`http`
`Firewall(config)# failover poll 3`
`Firewall(config)# failover`
	`Firewall(config)# interface gigabitethernet0`
	`Firewall(config-if)# description Outside`
	`  public network`
	`Firewall(config-if)# nameif outside`
	`Firewall(config-if)# security-level 0`
	`Firewall(config-if)# ip address 192.168.1.1`
	`  255.255.255.0 standby 192.168.1.2`
	`Firewall(config-if)# exit`
	`Firewall(config)# interface gigabitethernet1`
	`Firewall(config-if)# description Inside`
	`private network`
	`Firewall(config-if)# nameif inside`
	`Firewall(config-if)# security-level 100`
	`Firewall(config-if)# ip address 192.168.254.1`
	`  255.255.255.0 standby 192.168.254.2`
	`Firewall(config-if)# exit`
	`Firewall(config)# interface gigabitethernet2`
	`Firewall(config-if)# description Stateful`
	`  Failover link`
	`Firewall(config-if)# failover interface ip`
	`  stateful 192.168.199.1 255.255.255.0 standby`
	`  192.168.199.2`
	`Firewall(config-if)# exit`
	`Firewall(config)# failover link stateful`
	`  ethernet0`
	`Firewall(config)# failover replication http`
	`Firewall(config)# failover polltime unit msec`
	`  200 holdtime msec 800`
	`Firewall(config)# failover`

Additional configuration for the primary LAN-based failover unit is as follows:

PIX 6.3 Configuration	ASA Configuration

`Firewall(config)# nameif gb-`
`  ethernet3 lanfo security30`
`Firewall(config)# ip address`
`lanfo`
`  192.168.200.1 255.255.255.0`
`Firewall(config)# failover ip`
`  address lanfo 192.168.200.2`
`Firewall(config)# failover lan`
`unit primary`
`Firewall(config)# failover lan`
`  interface lanfo`
`Firewall(config)# failover lan`
`key myprivatekey`
`Firewall(config)# failover lan`
`  enable`
	`Firewall(config)# interface gigabitethernet3`
	`Firewall(config-if)# description LAN-based failover`
	`Firewall(config-if)# no shutdown`
	`Firewall(config-if)# exit`
	`Firewall(config)# failover interface ip lanfo`
	`  192.168.200.1 255.255.255.0 standby`
	`  192.168.200.2`
	`Firewall(config)# failover lan unit primary`
	`Firewall(config)# failover lan interface lanfo`
	`  gigabitethernet3`
	`Firewall(config)# failover lan myprivatekey`
	`Firewall(config)# failover lan enable`

Section 8-3

Now, a session is opened to the secondary failover unit, and the following additional configuration commands are added to it:

PIX 6.3 Configuration	ASA Configuration

Firewall(config)# **nameif gb-ethernet3**
  lanfo security30
Firewall(config)# **ip address lanfo**
  192.168.200.1 255.255.255.0
Firewall(config)# **failover ip**
address lanfo 192.168.200.2
Firewall(config)# **failover lan unit**
  secondary
Firewall(config)# **failover lan**
interface lanfo
Firewall(config)# **failover lan key**
  myprivatekey
Firewall(config)# **failover lan**
enable
	Firewall(config)# **interface**
	  gigabitethernet3
	Firewall(config-if)# **description LAN-based**
	  failover
	Firewall(config-if)# **no shutdown**
	Firewall(config-if)# **exit**
	Firewall(config)# **failover interface ip**
	  lanfo 192.168.200.1 255.255.255.0 standby
	  192.168.200.2
	Firewall(config)# **failover lan unit**
	  secondary
	Firewall(config)# **failover lan interface**
	  lanfo gigabitethernet3
	Firewall(config)# **failover key**
	  myprivatekey
	Firewall(config)# **failover lan enable**

Active-Standby Failover Example with FWSM

Now, suppose these firewalls are actually FWSMs. Suppose the inside interface uses VLAN 100, outside uses VLAN 200, stateful uses 300, and lanfo uses 400. The configuration for the primary FWSM in slot 3 would look like this, beginning with the necessary Catalyst 6500 commands:

```
Switch(config)# vlan 100,200,300,400
Switch(config)# firewall vlan-group 1 100,200,300,400
Switch(config)# firewall module 3 vlan-group 1
Switch(config)# exit
! Now open a session to the FWSM itself
Switch# session slot 3 processor 1
```

Next are the FWSM commands:

```
fwsm(config)# nameif vlan100 inside security100
fwsm(config)# ip address inside 192.168.254.1 255.255.255.0 standby 192.168.254.2
fwsm(config)# nameif vlan200 outside security0
fwsm(config)# ip address outside 192.168.1.1 255.255.255.0 standby 192.168.1.2
fwsm(config)# failover interface ip stateful 192.168.199.1 255.255.255.0 standby
   192.168.199.2
fwsm(config)# failover link stateful vlan 300
fwsm(config)# failover interface ip lanfo 192.168.200.1 255.255.255.0 standby
   192.168.200.2
fwsm(config)# failover lan unit primary
fwsm(config)# failover lan interface lanfo vlan 400
fwsm(config)# failover replication http
fwsm(config)# failover polltime unit msec 500 holdtime 3
fwsm(config)# failover
```

Then, on the secondary FWSM in the module 4 slot, the following configuration commands are entered, beginning with the Catalyst 6500 session. Note that the first two switch commands are entered again only if the two FWSMs are located in separate switch chassis. If the FWSMs are housed in the same switch chassis, the VLANs and the firewall VLAN group are already configured:

```
Switch(config)# vlan 100,200,300,400
Switch(config)# firewall vlan-group 1 100,200,300,400
Switch(config)# firewall module 4 vlan-group 1
Switch(config)# exit
! Now open a session to the FWSM itself
Switch# session slot 4 processor 1
[output omitted]
fwsm(config)# failover interface ip stateful 192.168.199.1 255.255.255.0 standby
  192.168.199.2
fwsm(config)# failover link stateful vlan 300
fwsm(config)# failover interface ip lanfo 192.168.200.1 255.255.255.0 standby
  192.168.200.2
fwsm(config)# failover lan unit secondary
fwsm(config)# failover lan interface lanfo vlan 400
fwsm(config)# failover
```

Active-Active Failover Example

Suppose a Cisco firewall is to be configured with multiple security contexts so that it can provide firewall services to two customers of a service provider. A total of three contexts are needed:

- admin
- CustomerA
- CustomerB

To enhance the availability of the firewall contexts, a second firewall is added to form a failover pair. Active-active failover is used so that one firewall has the active role for some contexts and the other firewall is active for a different set of contexts.

Figure 8-8 shows a basic diagram for this arrangement. The primary and secondary firewalls use LAN-based failover communication over their Ethernet0/0 interfaces. The firewalls send failover hello messages once every second and wait for 3 seconds before declaring their peer failed. Stateful failover carries connection state information between the firewalls over their GigabitEthernet1/2 interfaces.

TIP   This example uses interface names that are relevant to ASA platforms with a four-port GigabitEthernet module. The same example can apply to FWSM platforms, by substituting VLANs for physical interface names.

One path to the public network is provided over the firewalls' GigabitEthernet1/0 interfaces. This connection becomes the outside interface for each of the security contexts so that they share a common pipe to the public Internet.

Each security context has its own separate inside interface, which is carried as a VLAN over the GigabitEthernet1/1 trunking firewall interfaces. VLAN 10 is assigned to the admin context, VLAN 20 to the CustomerA context, and VLAN 30 to the CustomerB context.

Finally, two failover groups are used to allow the two firewalls to have differing roles in the contexts. Failover group 1 gives preference to the primary unit having the active role. The admin and CustomerA contexts are members of group 1. Failover group 2 gives preference to the secondary unit having the active role, where the CustomerB context is a member.

Figure 8-8 *Network Diagram for the Active-Active Example*

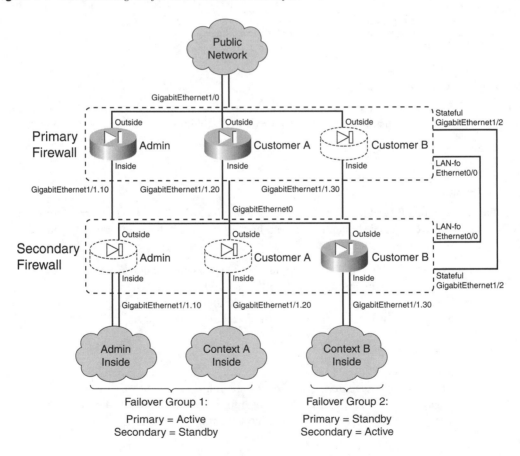

Remember that each interface of the primary firewall is "connected" to the corresponding interface of the secondary firewall. In other words, the two firewalls have their corresponding interfaces assigned to the same VLANs so that failover messages can be exchanged between the firewall units over each of their interfaces. This is required for failover operation.

Active-active failover can be difficult to visualize and configure. The configuration for this example is broken into several steps, as described in the following sections.

Primary Firewall Configuration

First, you need to configure the primary firewall. Remember that failover is configured in the system execution space of a multiple-context firewall.

1. Begin with only the interfaces needed for failover.

    The GigabitEthernet1/2 (stateful failover) and Ethernet0 (LAN-based failover) interfaces are needed. Their configuration is not necessary, because the actual **failover** commands remove any IP addressing or other parameters that might be assigned in interface configuration mode. They are shown here only for clarity:

    ```
    Firewall(config)# mode multiple
    [output omitted]
    ! Here, the system execution space is being configured
    !
    Firewall(config)# interface gigabitethernet1/2
    Firewall(config-if)# description Stateful failover interface
    Firewall(config-if)# exit
    Firewall(config)# interface ethernet0/0
    Firewall(config-if)# description LAN-based failover interface
    Firewall(config-if)# exit
    ```

2. Configure LAN-based failover:

    ```
    Firewall(config)# failover lan unit primary
    Firewall(config)# failover lan interface LAN-fo ethernet0/0
    Firewall(config)# failover interface ip LAN-fo 192.168.1.1 255.255.255.0
       standby 192.168.1.2
    Firewall(config)# failover polltime unit 1 holdtime 3
    Firewall(config)# failover key *****
    Firewall(config)# failover lan enable
    ```

3. Configure stateful failover:

    ```
    Firewall(config)# failover interface ip Stateful 192.168.2.1 255.255.255.0
       standby 192.168.2.2
    Firewall(config)# failover link Stateful gigabitethernet1/2
    ```

4. Define the failover groups:

    ```
    Firewall(config)# failover group 1
    Firewall(config-fover-group)# primary
    Firewall(config-fover-group)# preempt
    ```

```
Firewall(config-fover-group)# exit
Firewall(config)# failover group 2
Firewall(config-fover-group)# secondary
Firewall(config-fover-group)# preempt
Firewall(config-fover-group)# exit
```

5. Enable failover:

```
Firewall(config)# failover
```

Secondary Firewall Configuration

1. Begin with only the interfaces needed for failover.

   The GigabitEthernet1/2 (stateful failover) and Ethernet0/0 (LAN-based failover) interfaces are paired with identical interfaces on the primary firewall. Their configuration is not necessary; it is shown here only for clarity:

```
Firewall(config)# mode multiple
[output omitted]
! Here, the system execution space is being configured
!
Firewall(config)# interface gigabitethernet1/2
Firewall(config-if)# description Stateful failover interface
Firewall(config-if)# exit
Firewall(config)# interface ethernet0/0
Firewall(config-if)# description LAN-based failover interface
Firewall(config-if)# exit
```

2. Configure LAN-based failover.

   Here, the secondary unit begins its life in standby mode for all failover groups. Therefore, it knows to pick up the standby IP address for the LAN-based and stateful failover interfaces in the following commands:

```
Firewall(config)# failover lan unit secondary
Firewall(config)# failover lan interface LAN-fo ethernet0/0
Firewall(config)# failover interface ip LAN-fo 192.168.1.1 255.255.255.0
   standby 192.168.1.2
Firewall(config)# failover polltime unit 1 holdtime 3
Firewall(config)# failover key *****
Firewall(config)# failover lan enable
```

3. Configure stateful failover:

```
Firewall(config)# failover interface ip Stateful 192.168.2.1 255.255.255.0
   standby 192.168.2.2
Firewall(config)# failover link Stateful gigabitethernet1/2
```

4. Define the failover groups.

Although the failover groups could be explicitly configured here, as they were on the primary firewall unit, that is not really necessary. The failover group configuration is replicated to the secondary unit as soon as failover is enabled on each. The following commands become a part of the configuration:

```
Firewall(config)# failover group 1
Firewall(config-fover-group)# primary
Firewall(config-fover-group)# preempt
Firewall(config)# exit
Firewall(config)# failover group 2
Firewall(config-fover-group)# secondary
Firewall(config-fover-group)# preempt
Firewall(config)# exit
```

5. Enable failover:

```
Firewall(config)# failover
```

Allocating Interfaces to the Contexts

Configuration should continue on the primary firewall in the system execution space. As soon as failover is enabled on both firewalls and is operational, any remaining configuration commands are replicated to the secondary unit automatically. This saves time and effort over entering the same commands in the two firewalls manually.

1. Define physical interfaces in the system execution space.

Here, you identify the interfaces. You also configure the subinterfaces of GigabitEthernet1/1 with their VLAN numbers on the trunk. No IP addresses are assigned in the system execution space. Rather, the addressing is left up to the administrator of the context where each interface will be allocated:

```
Firewall(config)# interface gigabitethernet1/0
Firewall(config-if)# description Public Network for all contexts
Firewall(config-if)# exit
!
Firewall(config)# interface gigabitethernet1/1
Firewall(config-if)# description Trunk for non-public networks
Firewall(config-if)# exit
!
Firewall(config)# interface gigabitethernet1/1.10
Firewall(config-if)# description Private network for admin context
Firewall(config-if)# vlan 10
Firewall(config-if)# exit
!
Firewall(config)# interface gigabitethernet1/1.20
```

```
Firewall(config-if)# description Private network for CustomerA context
Firewall(config-if)# vlan 20
Firewall(config-if)# exit
!
Firewall(config)# interface gigabitethernet1/1.30
Firewall(config-if)# description Private network for CustomerB context
Firewall(config-if)# vlan 30
Firewall(config-if)# exit
```

  2. Allocate interfaces to the contexts and failover groups.

     For the admin context, you can allocate interfaces only with their physical interface names. For the CustomerA and CustomerB user contexts, however, you can assign logical names (intf0 and intf1) so that the physical identity remains hidden:

```
Firewall(config)# context admin
Firewall(config-ctx)# allocate-interface gigabitethernet1/0
Firewall(config-ctx)# allocate-interface gigabitethernet1/1.10
Firewall(config-ctx)# config-url flash:/admin.cfg
Firewall(config-ctx)# join-failover-group 1
Firewall(config-ctx)# exit
!
Firewall(config)# context CustomerA
Firewall(config-ctx)# description Virtual firewall for CustomerA
Firewall(config-ctx)# allocate-interface gigabitethernet1/0 intf0
Firewall(config-ctx)# allocate-interface gigabitethernet1/1.20 intf1
Firewall(config-ctx)# config-url flash:/CustomerA.cfg
Firewall(config-ctx)# join-failover-group 1
Firewall(config-ctx)# exit
!
Firewall(config)# context CustomerB
Firewall(config-ctx)# description Virtual firewall for CustomerB
Firewall(config-ctx)# allocate-interface gigabitethernet1/0 intf0
Firewall(config-ctx)# allocate-interface gigabitethernet1/1.30 intf1
Firewall(config-ctx)# config-url flash:/CustomerB.cfg
Firewall(config-ctx)# join-failover-group 2
Firewall(config-ctx)# exit
```

Configuring Interfaces in Each Context

After you have allocated the physical firewall interfaces to the security contexts, you must configure them for use by the contexts. You do this by opening a session to each context in turn. At this point, remember that the context is a virtual firewall, so each interface needs an IP address, a security level, and a name. Also remember that each context has its own concept of failover. Each interface needs a standby IP address, too.

1. Configure the admin context interfaces:

```
Firewall# change to context admin
Firewall/admin# configure terminal
Firewall/admin(config)# interface gigabitethernet1/0
Firewall/admin(config-if)# nameif outside
Firewall/admin(config-if)# security-level 0
Firewall/admin(config-if)# ip address 192.168.93.1 255.255.255.0 standby
  192.168.93.2
Firewall/admin(config-if)# exit
!
Firewall/admin(config)# interface gigabitethernet1/1.10
Firewall/admin(config-if)# nameif inside
Firewall/admin(config-if)# security-level 100
Firewall/admin(config-if)# ip address 192.168.1.1 255.255.255.0 standby
  192.168.1.2
Firewall/admin(config-if)# exit
Firewall/admin(config)# exit
```

2. Configure the CustomerA context interfaces:

```
Firewall/admin# changeto context CustomerA
Firewall/CustomerA# configure terminal
Firewall/CustomerA(config)# interface intf0
Firewall/CustomerA(config-if)# nameif outside
Firewall/CustomerA(config-if)# security-level 0
Firewall/CustomerA(config-if)# ip address 192.168.93.140 255.255.255.0
  standby 192.168.93.141
Firewall/CustomerA(config-if)# exit
!
Firewall/CustomerA(config)# interface intf1
Firewall/CustomerA(config-if)# nameif inside
Firewall/CustomerA(config-if)# security-level 100
Firewall/CustomerA(config-if)# ip address 192.168.200.10 255.255.255.0
  standby 192.168.200.11
Firewall/CustomerA(config-if)# exit
Firewall/CustomerA(config)# exit
```

3. Configure the CustomerB context interfaces:

```
Firewall/CustomerA# changeto context CustomerB
Firewall/CustomerB# configure terminal
Firewall/CustomerB(config)# interface intf0
Firewall/CustomerB(config-if)# nameif outside
Firewall/CustomerB(config-if)# security-level 0
Firewall/CustomerB(config-if)# ip address 192.168.93.150 255.255.255.0
  standby 192.168.93.151
Firewall/CustomerB(config-if)# exit
```

Section 8-3

```
!
Firewall/CustomerB(config)# interface intf1
Firewall/CustomerB(config-if)# nameif inside
Firewall/CustomerB(config-if)# security-level 100
Firewall/CustomerB(config-if)# ip address 192.168.220.10 255.255.255.0
  standby 192.168.220.11
Firewall/CustomerB(config-if)# exit
Firewall/CustomerB(config)# exit
```

8-4: Managing Firewall Failover

By nature, firewall failover is a feature that can take action automatically, based on whether two firewalls are operational and connected. You might want to monitor or troubleshoot the failover mechanism on a failover pair so that you can verify its operation. As well, there might be occasions when you need to manually force the failover action between the peers. The following sections cover these topics.

Displaying Information About Failover

When you connect to a firewall remotely, it is not always apparent which unit is the active one. Because the active unit configuration is replicated to the standby unit, the command-line prompt (and the underlying host name) is identical on both units. This can make interacting with the correct firewall very difficult.

After you connect to a firewall, use the **show failover** command to determine the state of that unit, as shown in the following example:

```
Firewall# show failover
Failover On
Cable status: Normal
Reconnect timeout 0:00:00
Poll frequency 15 seconds
        This host: Primary - Active
                Active time: 2421015 (sec)
                Interface stateful (192.168.199.1): Normal
                Interface dmz2 (127.0.0.1): Link Down (Shutdown)
                Interface outside (192.168.1.1): Normal
                Interface inside (192.168.254.1): Normal
        Other host: Secondary - Standby
                Active time: 0 (sec)
                Interface stateful (192.168.199.2): Normal
                Interface dmz2 (0.0.0.0): Link Down (Shutdown)
                Interface outside (192.168.1.2): Normal
                Interface inside (192.168.254.2): Normal
```

Remember that you should make configuration changes to only the active unit, because those changes are replicated in only one direction—active to standby. Active-active failover takes this one step further—configuration changes to the system execution space or the admin context must be made on the firewall unit that is active for failover group 1. If you attempt to configure the standby unit, the standby firewall displays a warning that the configurations are no longer synchronized.

In the case of active-active failover, this gets a little more complicated. Now, a firewall can be either the primary or secondary unit, but it can be active in some contexts while being standby in others. You can find out which failover group the firewall is active in by using the **show failover** command in the system execution space, as shown in the following example:

```
Firewall# show failover
Failover On
Cable status: N/A - LAN-based failover enabled
Failover unit Primary
Failover LAN Interface: Failover Ethernet0/2 (up)
Unit Poll frequency 3 seconds, holdtime 9 seconds
Interface Poll frequency 15 seconds
Interface Policy 1
Monitored Interfaces 3 of 250 maximum
Group 1 last failover at: 13:10:46 EST Dec 9 2004
Group 2 last failover at: 13:10:04 EST Dec 9 2004
  This host:    Primary
  Group 1       State:              Active
                Active time:        149706 (sec)
  Group 2       State:              Standby Ready
                Active time:        121650 (sec)
[output omitted]
  Other host:   Secondary
  Group 1       State:              Standby Ready
                Active time:        120936 (sec)
  Group 2       State:              Active
                Active time:        148995 (sec)
```

If you cannot enable failover, check the status of your firewall license with the **show activation-key** or **show version** command. The following example shows the results for an ASA firewall:

```
Firewall# show activation-key
Serial Number:  JHX1114L04Z
Running Activation Key: 0x7411c36d 0x639a94fa 0xa3f0b034 0x913c0374 0x3f3632ba
License Features for this Platform:
Maximum Physical Interfaces : Unlimited
Maximum VLANs               : 100
Inside Hosts                : Unlimited
Failover                    : Active/Active
VPN-DES                     : Enabled
VPN-3DES-AES                : Enabled
Security Contexts           : 5
GTP/GPRS                    : Enabled
VPN Peers                   : Unlimited
WebVPN Peers                : 2
Advanced Endpoint Assessment : Disabled
This platform has an ASA 5510 Security Plus license.
The flash activation key is the SAME as the running key.
Firewall#
```

Section 8-4

Displaying the Current Failover Status

You can use the following command to display a summary of the current failover status:

```
Firewall# show failover
```

The output from this command displays the configured failover state (on or off), along with failover cable status, the last failover date and time, the failover roles (primary or secondary) for both units, the firewall role (active or standby) for both units, the status of each configured interface, and the statistics for the stateful failover link (if configured).

An ASA or FWSM also presents this information for each failover group (1 and 2). Within each group, the status of each of the security contexts and its allocated interfaces are shown. For example, the system execution space on the primary firewall has the following output. Notice that at a glance, the shaded text gives a snapshot of every state and role involved in failover:

```
Firewall# show failover
Failover On
Cable status: N/A - LAN-based failover enabled
Failover unit Primary
Failover LAN Interface: Failover Ethernet2 (up)
Unit Poll frequency 3 seconds, holdtime 9 seconds
Interface Poll frequency 15 seconds
Interface Policy 1
Monitored Interfaces 3 of 250 maximum
Group 1 last failover at: 13:11:02 EST Dec 7 2004
Group 2 last failover at: 15:01:04 EST Dec 7 2004

  This host:    Primary
  Group 1       State:        Active
                Active time:  7536 (sec)
  Group 2       State:        Standby Ready
                Active time:  663 (sec)

                admin Interface outside (192.168.93.138): Normal
                CustomerA Interface outside (192.168.93.139): Normal
                CustomerA Interface inside (192.168.200.10): Normal
  (Not-Monitored)
                CustomerB Interface outside (192.168.93.143): Normal
                CustomerB Interface inside (192.168.220.11): Normal
  (Not-Monitored)

  Other host:   Secondary
  Group 1       State:        Standby Ready
                Active time:  0 (sec)
  Group 2       State:        Active
                Active time:  6879 (sec)

                admin Interface outside (128.163.93.141): Normal
                CustomerA Interface outside (128.163.93.142): Normal
                CustomerA Interface inside (192.168.200.11): Normal
  (Not-Monitored)
```

```
            CustomerB Interface outside (128.163.93.140): Normal
            CustomerB Interface inside (192.168.220.10): Normal
  (Not-Monitored)

Stateful Failover Logical Update Statistics
        Link : Failover Ethernet2 (up)
        Stateful Obj    xmit        xerr      rcv         rerr
        General         135508407   7         53412868    0
        sys cmd         266210      0         266207      0
        up time         14          0         0           0
        RPC services    0           0         0           0
        TCP conn        123228648   0         47758798    0
        UDP conn        663934      0         448445      0
        ARP tbl         6           0         0           0
        Xlate_Timeout   617643      0         556745      0

Logical Update Queue Information
                        Cur         Max       Total
        Recv Q:         0           35        7519538
        Xmit Q:         0           1         18562497
Firewall#
```

The **Stateful Failover Logical Update Statistics** represent the number of connection or table synchronization update messages that the firewall has transmitted and received. The **Logical Update Queue Information** shows the number of stateful update messages that have been queued as they have been transmitted to or received from the failover peer. Nonzero values mean that more updates have been queued than could be processed. A large value might indicate that the stateful failover bandwidth needs to be increased, usually by choosing a faster interface.

To see the failover status information for just one failover group, you can use the following command:

```
Firewall# show failover group {1 | 2}
```

On an ASA or FWSM, you can also get a quick summary of the failover status with the following command:

```
Firewall# show failover state
```

In the following example, the firewall is shown to be the primary unit with the active role, and the other peer is the secondary in standby. The configurations are synchronized, and the interface MAC addresses have been set according to the primary and secondary burned-in addresses. If one of the units had failed, a reason would be shown:

```
Firewall# show failover state
====My State===
Primary | Active |
====Other State===
Secondary | Standby |
====Configuration State===
        Sync Done
====Communication State===
        Mac set
========Failed Reason=============
My Fail Reason:
Other Fail Reason:
Firewall#
```

Section 8-4

Displaying the LAN-Based Failover Interface Status

An FWSM or an ASA cannot display LAN-based failover interface statistics. However, a firewall running PIX 6.3 displays this information if you use the following command:

Firewall# **show failover lan** [**detail**]

For example, in the following output, the LAN-based failover interface is called lan-fo. It uses 192.168.1.1 and 192.168.1.2 on the two peers:

```
Firewall# show failover lan
LAN-based Failover is Active
        interface lan-fo (192.168.1.1): Normal, peer (192.168.1.2): Normal
Firewall#
```

You could see much more detail about the interface activity by adding the **detail** keyword, as shown in the following example. Notice that statistics are kept for the number of failover messages sent, received, dropped, and so on, as well as the response times for message exchanges with the failover peer (the shaded text):

```
Firewall# show failover lan detail
LAN-based Failover is Active
This PIX is Primary
Command Interface is lan-fo
My Command Interface IP is 192.168.198.1
Peer Command Interface IP is 192.168.198.2
My interface status is Normal
Peer interface status is Normal
Peer interface down time is 0x0
Total cmd msgs sent: 107856, rcvd: 107845, dropped: 1, retrans: 8, send_err: 0
Total secure msgs sent: 147375, rcvd: 147301
bad_signature: 0, bad_authen: 0, bad_hdr: 0, bad_osversion: 0, bad_length: 0
Total failed retx lck cnt: 0
Total/Cur/Max of 52719:0:3 msgs on retransQ, 52718 ack msgs
Cur/Max of 0:7 msgs on txq
Cur/Max of 0:34 msgs on rxq
Number of blk allocation failure: 0, cmd failure: 0, Flapping: 0
Current cmd window: 3, Slow cmd Ifc cnt: 0
Cmd Link down: 17, down and up: 0, Window Limit: 17266
Number of fmsg allocation failure: 0, duplicate msgs: 0
Cmd Response Time History stat:
< 100ms:       52681
100 - 250ms:   12
250 - 500ms:   13
500 - 750ms:   12
750 - 1000ms:  0
1000 - 2000ms: 4
2000 - 4000ms: 1
> 4000ms:      3
Cmd Response Retry History stat:
Retry 0 = 52719, 1 = 4, 2 = 1, 3 = 1, 4 = 1
[output truncated]
```

Displaying a History of Failover State Changes

A firewall keeps a running history of each time its failover state changes. Although the history events are not recorded with a timestamp, the sequence of events can still be useful information. For example, if failover did not come up correctly, you could trace through the history to see the sequence of state changes and the cause for each. You can see the history with the following command:

```
Firewall# show failover history
```

For example, the following output shows the failover state change history for a firewall running in multiple-context mode. Failover groups 0 (for system execution space failover), 1, and 2 are listed, because failover operates independently in each group. This sequence of state changes occurred as failover was configured for the first time. During the **No Active unit found** changes, the secondary peer had not yet been configured for failover.

```
Firewall# show failover history
==============================================================================
  Group    From State              To State                Reason
==============================================================================
   0       Active Applying Config  Active Config Applied   No Active unit found
   0       Active Config Applied   Active                  No Active unit found
   1       Disabled                Negotiation             Failover state check
   2       Disabled                Negotiation             Failover state check
   2       Negotiation             Cold Standby            Detected an Active mate
   1       Negotiation             Just Active             No Active unit found
   1       Just Active             Active Drain            No Active unit found
   1       Active Drain            Active Applying Config   No Active unit found
   1       Active Applying Config  Active Config Applied   No Active unit found
   1       Active Config Applied   Active                  No Active unit found
   2       Cold Standby            Sync Config             Detected an Active mate
   2       Sync Config             Sync File System        Detected an Active mate
   2       Sync File System        Bulk Sync               Detected an Active mate
   2       Bulk Sync               Standby Ready           Detected an Active mate
   2       Standby Ready           Just Active             Set by the CI config cmd
   2       Just Active             Active Drain            Set by the CI config cmd
   2       Active Drain            Active Applying Config   Set by the CI config cmd
   2       Active Applying Config  Active Config Applied   Set by the CI config cmd
   2       Active Config Applied   Active                  Set by the CI config cmd
   2       Active                  Standby Ready           Set by the CI config cmd
==============================================================================
Firewall#
```

Debugging Failover Activity

Table 8-1 summarizes some of the commands you can use to generate debugging information about firewall failover operation.

Table 8-1 *debug Commands Relevant to Firewall Failover Operation*

Command	Display Function
debug fover cable	Failover cable status
debug fover {**rx** | **tx**}	Failover messages parsed or sent (serial cable only)
debug fover {**rxip** | **txip**}	Failover hello messages received or sent on all interfaces

continues

Table 8-1 *debug Commands Relevant to Firewall Failover Operation (Continued)*

debug fover fmsg	Stateful failover memory activity
**debug fover {get	put}**	Stateful failover packets received from or sent to the other unit (not available in PIX 7.x)
debug fover sync	Configuration command replication
debug fover switch	Health monitoring activity
debug fover ifc	Interface health polling

TIP Commands using the **debug** keyword produce real-time output for troubleshooting purposes. To see these messages, you must first enable logging output to the firewall console (**logging console**), to a Telnet or SSH session (**logging monitor**), to a logging buffer (**logging buffered**), or to a Syslog server (**logging host**). The **debug** output also must be sent to the Syslog destination with the **logging debug-trace** configuration command. See Chapter 10, "Firewall Logging," for more information.

Monitoring Stateful Failover

As soon as stateful failover is enabled, you should make sure your stateful failover interface is not being overrun with stateful information packets. In other words, verify that the stateful interface bandwidth is sufficient for the load. Otherwise, information about some active connections will not be passed from the active to the standby firewall. If a failover occurs, these unknown connections are terminated.

In single-context mode, you can make a quick manual estimate by using the **show traffic** command. Unfortunately, this command shows only cumulative values collected since the traffic counters were last cleared. For the packets-per-second and bytes-per-second values, a running average is computed since the counters were last cleared.

However, you can issue the **clear traffic** command on the active firewall to clear the counters, wait 10 seconds, and issue the **show traffic** command. You should do this during a peak load time so that you see a snapshot of the busiest stateful information exchange. The following example shows how this is done:

```
Firewall# clear traffic
[wait 10 seconds]
Firewall# show traffic
stateful:
        received (in 9.050 secs):
                3 packets        395 bytes
                0 pkts/sec       43 bytes/sec
        transmitted (in 9.050 secs):
                84 packets       98682 bytes
                9 pkts/sec       10904 bytes/sec
[output deleted]
```

In multiple-context mode (active-active failover), things get a little more difficult. The interface used for stateful failover is defined and configured only in the system execution space, where there is no **show traffic** command. (That command is available in each security context; however, the stateful failover interface is not!)

To gauge the stateful failover interface usage, you can use the **show interface** command instead. Issue that command and note the number of bytes shown. (This is a cumulative total, not a bytes-per-second rate.) Then, wait 10 seconds and issue the command again. Note the new byte count, subtract the two, and divide by 10. This gives you an estimate of the bytes per second being sent and received over the stateful interface.

You can also use ASDM to generate statistics or a utilization graph of a stateful LAN interface. Running the graph over a period of time shows you the maximum bit rate that has been used to transfer stateful information. Figure 8-9 shows a sample ASDM graph.

Figure 8-9   *Using ASDM to Gauge Stateful Failover Traffic*

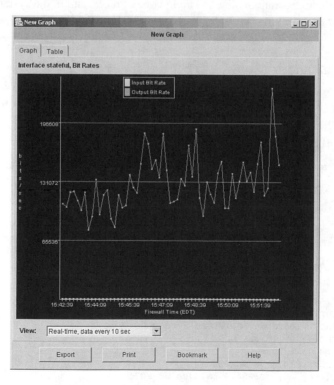

Finally, the firewall performance itself affects the stateful failover operation. As stateful messages are generated, they are put into 256-byte memory blocks and placed in a queue before being sent to the failover peer. If the firewall cannot generate and send the stateful messages as fast as they are needed, more memory blocks are used. Although the firewall can allocate more 256-byte blocks as needed, the supply of these blocks can be exhausted in an extreme case.

You can use the **show blocks** command as a gauge of the stateful failover performance. Over time, the 256-byte block "CNT" value should remain above 0. If it continues to hover around 0, the active firewall cannot keep the connection state information synchronized with the standby firewall. Most likely, a higher-performance firewall is needed.

Manually Intervening in Failover

When the firewalls in a failover pair detect a failure and take action, they do not automatically revert to their original failover roles. For example, if the primary firewall is active and then fails, it is marked as failed, and the secondary firewall takes over the active role. After the primary unit is repaired and returned to service, it does not automatically reclaim the active role (unless it has been configured to preempt active control).

You might occasionally find that you need to manually intervene in the failover process to force a role change or to reset a failover condition. The commands discussed in the following sections should be used from configuration mode in single-context mode and in the system execution space in multiple-context mode.

Forcing a Role Change

Ordinarily, the firewalls fail over to each other automatically, without any intervention. However, they do not automatically fail back to their original roles. If for some reason you need to force one unit to become active again, you can use the following privileged EXEC command:

```
Firewall# [no] failover active [group {1 | 2}]
```

You can also force a unit into standby mode with the **no failover active** command.

With active-active failover, you can specify the failover group (1 or 2) that will become active. For example, suppose the secondary firewall should be standby for failover group 1 and active for failover group 2. After a failure, it ends up in standby mode for both failover groups, as shown in the following output:

```
Firewall# show failover
Failover On
Cable status: N/A - LAN-based failover enabled
Failover unit Primary
Failover LAN Interface: Failover Ethernet0/2 (up)
Unit Poll frequency 3 seconds, holdtime 9 seconds
Interface Poll frequency 15 seconds
Interface Policy 2
Monitored Interfaces 3 of 250 maximum
Group 1 last failover at: 10:29:18 EST Jan 30 2005
Group 2 last failover at: 16:18:28 EST Mar 9 2005
  This host:    Secondary
  Group 1       State:          Standby Ready
                Active time:    3311601 (sec)
  Group 2       State:          Standby Ready
                Active time:    3304092 (sec)
```

To restore the secondary unit to the active role for failover group 2, you could take two different approaches:

- Force the primary unit (currently active) into the standby role by using the **no failover active group 2** command

- Force the secondary unit (currently standby) into the active role by using the **failover active group 2** command

Resetting a Failed Firewall Unit

If a firewall has been marked as failed but has been repaired or its connectivity restored, you might have to manually "unfail" it or reset its failover role. You can use the following privileged EXEC command:

Firewall# **failover reset** [**group** {**1** | **2**}]

You can use this command on either the active or failed unit. If it is issued on the active unit, the command is replicated to the failed unit, and only that unit's state is reset. In active-active failover, you can add the **group** keyword and failover group number for the firewall role to be reset.

Reloading a Hung Standby Unit

Sometimes, an active and standby firewall can communicate over a failover connection but cannot synchronize their failover operation. In this case, you can manually force the standby unit to reload and reinitialize its failover role with the following command:

Firewall# **failover reload-standby**

After the reload, it should resynchronize with the active unit.

Executing Commands on a Failover Peer

Although two firewalls can be configured as a failover pair, they still support their own administrative sessions independently. For example, you can connect to the active unit and enter commands, make configuration changes, and so on. The same is true of the standby unit, where you can connect and do everything except make configuration changes.

Sometimes you might find yourself connected to one unit when you would like to do something on the other unit. Normally you would have to open up an administrative connection to the other unit and enter your commands there. Beginning with ASA 8.0(1), you can open a single session and enter commands that are passed to the failover peer and evaluated there.

Use the following EXEC command to send a command string to the appropriate failover unit:

Firewall# **failover exec** {**active** | **standby** | **mate**} *cmd_string*

Regardless of the unit to which you are connected, you can send a command line, *cmd_string*, to any of the following failover pair units:

- **active**—The command is sent to the current active unit, where it is executed and also replicated to the standby unit.

- **standby**—The command is sent to the current standby unit, where it is executed; it is *not* replicated to the active unit.

- **mate**—The command is sent to the mate or peer of the unit, where the command is entered.

For example, suppose you are connected to the active unit, where you can display its activation key with the **show activation-key** command. Then, without opening a second connection to the standby unit, you can see the standby unit's flash file system by sending it the same command, too, as in the following example:

```
Firewall# show activation-key
Serial Number:  848020184
Running Activation Key: 0x7111c56d 0x689a94fa 0xa4f0b064 0x910c0474 0xcf36c2ba
Licensed features for this platform:
Maximum Physical Interfaces  : 6
Maximum VLANs                : 25
Inside Hosts                 : Unlimited
Failover                     : Active/Active
VPN-DES                      : Enabled
VPN-3DES-AES                 : Enabled
Cut-through Proxy            : Enabled
Guards                       : Enabled
URL Filtering                : Enabled
Security Contexts            : 5
GTP/GPRS                     : Enabled
VPN Peers                    : Unlimited
This platform has an Unrestricted (UR) license.
The flash activation key is the SAME as the running key.
Firewall#
Firewall# failover exec standby show activation-key
Serial Number:  857206105
Running Activation Key: 0xb116c169 0xd0f16030 0x44600c98 0xb138e8b0 0x8322dc9f
Licensed features for this platform:
Maximum Physical Interfaces  : 6
Maximum VLANs                : 25
Inside Hosts                 : Unlimited
Failover                     : Active/Active
VPN-DES                      : Enabled
VPN-3DES-AES                 : Enabled
Cut-through Proxy            : Enabled
Guards                       : Enabled
URL Filtering                : Enabled
Security Contexts            : 5
GTP/GPRS                     : Enabled
VPN Peers                    : Unlimited
This platform has an Unrestricted (UR) license.
The flash activation key is the SAME as the running key.
Firewall#
```

You should keep a couple things in mind about remotely executing commands:

- The command strings are sent over the LAN-based failover connection.

- The command strings are sent to the target failover unit, but the command output is always returned to the unit where the **failover exec** command was entered.

You can also use the **failover exec** command to remotely execute configuration commands. This can be handy if you need to make a small change, but are not currently connected to the appropriate unit. However, making configuration changes in this way is somewhat cumbersome.

You should never try to execute configuration commands remotely on a standby unit. Configuration changes must always be made on the active unit, while the failover feature takes care of replicating the changes to the standby unit automatically.

TIP   If you do decide to enter configuration commands remotely, be aware that the source and target firewalls each maintain their own command mode. For example, the firewall you enter the **failover exec** command into might be in configuration mode, but the target firewall is not necessarily in the same mode—it might be at the normal EXEC level prompt. In that case, the command you try to execute remotely might not work.

To see what mode the target firewall is currently at, use the **show failover exec** {**active** | **standby** | **mate**} command.

In multiple context mode, remote command execution takes place only in the context to which you are currently connected. In other words, the **changeto** command cannot be sent to a target firewall. To send a command to the target in a specific context, you have to first change to that context locally and then send the command.

8-5: Upgrading Firewalls in Failover Mode

Upgrading the operating system on a single standalone firewall is straightforward. You download a new image to the firewall, save the running configuration, and reload the firewall. The Auto Update feature can also be used to automate the upgrade process. Obviously, this should all be done during a scheduled maintenance time in your network, because the reload interrupts network connectivity.

A failover pair of firewalls is slightly more complicated, because both firewalls must be running exactly the same release of code at all times. If the code release differs between the two firewalls, failover is disabled. This causes each firewall to run independently, each thinking that the other has either failed or is incompatible for failover.

Firewall platforms running releases at or greater than FWSM 2.0(1) or PIX 7.0(1) are exceptions. These versions offer a "hitless upgrade" or "zero downtime upgrade" feature that allows failover to continue operating even if the two firewalls are running different releases of the software image. However, you should make sure the failover peers are upgrading in one of the following scenarios to achieve a zero downtime upgrade:

- Upgrade from one maintenance release to another (8.0[1] to 8.0[4], for example).

- Upgrade from one minor release to the next minor release increment (8.0[1] to 8.1[1], for example); don't skip minor releases.

- Upgrade from the last minor release of one major release to the first minor release of the next major release (7.2[4] to 8.0[1], for example).

Manually Upgrading a Failover Pair

In an active-standby pair, only one firewall is active, and both units must be running identical software releases. The only exception is during a zero downtime upgrade, where the firewalls might be running images with incrementally different release numbers.

In a nutshell, as long as one of the two firewalls is operating in active mode, it continues inspecting traffic and updating state information (connections, translations, and so on) to the standby unit. The idea is to juggle the active and standby roles so that the standby unit is always the one being upgraded. Whichever unit has the active role at any time will always have the newer, upgraded image and will continue to forward traffic and maintain the state information.

An active-active failover pair is only slightly different, because either unit might be running a failover group of security contexts in active mode. Here again, the idea is to move all active roles to one of the units—the primary unit—while upgrading the other.

You should carefully follow these basic steps for a zero downtime upgrade:

Step 1 Download the new image to both active and standby units.

Step 2 (Active-Active) Force all active roles onto the primary unit.

Step 3 Reload the standby unit to run the new image.

Step 4 Swap active and standby roles.

Step 5 Reload the new standby unit to run the new image.

Step 6 Swap active and standby roles again, to return the originally active unit to the active role.

You can use the following steps to upgrade the operating system on a failover pair:

1. Download the new OS image into both firewall units.

You can use any supported image transfer method, such as TFTP or FTP. Be certain to monitor the image file download to be certain that each firewall has written a complete new image into its flash memory. As soon as the OS image is stored in flash, you can see it in the flash file system directory, but you cannot view or verify it. You can either watch as it is being downloaded and written or watch as it is being run after a reload.

The OS image file is not automatically replicated from the active unit to the standby unit, or from the primary unit to the secondary unit in an active-active scenario. Instead, you must connect to each firewall and download the file.

Make sure the **boot system** command reflects the new image filename in flash memory so that the firewall boots the correct file after it reloads. This command is replicated to the standby unit as well, so both units boot from the same image filename and location.

2. Open a session to the active firewall unit.

While the two firewalls are operating as a failover pair, you cannot make configuration changes to each one separately. Configuration is allowed only on the active unit. However, you can download a new OS image without disrupting the failover status.

By keeping a session open to the active unit, you can keep any eye on firewall operation during the upgrade process. As well, you can control the failover roles and reload the standby unit remotely.

TIP   For the remainder of the steps in this upgrade process, you should stay connected to the unit that is currently active. From that unit, you can do all of the functions required during a zero downtime upgrade.

For an active-active failover pair, you should connect to the primary unit and stay connected there. In Step 3, the primary unit takes over the active role for all contexts, effectively becoming the active unit.

Section 8-5

Remember that both firewalls have the same host name, because it is replicated between them. Therefore, you cannot recognize the primary unit by its host name in the prompt. To determine which failover unit you are connected to (primary or secondary), use the **show failover** command on each. For example, if the active unit happens to be the primary unit, the firewall shows something like this:

```
Firewall# show failover
Failover On
Cable status: Normal
Reconnect timeout 0:00:00
Poll frequency 15 seconds
Last Failover at: 04:57:40 EST Sun Oct 26 2003
```

```
This host: Primary - Active
        Active time: 245010 (sec)
        Interface stateful (192.168.199.1): Normal
        Interface dmz2 (127.0.0.1): Link Down (Shutdown)
        Interface outside (192.168.110.65): Normal
        Interface inside (192.168.254.1): Normal
Other host: Secondary - Standby
        Active time: 0 (sec)
        Interface stateful (192.168.199.2): Normal
        Interface dmz2 (0.0.0.0): Link Down (Shutdown)
        Interface outside (192.168.110.71): Normal
        Interface inside (192.168.254.9): Normal
[output omitted]
Firewall#
```

It does not really matter whether the primary unit is in active or standby mode. You should only be concerned about connecting to the unit that is currently active, so you can upgrade the standy unit.

By looking at the **show failover** command output now, you can also verify that the failover pair is working properly. Failover must be working on both units to replicate enough dynamic information to have a zero downtime upgrade.

3. Save the running configuration on the primary unit:

```
Firewall# write memory
```

or

```
Firewall# copy running-config startup-config
```

Always make sure you have saved the current running configuration before a reload. The running configuration is dynamically updated from the active unit to the standby unit as commands are entered. However, you must manually save the running configuration to Flash with either of the preceding commands. Doing this causes the same command to be run on the standby unit as well.

On an active-active failover pair, where you have multiple security contexts, you should use the following command to save all context configurations:

```
Firewall# write memory all
```

Copying the running configuration to an external location is also a good idea. For example, you can copy it to a TFTP server with the **copy running-config tftp**:[[*//location*][*/pathname*]] command. In case the firewall pair has a catastrophic failure, you will have a copy of the configuration to load into a replacement unit.

4. (Active-Active only) Force all active roles onto the primary unit:

```
Firewall# failover active
```

The primary unit might currently have the active role for only some of the contexts; if so, the secondary unit has the active role for the remaining contexts. To perform a zero downtime upgrade, the primary unit must have the active role for *all* contexts.

When the **failover active** command is entered on the primary unit, it immediately assumes the active role for all configured contexts.

For the remainder of the upgrade process, the primary unit is referred to as the "active" unit and the secondary unit as the "standby" unit.

5. Force the standby unit to reload:

   Firewall# **failover reload-standby**

   From the active unit, you can reload the standby unit remotely without having to connect to it. As soon as the standby unit begins the reload procedure, you will not be able to watch it boot up unless you are connected to its console port.

6. Wait until the standby unit reloads.

   You should wait until you see that the standby unit is back in full operation and failover is working properly before moving on to the next step. You can do this by periodically checking the failover status with the **show failover** command.

7. Force the active unit to take the standby role:

   Firewall# **no failover active**

   On the active unit, this command forces it to immediately assume the standby failover role. The previous standby unit immediately assumes the active role.

   Now the two failover peers have exchanged roles—the unit with the upgraded image is now the active unit and carries on all firewall operations.

8. Reload the new standby unit:

   Firewall# **reload**

   On the new standby unit (the one that was originally active in Step 2), force a reload. Now that the other peer is running as the active unit, the new standby unit is free to be reloaded without impacting firewall operation. As soon as the standby unit is reloaded, it boots up with the upgraded image.

9. (Optional) Return the active role to the original firewall:

   Firewall# **failover active**

   At this point, the original failover roles have been reversed—the original active unit is now the standby unit. If you want to return the active role to the firewall that was originally active in Step 2, you can use the **failover active** command to force the roles to change immediately.

   For an active-active failover pair, you can use the **failover active group** *group_id* command to keep the active role for failover group *group_id* on the primary unit.

Section 8-5

You can also use the **no failover active group** *group_id* to move the active role for the failover group to the secondary unit.

TIP   You should always upgrade OS images in an incremental fashion so that the zero downtime upgrade feature can work properly. The previous procedure is meant to upgrade an increment from one maintenance release to another or from one minor release to another.

However, you can repeat the same procedure over and over if you need to upgrade to a code level that is several releases later. Make sure you use each pass through the upgrade procedure for each increment of the image release number.

Automatically Upgrading a Failover Pair

In Chapter 4, "Firewall Management," in Section "4-4: Automatic Updates with an Auto Update Server," firewalls can be configured to automatically poll and download updated image files from an Auto Updates Server (AUS). Normally, these are standalone firewalls, ones not operating as part of a failover pair.

Beginning with ASA 8.0(1), you can configure a failover pair of firewalls to work with AUS so that they both receive an updated image automatically. The firewalls must be operating in single-context mode to work with AUS.

To use AUS with failover, you should configure the Auto Update feature on the primary failover unit only. The primary unit handles all communication with the AUS and manages how the failover units are reloaded after they get their new image files. If the primary unit is not active at the time of an AUS poll, it automatically assumes the active role.

Normally, image files are not replicated as part of the failover process; image files must be downloaded to each failover unit separately. When AUS is used, however, the primary unit downloads an updated file to itself and then replicates it to the secondary unit automatically.

After an updated image file is downloaded to both of the failover units, the firewalls are reloaded under the following conditions:

- If the updated image file is an incremental upgrade, where a zero downtime upgrade is possible, then the standby unit is reloaded first. After it is back up, the failover roles are reversed, and the previously active unit is reloaded automatically.

- If a zero downtime upgrade is not possible, both units are reloaded at the same time. This results in an abrupt stop to traffic passing through the firewall pair.

Refer to Section 4-4 in Chapter 4 for complete information about configuring the Auto Update feature. Make sure you force the primary failover unit to take the active role if it is not already taking it. Then apply the configuration steps to the primary failover unit only; the configuration commands are then replicated to the secondary unit.

Refer to the following sections for information about these topics:

- **9-1: Firewall Load-Balancing Overview**—Explains how firewall load balancing works and the methods that are available to perform it.

- **9-2: Firewall Load-Balancing in Software**—Covers firewall load balancing with the Catalyst 6500 using the Cisco IOS software and its Server Load Balancing (SLB) feature.

- **9-3: Firewall Load-Balancing in Hardware**—Presents the methods to use the Catalyst 6500 Content Switching Module (CSM) for high-performance firewall load balancing.

- **9-4: Firewall Load-Balancing Appliance**—Covers firewall load balancing with the Cisco Content Services Switches (CSS 11000 and 11500 families).

CHAPTER 9

Firewall Load Balancing

In environments where network connectivity and security are vital, firewall availability becomes important. You can use the firewall failover feature to implement two firewalls as a failover pair. This increases the firewall availability, with the goal of having one of the two always up and operating correctly. Chapter 8, "Increasing Firewall Availability with Failover," covers firewall failover in greater detail.

However, firewall failover does not address distributing the traffic inspection load across the firewall platforms. Beginning with ASA 7.0 and FWSM 3.1 you can configure multiple contexts on each of the firewalls in a failover pair such that the contexts are distributed between them. This can divide the total inspection load between the two firewalls, but it is a manual configuration process that is not dynamic in nature. Even so, only two identical firewalls can be used together.

This chapter discusses the mechanisms you can use to distribute the traffic inspection load across any number of independent firewall platforms. The group of firewalls is organized into a logical *firewall farm*. Firewall load balancing is performed by external devices so that it is transparent to the firewalls themselves. As well, the firewalls can be a mixture of platforms offering different levels of performance.

9-1: Firewall Load-Balancing Overview

You can implement firewalls to provide security in several ways. Table 9-1 is a quick comparison between a single firewall, a firewall failover pair, and a firewall farm that uses Firewall Load Balancing (FWLB).

Table 9-1 *Comparison of Firewall Availability*

Attribute	Single Firewall	Firewall Failover	FWLB
Cost	Lower. Only one firewall unit is needed.	Medium. Two units are needed.	Higher. At least two firewall units are needed, along with load-balancing devices.
Firewall Points of Failure	One: the firewall itself.	None. The firewall pair can be physically separated.	None. All firewalls are grouped to make up a firewall farm.

continues

Table 9-1 *Comparison of Firewall Availability (Continued)*

Attribute	Single Firewall	Firewall Failover	FWLB
Performance	Limited to a single firewall.	Limited to a single firewall. Only one of the pair actively inspects traffic at any time.	Proportional to the number of firewall units. In theory, each can be used to its full capacity with ideal load balancing.
Load Balancing	None.	None. The active unit inspects all connections.	Connections are assigned to firewalls according to a hash function. All units can inspect traffic at the same time.
Reaction to a Firewall Failure	No traffic is forwarded or inspected.	All connections shift to the standby firewall.	New connections are assigned to other working firewalls in the farm.
Additional Hardware Needed	None.	None.	An FWLB device must be present on *every* side of the firewall farm. With the Catalyst 6500 Content Switching Module (CSM), a single CSM performs FWLB on *both* (or all) sides of a firewall farm.

To distribute connections among firewall farm members, FWLB requires an additional load-balancing function on *each side* of the firewall farm, as illustrated in Figure 9-1. This ensures that connections are distributed across the firewalls and that the inbound and outbound traffic for each connection is always sent to the same firewall.

Figure 9-1 *Firewall Load-Balancing Concept*

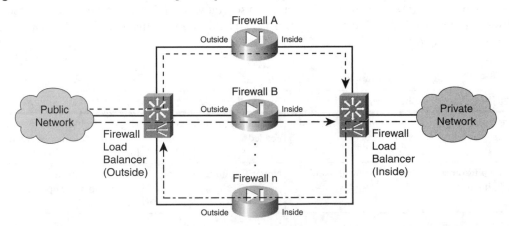

You can use the following methods to load-balance firewall traffic, in any combination:

- **Load-balancing software**—As packets are switched, they are inspected so that new connections can be forwarded through a firewall farm. The following attributes apply to software-based load balancing:

  — Cisco IOS software (native code only) can be used on the Catalyst 6500 switch platform for IOS Firewall Load Balancing (IOS FWLB), a subset of the Server Load Balancing (IOS SLB) feature.

  — Firewalls are configured as a firewall farm.

  — When traffic is routed through the firewall farm, connections are transparently distributed to individual firewalls.

  — See Section 9-2, "Firewall Load Balancing in Software," for complete information.

- **Load-balancing hardware**—Load-balancing devices appear as next-hop routers that distribute connections to members of a firewall farm. Firewall connections are load-balanced by embedded hardware with the following attributes:

  — The Cisco Catalyst 6500 Content Switching Module (CSM) can be used for firewall load balancing as a part of the Accelerated Server Load Balancing (ASLB) feature.

  — Firewalls are configured as normal server farms.

  — As traffic is received on an ingress virtual LAN (VLAN), the CSM transparently distributes connections to individual firewalls.

  — See Section 9-3, "Firewall Load Balancing in Hardware," for complete information.

- **Load-balancing appliances**—External content-switching appliances are placed on each side of a firewall farm. Connections are distributed among the members of the farm according to the following characteristics:

  — The Cisco Content Services Switch (CSS) family can be used for firewall load balancing.

  — Firewalls are configured individually; the CSS views them as a list of usable firewalls rather than a firewall farm.

  — The CSS distributes connections to firewalls according to the destination route and a hash algorithm based on IP addresses.

  — See Section 9-4, "Firewall Load-Balancing Appliance," for complete information.

TIP   You can mix different firewall load-balancing methods to distribute the load across a firewall farm. For example, you might use a CSM on the outside edge of the firewall farm to balance inbound connections and IOS FWLB on the inside to balance outbound connections.

Combinations of load-balancing technology are completely valid and can be chosen because of funding constraints or the placement of existing network hardware. In this case, however, you should be careful to configure the load balancer on each side of the firewall farm to have compatible and matching load-balancing algorithms and routing information. Otherwise, it is easy to get in a situation where certain firewalls in the farm are handed more connections than others.

As well, if the two load balancers are not configured with matching algorithms, connections might be handed off asymmetrically. The original traffic (forward direction) for a connection might be given to one firewall, and the return traffic is given to another firewall. Neither firewall would be able to inspect the complete connection, causing the connection to fail or become broken.

Remember that firewalls receive connection assignments in *both* directions from *both* load balancers. (This assumes that firewall load balancing occurs on only the inside and outside interfaces. You can also have firewall load balancers located on more than two interfaces, in the case of demilitarized zones [DMZs] and so on.)

9-2: Firewall Load-Balancing in Software

Firewall Load Balancing (FWLB) is used to balance traffic flows to one or more firewall farms. A firewall farm is a group of firewalls that are connected in parallel or that have their inside (protected) and outside (unprotected) interfaces connected to common network segments.

FWLB requires a load-balancing device to be connected to each side of the firewall farm. A firewall farm with inside and outside interfaces would then require two load-balancing devices—each making sure that traffic flows are directed toward the same firewall for the duration of the connection.

FWLB is performed in software on the Catalyst 6500 switch platform, only in native IOS (also called *supervisor IOS*). This is known as the IOS Server Load Balancing (IOS SLB or IOS FWLB) feature. If a Catalyst 6500 is already in place in a network, it can also be used as a firewall load-balancing device through further IOS configuration.

IOS FWLB works by acting as the gateway or next-hop address that routes traffic toward one or more firewalls. It computes a hash value on each new inbound traffic flow, based on the source and destination IP addresses and ports. This hash value determines which firewall will be used within the firewall farm. This is called a *route lookup*.

All the firewall interfaces grouped as a firewall farm *must* be located in a common Layer 2 VLAN and IP subnet. This is because the IOS FWLB device can modify only the Layer 2 information in packets passing through it. The IOS FWLB device substitutes the MAC address of the target firewall for the destination address in each packet.

IOS FWLB can detect a firewall failure by monitoring probe activity. Each probe is used to determine the state of every firewall in the farm.

You can add the Hot Standby Router Protocol (HSRP) to provide a *stateless backup* redundancy when multiple IOS FWLB devices are positioned on each side of the firewall farm. If one device fails, a redundant device can take over its function for the next inbound connection.

Multiple IOS FWLB devices can also use *stateful backup* for redundancy when they are placed together on the same side of a firewall farm. Backup devices keep state information dynamically and can take over immediately if a failure occurs.

TIP   You can mix different types of FWLB devices around a firewall farm. For example, an IOS FWLB (Catalyst 6500 native IOS) might balance traffic to the outside interfaces of a firewall farm, and an FWLB hardware platform handles traffic to the inside interfaces. In this case, it is not possible to provide either stateless or stateful backup, because the different types have different support for the backup protocols. To use these backup methods, you must use the same FWLB method on *both* sides of the firewall farm.

IOS FWLB Configuration Notes

IOS FWLB is configured in two halves. One FWLB device must be placed on the outside of the firewall farm, and another is placed on the inside. Each FWLB device distributes connections *toward the firewall*. Therefore, the outside FWLB balances connections going into the firewall farm's outside interfaces (inbound). The inside FWLB acts similarly for connections going into the firewall farm's inside interfaces (outbound).

Figure 9-2 illustrates this by showing two separate IOS FWLB devices on the two sides (inside and outside) of the firewall farm.

Figure 9-2 *IOS FWLB Placement Surrounding a Firewall Farm*

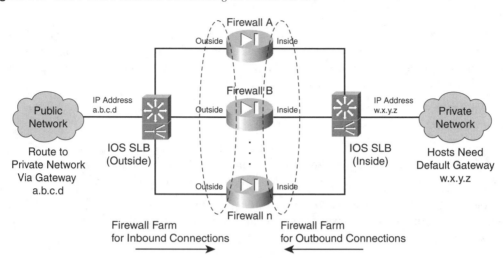

As soon as a new inbound connection is assigned to a firewall in the farm, how does the return traffic find its way back? For each connection, remember that both forward and reverse traffic *must* pass through the same firewall so that the stateful inspection can work properly. When the connection is assigned to a firewall in the forward direction, the FWLB device on the other side of the firewall farm simply relays the return traffic using that same firewall in the farm.

TIP   Some applications automatically open connections on other ports during their normal operation. A firewall might not follow these new connections as a part of its normal stateful inspection, except that the *fixup* or *inspection engine* feature allows it to inspect and track additional "helper" or "buddy" connections for some application protocols.

This concept must also be extended to FWLB. An IOS FWLB device uses *sticky connections* to keep any newly forming buddy connections heading toward the same firewall that has already been inspecting the original application connection. In other words, as soon as a connection has been opened and assigned to a firewall, any new connections between the same two hosts also are assigned to that firewall.

As you might expect, sticky connections must be supported on every FWLB device so that they can be properly inspected in every direction.

It is entirely possible to define more than one firewall farm on an IOS FWLB device. This would apply to networks that have several distinct firewall farms, each protecting a unique customer network, server farm, or other entity.

At this point, it might be tempting to try to use a single IOS FWLB platform to operate on both sides of one firewall farm. After all, it is possible to define two different firewall farms on an IOS FWLB device. Why not define an outside and an inside firewall farm, without going to the expense of using a second FWLB device? The problem with this idea is that it is not very secure. FWLB occurs on the same platform that performs routing on both the outside and inside networks. Therefore, it is all too easy for the Catalyst 6500 to route packets from outside to inside without even going through the firewall farm. In other words, it is possible to bypass the firewalls completely. Two physically separate IOS FWLB platforms should be used to completely isolate the two sides of the network.

The configuration steps are also presented here for one side of the firewall farm only (inside or outside). You need to repeat the sequence of steps for the IOS FWLB device on the other side of the firewall farm, too. Figure 9-3 illustrates this concept by separating the inside and outside FWLB devices. The top half of the figure shows how the outside IOS FWLB device should be configured to load-balance inbound connections to the firewall farm. The bottom half shows the inside FWLB device that handles the outbound connections.

If you have more protected networks (DMZs, for example), you can apply the same concepts to the other interfaces of the firewall farm. Follow the steps listed for the inside FWLB configuration for any other interfaces needed, because these are all more secure interfaces than the outside.

Figure 9-3 *Separating the Outside and Inside IOS FWLB Functions for Configuration*

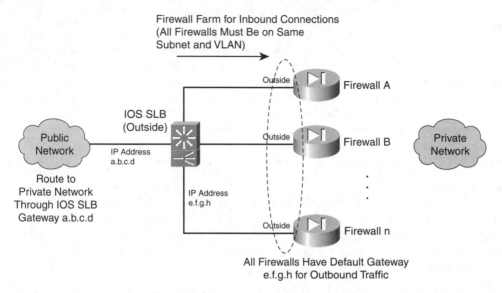

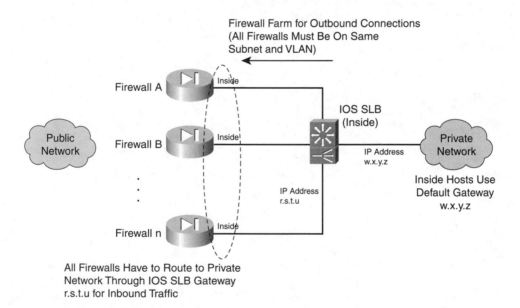

IOS FWLB Configuration

You can use the following steps to configure IOS FWLB on one device. Remember that FWLB requires a load-balancing device on each side of the firewall farm. Be sure to repeat the entire configuration process for the outside and inside IOS FWLB platforms.

1. Define connectivity away from the firewall farm:

```
Router(config)# vlan vlan-id
Router(config)# interface vlan vlan-id
Router(config-if)# ip address ip-address subnet-mask
Router(config-if)# no shutdown
```

The FWLB must be able to route packets to and from the network farthest from the firewall farm. For the outside FWLB device, this would be the public network. For the inside FWLB device, this would be the internal (secure) network.

You can use the commands shown to define a VLAN and then a switched virtual interface (SVI) so that the VLAN has a Layer 3 presence on the switch.

2. Define connectivity toward the firewall farm:

```
Router(config)# vlan vlan-id
Router(config)# interface vlan vlan-id

Router(config-if)# ip address ip-address subnet-mask
Router(config-if)# no shutdown
```

All firewalls in the firewall farm must have their outside interfaces residing on one VLAN, *vlan-id*, and their inside interfaces residing on another. Therefore, you need to define the VLAN on this side of the firewall, as well as its Layer 3 SVI presence.

TIP   An IOS FWLB device uses the IOS SLB feature. Therefore, it is also possible to use the inside FWLB device to load-balance traffic to server farms located on the secured inside network. Additional configuration is required to do this.

---

3. Define routes to any networks on the other side of the firewall farm:

```
Router(config)# ip route inside-network subnet-mask fw-outside-address
```

Here, the outside FWLB device must know about any networks that lie on the other side of the firewall farm. You can easily accomplish this by defining static routes that use the firewalls as the next hop. If you do not define these routes, the FWLB device has no idea where to find the inside protected networks.

The firewall farm itself has no single virtual IP address. Therefore, configure one of these static routes using each of the physical firewalls in the firewall farm as the gateway address.

NOTE   If multiple gateway addresses are configured for the same static route, does the Catalyst switch attempt to load-balance packets based on routing decisions rather than the FWLB algorithm? No, because the switch looks up the route only to find a next-hop address. Any of the firewall addresses are fine, because the FWLB algorithm still selects a target firewall and substitutes the destination MAC address according to the FWLB rules.

You define multiple routes so that every physical firewall is known as a next-hop gateway. In case one firewall is down or is removed from service in the firewall farm, a route can be found using the other firewalls.

---

4. Define a probe to detect a firewall failure.

   You should define a unique probe for each physical firewall in the firewall farm so that individual firewall failures can be detected. To do this, repeat Steps 4a through 4d for each firewall.

   a. Name the probe:

   ```
   Router(config)# ip slb probe name ping
   ```

   The probe is named *name* (a text string of up to 15 characters) and can be referenced by other FWLB commands. The probe uses **ping** (ICMP) packets to see if the target answers.

   b. Define a target address for the probe:

   ```
   Router(config-slb-probe)# address ip-address
   ```

   Ping requests are sent to the target address. If the target replies, it is assumed to be active and functional.

TIP   The probe's purpose is to detect whether a firewall in the firewall farm is alive. Therefore, you can choose a firewall's outside interface address as the target for the outside FWLB device. This determines if the outside interface is up and active. However, it does not determine if the firewall is inspecting traffic as it should.

You must also make sure that the firewall has been configured to allow ICMP packets to be received and answered by its own interface address.

---

c. (Optional) Set the time between probes:

```
Router(config-slb-probe)# interval seconds
```

Probes are sent toward the target at intervals of *seconds* (1 to 65535 seconds; the default is 1 second).

d. (Optional) Define the criteria for a failure:

```
Router(config-slb-probe)# faildetect retry-count
```

With IOS FWLB, a firewall is considered to have failed if *retry-count* (1 to 255; the default is 10) consecutive ping probes go unanswered.

5. Define the firewall farm:

```
Router(config)# ip slb firewallfarm firewallfarm-name
```

The collection of firewalls is referenced by *firewallfarm-name* (a text string of up to 15 characters).

6. Identify a firewall in the farm.

a. Define the firewall's IP address:

```
Router(config-slb-fw)# real ip-address
```

The firewall is directly connected (the same logical subnet) to the load-balancing device with an interface at IP address *ip-address*. For example, this is the outside firewall interface address when configuring the outside FWLB device.

b. Use a probe to detect a firewall failure:

```
Router(config-slb-fw-real)# probe probe-name
```

The probe that is defined by *probe-name* (a text string) is used periodically to see if the firewall has failed. A different probe is needed for each firewall, because the firewall's IP address is configured in the probe definition.

You can define more than one probe for a firewall by repeating this command. The firewall is declared down if it fails just one probe. A firewall must pass all probes to be recovered again.

c. Allow FWLB to begin using the firewall:

```
Router(config-slb-fw-real)# inservice
```

By default, FWLB does not use the real firewall unless it is placed in service. To remove a firewall from service, use the **no inservice** command.

d. Assign a relative weight to the firewall:

```
Router(config-slb-fw-real)# weight weighting-value
```

By default, each real firewall in the farm is given an equal weight so that the load balancing is symmetric. You can adjust the firewall weighting so that a firewall with more capacity or higher performance is given more connections than one with lesser capacity.

You can assign the real firewall a *weighting-value* (1 to 255; the default is 8) that is relative to the other real firewalls. A higher weighting results in more load given to the firewall.

7. (Optional; outside FWLB only) Define one or more flows that will be sent to the firewall farm:

```
Router(config-slb-fw)# access [source source-ip-address network-mask]
  [destination destination-ip-address network-mask]
```

When multiple firewall farms exist, traffic can be identified by address and sent through the appropriate firewall farm. A traffic flow is defined by its source and destination addresses and subnet masks.

If either the **source** or **destination** keywords are omitted, they default to 0.0.0.0 with a mask of 0.0.0.0, signifying all addresses and networks. This is the default behavior. In other words, the default assumes that only one firewall farm exists, and all inbound traffic is destined to pass through it.

For example, the following command could be used to route traffic destined for the network 192.168.77.0/24 through the firewall farm being configured:

```
Router(config-slb-fw)# access destination 192.168.77.0 255.255.255.0
```

8. (Optional) Choose an FWLB method:

```
Router(config-slb-fw)# predictor hash address [port]
```

By default, IOS FWLB computes a hash value from a flow's source and destination IP addresses to select a destination firewall. This usually works well, because the number of source hosts on the outside public network is quite large and causes the hash function to take on many different values.

If you find that the number of unique outside and inside addresses is small, the connections might not be balanced well across the members of the firewall farm. In this case, you can use the **port** keyword to use the source and destination addresses, as well as the source and destination TCP or UDP port numbers, in the selection decision. Port numbers vary greatly, so the chances of choosing a different firewall with each new connection are much greater.

9. (Optional) Use stateful backup to recover from a failure:

```
Router(config-slb-fw)# replicate casa listening-ip remote-ip port-number
  [interval] [password [0 | 7] password [timeout]]
```

The redundant FWLB devices use the Cisco Appliance Services Architecture (CASA) structure to exchange and replicate state information. This is sent from the *listening-ip* address (an interface on the local device) to the *remote-ip* address (an interface on the backup device) using *port-number* (1 to 65535). Replication messages are sent at *interval* seconds (1 to 300; the default is 10).

You can use a *password* (a text string; use 0 if it is unencrypted, the default, or 7 if it is encrypted) for MD5 authentication with the backup device. The optional *timeout* (0 to 65535 seconds; the default is 180 seconds) defines a time period when the password can be migrated from an old value to a new one. During this time, both old and new passwords are accepted.

For example, suppose CASA is first configured to use the password BigSecret with a timeout of 300 seconds (5 minutes) with the following command:

```
Router(config-slb-fw)# replicate casa 10.1.1.1 10.1.1.2 4000 password 0
  BigSecret 300
```

The password is migrated to NewBigSecret with the following command:

```
Router(config-slb-fw)# replicate casa 10.1.1.1 10.1.1.2 4000 password 0
  NewBigSecret 300
```

As soon as this command is entered, the local FWLB device begins to accept both BigSecret and NewBigSecret as passwords. After 300 seconds has elapsed, only the new NewBigSecret password is accepted.

10. (Optional) Adjust the TCP or UDP connection parameters:

```
Router(config-slb-fw)# {tcp | udp}
```

You might need to make adjustments to both TCP and UDP, depending on how connections should be handled. In this case, this command can be repeated to configure each independently.

   a.   (Optional; TCP only) Hold connections open after they are terminated:

```
Router(config-slb-fw-protocol)# delay duration
```

After a TCP connection is terminated, the connection context can be maintained for *duration* (1 to 600 seconds; the default is 10 seconds). This can be useful when packets arrive out of sequence and the connection is closed before the last missing data packet arrives.

   b.   (Optional; TCP only) Hold connections open after no activity:

```
Router(config-slb-fw-protocol)# idle duration
```

When an absence of packets is detected for a connection, the connection is kept open for *duration* (10 to 65535 seconds; the default is 3600 seconds, or 1 hour) before an RST is sent.

   c.   (Optional) Specify the maximum number of connections:

```
Router(config-slb-fw-protocol)# maxconns number
```

At any given time, the firewall is limited to *number* (1 to 4294967295; the default is 4294967295) of active connections.

   d.   (Optional) Assign subsequent connections from a source address to the same firewall:

```
Router(config-slb-fw-protocol)# sticky duration [netmask netmask]
```

For a given IP address, connections are assigned to the last-used firewall for *duration* (0 to 65535 seconds). A *netmask* can be given such that all source addresses within the mask are assigned to the same firewall.

Sticky connections are very useful for applications that open connections on other ports for control or data channels. Examples of this include FTP, H.323, and RTSP. The firewall must be able to inspect these additional connections too, so they must be sent through the same firewall.

11. Allow FWLB to begin using the firewall farm as a whole:

```
Router(config-slb-fw)# inservice
```

By default, FWLB does not use the firewall farm unless it is placed in service. To remove a firewall farm from service, use the **no inservice** command.

IOS Firewall Load-Balancing Example

FWLB requires two load-balancing devices:

- One located externally with respect to the firewall farm
- One located internally with respect to the firewall farm

Figure 9-4 shows a network diagram for this example. Note that this same example is also used in Section 9-3 to show how IOS FWLB and the CSM are configured in similar scenarios.

Figure 9-4 *Network Diagram for the IOS FWLB Example*

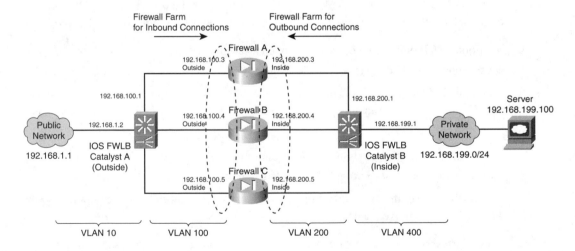

The firewall farm consists of three real firewalls.

The outside (unprotected) interfaces of the three firewalls are at 192.168.100.3, 192.168.100.4, and 192.168.100.5. On the outside, the default gateway to the public network is 192.168.1.1, and the external IOS FWLB device (Catalyst A) is at 192.168.1.2.

The inside (protected) interfaces of the three firewalls are at 192.168.200.3, 192.168.200.4, and 192.168.200.5. The internal IOS FWLB device performs firewall load balancing for outbound traffic to the firewall farm. On the internal secure network (192.168.199.0/24), one server is in use at 192.168.199.100. This server supports both inbound HTTP and Telnet connections.

Ping probes are used by both external and internal FWLB devices to test for firewall operation.

Basic Firewall Configuration

This section shows the firewall configurations first. Firewalls A and B are Firewall Services Modules (FWSM) installed in the Catalyst A chassis. Firewall C is an external Cisco Adaptive Security Application (ASA), connected to Catalyst A through a Gigabit Ethernet link. The configuration commands in this section give you a basic idea of all the pieces that must be configured for FWLB. Notice that all three firewalls have identical security policies configured. This is important, because any of the three firewalls could be assigned connections from any pair of inside and outside hosts:

```
Firewall(config)# hostname fwsm-a
fwsm-a(config)# nameif vlan100 outside security0
fwsm-a(config)# nameif vlan200 inside security100
fwsm-a(config)# ip address outside 192.168.100.3 255.255.255.0
fwsm-a(config)# ip address inside 192.168.200.3 255.255.255.0
fwsm-a(config)# icmp permit 192.168.100.0 255.255.255.0 outside
fwsm-a(config)# icmp permit 192.168.200.0 255.255.255.0 inside
fwsm-a(config)# static (inside,outside) 192.168.199.0 192.168.199.0 netmask
  255.255.255.0 0 0
fwsm-a(config)# object-group icmp-type ICMP
fwsm-a(config-icmp)# icmp-object echo
fwsm-a(config-icmp)# icmp-object echo-reply
fwsm-a(config-icmp)# icmp-object time-exceeded
fwsm-a(config-icmp)# icmp-object unreachable
fwsm-a(config-icmp)# exit
fwsm-a(config)# access-list acl_out permit tcp any host 192.168.199.100 eq telnet
fwsm-a(config)# access-list acl_out permit tcp any host 192.168.199.100 eq www
fwsm-a(config)# access-list acl_out permit icmp any host 192.168.199.100
  object-group ICMP
fwsm-a(config)# access-list acl_in permit tcp 192.168.199.0 255.255.255.0 eq
  telnet any
fwsm-a(config)# access-list acl_in permit tcp 192.168.199.0 255.255.255.0 eq www
  any
fwsm-a(config)# access-list acl_in permit icmp 192.168.199.0 255.255.255.0 any
  object-group ICMP
fwsm-a(config)# access-list acl_in permit icmp 192.168.200.0 255.255.255.0 any
  object-group ICMP
fwsm-a(config)# access-group acl_out in interface outside
```

```
fwsm-a(config)# access-group acl_in in interface inside
fwsm-a(config)# route outside 0.0.0.0 0.0.0.0 192.168.100.1 1
fwsm-a(config)# route inside 192.168.199.0 255.255.255.0 192.168.200.1 1
```

```
Firewall(config)# hostname fwsm-b
fwsm-b(config)# nameif vlan100 outside security0
fwsm-b(config)# nameif vlan200 inside security100
fwsm-b(config)# ip address outside 192.168.100.4 255.255.255.0
fwsm-b(config)# ip address inside 192.168.200.4 255.255.255.0
fwsm-b(config)# icmp permit 192.168.100.0 255.255.255.0 outside
fwsm-b(config)# icmp permit 192.168.200.0 255.255.255.0 inside
fwsm-b(config)# static (inside,outside) 192.168.199.0 192.168.199.0 netmask
  255.255.255.0 0 0
fwsm-b(config)# object-group icmp-type ICMP
fwsm-b(config-icmp)# icmp-object echo
fwsm-b(config-icmp)# icmp-object echo-reply
fwsm-b(config-icmp)# icmp-object time-exceeded
fwsm-b(config-icmp)# icmp-object unreachable
fwsm-b(config-icmp)# exit
fwsm-b(config)# access-list acl_out permit tcp any host 192.168.199.100 eq telnet
fwsm-b(config)# access-list acl_out permit tcp any host 192.168.199.100 eq www
fwsm-b(config)# access-list acl_out permit icmp any host 192.168.199.100
  object-group ICMP
fwsm-b(config)# access-list acl_in permit tcp 192.168.199.0 255.255.255.0 eq
  telnet any
fwsm-b(config)# access-list acl_in permit tcp 192.168.199.0 255.255.255.0 eq www
  any
fwsm-b(config)# access-list acl_in permit icmp 192.168.199.0 255.255.255.0 any
  object-group ICMP
fwsm-b(config)# access-list acl_in permit icmp 192.168.200.0 255.255.255.0 any
  object-group ICMP
fwsm-b(config)# access-group acl_out in interface outside
fwsm-b(config)# access-group acl_in in interface inside
fwsm-b(config)# route outside 0.0.0.0 0.0.0.0 192.168.100.1 1
fwsm-b(config)# route inside 192.168.199.0 255.255.255.0 192.168.200.1 1
```

```
Firewall(config)# hostname asa-c
asa-c(config)# interface gb-ethernet0 1000full
asa-c(config)# interface gb-ethernet1 1000full
asa-c(config)# nameif gb-ethernet0 outside security0
asa-c(config)# nameif gb-ethernet1 inside security100
asa-c(config)# ip address outside 192.168.100.5 255.255.255.0
asa-c(config)# ip address inside 192.168.200.5 255.255.255.0
asa-c(config)# icmp permit 192.168.100.0 255.255.255.0 outside
asa-c(config)# icmp permit 192.168.200.0 255.255.255.0 inside
asa-c(config)# static (inside,outside) 192.168.199.0 192.168.199.0 netmask
  255.255.255.0 0 0
asa-c(config)# object-group icmp-type ICMP
asa-c(config-icmp)# icmp-object echo
asa-c(config-icmp)# icmp-object echo-reply
asa-c(config-icmp)# icmp-object time-exceeded
asa-c(config-icmp)# icmp-object unreachable
asa-c(config-icmp)# exit
asa-c(config)# access-list acl_out permit tcp any host 192.168.199.100 eq telnet
asa-c(config)# access-list acl_out permit tcp any host 192.168.199.100 eq www
```

```
asa-c(config)# access-list acl_out permit icmp any host 192.168.199.100
  object-group ICMP
asa-c(config)# access-list acl_in permit tcp 192.168.199.0 255.255.255.0 eq telnet
  any
asa-c(config)# access-list acl_in permit tcp 192.168.199.0 255.255.255.0 eq www
  any
asa-c(config)# access-list acl_in permit icmp 192.168.199.0 255.255.255.0 any
  object-group ICMP
asa-c(config)# access-list acl_in permit icmp 192.168.200.0 255.255.255.0 any
object-group ICMP
asa-c(config)# access-group acl_out in interface outside
asa-c(config)# access-group acl_in in interface inside
asa-c(config)# route outside 0.0.0.0 0.0.0.0 192.168.100.1 1
asa-c(config)# route inside 192.168.199.0 255.255.255.0 192.168.200.1 1
```

Outside IOS FWLB Configuration

This section shows the configuration for the outside load-balancing device. Notice that this is all done from the Catalyst 6500 (Catalyst A) command-line interface (CLI), because the switch Supervisor performs both the multilayer switching and IOS FWLB functions.

First, here are the preliminary commands to define VLANs and connectivity:

```
Switch(config)# hostname CatalystA
! Define the VLANs
CatalystA(config)# vlan 10
CatalystA(config-vlan)# name Public-Network
CatalystA(config-vlan)# vlan 100
CatalystA(config-vlan)# name FW-outside
CatalystA(config-vlan)# vlan 200
CatalystA(config-vlan)# name FW-inside
CatalystA(config-vlan)# exit
! Pass the VLANs to the two FWSMs
CatalystA(config)# firewall module 3 vlan-group 1
CatalystA(config)# firewall module 4 vlan-group 1
CatalystA(config)# firewall vlan-group 1  100,200
! Set up a trunk to the inside IOS FWLB Catalyst
CatalystA(config)# interface GigabitEthernet8/1
CatalystA(config-if)# description Inside networks for IOS FWLB Catalyst B
CatalystA(config-if)# no ip address
CatalystA(config-if)# switchport
CatalystA(config-if)# switchport trunk encapsulation dot1q
CatalystA(config-if)# switchport trunk native vlan 2
CatalystA(config-if)# switchport trunk allowed vlan 200
CatalystA(config-if)# switchport trunk on
CatalystA(config-if)# switchport mode trunk
! Set up the connection to PIX Firewall-C
CatalystA(config-if)# interface GigabitEthernet8/2
CatalystA(config-if)# description PIX-C outside
CatalystA(config-if)# no ip address
CatalystA(config-if)# switchport
CatalystA(config-if)# switchport access vlan 100
```

```
CatalystA(config-if)# switchport mode access
CatalystA(config-if)# spanning-tree portfast
! Define the IOS FWLB presence on VLAN 100
CatalystA(config-if)# interface Vlan100
CatalystA(config-if)# ip address 192.168.100.1 255.255.255.0
! Define the IOS FWLB presence on the public network
CatalystA(config-if)# interface Vlan10
CatalystA(config-if)# ip address 192.168.1.2 255.255.255.0
CatalystA(config-if)# exit
! Now define a way to get out to the public network
CatalystA(config)# ip default-gateway 192.168.1.1
CatalystA(config)# ip route 0.0.0.0 0.0.0.0 192.168.1.1
! For the internal (secure) network, define a route that uses each firewall
CatalystA(config)# ip route 192.168.199.0 255.255.255.0 192.168.100.3
CatalystA(config)# ip route 192.168.199.0 255.255.255.0 192.168.100.4
CatalystA(config)# ip route 192.168.199.0 255.255.255.0 192.168.100.5
```

Next, here are the actual IOS FWLB configuration commands:

```
! Define a ping probe for firewall A outside
CatalystA(config)# ip slb probe FW-A ping
CatalystA(config-slb-probe)# address 192.168.100.3
CatalystA(config-slb-probe)# interval 10
CatalystA(config-slb-probe)# faildetect 2
CatalystA(config-slb-probe)# exit
! Define a ping probe for firewall B outside
CatalystA(config)# ip slb probe FW-B ping
CatalystA(config-slb-probe)# address 192.168.100.4
CatalystA(config-slb-probe)# interval 10
CatalystA(config-slb-probe)# faildetect 2
CatalystA(config-slb-probe)# exit
! Define a ping probe for firewall C outside
CatalystA(config)# ip slb probe FW-C ping
CatalystA(config-slb-probe)# address 192.168.100.5
CatalystA(config-slb-probe)# interval 10
CatalystA(config-slb-probe)# faildetect 2
CatalystA(config-slb-probe)# exit
!
! Define the actual firewall farm
CatalystA(config)# ip slb firewallfarm FW-INBOUND
CatalystA(config-slb-fw)# inservice
! Firewall A
CatalystA(config-slb-fw)# real 192.168.100.3
CatalystA(config-slb-fw-real)# probe FW-A
CatalystA(config-slb-fw-real)# inservice
CatalystA(config-slb-fw-real)# exit
! Firewall B
CatalystA(config-slb-fw)# real 192.168.100.4
CatalystA(config-slb-fw-real)# probe FW-B
CatalystA(config-slb-fw-real)# inservice
```

```
CatalystA(config-slb-fw-real)# exit
! Firewall C
CatalystA(config-slb-fw)# real 192.168.100.5
CatalystA(config-slb-fw-real)# probe FW-C
CatalystA(config-slb-fw-real)# inservice
CatalystA(config-slb-fw-real)# exit
!
```

Inside IOS FWLB Configuration

This section covers the configuration for the inside load-balancing device (Catalyst B).

First, here are the commands to define VLANs and connectivity:

```
Switch(config)# hostname CatalystB
! Define the VLANs
CatalystB(config)# vlan 200
CatalystB(config-vlan)# name FW-inside
CatalystB(config-vlan)# vlan 400
CatalystB(config-vlan)# name Internal-Network
CatalystB(config-vlan)# exit
! Set up a trunk to the outside Catalyst
CatalystB(config)# interface GigabitEthernet8/1
CatalystB(config-if)# description Inside networks from IOS FWLB Catalyst A
CatalystB(config-if)# no ip address
CatalystB(config-if)# switchport
CatalystB(config-if)# switchport trunk encapsulation dot1q
CatalystB(config-if)# switchport trunk native vlan 2
CatalystB(config-if)# switchport trunk allowed vlan 200
CatalystB(config-if)# switchport trunk on
CatalystB(config-if)# switchport mode trunk
! Set up the connection to ASA Firewall-C
CatalystB(config-if)# interface GigabitEthernet8/2
CatalystB(config-if)# description PIX-C inside
CatalystB(config-if)# no ip address
CatalystB(config-if)# switchport
CatalystB(config-if)# switchport access vlan 200
CatalystB(config-if)# switchport mode access
CatalystB(config-if)# spanning-tree portfast
! Define the IOS FWLB presence on VLAN 200
CatalystB(config-if)# interface Vlan200
CatalystB(config-if)# ip address 192.168.200.1 255.255.255.0
! Define the IOS FWLB presence on the inside (secure) network
CatalystB(config-if)# interface Vlan400
CatalystB(config-if)# ip address 192.168.199.1 255.255.255.0
CatalystB(config-if)# exit
! Now define a way to get out to the public network
! Define default routes that use each firewall's inside interface as a gateway
CatalystB(config)# ip route 0.0.0.0 0.0.0.0 192.168.200.3
CatalystB(config)# ip route 0.0.0.0 0.0.0.0 192.168.200.4
CatalystB(config)# ip route 0.0.0.0 0.0.0.0 192.168.200.5
```

Next, here are the actual IOS FWLB commands:

```
! Define a ping probe for firewall A inside
CatalystB(config)# ip slb probe FW-A ping
CatalystB(config-slb-probe)# address 192.168.200.3
CatalystB(config-slb-probe)# interval 10
CatalystB(config-slb-probe)# faildetect 2
CatalystB(config-slb-probe)# exit
! Define a ping probe for firewall B inside
CatalystB(config)# ip slb probe FW-B ping
CatalystB(config-slb-probe)# address 192.168.200.4
CatalystB(config-slb-probe)# interval 10
CatalystB(config-slb-probe)# faildetect 2
CatalystB(config-slb-probe)# exit
! Define a ping probe for firewall C inside
CatalystB(config)# ip slb probe FW-C ping
CatalystB(config-slb-probe)# address 192.168.200.5
CatalystB(config-slb-probe)# interval 10
CatalystB(config-slb-probe)# faildetect 2
CatalystB(config-slb-probe)# exit
!
! Define the actual firewall farm
CatalystB(config)# ip slb firewallfarm FW-OUTBOUND
CatalystB(config-slb-fw)# inservice
! Firewall A
CatalystB(config-slb-fw)# real 192.168.200.3
CatalystB(config-slb-fw-real)# probe FW-A
CatalystB(config-slb-fw-real)# inservice
CatalystB(config-slb-fw-real)# exit
! Firewall B
CatalystB(config)# real 192.168.200.4
CatalystB(config-slb-fw-real)# probe FW-B
CatalystB(config-slb-fw-real)# inservice
CatalystB(config-slb-fw-real)# exit
! Firewall C
CatalystB(config)# real 192.168.200.5
CatalystB(config-slb-fw-real)# probe FW-C
CatalystB(config-slb-fw-real)# inservice
CatalystB(config-slb-fw-real)# exit
!
```

Displaying Information About IOS FWLB

Table 9-2 lists the switch commands you can use to display helpful information about IOS firewall load-balancing configuration and status.

Table 9-2 *Commands to Display IOS FWLB Configuration and Status*

Command Syntax	Display Function
Router# **show ip slb firewallfarms** [**detail**]	Firewall farm status
Router# **show ip slb reals**	Status of firewalls in a farm

Table 9-2   *Commands to Display IOS FWLB Configuration and Status (Continued)*

Command Syntax	Display Function
Router# **show ip slb reals** [**sfarm** *firewall-farm-name*] **detail**	Firewall weight and connection counters
Router# **show ip slb conn** [**firewall** *firewallfarm-name*] [**detail**]	Load-balancing connections to firewalls
Router# **show ip slb probe** [**name** *probe_name*] [**detail**]	Probes
Router# **show ip slb sticky**	Sticky connections

IOS FWLB Output Example

For the sample network shown in Figure 9-4, the outside firewall farm status is as follows:

```
Router# show ip slb firewallfarms name FW-INBOUND

firewall farm    hash       state        reals
------------------------------------------------
FW-INBOUND       IPADDR     INSERVICE    3

Router# show ip slb firewallfarms name FW-INBOUND detail
FW-INBOUND, hash = IPADDR, state = INSERVICE, reals = 3
  FirewallTCP7:
    sticky: <none>
    idle = 3600, delay = 10, syns = 11, syn drop = 0
    maxconns = 4294967295, conns = 11, total conns = 11
  FirewallDG8:
    sticky: <none>
    idle = 3600
    maxconns = 4294967295, conns = 0, total conns = 2653
  Real firewalls:
    192.168.100.3, weight = 8, OPERATIONAL, conns = 3
    192.168.100.4, weight = 8, OPERATIONAL, conns = 5
    192.168.100.5, weight = 8, OPERATIONAL, conns = 3
  Total connections = 11
```

Here, the firewall farm FW-INBOUND has three "real" firewalls, each weighted equally using a hash algorithm based on IP addresses. Notice that after 11 connections (most from different source addresses to a single destination address), the connection load has been distributed rather equally across all the firewalls in the farm.

The sections of output beginning with FirewallTCP7 and FirewallDG8 show parameters set for the TCP and UDP protocols (DG stands for datagram).

To see a detailed history of each firewall's activity within the firewall farm, enter the following command to get the resulting output:

```
Router# show ip slb reals sfarm FW-INBOUND
real                    farm name         weight   state          conns
```

```
-----------------------------------------------------------------
192.168.100.3        FW-INBOUND      8       OPERATIONAL    4
192.168.100.4        FW-INBOUND      8       OPERATIONAL    6
192.168.100.5        FW-INBOUND      8       OPERATIONAL    5

Router# show ip slb reals sfarm FW-INBOUND detail
192.168.100.3, FW-INBOUND, state = OPERATIONAL, type = firewall
  conns = 4, dummy_conns = 0, maxconns = 4294967295
  weight = 8, weight(admin) = 8, metric = 0, remainder = 0
  total conns established = 99036, hash count = 3
  server failures = 0
  interface Vlan100, MAC 000b.46b3.4e40

192.168.100.4, FW-INBOUND, state = OPERATIONAL, type = firewall
  conns = 6, dummy_conns = 0, maxconns = 4294967295
  weight = 8, weight(admin) = 8, metric = 0, remainder = 0
  total conns established = 99383, hash count = 10
  server failures = 0
  interface Vlan100, MAC 000b.5f0c.8ac0

192.168.100.5, FW-INBOUND, state = OPERATIONAL, type = firewall
  conns = 5, dummy_conns = 0, maxconns = 4294967295
  weight = 8, weight(admin) = 8, metric = 0, remainder = 0
  total conns established = 99532, hash count = 3
  server failures = 0
  interface Vlan100, MAC 0090.2744.5c66
```

To check on the progress of the firewall probes, you might enter the following command to get the resulting output:

```
Router# show ip slb probe
Server:Port        Target:Port          State        Outages  Current  Cumulative
---------------------------------------------------------------------------------
192.168.100.3:0    192.168.100.3:0      OPERATIONAL 0         never    00:00:00
192.168.100.4:0    192.168.100.4:0      OPERATIONAL 0         never    00:00:00
192.168.100.5:0    192.168.100.5:0      OPERATIONAL 0         never    00:00:00
Router#
Router# show ip slb probe detail
FW-A, ping, address = 192.168.100.3, interval = 10, faildetect = 2
  FW-INBOUND, type = firewall
    target = 192.168.100.3:0, real = 192.168.100.3:0, virtual = 0.0.0.0:0 ALL
      state = OPERATIONAL, status = 33, operation id = 25
      outages = 0, failures = 374, successes = 98690, tests = 376
      current = never, cumulative = 00:00:00
FW-B, ping, address = 192.168.100.4, interval = 10, faildetect = 2
  FW-INBOUND, type = firewall
    target = 192.168.100.4:0, real = 192.168.100.4:0, virtual = 0.0.0.0:0 ALL
      state = OPERATIONAL, status = 33, operation id = 26
      outages = 0, failures = 806, successes = 98604, tests = 808
      current = never, cumulative = 00:00:00
FW-C, ping, address = 192.168.100.5, interval = 10, faildetect = 2
  FW-INBOUND, type = firewall
    target = 192.168.100.5:0, real = 192.168.100.5:0, virtual = 0.0.0.0:0 ALL
      state = OPERATIONAL, status = 33, operation id = 27
```

```
            outages = 0, failures = 995, successes = 98565, tests = 996
            current = never, cumulative = 00:00:00
    Router#
```

In the shaded portions, for example, probe FW-A sent to Firewall A (192.168.100.3) has succeeded 98,690 times and had 374 failures. The probe has been sent at 10-second intervals, causing the firewall to be declared in failure after two missed probes.

Sometimes, you might need to figure out which firewall in the farm is handling a specific flow or connection. For example, suppose a series of Telnet connections have been opened from a variety of client addresses, all to the same server. You can see the active connections with the output from the **show ip slb conn** command. Each active connection is listed, along with the "real" server or firewall that is handling that connection:

```
Router# show ip slb conn
vserver          prot client               real               state    nat
----------------------------------------------------------------------------
FirewallTCP7     TCP  10.1.17.4:23          192.168.100.3      ESTAB    none
FirewallTCP7     TCP  10.1.17.5:23          192.168.100.4      ESTAB    none
FirewallTCP7     TCP  10.1.17.9:23          192.168.100.5      ESTAB    none
FirewallTCP7     TCP  10.1.17.8:23          192.168.100.4      ESTAB    none
FirewallTCP7     TCP  10.1.17.6:23          192.168.100.5      ESTAB    none
FirewallTCP7     TCP  10.1.17.7:23          192.168.100.3      ESTAB    none
FirewallTCP7     TCP  10.1.17.11:23         192.168.100.4      ESTAB    none
FirewallTCP7     TCP  10.1.17.10:23         192.168.100.3      ESTAB    none
FirewallTCP7     TCP  10.1.17.229:3580      192.168.100.4      ESTAB    none
Router#
```

9-3: Firewall Load-Balancing in Hardware

FWLB is used to balance traffic flows to one or more firewall farms. A firewall farm is a group of firewalls that are connected in parallel or that have their inside (protected) and outside (unprotected) interfaces connected to common network segments.

FWLB requires a load-balancing device to be connected to each side of the firewall farm. A firewall farm with inside and outside interfaces would then require two load-balancing devices—each making sure that traffic flows are directed toward the same firewall for the duration of the connection.

FWLB can be performed in hardware with a CSM on the Catalyst 6500 switch platform. The CSM is a very robust and high-performance device, using the ASLB features to distribute connections to both server and firewall farms.

The CSM has no *firewall farm* concept. Rather, it treats a firewall farm as a regular server farm where the physical firewalls are configured as real servers in the farm. The CSM itself has logical interfaces that are configured as the gateway or next-hop addresses toward and away from a firewall farm.

To load-balance traffic, the CSM is configured with a *virtual server* that represents the firewall farm. As new traffic flows arrive at the virtual server, the CSM computes a hash value according to a predefined algorithm. This hash value determines which firewall is used within the firewall farm.

The CSM is flexible with how firewalls are connected and where they are located. Firewalls can reside on a single VLAN or subnet, or they can each reside on a unique subnet. As well, the firewalls can be more than one router hop away from the CSM.

The CSM can operate in the following modes, based on its placement between a firewall farm and the clients:

- **Single subnet (bridge) mode**—The clients and the firewall farm members all reside on one common IP subnet. However, each side of the CSM (client and server) must be assigned to unique VLANs that share the same IP subnet. The CSM distributes inbound connections to the firewalls by substituting the destination MAC address to match the next firewall to be used while bridging the packets from the client to the server VLAN.

  This mode can be useful when you need to implement load-balancing needs in an existing network where it is not feasible to move the clients or the firewalls to different IP subnets. In other words, it is not possible to wedge a router between the clients and the firewalls. Instead, transparent or "stealth" Layer 2 firewalls are used in the firewall farm.

- **Secure (router) mode**—The clients and the firewall farm members are located on different IP subnets and VLANs. In this case, traditional Layer 3 or "routed mode" firewalls are used in the firewall farm.

  The CSM distributes inbound connections to the firewalls by forwarding the packets just as a router would do. The CSM maintains an Address Resolution Protocol (ARP) cache of all the firewalls and substitutes the destination MAC address to point to the appropriate firewall.

  Because the client and firewall farm IP subnets are different, the CSM must know enough routing information to distribute and forward connections to the firewalls. This becomes especially important when the firewalls are located more than one router hop away from the CSM.

CSM FWLB can detect a firewall failure by monitoring probe activity. One probe is configured and is used on all members of the firewall farm in succession. The CSM automatically inserts the target IP address of each firewall. The CSM also periodically gathers ARP data from each firewall and uses that information to detect firewall failures.

Multiple CSM FWLB devices can also use *stateful backup* for redundancy. Backup devices keep state information dynamically and can take over immediately if a failure occurs.

NOTE   The CSM is a standalone device installed in a Catalyst 6500 chassis. The CSM interfaces with the switch through a 6-Gbps channel that acts as a trunk carrying multiple VLANs. As soon as packets are handed off to the CSM, they are effectively isolated from the switch until the CSM sends them back.

As you might expect, FWLB can be performed by two separate CSMs, in either one or two physical switch chassis. However, the CSM architecture also allows FWLB using only a single CSM in one switch chassis. You can configure many separate virtual servers and firewall farms within one CSM so that all the FWLB devices needed to surround a firewall farm can be present in that CSM. This makes high-performance FWLB more cost-effective but limits the redundancy to a single CSM.

FWLB in Hardware Configuration Notes

FWLB is configured in two halves. One FWLB device must be placed on the outside of the firewall farm, and another is placed on the inside. Each FWLB device distributes connections *toward the firewall*. Therefore, the outside FWLB balances connections going into the firewall farm's outside interfaces (inbound). The inside FWLB acts similarly for connections going into the firewall farm's inside interfaces (outbound).

The CSM is configured differently from IOS FWLB because it supports only generic server farms that act as firewall farms. A virtual server and its server farm must be configured for each direction in which packets will be sent. Therefore, on each side of the firewall, you must configure the CSM with two virtual servers that either load-balance or just forward traffic in the inbound and outbound directions.

This might sound a bit complicated, but it really is not. Figure 9-5 shows how CSM FWLB devices use the various virtual servers. (For the purposes of this discussion, assume that two separate CSMs are being used.) On the outside of the firewall farm, that CSM needs one virtual server to distribute connections into a firewall farm's outside interfaces in the inbound direction. A second "generic" virtual server takes care of the outbound traffic coming from the firewall farm. This virtual server is actually a simple traffic forwarder that makes no load-balancing decisions.

Figure 9-5 *CSM FWLB Operation Surrounding a Firewall Farm*

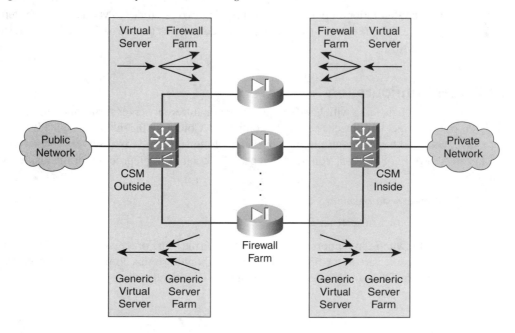

The inside CSM also has two virtual servers:

- One virtual server simply forwards inbound traffic toward the internal secure network.

- One virtual server is a true load balancer that distributes outbound connections to the firewalls' inside interfaces.

TIP   If only one CSM can be used to provide FWLB around a firewall farm, how much network functionality can be put into a single Catalyst 6500 chassis? Plenty! That chassis can contain the usual Supervisor and line cards, along with the CSM, and up to four FWSMs. In other words, the outside public network and the inside secure network can exist on that switch as separate isolated VLANs, and the CSM provides robust load balancing to multiple high-performance firewall modules—all without compromising security.

The following sections present configuration steps for only one side (inside or outside) of the firewall farm. You need to repeat the sequence of steps for the FWLB functions on the other side of the firewall farm, too, assuming that you are working with firewalls that have dual (outside and inside) interfaces.

If you have more protected networks (DMZs, for example), you can apply the same concepts to the firewall farm's other interfaces. Follow the steps listed for the inside FWLB configuration for any other interfaces needed, because these are all more secure interfaces than the outside.

Also notice that the configuration steps assume you are using two separate CSMs. These same steps easily apply to a single CSM scenario just by using all the commands (inside and outside FWLB) to configure that one CSM.

CSM FWLB Configuration

Because firewall load balancing with CSMs requires several different server farms and virtual servers, it is easy to forget what pieces need to be configured. Configure the inside and outside CSMs one at a time, and keep track of your progress in each by following the virtual servers and server farms that are shown in Figure 9-5. You need to repeat this configuration process for the inside and outside CSM.

1. Enter CSM server load-balancing mode:

```
Switch(config)# ip slb mode csm
```

A Catalyst 6500 switch can support SLB functionality on the route processor (RP) or Supervisor in the native IOS software. If a CSM is installed, you should use this command to convert the switch to using the CSM for all the SLB configuration commands.

After you issue this command, the switch needs to be reloaded, and all existing IOS SLB commands are automatically removed.

2. Select the CSM module:

    ```
    Switch(config)# module csm slot-number
    ```

    The native IOS CLI begins CSM configuration mode for the CSM located at *slot-number* in the switch chassis. To end this mode, use the **exit** command. To find the appropriate slot number, use the **show module all** command.

3. Define connectivity away from the firewall farm.

    a. Identify the outside network VLAN:

        ```
        Switch(config-module-csm)# vlan vlan-id client
        ```

        The VLAN number is given as *vlan-id* (2 to 4095; VLAN 1 cannot be used). This VLAN must already be defined on the switch. Defining the VLAN as **client** means that the CSM expects new inbound connections to originate from clients there. These connections are distributed into a server-type VLAN where the firewall farm is located.

    TIP   The CSM does not have a special configuration mode for firewall farms or FWLB. When configuring a CSM for FWLB, always consider the client-side VLAN of the CSM to be away from the firewalls. The server-side VLAN of the CSM is always closest or directly connected to the firewall farms.

    ---

    b. Assign a primary IP address:

        ```
        Switch(config-slb-vlan-client)# ip address ip-address netmask
        ```

        One IP address can be defined per VLAN on the CSM. This address is used as the next-hop gateway for inbound traffic, as well as for management traffic (probes, for example) and ARP requests.

    TIP   For the outside CSM, make sure the hosts or routers on the outside public (unsecure) network use this address as their next-hop gateway to reach the inside (secure) network. Likewise, for the inside CSM, make sure the inside (secure) hosts and routers use this address as their default gateway to the public network.

    ---

    c. (Outside CSM only) Define a default gateway:

        ```
        Switch(config-slb-vlan-client)# gateway ip-address
        ```

A next-hop default gateway or router address is given by *ip-address*. You can repeat this command to define up to 7 gateways per VLAN, or 255 gateways per CSM. Gateways are usually used on the client-side VLAN to forward outbound traffic to the next-hop router in the public network.

d. Exit client VLAN mode:

```
Switch(config-slb-vlan-client)# exit
```

4. Define connectivity toward the firewall farm.

a. Identify the nearest firewall farm VLAN:

```
Switch(config-module-csm)# vlan vlan-id server
```

This is the VLAN that is used to connect this CSM to the firewalls in the firewall farm. The VLAN number is given as *vlan-id* (2 to 4095; VLAN 1 cannot be used). This VLAN must already be defined on the switch. Defining the VLAN as **server** means that the CSM distributes new connections to firewall "servers" in the firewall farm.

TIP   The firewalls in a firewall farm can all be located on the same IP subnet and VLAN as the CSM. In this case, only one server VLAN needs to be defined on the CSM.

Having each firewall located on a separate IP subnet and VLAN is also valid. This can occur when the firewalls are located in different geographic locations or when they need to be logically isolated from each other. In this case, you need to create a server VLAN for each firewall in the farm. Each server VLAN is assigned an IP address that correlates to a specific firewall's interface.

---

b. Assign a primary IP address:

```
Switch(config-slb-vlan-server)# ip address ip-address netmask
```

One IP address can be defined per VLAN on the CSM. For the outside CSM, this address is used as the next-hop gateway for outbound traffic from the firewalls. Likewise, for the inside CSM, this address is the next hop for inbound traffic from the firewalls. The CSM also uses this address as a source address when it generates management traffic (probes, for example) and ARP requests.

TIP   Make sure all the firewalls in the farm are configured with the outside CSM's server-side VLAN IP address as their default gateway. The firewalls should also have the inside CSM's server-side address as their next-hop gateway to reach the inside (secure) networks.

That way, the firewalls can easily forward packets to the appropriate CSM, which in turn forwards them to the public or secure network.

c. (Optional) Define additional IP addresses:

```
Switch(config-slb-vlan-server)# alias ip-address netmask
```

You can define an additional IP address and subnet on a server-side VLAN if necessary. This is similar to configuring a secondary IP address on a router interface. By repeating this command, you can add up to 255 additional addresses to a VLAN.

d. (Optional) Define static routes to reach distant networks:

```
Switch(config-slb-vlan-server)# route ip-address netmask gateway
  gw-ip-address
```

You can define a static route when the CSM needs to know how to reach firewalls that are more than one router hop away. Define the route by the network *ip-address* and *netmask* using next-hop gateway address *gw-ip-address*. The gateway must reside on the same local network as the CSM server VLAN.

You do not need to use this command if each firewall is connected to the same IP subnet as a CSM server VLAN. In this case, no routing information is needed to reach the firewalls.

5. Define a probe for a firewall farm:

```
Switch(config-module-csm)# probe probe-name icmp
```

The probe is named *probe-name* (a text string of up to 15 characters) and can be referenced by other FWLB commands.

TIP   You do not have to configure a target IP address for a CSM probe. Rather, the CSM uses the probe definition and substitutes each firewall's IP address from the firewall farm. Every firewall is automatically probed in this fashion.

Notice that this makes detecting complete firewall operation somewhat difficult. Ideally, you should send and receive ICMP packets that have passed all the way through a firewall to be sure it is completely functional. You normally use a target address of the far-side firewall interface or another device on the other side. This isn't possible on the CSM; only the nearest firewall interface (the one configured in the firewall farm) is probed. At the least, if ICMP replies are received, you can safely assume that the firewall's outside interface is up and running.

Section 9-3

TIP   The CSM is somewhat unique with regard to probes. Even if no probes are defined and configured, it uses ARP requests that it regularly sends every 5 minutes to determine if each firewall in a farm is alive. If the firewall does not send an ARP reply, it is marked as failed. Although this is automatic, it is not very timely, because 5 minutes could pass before the CSM realizes there is a problem with a firewall. During that time, new connections could have been assigned to the dead firewall.

You should always define and use a probe for each firewall farm. Although you cannot configure the target IP addresses used by probes, you can tune the probe interval and the number of retries before a failure is declared.

---

   a. (Optional) Set the amount of time between probes:

   ```
   Switch(config-slb-probe-icmp)# interval seconds
   ```

   Probes are sent toward the target at intervals of *seconds* (5 to 65535 seconds; the default is 120 seconds).

   b. (Optional) Set how long to wait for a probe reply:

   ```
   Switch(config-slb-probe-icmp)# receive receive-timeout
   ```

   The CSM waits *receive-timeout* (1 to 65535 seconds; the default is 10 seconds) for an ICMP reply to be received before considering the probe failed.

   c. (Optional) Define the criteria for a failure:

   ```
   Switch(config-slb-probe-icmp)# retries retry-count
   ```

   With a CSM, the target has failed if *retry-count* (0 to 65535; the default is 3) probes go unanswered.

   d. (Optional) Wait to retry a failed firewall:

   ```
   Switch(config-slb-probe-icmp)# failed failed-interval
   ```

   After a CSM has determined that a firewall has failed, it waits *failed-interval* (5 to 65535 seconds; the default is 300 seconds) before sending another probe.

6. Define the firewall farm.

   a. Assign a name to the firewall farm:

   ```
   Switch(config-module-csm)# serverfarm serverfarm-name
   ```

   The CSM views a firewall farm as just another form of a server farm, referenced by *serverfarm-name* (a text string of up to 15 characters).

b. Identify one or more firewalls in the farm:

```
Switch(config-slb-sfarm)# real ip-address
Switch(config-slb-real)# inservice
```

The firewall interface nearest to the CSM can be found at IP address *ip-address*. By default, the CSM does not use the firewall unless it is placed in service with the **inservice** command. To remove a firewall from service, use the **no inservice** command.

c. Choose a firewall load-balancing method:

```
Switch(config-slb-sfarm)# predictor hash address {source |
  destination} 255.255.255.255
```

On a CSM located outside relative to the firewall farm (the unsecure side), the algorithm should use only the **source** addresses. On an inside CSM, the **destination** hash algorithm should be used. Here, you should set the netmask option to 255.255.255.255 so that all address bits are used in the hash algorithm.

In this fashion, inbound and outbound connections are distributed according to the largest and most diverse population of addresses—those found on the public network.

TIP   The CSM has a very robust load-balancing capability that can be based on source or destination addresses, a round-robin fashion, or the actual connection loads on each firewall. For firewall load balancing, the source and destination address hashes are the most useful and predictable.

You might be inclined to use one of the more dynamic hash algorithms so that the firewalls are loaded evenly. These algorithms include *weighted round robin*, which assigns a number of new connections to one firewall before moving on to the next one, and *weighted least connections*, which assigns new connections to the firewall that is least used at any given time. Or you might have a mix of firewall models in a firewall farm, where some have a higher throughput than others and should be used more.

In any event, the dynamic hash algorithms do not lend themselves to FWLB because multiple FWLB devices always surround a firewall farm. The outside FWLB device can do a nice, accurate job of evenly distributing the load to the outside of the firewall farm, but its information about the firewall loads, weighting, and number of active connections is not passed to the inside FWLB device. The same is true of the inside FWLB device. This makes it possible for some firewalls to be overloaded by a combination of inside and outside FWLB devices while others are underutilized.

---

d. Disable server NAT:

```
Switch(config-slb-sfarm)# no nat server
```

By default, server NAT is enabled for a CSM server farm (including a firewall farm). However, NAT is never needed when load-balancing to firewalls. The FWLB device should just pass IP addresses through unaltered.

e. Use one or more probes to detect failures within the firewall farm:

```
Switch(config-slb-sfarm)# probe probe-name
```

The probe that is defined by *probe-name* (a text string) is used to periodically check each firewall in the firewall farm. The probe inherits each firewall's IP address from the list of real servers to use as a target address. You can define more than one probe, but a firewall is declared down if it fails just one probe. A firewall must pass all probes to be recovered again.

7. Define a virtual server to handle traffic toward the firewall farm.

a. Name the virtual server:

```
Switch(config-module-csm)# vserver virtual-server-name
```

The virtual server is given the name *virtual-server-name* (a text string of up to 15 characters).

b. Assign the virtual server to a firewall server farm:

```
Switch(config-slb-vserver)# serverfarm serverfarm-name
```

FWLB uses the virtual server as the front end for the server farm named *serverfarm-name* (a text string of up to 15 characters).

c. Define the virtual server's IP address:

```
Switch(config-slb-vserver)# virtual ip-address [network-mask] any
```

The virtual server appears as IP address *ip-address* (the default is 0.0.0.0) with *network-mask* (the default is 255.255.255.255; 1 bits match, and 0 is a wildcard). In the default case (0.0.0.0 255.255.255.255), no destination addresses are ever matched, so no traffic is accepted.

In most cases, you can just define the virtual server to accept any destination (0.0.0.0 0.0.0.0), as long as you specify the ingress VLAN in Step 7d. The **any** keyword allows all protocols to be load-balanced.

However, it is good practice to be more specific by defining the virtual server to accept only the IP subnets that are behind the firewall farm on the inside (secure) network.

d. (Optional) Allow traffic only from a source VLAN to use the virtual server:

```
Switch(config-slb-vserver)# vlan vlan-number
```

By default, traffic from all VLANs is allowed to reach the firewalls through the virtual server. To restrict the access, specify a *vlan-number* (2 to 4095) that is to be allowed. This is usually the CSM VLAN that connects away from the firewalls. After it is defined, all other VLANs are restricted from accessing the virtual server.

e. Allow FWLB to begin using the virtual server:

```
Switch(config-slb-vserver)# inservice
```

By default, FWLB does not use the virtual server unless it is placed in service. To remove a virtual server from service, use the **no inservice** command.

f. (Optional) Use SLB stateful backup:

```
Switch(config-slb-vserver)# replicate csrp {sticky | connection}
```

CSM replicates its connection information using Content Switching Replication Protocol (CSRP). You can replicate the **sticky** connection database or the regular **connection** database. To replicate both, choose each one in a separate **replicate csrp** command.

8. Define a generic server farm for traffic away from the firewall farm.

a. Assign a name to the generic server farm:

```
Switch(config-module-csm)# serverfarm serverfarm-name
```

The CSM sees the network away from the firewall farm as a server farm. Here, the server farm represents the Internet or public network to the outside CSM and the internal (secure) network to the inside CSM.

TIP You must also configure traffic away from the firewall farm for load balancing with a generic **serverfarm** having no real servers. Instead, a generic virtual server is used to forward all traffic through the generic server farm according to the CSM's internal routing tables.

---

b. (Optional) Choose a load-balancing method:

```
Switch(config-slb-sfarm)# predictor forward
```

Here, the algorithm uses only **forward** mode without computing hash values. This merely forwards traffic destined away from the firewall farm according to the CSM's internal routing table.

c. Disable server NAT:

```
Switch(config-slb-sfarm)# no nat server
```

By default, server NAT is enabled for a CSM server farm. In the case of firewall load balancing, NAT is not required, because packets should be presented to and from the firewalls unaltered.

9. Define a generic virtual server for traffic away from the firewall farm.

   a. Name the virtual server:

   ```
   Switch(config-module-csm)# vserver virtual-server-name
   ```

   The virtual server is given the name *virtual-server-name* (a text string of up to 15 characters).

   b. Assign the virtual server to the generic server farm:

   ```
   Switch(config-slb-vserver)# serverfarm serverfarm-name
   ```

   FWLB uses the virtual server as the front end for the generic server farm named *serverfarm-name* (a text string of up to 15 characters).

   c. Let the virtual server accept all outbound traffic:

   ```
   Switch(config-slb-vserver)# virtual 0.0.0.0 0.0.0.0 any
   ```

   The virtual server matches any destination IP address so that traffic gets forwarded away from the firewall farm.

   d. (Optional) Allow traffic only from a source VLAN to use the virtual server:

   ```
   Switch(config-slb-vserver)# vlan vlan-number
   ```

   By default, traffic from all VLANs is forwarded out through the virtual server. To restrict the access, specify a *vlan-number* (2 to 4095) that is to be allowed. This is usually the CSM VLAN that connects to the firewall farm. After it is defined, all other VLANs are restricted from accessing the virtual server.

   e. (Optional) Use sticky connections to maintain client/server firewall mapping:

   ```
   Switch(config-slb-vserver)# sticky duration [group group-id]
     [netmask netmask] [source | destination | both]
   Switch(config-slb-vserver)# reverse-sticky group-id
   ```

   After a CSM builds a connection from a client to a real server (firewall) through a virtual server, it can make the connection "sticky" to permit subsequent client/server connections to use the same firewall. This is important for some applications, where one connection sets up the appropriate conditions for a second connection. This is commonly done with protocols such as H.323, where "buddy" ports or additional connections are negotiated and initiated.

You can enable sticky connections with the **sticky** command, where connections are held in the sticky database for *duration* (1 to 65535 minutes). By using the **group** keyword, you can organize the connections in the database as groups if certain types of connections should be held together. The *group-id* is 0 by default, but it can be 1 to 255.

Connections are flagged as "sticky" according to IP address criteria. You can provide a subnet mask designation with **netmask** *netmask*, where 1 bits signify the address bits that are eligible for stickiness. The actual address used can be **source**, **destination**, or **both**.

With firewall load balancing, sticky connections usually need to be extended further. This is because a CSM is configured with two virtual servers—one to load-balance connections toward the firewall farm and another to load-balance connections away from the firewall farm. In practice, these virtual servers work independently so that connections that are marked sticky through one virtual server do not appear sticky to the other virtual server.

To remedy this, you can enable reverse sticky connections with the **reverse-sticky** command. This is done on a per-group basis, where *group-id* (0 to 255) identifies the group created with the **sticky** command. As connections are load-balanced and made sticky in one direction, sticky entries are automatically made for them in the reverse direction. In effect, this provides a common sticky database for all the virtual servers.

f.   Allow FWLB to begin using the virtual server:

```
Switch(config-slb-vserver)# inservice
```

By default, the virtual server is not used until it is placed in service. To remove a virtual server from service, use the **no inservice** command.

CSM Firewall Load-Balancing Example

The network from the example in Section 9-2 is reused here so that you can get a feel for the difference between IOS FWLB and CSM configurations.

To perform firewall load balancing, you need two load-balancing devices:

- One located externally with respect to the firewall farm
- One located internally with respect to the firewall farm

Figure 9-6 shows a network diagram for this example using CSMs as FWLB devices. Remember that in the case of CSMs, you have the flexibility to use two separate modules (in the same or different chassis) on each side of the firewall farm or a single CSM that simply connects to both sides of the firewall farm.

Figure 9-6 *Network Diagram for the CSM FWLB Example*

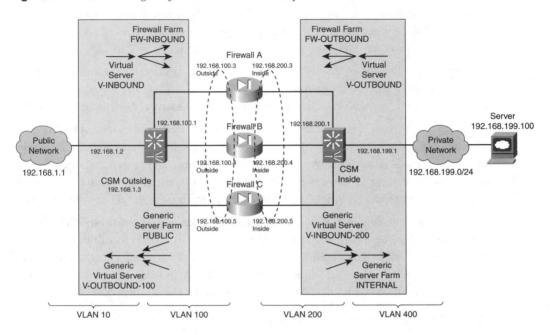

The firewall farm consists of three real firewalls.

The outside (unprotected) interfaces of the three firewalls are at 192.168.100.3, 192.168.100.4, and 192.168.100.5. On the outside, the default gateway to the public network is 192.168.1.1, and the external CSM FWLB device (Catalyst A) is at 192.168.1.2.

The inside (protected) interfaces of the three firewalls are at 192.168.200.3, 192.168.200.4, and 192.168.200.5. The internal CSM FWLB device performs firewall load balancing for outbound traffic to the firewall farm. On the internal secure network (192.168.199.0/24), one server is in use at 192.168.199.100. This server supports both inbound HTTP and Telnet connections.

Ping probes are used by both external and internal FWLB devices to test for firewall operation.

CSM Components Needed

Before we look at the actual configuration commands, you should understand the many logical pieces of the two CSMs that are used for FWLB. Remember that the CSM thinks of everything in terms of a server farm and its virtual server front end.

For the outside CSM, keep in mind that both inbound (toward the firewall farm and the inside secure network) and outbound (away from the firewall farm, toward the public network) connections exist. You need a server farm and virtual server pair in each of these directions. These are labeled as follows:

- Inbound connections:

    — **FW-INBOUND**—The server farm composed of individual firewalls ("real servers") and their outside interfaces.

    — **V-INBOUND**—The virtual server that distributes inbound connections among the firewall farm.

- Outbound connections:

    — **PUBLIC**—A generic server farm that simply forwards all traffic toward the public network.

    — **V-OUTBOUND-100**—The virtual server that accepts outbound connections from VLAN 100 (outside interfaces of the firewall farm).

The inside CSM is very similar, requiring the following inbound and outbound pairs of server farms and virtual servers:

- Inbound connections:

    — **INTERNAL**—A generic server farm that simply forwards all traffic toward the internal (secure) network.

    — **V-INBOUND-200**—The virtual server that accepts inbound connections from VLAN 200 (inside interfaces of the firewall farm).

- Outbound connections:

    — **FW-OUTBOUND**—The server farm composed of individual firewalls ("real servers") and their inside interfaces.

    — **V-OUTBOUND**—The virtual server that distributes outbound connections among the firewall farm.

Basic Firewall Configuration

This section begins with the firewall configurations. Firewalls A and B are FWSMs installed in the Catalyst A chassis. Firewall C is an external Cisco ASA connected to Catalyst A through a Gigabit Ethernet link. These configuration commands are shown here to give you a basic idea of all the pieces that must be configured for FWLB. Notice that all three firewalls have identical security policies configured. This is important, because any of the three firewalls could be assigned connections from any pair of inside and outside hosts.

```
Firewall(config)# hostname fwsm-a
fwsm-a(config)# nameif vlan100 outside security0
fwsm-a(config)# nameif vlan200 inside security100
fwsm-a(config)# ip address outside 192.168.100.3 255.255.255.0
fwsm-a(config)# ip address inside 192.168.200.3 255.255.255.0
fwsm-a(config)# icmp permit 192.168.100.0 255.255.255.0 outside
fwsm-a(config)# icmp permit 192.168.200.0 255.255.255.0 inside
fwsm-a(config)# static (inside,outside) 192.168.199.0 192.168.199.0 netmask
  255.255.255.0 0 0
```

```
fwsm-a(config)# object-group icmp-type ICMP
fwsm-a(config-icmp)# icmp-object echo
fwsm-a(config-icmp)# icmp-object echo-reply
fwsm-a(config-icmp)# icmp-object time-exceeded
fwsm-a(config-icmp)# icmp-object unreachable
fwsm-a(config-icmp)# exit
fwsm-a(config)# access-list acl_out permit tcp any host 192.168.199.100 eq telnet
fwsm-a(config)# access-list acl_out permit tcp any host 192.168.199.100 eq www
fwsm-a(config)# access-list acl_out permit icmp any host 192.168.199.100
  object-group ICMP
fwsm-a(config)# access-list acl_in permit tcp 192.168.199.0 255.255.255.0 eq
  telnet any
fwsm-a(config)# access-list acl_in permit tcp 192.168.199.0 255.255.255.0 eq www
  any
fwsm-a(config)# access-list acl_in permit icmp 192.168.199.0 255.255.255.0 any
  object-group ICMP
fwsm-a(config)# access-list acl_in permit icmp 192.168.200.0 255.255.255.0 any
  object-group ICMP
fwsm-a(config)# access-group acl_out in interface outside
fwsm-a(config)# access-group acl_in in interface inside
fwsm-a(config)# route outside 0.0.0.0 0.0.0.0 192.168.100.1 1
fwsm-a(config)# route inside 192.168.199.0 255.255.255.0 192.168.200.1 1
```

```
Firewall(config)# hostname fwsm-b
fwsm-b(config)# nameif vlan100 outside security0
fwsm-b(config)# nameif vlan200 inside security100
fwsm-b(config)# ip address outside 192.168.100.4 255.255.255.0
fwsm-b(config)# ip address inside 192.168.200.4 255.255.255.0
fwsm-b(config)# icmp permit 192.168.100.0 255.255.255.0 outside
fwsm-b(config)# icmp permit 192.168.200.0 255.255.255.0 inside
fwsm-b(config)# static (inside,outside) 192.168.199.0 192.168.199.0 netmask
  255.255.255.0 0 0
fwsm-b(config)# object-group icmp-type ICMP
fwsm-b(config-icmp)# icmp-object echo
fwsm-b(config-icmp)# icmp-object echo-reply
fwsm-b(config-icmp)# icmp-object time-exceeded
fwsm-b(config-icmp)# icmp-object unreachable
fwsm-b(config-icmp)# exit
fwsm-b(config)# access-list acl_out permit tcp any host 192.168.199.100 eq telnet
fwsm-b(config)# access-list acl_out permit tcp any host 192.168.199.100 eq www
fwsm-b(config)# access-list acl_out permit icmp any host 192.168.199.100
  object-group ICMP
fwsm-b(config)# access-list acl_in permit tcp 192.168.199.0 255.255.255.0 eq
  telnet any
fwsm-b(config)# access-list acl_in permit tcp 192.168.199.0 255.255.255.0 eq www
  any
fwsm-b(config)# access-list acl_in permit icmp 192.168.199.0 255.255.255.0 any
  object-group ICMP
fwsm-b(config)# access-list acl_in permit icmp 192.168.200.0 255.255.255.0 any
  object-group ICMP
fwsm-b(config)# access-group acl_out in interface outside
fwsm-b(config)# access-group acl_in in interface inside
fwsm-b(config)# route outside 0.0.0.0 0.0.0.0 192.168.100.1 1
```

```
fwsm-b(config)# route inside 192.168.199.0 255.255.255.0 192.168.200.1 1
```

```
Firewall(config)# hostname asa-c
asa-c(config)# interface gb-ethernet0 1000full
asa-c(config)# interface gb-ethernet1 1000full
asa-c(config)# nameif gb-ethernet0 outside security0
asa-c(config)# nameif gb-ethernet1 inside security100
asa-c(config)# ip address outside 192.168.100.5 255.255.255.0
asa-c(config)# ip address inside 192.168.200.5 255.255.255.0
asa-c(config)# icmp permit 192.168.100.0 255.255.255.0 outside
asa-c(config)# icmp permit 192.168.200.0 255.255.255.0 inside
asa-c(config)# static (inside,outside) 192.168.199.0 192.168.199.0 netmask
  255.255.255.0 0 0
asa-c(config)# object-group icmp-type ICMP
asa-c(config-icmp)# icmp-object echo
asa-c(config-icmp)# icmp-object echo-reply
asa-c(config-icmp)# icmp-object time-exceeded
asa-c(config-icmp)# icmp-object unreachable
asa-c(config-icmp)# exit
asa-c(config)# access-list acl_out permit tcp any host 192.168.199.100 eq telnet
asa-c(config)# access-list acl_out permit tcp any host 192.168.199.100 eq www
asa-c(config)# access-list acl_out permit icmp any host 192.168.199.100
  object-group ICMP
asa-c(config)# access-list acl_in permit tcp 192.168.199.0 255.255.255.0 eq telnet
  any
asa-c(config)# access-list acl_in permit tcp 192.168.199.0 255.255.255.0 eq www
  any
asa-c(config)# access-list acl_in permit icmp 192.168.199.0 255.255.255.0 any
  object-group ICMP
asa-c(config)# access-list acl_in permit icmp 192.168.200.0 255.255.255.0 any
  object-group ICMP
asa-c(config)# access-group acl_out in interface outside
asa-c(config)# access-group acl_in in interface inside
asa-c(config)# route outside 0.0.0.0 0.0.0.0 192.168.100.1 1
asa-c(config)# route inside 192.168.199.0 255.255.255.0 192.168.200.1 1
```

Outside CSM FWLB Configuration

This section shows the configuration for the outside CSM. Notice that this is all done from the Catalyst 6500 CLI, because the commands pertaining to the CSM are automatically downloaded to it. This section begins with the preliminary commands to define VLANs and connectivity. Notice that the Catalyst switch handles routing only from the public network to the outside CSM. The outside and inside CSMs handle all other traffic forwarding from VLAN 10 on to the inside (secure) network. This effectively isolates the inside and outside networks, although they might be present in the same switch chassis.

```
Switch(config)# hostname CatalystA
! Define the VLANs
CatalystA(config)# vlan 10
CatalystA(config-vlan)# name Public-Network
CatalystA(config)# vlan 100
CatalystA(config-vlan)# name FW-outside
```

```
CatalystA(config)# vlan 200
CatalystA(config-vlan)# name FW-inside
CatalystA(config)# vlan 400
CatalystA(config-vlan)# name Internal-Network
! Pass the VLANs to the two FWSMs
CatalystA(config)# firewall module 3 vlan-group 1
CatalystA(config)# firewall module 4 vlan-group 1
CatalystA(config)# firewall vlan-group 1  100,200
! Set up the outside connection to PIX Firewall-C
CatalystA(config)# interface GigabitEthernet8/1
CatalystA(config-if)# description PIX-C outside
CatalystA(config-if)# no ip address
CatalystA(config-if)# switchport
CatalystA(config-if)# switchport access vlan 100
CatalystA(config-if)# switchport mode access
CatalystA(config-if)# spanning-tree portfast
! Define the Catalyst presence only on VLAN 10; CSM will handle everything beyond
! this
CatalystA(config-if)# interface Vlan10
CatalystA(config-if)# ip address 192.168.1.2 255.255.255.0
! Now define a way to get out to the public network
CatalystA(config)# ip default-gateway 192.168.1.1
CatalystA(config)# ip route 0.0.0.0 0.0.0.0 192.168.1.1
! For the internal (secure) network, define a route that points to the outside CSM
CatalystA(config)# ip route 192.168.199.0 255.255.255.0 192.168.1.1
```

Now, the actual outside CSM commands are addressed. The **ip slb mode csm** command should already be used to force the switch to perform all SLB functions on the CSM instead of using the route processor. (Remember that a CSM performs generic SLB; FWLB is possible by having SLB on each side of a firewall farm.)

```
! Configure the outside CSM on CatalystA
CatalystA(config)# module ContentSwitchingModule 7
CatalystA(config-module-csm)# vlan 10 client
CatalystA(config-slb-vlan-client)# ip address 192.168.1.3 255.255.255.0
CatalystA(config-slb-vlan-client)# gateway 192.168.1.2
CatalystA(config-slb-vlan-client)# exit
!
CatalystA(config-module-csm)# vlan 100 server
CatalystA(config-slb-vlan-server)# ip address 192.168.100.1 255.255.255.0
CatalystA(config-slb-vlan-server)# exit
!
! Define a probe to detect failures within the firewall farm
CatalystA(config-module-csm)# probe FARM-PROBE-OUTSIDE icmp
CatalystA(config-slb-probe-icmp)# interval 15
CatalystA(config-slb-probe-icmp)# exit
!
! Define the inbound firewall farm
CatalystA(config-module-csm)# serverfarm FW-INBOUND
CatalystA(config-slb-sfarm)# no nat server
CatalystA(config-slb-sfarm)# no nat client
CatalystA(config-slb-sfarm)# probe FARM-PROBE-OUTSIDE
```

```
CatalystA(config-slb-sfarm)# predictor hash address source
CatalystA(config-slb-sfarm)# real 192.168.100.3
CatalystA(config-slb-real)# inservice
CatalystA(config-slb-real)# exit
CatalystA(config-slb-sfarm)# real 192.168.100.4
CatalystA(config-slb-real)# inservice
CatalystA(config-slb-real)# exit
CatalystA(config-slb-sfarm)# real 192.168.100.5
CatalystA(config-slb-real)# inservice
CatalystA(config-slb-real)# exit
!
! Define the front end of the inbound FW farm
CatalystA(config-module-csm)# vserver V-INBOUND
CatalystA(config-slb-vserver)# virtual 0.0.0.0 0.0.0.0 any
CatalystA(config-slb-vserver)# vlan 10
CatalystA(config-slb-vserver)# serverfarm FW-INBOUND
CatalystA(config-slb-vserver)# inservice
CatalystA(config-slb-vserver)# exit
!
! Define the outbound forwarder
CatalystA(config-module-csm)# serverfarm PUBLIC
CatalystA(config-slb-sfarm)# no nat server
CatalystA(config-slb-sfarm)# no nat client
CatalystA(config-slb-sfarm)# predictor forward
CatalystA(config-slb-sfarm)# exit
!
! Define the front end to the outbound forwarder
CatalystA(config-module-csm)# vserver V-PUBLIC-100
CatalystA(config-slb-vserver)# virtual 0.0.0.0 0.0.0.0 any
CatalystA(config-slb-vserver)# vlan 100
CatalystA(config-slb-vserver)# serverfarm PUBLIC
CatalystA(config-slb-vserver)# inservice
!
```

Inside CSM Configuration

This section covers the configuration for the inside CSM. At this point, you should notice that you are still configuring things on Catalyst A. Only one physical CSM acts as both outside and inside FWLB devices.

First, here are the commands to define VLANs and connectivity:

```
! Set up the inside connection to ASA Firewall-C
CatalystA(config)# interface GigabitEthernet8/2
CatalystA(config-if)# description PIX-C inside
CatalystA(config-if)# no ip address
CatalystA(config-if)# switchport
CatalystA(config-if)# switchport access vlan 200
CatalystA(config-if)# switchport mode access
CatalystA(config-if)# spanning-tree portfast
! Set up the inside connection the example server 192.168.199.100
CatalystA(config)# interface GigabitEthernet8/3
```

```
CatalystA(config-if)# description Inside Server
CatalystA(config-if)# no ip address
CatalystA(config-if)# switchport
CatalystA(config-if)# switchport access vlan 400
CatalystA(config-if)# switchport mode access
CatalystA(config-if)# spanning-tree portfast
```

Next are the actual inside CSM commands:

```
! Configure the inside CSM (also on CatalystA)
CatalystA(config)# module ContentSwitchingModule 7
CatalystA(config-module-csm)# vlan 400 client
CatalystA(config-slb-vlan-client)# ip address 192.168.199.1 255.255.255.0
CatalystA(config-slb-vlan-client)# exit
!
CatalystA(config-module-csm)# vlan 200 server
CatalystA(config-slb-vlan-server)# ip address 192.168.200.1 255.255.255.0
CatalystA(config-slb-vlan-server)# exit
!
! Define a probe to detect failures within the firewall farm
CatalystA(config-module-csm)# probe FARM-PROBE-INSIDE icmp
CatalystA(config-slb-probe-icmp)# interval 15
!
! Define the outbound firewall farm
CatalystA(config-module-csm)# serverfarm FW-OUTBOUND
CatalystA(config-slb-sfarm)# no nat server
CatalystA(config-slb-sfarm)# no nat client
CatalystA(config-slb-sfarm)# probe FARM-PROBE-INSIDE
CatalystA(config-slb-sfarm)# predictor hash address destination
CatalystA(config-slb-sfarm)# real 192.168.200.3
CatalystA(config-slb-real)# inservice
CatalystA(config-slb-real)# exit
CatalystA(config-slb-sfarm)# real 192.168.200.4
CatalystA(config-slb-real)# inservice
CatalystA(config-slb-real)# exit
CatalystA(config-slb-sfarm)# real 192.168.200.5
CatalystA(config-slb-real)# inservice
CatalystA(config-slb-real)# exit
!
! Define the front end of the outbound FW farm
CatalystA(config-module-csm)# vserver V-OUTBOUND
CatalystA(config-slb-vserver)# virtual 0.0.0.0 0.0.0.0 any
CatalystA(config-slb-vserver)# vlan 400
CatalystA(config-slb-vserver)# serverfarm FW-OUTBOUND
CatalystA(config-slb-vserver)# inservice
CatalystA(config-slb-vserver)# exit
!
! Define the inbound forwarder
CatalystA(config-module-csm)# serverfarm INTERNAL
CatalystA(config-slb-sfarm)# no nat server
CatalystA(config-slb-sfarm)# no nat client
CatalystA(config-slb-sfarm)# predictor forward
CatalystA(config-slb-sfarm)# exit
```

```
!
! Define the front end to the inbound forwarder
CatalystA(config-module-csm)# vserver V-INBOUND-200
CatalystA(config-slb-vserver)# virtual 192.168.199.100 255.255.255.255 any
CatalystA(config-slb-vserver)# vlan 200
CatalystA(config-slb-vserver)# serverfarm INTERNAL
CatalystA(config-slb-vserver)# inservice
!
```

Displaying Information About CSM FWLB

You can use the switch commands listed in Table 9-3 to display helpful information about a CSM FWLB configuration and its status.

Table 9-3 *Commands to Display CSM FWLB Configuration and Status*

Command Syntax	Display Function
Switch# **show module csm** *slot* **serverfarms** [**name** *serverfarm-name*] [**detail**] or Switch# **show module csm** *slot* **vserver** [**detail**]	Firewall farm status
Switch# **show module csm** *slot* **real** [**sfarm** *sfarm-name*]	Status of firewalls in a farm
Switch# **show module csm** *slot* **conns** [**vserver** *virtserver-name*] [**client** *ip-address*] [**detail**]	Load-balancing connections to firewalls
Switch# **show module csm** *slot* **probe icmp** [**name** *probe_name*] [**detail**]	Probe information
Switch# **show module csm** *slot* **sticky** [**groups** | **client** *ip_address*]	Sticky connections

CSM FWLB Output Example

For the network shown in Figure 9-6, you can display the status of the inside (outbound) firewall farm as follows:

```
Switch# show module csm 7 reals
real                    server farm     weight  state         conns/hits
- - - - - - - - - - - - - - - - - - - - - - - - - - - - - - - - - - - - - - - - - - -
192.168.200.3           FW-OUTBOUND     8       OPERATIONAL   0
192.168.200.4           FW-OUTBOUND     8       OPERATIONAL   0
192.168.200.5           FW-OUTBOUND     8       FAILED        0
Switch#
```

Notice that two of the three firewalls are working, but the third is in a **FAILED** state. It has not answered probes or ARP requests from the CSM.

Now, suppose the third firewall is restored to service. You can use the same command to watch the connection load that has been distributed to each firewall. Remember that the number of connections shown represents only the new connections that have originated on one side of the firewall farm. The return traffic for those connections is always forwarded back through the same firewalls, so it is not recorded as additional connections.

For example, the **show module csm** *mod* **reals** command has been issued after each new outbound connection. Here, the destination IP addresses have been incremented just to show how the connections build and are distributed among the firewalls in the farm:

```
Switch# show module csm 7 reals
real                    server farm      weight  state         conns/hits
-----------------------------------------------------------------------
192.168.200.3           FW-OUTBOUND      8       OPERATIONAL   0
192.168.200.4           FW-OUTBOUND      8       OPERATIONAL   0
192.168.200.5           FW-OUTBOUND      8       OPERATIONAL   0
Switch# show module csm 7 reals
real                    server farm      weight  state         conns/hits
-----------------------------------------------------------------------
192.168.200.3           FW-OUTBOUND      8       OPERATIONAL   1
192.168.200.4           FW-OUTBOUND      8       OPERATIONAL   0
192.168.200.5           FW-OUTBOUND      8       OPERATIONAL   0
Switch# show module csm 7 reals
real                    server farm      weight  state         conns/hits
-----------------------------------------------------------------------
192.168.200.3           FW-OUTBOUND      8       OPERATIONAL   1
192.168.200.4           FW-OUTBOUND      8       OPERATIONAL   1
192.168.200.5           FW-OUTBOUND      8       OPERATIONAL   0
Switch# show module csm 7 reals
real                    server farm      weight  state         conns/hits
-----------------------------------------------------------------------
192.168.200.3           FW-OUTBOUND      8       OPERATIONAL   1
192.168.200.4           FW-OUTBOUND      8       OPERATIONAL   1
192.168.200.5           FW-OUTBOUND      8       OPERATIONAL   1
Switch# show module csm 7 reals
real                    server farm      weight  state         conns/hits
-----------------------------------------------------------------------
192.168.200.3           FW-OUTBOUND      8       OPERATIONAL   2
192.168.200.4           FW-OUTBOUND      8       OPERATIONAL   1
192.168.200.5           FW-OUTBOUND      8       OPERATIONAL   1
```

As long as the destination addresses are increasing by 1, the connections are distributed in a round-robin fashion. In actual use, the source and destination addresses can vary greatly, causing the hash algorithm to distribute the connections in an unpredictable fashion. The idea is that there should be a large distribution of address values, causing the connections to be distributed more or less equally among the firewalls.

The CSM must also build an ARP cache so that it can communicate with other devices. To display the MAC and IP address associations it has built, you can use the **show module csm** *mod* **arp** command:

```
Switch# show module csm 7 arp
Internet Address  Physical Interface  VLAN    Type      Status
-----------------------------------------------------------------
 192.168.199.1    00-02-FC-E0-7E-B2   400     --SLB--   local
```

```
  192.168.200.1     00-02-FC-E0-7E-B2    200        --SLB--     local
  192.168.200.3     00-0B-46-B3-4E-40    200        REAL        up(0 misses)
  192.168.200.4     00-0B-5F-0C-8A-C0    200        REAL        up(0 misses)
  192.168.200.5     00-90-27-6C-3D-0A    200        REAL        up(0 misses)
  192.168.199.100   00-50-E2-C6-F6-80    400        LEARNED     up(0 misses)
Switch#
```

The **--SLB--** entries are the CSM VLAN interfaces, the **REAL** entries are the configured firewall addresses, and the **LEARNED** entries have been learned from traffic on a VLAN.

To see a quick summary of how the CSM probes have been configured, use the **show module csm** *mod* **probe icmp** command:

```
Switch# show module csm 7 probe icmp
probe                 type      interval retries failed  open   receive
-------------------------------------------------------------------------
FARM-PROBE-INSIDE     icmp      10       2       300            10
Switch#
```

Here, the probe is using ICMP at 10-second intervals. The probe waits 10 seconds to receive a reply and declares the firewall failed after two probes go unanswered. Finally, as soon as a firewall is in the failed state, the CSM waits 300 seconds before trying to probe again.

You might also be interested in monitoring the connections that are load-balanced by a CSM. The **show module csm** *mod* **conns** command displays a list of the active connections:

```
Switch# show module csm 7 conns
      prot vlan source                 destination            state
-------------------------------------------------------------------------
In   TCP  400  192.168.199.100:13825    10.1.17.9:23          ESTAB
Out  TCP  200  10.1.17.9:23           192.168.199.100:13825 ESTAB

In   TCP  400  192.168.199.100:13313    10.1.17.8:23          ESTAB
Out  TCP  200  10.1.17.8:23           192.168.199.100:13313 ESTAB

In   TCP  400  192.168.199.100:12801    10.1.17.7:23          ESTAB
Out  TCP  200  10.1.17.7:23           192.168.199.100:12801 ESTAB

In   TCP  400  192.168.199.100:11265    10.1.17.4:23          ESTAB
Out  TCP  200  10.1.17.4:23           192.168.199.100:11265 ESTAB
```

Each is shown with the **In** and **Out** VLANs, so you can see the connection traffic in both directions. Notice that the CSM does not have a way to display a connection and the firewall that has been assigned to handle it.

9-4: Firewall Load-Balancing Appliance

A Cisco CSS acts as a multilayer switch and performs FWLB as well as many other types of content processing. A CSS interface can carry a single VLAN or a trunk with multiple VLANs.

A CSS unit must be placed on each side of a firewall farm so that connections are load-balanced to the firewalls in each direction. Firewalls are defined individually rather than as a distinct firewall farm.

The CSS performs a route lookup on each inbound connection to determine the possible firewalls that can be used. The CSS then computes the exclusive OR (XOR) of the source and destination IP addresses as a hash value to select which firewall will receive the connection.

Keepalives (custom ICMP packets) are sent from one CSS to the other at regular intervals. If keepalives are not received from the opposite CSS through a firewall, that firewall is declared dead (failed).

CSS FWLB Configuration

You can use the following steps to configure FWLB on one CSS device. Remember that FWLB requires a load-balancing device on each side of the firewall farm. Be sure to repeat the entire configuration process for the outside and inside CSS FWLB platforms.

1. Configure each CSS physical interface.

    a. Select the interface:

       ```
       (config) interface interface_name
       ```

    b. Configure trunking mode (one or multiple VLANs):

       ```
       (config-if) bridge vlan vlan-id
       ```

       or

       ```
       (config-if) trunk
       ```

       To carry only one VLAN on the interface, use the **bridge vlan** *vlan-id* command. The interface is assigned to VLAN number *vlan-id* (1 to 4094; the default is 1). The CSS performs Layer 2 bridging between interfaces with the same VLAN assignments.

       To carry multiple VLANs on the interface, you can configure it as an 802.1Q trunk. Use the **trunk** command.

    c. (Optional; trunk only) Identify each VLAN to be trunked:

       ```
       (config-if) vlan vlan-id
       ```

       VLAN number *vlan-id* (1 to 4094) is encapsulated on the trunk link. To identify the VLAN as the native VLAN (unencapsulated or untagged frames), follow this with the **default-vlan** command.

2. Assign IP addresses to the CSS VLANs.

    a. Define a logical circuit:

       ```
       (config) circuit circuit_name
       ```

Here, the circuit represents a logical interface within the CSS. You can see a list of available circuit names with the **circuit ?** command. Generally, *circuit_name* is a VLAN that has been configured in the CSS, of the form **VLAN** *vlan-id*.

b. Assign an IP address:

```
(config-circuit) ip address ip_address subnet_mask
(config-circuit-ip) enable
```

3. (Optional) Define a default route toward the public network:

```
(config) ip route 0.0.0.0 0.0.0.0 next-hop-address
```

On the outside CSS unit, you should configure a default route so that traffic can be forwarded to and from the public network. The *next-hop-address* is the IP address of the nearest router in the public network.

4. Define each firewall in the firewall farm:

```
(config) ip firewall index local_firewall_address remote_firewall_address
  remote_css_address
```

You must assign each firewall in the farm a unique arbitrary *index* number (1 to 254). The firewall must have the same index configured in both inside and outside CSS units.

You must also define the firewall in terms of its IP addresses. The *local_firewall_address* is the address of the interface nearest to the CSS, and the *remote_firewall_address* is the address nearest to the CSS on the other side of the firewall. The other CSS unit must also be defined by its IP address *remote_css_address*. (The remote-side IP addresses are defined here because of how the CSS detects firewall failures.)

5. Define static routes to reach beyond the firewall farm:

```
(config) ip route ip_address subnet_mask firewall index distance
```

The CSS on one side of the firewall farm needs to know about any networks that are located on the other side. You can define a static route to the network *ip_address* with a subnet mask *subnet_mask* (either in dotted-decimal or /*n* prefix length notation). This route can be reached through the firewall with an index number *index* (1 to 254).

You can also assign an administrative distance to the route to adjust whether static or dynamic routes are more preferable. You can also use the *distance* (1 to 254; the default is 1; lower is more preferable) to differentiate between two or more sets of firewalls.

For example, if you normally expect traffic to pass through one firewall farm (indices 1 through *n*), you could use a distance of 1. Then define other static routes to the same destination network, but point to a different firewall and use a higher distance. The route (and firewalls) with the lower distance is used unless all of them have failed.

6. (Optional) Adjust the keepalive timing:

```
(config) ip firewall timeout seconds
```

Section 9-4

Each CSS unit expects to receive keepalive probes at regular intervals from the CSS on the other side of the firewall farm. The keepalive probes are sent every *seconds* (3 to 16; the default is 3 seconds) and are expected to be received every *seconds*.

TIP	You must configure the keepalive timeout interval identically for the CSS units on both sides of the firewall farm. With identical configurations, both units correctly detect a failed keepalive from each other at the same time. At that time, each unit declares its side of the firewall to be dead, and subsequent connections are assigned to another firewall. Otherwise, if both units do not detect the same failure, connections could be improperly assigned to the firewalls in an asymmetric fashion.

TIP	Each CSS sends an ICMP packet as a keepalive to the target address of the opposing CSS unit. Each CSS also substitutes the destination MAC address of the specific firewall that is being tested so that the keepalive probe passes through that firewall.
	For this reason, you must make sure that each firewall in the firewall farm is configured to pass ICMP packets between the two CSS IP addresses. The ICMP packets (both echo and echo-reply) must be able to pass through the firewall in both directions (outside to inside and inside to outside).

CSS Appliance Firewall Load-Balancing Example

The network from the example in Section 9-2 is reused here so that you can get a feel for the difference between IOS FWLB, CSM FWLB, and CSS FWLB configurations.

Performing FWLB using this method requires two CSS load-balancing devices:

- One located externally with respect to the firewall farm
- One located internally with respect to the firewall farm

Figure 9-7 shows a network diagram for this example.

Figure 9-7 *Network Diagram for the CSS FWLB Example*

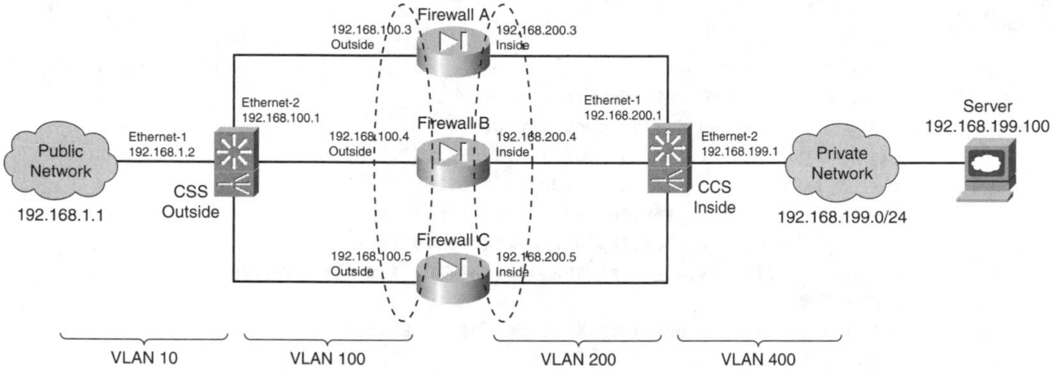

The firewall farm consists of three real firewalls.

The outside (unprotected) interfaces of the three real firewalls are at 192.168.100.3, 192.168.100.4, and 192.168.100.5. On the outside, the default gateway to the public network is 192.168.1.1, and the outside CSS unit is at 192.168.1.2.

The inside (protected) interfaces of the three real firewalls are at 192.168.200.3, 192.168.200.4, and 192.168.200.5. The inside CSS unit performs firewall load balancing for outbound traffic to the firewall farm. On the internal secure network (192.168.199.0/24), one server is in use at 192.168.199.100. This server supports both inbound HTTP and Telnet connections.

Basic Firewall Configuration

This section begins with coverage of the firewall configurations. Firewalls A and B are FWSMs installed in the Catalyst A chassis. Firewall C is an external Cisco PIX Firewall, connected to Catalyst A through a Gigabit Ethernet link. This section shows the configuration commands to give you a basic idea of all the pieces that must be configured for FWLB using an FWLB appliance. Notice that all three firewalls have identical security policies configured. This is important because any of the three firewalls could be assigned connections from any pair of inside and outside hosts.

Notice also that access list rules have been configured to allow the inside and outside CSS units to pass ICMP packets between each other. This is important to allow each CSS to monitor the health of each firewall:

```
Firewall(config)# hostname fwsm-a
fwsm-a(config)# nameif vlan100 outside security0
fwsm-a(config)# nameif vlan200 inside security100
fwsm-a(config)# ip address outside 192.168.100.3 255.255.255.0
fwsm-a(config)# ip address inside 192.168.200.3 255.255.255.0
fwsm-a(config)# icmp permit 192.168.100.0 255.255.255.0 outside
fwsm-a(config)# icmp permit 192.168.200.0 255.255.255.0 inside
fwsm-a(config)# static (inside,outside) 192.168.199.100 192.168.199.100 netmask
  255.255.255.255 0 0
fwsm-a(config)# static (inside,outside) 192.168.200.1 192.168.200.1 netmask
  255.255.255.255 0 0
fwsm-a(config)# static (inside,outside) 192.168.100.1 192.168.100.1 netmask
  255.255.255.255 0 0
fwsm-a(config)# object-group icmp-type ICMP
fwsm-a(config-icmp)# icmp-object echo
fwsm-a(config-icmp)# icmp-object echo-reply
fwsm-a(config-icmp)# icmp-object time-exceeded
fwsm-a(config-icmp)# icmp-object unreachable
fwsm-a(config-icmp)# exit
fwsm-a(config)# access-list acl_out permit icmp host 192.168.100.1 host
  192.168.200.1
fwsm-a(config)# access-list acl_out permit tcp any host 192.168.199.100 eq telnet
fwsm-a(config)# access-list acl_out permit tcp any host 192.168.199.100 eq www
fwsm-a(config)# access-list acl_out permit icmp any host 192.168.199.100
  object-group ICMP
fwsm-a(config)# access-list acl_in permit ip 192.168.199.100 255.255.255.255 any
fwsm-a(config)# access-list acl_in permit icmp host 192.168.200.1 host
  192.168.100.1
fwsm-a(config)# access-group acl_out in interface outside
fwsm-a(config)# access-group acl_in in interface inside
fwsm-a(config)# route outside 0.0.0.0 0.0.0.0 192.168.100.1 1
fwsm-a(config)# route inside 192.168.199.0 255.255.255.0 192.168.200.1 1
Firewall(config)# hostname fwsm-b
fwsm-b(config)# nameif vlan100 outside security0
fwsm-b(config)# nameif vlan200 inside security100
fwsm-b(config)# ip address outside 192.168.100.4 255.255.255.0
fwsm-b(config)# ip address inside 192.168.200.4 255.255.255.0
fwsm-b(config)# icmp permit 192.168.100.0 255.255.255.0 outside
fwsm-b(config)# icmp permit 192.168.200.0 255.255.255.0 inside
fwsm-b(config)# static (inside,outside) 192.168.199.100 192.168.199.100 netmask
  255.255.255.0 0 0
fwsm-b(config)# static (inside,outside) 192.168.200.1 192.168.200.1 netmask
  255.255.255.255 0 0
fwsm-b(config)# static (inside,outside) 192.168.100.1 192.168.100.1 netmask
  255.255.255.255 0 0
```

```
object-group icmp-type ICMP
fwsm-a(config-icmp)# icmp-object echo
fwsm-a(config-icmp)# icmp-object echo-reply
fwsm-a(config-icmp)# icmp-object time-exceeded
fwsm-a(config-icmp)# icmp-object unreachable
fwsm-a(config-icmp)# exit
fwsm-b(config)# access-list acl_out permit icmp host 192.168.100.1 host
  192.168.200.1
fwsm-b(config)# access-list acl_out permit tcp any host 192.168.199.100 eq telnet
fwsm-b(config)# access-list acl_out permit tcp any host 192.168.199.100 eq www
fwsm-b(config)# access-list acl_out permit icmp any host 192.168.199.100
  object-group ICMP
fwsm-b(config)# access-list acl_in permit ip 192.168.199.100 255.255.255.255 any
fwsm-b(config)# access-list acl_in permit icmp host 192.168.200.1 host
  192.168.100.1
fwsm-b(config)# access-group acl_out in interface outside
fwsm-b(config)# access-group acl_in in interface inside
fwsm-b(config)# route outside 0.0.0.0 0.0.0.0 192.168.100.1 1
fwsm-b(config)# route inside 192.168.199.0 255.255.255.0 192.168.200.1 1
```

```
Firewall(config)# hostname asa-c
asa-c(config)# interface gb-ethernet0 1000full
asa-c(config)# interface gb-ethernet1 1000full
asa-c(config)# nameif gb-ethernet0 outside security0
asa-c(config)# nameif gb-ethernet1 inside security100
asa-c(config)# ip address outside 192.168.100.5 255.255.255.0
asa-c(config)# ip address inside 192.168.200.5 255.255.255.0
asa-c(config)# icmp permit 192.168.100.0 255.255.255.0 outside
asa-c(config)# icmp permit 192.168.200.0 255.255.255.0 inside
asa-c(config)# static (inside,outside) 192.168.199.100 192.168.199.100 netmask
  255.255.255.0 0 0
asa-c(config)# static (inside,outside) 192.168.200.1 192.168.200.1 netmask
  255.255.255.255 0 0
asa-c(config)# static (inside,outside) 192.168.100.1 192.168.100.1 netmask
  255.255.255.255 0 0
asa-c(config)# object-group icmp-type ICMP
asa-c(config-icmp)# icmp-object echo
asa-c(config-icmp)# icmp-object echo-reply
asa-c(config-icmp)# icmp-object time-exceeded
asa-c(config-icmp)# icmp-object unreachable
asa-c(config-icmp)# exit
asa-c(config)# access-list acl_out permit icmp host 192.168.100.1 host
  192.168.200.1
asa-c(config)# access-list acl_out permit tcp any host 192.168.199.100 eq telnet
asa-c(config)# access-list acl_out permit tcp any host 192.168.199.100 eq www
asa-c(config)# access-list acl_out permit icmp any host 192.168.199.100
  object-group ICMP
asa-c(config)# access-list acl_in permit ip 192.168.199.100 255.255.255.255 any
asa-c(config)# access-list acl_in permit icmp host 192.168.200.1 host
  192.168.100.1
```

Section 9-4

```
asa-c(config)# access-group acl_out in interface outside
asa-c(config)# access-group acl_in in interface inside
asa-c(config)# route outside 0.0.0.0 0.0.0.0 192.168.100.1 1
asa-c(config)# route inside 192.168.199.0 255.255.255.0 192.168.200.1 1
```

Outside CSS FWLB Configuration

The outside CSS unit is configured with three firewalls and three static routes. Notice that each of the static routes lists the internal (secure) network as the destination and has each firewall as a next-hop gateway address. Firewall keepalive probes are sent and are expected every 3 seconds by default. The configuration commands are as follows:

```
(config) interface ethernet-1
(config-if) description "Outside public network"
(config-if) bridge vlan 10
(config) circuit VLAN10
(config-circuit) description "Circuit to the outside network"
(config-circuit) ip address 192.168.1.2 255.255.255.0
(config-circuit-ip) enable
(config) interface ethernet-2
(config-if) description "Firewall farm outside"
(config-if) bridge vlan 100
(config) circuit VLAN100
(config-circuit) description "Circuit to the firewall farm"
(config-circuit) ip address 192.168.100.1 255.255.255.0
(config-circuit-ip) enable
(config) ip route 0.0.0.0 0.0.0.0 192.168.1.1

(config) ip firewall 1 192.168.100.3 192.168.200.3 192.168.200.1
(config) ip firewall 2 192.168.100.4 192.168.200.4 192.168.200.1
(config) ip firewall 3 192.168.100.5 192.168.200.5 192.168.200.1
(config) ip route 192.168.199.0 255.255.255.0 firewall 1 1
(config) ip route 192.168.199.0 255.255.255.0 firewall 2 1
(config) ip route 192.168.199.0 255.255.255.0 firewall 3 1
(config) ip route 192.168.200.0 255.255.255.0 firewall 1 1
(config) ip route 192.168.200.0 255.255.255.0 firewall 2 1
(config) ip route 192.168.200.0 255.255.255.0 firewall 3 1
```

Inside CSS FWLB Configuration

The inside CSS unit is also configured with the inside addresses of the three firewalls. Notice this time that three static routes have been configured as default routes to reach the outside public network. Each one has a different firewall as a next-hop gateway address. Firewall keepalive probes are sent and are expected every 3 seconds by default. The configuration commands are as follows:

```
(config) interface ethernet-1
(config-if) description "Firewall farm inside"
(config-if) bridge vlan 200
(config) circuit VLAN200
(config-circuit) description "Circuit to the firewall farm"
(config-circuit) ip address 192.168.200.1 255.255.255.0
```

```
(config-circuit-ip) enable
(config) interface ethernet-2
(config-if) description "Inside private network"
(config-if) bridge vlan 400
(config) circuit VLAN400
(config-circuit) description "Circuit to the inside network"
(config-circuit) ip address 192.168.199.1 255.255.255.0
(config-circuit-ip) enable

(config) ip firewall 1 192.168.200.3 192.168.100.3 192.168.100.1
(config) ip firewall 2 192.168.200.4 192.168.100.4 192.168.100.1
(config) ip firewall 3 192.168.200.5 192.168.100.5 192.168.100.1
(config) ip route 0.0.0.0 0.0.0.0 firewall 1 1
(config) ip route 0.0.0.0 0.0.0.0 firewall 2 1
(config) ip route 0.0.0.0 0.0.0.0 firewall 3 1
```

Displaying Information About CSS FWLB

Table 9-4 lists the CSS commands that you can use to display helpful information about CSS FWLB configuration and status.

Table 9-4 *Commands to Display CSS FWLB Configuration and Status*

Command Syntax	Display Function
`show ip firewall`	Firewall status
`show ip routes firewall`	Static routes to firewalls
`show flows` [*source_address* [*destination_address*]]	Load-balancing connections to firewalls

Refer to the following sections for information about these topics:

- **10-1: Managing the Firewall Clock**—Discusses ways to set and maintain the firewall's internal clock so that events and messages can have accurate time stamps.

- **10-2: Generating Logging Messages**—Explains how firewalls generate logging messages and how you can configure them to do that.

- **10-3: Fine-Tuning Logging Message Generation**—Covers the configuration steps that can be used to enable or disable specific logging messages or change their severity levels. This section also discusses how to configure access list activity logging.

- **10-4: Analyzing Firewall Logs**—Provides an overview of how you can approach collecting and analyzing the logging messages that firewalls produce.

CHAPTER 10

Firewall Logging

Cisco firewalls and security appliances can be configured to generate an audit trail of messages describing their activities. Firewall logs can be collected and analyzed to determine what types of traffic have been permitted or denied, what users have accessed various resources, and so on.

This chapter presents the tasks that are necessary to begin generating and collecting logging messages.

10-1: Managing the Firewall Clock

A Cisco firewall keeps an internal clock that can be used for Syslog time stamps, certificate time stamps, and so on. The clock is powered by a battery in the absence of regular power.

The internal clock is always based on Coordinated Universal Time (UTC). UTC was previously known as Greenwich Mean Time (GMT).

You can set the system time using two different approaches:

- **Manually**—You set the time and date on the firewall along with the time zone and specify whether to observe daylight savings time. With manual configuration, the firewall clock is only as accurate as the internal clock hardware.

- **Using Network Time Protocol (NTP)**—This is a protocol defined by RFC 1305 that provides a mechanism for the devices in the network to get their time from an NTP server. With NTP, all the devices are synchronized to a common, trusted source and keep very accurate time.

NTP uses the concept of *stratum* to determine how close an NTP server is to an authoritative time source (an atomic or radio clock). Stratum 1 means that an NTP server is directly connected to an authoritative time source. NTP also compares the times reported from all configured NTP peers and does not listen to a peer that has a significantly different time.

NTP associations with other NTP peers can be protected through an encrypted authentication.

TIP   NTP version 3 is based on RFC 1305 and uses UDP port 123. Information about public NTP servers and other NTP subjects can be found at http://www.ntp.org.

You can also use a commercial product as your own stratum 1 time source. For example, Symmetricom (http://www.ntp-systems.com/products.asp) offers several NTP time servers that are based on Global Positioning Satellite (GPS) signals.

Setting the Clock Manually

1. (Optional) Identify the time zone:

   ```
   Firewall(config)# clock timezone zone-name hours [minutes]
   ```

   zone-name is the time zone (an arbitrary text string such as EST) and is *hours* (0 to 12 or 0 to 12) and optionally *minutes* offset from UTC. For example, Eastern Standard Time in the U.S. is 5 hours behind UTC and would be configured as follows:

   ```
   Firewall(config)# clock timezone EST -5
   ```

2. (Optional) Set daylight savings time (DST or summer time) parameters.

   a. Use the following command if daylight savings time recurs at regular intervals:

   ```
   Firewall(config)# clock summer-time zone recurring [week weekday month
     hh:mm week weekday month hh:mm] [offset]
   ```

   If daylight savings time begins and ends on a certain day and week of a month, you can use this command. The name of the daylight savings time zone is given as *zone* (an arbitrary name or abbreviation, such as EDT). The week number *week* (1 to 4 or the words "first" and "last"), the name of the *weekday*, the name of the *month* (only the first three letters matter), and the time *hh:mm* in 24-hour format can all be given to start and stop daylight savings time. The *offset* value gives the number of minutes to add during daylight savings time (the default is 60 minutes).

   For example, until 2007, daylight savings time in the United States began at 2 a.m. on the first Sunday in April and ended at 2 a.m. on the last Sunday in October. That recurring DST schedule could be defined with this command:

   ```
   Firewall(config)# clock summer-time EDT recurring first Sunday april
     2:00 last Sunday oct 2:00
   ```

   Beginning in 2007, the United States began using a modified schedule where DST starts at 2 a.m. on the second Sunday in March and ends at 2 a.m. on the first Sunday in November. The modified DST schedule could be defined with the following command:

   ```
   Firewall(config)# clock summer-time EDT recurring second sunday march
     2:00 first sunday nov 2:00
   ```

| TIP | You can use the **recurring** keyword with no other arguments for any of the U.S. and Canadian time zones. The correct begin and end dates are used automatically. For the preceding example, you could define daylight savings time as follows: |

```
Firewall(config)# clock summer-time EDT recurring
```

Be aware that this default recurring schedule is based on the U.S. DST standard that was in effect when the firewall code was released. For example, ASA release 7.2(1) uses the default DST based on the older April/October schedule, while releases 7.2(1)27 and later use the newer March/November schedule.

To make sure your firewall is using the current or correct DST schedule, do not use the default schedule; rather, you should enter the **clock summer-time** command with specific dates and times.

b. If daylight savings time occurs at specific times, you can use the following command to specify the exact date and time that daylight savings time begins and ends in a given year:

```
Firewall(config)# clock summer-time zone date {day month | month day}
  year hh:mm {day month | month day} year hh:mm [offset]
```

This command is useful if the begin and end times change from year to year. Specify the year number as *year* (four digits, 1993 to 2035).

3. Set the firewall clock:

```
Firewall(config)# clock set hh:mm:ss {day month | month day} year
```

The clock is set when this command is executed. The time is given in 24-hour format, *day* is the day number (1 to 31), *month* is the name of the month (only the first three letters are needed), and *year* is the full four-digit year. The *day* and *month* parameters can be reversed, according to what is customary.

4. Verify the clock:

```
Firewall# show clock [detail]
```

The current time and date are shown. If you use the **detail** keyword, the source of the time ("hardware calendar" is the internal battery-operated clock) and any daylight savings time definitions are shown, as in this example:

```
Firewall# show clock detail
00:04:48.218 EDT Mon Mar 19 2007
Time source is hardware calendar
Summer time starts 02:00:00 EST Sun Mar 11 2007
Summer time ends 02:00:00 EDT Sun Nov 4 2007
Firewall#
```

Setting the Clock with NTP

TIP   In ASA multiple-context mode, NTP must be configured on the system execution space only. All the other contexts (both admin and user) obtain their clock information from the system execution space, because all the contexts exist in the same physical firewall. You can use the **changeto system** command to move your session into the system execution space before using the following configuration steps.

The Firewall Services Module (FWSM) does not have a standalone clock, and it does not support NTP. Because it is a module inside a Catalyst 6500 chassis, it relies on the switch clock instead. Therefore, you should make sure the switch Supervisor has been configured for NTP as an accurate clock source.

---

1. (Optional) Use NTP authentication.

   a.   Define an authentication key:

   ```
   Firewall(config)# ntp authentication-key key-number md5 value
   ```

   An MD5 authentication key numbered *key-number* (1 to 4294967295) is created. The key is given a text-string *value* of up to eight cleartext characters. After the configuration is written to Flash memory, the key value is displayed in its encrypted form.

   You can repeat this command to define additional keys if needed.

   b.   (Optional) Identify a key to expect from all defined NTP servers:

   ```
   Firewall(config)# ntp trusted-key key-number
   ```

   Remote NTP peers must authenticate themselves with the firewall using the authentication key numbered *key-number* (1 to 4294967295), as defined in Step 1a. If this command is used, any NTP server must supply this key to the firewall before its time update information is accepted. You can repeat this command to identify additional keys to expect. (Trusted keys can also be defined on a per-server basis in Step 2.)

   c.   Enable NTP authentication:

   ```
   Firewall(config)# ntp authenticate
   ```

2. Specify an NTP server:

   ```
   Firewall(config)# ntp server ip-address [key number] [source if-name]
      [prefer]
   ```

   The NTP peer (server) is identified at *ip-address*. If you are using NTP authentication, you can use the **key** keyword to identify which authentication key to expect from this server. (See

Step 1a.) By default, the firewall sends NTP packets on the interface derived from its routing table. You can specify an interface to use with the **source** keyword and the interface named *if-name* (**outside** or **inside**, for example).

You can repeat this command to define more than one NTP server. If one server is down or unavailable, a second or third server could be used to synchronize time. You can use the **prefer** keyword to indicate one NTP server that is preferred if multiple NTP servers are configured.

TIP   Actually, a firewall using NTP can use its associations with several servers to derive a more accurate idea of the time. If possible, you should configure a minimum of three different NTP servers so that your firewall can determine if any one of them is inaccurate.

---

3. Verify NTP operation.

PIX 6.3	Firewall# **show ntp**
ASA, FWSM	Firewall# **show running-config ntp**

This command displays the commands but not any information about NTP operation, as in this example:

```
Firewall# show running-config ntp
ntp authentication-key 1 md5 *
ntp authentication-key 2 md5 *
ntp authenticate
ntp server 192.168.254.4 key 1 source inside prefer
ntp server 192.168.254.3 key 2 source inside
Firewall#
```

Notice that the MD5 hash keys are automatically hidden from being displayed in the configuration. Instead, only an asterisk is shown.

a. Verify the current NTP status:

```
Firewall# show ntp status
```

NTP should be in the synchronized state if the firewall has successfully authenticated and exchanged information with at least one NTP server. This command shows this in the first line of output, as shown in the following example. Notice that the firewall has become a stratum 4 time source itself, deriving its time information from a higher (lower-stratum) authority:

```
Firewall# show ntp status
Clock is synchronized, stratum 4, reference is 192.168.254.4
nominal freq is 99.9984 Hz, actual freq is 99.9984 Hz, precision is 2**6
```

```
reference time is c34d3659.655d8a23 (14:28:25.395 EST Fri Oct 31 2003)
clock offset is 10.8642 msec, root delay is 87.74 msec
root dispersion is 15927.54 msec, peer dispersion is 15875.02 msec
Firewall#
```

If the clock is unsynchronized, the firewall has not yet authenticated or synchronized its time clock with an NTP server. Keep checking the status every minute or so to see if the clock becomes synchronized. If it does not, confirm your NTP configuration and authentication keys.

b. View all NTP server associations:

```
Firewall# show ntp associations [detail]
```

The firewall clock becomes synchronized with only one NTP server. However, it keeps an association with each NTP server that is configured. NTP continuously compares clock information from all known servers so that it can maintain the most accurate time. In the following example, the firewall has associations with two NTP servers:

```
Firewall# show ntp associations
      address          ref clock      st  when  poll reach  delay  offset
      disp
*~192.168.254.4    198.82.162.213    3    21    64    3    14.8   10.86
      7889.6
+~192.168.254.3    198.82.162.213    3    10    64    3    2.5    0.31
      7881.1
 * master (synced), # master (unsynced), + selected, - candidate,
 ~ configured
Firewall#
```

Notice that the two NTP servers are shown (each is stratum 3 in the **st** column), along with the reference clock that each uses. Here, 192.168.254.4 has become the preferred, or "master," source of synchronization, designated by the * flag. The 192.168.254.3 server is marked with +, indicating that it is selected for possible synchronization.

If you find that some of the server addresses are not selected or synchronized, you can get more information about the failed associations by adding the **detail** keyword.

TIP   If you are having trouble getting a firewall to synchronize its clock, you can use the **debug ntp authentication** EXEC command (if the NTP server requires authentication) or the **debug ntp** {**events** | **select** | **sync**} command to watch the exchange of NTP information. The debug output is shown only in the "debug trace" channel, which is usually the first Telnet or SSH session active on the firewall. If there are no Telnet or SSH sessions, the output is sent to the console.

10-2: Generating Logging Messages

The firewall uses logging to send system messages to one or more logging destinations, where they can be collected, archived, and reviewed.

Messages are generated according to a *severity level*, specified by a number (0 through 7) or a keyword, as shown in Table 10-1.

Table 10-1   *System Message Severity Levels*

Severity Level	Description
0: emergencies	The system is unusable
1: alerts	Immediate action is required
2: critical	A critical condition exists
3: errors	Error message
4: warnings	Warning message
5: notifications	A normal but significant condition
6: informational	Information message
7: debugging	Debug output and very detailed logs

Logging messages can be sent to any of the following destinations:

- The firewall console
- Telnet or SSH sessions to the firewall
- A temporary buffer internal to the firewall
- SNMP management stations
- Syslog servers
- Firewall management applications such as Cisco Adaptive Security Device Manager (ASDM) and Cisco PIX Device Manager (PDM)
- E-mail addresses (ASA 7.0 and above, FWSM 3.1[1] and above)
- An FTP server (ASA 7.0 and above, FWSM 3.1[1] and above)
- Firewall flash (ASA 7.0 and above, FWSM 3.1[1] and above)

The logging level can be set to determine which messages should be sent to each of the destinations. When you set a severity level for a destination, all messages with a lower severity level are also sent.

Alternatively, you can adjust the severity level for the logging destination so that a lower value is used. This reduces the number and type of messages produced but also reduces the amount of useful information that can be collected and analyzed.

You should always add time stamps to Syslog messages to help in real-time debugging and management. The firewall can add time stamps as messages are generated, or a Syslog server can add time stamps as messages are received.

TIP   You should have all your network devices use a common time reference point so that all the time stamps on all logging messages are synchronized. You can do this by configuring firewalls, routers, and switches to use one or more authoritative NTP servers as a time source.

If you have some NTP servers inside your network, each network device can synchronize time with them. However, if you intend to use NTP servers on the public Internet, you should use a hierarchical approach. Select two routers within your network to synchronize time with the Internet servers. Optimally, each router should peer with three unique time sources so that none of them are duplicated.

Then point all your inside devices to synchronize time with the routers. The idea is to contain the bulk of NTP synchronizations within your network rather than have a multitude of hosts peering with the Internet servers.

You can configure a unique "device ID" so that logging messages from a firewall can be readily identified. This becomes important when one Syslog server collects messages from many different firewalls, routers, and switches.

Figure 10-1 shows each of the logging severity levels, along with a general list of the types of messages generated. Each level also includes every level below it. The higher the severity level, the more types of messages that are included.

System messages are logged in either the default or EMBLEM format. Figure 10-2 shows the default message format. Each message has the following fields:

- **Time stamp**—The date and time from the firewall clock. The default is no time stamp.

- **Device ID**—Added to uniquely identify the firewall generating the message. Can be the firewall's host name, an interface IP address, or an arbitrary text string. The default is no device-id.

- **Message ID**—Always begins with **%PIX-**, **%ASA-**, or **%FWSM-**, followed by the severity level and the six-digit message number.

- **Message text**—A description of the event or condition that triggered the message.

The EMBLEM format is used primarily for the CiscoWorks Resource Manager Essentials (RME) Syslog analyzer. This format matches the Cisco IOS Software Syslog format produced by routers and switches. It is available only to UDP Syslog servers.

Figure 10-1 *Syslog Severity Levels and Their Messages*

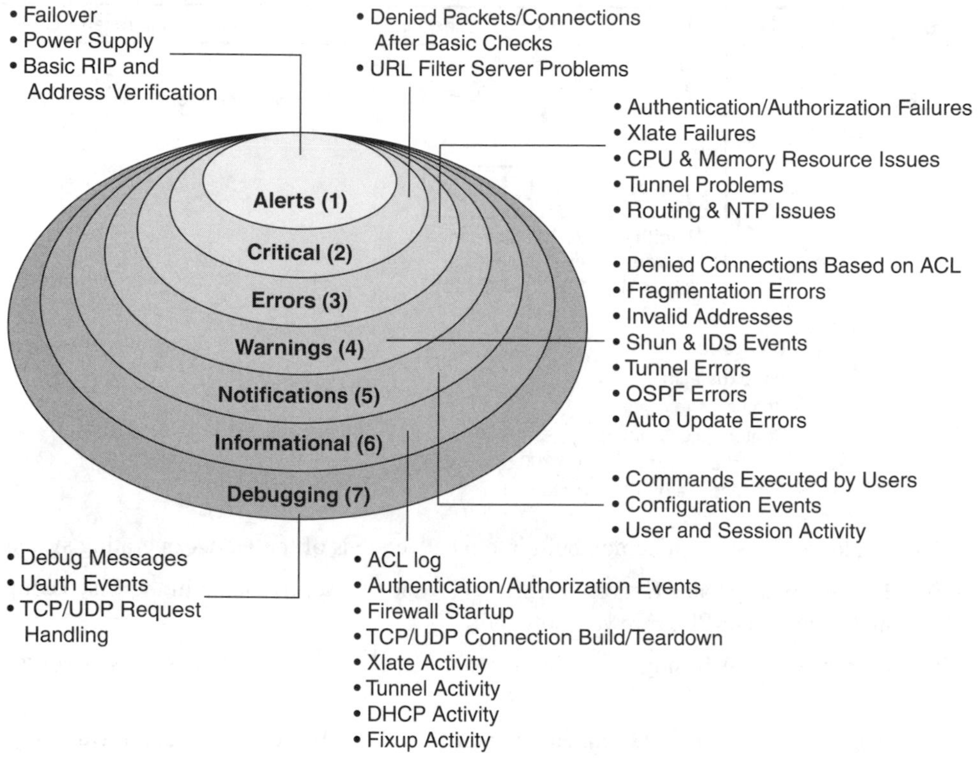

- Failover
- Power Supply
- Basic RIP and Address Verification

- Denied Packets/Connections After Basic Checks
- URL Filter Server Problems

- Authentication/Authorization Failures
- Xlate Failures
- CPU & Memory Resource Issues
- Tunnel Problems
- Routing & NTP Issues

- Denied Connections Based on ACL
- Fragmentation Errors
- Invalid Addresses
- Shun & IDS Events
- Tunnel Errors
- OSPF Errors
- Auto Update Errors

Alerts (1)
Critical (2)
Errors (3)
Warnings (4)
Notifications (5)
Informational (6)
Debugging (7)

- Commands Executed by Users
- Configuration Events
- User and Session Activity

- Debug Messages
- Uauth Events
- TCP/UDP Request Handling

- ACL log
- Authentication/Authorization Events
- Firewall Startup
- TCP/UDP Connection Build/Teardown
- Xlate Activity
- Tunnel Activity
- DHCP Activity
- Fixup Activity

Section 10-2

NOTE By default, logging to a Syslog server uses UDP port 514. You can also select TCP along with a specific port number for reliable logging. Sending logging messages via SNMP traps uses UDP port 162. UDP is usually used as an efficient, "best-effort" method. TCP can be used when Syslog collection is a vital part of enterprise security, because its delivery is reliable.

The six-digit message numbers are arbitrarily defined by Cisco and uniquely identify each logging message. You can look up message numbers and their meanings in Appendix B, "Security Appliance Logging Messages."

Syslog Server Suggestions

To make full use of the logging messages generated by a firewall, you need a Syslog server application running somewhere in your network. Some recommendations for Syslog servers are as follows:

- **Kiwi Syslog Daemon**—A commercial Syslog server for Windows-based platforms, available at http://www.kiwisyslog.com

Figure 10-2 *Firewall Logging Message Format*

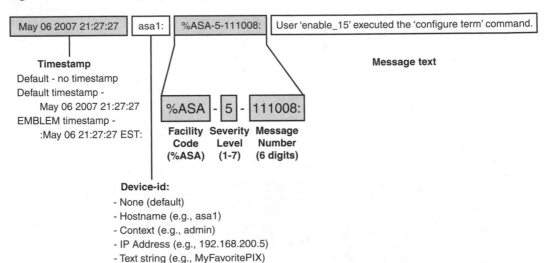

- **UNIX syslogd**—A Syslog daemon built into most versions of the UNIX operating system
- **Cisco PIX Firewall Syslog Server (PFSS)**—A Syslog server available in the Cisco.com Software Center under PIX Firewall Software
- **CiscoWorks 2000**—A Syslog server built into the RME module of the base CiscoWorks 2000 package
- **CiscoWorks VPN/Security Management Solution (VMS)**—A Syslog server available as a part of the Monitoring Center for Security component of VMS
- **Syslog server**—Available as a part of the Network Security Analyzer and FirewallAnalyzer products from eIQnetworks at http://www.eiqnetworks.com
- **Sawmill**—A Syslog server and analysis application that runs on a wide variety of platforms, available from FlowerFire at http://www.sawmill.net

If you have a large network with firewalls that generate a large amount of Syslog information, an average Syslog server software application might become overwhelmed with the load. The end result is that logging messages are lost or that the Syslog server runs out of storage space.

In this case, you should consider moving the Syslog resources to a hardware platform. Some examples of hardware appliances are as follows:

- **Cisco CS-MARS**—Appliances that offer Syslog collection and analysis, along with many other security analysis and mitigation features, at a high volume. Available from Cisco Systems at http://www.cisco.com/en/US/products/ps6241/index.html.
- **LogLogic**—Appliances that offer real-time Syslog collection and analysis in a high volume environment. Available from LogLogic at http://www.loglogic.com.

- **Network Intelligence Engine**—Appliances that collect, analyze, and manage Syslog messages at a high volume. Available from Network Intelligence Corporation at http://www.network-intelligence.com.

Logging Configuration

A firewall can be configured to send logging information to one or more destinations. In PIX 6.3 and FWSM 2.2, each destination can have only one severity level associated with it, so only messages at or below that severity level are actually sent.

This tends to limit any customization if you need to filter or collect only specific types of information at a destination. For example, if you set a Syslog server destination to collect messages at or below the "notifications" level, you cannot collect any useful information from messages that have a default severity of "informational."

To get around this, you can adjust the default severity level of individual logging message IDs. Suppose your destination is configured to collect at level "notifications." There might be some useful messages that have a default level of "informational" or "debugging" that would not be sent to that destination because their default severity levels are greater than that of the destination. You can change those message IDs to have a new severity level of "notifications" so that they are sent too.

Firewall releases beginning with ASA 7.0 and FWSM 3.1(1) include more flexible logging functionality. As before, each logging destination can have one overall severity threshold. If any message is generated, it is sent only if its severity level is at or below this threshold.

However, logging destinations can have a severity threshold that is dependent on several conditions. Think of this as defining a *logging policy* for a destination, where you can pick and choose messages to be collected based on certain criteria. For each destination, you can assign *one* of the following:

- An overall severity level threshold
- A logging policy, defined as a "logging list"

The logging list is made up of one or more policy statements. When a logging message is generated, it is sent if any policy statement is matched. A logging list can be made up of any of the following:

- A severity level threshold for specific classes of messages
- An overall severity level threshold
- Specific logging message IDs to match against

In addition, you can configure messages from a predefined class of messages to appear at one or more destinations at configurable severity levels. Any message within the logging class is sent to a destination if it is at or below the severity level threshold configured for that destination.

You can use the following predefined classes of logging messages:

- **auth**—User authentication messages
- **bridge**—Transparent firewall messages

- **ca**—PKI certificate authority messages
- **citrix**—Citrix client messages
- **config**—Firewall configuration and EXEC commands via the command-line interface (CLI)
- **csd**—Cisco Secure Desktop messages
- **dap**—Dynamic Access Policy messages
- **eap**—EAP for Network Admission Control messages
- **eapoudp**—EAP over UDP for Network Admission Control messages
- **eigrp**—EIGRP routing protocol messages
- **email**—E-mail proxy messages
- **ha**—Failover messages
- **ids**—Intrusion Detection System messages
- **ip**—TCP/IP inspection messages
- **nac**—Network Admission Control messages
- **nacpolicy**—NAC policy messages
- **nacsettings**—NAC policy settings messages
- **np**—Network processor messages
- **ospf**—OSPF routing messages
- **rip**—RIP routing messages
- **rm**—Firewall Resource Manager messages
- **session**—Firewall user session messages
- **snmp**—SNMP messages
- **ssl**—SSL stack messages
- **svc**—SSL VPN client messages
- **sys**—System messages
- **vm**—VLAN mapping messages
- **vpdn**—PPTP and L2TP session messages
- **vpn**—IKE and IPSec messages
- **vpnc**—VPN client messages
- **vpnfo**—VPN failover messages
- **vpnlb**—VPN load-balancing messages
- **webfo**—WebVPN failover messages
- **webvpn**—WebVPN client messages

Logging policies and logging class definitions are configured in Steps 2 and 3, respectively.

Configuring Basic Logging Parameters

Before you configure a firewall to send logging messages to specific destinations, you should configure some basic logging parameters. Use the following configuration steps to prepare the firewall:

1. Enable message logging:

ASA, FWSM	`Firewall(config)# logging enable`
PIX 6.3	`Firewall(config)# logging on`

By default, logging is globally disabled, even if it is configured for one or more destinations. To begin logging, you must use this command.

2. (Optional) Limit the rate at which logging messages are generated:

ASA, FWSM	`Firewall(config)# logging rate-limit {unlimited I number [interval]}` `{level level I message message_id}`
PIX 6.3	—

You can rate-limit messages being generated at a specific severity level by using the level keyword, where *level* is **emergencies (0)**, **alerts (1)**, **critical (2)**, **errors (3)**, **warnings (4)**, **notifications (5)**, **informational (6)**, or **debugging (7)**. Note that this affects messages only at the severity level specified. Messages at lower or higher levels are not rate-limited.

You can also rate-limit specific messages being generated with the **message** keyword, where *message_id* is a six-digit number (as defined in Appendix B).

Logging messages meeting these criteria are sent at a maximum of *number* (0 to 2147483647, where 0 is unlimited) messages per *interval* (0 to 2147483647) seconds. The interval defaults to 1 second if not specified. By default, rate limiting is unlimited on all platforms.

For example, the following commands limit all debugging (severity level 7) messages so that up to 50 message per second are generated. In addition, message ID 106015 (deny TCP/no connection) is limited to 10 messages per second.

```
Firewall(config)# logging rate-limit 50 1 level debugging
Firewall(config)# logging rate-limit 10 1 message 106015
```

NOTE   Rate limiting is applied to a severity level or message ID. It is not applied to a destination. Therefore, rate limiting affects the volume of messages being sent to *all* configured destinations.

---

3. Define a logging policy with an event list.

The event list is defined by its name and can consist of one or more **logging list** commands. Logging messages are matched against the event list as they are generated. If a match is found, the message is allowed to be sent.

Logging lists can be configured with the commands shown in this step. A logging list policy is actually applied when the severity level is configured for a specific logging destination in Steps 4 through 9 in this list.

TIP If a logging list has been configured and applied to a destination, it cannot be modified until it is removed or unbound from the destination. You can unbind a logging list by reissuing the **logging** *destination level* command, omitting the logging list name.

---

a. (Optional) Match against a severity level:

ASA, FWSM	Firewall(config)# **logging list** *event_list* **level** *level* [**class** *event_class*]
PIX 6.3	—

The event list named *event_list* matches any Syslog message at or below one of the following severity *level* keywords or numbers: **emergencies (0)**, **alerts (1)**, **critical (2)**, **errors (3)**, **warnings (4)**, **notifications (5)**, **informational (6)**, or **debugging (7)**.

You can also narrow the matching criteria by using a predefined "class" of Syslog message types. Use the **class** keyword with one of the following *event_class* names: **auth**, **bridge**, **ca**, **config**, **ha**, **ids**, **ip**, **np**, **ospf**, **rip**, **rm**, **session**, **snmp**, **sys**, **vpdn**, **vpn**, **vpnc**, **vpnfo**, **vpnlb**, or **webvpn**.

For example, the following commands can be used to match all logging messages at the notifications level and all IP-related messages (xlate and conn build/teardown and ACL activity) at the debugging level. Now the destination can collect various types of messages from multiple severity levels.

```
Firewall(config)# logging list MyList level notifications
Firewall(config)# logging list MyList level debugging class ip
```

b. (Optional) Match specific Syslog message IDs:

ASA, FWSM	Firewall(config)# **logging list** *event_list* **message** *start*[*-end*]
PIX 6.3	—

The event list named *event_list* matches any of the Syslog messages defined by the ID range *start* to *end* (100000 to 999999). If no *end* value is given, *start* defines a single message ID.

For example, suppose the logging list **xlate-log** is used to log messages related to address translation. Message 202001 (**out of translation slots**) and messages 305009 through 305011 (**translations built and torn down**) can be used to collect an audit trail of dynamic xlate entries (using the following commands) so that inside users can be associated with PAT addresses at any given time:

```
Firewall(config)# logging list xlate-log message 202001
Firewall(config)# logging list xlate-log message 305009-305011
```

4. (ASA and FWSM) Define destinations for a logging class of messages:

ASA, FWSM	Firewall(config)# **logging class** *event_class destination level* [*destination level*] [*destination level*] ...
PIX 6.3	—

You can configure a predefined class of logging messages to be sent to one or more logging destinations, each having a unique severity threshold. The class is identified by one of the following *event_class* names: **auth**, **bridge**, **ca**, **citrix**, **config**, **csd**, **dap**, **eap**, **eapoudp**, **eigrp**, **email**, **ha**, **ids**, **ip**, **nac**, **nacpolicy**, **nacsettings**, **np**, **ospf**, **rip**, **rm**, **session**, **snmp**, **ssl**, **svc**, **sys**, **vm**, **vpdn**, **vpn**, **vpnc**, **vpnfo**, **vpnlb**, **webfo**, or **webvpn**.

You can define one or more destinations and severity threshold pairs for the class using a single command line. Each *destination* must be one of the following keywords: **console** (firewall console), **monitor** (Telnet or SSH session), **buffered** (memory buffer), **trap** (Syslog servers), **history** (SNMP traps), **mail** (SMTP), **pdm** (PDM application for PIX 6.3), or **asdm** (ASDM application for ASA or FWSM). The destination will be configured in subsequent sections in this chapter.

Each severity *level* must be one of the following keywords or numbers: **emergencies (0)**, **alerts (1)**, **critical (2)**, **errors (3)**, **warnings (4)**, **notifications (5)**, **informational (6)**, or **debugging (7)**.

For example, in the following command, high-availability messages of severity 1 (alerts) are sent to the trap destination, and severity 7 (debugging) messages are sent to the logging buffer:

```
Firewall(config)# logging class ha trap alerts buffered debugging
```

Log to an Interactive Firewall Session

To view logging messages when you open console, SSH, and Telnet sessions to the firewall itself, use the following configuration steps.

1. (Optional) Log to the firewall console:

ASA, FWSM	Firewall(config)# **logging console** {*level* | *event-list*}
PIX 6.3	Firewall(config)# **logging console** *level*

If you have a terminal emulator connected to the firewall console, you might want to see logging messages as they are generated. Messages are displayed if they are at or below the specified severity *level*: **emergencies (0)**, **alerts (1)**, **critical (2)**, **errors (3)**, **warnings (4)**, **notifications (5)**, **informational (6)**, or **debugging (7)**.

On an ASA or FWSM, you can also use a policy to select which messages are displayed. Messages that are matched by the event list named *event-list* (defined in Step 2) are forwarded to the logging destination. Keep in mind that multiple-context mode still has only one physical console port. Therefore, it does not make sense to enable console logging for a user context, because those contexts do not have a usable console.

CAUTION   You should send logging messages to the serial console only if the firewall is lightly loaded or in a test environment. Messages are displayed at a relatively low speed (9600 baud); if many messages are generated, the backlog of messages can cause the firewall to have slow response. As well, you lose interactive control at the console while the messages are being displayed.

For these reasons, console logging is disabled by default.

2. (Optional) Log to Telnet or SSH sessions on the firewall:

ASA, FWSM	Firewall(config)# **logging monitor** {*level*	*event-list*}
PIX 6.3	Firewall(config)# **logging monitor** *level*

If you have a remote firewall Telnet or SSH session open, you might want to see logging messages as they are generated. Messages are displayed if they are at or below the specified severity *level*: **emergencies (0)**, **alerts (1)**, **critical (2)**, **errors (3)**, **warnings (4)**, **notifications (5)**, **informational (6)**, or **debugging (7)**.

To see the logging messages in the current session as they are generated, use the **terminal monitor** EXEC command. (In PIX 6.3, you must be in configuration mode to use this command. In addition, the most recently initiated Telnet session receives the session logging output by default, because **terminal monitor** mode is active until it is disabled.) To stop seeing the messages, use the EXEC command **terminal no monitor**.

With an ASA or FWSM, you can also use a policy to select which messages are displayed. Messages that are matched by the event list named *event-list* (defined in Step 2 of the "Configuring Basic Logging Parameters" section) are forwarded to the logging destination.

CAUTION   You should avoid sending logging messages to Telnet and SSH sessions on a highly utilized production firewall. Although logging messages can be sent to interactive sessions more efficiently than the firewall console, the firewall can still become backlogged with messages to send. Therefore, monitor (session) logging is disabled by default.

Log to the Firewall's Internal Buffer

Internal buffered logging uses a 4096-byte circular memory buffer to store the most recent messages. The actual number of logging messages stored depends on the length of each message. For example, one full buffer might contain only 32 messages if those lines of message text are very long.

The logging buffer can be handy if you do not have access to a Syslog server or if the Syslog server is unavailable. The logging buffer is the most efficient way to collect some messages for troubleshooting or to inspect specific activity without having to sift through massive Syslog server logs. You might want to see only certain types of messages that are being generated, even though a wide variety of logging messages are being sent to a Syslog server.

In addition, the logging buffer is much more efficient than sending logging output to the firewall console or a Telnet or SSH session. Think of the logging buffer as a small collector for occasional use.

1. Set the buffer logging level:

ASA, FWSM	Firewall(config)# **logging buffered** {*level*	*event-list*}
PIX 6.3	Firewall(config)# **logging buffered** *level*

The firewall keeps a circular buffer in memory that can hold the most recent logging messages. Messages are sent to the buffer if they are at or below the specified severity *level*: **emergencies (0)**, **alerts (1)**, **critical (2)**, **errors (3)**, **warnings (4)**, **notifications (5)**, **informational (6)**, or **debugging (7)**.

Beginning in ASA 7.0 and FWSM 3.1(1), you can also use a policy to select which messages are displayed. Messages that are matched by the event list named *event_list* (defined in Step 3 of the "Configuring Basic Logging Parameters" section) are forwarded to the logging destination.

By default, the buffer is 4096 bytes long and can hold about 100 messages. You can adjust the size of the buffer if needed. You can use the **logging buffer-size** *bytes* command to size the buffer to 4096 to 1048576 bytes.

To see the buffered messages, use the EXEC command **show logging**. Remember that the buffer is circular, so it never overflows and never needs clearing. However, you can clear the buffer with the **clear logging buffer** command if you need to see only the most recent messages collected after a certain point.

2. (Optional) Copy the buffer via FTP if it fills and wraps:

ASA, FWSM	Firewall(config)# **logging ftp-bufferwrap** Firewall(config)# **logging ftp-server** *ftp_server path username password*
PIX 6.3	—

When the circular logging buffer is full (is getting ready to wrap around itself), the firewall can copy a snapshot of it to an FTP server at IP address *ftp_server*. The firewall connects to the server using *username* and *password*.

The buffer contents are uploaded as a file stored at the path name *path*. The path name is relative to the username's directory on the server. For example, to save the log file into user hucaby's home directory, you can use the "." current directory path name. The firewall automatically names the log file in the form LOG-*YYYY-MM-DD-HHMMSS*.TXT (where *YYYY-MM-DD* represents the date and *HHMMSS* represents the time). The log file is always the total size of the logging buffer (4096 bytes by default).

For example, you could use the following commands to force the logging buffer contents to be uploaded to an FTP server into the home directory of user pixadmin:

```
Firewall(config)# logging ftp-bufferwrap
Firewall(config)# logging ftp-server 192.168.199.10 pixadmin  bigsecretpw
```

TIP   If you experience problems getting the firewall to successfully upload log files to the FTP server, you might see the following error messages:

```
Firewall/admin# ERROR: ftp write to server 192.168.3.14 failed:
%ASA-3-414001: Failed to save logging buffer to FTP server 192.168.3.14
  using filename LOG-2007-05-06-010113.TXT on interface inside:
```

You can use the **debug ftp client** command to see debugging output as the firewall attempts to upload its log files. Make sure you have a logging destination configured for the debugging severity, as well as for the debug-trace output.

From this information, you should be able to see where the process fails. Consider the following example, in which the firewall successfully logs into the FTP server but the server rejects the log file path name because it is not relative to the user's directory:

```
Firewall# debug ftp client
[time passes until buffer wraps]
%ASA-7-711001: Writing /pix-log-snapshot/LOG-2007-05-06-010703.TXT
%ASA-7-711001: FTP: 220 pi FTP server ready.
%ASA-7-711001: FTP: ---> USER pixadmin
%ASA-7-711001: FTP: 331 Password required for pixadmin.
%ASA-7-711001: FTP: ---> PASS *
%ASA-7-711001: FTP: 230 User pixadmin logged in.
%ASA-7-711001: FTP: ---> TYPE I
%ASA-7-711001: FTP: 200 Type set to I.
%ASA-7-711001: FTP: ---> PORT 192,168,93,135,4,100
%ASA-7-711001: FTP: 200 PORT command successful.
%ASA-7-711001: FTP: ---> STOR /pix-log-snapshot/LOG-2007-05-06-010703.TXT
%ASA-7-711001: FTP: 553 /pix-log-snapshot/LOG-2007-05-06-010703.TXT: No
  such file or directory.
%ASA-7-711001: FTP: ---> QUIT
%ASA-3-414001: Failed to save logging buffer to FTP server 192.168.3.14
  using filename LOG-2007-05-06-010703.TXT on interface inside:
%ASA-7-711001: FTP: 221 Goodbye.
```

---

3. (Optional) Copy the buffer to Flash if it fills and wraps:

ASA, FWSM	`Firewall(config)# logging flash-bufferwrap`
	`Firewall(config)# logging flash-minimum-free kbytes_free`
	`Firewall(config)# logging flash-maximum-allocation kbytes_max`

PIX 6.3	—

When the circular logging buffer gets ready to wrap, the firewall can copy a snapshot of it into a file on the Flash file system. The firewall automatically names the log file in the Syslog Flash directory using a filename of the form LOG-*YYYY-MM-DD-HHMMSS*.TXT (where *YYYY-MM-DD* represents the date and *HHMMSS* represents the time). The log file is always the total size of the logging buffer (4096 bytes by default).

As more log files are saved, more space in the Flash file system is used up. With the **flash-maximum-allocation** keyword, you can limit the total space reserved for log files to *kbytes_max* (4 to 15750 KB). The **flash-minimum-free** keyword specifies how much Flash memory must be free before log files can be saved, as *kbytes_free* (0 to 15750 KB).

TIP   Flash-related logging buffer commands are available only in ASA and FWSM platforms running in single-context mode. If multiple contexts are being used, only the system execution space has access to the Flash file system. However, its logging capability is very limited because most of the firewall activity occurs in other contexts.

In single-context mode, you can manually save the current buffer contents into Flash by using the following command in privileged EXEC mode:

`Firewall# logging savelog [savefile]`

The log file is saved in the Syslog directory of the Flash file system. You can specify a filename *savefile* for it. Otherwise, the default filename template LOG-*YYYY-MM-DD-HHMMSS*.TXT is used (where *YYYY-MM-DD* represents the current date and *HHMMSS* represents the current time).

Log to an SNMP Management Station

You can use the following configuration steps to send firewall logging messages to an SNMP network management station. Messages are sent as SNMP traps.

1. Configure a destination for SNMP traps:

ASA, FWSM	`Firewall(config)# snmp-server host [if_name] ip_addr trap` `[community string] [version version] [udp-port port]`
PIX 6.3	`Firewall(config)# snmp-server host [if_name] ip_addr trap`

The SNMP management station is located on the firewall interface named *if_name* (**inside**, for example) at IP address *ip_addr*.

Section 10-2

2. Enable traps to be sent by SNMP:

ASA, FWSM	Firewall(config)# **snmp-server enable traps {all	syslog}**
PIX 6.3	Firewall(config)# **snmp-server enable traps**

By default, all trap types are sent. ASA and FWSM allow specific types of traps to be sent, as described in Chapter 4, "Firewall Management," in Section "4-7: Monitoring a Firewall with SNMP." Only the **all** and **syslog** trap types are shown here, because either is sufficient for the purpose of sending Syslog messages as SNMP traps.

3. Enable traps containing logging messages to be sent:

ASA, FWSM	Firewall(config)# **logging history {*level*	*event-list*}**
PIX 6.3	Firewall(config)# **logging history** *level*

Logging messages can be sent as SNMP traps to any configured SNMP management station. Messages are sent if they are at or below the specified severity *level*: **emergencies (0)**, **alerts (1)**, **critical (2)**, **errors (3)**, **warnings (4)**, **notifications (5)**, **informational (6)**, or **debugging (7)**. Each message is sent in a separate SNMP trap packet.

With ASA or FWSM, you can also use a policy to select which messages are displayed. Messages that are matched by the *event list* named event-list (defined in Step 2 of the "Configuring Basic Logging Parameters" section) are forwarded to the logging destination.

Logging to a Syslog Server

Use the following configuration steps to send firewall logging messages to one or more Syslog servers.

1. Set the logging level:

ASA, FWSM	Firewall(config)# **logging trap {*level*	*event-list*}**
PIX 6.3	Firewall(config)# **logging trap** *level*

Messages are sent to any configured Syslog servers if they are at or below the specified severity *level*: **emergencies (0)**, **alerts (1)**, **critical (2)**, **errors (3)**, **warnings (4)**, **notifications (5)**, **informational (6)**, or **debugging (7)**.

With ASA and FWSM, you can also use a policy to select which messages are displayed. Messages that are matched by the event list named *event-list* (defined in Step 3 of the "Configuring Basic Logging Parameters" section) are forwarded to the logging destination.

NOTE   You might find it confusing that logging messages sent as SNMP traps are configured using **logging history** and messages sent as Syslog packets are configured using **logging trap**. Unfortunately, the term "trap" has a different meaning here.

---

2. (Optional) Identify the firewall in Syslog messages:

ASA, FWSM	Firewall(config)# **logging device-id** {**context-name** | **hostname** | **ipaddress** *if_name* | **string** *text*}
PIX 6.3	Firewall(config)# **logging device-id** {**hostname** | **ipaddress** *if_name* | **string** *text*}

A Syslog server usually records the originating IP address along with each message received. However, you can define one unique identifier for your firewall that also appears in the text of each Syslog message. (This identifier does not appear in EMBLEM formatted messages.)

The identifier can be the firewall's host name (defined with the **hostname** configuration command), the IP address of a specific firewall interface named *if_name* ("inside" or "outside," for example), or an arbitrary *text* string (up to 16 characters). With an ASA or FWSM operating in multiple-context mode, the name of the firewall context can also be sent.

For example, the following firewall is named InnerSanctum. It identifies itself using its host name:

```
Firewall(config)# hostname InnerSanctum
Firewall(config)# logging device-id hostname
```

3. Identify a Syslog server destination:

ASA, FWSM	Firewall(config)# **logging host** *if_name ip_address* [*protocol/port*] [**format emblem**]
PIX 6.3	Firewall(config)# **logging host** *if_name ip_address* [*protocol/port*] [**format emblem**]

Syslog messages are sent out the firewall interface named *if_name* ("inside" or "outside," for example) to the Syslog server located at IP address *ip_address*.

By default, messages are sent using UDP port 514. You can use the *protocol* field to specify either **udp** or **tcp** (or as a protocol number, **17** or **6**, respectively). Define the port number to use with the *port* field, a number from 1025 to 65535. Because TCP Syslog does not use a standard port, you always have to specify one.

Obviously, the Syslog server must be configured to listen on the matching protocol and port number.

You can use the **format emblem** keywords to send logging messages in the EMBLEM format.

The firewall in the following example sends its trap logging messages to the Syslog server using the default UDP port 514:

```
Firewall(config)# logging host inside 192.168.199.70
```

This command can be repeated to define multiple Syslog servers.

NOTE   Keep in mind that the firewall sends a copy of each Syslog message generated to *each* of the configured Syslog servers. If your firewall is heavily utilized and is configured to generate high-severity messages to multiple Syslog servers, its performance can be affected.

Normally, Syslog messages are sent using UDP port 514. This provides an easy way to send messages in a best-effort fashion. The firewall has no idea if the messages are being received by the Syslog server, much less if there is actually a Syslog server at the address.

Some environments require strict collection of security information. In this case, you should use TCP to send Syslog messages, usually over port 1470.

The firewall opens and maintains a TCP connection with the Syslog server. As long as this connection stays open, the firewall can be certain that the messages are being reliably received.

In fact, the TCP Syslog method is designed to be so reliable that the firewall's operation becomes dependent upon the TCP Syslog connection. The TCP connection closes only if the Syslog server becomes unavailable or if its logging storage space becomes full.

By default, if the TCP connection closes for any reason, the firewall immediately stops forwarding all traffic through itself. You can realize that this has happened in several ways:

— Traffic is no longer passing through the firewall, and users are calling to complain.

— The firewall generates a "201008: The PIX is disallowing new connections" logging message. (Naturally, if the Syslog server connection is broken, you will not be able to see this message on the Syslog server. Instead, you might find it in the logging buffer on the firewall with the **show logging** command.)

— The **show logging setting** command shows the Syslog server as "disabled," as in the following example.

```
Firewall# show logging setting
Syslog logging: enabled
    Facility: 20
    Timestamp logging: enabled
    Standby logging: disabled
    Console logging: disabled
    Monitor logging: disabled
    Buffer logging: level informational, 716 messages logged
    Trap logging: level informational, 162 messages logged
        Logging to inside 172.21.4.1 tcp/1470 disabled
    History logging: disabled
    Device ID: hostname "Firewall"
```

If this condition occurs, check the Syslog server and determine the source of the problem. Even after the Syslog service is restored, the firewall will still show the server as disabled. To re-

enable it, you have to reconfigure the TCP Syslog connection manually by re-entering the
logging host *if_name ip_address* **tcp**/*port* configuration command.

TIP   With ASA and FWSM, you can use the following command to allow traffic to pass and
firewall operation to continue, even if a TCP Syslog server is down:

```
Firewall(config)# logging permit-hostdown
```

---

4. (Optional) Tune the Syslog transmission queue.

    As Syslog messages are generated, they are placed in a queue for transmission. If messages are
    being generated faster than they can be sent, the logging queue begins to fill. By default, a
    firewall queues up to 512 messages. As soon as this threshold is reached, any new messages are
    simply dropped and are not sent.

    You can see information about the logging queue with the following EXEC command:

    ```
    Firewall# show logging queue
    ```

    The output from this command displays the size of the queue, along with the current queue
    depth and the high-water mark. If the **msgs most on queue** value is 512, the queue filled up at
    some point, and messages have been lost. In the following example, a high volume of logging
    messages is being generated, but they are being transmitted fast enough that the queue has never
    filled.

    ```
    Firewall# show logging queue
            Logging Queue length limit : 512 msg(s)
            Current 0 msg on queue, 136 msgs most on queue
    Firewall#
    ```

    If you find that the logging queue is consistently full ("512 msgs most on queue"), you can tune
    the queue's size. Use the following configuration command:

    ```
    Firewall(config)# logging queue queue_size
    ```

    The queue holds *queue_size* messages (0 to 8192; 0 = unlimited up to available memory). You
    can use the **show blocks** EXEC command to see how much memory is available before tuning
    the queue. Syslog messages use 256-byte blocks of memory. Be careful not to allocate too much
    of this memory to the logging queue, because the 256-byte blocks are also used for stateful
    failover message queuing.

5. (Optional) Add time stamps to Syslog messages:

    ```
    Firewall(config)# logging timestamp
    ```

    By default, Syslog messages are sent with no indication of the date or time at which they occurred.
    In this case, the Syslog server should add its own time stamps to the messages as they are received.
    Make sure the Syslog server synchronizes its clock with a known and accurate source.

The **logging timestamp** command causes the firewall to add a time stamp to each Syslog message before it is sent. The firewall should have its clock set and time synchronized to a known and accurate source—preferably an NTP server that is common to all devices on your network.

TIP   If the **logging timestamp** command is used to make the firewall add time stamps, it is also possible that the Syslog server is configured to add its own time stamps. This can result in logging messages that have double time stamps in the text. Many Syslog servers can be configured to detect this and strip the extra time stamp automatically.

---

6. (Optional) Set the Syslog facility:

   `Firewall(config)# logging facility facility`

   Syslog servers can collect logging messages from a variety of sources. Messages are marked with a *facility* number (0 to 23), allowing the Syslog server to classify and store messages from similar sources.

   Facility numbers correspond to the UNIX-based Syslog facility names as follows: 0 (Kern), 1 (User), 2 (Mail), 3 (Daemon), 4 (Auth), 5 (Syslog), 6 (Lpr), 7 (News), 8 (UUCP), 9 (Cron), 10 to 15 (System0 to System5), 16 to 23 (Local0 to Local7).

   The default facility, 20, is also known as the Local4 facility. This is usually expected by most Syslog server implementations.

7. (Optional) Generate Syslog messages from the standby failover unit:

   `Firewall(config)# logging standby`

   Normally, only the active firewall unit in an active/passive failover pair generates Syslog messages. If your environment needs strict collection of logging information, you can use this command to cause the standby firewall to generate Syslog messages too.

   The standby firewall can generate the same Syslog messages as the active unit only because the same state information is passed from the active unit to the passive unit. This doubles the number of messages sent to the Syslog server(s), and each message is duplicated. However, if the active unit fails, any messages that were queued might be lost. The standby unit continues sending those messages as if nothing happened.

Logging to a Secure Syslog Server Using SSL

By using a TCP connection to a Syslog server, logging messages can be sent and collected reliably. However, the logging information is sent in cleartext. If someone can intercept the Syslog packets, they can easily examine the logging messages to learn sensitive information such as usernames that have authenticated, collections that are permitted or blocked by the firewall, and so on. The more information an unauthorized user can gather about the secure part of your network, the easier it is for them to find ways to exploit that information.

If your Syslog server is located on a protected network, then the stream of logging messages stays within the boundary of your firewall. Ideally, a Syslog server should be located on a private management network, so that the firewall can strictly limit access to the server and the data being sent to it.

However, this is not always possible or practical. Beginning with ASA 8.0, you can configure the firewall to send its logging messages through a Secure Socket Layer (SSL) tunnel to a Syslog server. The SSL tunnel takes care of encrypting the logging messages and maintaining their integrity until they reach the Syslog server. Now you can locate the Syslog server anywhere on the network without worrying about sensitive logging information being exposed.

Most Syslog servers can collect logging messages over normal UDP and TCP connections, but they do not have the capability to use an SSL tunnel. Fortunately, you can add a "shim" or an additional piece of software that sits between the SSL tunnel and the Syslog server, passing data between the two. You can use any SSL tunneling software, such as the following free open source packages:

- **Stunnel**—Universal SSL Wrapper at http://www.stunnel.org, as source code and Windows binaries

- **OpenSSL**—The OpenSSL Project at http://www.openssl.org, as source code only. You can find precompiled Windows binaries at the Win32 OpenSSL Installation Project, http://www.slproweb.com/products/Win32OpenSSL.html

Figure 10-3 shows how the secure Syslog configuration works. The firewall is configured to send logging information to a secure Syslog server destination over a TCP port that you define. In the figure, secure Syslog is using TCP port 60514.

Figure 10-3 *Communication Between a Firewall and a Secure Syslog Server*

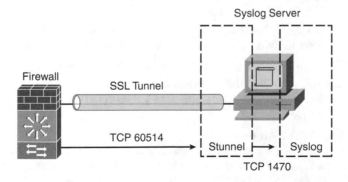

On the Syslog server, the SSL software is installed and configured to receive SSL traffic over the same TCP port that the firewall is using (TCP 60514, for example). The software unencrypts the TCP Syslog packets from the SSL tunnel and relays them to the Syslog application's TCP port (TCP 1470).

As with a regular TCP Syslog connection, the firewall monitors the status of the Syslog server by the TCP connection status. If the connection goes down, the firewall tries to bring it back up five times.

If it still is not successful, the firewall marks the Syslog server as being disabled. You can re-enable the server only by manually re-entering it into the firewall configuration.

Use the following steps to add SSL capability to your Syslog server and to configure the firewall for secure Syslog operation.

1. Install and configure the SSL tunnel software.

   a. Edit the SSL software configuration file.

      After the SSL software package is installed, you should find a configuration file in the installation directory. For example, the Stunnel package uses a file called *stunnel.conf*. On a Windows platform, you can find the file in C:\Program Files\stunnel\stunnel.conf. Add the following lines to define the secure Syslog SSL tunnel:

```
[ssyslog]
accept = 60514
connect = 1470
```

      Here, the "accept" port is the TCP port used for the SSL tunnel (60514, for example), and "connect" is the TCP port used by the Syslog software (1470). Make sure you do not begin the lines with a semicolon; otherwise, they are ignored as comment lines.

      Save the configuration file into its original location and name.

   b. Obtain an SSL certificate for the SSL software.

      The SSL software acts as an SSL server, whereas the firewall acts as an SSL client. Therefore, the server must have a valid SSL certificate from a trusted certificate authority before the firewall can bring up an SSL connection to it. The Stunnel package comes with a default certificate in the *stunnel.pem* file, but it should never be used in a production environment. The same certificate is given out to everyone who downloads and installs the package. Anyone who has the package can use the private key found in the *stunnel.pem* file and can potentially intercept your "secure" Syslog traffic.

      Instead, you should request a new SSL certificate from a trusted source. The certificate contents can be pasted into the *stunnel.pem* file, replacing the old certificate. Be sure to include the surrounding "-----BEGIN/END CERTIFICATE-----" lines, as shown in the following example:

```
-----BEGIN CERTIFICATE-----
MIIClTCCAf6gAwIBAgIJANtC9yI81EYQMA0GCSqGSIb3DQEBBAUAMIGAMQswCQYD
VQQGEwJVUzERMA8GA1UECBMIS2VudHVja3kxEjAQBgNVBAcTCUxleGluZ3RvbjET
MBEGA1UEChMKTXkgQ29tcGFueTEZMBcGA1UECxMQVGVzdCBFbmdpbmVlcmluZzEa
MBgGA1UEAxMRd3d3Lm15Y29tcGFueS5jb20wHhcNMDcwMzIwMDM0OTU2WhcNMDgw
MzE5MDM0OTU2WjCBgDELMAkGA1UEBhMCVVMxETAPBgNVBAgTCEtlbnR1Y2t5MRIw
EAYDVQQHEwlMZXhpbmd0b24xEzARBgNVBAoTCk15IENvbXBhbnkxGTAXBgNVBAsT
EFRlc3QgRW5naW5lZXJpbmcxGjAYBgNVBAMTEXd3dy5teWNvbXBhbnkuY29tMIGf
MA0GCSqGSIb3DQEBAQUAA4GNADCBiQKBgQDo2eenyqOXltzK/XvV99lrQUHt42SC
afE+uRDIG9nbpGw/3UjPxhKAhM4JCgb6FqtLXAqS0LNTVf4W5u2dJo0WM2rQS12P
```

```
bIm4yYlftU8prCTTvxYYuWD+ceZqwc0pSWk//BDOKjOHWBSyfp4aW/uoELcGtUEB
uoV83CwLPBehDQIDAQABoxUwEzARBglghkgBhvhCAQEEBAMCBkAwDQYJKoZIhvcN
AQEEBQADgYEArUYe/jVl/n0iwVdZNhfl6DySYvpa6u4x/Gn86TsWzPTJ8waR0Y+n
fIKb9in1Et8DdFRBOKejhCnGflw857HHFvXFqI5KBAzFyZ28FeGnnt7SP3Wlwfo5
QCNkvzEc/iB4EFKBZ7y0OQsz7xodty4ptRS4icwMA+kiAJUMmk7NhyM=
-----END CERTIFICATE-----
```

c. Start the SSL software.

The SSL software can run as a service so that it is always available to incoming tunnel requests. On a Windows platform, the software can also run as a regular application that you start manually.

2. Configure secure logging on the firewall.

By default, the firewall does not know about any trusted certificate authorities. This means it will not be able to validate the SSL certificate it receives from the Syslog server's SSL software. You have to manually configure a certificate authority (CA) trustpoint and its self-signed certificate with the following steps:

a. Define a CA trustpoint:

```
Firewall(config)# crypto ca trustpoint name
```

A trustpoint is simply a definition of the CA that the firewall should trust as it validates certificates from SSL servers. The *name* is arbitrary.

b. Use manual CA enrollment:

```
Firewall(config-ca-trustpoint)# enrollment terminal
Firewall(config-ca-trustpoint)# exit
```

Although the firewall can enroll with a CA automatically through an enrollment protocol, you need to enter the CA certificate manually. Here, the **terminal** keyword denotes the use of a terminal session (Telnet or SSH) with the firewall.

c. Import the SSL software's certificate:

```
Firewall(config)# crypto ca authenticate name
```

The firewall authenticates the CA trustpoint named *name* by allowing you to enter the certificate contents interactively. When you are prompted to enter the CA certificate contents, you can paste in the same lines of content you pasted into the SSL software certificate file in Step 1b. Here, the certificate can be pasted with or without the surrounding "-----BEGIN/END CERTIFICATE-----" lines. After pasting the contents into the terminal session, be sure to type the word **quit** as the last line before pressing the **Enter** key.

In the following example, a CA trustpoint named **syslogCA** is defined and its certificate entered:

```
Firewall(config)# crypto ca trustpoint syslogCA
```

```
Firewall(config-ca-trustpoint)# enrollment terminal
Firewall(config-ca-trustpoint)# exit

Firewall(config)#crypto ca authenticate test
Enter the base 64 encoded CA certificate.
End with the word "quit" on a line by itself
-----BEGIN CERTIFICATE-----
MIIClTCCAf6gAwIBAgIJANtC9yI81EYQMA0GCSqGSIb3DQEBBAUAMIGAMQswCQYD
VQQGEwJVUzERMA8GA1UECBMIS2VudHVja3kxEjAQBgNVBAcTCUxleGluZ3RvbjET
MBEGA1UEChMKTXkgQ29tcGFueTEZMBcGA1UECxMQVGVzdCBFbmdpbmVlcmluZzEa
MBgGA1UEAxMRd3d3Lm15Y29tcGFueS5jb20wHhcNMDcwMzIwMDM0OTU2WhcNMDgw
MzE5MDM0OTU2WjCBgDELMAkGA1UEBhMCVVMxETAPBgNVBAgTCEtlbnR1Y2t5MRIw
EAYDVQQHEwlMZXhpbmd0b24xEzARBgNVBAoTCk15IENvbXBhbnkxGTAXBgNVBAsT
EFRlc3QgRW5naW5lZXJpbmcxGjAYBgNVBAMTEXd3dy5teWNvbXBhbnkuY29tMIGf
MA0GCSqGSIb3DQEBAQUAA4GNADCBiQKBgQDo2eenyqOXltzK/XvV99lrQUHt42SC
afE+uRDIG9nbpGw/3UjPxhKAhM4JCgb6FqtLXAqS0LNTVf4W5u2dJo0WM2rQS12P
bIm4yYlftU8prCTTvxYYuWD+ceZqwc0pSWk//BDOKjOHWBSyfp4aW/uoELcGtUEB
uoV83CwLPBehDQIDAQABoxUwEzARBglghkgBhvhCAQEEBAMCBkAwDQYJKoZIhvcN
AQEEBQADgYEArUYe/jVl/n0iwVdZNhfl6DySYvpa6u4x/Gn86TsWzPTJ8waR0Y+n
fIKb9in1Et8DdFRBOKejhCnGflw857HHFvXFqI5KBAzFyZ28FeGnnt7SP3Wlwfo5
QCNkvzEc/iB4EFKBZ7y00Qsz7xodty4ptRS4icwMA+kiAJUMmk7NhyM=
-----END CERTIFICATE-----
quit

INFO: Certificate has the following attributes:
Fingerprint:    4097e286 8f4425db 36ddae78 f750d6d8
Do you accept this certificate? [yes/no]: yes
Trustpoint CA certificate accepted.

% Certificate successfully imported
Firewall(config)#
```

d.   Define the SSL trustpoint:

```
Firewall(config)# ssl trust-point name if_name
```

So, the CA trustpoint named *name* is used as the trusted CA for the firewall's SSL connection. The trustpoint (secure Syslog server) can be found on the firewall interface named *if_name*. For example, if your secure Syslog server is located on the outside interface, you could use the following command:

```
Firewall(config)# ssl trust-point syslogCA outside
```

e.   Configure a secure Syslog server destination:

```
Firewall(config)# logging host if_name ip_address tcp/port secure
```

The firewall begins sending logging messages to the Syslog server located on the firewall interface *if_name* at IP address *ip_address*. Instead of using a normal TCP connection, the **secure** keyword tells the firewall to attempt to bring up an SSL tunnel to the TCP destination port number you specify.

As an example, the Syslog server is located on the outside interface at 172.21.4.37 and uses SSL tunneling software configured for TCP port 60514. To configure this setup, you would enter the following command:

```
Firewall(config)# logging host outside 172.21.4.37 tcp/60514 secure
```

CAUTION   As with a regular TCP Syslog destination, the firewall's default behavior is to stop passing traffic through itself if the TCP connection fails for any reason. You might want to disable this feature while you build and test the secure Syslog server configuration so that you do not interrupt your production firewall traffic inadvertently. You can use the following command to force the firewall to continue forwarding traffic even if the secure Syslog TCP connection fails:

```
Firewall(config)# logging permit-hostdown
```

---

3. Verify the secure Syslog operation.

    You can verify that the SSL connection to the secure Syslog server is operational by using the **show logging setting** command. In the following example, the Syslog server destination is shown to be up and active by the "SECURE" status:

```
Firewall# show logging setting
Syslog logging: enabled
    Facility: 20
    Timestamp logging: enabled
    Standby logging: disabled
    Deny Conn when Queue Full: disabled
    Console logging: disabled
    Monitor logging: level debugging, 93799 messages logged
    Buffer logging: level debugging, 93799 messages logged
    Trap logging: level debugging, facility 20, 93799 messages logged
        Logging to outside 172.21.4.217 tcp/60514 SECURE
    History logging: disabled
    Device ID: disabled
    Mail logging: disabled
    ASDM logging: level informational, 176 messages logged
Firewall#
```

Section 10-2

If the SSL tunnel is not successful, the firewall makes five attempts at bringing the tunnel up before declaring the server to be disabled. In that case, you could see the logging destination status shown as an attempt number or "disabled," as in the following lines from the **show logging setting** command output:

```
Firewall# show logging setting
Syslog logging: enabled
    Facility: 20
    Timestamp logging: enabled
    Standby logging: disabled
    Deny Conn when Queue Full: disabled
    Console logging: disabled
    Monitor logging: level debugging, 10730084 messages logged
    Buffer logging: level debugging, 10730084 messages logged
    Trap logging: level debugging, facility 20, 10730084 messages logged
        Logging to outside 172.21.4.37 tcp/60514 SECURE retry: Attempt 2
    History logging: disabled
    Device ID: disabled
    Mail logging: disabled
    ASDM logging: level informational, 1950 messages logged
Firewall# show logging setting
Syslog logging: enabled
    Facility: 20
    Timestamp logging: enabled
    Standby logging: disabled
    Deny Conn when Queue Full: disabled
    Console logging: disabled
    Monitor logging: level debugging, 10730091 messages logged
    Buffer logging: level debugging, 10730091 messages logged
    Trap logging: level debugging, facility 20, 10730091 messages logged
        Logging to outside 172.21.4.37 tcp/60514 SECURE disabled
    History logging: disabled
    Device ID: disabled
    Mail logging: disabled
    ASDM logging: level informational, 1950 messages logged
Firewall#
```

You can also see evidence of the SSL tunnel process by looking through the firewall's logging buffer. In the following example, the firewall has attempted to bring up the SSL tunnel and to validate the Syslog server's SSL certificate. The tunnel is successful, as shown by the final "Device completed SSL handshake with server" message.

```
%ASA-6-725001: Starting SSL handshake with server outside:172.21.67.252/1041 for
TLSv1 session.
%ASA-7-725009: Device proposes the following 4 cipher(s) to server
outside:172.21.4.37/1041
%ASA-7-725011: Cipher[1] : RC4-SHA
```

```
%ASA-7-725011: Cipher[2] : AES128-SHA
%ASA-7-725011: Cipher[3] : AES256-SHA
%ASA-7-725011: Cipher[4] : DES-CBC3-SHA
%ASA-7-725013: SSL Server outside:172.21.4.37/1041 choose cipher : RC4-SHA
%ASA-7-717025: Validating certificate chain containing 1 certificate(s).
%ASA-7-717029: Identified client certificate within certificate chain. serial number:
00DB42F7223CD44610, subject name: cn=www.mycompany.com,ou=Test Engineering,o=My
Company,l=Lexington,st=Kentucky,c=US.
%ASA-6-717022: Certificate was successfully validated. Certificate is resident and
trusted, serial number: 00DB42F7223CD44610, subject name:
cn=www.mycompany.com,ou=Test
Engineering,o=My Company,l=Lexington,st=Kentucky,c=US.
%ASA-6-717028: Certificate chain was successfully validated with revocation status
check.
%ASA-6-725002: Device completed SSL handshake with server outside:172.21.4.37/1041
```

Logging to an E-mail Address

When logging messages are generated, they can be sent to an e-mail address. Each message is sent as a single e-mail message.

You can configure the "From" and "To" addresses for the resulting e-mails. The firewall always sends these with the subject line "ASA Alert (*hostname*)" or "FWSM Alert (*hostname*)." The actual e-mail message has the following format:

```
Date: Sun, 6 May 2007 16:17:43 Eastern
From: firewall@mycompany.com
To: hucaby@mycompany.com
Subject: ASA Alert (Firewall-c)
<165>May 06 2007 16:17:43  admin : %ASA-2-106001: Inbound TCP connection denied from
172.16.89.4/1489 to 172.21.2.200/23 flags INVALID on interface outside
```

In this example, the firewall has added its own time stamp and the originating context name (admin in multiple-context mode) to the logging message text.

Use the following configuration steps to begin sending logging messages to one or more email destinations.

1. Set the mail logging level:

ASA, FWSM	Firewall(config)# **logging mail** {*level* | *event-list*}
PIX 6.3	—

Messages are sent to any configured e-mail recipient addresses if they are at or below the specified severity *level*: **emergencies (0)**, **alerts (1)**, **critical (2)**, **errors (3)**, **warnings (4)**, **notifications (5)**, **informational (6)**, or **debugging (7)**. The ASA and FWSM also let you use a policy to select which messages are sent. Messages that are matched by the event list named *event-list* (defined in Step 3 of the "Configuring Basic Logging Parameters" section) are forwarded to the logging destination.

2. Identify an SMTP server for e-mail delivery:

ASA, FWSM	`Firewall(config)# `**`smtp-server`**` server_primary [server_secondary]`
PIX 6.3	—

The firewall sends all its mail logging messages to an SMTP server, which should relay the mail to the appropriate recipients. Up to two servers can be identified, either by IP address or host name. The firewall first tries to send to *server_primary*. If that fails, it tries *server_secondary*.

NOTE   If you use a host name, a matching **name** command must already be configured so that the name can be resolved to an IP address. This is because the firewall will not resolve names through an external DNS server. Instead, resolution must happen internally.

Even if you supply a host name with the **smtp-server** command, the IP address is substituted in the actual running-config.

---

3. Assign a sender address for the messages:

ASA, FWSM	`Firewall(config)# `**`logging from-address`**` from_email_address`
PIX 6.3	—

Mail messages are sent with an arbitrary e-mail source address of *from_email_address*. This address is not automatically verified or resolved; instead, it is just copied into the resulting message and sent to the SMTP server. The address can be fictitious, because it is not necessary or possible to reply to that address. In the following sample command, logging messages appear to be sent from myasa@mycompany.com:

```
Firewall(config)# logging from-address myasa@mycompany.com
```

4. Identify the e-mail recipient:

ASA, FWSM	`Firewall(config)# `**`logging recipient-address`**` to_email_address` [**`level`** `level`]
PIX 6.3	—

Logging messages are sent to the recipient address *to_email_address*. This can be an actual person's address or the address of a system that can automatically distribute the e-mail message to any number of recipients. You can repeat this command to define multiple recipient addresses.

Each mail logging recipient can have a unique severity level associated with it, specified as *level*: **emergencies (0)**, **alerts (1)**, **critical (2)**, **errors (3)**, **warnings (4)**, **notifications (5)**, **informational (6)**, or **debugging (7)**. If a message is at or below the recipient's severity level, it is sent. However, the **logging mail** *level* command sets the highest possible severity that can be sent to any e-mail recipient.

> **CAUTION**   Be careful when you set a mail logging severity level. Remember that *each* relevant
> logging message is sent as a separate e-mail message. A highly utilized firewall or a
> severity level that is too great can quickly overload a recipient's mailbox. In addition,
> it can overload the firewall's SMTP queue to the point that new logging messages are
> dropped. The firewall reminds you of this potential, as the following example
> demonstrates:
>
> ```
> Firewall(config)# logging recipient-address hucaby@mycompany.com level
> informational
> WARNING: SMTP logging is very inefficient.  At this severity level,
>          a large number of syslogs might overwhelm the SMTP
>          input queue, resulting in dropped messages.
> Firewall(config)#
> ```

Logging to an ASDM Management Application

A firewall can feed logging messages to one or more ASDM sessions. Messages are kept in a buffer until they are requested by an ASDM session. The messages are transferred to ASDM over an SSL connection rather than as traditional Syslog packets.

Use the following steps to configure ASDM logging on your firewall.

1. (Optional) Set the buffer size for ASDM messages:

ASA, FWSM	`Firewall(config)# `**`logging asdm-buffer-size`** *`num_of_msgs`*
PIX 6.3	—

    By default, the buffer holds 100 messages. You can adjust the buffer size to *num_of_msgs* (100 to 512 messages).

2. Set the ASDM logging level:

ASA, FWSM	`Firewall(config)# `**`logging asdm`** {*`level`* | *`event-list`*}
PIX 6.3	—

    Messages are buffered for ASDM if they are at or below the specified severity *level*: **emergencies (0)**, **alerts (1)**, **critical (2)**, **errors (3)**, **warnings (4)**, **notifications (5)**, **informational (6)**, or **debugging (7)**.

    On an ASA or FWSM, you can also use a policy to select which messages are displayed. Messages that are matched by the event list named *event-list* (defined in Step 3 of the "Configuring Basic Logging Parameters" section) are buffered for ASDM use.

Verifying Message Logging Activity

Use the **show logging** command to verify where logging messages are being sent. The first few lines of output display message counters for every possible logging destination.

The firewall in the following example has sent 117 messages to the console, 408,218 messages to the internal buffer (only 4096 bytes of the most recent messages are kept), and 1,852,197 messages to the Syslog host at 192.168.199.200. You can also verify each destination's severity level.

```
Firewall# show logging
Syslog logging: enabled
    Facility: 20
    Timestamp logging: enabled
    Standby logging: disabled
    Console logging: level warnings, 117 messages logged
    Monitor logging: level errors, 0 messages logged
    Buffer logging: level informational, 408218 messages logged
    Trap logging: level informational, 1852197 messages logged
        Logging to outside 192.168.199.200
    History logging: disabled
    Device ID: hostname "Firewall"
```

ASA and FWSM platforms provide some additional information, along with the settings of any additional logging destinations. The **show logging setting** command displays the same type of information without showing the logging buffer contents, as demonstrated in the following example:

```
Firewall/admin# show logging setting
Syslog logging: enabled
    Facility: 20
    Timestamp logging: enabled
    Standby logging: disabled
    Deny Conn when Queue Full: disabled
    Console logging: disabled
    Monitor logging: disabled
    Buffer logging: list MyFilter, class config ip np session sys, 6756 messages
  logged
    Trap logging: level debugging, facility 20, 259799 messages logged
        Logging to outside syslog.mycompany.com
    History logging: disabled
    Device ID: context name "admin"
    Mail logging: level critical, 166 messages logged
    ASDM logging: level informational, 246891 messages logged
Firewall/admin#
```

ASA and FWSM platforms also let you add message filters and classes to any logging destination. The preceding example shows how an event list called **MyFilter** is being used on the logging buffer. Notice that buffered logging is being performed for the event classes called **config**, **ip**, **np**, **session**, and **sys**.

Also notice that the firewall is using its context name "admin" as a device ID. Settings and counters are also shown for the other logging destinations, mail logging and ASDM logging.

Manually Testing Logging Message Generation

If it is not apparent that the firewall is sending Syslog messages, you can use another method to force messages to be sent while watching them being received at the destination. First, make sure the logging destination has been configured for severity level 4 or greater. Then, from enable mode in a session, run the following EXEC commands with a bogus or unused IP address:

```
Firewall# shun ip-address
Firewall# no shun ip-address
```

This creates and deletes a temporary shun on the nonexistent address. This command is handy because it is the only one that generates simple Syslog messages at a very low severity level (level 4, warnings) without a complex scenario. You should see something similar to the following logging messages displayed at the appropriate logging destination:

```
%ASA-4-401002: Shun added: 10.1.1.1 0.0.0.0 0 0
%ASA-4-401003: Shun deleted: 10.1.1.1
```

TIP   You can view the firewall's internal logging buffer with the **show logging** EXEC command. Only the most recent messages still remaining in the buffer are shown.

ASA and FWSM platforms add both time stamps (if configured to do so) and the complete **%ASA**-*severity-messageID* or **%FWSM**-*severity-messageID* prefix to each message in the buffer. PIX 6.3 does not add the prefix or time stamps. Only the six-digit message number and the message text are shown.

To clear the internal logging buffer, you can use the **clear logging buffer** (ASA or FWSM) or the **clear logging** (PIX 6.3) command.

10-3: Fine-Tuning Logging Message Generation

After you have chosen and configured severity levels for logging destinations, you should make sure you are receiving only necessary messages. In other words, do not choose a severity level that can produce an abundance of messages that will be ignored. Always keep in mind that a Syslog server must receive and archive every message sent to it. Storage space is at a premium, especially when logs continuously grow over time.

Here are rules of thumb to follow when choosing a severity level:

- If only firewall error conditions should be recorded and no one will regularly view the message logs, choose severity level 3 (errors).

- If you are primarily interested in seeing how traffic is being filtered by the firewall access lists, choose severity level 4 (warnings).

- If you need an audit trail of firewall users and their activity, choose severity level 5 (notifications).

- If you will be using a firewall log analysis application, you should choose severity level 6 (informational). This is the only level that produces messages about connections that are created, as well as the time and data volume usage.

- If you need to use any **debug** command to troubleshoot something on the firewall, choose a destination with severity level 7 (debugging). You can use the **logging debug-trace** command to force debug output to be sent to a logging destination for later review. All Syslog messages containing debug output use message ID 711001 at a default severity level of 7.

Pruning Messages

If you find that a severity level meets your needs but generates some unnecessary messages, you can "prune" those messages and keep them from being generated at all. Locate the message from an actual Syslog capture, from the lists of messages in this section, or from the message listing in Appendix B. Next, disable the message based on its six-digit message number with the following configuration command:

```
Firewall(config)# no logging message message-number
```

You can see a listing of all the disabled logging messages with the following EXEC command:

```
Firewall# show logging message
```

To re-enable a disabled message, you can use the **logging message** *message-number* configuration command. To return all messages to their default levels on an ASA or FWSM, you can use the **clear configure logging disabled** configuration command.

Changing the Message Severity Level

Recall that each logging message has a default severity level associated with it. You can change that default behavior so that a message is sent based on a configurable severity level instead. This might be useful if you choose a severity level for a logging destination that includes most (but not all) of the messages that are interesting to you. For the messages that have a higher default level and that will not be sent, you can reconfigure their level to a lower value.

To change a message's severity level, use the following configuration command:

```
Firewall(config)# logging message message-number [level level]
```

Here, the message is identified by its six-digit *message-number* or Syslog ID and is assigned a new severity *level* (0 to 7). To see a message's current severity level, you can use the following EXEC command:

```
Firewall# show logging message {message-number | all}
```

The **all** keyword causes the state of all known or supported logging messages to be listed. Otherwise, you can specify the six-digit *message-number* to see the state of a specific message. The output shows the default severity level, the newly configured severity level (if any), and whether the message is enabled.

For example, suppose a firewall administrator wants to completely disable Syslog message 111008 while changing the severity of message 111009 from its default (debugging) to notifications. You could use the following commands to accomplish and verify this:

```
Firewall/admin(config)# logging message 111009 level notifications
Firewall/admin(config)# no logging message 111008
Firewall/admin(config)# exit
Firewall/admin# show logging message
syslog 111009: default-level debugging, current-level notifications (enabled)
syslog 111008: default-level notifications (disabled)
Firewall/admin#
```

Access List Activity Logging

By default, logging message 106023 (default severity level 4, warnings) is generated when a **deny** access list entry is matched with a traffic flow. Only the overall ACL is listed in the message, with no reference to the actual denying ACL entry, as in the following example:

```
%ASA-4-106023: Deny tcp src outside:220.163.33.180/18909 dst inside:
  10.10.95.23/8039 by access-group "acl_outside"
```

You can log messages when specific access control entries (ACEs, or individual permit/deny statements within an ACL) permit or deny a traffic flow by adding the **log** keyword to an ACE.

You can also log the rate at which traffic flows match specific access list entries. This can be useful to gauge the volume of attacks or exploits that are occurring over time.

After a traffic flow triggers an ACE configured for logging, the firewall keeps the flow in a cached list. If the reporting interval completes and there are no additional occurrences of the same flow, the cached entry is deleted, and the flow's hit count becomes 0.

You can set the logging severity level on a per-ACE basis if needed. Otherwise, severity level 6 is the default.

TIP ACE logging generates logging message 106100 (default severity level 6), which has the following format:

```
%ASA-6-106100: access-list acl_ID {permitted | denied | est-allowed}
  protocol interface_name/source_address(source_port) ->
  interface_name/dest_address(dest_port) hit-cnt number ({first hit |
  number-second interval})
```

The ACL name *acl_ID* is shown to have permitted or denied a traffic flow. The specific traffic flow is defined as a *protocol* (UDP or TCP, for example), from the source (firewall interface name, IP address, and port) to the destination (firewall interface name, IP address, and port).

If this is the first packet in a flow, the hit count is 1, followed by the "first hit" flag. If the traffic flow has already been seen and is being tracked, this logging message

Section 10-3

appears at intervals defined along with the ACE **log** keyword. The hit count reflects how many times the same flow has been attempted, and the hit count interval is shown as a *number* of seconds. Using the hit count and interval timing values allows you to calculate the flow rate that is occurring.

1. Configure logging on specific access list entries:

ASA, FWSM	Firewall(config)# **access-list** *acl_name* [**extended**] {**permit** ǀ **deny**} ... **log** [*level*] [**interval** *seconds*]
PIX 6.3	Firewall(config)# **access-list** *acl_name* {**permit** ǀ **deny**} ... **log** [*level*] [**interval** *seconds*]

Enter the access list entry normally, but add the **log** keyword at the end. If you want to log activity on this entry at a severity level other than 6, specify the *level* (1 to 7) too.

As soon as a traffic flow triggers this ACE, the hit count begins to increment with each new occurrence of the same flow. Nonzero hit counts are reported with a logging message at intervals of *seconds* (1 to 600; the default is 300 seconds or 5 minutes).

TIP   If you already have an access list configured and in place on a firewall, you can safely add the logging capability to any number of ACEs within it. In other words, when **log** and its associated fields are added to an existing ACE, the ACE remains in its current location in the list sequence; it is not moved to the end of the list. In addition, you do not have to remove the ACE before configuring the **log** options. Simply re-enter the existing ACE and add the **log** keyword and options.

In the following example, an existing ACL called acl_out is being used on a production firewall. The third ACE needs to have logging added to it at severity level 4. Notice that after the ACE command is re-entered with **log 4** added, it stays in the third ACE position and becomes active immediately.

```
Firewall# show running-config
[output omitted]
access-list acl_out permit icmp any any
access-list acl_out permit tcp any host 192.168.199.100 eq telnet
access-list acl_out permit tcp any host 192.168.199.100 eq www
access-list acl_out permit icmp any host 192.168.199.100
[output omitted]
Firewall(config)# access-list acl_out permit tcp any host 192.168.199.100
  eq www log 4
Firewall# show running-config
[output omitted]
access-list acl_out permit icmp any any
access-list acl_out permit tcp any host 192.168.199.100 eq telnet
access-list acl_out permit tcp any host 192.168.199.100 eq www log 4
access-list acl_out permit icmp any host 192.168.199.100
[output omitted]
```

To disable message ID 106100 logging on an ACE, re-enter the command with the **log default** keywords appended. For example, the preceding shaded command would be re-entered as

```
Firewall(config)# access-list acl_out permit tcp any host 192.168.199.100
  eq www log default
```

You can also re-enter the ACE with the **log disable** keywords to completely disable all ACE logging (both message IDs 106100 and 106023). In this case, the sample command would be re-entered as

```
Firewall(config)# access-list acl_out permit tcp any host 192.168.199.100
  eq www log disable
```

2. Limit the volume of deny messages.

   a.   Limit the number of deny flows that are tracked:

   ```
   Firewall(config)# access-list deny-flow-max n
   ```

   Each unique traffic flow that is denied by an ACE configured for logging is added to a cached list of tracked flows. This usually is not a problem unless something like a denial-of-service attack causes a very large number of flows to be denied and tracked.

   The firewall limits the maximum number of denied flows it tracks. By default, the maximum number is based on the available firewall memory: 4096 (64 MB or more), 1024 (16 MB or more), or 256 (less than 16 MB).

   You can change this to a lower maximum number of flows by specifying *n* (1 to the default maximum).

   b.   (Optional) Send an alert when the number of tracked flows is too high:

   ```
   Firewall(config)# access-list alert-interval seconds
   ```

   When the maximum number of tracked flows is reached, the firewall generates logging message 106101. By default, this message is limited to appearing only every 300 seconds (5 minutes). You can change the alert interval to *seconds* (1 to 3600 seconds).

10-4: Analyzing Firewall Logs

The most important thing you can do with a firewall is collect and analyze its Syslog information.

Firewall logs should be inspected on a regular basis. Always make sure the Syslog collector or server is configured to archive older information and that disk space is not completely consumed.

The Syslog collector or server should be sized according to the following parameters:

- The number of firewalls and other network devices sending Syslog messages to the Syslog server
- The number of Syslog events per second (usually called EPS) generated by all devices
- How long Syslog information should be kept available

Consider the type of information you want to get from your firewall logs. Here are some examples:

- **Connections permitted by firewall rules**—Glancing through these messages can help you spot "holes" that remain open in your security policies.

- **Connections denied by firewall rules**—You can instantly see what types of activity are being directed toward your secured inside network.

- **Denied rule rates**—Using the ACE deny rate logging feature can show attacks that are occurring against your firewall.

- **User activity**—Firewall user authentication and command usage can all be logged, providing an audit trail of security policy changes.

- **Cut-through-proxy activity**—As end users authenticate and pass through the firewall, their activity can be logged for a general audit trail.

- **Bandwidth usage**—Firewall logs can show each connection that was built and torn down, as well as the duration and traffic volume used. This can be broken down by connection, user, department, and so on.

- **Protocol usage**—Firewall logs can show the protocols and port numbers that are used for each connection.

- **Intrusion Detection System (IDS) activity**—A firewall can be configured with a set of IDS signatures and can log attacks that occur.

- **Address translation audit trail**—If Network Address Translation (NAT) or Port Address Translation (PAT) is being used, the firewall logs can keep records of each translation that is built or torn down. This can be useful if you receive a report of malicious activity coming from inside your network toward the outside world. You can backtrack to find which internal user had a specific global IP address at a specific time.

You can scan the flat or raw Syslog data yourself to discover quite a few curious events or trends. However, if your firewall generates a large amount of logging information, you might want to invest in a firewall log analysis tool.

You should choose a logging analysis application that is tailored for firewalls so that the connection and ACL messages (among many others) can be fully interpreted and utilized. The following are some firewall logging analysis applications:

- CS-MARS from Cisco Systems (http://www.cisco.com)
- LogLogic Log Management and Intelligence Platform from LogLogic (http://www.loglogic.com)
- Network Intelligence Engine from Network Intelligence (http://www.network-intelligence.com)
- Network Security Analyzer and FirewallAnalyzer Enterprise from eIQnetworks (http://www.eiqnetworks.com)
- Sawmill Log Analyzer from FlowerFire (http://www.sawmill.net)
- CiscoWorks VPN and Security Management Solution (VMS) and Security Information Management Solution (SIMS) from Cisco Systems (http://www.cisco.com)

Consider the volume of Syslog information your firewalls and other network devices will generate. Syslog collection and analysis tools must be able to handle a sustained number of events per second so that no logging information is missed. They must also be able to store Syslog data over a reasonable period of time so that you can come back and analyze information from the recent past.

You can get an idea of how many events per second a firewall generates without having a Syslog collector already in place. You can use the firewall's internal logging buffer as a gauge. Follow these steps:

1. Enable logging to the buffer at a severity level:

   ```
   Firewall(config)# logging buffered level
   ```

   Here, the severity level is set to *level* (0 to 7): **emergencies (0)**, **alerts (1)**, **critical (2)**, **errors (3)**, **warnings (4)**, **notifications (5)**, **informational (6)**, or **debugging (7)**. The higher the level, the more messages (and types of messages) that are generated.

   Set this to the level you think will generate the logging messages you are most interested in recording. When this command is executed, logging to the buffer begins immediately.

2. Read the logging buffer counter as a baseline:

   ```
   Firewall# show logging
   ```

   Note when you issue this command. This begins the time period during which buffered logging is monitored.

   The "*n* messages logged" counters cannot be reset while the firewall is operational. Therefore, you can take a reading of the buffer logging message counter now as a starting point. The logging counters are shown in the first few lines of output. For ASA and FWSM platforms, you can use the **show logging setting** command to omit any output except settings and counters.

   In the following example, the firewall begins with 460,864 messages that have already been sent to the buffer, because buffered logging has been active in the past.

```
Firewall# show logging setting
Syslog logging: enabled
    Facility: 20
    Timestamp logging: disabled
    Standby logging: disabled
    Console logging: disabled
    Monitor logging: disabled
    Buffer logging: level informational, 460864 messages logged
    Trap logging: level warnings, 1882119 messages logged
        Logging to outside 192.168.254.100
    History logging: disabled
    Device ID: disabled
```

3. Wait 60 seconds and then see how many messages were sent to the buffer:

```
Firewall# show logging setting
```

Note the number of buffer messages logged now, and calculate the difference between this and the baseline number from Step 2. This is the number of messages generated at the desired severity level over the span of 60 seconds. Divide that by 60, and you have an estimate of events or messages per second (EPS).

In the following example, the firewall begins with 438,113 buffered messages. After 1 minute of buffered logging at severity level 6 (informational), the counter has risen to 460,864. Therefore, 460,864 minus 438,113 equals 22,751 messages in one minute, or 379 messages per second.

```
Firewall# config term
Firewall(config)# logging buffered informational
Firewall(config)# exit
Firewall# show logging setting
Syslog logging: enabled
    Facility: 20
    Timestamp logging: disabled
    Standby logging: disabled
    Console logging: disabled
    Monitor logging: disabled
    Buffer logging: level warnings, 438113 messages logged
    Trap logging: level warnings, 1882092 messages logged
        Logging to outside 192.168.254.100
    History logging: disabled
    Device ID: disabled
 [after one minute]
```

```
Firewall# show logging setting
Syslog logging: enabled
    Facility: 20
    Timestamp logging: disabled
    Standby logging: disabled
    Console logging: disabled
    Monitor logging: disabled
    Buffer logging: level informational, 460864 messages logged
  Sample Breakdown of Received Syslog Messages by Severity Level
 Trap logging: level warnings, 1882119 messages logged
        Logging to outside 192.168.254.100
    History logging: disabled
    Device ID: disabled
```

As you might expect, higher severity levels generate more logging messages. This is because the firewall reports on more types of normal activity. Higher severity levels actually mean that the events reported are less severe (more normal). Figure 10-4 shows a sample breakdown of the Syslog severity levels in messages that were collected over an hour from a firewall supporting an enterprise of several thousand users. Notice how the number of Local4.Critical (level 2) messages are few, progressing to the very large number of Local4.Info (level 6) messages.

Figure 10-4 *Sample Breakdown of Received Syslog Messages by Severity Level*

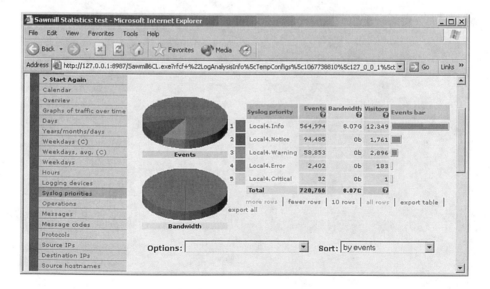

Refer to the following sections for information about these topics:

- **11-1: Checking Firewall Vital Signs**—Discusses methods you can use to diagnose a firewall's health. System resources, logging output, throughput, failover, interface operation, and packet queuing are all covered.

- **11-2: Watching Data Pass Through a Firewall**—Covers ways that packets can be logged or captured as they pass through a firewall or through its interfaces.

- **11-3: Verifying Firewall Connectivity**—Provides a set of basic approaches to verify working communication through a firewall.

CHAPTER 11

Verifying Firewall Operation

In the course of configuring and using a firewall, it is important to follow the appropriate security policies and offer the proper connectivity to the user community, all while making sure the firewall is operating properly.

A firewall's operation has many aspects, so it can be difficult to assess its health. When users call to complain about slow or lost connectivity, you should be able to decide if the problem is in the firewall or somewhere else.

This chapter presents several ways you can check a firewall's operation. This chapter also covers data-capture methods so that you can verify if data is passing through a firewall as expected.

11-1: Checking Firewall Vital Signs

After a firewall is put into production, it is important to know how to check its health. You can proactively monitor various resources and statistics in an effort to determine when the firewall has a problem or becomes underpowered. As well, when users complain of problems or slow response times, you should be able to look into some of the firewall's inner workings to quickly spot issues.

How a firewall will behave under the load of a production network with real users and real applications is difficult to predict. When a problem is reported, you can rely on many of the available firewall statistics to see what is wrong. However, those numbers do not mean much if you do not have anything to compare them against.

You should make every effort to determine a baseline or average for several firewall parameters. Do this while the firewall is operating normally and all users are satisfied with its performance. Monitor the following statistics periodically so that you get an idea about their values and how they change during a business day or week:

- CPU utilization
- Memory usage
- Xlate table size
- Conn table size

- Firewall throughput
- Failover activity and synchronization rates (if applicable)

The following sections show you how to monitor these functions.

Using the Syslog Information

Firewalls normally stay busy silently inspecting traffic, denying some packets and forwarding others. The only way to "feel the pulse" of your firewall, to see what it has been doing, is to look back through the Syslog messages it has generated.

You can view the most recent Syslog information, whether or not you have a Syslog server set up. You can enable buffered logging with the **logging buffered** *level configuration* command and view the buffer with the **show logging** command. However, only the most recent messages are kept in the buffer. On a busy firewall, the buffer can be completely overwritten in only a few seconds, so you might not be able to find the information you need.

Instead, you should seriously consider setting up machines to collect Syslog messages from every firewall in your network. Syslog information gives a very useful historic record in the following ways:

- **Troubleshooting information**—Events in the life of the firewall itself (reloads, failovers, memory shortages, and so on) are recorded, along with the reasons some packets were denied or dropped.

- **Performance and activity**—Address translations and connections are recorded as they are created and torn down. The duration (both time and data volume) of each connection is also recorded so that an analysis of data throughput can be computed over time.

- **Security audit trail**—The results of user authentication can be recorded for a historical record or for usage information. Address translation and connection information can be recorded and used as evidence when someone from the outside attempts malicious activity.

The same can be recorded for internal users attempting similar activity toward the outside world. In the case of port address translation (PAT), the Syslog record is the only evidence that can be used to backtrack from the outside to find which internal user was using the PAT global address at a certain date and time.

TIP   When you set up a Syslog server, make sure you have a system (both hardware and the Syslog software) that can handle the appropriate Syslog message rate sent by the firewall(s). This rate varies according to the firewall's connection load. More importantly, it varies according to the Syslog severity level configured on the firewall.

Refer to Chapter 10, "Firewall Logging," for detailed information about Syslog planning and analysis.

After you configure a firewall to send Syslog information to a server or memory buffer, you should verify its operation. You can use the **show logging** command for this, paying attention to the first dozen lines of output. Look at each type of logging to see if the appropriate ones are enabled and if they are set to the correct severity level. In particular, you should see a count of the total number of messages sent to each enabled destination. In the following example, both buffer and trap (Syslog server) logging are enabled and active:

```
Firewall# show logging
Syslog logging: enabled
    Facility: 20
    Timestamp logging: disabled
    Standby logging: disabled
    Console logging: disabled
    Monitor logging: disabled
    Buffer logging: level warnings, 5526712 messages logged
    Trap logging: level warnings, 6933062 messages logged
        Logging to outside 192.168.2.142
    History logging: disabled
    Device ID: disabled
    Mail logging: disabled
    ASDM logging: level informational, 128765 messages logged
21.68.65/47808 to 1.0.0.0/0
500004: Invalid transport field for protocol=17, from 172.29.68.65/47808 to
    1.0.0.0/0
[logging buffer output omitted]
```

Notice that the total numbers of buffer and trap logging messages are different. This is because each logging method is configured independently. For example, trap logging might have been enabled at an earlier date than buffer logging. Otherwise, each logging method can be configured with a different severity level threshold, causing each one to generate a different type and volume of message.

Checking System Resources

A firewall inspects traffic and performs its functions by using a combination of system resources. From a hardware standpoint, these resources are very straightforward and include the CPU and system memory. The following sections analyze these resources.

Firewall CPU Load

You get a general idea about the processing load on a Cisco firewall by using the **show cpu usage** command. For example, the following firewall appliance has a 5-second average of 27 percent. The command output also shows that the CPU is under a consistent load of about 24 percent:

```
Firewall# show cpu usage
CPU utilization for 5 seconds = 27%; 1 minute: 25%; 5 minutes: 24%
Firewall#
```

As a rule of thumb, the CPU utilization should stay below an average of 80 percent. The utilization might spike or temporarily peak at a greater value, as seen in the short-term 5-second utilization. This is normal behavior, because the CPU could be processing a periodic task or a short burst of traffic.

In extreme situations, you might see Syslog message ID 211003 (**ASA-3-211003**, for example) being generated. This message is sent when the firewall CPU has consistently been at 100 percent.

If the CPU stays above 80 percent during a time you consider to be a normal traffic load, without a significant attack occurring, you should consider upgrading the firewall or lightening its traffic load. Some of the possibilities for doing so are as follows:

- Replace the firewall with a higher-performance model.

- Implement firewall load balancing so that the traffic load is balanced across two or more firewall platforms. Refer to Chapter 9, "Firewall Load Balancing," for detailed coverage.

- Make configuration changes to reduce the firewall's processing load; remove any unnecessary activities it is performing.

TIP   If your firewall is configured to run multiple security contexts, remember that these "virtual firewalls" are all being emulated by one firewall platform. If the CPU usage is running high, you might have too many different contexts configured or too many contexts that are heavily used. You can get an idea of the breakdown of CPU resources across the contexts with the **show cpu usage context all** command, as in the following example:

```
Firewall# show cpu usage
CPU utilization for 5 seconds = 86%; 1 minute: 84%; 5 minutes: 83%
Firewall# show cpu usage context all
  5 sec        1 min        5 min       Context Name
  2.2%         2.5%         2.4%        system
  1.0%         1.1%         1.0%        admin
  54.6%        52.2%        53.1%       CustomerA
  27.3%        27.2%        25.6%       CustomerB
  0.9%         1.0%         0.9%        Test
Firewall#
```

The utilization values from the first command are totals for the sum of the context values from the second command. In this example, the CustomerA context is using the most CPU resources and is a good candidate for being moved onto its own firewall platform. With active-active failover, you can assign contexts individually to each of the physical firewalls in a pair to distribute the active roles evenly according to their CPU loads.

To find out more about which activities are taxing the CPU, you can try to track down the most-used processes. The firewall's CPU continuously performs a number of different tasks, such as processing inbound packets; inspecting ICMP, UDP, and TCP traffic; interacting with the console and user sessions; maintaining failover communication; operating routing protocols; and so on.

In addition, a large number of tasks involve maintaining timers. When xlate and conn entries are created, timers must be started; when the various timers expire, those entries must be deleted. You also can time and control authenticated user sessions. Each of these timer functions has its own process, requiring periodic attention from the CPU. In fact, a process runs continuously just to keep the CPU utilization values computed and updated!

To see the entire list of active firewall processes, you can use the **show processes** command. Unless you are a Cisco Technical Assistance Center (TAC) engineer, the only interesting information is found in the following columns:

- **Process**—Displays a descriptive name for the process, such as update_cpu_usage, that computes the values for the **show cpu usage** command.

- **Runtime**—Lists the actual amount of time the CPU has spent on each process, in milliseconds. The runtime values begin at 0 when the firewall is first booted and accumulate until it is powered down or reloaded.

NOTE   Each line of the **show processes** command begins with three flag characters that give more information about the process. The first character denotes the process priority; it can be one of the following: **D** (dead), **L** (low), **M** (medium), or **C** (critical).

The second character denotes the process state: **r** (ready to run), **s** (sleeping), **x** (dead), **w** (idle), or * (running).

For example, the following processes are running at medium and critical priority, respectively:

```
Mrd 003cb154 013ab118 00d9d580    9130720 013a9190 7660/8192 557poll
Csi 0071b139 01d48580 00d9d490          0 01d46618 7340/8192 update
 _cpu_usage
```

Now suppose you see that the CPU utilization is running a consistent 25 percent, and you want to know why. Although it is somewhat involved, you can discover which processes are "hogging" the CPU by following these steps:

1. Run the **show** processes command. Copy the output and paste it to another location, such as Windows Notepad.

2. Wait about a minute, and run the **show processes** command again. Copy and paste this output into another location.

3. For each process listed, subtract the most recent runtime from the first runtime shown. The result is the number of milliseconds the CPU spent on that process during the last minute.

You can use a spreadsheet application such as Microsoft Excel to quickly compute the runtime difference on all the processes. Table 11-1 shows an example of most processes running on a Firewall

Services Module (FWSM) platform. The actual runtime difference is shown in the rightmost column. Shaded rows denote processes that have a non-zero CPU usage within the last 60 seconds.

Table 11-1 *Computing Actual Firewall Process Runtimes*

Process Name	Runtime t=0	Runtime t=60 seconds	Msec CPU in 1 minute
block_diag	0	0	0
Dispatch Unit	1702268213	1702293806	25593
Reload ControlThread	0	0	0
aaa	0	0	0
dbgtrace	0	0	0
ibm_4gs3_connstate_thread	0	0	0
Chunk Manager	0	0	0
PIX Garbage Collector	306806	306815	9
route_process	8618	8618	0
IP Address Assign	0	0	0
QoS Support Module	0	0	0
Client Update Task	0	0	0
Checkheaps	5343627	5343707	80
Session Manager	1230	1230	0
uauth	6977	6977	0
Uauth_Proxy	0	0	0
SMTP	0	0	0
Logger	25660105	25660528	423
Thread Logger	0	0	0
vpnlb_thread	0	0	0
ScpIncomingThread	3818	3818	0
ScpManagerThread	1097120	1097136	16
tcp_fast	10	10	0
tcp_slow	2385	2387	2
udp_timer	0	0	0
ScpSendReqThread	81109	81110	1
arp_timer	39399	39400	1

Table 11-1 *Computing Actual Firewall Process Runtimes (Continued)*

Process Name	Runtime t=0	Runtime t=60 seconds	Msec CPU in 1 minute
FragDBGC	33597	33598	1
arp_forward_thread	0	0	0
snp_timer_thread	969661792	969676395	14603
ScpPollingThread	572	572	0
doorbell_poll	16495	16495	0
np/wrapper	1541636	1541722	86
route resend process	188	188	0
arp resend thread	2875	2875	0
arp send process	187304	187305	1
mfib send process	0	0	0
np_cls_download_process	19538	19538	0
CTCP Timer process	0	0	0
IPSec message handler	0	0	0
CTM message handler	82172	82173	1
L2TP data daemon	0	0	0
L2TP mgmt daemon	0	0	0
ppp_timer_thread	3884	3884	0
vpnlb_timer_thread	13312	13312	0
tmatch compile thread	22	22	0
Crypto PKI RECV	0	0	0
Crypto CA	0	0	0
xlate clean	7110	7110	0
maintain random data	5336	5336	0
Host object cleaner	111895	111896	1
perfmon	27616	27616	0
IKE Timekeeper	0	0	0
IKE Daemon	0	0	0
url_filter	0	0	0
Dns	0	0	0
activex	0	0	0

continues

Section 11-1

Table 11-1 *Computing Actual Firewall Process Runtimes (Continued)*

Process Name	Runtime t=0	Runtime t=60 seconds	Msec CPU in 1 minute
Java	0	0	0
domain	0	0	0
http	0	0	0
h323_h225	8395	8395	0
h323_ras	238	238	0
Ils	0	0	0
sunrpc	0	0	0
Rpc	0	0	0
Rsh	160	160	0
Rtsp	14648231	14648963	732
Smtp	0	0	0
sqlnet	74078	74078	0
Sip	614	614	0
skinny	5553	5554	1
sunrpc_udp	0	0	0
rpc_udp	0	0	0
xdmcp	0	0	0
udp_sip	139381	139390	9
netbios	0	0	0
ctiqbe	0	0	0
ftp_filter_command	0	0	0
https_filter	0	0	0
Mgcp	0	0	0
Tftp	0	0	0
Snmp	0	0	0
Pptp	0	0	0
Gtp	0	0	0
Fast_fixup	20734098	20734692	594
Pkt	19312	19313	1
syslog_entry	42680361	42680935	574

Firewall Memory

Cisco firewalls base their entire operation on the use of internal random-access memory (RAM). This memory can be broken up and allocated for many processes and other uses. Some examples of memory usage are as follows:

- **OS image**—A firewall's operating system image is stored in Flash (nonvolatile) memory. When the firewall is first powered up or reloaded, a small bootstrap executable copies the image from Flash into RAM. From that point on, the CPU runs the image from RAM.

- **Configuration**—A firewall's configuration is stored in Flash (nonvolatile) memory with the write mem command. When the firewall boots, the configuration file is copied from Flash to RAM, where each command is executed.

- **ACLs**—Access lists are compiled into a turbo access control list (ACL) or a compact and deterministic form, and the results are stored in an area of RAM separate from the running configuration.

- **Downloadable ACLs**—If the firewall is configured to accept per-user ACLs that are downloaded from an authentication server, the contents of those dynamic ACLs are stored in memory.

- **Interactive processes**—Management sessions through the console, Telnet, and SSH can all require memory. For example, when a command's output is filtered with the l include keywords, the original output is buffered in memory before being filtered to the session. Other processes include user authentication (uauth), content filtering, and VPN security associations (SA).

- **Routing information**—The firewall maintains its own "routing table" in memory so that it can make packet-forwarding decisions. Routes are learned through static route configuration and through dynamic routing protocols such as Routing Information Protocol (RIP) and Open Shortest Path First (OSPF). The firewall also maintains an Address Resolution Protocol (ARP) cache in memory for MAC-to-IP address resolution.

- **Capture sessions**—Each active capture session is immediately allocated a block of 512 KB of memory to use as a packet-capture buffer. The capture buffer can be resized through the use of the **capture** command.

- **Xlate table entries**—As address translations are created, they are added to the xlate table in memory.

- **Conn table entries**—As connections are established through the firewall, they are added to the conn table in memory.

- **Packets awaiting stateful inspection**—As packets are pulled from interface queues, they are stored in memory. The firewall CPU works through this packet buffer as it inspects the traffic with its fixup procedures.

From a monitoring standpoint, firewall memory is organized in two ways:

- **Main memory**—The entire contents of the firewall's RAM memory.

- **Blocks**—Portions of main memory that are allocated as pools of fixed-size entries. Each size block is used for a specific purpose.

Likewise, you have two ways to query a firewall's memory usage. To see the utilization of the firewall's main memory, you can use the **show memory** command. The following example shows a firewall to have 256 MB of RAM, 85 MB of which is in use, and about 183 MB of memory that is still free. The percentage values are shown as a quick gauge.

```
Firewall# show memory
Free memory:        183131072 bytes (68%)
Used memory:         85304384 bytes (32%)
-------------       ----------------
Total memory:       268435456 bytes (100%)
Firewall#
```

You can use the **show memory detail** command to display statistics about how the firewall memory has been fragmented during allocations. However, this information is useful mainly to Cisco TAC engineers.

You can also see how the firewall is managing its block memory with the **show blocks** command. Consider the following block statistics as an example:

```
Firewall# show blocks
  SIZE    MAX    LOW    CNT
     4    100     93     99
    80    100     98    100
   256   1100   1025   1036
  1550   2688   1912   1920
  2560     40     40     40
  4096     30     30     30
  8192     60     60     60
 16384    100    100    100
 65536     10     10     10
Firewall#
```

Notice that statistics are shown for each different block size, ranging from 4-byte blocks up to 65,536-byte blocks. Table 11-2 lists the possible block sizes and their purposes.

Table 11-2 *Firewall Memory Blocks and Their Uses*

Size in Bytes	Description
4	A general-purpose "scratch pad" for a variety of housekeeping functions: DNS, ISAKMP, URL filtering, uauth, H.323, TFTP, and some TCP uses
80	Failover "hello" messages between failover units TCP ACK packets that are sent during TCP intercept (limiting embryonic connections)
256	Syslog messages Stateful failover updates TCP
1550	Queue for Ethernet packets awaiting inspection (10/100 and Gigabit Ethernet interfaces other than i82543) Buffer for URL-filtering packets

Table 11-2 *Firewall Memory Blocks and Their Uses (Continued)*

Size in Bytes	Description
2560	IKE messages
4096	QoS metrics
8192	QoS metrics
16384	Queue for Gigabit Ethernet packets awaiting inspection (64-bit 66-MHz i82543 interfaces only)
65536	QoS metrics

A firewall begins by allocating a default number of each block size when it boots up. The default number of blocks in each size varies with the firewall model, the number and type of interfaces, and the amount of available memory. For example, a firewall might begin by allocating 1,444 1550-byte blocks.

During operation, a firewall might use most or all of the blocks of a certain size. This might occur if Ethernet packets arrive faster than they can be inspected and processed. When the number of blocks approaches 0, the firewall attempts to allocate more blocks of that size from the available memory.

The output from the **show blocks** command reports the current state of each block size. The count labels, **MAX**, **LOW**, and **CNT**, are not very intuitive; you should think of these in relation to blocks that are *available*, not blocks that are used. The count labels have the following meanings:

- **MAX**—The maximum number of blocks that are available for use. The maximum can increase if additional blocks are allocated at some point.
- **LOW**—The lowest number of blocks that have been available since the firewall was booted.
- **CNT**—The number of blocks currently available for use.

You can use the **clear blocks** command to return the maximum number of available blocks to the system defaults and to set the low block counts to the currently available values. This command can be useful if you notice that an extraordinary number of blocks have been allocated and you want to bring the firewall block allocation closer to its default state without a reboot.

Normally, you should not see any of the **CNT** values staying at 0. If some values do tend to remain at 0, the firewall cannot allocate any more memory to the block size shown.

TIP   Notice that some firewalls set aside memory blocks for Ethernet (1550-byte) and Gigabit Ethernet (16384-byte). Why is there a difference? The 1550-byte blocks are used for traditional Ethernet, for both 10/100 and lower-performance Gigabit Ethernet interfaces. The maximum transmission unit (MTU) for Ethernet is 1500 bytes.

The 16384-byte blocks are reserved for firewalls that have higher-performance Gigabit Ethernet interfaces installed. These interfaces also use an MTU of 1500 bytes. However, the firewall can achieve better performance by moving the 1500-byte packets into and out of the interface in large numbers. In other words, the best performance is obtained when about ten packets are moved at a time.

To see what types of interface controllers your firewall has, you can use the **show interface** command. You can focus on the controller hardware by filtering the output with the **show interface | include (line protocol | Hardware)** command, as shown in this example:

```
Firewall# show interface | include (line protocol | Hardware)
Interface Ethernet0/0 "outside", is up, line protocol is up
  Hardware is i82546GB rev03, BW 100 Mbps, DLY 100 usec
Interface Ethernet0/1 "", is up, line protocol is up
  Hardware is i82546GB rev03, BW 100 Mbps, DLY 100 usec
Interface Ethernet0/2 "", is up, line protocol is up
  Hardware is i82546GB rev03, BW 100 Mbps, DLY 100 usec
Interface Ethernet0/3 "dmz", is administratively down, line protocol is up
  Hardware is i82546GB rev03, BW 100 Mbps, DLY 100 usec
Interface Management0/0 "management", is administratively down, line protocol
is down
  Hardware is i82557, BW 100 Mbps, DLY 100 usec
Interface Redundant1 "inside", is up, line protocol is up
  Hardware is i82546GB rev03, BW 100 Mbps, DLY 100 usec
Firewall#
```

Checking Stateful Inspection Resources

As a firewall inspects and passes traffic, it maintains two tables of entries: address translations (xlates) and connections (conns). You can get an idea of the inspection load by looking at the size of these tables.

Xlate Table Size

To see the translation table size, use the following command:

```
Firewall# show xlate count
```

The output from this command shows the current number of xlates in use and the maximum number that have been built since the firewall was booted. The firewall in the following example currently has built 15,273 translations. At some time in the past, a maximum of 22,368 xlates were in use:

```
Firewall# show xlate count
15273 in use, 22368 most used
Firewall#
```

The xlate count is the sum of both static xlates (from the **static** command) and dynamic xlates (from **nat** and **global** commands).

When you see the xlate count, it might not be obvious whether there are too many translations. When a host passes through the firewall, it can use only one translation if it falls within a static mapping. If a host triggers a dynamic translation, the firewall creates one xlate for every unique PAT connection.

In other words, it is not possible to estimate or calculate ahead of time the number of xlates that will be used. Instead, be sure to look at the xlate count periodically so that you can get an average baseline value. Then, if you see the xlate count jump to a much higher value later, you can assume that something is wrong. In that case, your firewall could be faced with building xlates during an attack of malicious activity.

Conn Table Size

A firewall creates and tears down connection entries for UDP and TCP connections between pairs of hosts. You can get connection statistics with the following command:

```
Firewall# show conn count
```

The output of this command shows the current number of connections in use and the maximum number of connections that have been built since the firewall was booted. The firewall in the following example has 4495 connections currently in its conn table, and it has had up to 577,536 simultaneous connections in the past!

```
Firewall# show conn count
4495 in use, 577536 most used
Firewall#
```

The conn count is the sum of all types of connections. The count fluctuates as connections are built and torn down. Again, you should periodically use this command to get a feel for the average number of connections your network uses. If the conn count is excessive, as in the maximum number in the preceding example, an attack is likely in progress. If you have a failover pair of firewalls, should not the xlate and conn counts be identical in each unit? The xlate and conn entries are replicated only from the active unit to the standby unit if you have configured stateful failover. Otherwise, the active unit shows positive counts for both xlates and conns, but the standby unit shows counts of 0.

Also, it is not unusual for the active and standby table counts to be quite different, even when stateful failover is being used. The entire xlate and conn tables are not replicated between the units. Rather, only *new* entries (either created or torn down) are replicated.

If the stateful failover link goes down, the standby unit misses new table entries. When the link comes back up, only new entries from that point on are received. If the standby unit loses power or reboots, its entire xlate and conn tables are lost. When it comes back up, it receives the continual flow of only *new* entries—not the entire contents of the tables. Existing conn table entries from the active unit are replicated to the standby unit only if they are actively passing data. Existing connections that are idle are not replicated.

Also, the two units might show a disproportionate number of conn table entries if HTTP replication is not enabled between the failover pair. In this case, the active unit maintains HTTP connection entries but does not replicate those to the standby unit.

A failover pair has been configured for stateful failover in the following example. Somewhere along the way, the standby unit lost power and was rebooted. Notice that the table counts are quite different; the standby unit lost its tables and has received only new table changes, and HTTP replication has not been configured on the failover pair. The active unit is shown first, followed by the standby unit.

```
[Active unit]
Firewall# show conn count
4263 in use, 577536 most used
Firewall# show xlate count
15166 in use, 22368 most used
Firewall#

[Standby unit]
Firewall# show conn count
686 in use, 690 most used
Firewall# show xlate count
659 in use, 665 most used
Firewall#
```

Checking Firewall Throughput

Many of the firewall statistics that you might display are based on incrementing counters or "snapshot" values. These give you an idea of the *volume* of activity over a long period of time, but not of the *rate*. For example, to gauge your firewall's throughput, you might want to see the number of bytes per second being forwarded on an interface or the number of TCP connections per second that are being inspected.

A Cisco firewall keeps several running statistics that you can display. You also can use an external application to perform some analysis on firewall counters and messages. The following sections describe several ways to show the firewall throughput.

ASDM

The Adaptive Security Device Manager (ASDM) default view shows several useful throughput calculations. Figure 11-1 shows a sample ASDM display, where you can determine the following throughput measures:

- Current interface throughput, in kbps, is shown in the upper-right portion of the display. This is the aggregate or total of input and output rates. (You can select an interface to see the current input and output throughput values.)
- UDP and TCP connections per second, in the middle-right portion of the display.

- A history of the first (lowest-numbered) interface throughput, in kbps, shown in the lower right of the display. Separate graphs are shown for input and output throughput. Figure 11-1 shows a graph of the "outside" interface activity.

Figure 11-1 *A Sample ASDM Display of Firewall Throughput*

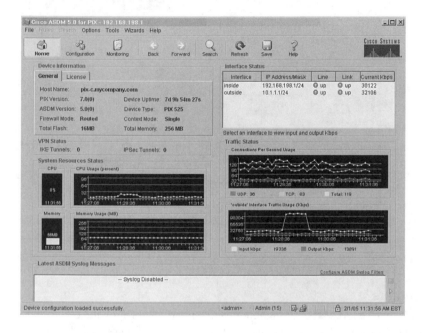

Syslog

Some Syslog analysis applications can parse the history of Syslog messages generated by a firewall. If the firewall is configured to report about connections being set up and torn down (logging severity level 6, *informational*, by default), the Syslog analyzer can calculate the number of connections per second, the interface data rate per second, and so on.

For example, a Syslog analysis tool is used to present information about the bandwidth being passed through firewall interfaces. Figure 11-2 shows a graph of utilization per unit time, as "bandwidth usage per hour." In this case, rather than showing the throughput for an individual interface, the total aggregate bandwidth for all interfaces is shown over time.

Figure 11-2 *An Example of Firewall Throughput Reporting by Syslog Analysis*

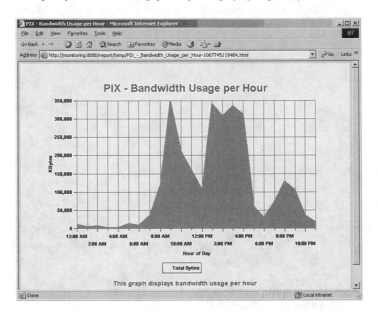

Traffic Counters

Cisco firewalls can report traffic throughput on each interface through the command-line interface (CLI). This can be handy if you are connected to a firewall over a console, Telnet, or Secure Shell (SSH) session, and you want to check the throughput.

The firewall keeps running counters of input and output data on each interface while it is operational. These counters begin at bootup or at the last counter reset, and they accumulate until you issue the command to display them. The firewall also computes the average throughput in bytes per second, but this is based on the *total* time elapsed since the counters were last reset.

To see the traffic counters and throughput information, follow these steps:

1. (Optional) Reset the traffic counters:

   ```
   Firewall# clear traffic
   ```
   The data counters, rates, and elapsed time values are reset to 0 for each interface. This step is important so that you establish a time frame for taking throughput measurements.

NOTE   If you do not begin by resetting the counters, you might end up displaying traffic statistics that have been running for a very long time, as in this example:

```
Firewall# show traffic
```

```
outside:
        received (in 509866.850 secs):
                785027658 packets      2630237219 bytes
                1000 pkts/sec   5007 bytes/sec
        transmitted (in 509866.850 secs):
                640777558 packets       494377136 bytes
                1004 pkts/sec   0 bytes/sec
inside:
        received (in 509866.850 secs):
                642131249 packets      1622203492 bytes
                1006 pkts/sec   3004 bytes/sec
        transmitted (in 509866.850 secs):
                770623656 packets      1358715766 bytes
                1005 pkts/sec   2007 bytes/sec
```

The counters have been accumulating for 509,866 seconds, or about 5.9 days. Because the data throughput values fluctuate all the time, this is not an accurate estimate of the current throughput.

2. Wait, and then display the traffic statistics:

    Firewall# **show traffic**

    You should wait a few seconds or even a minute before displaying the traffic statistics. The byte and packet counters shown will have accumulated over that time. The byte and packet rates (per second) will be calculated as an average over that time.

    For example, the following firewall's statistics were shown after 70 seconds had elapsed. Its outside interface (Gigabit Ethernet) received an average of 2,826,360 bytes per second over those 70 seconds.

```
Firewall# show traffic
stateful:
        received (in 70.750 secs):
                15 packets      1560 bytes
                0 pkts/sec      22 bytes/sec
        transmitted (in 70.750 secs):
                1096 packets    1307978 bytes
                15 pkts/sec     18487 bytes/sec
outside:
        received (in 70.750 secs):
                258717 packets  199964989 bytes
                3656 pkts/sec   2826360 bytes/sec
        transmitted (in 70.750 secs):
                210554 packets  48903164 bytes
                2976 pkts/sec   691210 bytes/sec
inside:
        received (in 70.750 secs):
                210849 packets  53713701 bytes
                2980 pkts/sec   759204 bytes/sec
```

```
        transmitted (in 70.750 secs):
                256901 packets  166768097 bytes
                3631 pkts/sec   2357146 bytes/sec
Firewall#
```

On an ASA platform, the **show traffic** command also breaks down the traffic statistics based on logical interfaces and on the aggregate performance of physical interfaces. For example, a firewall might have two physical interfaces, *GigabitEthernet1/0* and *GigabitEthernet1/1*. You can assign each of these a logical name such as **outside** or **inside**.

In addition, you can configure the physical interface to trunk multiple VLANs; each VLAN subinterface (*GigabitEthernet1/0.1*, for example) can become a unique logical interface (*dmz*, *intf3*, and so on) while remaining a part of the aggregate physical interface.

In the following example, logical interfaces *outside*, *inside*, and *Test* are mapped from physical interfaces *GigabitEthernet1/0*, *GigabitEthernet1/1.1*, and *GigabitEthernet1/1.2*, respectively.

```
Firewall# show traffic
outside:
        received (in 2701.540 secs):
                15754 packets   12405921 bytes
                5 pkts/sec      4592 bytes/sec
        transmitted (in 2701.540 secs):
                1447 packets    126813 bytes
                0 pkts/sec      46 bytes/sec
inside:
        received (in 2701.550 secs):
                1533 packets    132357 bytes
                0 pkts/sec      48 bytes/sec
        transmitted (in 2701.550 secs):
                15936 packets   12364101 bytes
                5 pkts/sec      4576 bytes/sec
Test:
        received (in 2701.550 secs):
                185 packets     19980 bytes
                0 pkts/sec      7 bytes/sec
        transmitted (in 2701.550 secs):
                276 packets     29808 bytes
                0 pkts/sec      11 bytes/sec
----------------------------------------
Aggregated Traffic on Physical Interface
----------------------------------------
GigabitEthernet1/0:
        received (in 2705.540 secs):
                15782 packets   12706533 bytes
                5 pkts/sec      4696 bytes/sec
```

```
         transmitted (in 2705.540 secs):
                 1447 packets    157397 bytes
                 0 pkts/sec      58 bytes/sec
GigabitEthernet1/1:
         received (in 2705.540 secs):
                 1541 packets    171097 bytes
                 0 pkts/sec      63 bytes/sec
         transmitted (in 2705.540 secs):
                 15959 packets   12695684 bytes
                 5 pkts/sec      4692 bytes/sec
Firewall#
```

Aggregate interface performance also comes into play for firewalls that are configured for multiple-context security mode. Each context has its own set of logical interfaces (*inside* and *outside*, for example) that are mapped from a physical interface or subinterface in the system execution space. From any user context, **show traffic** shows only the logical interfaces used by that context. However, the system execution space shows a breakdown that includes the aggregate physical interfaces.

Perfmon Counters

A Cisco firewall also keeps statistics about its stateful inspection performance. These values are called performance monitors or *perfmon*. From this information, you can get a good idea about the types of traffic passing through the firewall. You can also use the displayed rates to see a load distribution of the inspection or fixup processes.

To configure and view the performance statistics, follow these steps:

1. (Optional) Set the perfmon calculation interval:

    Firewall(config)# **perfmon interval** *seconds*

    Perfmon statistics are calculated and optionally reported at intervals of *seconds* (the default is 120 seconds). This means the results are computed as averages over this interval of time.

2. (Optional) Automatically display perfmon results on the firewall console:

    Firewall(config)# **perfmon {verbose | quiet}**

    By default, a firewall displays perfmon information only when a command is entered manually, as **quiet** mode.

    The firewall can automatically display the perfmon statistics at each interval of time if you use the **verbose** keyword. As soon as this is enabled, the results are displayed only on the firewall console—not on any active Telnet or SSH sessions. This might be handy if you have a terminal connected to the console and you want to see the firewall performance continually updated on the screen. However, if you choose too short an interval, the console connection can become very congested with new perfmon information. As a result, you might not be able to interact with the firewall over the console connection.

3. Display the perfmon statistics:

```
Firewall# show perfmon
```

Firewall performance is reported in several groups, with the following labels:

— **New xlate entry creation**—"Xlates"

— **New connection entry creation**—"Connections" (the total of all connection types), "TCP Conns," and "UDP Conns"

— **Web content filtering**—"URL Access" (new URLs being requested; reported even if Websense or N2H2 servers are not being used) and "URL Server Req" (new Websense and N2H2 server requests)

— **Fixups**—"TCP Fixup" (new TCP packets inspected), "TCPIntercept" (TCP intercept or embryonic connection inspections if an embryonic connection limit is set), "HTTP Fixup" (new HTTP packets inspected), and "FTP Fixup" (new FTP packets inspected)

— **User authentication**—"AAA Authen" (uauth authentication requests processed), "AAA Author" (uauth authorization requests), and "AAA Account" (uauth accounting requests)

In the following example, the firewall has just created 107 new TCP connections, inspected 6196 TCP packets, and inspected 2631 HTTP packets, all in the previous second:

```
Firewall# show perfmon
PERFMON STATS:     Current      Average
Xlates              53/s          0/s
Connections        146/s          0/s
TCP Conns          107/s          0/s
UDP Conns           38/s          0/s
URL Access          79/s          0/s
URL Server Req       0/s          0/s
TCP Fixup         6196/s          0/s
TCPIntercept         0/s          0/s
HTTP Fixup        2631/s          0/s
FTP Fixup            3/s          0/s
AAA Authen           0/s          0/s
AAA Author           0/s          0/s
AAA Account          0/s          0/s
Firewall#
```

The **Current** values are calculated as the number of operations over the last second before the command was issued. The **Average** values are calculated as an average over the perfmon reporting interval, or the last 120 seconds by default. (Because of a cosmetic bug in some platforms, all the average values might be shown as **0/s**.)

TIP	If you are unsure of the perfmon settings, you can use the **perfmon settings** command to see them. Notice that this command does not use a **show** keyword, like most other EXEC firewall commands. The perfmon interval and reporting mode are shown.

Checking Inspection Engine and Service Policy Activity

In ASA and FWSM, application inspection is performed by independent inspection engines that are referenced in service policies. You can get information about the activity of the various inspection engines by displaying the active service policies.

One service policy can be applied to a firewall interface to define the actions to take on matching traffic in the inbound and outbound directions. A default service policy also is configured by default and is applied to all firewall interfaces. Any traffic not matched by an interface service policy is matched by the default global service policy.

You can use the following command to display all active service policy statistics:

```
Firewall# show service-policy
```

The modular policy configuration of each service policy is shown. This includes the target interface, the service policy name, the class map used to match traffic, and each policy action.

For each inspection engine, the number of packets inspected, dropped, and dropped with reset are shown. Packets are counted only in the service policy where they are matched and inspected. The default global service policy matches all packets that are not matched elsewhere.

In the following example, notice the packet counts for HTTP traffic and how each service policy has matched a different set of packets to inspect. The output of this command gives you a quick snapshot of all the inspections and actions that have been configured on the firewall and are actually being used.

```
Firewall# show service-policy
Global policy:
  Service-policy: global_policy
    Class-map: inspection_default
      Inspect: dns maximum-length 512, packet 363, drop 0, reset-drop 0
      Inspect: ftp, packet 0, drop 0, reset-drop 0
      Inspect: h323 h225, packet 0, drop 0, reset-drop 0
      Inspect: h323 ras, packet 0, drop 0, reset-drop 0
      Inspect: rsh, packet 0, drop 0, reset-drop 0
      Inspect: rtsp, packet 26601, drop 0, reset-drop 0
      Inspect: esmtp, packet 1668, drop 0, reset-drop 0
      Inspect: sqlnet, packet 0, drop 0, reset-drop 0
      Inspect: skinny, packet 0, drop 0, reset-drop 0
      Inspect: sunrpc, packet 0, drop 0, reset-drop 0
      Inspect: xdmcp, packet 0, drop 0, reset-drop 0
      Inspect: sip, packet 0, drop 0, reset-drop 0
      Inspect: netbios, packet 0, drop 0, reset-drop 0
      Inspect: tftp, packet 0, drop 0, reset-drop 0
```

```
        Inspect: http, packet 36614, drop 0, reset-drop 0
        Inspect: icmp, packet 3911, drop 0, reset-drop 0
        Inspect: icmp error, packet 171, drop 0, reset-drop 0
    Class-map: asa_class_tftp
        Inspect: tftp, packet 0, drop 0, reset-drop 0
Interface outside:
  Service-policy: test-policy
    Class-map: test
      Inspect: http, packet 369, drop 0, reset-drop 0
      Priority:
        Interface outside: aggregate drop 0, aggregate transmit 0
Interface inside:
  Service-policy: PolicyA
    Class-map: http_class
      Inspect: http test_http, packet 99400, drop 41, reset-drop 0
    Class-map: ftp_class
      Inspect: ftp strict Filter_ftp, packet 696, drop 0, reset-drop 0
    Class-map: test
      Priority:
        Interface inside: aggregate drop 0, aggregate transmit 0
Firewall#
```

Checking Failover Operation

If you have a failover pair of firewalls, you should periodically check to see that the failover mechanisms are actually working properly. Use the techniques described in the following sections to gauge the failover performance.

Verifying Failover Roles

First, you should verify that the active failover unit is indeed the one you are expecting. When a failover pair is initially configured for failover, only one of them becomes the active unit. The other assumes the standby (passive) mode. If a failover occurs, the two units swap roles.

Recall that the two failover units also have a "primary" and "secondary" designation. This has nothing to do with the actual failover operation, other than to distinguish one unit from the other. Usually, the secondary unit is purchased with a Failover license at a lower price.

Why are the failover units hard to distinguish from each other? The active unit always uses the active IP addresses on its interfaces, and the standby unit uses the standby IP addresses. As soon as a failover happens, the two units swap IP addresses. (Keep in mind that the same thing happens with MAC addresses.) This means if you open a Telnet or SSH session to the active IP address on an interface, you will not know which physical unit answers. To make matters more difficult, both failover units also have the same host name and command-line prompt!

After you open a session, you can use the **show failover** command to learn the identity of the physical unit (primary or secondary), as well as its current failover role (active or standby).

For example, suppose a failover pair is configured with an inside active address of 192.168.254.1 and an inside standby address of 192.168.254.2. When failover is first enabled, the primary unit takes on the active failover role.

An SSH session is opened to the active address 192.168.254.1. You would use the **show failover** command to see which unit is currently active:

```
Firewall# show failover
Failover On
Cable status: Normal
Reconnect timeout 0:00:00
Poll frequency 15 seconds
Last Failover at: 08:34:03 EST Sun Dec 28 2003
        This host: Primary - Active
                Active time: 7304955 (sec)
                Interface stateful (192.168.199.1): Normal
                Interface dmz2 (127.0.0.1): Link Down (Shutdown)
                Interface outside (172.16.110.65): Normal
                Interface inside (192.168.254.1): Normal
        Other host: Secondary - Standby
                Active time: 2770785 (sec)
                Interface stateful (192.168.199.2): Normal
                Interface dmz2 (0.0.0.0): Link Down (Shutdown)
                Interface outside (172.16.110.66): Normal
                Interface inside (192.168.254.2): Normal
[output deleted]
```

In the highlighted output, it is easy to see that failover is enabled (on), that the host to which you are connected is the primary unit, and that it has the active role. Notice that the pair of units is polling each other every 15 seconds (the default). This means that it takes up to two or three poll intervals (30 to 45 seconds) for one unit to detect that the other unit has failed.

You can also use this command to quickly see the status of every firewall interface—on both units at the same time. For each interface that is being used, you should see the **Normal** status listed. If you see **Waiting**, one of the units has missed one hello message from the other and suspects there might be a problem. **Testing** means that three hellos have been missed, so the interface is currently going through a series of tests. If the tests fail, the interface is marked as **Failed**.

Verifying Failover Communication

If failover is enabled, you might want to verify that the two units are communicating properly over the failover links. Cisco firewalls can exchange failover information in three ways:

- **Failover cable**—An asynchronous serial data cable (DB-9 connectors) can connect two PIX units. Failover information is exchanged at 115,200 kbps.

- **LAN-based failover**—A firewall interface (a physical Fast or Gigabit Ethernet interface only) is used to exchange data between the units. This allows the failover units to be geographically separated.

- **Stateful failover**—Information about new connections, xlates, and uauth entries is sent from the active unit to the standby unit. The standby unit receives these updates so that it can perform a stateful failover when assuming the active role. (Stateful failover can be used in addition to the failover cable or LAN-based failover.)

If a failover cable is being used, look for the cable status in the **show failover** command output:

```
Firewall# show failover
Failover On
Cable status: Normal
Reconnect timeout 0:00:00
Poll frequency 15 seconds
Last Failover at: 08:34:03 EST Sun Dec 28 2004
        This host: Primary - Active
[output deleted]
```

In this example, the cable is in place and the status is **Normal**. This means the two units are exchanging failover information successfully. With the failover cable, each unit can also determine if the other unit is powered on. If the companion unit has lost power, the cable status shows **other side is powered off**.

TIP   Keep in mind that the failover cable itself determines which unit is primary and which is secondary. One end of the cable is labeled "primary" and should be plugged into the unit that has the primary firewall license. Obviously, the other end of the cable plugs into the secondary unit, usually the one with the failover license.

If you are using LAN-based failover, the status of the failover cable is irrelevant. The status of the interface dedicated to LAN-based failover communication, however, is important. The primary and secondary failover units are identified through configuration commands.

With PIX 6.3, rather than sifting through output showing the status of the LAN-based interface, you can quickly see the status with the **show failover lan** command. In the following example, the **dmz** interface is being used for failover communication. The failover peer at each end of the LAN connection is seen to be **Normal**.

```
Firewall# show failover lan
Lan Based Failover is Active
   interface dmz (192.168.1.1): Normal, peer (192.168.1.2): Normal
```

ASA and FWSM platforms do not have this command. Instead, look at the first few lines of the **show failover** command output:

```
Firewall# show failover
Failover On
Cable status: N/A - LAN-based failover enabled
Failover unit Primary
Failover LAN Interface: Failover Ethernet2 (up)
Unit Poll frequency 3 seconds, holdtime 9 seconds
Interface Poll frequency 15 seconds
[output omitted]
```

> **NOTE**   Unlike with the failover cable, it is not possible to detect the power status of the other
> unit with LAN-based failover. The cable carries a power signal from each unit so that
> it is easy to sense a loss of power. No power signals can be carried over a LAN-based
> failover connection, simply because only IP packets can be exchanged between the two
> units. If one unit has lost power, nothing in the IP failover packets indicates that. The
> other unit notices only the absence of failover packets.

In PIX 6.3, you can also use the **show failover lan detail** command to add a generous amount of
debugging information. Most of the output messages are coded values that are not intuitive.
However, you can see failover message counters and retransmission queue statistics that show how
congested the LAN-based failover link has been.

If you are concerned about two firewalls failing over with little impact to a production network, you
have likely configured stateful failover. This type of failover works in conjunction with a failover
cable or LAN-based failover. The basic housekeeping functions are communicated over the cable or
the LAN interface, and the stateful interface is reserved for sending dynamic updates about
connection or translation entries.

If it works properly, stateful failover keeps the standby unit fully informed about the state of every
active TCP and UDP connection in the active unit. In addition, the xlate table entries and ARP table
entries are replicated. Should the standby unit need to take over, it already has the stateful
information and can preserve existing connections during the failover transition.

A failover pair keeps detailed statistics about the stateful information exchange. You will find this at
the end of the **show failover** command output. You should only be concerned about verifying
effective stateful updates so that the two firewall units stay synchronized at all times.

For example, the active unit shows the following output from the **show failover** command:

```
Firewall# show failover
Failover On
Cable status: N/A - LAN-based failover enabled
Failover unit Primary
Failover LAN Interface: Failover Ethernet2 (up)
Unit Poll frequency 3 seconds, holdtime 9 seconds
Interface Poll frequency 15 seconds
Interface Policy 2
Monitored Interfaces 3 of 250 maximum
Group 1 last failover at: 10:29:18 EST Jan 30 2005
Group 2 last failover at: 10:29:27 EST Jan 30 2005
Stateful Failover Logical Update Statistics
        Link : Failover Ethernet2 (up)
        Stateful Obj   xmit       xerr        rcv         rerr
        General        0          0           0           0
        sys cmd        13531      0           13531       0
        up time        0          0           0           0
```

```
   RPC services    0          0          0          0
   TCP conn        0          0          0          0
   UDP conn        0          0          0          0
   ARP tbl         29         0          0          0
   Xlate_Timeout   0          0          0          0


   Logical Update Queue Information
                   Cur     Max      Total
   Recv Q:         0       1        13531
   Xmit Q:         0       1        13573
```
Firewall#

Here, the number of these types of replicated stateful messages are shown:

- **General**—The total number of stateful messages
- **sys cmd**—System commands that have been replicated to the other unit
- **up time**—Uptime reports (the elapsed time since the unit has been booted)
- **RPC services**—Remote Procedure Call entry updates
- **xlate**—Translation or xlate table entry updates (PIX 6.3 only—not shown in the preceding output)
- **TCP conn**—Conn table TCP connection entry updates
- **UDP conn**—Conn table UDP connection entry updates
- **ARP tbl**—ARP table entry updates
- **L2BRIDGE tbl**—MAC address table entry updates (ASA transparent firewall mode only—not shown in the preceding output)
- **RIP Tbl**—RIP route advertisement updates (PIX 6.3 only—not shown in the preceding output)
- **Xlate Timeout**—Xlate entries removed after timeout (ASA and FWSM)

The **xmit** and **rcv** columns show how many of each message type have been transmitted or received by this firewall, respectively. While the unit is in active mode, you should see the transmit counters increasing much more than the receive counters. This is because the active unit is tasked with keeping the standby unit updated.

The **xerr** and **rerr** columns show the number of transmit and receive errors encountered while exchanging messages. If you find a large number of transmit errors, the sending firewall unit could not successfully send failover messages because of network congestion or a slow LAN interface. Receive errors indicate failover messages that arrived corrupted.

Determining If a Failover Has Occurred

If a failover pair of firewalls is operating correctly, and stateful failover is being used to synchronize the state information, you might never realize when a failover takes place. How can you determine if the units have failed over?

You can use the **show failover** command to see a record of the last failover event. The output from this command displays the date and time, along with the total amount of time that each unit has assumed the active role. In the following example, the failover occurred on December 28 at 8:34:03 a.m. Be aware that you must have already set the firewall clock (both active and standby units) or have configured the units to use Network Time Protocol (NTP). Otherwise, the failover time stamp will be incorrect, and you will have no idea when it actually occurred.

```
Firewall# show failover
Failover On
Cable status: N/A - LAN-based failover enabled
Failover unit Primary
Failover LAN Interface: Failover Ethernet2 (up)
Unit Poll frequency 3 seconds, holdtime 9 seconds
Interface Poll frequency 5 seconds, holdtime 25 seconds
Interface Policy 2
Monitored Interfaces 4 of 250 maximum
Version: Ours 8.0(1), Mate 8.0(1)
Last Failover at: 08:34:03 EST Thu Dec 28 2006
        This host: Primary - Active
                Active time: 7304955 (sec)
                Interface stateful (192.168.199.1): Normal
                Interface dmz2 (127.0.0.1): Link Down (Shutdown)
                Interface outside (172.16.110.65): Normal
                Interface inside (192.168.254.1): Normal
        Other host: Secondary - Standby
                Active time: 2770785 (sec)
                Interface stateful (192.168.199.2): Normal
                Interface dmz2 (0.0.0.0): Link Down (Shutdown)
                Interface outside (172.16.110.66): Normal
                Interface inside (192.168.254.2): Normal
[output deleted]
```

At this point, you should also take note of the failover roles. When this command was entered, the primary unit was in the active role. This means that when the failover occurred, the other unit (the secondary) was active.

The **Active time** values only serve to give you an idea of how much time each unit has spent in the active role. This is the total cumulative active time since the last reboot—not the amount of time the unit has been active since the last failover. In the sample output, the two units might have failed over more than once. Only the *last* failover event is noted, and you have no knowledge of any previous ones. Therefore, these units might have traded roles and accumulated active duty time on several occasions.

If Syslog messages have been generated and recorded, you can find a detailed record of each failover and the symptoms surrounding it, complete with time stamps.

Determining the Cause of a Failover

Now consider the importance of knowing *why* a failover has happened. For a failover to be triggered, one or both firewalls must have detected a problem—either the other unit was unresponsive with failover polls, or an interface had a problem. If a problem exists, you should try to identify it and get it fixed; otherwise, you might be left with only one working firewall out of the pair. In addition, the same problem could recur, causing the firewalls to failover again.

TIP   For proper failover operation, each firewall unit must be able to send failover messages to the other unit on *every* useable or monitored interface. This means you should make sure each interface on the primary unit can reach each corresponding interface on the secondary unit. A failure of just one interface can trigger a failover condition. (In ASA and FWSM, you can configure a failover policy that triggers a failover when the number of failed monitored interfaces increases above a threshold.)

If you have firewall interfaces that are not being used, make sure you shut down those interfaces with the **interface** *hardware_id* **shutdown** configuration command (PIX 6.3) or the **shutdown** interface configuration command (ASA, FWSM). You should also make sure that unused interfaces do not have a valid IP address configured. You can use the **ip address** *interface* **0.0.0.0 255.255.255.255** configuration command. If any unused interface is left enabled, it could inadvertently trigger a failover just from a lack of connectivity between the failover units.

You can diagnose the cause of a failover event using one of the following two methods:

- The status of interfaces reported by the **show failover** command
- Failover messages recorded in the Syslog history

If a firewall interface fails for some reason, it might trigger a failover. However, if the interface becomes usable again, it is shown as **Normal** in the **show failover** output. If it fails and stays failed, you can use that command to find the broken interface, even at a later date.

The most detailed way to track down the failure is to sift through the Syslog message history. A Syslog server is a must here, because the failover event might be buried within many thousands or millions of other Syslog messages. The firewall logging buffer simply is not large enough to store a long history of messages.

Usually, only the active failover unit is configured to generate "trap" (Syslog) logging to a Syslog server. The standby unit can generate its own Syslog messages, but that causes both units to send duplicate messages to the server. That doubles the amount of message storage required and is usually considered redundant.

Therefore, begin by finding the date and time of the failover event with the **show failover** command. This gives you a window of time to use when searching through the archived Syslog data.

Failover messages are generated with the identity of the sending firewall unit embedded in the message text: **(Primary)** or **(Secondary)**. This is important, because it uniquely identifies which physical firewall unit is reporting the failover activity. If logging from the standby unit has not been enabled, you can conclude that any messages found must have come from the unit that was *active* at that time.

The active unit messages found on the Syslog server tell only half of the failover story; to find the standby unit's testimony, you have to look elsewhere. For this, it is handy to enable buffered logging in addition to trap (Syslog) logging on the active unit. Unlike trap logging, when buffered logging is enabled, it is enabled on both the active and standby units.

Therefore, the standby unit (after failover) has in its logging buffer a brief record of the failover. In fact, the failover messages are the very last messages recorded in the buffer. Why? This is because that unit was active up until the failover. It would have recorded all sorts of Syslog messages in its buffer, because they were also sent to the Syslog server. Any failover messages would be recorded there, up until the unit switched to standby mode. Then the unit becomes passive and does not really generate any further Syslog messages.

Therefore, use the search terms **Primary** or **Secondary** when you search through the Syslog messages. Then go to the standby unit (after failover) and get a record of its logging buffer with the **show logging** command.

An Example of Finding the Cause of a Failover

A failover has occurred within a pair of Cisco Firewalls. From the **show failover** command, you find this time stamp:

```
Firewall# show failover
Failover On
Cable status: Normal
Reconnect timeout 0:00:00
Poll frequency 15 seconds
Last Failover at: 08:34:03 EST Mon Apr 23 2007
        This host: Primary - Active
             Active time: 7319775 (sec)
```

On the Syslog server, you perform a search for the terms **Primary** and **Secondary** in the message text around that time frame. You are looking for any failover messages that might have been sent by the primary or secondary firewall units. Here are the results of the search:

```
Apr 23 2007 8:34AM Firewall LOCAL4  ALERT %ASA-1-104001: (Primary) Switching to
   ACTIVE - mate want me Active.
Apr 23 2007 8:34AM Firewall LOCAL4  ALERT %ASA-1-105003: (Primary) Monitoring on
   interface 3 waiting
Apr 23 2007 8:34AM Firewall  LOCAL4  ALERT %ASA-1-105003: (Primary) Monitoring on
   interface 0 waiting
Apr 23 2007 8:34AM Firewall  LOCAL4  ALERT %ASA-1-105004: (Primary) Monitoring on
   interface 3 normal
Apr 23 2007 8:34AM Firewall  LOCAL4  ALERT %ASA-1-105004: (Primary) Monitoring on
   interface 0 normal
```

```
Apr 23 2007 9:09AM Firewall  LOCAL4  ALERT %ASA-1-105008: (Primary) Testing
    Interface 2
Apr 23 2007 9:09AM Firewall  LOCAL4  ALERT %ASA-1-105009: (Primary) Testing on
    interface 2 Passed
Apr 23 2007 9:09AM Firewall  LOCAL4  ALERT %ASA-1-105008: (Primary) Testing
    Interface 2
Apr 23 2007 9:09AM Firewall  LOCAL4  ALERT %ASA-1-105009: (Primary) Testing on
    interface 2 Passed
Apr 23 2007 9:10AM Firewall  LOCAL4  ALERT %ASA-1-105008: (Primary) Testing
    Interface 2
Apr 23 2007 9:10AM Firewall  LOCAL4  ALERT %ASA-1-105009: (Primary) Testing on
    interface 2 Passed
Apr 23 2007 9:10AM Firewall  LOCAL4  ALERT %ASA-1-105008: (Primary) Testing
    Interface 2
Apr 23 2007 9:10AM Firewall  LOCAL4  ALERT %ASA-1-105009: (Primary) Testing on
    interface 2 Passed
Apr 23 2007 9:10AM Firewall  LOCAL4  ALERT %ASA-1-105004: (Primary) Monitoring on
    interface 2 normal
```

From this record, it is evident that something began to happen at 8:34 a.m. on April 23. The primary unit reports that the other unit ("mate") has decided that it should assume the active role. Obviously, before this time, the primary unit had been in the standby role.

When the primary unit becomes active, it begins to monitor on several interfaces, determining if the interfaces are working properly and if it can detect the other unit on them too. Notice that at 9:09 a.m., it begins several testing phases on interface 2. Evidently, interface 2 (missing from the earlier monitor tests) had a problem from 8:34 until 9:09.

You still do not know what triggered the failover, because you have a record only from the unit that had just become active at that time. That also means that the other unit, which had been active before the failover, was generating other Syslog messages before the failover. However, the failover caused it to enter the standby mode, so no further Syslog information was sent to the server.

As a last step, you connect to that unit (currently in standby mode) and have a look at its logging buffer:

```
Firewall# show logging
Syslog logging: enabled
    Facility: 20
    Timestamp logging: disabled
    Standby logging: disabled
    Console logging: disabled
    Monitor logging: disabled
    Buffer logging: level warnings, 553574 messages logged
    Trap logging: level warnings, 553574 messages logged
        Logging to inside 192.168.100.100
    History logging: disabled
    Device ID: disabled
305006: Dst IP is network/broadcast IP, translation creation failed for icmp src
    outside:64.170.37.34 dst inside:169.163.69.0 (type 8, code 0)
305006: Dst IP is network/broadcast IP, translation creation failed for icmp src
    outside:64.170.37.34 dst inside:169.163.69.0 (type 8, code 0)
500004: Invalid transport field for protocol=17, from 172.21.68.65/47808 to
    1.0.0.0/0
```

```
[output deleted]
411002: Line protocol on Interface outside, changed state to down
105007: (Secondary) Link status 'Down' on interface 2
104002: (Secondary) Switching to STNDBY - interface check, mate is healthier
105003: (Secondary) Monitoring on interface 3 waiting
105003: (Secondary) Monitoring on interface 0 waiting
105004: (Secondary) Monitoring on interface 3 normal
105004: (Secondary) Monitoring on interface 0 normal
105006: (Secondary) Link status 'Up' on interface 2
105003: (Secondary) Monitoring on interface 2 waiting
105004: (Secondary) Monitoring on interface 2 normal
Firewall#
```

Aha! The buffered record shows that the "outside" interface went down, triggering the failover. This unit decided that because its own interface went down hard, it should immediately relinquish the active role.

Unfortunately, logging time stamps were not configured, so the firewall did not add any date and time information to the messages in its own buffer. (This is true only for ASA or FWSM; PIX and early FWSM releases do not add time stamps to buffered logging messages.) This does not really matter, because these are the final recorded messages and must have occurred right before the last time the unit entered the standby role.

Intervening in a Failover Election

Cisco firewalls do not toggle their roles as failures come and go. For example, if an active unit fails, it automatically enters the standby role. Even if its failure is cured, it does not resume its former active role.

The idea is that after a failure has taken place, a network administrator needs to diagnose the problem and fix it. After a failed firewall unit is repaired, you have to manually inform the pair that they need to reset the failed condition in their failover status. When a problem is resolved on a failed standby unit, you can use the **failover reset** command on the active unit. Both units recognize that the standby unit has become "unfailed" and resume normal failover communication.

Sometimes you might need to manually toggle the roles. This might be necessary if you need to perform some maintenance on one unit, but it is unfortunately already in the active role. You can approach this in two ways:

- Use the **no failover active** command on the *active* unit. It immediately relinquishes the active role to its failover peer.
- Use the **failover active** command on the *standby* unit to force it to immediately assume the active role.

Checking Firewall Interfaces

You can use the **show traffic** command to see throughput information about firewall interfaces, but you can monitor other interface statistics as well. You can use the **show interface** command to see a wealth of information about the interface operation, many types of error conditions, and packet buffering.

As with the Cisco IOS Software, the **show interface** command can produce such a condensed dump of interface parameters that it becomes difficult to interpret. To make this easier, think of the command output as being broken into various sections.

Figure 11-3 shows an example of the **show interface** command on an ASA platform. Other software releases show similar information but are organized slightly differently. Only the "outside" interface is shown, for clarity. If you just glance through the lines of output looking for any glaring error condition you are unlikely to find anything but a collection of numbers.

Figure 11-3 *A Breakdown of Information Presented by the* ***show interface*** *Command*

```
Firewall# show interface
```

Interface name and status

```
Interface GigabitEthernet1/0 "outside", is up, line protocol is up
```

Interface control

```
  Hardware is VCS7380 rev01, BW 1000 Mbps, DLY 10 usec
    Auto-Duplex(Full-duplex), Auto-Speed(1000 Mbps)
```

Interface addresses

```
    MAC address 0003.4725.2e32, MTU 1500
    IP address 192.168.254.1, subnet mask 255.255.255.0
```

Inbound packet statistics

```
    74613701 packets input, 50030269037331 bytes, 258406 no buffer
    Received 1375986 broadcasts, 0 runts, 0 giants
    46 input errors, 0 CRC, 46 frame, 0 overrun, 0 ignored, 0 abort
    0 L2 decode drops
```

Outbound packet statistics

```
    2349219007 packets output, 7440196846237 bytes, 0 underruns
    0 output errors, 0 collisions, 0 interface resets
    0 babbles, 0 late collisions, 27 deferred
    0 lost carrier, 0 no carrier
```

Packet queue status

```
    input queue (curr/max blocks): hardware (0/25) software (0/0)
    output queue (curr/max blocks): hardware (3/122) software (0/0)
```

Traffic statistics

```
  Traffic Statistics for "outside":
        74613701 packets input, 50030269037331 bytes
        2349219007 packets output, 7440196846237 bytes
        1765234 packets dropped
      1 minute input rate 4013 pkts/sec,  2247280 bytes/sec
      1 minute output rate 3862 pkts/sec,  2170444 bytes/sec
      1 minute drop rate, 1 pkts/sec
      5 minute input rate 6107 pkts/sec,  3432134 bytes/sec
      5 minute output rate 4525 pkts/sec,  2543050 bytes/sec
      5 minute drop rate, 1 pkts/sec
```

As the figure shows, the lines of output are organized into groups of related information. Each of these groups is explained in detail in the following sections to correspond with the figure. The parameters in each group appear in table format for quick reference. The sample values in Figure 11-3 are shown, along with an explanation of the parameter.

Interface Name and Status

Table 11-3 describes the interface name and status information displayed by the **show interface** command as depicted in Figure 11-3.

Table 11-3 *show interface Command Output: Interface Name and Status Information*

Parameter	Sample Value	Description
Hardware interface	GigabitEthernet1/0	The physical interface names listed by the **show version** command.
Interface name	Outside	An arbitrary name configured by the **nameif** command.
Interface status	Up	The interface is enabled (not shut down).
Line protocol	Up	The Gigabit Ethernet link is established or up.

Interface Control

Table 11-4 describes the interface control information displayed by the **show interface** command as depicted in Figure 11-3.

Table 11-4 *show interface Command Output: Interface Control Information*

Parameter	Sample Value	Description
Hardware	VCS7380 rev01	The interface controller on a Gigabit Ethernet interface.
BW	1000 Mbps	The interface bandwidth (1 Gbps in this case).
DLY	10 μsec	The interface delay, measured in microseconds (10 μsec in this case). The delay is one component in the metric calculation for routes in EIGRP.
Duplex mode	(Full-duplex)	The current mode can be full or half. If autonegotiation is configured, this appears as **Auto-Duplex(Full-duplex)**. This is configured with the **interface** (PIX 6.3) or **duplex** (ASA) command.
Speed	Auto-Speed(1000 Mbps)	The autonegotiated speed is 1 Gbps. This is configured with the **interface** (PIX 6.3) or **speed** (ASA) command.

The interface bandwidth or speed shown should match that of the network device on the other end of the connection.

However, be aware of problems caused by duplex mode configuration. Duplex mode must be configured identically on the firewall and the network device to which it connects. Duplex mode can be autonegotiated only if the other end of the connection is also set to autonegotiate. Otherwise, autonegotiation is unable to "sense" what mode the other side is using, and duplex mode defaults to half-duplex.

TIP   You can use the interface information to troubleshoot duplex mismatch problems. First, look at the duplex setting that is reported. If the interface is set to **Auto-duplex** and the actual mode is half-duplex, most likely the far end of the connection is not configured for autonegotiation. The firewall then attempts to negotiate duplex mode and falls back to half-duplex as a default.

In addition, nonzero values for collisions, late collisions, and output errors can also indicate a duplex mismatch. If one end is using full-duplex mode and the other end half-duplex mode, there is a good chance that the two devices will attempt to transmit at the same time and cause a frame collision. The resulting data becomes scrambled and appears as an output error.

Best practice is to hard-code or configure specific interface speed and duplex settings to avoid any problems with misconfiguration or autonegotiation.

Interface Addresses

Table 11-5 describes the interface address information displayed by the **show interface** command as depicted in Figure 11-3.

Table 11-5   **show interface** *Command Output: Interface Address Information*

Parameter	Sample Value	Description
MAC address	0003.4725.2e32	The interface MAC address
MTU	MTU 1500	The maximum transmission unit—the largest packet that can be transmitted or received over the interface
IP address	192.168.254.1	The interface IP address
Subnet mask	255.255.255.0	The interface subnet mask

The MAC address shown is the burned-in address (BIA) that is preprogrammed on the interface. If failover is enabled, the MAC address changes according to the firewall's failover role. The active unit always takes on the MAC address of the primary unit's interface BIA. The standby unit always takes on the MAC address defined for the secondary unit. You can also configure both units to have specific MAC addresses with the **failover mac address** command.

The IP address shown is the address configured for the interface. If failover is enabled, the active unit takes on the IP address configured for the primary unit's interface. The standby unit takes on the IP address configured for the secondary unit's interface.

The MTU value shown defaults to 1500 bytes for Ethernet interfaces and can be configured with the **mtu** command. In ASA, the interface MTU is shown as **MTU not set** if the interface is shut down or if it has not been configured with a logical name with the **nameif** command.

Inbound Packet Statistics

Table 11-6 describes the packet statistics information displayed by the **show interface** command as depicted in Figure 11-3.

Each of these counters is accumulated from the time the firewall was booted or from the time the interface counter was last cleared with the **clear interface** [*if_name*] [**stats**] command.

Table 11-6   *show interface Command Output: Inbound Packet Statistics*

Counter	Sample Value	Description
Packets input	74613701	The number of packets received on the interface.
Bytes input	50030269037331	The number of bytes received on the interface.
No buffer	258406	The number of packets that could not be transferred from the interface to the CPU. No buffer space (packet-sized blocks) was available to queue these packets, so they were dropped.
Received broadcasts	1375986	The number of broadcast packets received.
Runts	0	The number of received packets that were dropped because they were smaller than the minimum Ethernet packet size (64 bytes).
Giants	0	The number of received packets that were dropped because they were larger than the interface's MTU (1500 bytes is the default).
Input errors	46	Usually a catchall count of any of the five errors listed next.
CRC	0	The number of whole packets received whose cyclic redundancy check (CRC) value differed from the expected value. This can indicate that corrupted data is being transmitted from the far end.
Frame	46	The number of incomplete packets received. These packets can also show a CRC error. They are truncated because of packet collisions or a duplex mismatch.
Overrun	0	The number of times the inbound interface controller could not even queue a packet because packets were arriving too fast to be handled. If this count increases, it indicates slowness within the network interface card (NIC), not with the firewall CPU.
Ignored	0	The number of times a packet was ignored by the interface controller because its packet buffer was too full.

continues

Table 11-6 *show interface Command Output: Inbound Packet Statistics (Continued)*

Counter	Sample Value	Description
Abort	0	The number of packets that were dropped because their processing was aborted for some reason.
L2 decode drops	0	The number of packets dropped because of a Layer 2 problem— either the packet arrived on a VLAN that was not configured on the interface or the interface was not configured with a name yet (via the **nameif** command).

The **overrun**, **ignored**, and **abort** input errors are traditional values that have been carried over from Cisco IOS Software on routers. You typically do not see these error counts increase because of the firewall queuing strategy. This is described further in the "Packet Queue Status" section a bit later.

Outbound Packet Statistics

Table 11-7 describes the outbound packet statistical information displayed by the **show interface** command as depicted in Figure 11-3.

Each of these outbound counters is accumulated from the time the firewall was booted or from the time the interface counter was last cleared with the **clear interface** [*if_name*] [**stats**] command.

Table 11-7 *show interface Command Output: Outbound Packet Statistics*

Counter	Sample Value	Description
Packets output	2349219007	The total number of packets transmitted on the interface.
Bytes	7440196846237	The total number of bytes transmitted on the interface.
Underruns	0	The number of times the interface has transmitted a packet faster than the CPU could keep up. In this case, the interface did not have a complete packet or group of packets to send.
Output errors	0	The number of frames that could not be sent because too many collisions occurred.
Collisions	0	The number of times a collision occurred when a packet was trying to be sent, causing the packets to be retransmitted. Collisions are expected on a half-duplex connection.
Late collisions	0	The number of times a collision occurred but the other stations did not adhere to the normal collision back-off window. Therefore, these packets were lost because the buffer was already freed. You might see late collisions on a half-duplex connection.
Deferred	27	The number of times a packet could not be sent because the interface was already busy transmitting.

You might also see the counters listed in Table 11-8 displayed, depending on the firewall platform and the type of connection.

Table 11-8 *show interface Command Output: Additional Interface Statistics*

Counter	Description
Interface resets	The number of times the interface was reset or reinitialized. This can happen if the interface is shut down and brought back up or if something prevents the firewall from transmitting on the interface for more than 3 seconds.
Babbles	The number of times a packet could not be sent because another station was transmitting out of turn for longer than the length of a packet. This term normally is not used by Cisco firewalls.
Lost carrier	The number of times the Ethernet carrier signal was lost while a packet was being sent. The carrier signal is essential to bringing the link up and to coordinating transmission on a half-duplex connection.
No carrier	The number of times the Ethernet carrier signal was not detected when a packet needed to be sent. This term normally is not used by Cisco firewalls.

In ASA or FWSM multiple-context security mode, the **show interface** command presents a shortened amount of information when it is used from a user context. For example, the following output was produced from the admin context:

```
Firewall/admin# show interface outside
Interface Ethernet0 "outside", is up, line protocol is up
        MAC address 00a0.c900.0101, MTU 1500
        IP address 192.168.93.138, subnet mask 255.255.255.128
        Received 7299 packets, 787753 bytes
        Transmitted 7398 packets, 790589 bytes
        Dropped 0 packets
Firewall/admin#
```

Notice that user context interfaces are known only by their logical names (**outside**, for example). As well, only the addressing and data counter information is shown. The interface error counters are reserved for the system execution space, where the actual physical interfaces are configured.

When an interface is configured as a VLAN trunk, you might see some additional information from the **show interface** command. For example, the following information might be shown:

```
Received 214095 VLAN untagged packets, 174551017 bytes
        Transmitted 103055 VLAN untagged packets, 10106195 bytes
        Dropped 1456 VLAN untagged packets
```

Here, **VLAN untagged packets** represents packets that are sent or received over the native (untagged) VLAN on the 802.1Q trunk.

PIX 6.3 can produce the following output for a trunk interface, including a breakdown of traffic activity on specific VLANs:

```
279 aggregate VLAN packets input, 110463 bytes
     87 aggregate VLAN packets output, 6412 bytes
     8 vlan41 packets input, 540 bytes
     0 vlan41 packets output, 0 bytes
     0 invalid VLAN ID errors, 6 native VLAN errors
```

On ASA and FWSM platforms, if an interface is not completely configured, you might see some additional information. If the **nameif** command has not yet been used to assign a logical name to an interface, the following line is shown from the **show interface** command:

```
Available but not configured via nameif
```

Finally, in multiple-context security mode, physical interfaces must be mapped from the system execution space to the appropriate user contexts. If an interface has not been mapped with the **allocate-interface** context configuration command, the following line is shown:

```
Available for allocation to a context
```

Traffic Statistics

Beginning in ASA 7.2(1), the **show interface** command displays traffic statistics based on input and output activity, in addition to the interface counters. The bottom of Figure 11-3 demonstrated this information earlier; however, the example that follows also shows this information:

```
Traffic Statistics for "outside":
     74613701 packets input, 50030269037331 bytes
     2349219007 packets output, 7440196846237 bytes
     1765234 packets dropped
  1 minute input rate 4013 pkts/sec,  2247280 bytes/sec
  1 minute output rate 3862 pkts/sec,  2170444 bytes/sec
  1 minute drop rate, 31 pkts/sec
  5 minute input rate 6107 pkts/sec,  3432134 bytes/sec
  5 minute output rate 4525 pkts/sec,  2543050 bytes/sec
  5 minute drop rate, 17 pkts/sec
```

The traffic statistics are first shown as cumulative totals, in bytes and packets. The input, output, and drop rates are shown in bytes per second or packets per second.

Packet Queue Status

A Cisco firewall uses several different buffers or queues as it handles packets in a network. To monitor a firewall's performance, it is a good idea to become familiar with the buffering process and statistics.

Figure 11-4 illustrates how packets arriving on an interface are queued for inspection and how other inspected packets are queued for transmission on the interface.

Figure 11-4 *Firewall Interface Packet Queues*

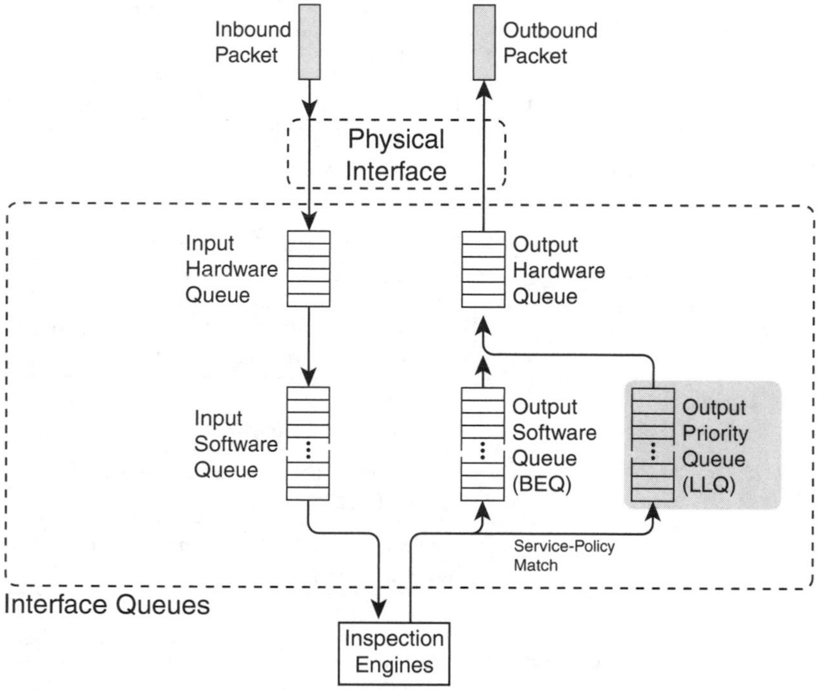

Each firewall interface has its own inbound and outbound queues, arranged as a *hardware queue* and a *software queue* in each direction. In ASA platforms, the outbound software queue is known as the *best-effort queue* (BEQ). Each interface also has an outbound priority queue, the *low-latency queue* (LLQ), that can be used to forward high-priority traffic. The LLQ is always serviced before the BEQ.

Basically, incoming packets arrive from the physical interface and go into a hardware interface queue (if one is present) on the firewall platform. If that queue overflows before packets can be emptied for inspection, new packets are pushed into the input software queue.

In the outbound direction, the process is similar but reversed. As packets are inspected and approved for forwarding, they are moved into an output queue. In PIX 6.3 and earlier, packets were copied right into the output hardware queue if there was room. If not, they went into the output software queue. All packet delivery was done on a best-effort basis, with no quality of service possible.

On ASA platforms, outbound packets can be moved into an output BEQ or an output LLQ, depending on the results of a service policy. If priority queuing is enabled, packets are always pulled from the LLQ before the BEQ is serviced. If priority queuing is not enabled, all outbound packets go into the BEQ.

Hardware and software queue statistics are reported through the **show interface** command, as in the following example from the "Packet Queue Status" section of Figure 11-3:

```
input queue (curr/max blocks): hardware (0/25) software (0/0)
output queue (curr/max blocks): hardware (3/122) software (0/0)
```

Each firewall interface has both input and output queues; the current state of the queues is displayed as a ratio of current/maximum blocks used. Table 11-9 lists the values reported in the preceding command output and describes each value.

Table 11-9   *show interface Command Output: Packet Queue Status Information*

Parameter	Sample Value	Description
Input queue hardware	0/25	No packets are currently in the hardware queue. 25 packets are the most that have ever been in the queue.
Input queue software	0/0	No packets are currently in the software queue. The queue has always been empty.
Output queue hardware	3/122	Three packets are currently in the hardware queue. It has held up to 122 packets in the past.
Output queue software	0/0	No packets are currently in the software queue. The queue has always been empty.

It is common to see the hardware queue (either input or output) reported to have activity. You should see a nonzero number for the maximum queue level when the hardware queue has been used. However, you should see nonzero values for the software queue only when the hardware queue has been full sometime in the past. This is not necessarily a bad thing.

If you see large values reported for a software queue, and the current number consistently stays close to the maximum number, your firewall CPU is having trouble keeping up with the interface load.

TIP   Fast Ethernet firewall interfaces (10/100) always report an inbound hardware queue statistic of 128/128. As well, you always see some inbound software queue activity. This indicates that this type of interface does not use a hardware queue. Instead, all inbound packets are copied into the software queue directly.

This is not true for the Fast Ethernet outbound queues, which use both hardware and software queues.

Outbound priority queues are available only beginning with ASA software release 7.0(1). The **show interface** command does not report on the outbound priority queue. Instead, you can use the following command to view output queue statistics:

```
Firewall# show priority-queue statistics [if_name]
```

This command displays the current statistics about both the priority queue (LLQ) and the best-effort queue (BEQ) of a firewall interface. These are shown as the queue type in the command output. If no interface name is given, all interfaces are shown.

For example, the following statistics resulted from a firewall's *outside* interface:

```
Firewall# show priority-queue statistics outside
Priority-Queue Statistics interface outside
Queue Type        = BE
Packets Dropped   = 0
Packets Transmit  = 132213
Packets Enqueued  = 0
Current Q Length  = 0
Max Q Length      = 0

Queue Type        = LLQ
Packets Dropped   = 0
Packets Transmit  = 1826
Packets Enqueued  = 5
Current Q Length  = 0
Max Q Length      = 32
Firewall#
```

Table 11-10 lists the fields displayed in the command output. The descriptions pertain to the priority queue.

Table 11-10 *show priority-queue statistics Command Output: Packet Queue Status Information*

Parameter	Sample Value	Description
Queue Type	LLQ	The low-latency queue (LLQ), also called the priority queue
Packets Dropped	0	Packets that were dropped because the priority queue was full
Packets Transmit	1826	Packets that were candidates for the priority queue and were successfully transmitted (cumulative total)
Packets Enqueued	5	The running total of packets that have been placed in the priority queue
Current Q Length	0	The current priority queue depth, or the number of packets currently in the priority queue
Max Q Length	32	The largest number of packets stored in the priority queue since the last reboot or **clear priority-queue statistics** command

Sometimes you might see a larger number in the Packets Transmit counter than the Packets Enqueued counter. That might seem odd, because outbound priority packets should be put into the LLQ before being transmitted. The difference is that some firewall platforms can write priority packets into the output hardware queue directly, so they do not actually pass through the LLQ first.

11-2: Watching Data Pass Through a Firewall

Sometimes you might want to know what sort of traffic has passed through a firewall to reach a certain host. At other times, you might need to troubleshoot why traffic is not being forwarded through the firewall. In this case, you would want to verify that packets arrived on one firewall interface but did not go out another interface.

You can use two methods to watch or verify that packets have passed through a firewall:

- **Capture session**—Packets passing through an interface and matching given conditions are captured in a buffer and can be displayed later.

- **Debug packet**—Packets matching conditions defined in a **debug** command are reported as they pass through the firewall.

NOTE Beginning with ASA 7.0(1), the debug packet method is no longer supported.

These methods require different configuration steps, and each affects the firewall resources in different ways. Table 11-11 compares the capture and debug packet methods.

Table 11-11 *Verifying That Packets Have Passed Through a Firewall: Capture Session Versus Debug Packet*

Capture Session	Debug Packet
Packets (or portions of packets) are captured and stored in a memory buffer.	Packets are reported but not captured. Reports are sent to the active debug trace channel (Telnet, SSH, or console).
Captured packets are displayed later.	Packet reports are displayed in real time.
Packets are identified for capture by an interface, an EtherType, or an access list.	Packets are identified for debugging by parameters in the **debug packet** command.
Many capture sessions can be configured and enabled.	Only one debug packet session can be configured at a time.
A capture session is bound to a firewall interface. Only packets passing through that interface can be captured.	A debug packet session reports on matching packets as they are inspected and moved through a firewall interface.
Capture sessions do not adversely affect firewall CPU resources.	A debug packet session can be very taxing on the firewall CPU and packet throughput.
By default, each capture session uses a 512-KB buffer in the firewall memory.	A debug packet session does not require a block of firewall memory.

Using Capture

You can define one or more capture sessions on a firewall, each operating independently. Captured packets are stored in a memory buffer and can be viewed much like a protocol analyzer or sniffer trace.

Defining a Capture Session

Two basic steps are involved in defining a capture session:

1. Configure an access list to identify the interesting traffic for capture.

2. Define the actual capture session.

An access list is used to pick out specific traffic passing through a firewall interface. You can set up a capture session that does not use an access list at all, but it then captures all traffic passing through.

You can configure the access list by entering one or more access control entry (ACE) statements with the following configuration command:

```
Firewall(config)# access-list acl_id [line line-num] [extended] permit protocol
  {source_addr  source_mask [operator sport] [destination_addr destination_mask
  [operator dport]]
```

The access list is used to flag packets for capture—not to permit or deny them from passing through the interface. Therefore, only the **permit** keyword is useful here. An implicit **deny** statement is at the end of the access list, which causes all other traffic to pass without being captured.

The matched *protocol* can be **ip** (any IP protocol), **tcp** (6), **udp** (17), **ah** (51), **eigrp** (88), **esp** or **ipsec** (50), **gre** or **pptp** (47), **igmp** (2), **igrp** (9), **ipinip** (4), **nos** (94), **ospf** (89), **pcp** (108), **pim** (103), **snp** (109), **icmp** (1), **icmp6** (58), or a number from 1 to 255.

Source and destination addresses can be explicit IP addresses or subnets, and the masks are regular subnet masks. If you need to specify addresses, be sure the addresses are relevant with respect to NAT. A capture session can monitor inbound traffic on an interface *before* NAT is performed, and it can monitor outbound traffic *after* NAT is performed.

If you need to match against a source or destination port number, you can add an optional *operator*: **lt** (less than), **gt** (greater than), **eq** (equal to), **neq** (not equal to), or **range** (lies between two port limits). The operator compares the port number to the value given by *port* (a single decimal number; for a range, give two numbers for lower and upper limits).

TIP   You might find it handy to include something like **cap** in the access list name, as in **acl_cap_testprobe**. This way, you can guess that the ACL has a special purpose just by looking at its name.

Section 11-2

To define and start a capture session on a firewall interface, you can use the following privileged EXEC command:

```
Firewall# capture capture_name [access-list acl_name] [ethernet-type type]
  [interface if-name] [buffer bytes] [circular-buffer] [packet-length bytes]
```

The capture session is named *capture_name* (an arbitrary text string). The access list named *acl_name* is used to identify packets to be captured. If an access list is not used or defined, all IP packets are matched. However, you should use an access list to specifically match traffic with respect to NAT.

You can define the protocol to capture in the access list. You can also specify an Ethernet type code in the **capture** command instead if you need to capture a protocol that the ACL does not support. By default, all Ethernet types are flagged for capture. You can specify one as type using one of these values: **arp** (ARP requests and replies), **ip** (TCP/IP), **pppoe** (PPP over Ethernet), **pppoed** (PPP over Ethernet Discovery), **ip6** (IP version 6), **ipx** (Novell IPX), or **rarp** (Reverse ARP).

You should specify which interface the capture session will monitor with the **interface** keyword and the interface *if-name* (defined with the **nameif** command).

TIP On a FWSM platform, the capture feature is somewhat broken until release 3.2. You can define a capture session and apply it to a VLAN interface, but the FWSM captures only packets coming into the interface—outbound packets are not captured at all.

You can also use an external protocol analyzer or "sniffer" to capture all traffic going to and from a FWSM interface. A VLAN ACL (VACL) capture is used on the Catalyst 6500 to intercept packets as they pass between the switch backplane to the FWSM. See the section "Capturing FWSM Packets Inside the Switch" in this chapter for more information.

You can also make adjustments to the capture buffer. By default, the capture session buffer is 512 KB in the main firewall memory. With the **buffer** keyword, the buffer can be resized to bytes. By default, the capture session stops when the buffer is full. However, you can use the **circular-buffer** keyword to allow the capture to work continuously; when the buffer fills, the capture stores the next packet at the beginning of the buffer.

By default, up to 68 bytes of each captured packet are stored in the buffer. You can change this limit with the **packet-length** keyword to *bytes* (up to the MTU or maximum packet size). The default value gives enough information to include the IP and upper-layer protocol headers. Be aware that if you increase the packet length, you can view the contents of captured packets, including any cleartext user IDs, passwords, or other confidential information.

Beginning with ASA 7.0(1), you can add the **type** keyword to specify a type of data to capture. The following command syntax is used:

```
Firewall# capture capture_name type {raw-data | isakmp | asp-drop drop-reason}
  [buffer bytes] [circular-buffer] [packet-length bytes]
```

The **raw-data** type is used in capture sessions by default, even when the **type** keyword is unavailable. In other words, raw IP packets can be captured. You can also capture certain VPN traffic by specifying **type isakmp**.

Another novel feature involves capturing packets that are dropped rather than forwarded through the firewall. This allows you to analyze the contents of dropped packets so that you can see exactly why the packet was dropped. No other capture filtering by access list or interface is necessary, because packets can be dropped for a wide variety of reasons.

You can use the **type asp-drop** keywords along with one of the *drop-reason* keywords listed in Table 11-12.

Table 11-12 *drop-reason Keywords for the **capture type asp-drop** Command*

drop-reason Keyword	Description
acl-drop	Flow is denied by the access rule
all	All packet drop reasons
bad-crypto	Bad crypto return in packet
bad-ipsec-natt	Bad IPSec NAT-T packet
bad-ipsec-prot	IPSec is not AH or ESP
bad-ipsec-udp	Bad IPSec UDP packet
bad-tcp-cksum	Bad TCP checksum
bad-tcp-flags	Bad TCP flags
ctm-error	Crypto Transform Manager (CTM) returned an error
dns-guard-app-id-not-match	DNS Guard application ID did not match
dns-guard-out-of-app-id	DNS Guard out of application ID
dst-l2_lookup-fail	Destination MAC L2 lookup failed
flow-expired	Expired flow
fo-standby	Dropped by the standby unit
ids-fail-close	IDS card is down
ids-request	IDS Module requested a drop
ifc-classify	Virtual firewall classification failed
inspect-dns-app-id-not-match	DNS Inspect application ID did not match

continues

Table 11-12 *drop-reason Keywords for the **capture type asp-drop** Command (Continued)*

drop-reason Keyword	Description
inspect-dns-invalid-domain-label	DNS Inspect invalid domain label
inspect-dns-invalid-pak	DNS Inspect invalid packet
inspect-dns-out-of-app-id	DNS Inspect out of application ID
inspect-dns-pak-too-long	DNS Inspect packet was too long
inspect-icmp-app-id-not-match	ICMP Inspect application ID did not match
inspect-icmp-error-no-existing-conn	ICMP Error Inspect had no existing connection
inspect-icmp-out-of-app-id	ICMP Inspect out of application ID
inspect-icmpv6-error-invalid-pak	ICMPv6 Error Inspect invalid packet
inspect-icmpv6-error-no-existing-conn	ICMPv6 Error Inspect had no existing connection
intercept-unexpected	Unexpected packet was intercepted
interface-down	Interface is down
invalid-app-length	Invalid application length
invalid-encap	Invalid encapsulation
invalid-ethertype	Invalid EtherType
invalid-ip-addr	Invalid IP address
invalid-ip-header	Invalid IP header
invalid-ip-length	Invalid IP length
invalid-ip-option	IP option configured drop
invalid-tcp	Invalid TCP packet
invalid-tcp-hdr-length	Invalid TCP length
invalid-udp-length	Invalid UDP length
ip-fragment	IP fragment unsupported
ipsec-clearpkt-notun	IPSec clear packet with no tunnel
ipsec-ipv6	IPSec via IPv6
ipsec-need-sa	IPSec SA not negotiated yet
ipsec-spoof	IPSec spoof detected
ipsec-tun-down	IPSec tunnel is down
ipsecudp-keepalive	IPSec/UDP keepalive message
ipv6_fp-security-failed	IPv6 fastpath security checks failed
ipv6_sp-security-failed	IPv6 slowpath security checks failed

Table 11-12 *drop-reason Keywords for the **capture type asp-drop** Command (Continued)*

drop-reason Keyword	Description
l2_acl	Fast Path (FP) L2 rule drop
l2_same-lan-port	L2 source/destination same LAN port
large-buf-alloc-fail	Fast Path (FP) large buffer allocation failed
loopback-buffer-full	Loopback buffer is full
lu-invalid-pkt	Invalid failover logical update (LU) packet
natt-keepalive	NAT-T keepalive message
no-adjacency	No valid adjacency
no-mcast-entry	Fast Path (FP) has no multicast entry
no-mcast-intrf	Fast Path (FP) has no multicast output interface
no-punt-cb	No registered punt callback
no-route	No route to host
np-sp-invalid-spi	Invalid SPI
punt-rate-limit	Punt rate limit exceeded
queue-removed	Queued packet dropped
rate-exceeded	QoS rate exceeded
rpf-violated	Reverse-path verify failed
security-failed	Early security checks failed
send-ctm-error	Send to Crypto Transform Manager (CTM) returned an error
tcp-3whs-failed	TCP failed three-way handshake
tcp-ack-syn-diff	TCP ACK in SYNACK invalid
tcp-acked	TCP duplicate and has been ACKed
tcp-bad-option-len	Bad option length in TCP
tcp-bad-option-list	TCP option list invalid
tcp-bad-sack-allow	Bad TCP SACK ALLOW option
tcp-bad-winscale	Bad TCP window scale value
tcp-buffer-full	TCP packet buffer full
tcp-conn-limit	TCP connection limit reached
tcp-data-past-fin	TCP data send after FIN
tcp-discarded-ooo	TCP packet out of order
tcp-dual-open	TCP dual open denied

continues

Section 11-2

Table 11-12 *drop-reason Keywords for the **capture type asp-drop** Command (Continued)*

drop-reason Keyword	Description
tcp-fo-drop	TCP replicated flow packet drop
tcp-invalid-ack	TCP invalid ACK
tcp-mss-exceeded	TCP MSS was too large
tcp-mss-no-syn	TCP MSS option on non-SYN
tcp-not-syn	First TCP packet not SYN
tcp-paws-fail	TCP packet failed Protect Against Wrapped Sequence numbers (PAWS) test
tcp-reserved-set	TCP reserved flags set
tcp-rst-syn-in-win	TCP RST/SYN in window
tcp-rstfin-ooo	TCP RST/FIN out of order
tcp-seq-past-win	TCP packet SEQ past window
tcp-seq-syn-diff	TCP SEQ in SYN/SYN-ACK invalid
tcp-syn-data	TCP SYN with data
tcp-syn-ooo	TCP SYN on established connection
tcp-synack-data	TCP SYN-ACK with data
tcp-synack-ooo	TCP SYN-ACK on established connection
tcp-tsopt-notallowed	TCP time stamp not allowed
tcp-winscale-no-syn	TCP window scale on non-SYN
unable-to-add-flow	Flow hash full
unable-to-create-flow	Out of flow cache memory
unimplemented	Slow path unimplemented
unsupport-ipv6-hdr	Unsupported IPv6 header
unsupported-ip-version	Unsupported IP version

As a simple example, the following capture session is created to capture all packets that have been dropped by an interface access list:

```
Firewall# capture ACLdroptest type asp-drop acl-drop
```

An inbound SMTP session is attempted from an outside host, which is blocked by an access list applied to the outside interface. First, the following Syslog messages were collected for the failed session:

```
Feb 08 2007 00:25:41  single_vf : %PIX-4-106023: Deny tcp src
  outside:172.21.4.48/3407 dst inside:172.16.1.5/25 by access-group "acl_outside"
```

```
Feb 08 2007 00:25:44  single_vf : %PIX-4-106023: Deny tcp src
  outside:172.21.4.48/3407 dst inside: 172.16.1.5/25 by access-group "acl_outside"
Feb 08 2007 00:25:50  single_vf : %PIX-4-106023: Deny tcp src
  outside:172.21.4.48/3407 dst inside: 172.16.1.5/25 by access-group "acl_outside"
```

The denied packets can be correlated to the following packets in the capture session:

```
Firewall# show capture test
3 packets captured
   1: 00:25:41.114312 172.21.4.48.3407 > 172.16.1.5.25: S 3520305660:3520305660(0)
  win 65520 <mss 1260,nop,nop,sackOK>
   2: 00:25:44.026197 172.21.4.48.3407 > 172.16.1.5.25: S 3520305660:3520305660(0)
  win 65520 <mss 1260,nop,nop,sackOK>
   3: 00:25:50.122659 172.21.4.48.3407 > 172.16.1.5.25: S 3520305660:3520305660(0)
  win 65520 <mss 1260,nop,nop,sackOK>
3 packets shown
Firewall#
```

TIP   You can repeat these steps to define several capture sessions. You can assign multiple capture sessions to the same interface. You also can reuse an ACL in multiple capture sessions if needed. Each capture session is independent and captures its own data in a separate capture buffer.

You can use multiple capture sessions to troubleshoot difficult problems in which the firewall is not forwarding traffic for some reason. Configure one capture session on one interface and a similar capture session on another interface. Use the same access list in both capture sessions. Then you can see traffic arriving on one interface but not appearing on the other.

Aside from the normal traffic inspection engines, access lists, and service policies that might be dropping the packets, consider other information contained in the capture buffer. Be sure to look for packet-related parameters such as the do not fragment (DF) bit or the TCP maximum segment size (MSS) that could be causing packets to be silently dropped.

Getting Results from a Capture Session

After you have defined a capture session, you need to monitor it for activity and retrieve the captured data. If you have defined several capture sessions, you might have trouble remembering which one is performing a certain function. You can list the current capture sessions with the following command:

```
Firewall# show capture
```

For example, the firewall used in the following **show capture** output has three capture sessions defined:

```
Firewall# show capture
capture Aserver-out access-list interface outside
```

```
capture Aserver-in access-list interface inside
capture A-trunk interface outside
```

Notice that one session is bound to the inside interface, and two other separate sessions are active on the outside interface.

You can display the contents of a capture session buffer at any time, even if the capture is still active. To view the buffer contents from a console, Telnet, or SSH session, you can use the following command:

PIX 6.3	Firewall# **show capture** *capture_name* [**access-list** *acl_name*] [**detail**] [**dump**]
ASA, FWSM	Firewall# **show capture** *capture_name* [**access-list** *acl_name*] {**detail** | **dump** | **decode**} [**packet-number** *packet*] [**count** *count*]

A summary of each packet saved in the capture buffer named *capture_name* is displayed, even though the capture session is still active. You can also configure another access list named *acl_name* ahead of time and use that ACL as a display filter. Only packets that are permitted by the display filter access list are displayed.

With ASA and FWSM platforms, you can use the **decode** keyword to display captured packets in an abbreviated form. This is the default display format. You can also display a subset of captured packets. You can use the **packet-number** keyword to specify packet number *packet* as the first to display. You can also use the **count** keyword to set the number of packets to display as *count*.

For example, you could use the following command to display packets 100 through 157 in the capture buffer:

Firewall# **show capture test packet-number 100 count 57**

The top portion of Figure 11-5 shows an example of a TCP packet displayed from the capture session named "test." Only the basic IP and TCP information is shown. This format is useful if you are looking at a list of packets as a record of traffic flow.

To see more detail about the captured packets, you can add the **detail** keyword to the **show capture** command. The same sample packet is shown in the middle of Figure 11-5. Here, the source and destination MAC addresses are shown along with the IP addresses. Many IP and TCP fields contained in the packet are also shown.

Until this point, only the packet header information has been displayed. You can also see the contents of the packet payload (up to *packet-length* bytes, as given in the **capture** command) by using the **dump** keyword. The bottom portion of Figure 11-5 shows the sample packet in the dump format. The captured IP packet contents are shown as a hexadecimal decode, along with the ASCII equivalent of each byte.

Figure 11-5 *Examples of Different show capture Output Formats*

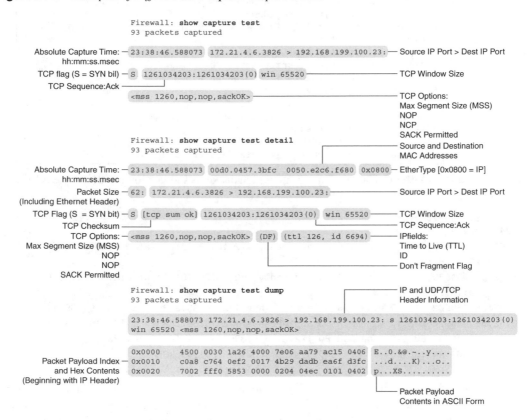

Using a Capture Session to Display Trunk Contents

You can also use a capture session to capture and decode packets traveling over a trunking interface. In the following example, interface ethernet0 is configured as an 802.1Q trunk, passing VLANs 41 (interface dmz3) and 998 (interface outside). A capture session named "trunk-test" is enabled on the outside interface, with no access list as a filter:

PIX 6.3	`Firewall(config)# interface ethernet0 auto`
	`Firewall(config)# interface ethernet0 vlan41 physical`
	`Firewall(config)# interface ethernet0 vlan998 logical`
	`Firewall(config)# nameif vlan998 outside security0`
	`Firewall(config)# nameif vlan41 dmz3 security20`
	`Firewall(config)# exit`
	`Firewall# capture trunk-test interface outside`

```
ASA     Firewall(config)# interface ethernet0
        Firewall(config-if)# no shutdown
        Firewall(config-if)# interface ethernet0.41
        Firewall(config-if)# vlan 41
        Firewall(config-if)# nameif dmz3
        Firewall(config-if)# security-level 20
        Firewall(config-if)# interface ethernet0.998
        Firewall(config-if)# vlan 998
        Firewall(config-if)# nameif outside
        Firewall(config-if)# security-level 0
        Firewall(config-if)# exit
        Firewall(config)# exit
        Firewall# capture trunk-test interface outside
```

When the capture buffer is displayed, notice how each packet is shown along with its 802.1Q VLAN number tag:

```
Firewall# show capture trunk-test
4434 packets captured
00:52:55.034116 802.1Q vlan#998 P0 arp reply 172.16.89.191 is-at 0:d:28:a7:83:80
  (0:d:28:a7:83:80)
00:52:55.034589 802.1Q vlan#998 P0 arp reply 172.16.89.191 is-at 0:c:30:10:26:0
  (0:c:30:10:26:0)
00:52:55.860902 802.1Q vlan#998 P0 arp who-has 172.16.89.253 tell 128.163.89.11
00:52:55.860978 802.1Q vlan#998 P0 arp who-has 172.16.89.254 tell 128.163.89.11
00:53:01.841844 802.1Q vlan#998 P0 172.21.4.6.3862 > 172.16.89.161.23: S
  2411823264:2411823264(0) win 65520 <mss 1260,nop,nop,sackOK>
[output deleted]
```

Some firewall documentation explains that you should configure the capture session to collect only VLAN or 802.1Q EtherTypes by adding the **vlan** or **802.1q** keywords, respectively. As of PIX 6.3(3), this is not necessary. The firewall interprets the 802.1Q encapsulation correctly with a normal capture session definition.

Copying Capture Buffer Contents

Sometimes you might find that viewing the contents of a capture buffer from a command-line interface (CLI) becomes too cumbersome or confusing. This can happen when the capture buffer becomes very large—too large to navigate with CLI commands or display filters.

At other times, the capture buffer might contain useful information that deserves further review. For example, you might have a PC-based tool that can import captured data for viewing and analysis. You also might want to archive the capture buffer for future use. You can extract a capture buffer from a firewall in several ways, as discussed in the following sections.

Copying to an External TFTP Server

You can copy a capture session to a Trivial File Transfer Protocol (TFTP) server with the following command:

```
Firewall# copy capture:capture-name tftp://server/path [pcap]
```

The entire buffer from the capture session named *capture-name* is copied to the TFTP server at IP address *server* into the file and directory defined by *path*, which is relative to the TFTP server's root directory.

In the following, the capture session named bigtest is copied to the TFTP server at 192.168.254.10 as file bigtest in the TFTP root directory:

```
Firewall# copy capture:bigtest tftp://192.168.254.10/bigtest
```

The resulting capture file contains the same text that is seen with the **show capture** command. You can also save the capture buffer in the PCAP format, which can be imported into many network analysis tools. To do this, add the **pcap** keyword.

TIP   The PCAP capture file format is used by the tcpdump analysis utility. It can be imported directly into the Wireshark (formerly Ethereal) network analysis application. It can also be converted and imported into other commercial network analysis tools. You can go to http://www.tcpdump.org for more information about tcpdump and PCAP. See http://www.wireshark.org (formerly http://www.ethereal.com) for more about the Wireshark application.

Copying the Capture Buffer to a Web Browser

From a web browser, you can display a capture buffer as if you had used the **show capture** command. You also can download the capture buffer in PCAP format and save it as a file—all without leaving your web browser and without needing a TFTP server running on your PC. Follow these steps to accomplish this:

1. Enable the HTTP server on the firewall:

   ```
   Firewall(config)# http ip-address subnet-mask interface
   Firewall(config)# http enable
   ```

   The firewall's HTTP server allows connections from the *ip-address* and *subnet-mask* locations, originating on the firewall interface named *interface*. Usually, it is best to enable HTTP access only on a secure or trusted interface.

2. Open a web browser to this URL:

   ```
   https://firewall_address/capture/capture_name[/pcap]
   ```

   The capture web page is found at the firewall interface given by IP address *firewall-address*. The capture session named *capture_name* is downloaded to the browser window, as if you had used the **show capture** firewall command. As soon as the text is displayed, you can save it in a file through your browser application.

Figure 11-6 shows the capture session named **Aserver-in** from the firewall at 192.168.254.1 displayed in a browser window.

Section 11-2

Figure 11-6 *Displaying a Capture Buffer in a Web Browser*

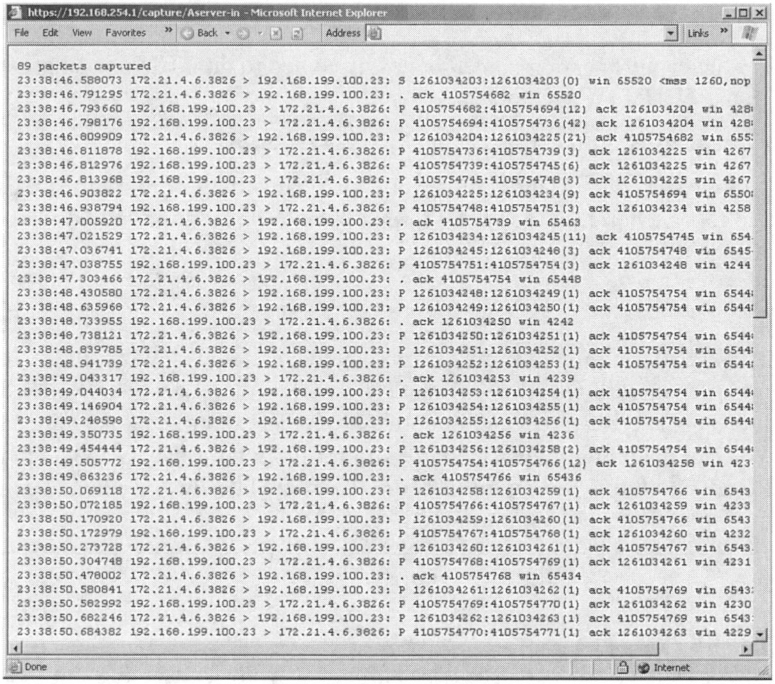

You can also use the web browser to download the capture buffer as a file in PCAP format. To do this, add the **/pcap** keyword to the end of the URL. This time, the browser automatically fetches the capture file rather than displaying the capture text. Figure 11-7 shows an example of saving the capture session named **icmp** from the firewall at 192.168.254.1 to the local machine. Notice that the browser saves the capture data to a file called **pcap** by default. You can change the filename and location through the web browser's file download dialog box.

As soon as you have the capture file downloaded in PCAP format, you can use a network analysis tool to examine and interpret the contents. For example, Wireshark is a free network protocol analyzer (http://www.wireshark.org) that can import PCAP files directly. Figure 11-8 shows how Wireshark (Ethereal) has been used to open the sample Aserver-in capture file.

Likewise, you can use other commercial protocol analyzers as long as they can convert or import the PCAP file format. Figures 11-9 and 11-10 show how the OmniPeek protocol analyzer (http://www.wildpackets.com) can be used to convert and import the capture file. Notice that the ProConvert tool is used first to convert the PCAP (tcpdump) file into OmniPeek or EtherPeek format.

Figure 11-7 *Downloading a Capture Buffer Through a Web Browser*

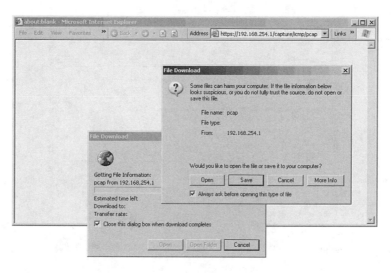

Figure 11-8 *A Sample Capture Buffer Opened in Wireshark*

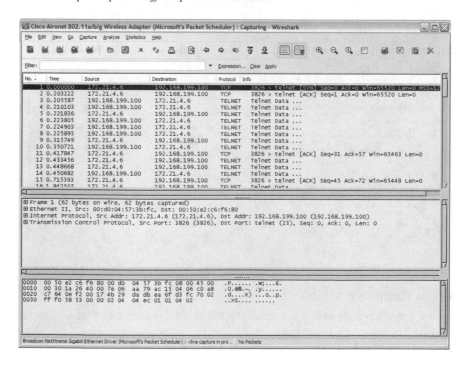

Figure 11-9 *Using the WildPackets ProConvert Capture Conversion Utility*

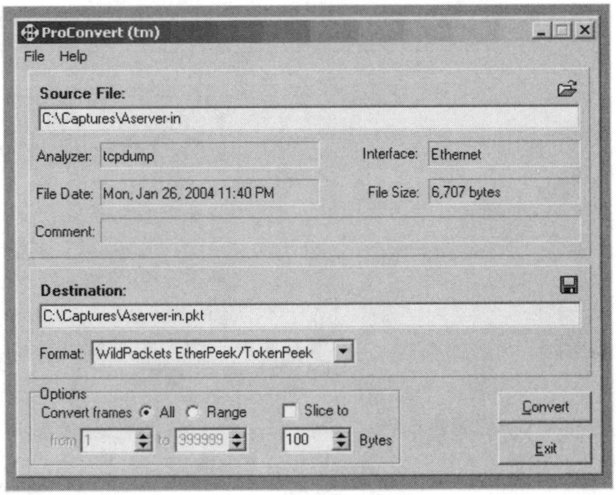

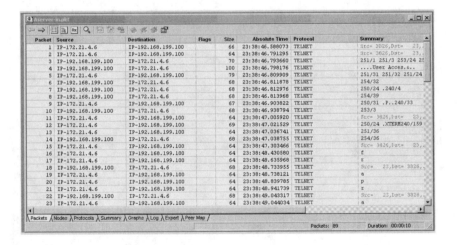

Figure 11-10 *A Sample Capture Buffer Opened in OmniPeek*

Controlling a Capture Session

After a capture session is defined and activated, you might need to stop it as soon as some interesting data is captured. You might also want to clear the buffer so that new data can be captured in an empty buffer. When you are finished with a capture session, you need to delete it.

You can use the following commands (Table 11-13) to control an existing capture session:

Table 11-13 *Commands to Control a Data Capture Session*

Firewall# **clear capture** *capture_name*	Empties the capture buffer and retains the session
Firewall# **no capture** *capture_name* **interface** *if_name*	Stops the capture, detaches it from the interface, and retains the capture session and buffer
Firewall# **no capture** *capture_name* **access-list** *acl_name*	Stops the capture, detaches the access list from it, and retains the capture session and buffer
Firewall# **no capture** *capture_name*	Deletes a capture session and the capture buffer

A Capture Example

A firewall separates a web server on the inside from a user on the outside. The web server has worked correctly in the past, but users are calling to complain that they cannot get the server to respond with valid browser content. Naturally, the user believes the firewall is to blame!

You find that you can ping both the user and the web server from the firewall. As well, the outside user can ping the web server through the firewall. After inspecting the firewall configuration, you also find that the address translation and access list definitions look correct. You also spend some time searching the Syslog archives for any messages that might indicate that the firewall is somehow blocking the HTTP connections. Unfortunately, you do not see anything interesting.

The capture feature can provide some low-level data about this problem. Because you can configure multiple capture sessions, it is wise to capture this traffic flow on both the outside and inside interfaces. If you can see what packets have arrived on both sides of the firewall, you are more likely to see the traffic from the firewall's perspective.

First, you configure two access lists—one for each firewall interface, configured to permit traffic between the user's PC and the web server. These access lists will trigger the capture for packets that match the permit statements.

Figure 11-11 shows a simple network diagram of this scenario. The web server is at 172.19.32.9 (the local address) on the inside, and it has a static translation to 10.4.4.10 (the global address) on the outside. The user PC is at 10.4.4.33 on the outside.

You define the following access lists:

```
Firewall(config)# access-list cap_outside permit ip any host 10.4.4.10
Firewall(config)# access-list cap_outside permit ip host 10.4.4.10 any

Firewall(config)# access-list cap_inside permit ip any host 172.19.32.9
Firewall(config)# access-list cap_inside permit ip host 172.19.32.9 any
```

Figure 11-11 *A Network Diagram for the Capture Example*

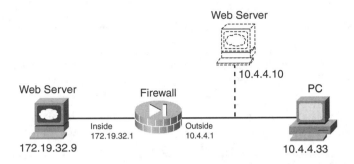

Next, you define and enable the two capture sessions:

```
Firewall# capture web_inside access-list cap_inside interface inside
Firewall# capture web_outside access-list cap_outside interface outside
```

Now you instruct the user to try opening a web browser to the web server's URL. As soon as that happens, you can display the contents of both capture buffers as follows:

```
Firewall# show capture web_outside
2 packets captured
19:24:27.241885 10.4.4.33.1193 > 10.4.4.10.80: S 3375443541:3375443541(0) win 4096
  <mss 1460>
19:24:27.242403 10.4.4.10.80 > 10.4.4.33.1193: R 917139784:917139784(0) ack
  3375443542 win 0
```

Here, only two packets are seen at the firewall's outside interface:

- A packet from the user's PC to the web server (TCP port 80) with the TCP SYN flag set (**S**).

- A reply from the web server address to the user's PC.

Why are there only two packets when there should be at least a three-way TCP handshake? A clue is present, because the return packet has the TCP RST flag set (**R**). Something has caused the connection to be reset before it has been established.

A look at the capture on the inside interface might provide some evidence about who is resetting the HTTP connections:

```
Firewall# show capture web_inside
2 packets captured
19:23:56.171469 10.4.4.33.1192 > 172.19.32.9.80: S 2178639828:2178639828(0) win
  4096 <mss 1380>
19:23:56.171759 172.19.32.9.80 > 10.4.4.33.1192: R 0:0(0) ack 2178639829 win 0
```

Again, only two packets are seen at the inside interface. The reply packet that has reset the connection did indeed come from the web server's IP address on the inside. In fact, the RST flag (**R**) was already set when the packet arrived at the firewall's inside interface. Therefore, you can conclude that something is misconfigured on the web server that causes it to deny or reset every HTTP connection. The problem is not within the firewall.

Using the ASDM Packet Capture Wizard

You can also set up packet captures in ASDM using the Packet Capture Wizard. The ASA must be running release 8.0(1) or later, as well as ASDM release 6.0(1) or later. The wizard configures capture sessions that are identical to the **capture** command in the CLI, except that a GUI front end is used instead.

The Packet Capture Wizard sets up two separate capture sessions—one on the ingress side of the firewall and one on the egress side. Each session captures traffic in both directions, giving you data as it enters and exits the firewall.

To use the Packet Capture Wizard, click on the **Wizards** menu in ASDM and then select **Packet Capture Wizard**. Use the following steps to configure a capture session:

1. A new window describing the six steps of the wizard appears. Click the **Next** button.

2. Enter the ingress traffic information, as shown in Figure 11-12. This includes the ingress interface (outside in the example), source and destination addresses and subnet masks, and the protocol. In the example, traffic from any address to the host at 172.21.67.101 will be captured. Click the **Next>** button.

Figure 11-12 *Entering Ingress Traffic Information in the Packet Capture Wizard*

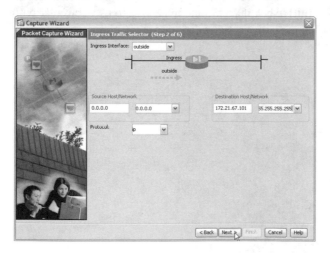

3. Enter the egress traffic information, as shown in Figure 11-13. This includes the egress interface (inside in the example) and the source and destination addresses and subnet masks. In the example, traffic from any address to the host at 192.168.100.101 will be captured. The firewall has already been configured with a static address translation of 172.21.67.101 on the outside to 192.168.100.101 on the inside.

Figure 11-13 *Entering Egress Traffic Information in the Packet Capture Wizard*

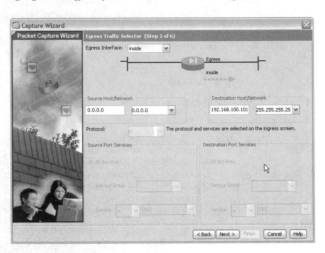

4. Enter the capture buffer parameters, as shown in Figure 11-14. The maximum packet size (1522 in the example) and capture buffer size (524,288 bytes in the example) are given here. Check the **Use circular buffer** box if you want the capture to use a circular buffer. By default, the capture stops when the buffer is full. Click **Next>**.

Figure 11-14 *Tuning the Capture Buffer in the Packet Capture Wizard*

5. Click **Next>** in the Summary window, which shows all of the CLI commands that will be added to the firewall configuration to build the packet capture.

6. Start the capture by clicking the **Start** button. The **Run Captures** window remains mostly empty while the capture is running. To see the results in the capture buffers, click on the **Get Capture Buffer** button, as shown in Figure 11-15.

Figure 11-15 *Displaying the Capture Buffers*

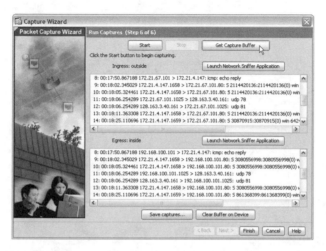

The capture buffer for the ingress capture session is shown in the topmost box, whereas the egress session is shown in the bottom box.

7. Save the capture buffers by clicking on the **Save captures** button. From the screen shown in Figure 11-16, select **ASCII** to save the capture in plaintext or **PCAP** to save it in a standard format that Ethereal or Wireshark can decode.

Click on **Save ingress capture** or **Save egress capture** to begin saving the capture buffer to a file on your local machine.

8. Load the capture into a network analyzer application by clicking on the **Launch Network Sniffer Application** button (shown previously in Figure 11-15). By default, ASDM expects to find Ethereal or Wireshark installed on your local PC at the following pathname:

C:\Program Files\Ethereal\ethereal.exe

TIP   If you do not have Ethereal or Wireshark installed, you can configure the wizard to use a different PCAP-compliant network analyzer application. Go to **Tools > Preferences**, and choose the location of the application's startup file in the Network Sniffer Application box.

Figure 11-16 *Saving the Capture Buffers*

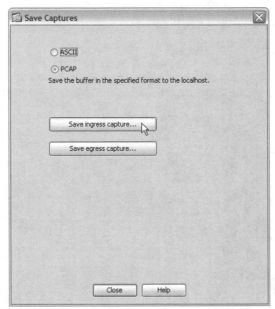

Capturing FWSM Packets Inside the Switch

Sometimes you might need to use an external network analyzer or application. With an ASA or PIX, you have physical interfaces to work with, which can be mirrored on a switch port where they terminate.

With a FWSM, however, the firewall is embedded in a Catalyst 6500 chassis, and you have no physical interfaces to mirror. The FWSM is based around virtual LAN (VLAN) interfaces within the chassis, which can be more difficult to access.

To intercept traffic within a VLAN inside a switch chassis you have two options:

- **SPAN sessions**—Switched Port Analyzer (SPAN) mirrors frames passing through a source interface onto a destination interface, where a sniffer is connected.

- **VACL captures**—A VLAN access list is used to identify interesting traffic on a source VLAN and copy it to a destination capture interface, where a sniffer is connected.

In Figure 11-17, a sniffer is connected to interface GigabitEthernet 2/1. From that location, you can capture frames from any VLAN within the switch—particularly the VLANs that interface with the FWSM.

Figure 11-17   *An Example Scenario for Capturing FWSM Packets*

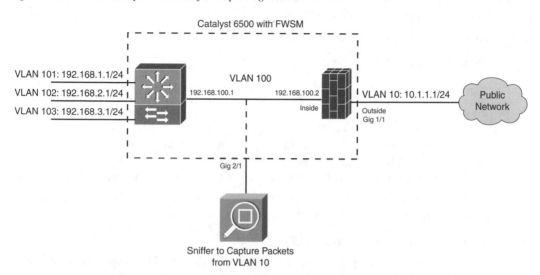

Sniffer to Capture Packets
from VLAN 10

First, consider an example SPAN session configuration. You can monitor traffic on a whole VLAN (and all active switch interfaces assigned to that VLAN), or you can monitor individual physical switch interfaces. For the FWSM outside interface in Figure 11-17, you could use interface GigabitEthernet1/1 as the source because VLAN 10 is accessible there.

For a VLAN that is entirely contained within the switch, such as the FWSM inside interface on VLAN 100, you would have to use VLAN 100 as the source. VLAN 100 is not accessible on any physical switch interface.

Suppose you want to capture packets from the FWSM inside interface on VLAN 100. The SPAN session could be configured with the following commands:

```
Switch(config)# monitor session 1 source vlan 100 both
Switch(config)# monitor session 1 destination interface gigabitethernet2/1
```

Now, all traffic entering or leaving the switch on interface GigabitEthernet 1/1 is mirrored to GigabitEthernet2/2 (the **both** keyword mirrors traffic in both directions from the source interface).

To capture packets on the FWSM outside interface, you could use either VLAN 10 or GigabitEthernet1/1 as the source.

As soon as your packet capture is complete, do not forget to tear down the VACL capture with the following command:

```
Switch(config)# no monitor session 1
```

With a SPAN session, all packets from the source are mirrored to the destination. The sniffer or network analyzer is responsible for filtering the mirrored packets, if you need to pinpoint specific types of traffic. With a VACL capture, you can configure an access list on the switch to identify only interesting traffic that is sent on to a capture interface. In a high-traffic volume VLAN, this can greatly reduce the amount of captured data you have to examine.

You can configure a VACL capture with the following steps:

1. Configure an access list to identify captured traffic:

   ```
   Switch(config)# ip access-list extended acl_name
   Switch(config-ext-nacl)# permit protocol source [source_port] destination [dest_port]
   [arguments]
   Switch(config-ext-nacl)# exit
   ```

   The access list identifies only interesting traffic; it does not actually permit or deny the traffic from passing through the switch. The **permit** keyword is used to flag matching packets for capture. You can repeat the **permit** command to identify more interesting traffic to be captured.

   You can use the **deny** keyword to exempt matching traffic from capture, if needed. A hidden **deny ip any any** statement is always implicit at the end of the access list.

2. Configure an access list to match all traffic.

   A second ACL must be configured to match all traffic on the VLAN. This will be used in Step 3 to make sure that non-captured traffic is still forwarded normally by the switch.

   ```
   Switch(config)# ip access-list extended match_any
   Switch(config-ext-nacl)# permit ip any any
   Switch(config-ext-nacl)# exit
   ```

3. Define a VLAN access map to handle the VLAN traffic:

   ```
   Switch(config)# vlan access-map vacl_name 10
   Switch(config-access-map)# match ip address acl_name
   Switch(config-access-map)# action forward capture
   Switch(config-access-map)# vlan access-map vacl_name  20
   Switch(config-access-map)# match ip address match_any
   Switch(config-access-map)# action forward
   Switch(config-access-map)# exit
   ```

   Here, the access list named *acl_name*, defined in Step 1, is used to match interesting traffic. The **action forward capture** command causes the interesting traffic to be forwarded through the switch normally (**forward**), as well as copied to the destination capture interface (**capture**).

   The second **vlan access-map** command identifies any traffic and causes it to be forwarded normally (**action forward**) without being captured.

4. Apply the VACL to a specific VLAN:

   ```
   Switch(config)# vlan filter vacl_name  vlan-list vlan_number
   ```

   The VACL is applied to VLAN number *vlan_number* immediately after this command is entered. From this point on, the VACL copies the interesting traffic from the VLAN to the destination interface that is identified in the following step.

5. Identify the destination capture interface:

```
Switch(config)# interface type mod/num
Switch(config-if)# switchport
Switch(config-if)# no ip address
Switch(config-if)# switchport access vlan vlan_number
Switch(config-if)# switchport mode access
Switch(config-if)# switchport capture
Switch(config-if)# exit
```

The switch interface should be assigned to the monitored VLAN number with the **switchport access vlan** command. The **switchport capture** command begins the VACL capture operation, allowing captured packets to be sent out the interface.

As a complete example for Figure 11-17, only traffic going to and from the host at 192.168.2.24 as seen on VLAN 100 should be identified for capture. All other traffic on VLAN 100 should be forwarded normally. You could use the following configuration commands to set up the VACL capture on the switch:

```
Switch(config)# ip access-list extended match_cap
Switch(config-ext-nacl)# permit ip any host 192.168.2.24
Switch(config-ext-nacl)# permit ip host 192.168.2.24 any
Switch(config-ext-nacl)# exit
Switch(config)# ip access-list extended match_any
Switch(config-ext-nacl)# permit ip any any
Switch(config-ext-nacl)# exit
Switch(config)# vlan access-map vacl_cap 10
Switch(config-access-map)# match ip address match_cap action forward capture
Switch(config-access-map)# exit
Switch(config)# vlan access-map vacl_cap 20
Switch(config-access-map)# match ip address cap_any action forward
Switch(config-access-map)# exit
Switch(config)# vlan filter vacl_cap vlan-list 100
Switch(config)# interface GigabitEthernet2/1
Switch(config-if)# switchport
Switch(config-if)# no ip address
Switch(config-if)# switchport access vlan 100
Switch(config-if)# switchport mode access
Switch(config-if)# switchport capture
Switch(config-if)# exit
```

Using Debug Packet

In FWSM 2.3 and PIX 6.3, you can enable a single debug packet session so that the firewall reports how it has handled packets from specific traffic flows. This feature is not available beginning with ASA 7.0(1) and FWSM 3.1(1).

Only the debug messages are displayed to the trace channel, or the first active Telnet session open to the firewall. No packets are captured or stored during the debug packet session. However, the packet header and upper-layer protocol headers are shown in the debug messages. As well, up to 50 bytes of the packet payload contents are displayed in hex and ASCII.

TIP   A debug session can impact the performance of a busy firewall. The firewall must match packets as it inspects them and generate the appropriate debug information. Obviously, adding this process can also add significant delays to the firewall's throughput. Because debug output is also sent to a management session interactively, as matching packets are forwarded, a terminal session can become so congested with output that it becomes unusable.

As soon as the debug output begins, be ready to stop it by entering the **no debug packet** *interface-name* command.

If your terminal session is unresponsive and you cannot enter the command, start a new terminal session (preferably through Telnet or SSH) and enter the command from there.

Be aware that the **no debug all** and **undebug all** commands have no effect on the debug packet session. Debug packet is a special type of debug session and must be disabled explicitly.

You can define and activate a packet debug session with the following command:

```
Firewall# debug packet if_name [src source_ip [netmask mask]] [dst dest_ip
  [netmask mask]] [[proto icmp] | [proto {tcp | udp} [sport src_port] [dport
  dest_port]] [rx | tx | both]
```

The debug process displays only packets matching a set of parameters. The packets also must pass through the firewall interface named *if_name* (**outside**, for example) in the receive direction (**rx**, or inbound), the transmit direction (**tx**, or outbound), or either direction (**both**, inbound or outbound).

You can (and should) be as specific as possible in identifying the debugged traffic. You can use the **src** and **dst** keywords to specify the source address and destination address, respectively. If you also provide a netmask, it follows the normal subnet mask format (a 1 bit matches, and a 0 bit is a wildcard). You can match a protocol as ICMP (**proto icmp**), UDP (**proto udp**), or TCP (**proto tcp**), and the source and destination port numbers (**sport** and **dport**) if needed.

You can select the traffic direction, relative to the interface if_name, as receive only (**rx**), transmit only (**tx**), or in both directions (**both**).

As a simple example, the following **debug packet** command is used to verify how a firewall handles an ICMP echo request from a host on the outside (172.21.4.6) to a host on the inside (global address 10.63.89.161, local address 192.168.199.100):

```
Firewall# debug packet outside dst 10.63.89.161 both
--------- PACKET ---------
-- IP --
172.21.4.6==>10.63.89.161
ver = 0x4     hlen = 0x5    tos = 0x0    tlen = 0x3c
id = 0xf3a8     flags = 0x0    frag off=0x0
ttl = 0x7e     proto=0x1    chksum = 0xbeb8
```

```
-- ICMP --
type = 0x8    code = 0x0    checksum=0x485c
identifier = 0x400    seq = 0x100
-- DATA --
00000010:                                      61 62 63 64 |          abcd
00000020: 65 66 67 68 69 6a 6b 6c 6d 6e 6f 70 71 72 73 74 | efghijklmnopqrst
00000030: 75 76 77 61 62 63 64 65 66 67 68 69 a1           | uvwabcdefghi.
--------- END OF PACKET ---------

--------- PACKET ---------
-- IP --
172.21.4.6==>192.168.199.100
ver = 0x4    hlen = 0x5    tos = 0x0    tlen = 0x3c
id = 0xf3a8    flags = 0x0    frag off=0x0
ttl = 0x7e    proto=0x1    chksum = 0x10f0
-- ICMP --
type = 0x8    code = 0x0    checksum=0x485c
identifier = 0x400    seq = 0x100
-- DATA --
00000010:                                      61 62 63 64 |          abcd
00000020: 65 66 67 68 69 6a 6b 6c 6d 6e 6f 70 71 72 73 74 | efghijklmnopqrst
00000030: 75 76 77 61 62 63 64 65 66 67 68 69 a1           | uvwabcdefghi.
--------- END OF PACKET ---------

--------- PACKET ---------
-- IP --
192.168.199.100==>172.21.4.6
ver = 0x4    hlen = 0x5    tos = 0x0    tlen = 0x3c
id = 0xf3a8    flags = 0x0    frag off=0x0
ttl = 0xff    proto=0x1    chksum = 0x8fef
-- ICMP --
type = 0x0    code = 0x0    checksum=0x505c
identifier = 0x400    seq = 0x100
-- DATA --
00000010:                                      61 62 63 64 |          abcd
00000020: 65 66 67 68 69 6a 6b 6c 6d 6e 6f 70 71 72 73 74 | efghijklmnopqrst
00000030: 75 76 77 61 62 63 64 65 66 67 68 69 a1           | uvwabcdefghi.
--------- END OF PACKET ---------
Firewall# no debug packet outside
```

Notice that the first inbound packet is destined for the global address of the internal host. The firewall displays the second packet when it performs the address translation, with a new destination of the local address. The third packet is the echo reply from the internal host.

11-3: Verifying Firewall Connectivity

When you install a firewall or make configuration changes to one, you might need to verify that it can communicate on all its interfaces. Users might also report problems they experience when trying to pass through the firewall. You need a logical approach to verifying the firewall's operation and troubleshooting its connectivity.

You can follow these basic steps to verify that a firewall can communicate with its neighboring networks:

Step 1   Test with ping packets.

Step 2   Check the ARP cache.

Step 3   Check the routing table.

Step 4   Use **traceroute** to verify the forwarding path.

Step 5   Check the access lists.

Step 6   Verify address translation operation and connection tables.

Step 7   Look for active shuns.

Step 8   Check user authentication.

Step 9   See what has changed.

Each of these steps is discussed fully in the sections to follow.

TIP   In case you need to open a case with the Cisco TAC, you can gather all the necessary information from your firewall with one command. Configure your terminal emulator to log the session to a file, and issue the **show tech-support** command. The saved file can be uploaded or sent to the TAC engineer.

You can also use the Packet Tracer feature to verify many of the same firewall mechanisms. This is available on ASA platforms beginning with release 7.2(1). Through ASDM, you can start the Packet Tracer tool, which moves virtual trace packets through each of the following firewall operations:

- **Flow Lookup**—Checks for existing xlate and conn entries
- **UN-NAT**—Checks for address translation entries
- **Access List Lookup**—Checks for any applicable ACL entries
- **IP Options Lookup**—Checks handling of IP options in the ingress packet
- **NAT**—Checks the Reverse Path Forwarding (RPF) information
- **NAT**—Checks for host connection limits
- **IP Options Lookup**—Checks handling of IP options in egress packet
- **Flow Creation**—Creates new xlate and conn entries, if needed
- **Route Lookup**—Checks for a route to the destination address

TIP   Notice that the Packet Tracer tool does not include tests from any of the firewall's inspection engines. This is because only a single packet is used for the test.

To start Packet Tracer, click on the **Tools** menu in ASDM and select **Packet Tracer.** A new Packet Tracer window appears, as shown in Figure 11-18, containing a string of symbols representing each firewall function to be tested. To begin a Packet Trace, use the following steps:

Figure 11-18   *Entering Information into the Packet Tracer Tool*

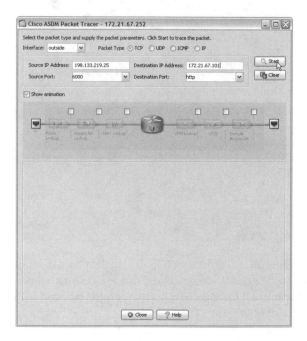

1. Choose the ingress interface, where the packet enters the firewall. At the upper-left corner of the window, select an interface name from the drop-down menu.

2. Select the Packet Type—TCP, UDP, ICMP, or IP—from the list across the top of the window.

3. Enter the Source IP Address and Source Port.

4. Enter the Destination IP Address and Destination Port.

5. Click the **Start** button. Packet Tracer animates a packet as it moves from function to function. When the trace is complete, the results are shown in the bottom half of the window.

If the trace is successful, the packet is able to enter and exit the firewall. You see green check marks in the **Action** column next to each successful phase. As well, the **Results** section shows the ingress and egress interfaces. The outcome of each phase is shown in a collapsed list, as shown in Figure 11-19. You can click on the plus sign next to any Phase to see more detailed information about the test.

Figure 11-19 *A Successful Packet Tracer Test*

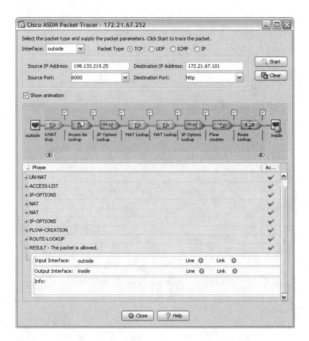

If the trace is not successful, you see red X symbols next to the phase that failed or denied the packet. In Figure 11-20, a packet trace has been configured to use a destination port of sqlnet, arriving on the outside interface. The firewall has an access list that permits inbound HTTP (TCP port 80) traffic, but denies inbound SQLNet (TCP port 1433).

TIP The Packet Tracer tool creates a virtual packet based on the protocol, address, and port information you provide. The virtual packet is passed through each of the firewall functions, as if a real packet were being handled. This means that you see syslog information being generated as the trace progresses. The firewall removes the virtual packet as soon as it is queued in the egress interface buffer for transmission.

You can also use the Packet Tracer tool from the CLI with the following syntax:

```
Firewall# packet-tracer input if_name {tcp | udp | icmp | ip} source_addr
source_port  dest_addr  dest_port  [detailed] [xml]
```

The output shows each of the firewall test phases, along with the results. The **xml** keyword produces an XML output version of the results; this is meant for ASDM, which translates XML into the graphical results.

Figure 11-20 *An Example of a Failed Packet Trace*

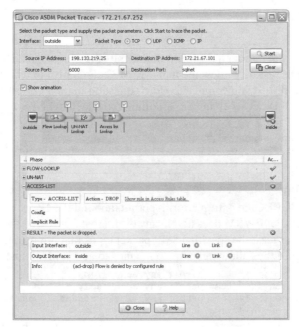

Step 1: Test with Ping Packets

If you know that some hosts on one interface are having trouble reaching hosts on another interface, you can begin troubleshooting with the most basic tool, the ping or ICMP echo.

You should begin by testing with ping packets from the firewall itself to hosts on each side. From a management session, you can use this command:

PIX 6.3	Firewall# **ping** [*if_name*] *host*
ASA, FWSM	Firewall# **ping** [*if_name*] *host* [**data** *pattern*] [**repeat** *count*] [**size** *bytes*] [**timeout** *seconds*] [**validate**]

The destination address is *host*, an IP address or a hostname. If a hostname is given, the firewall must also be configured to use an external DNS to resolve the IP address.

If the firewall can find a routing table entry for the destination, it can figure out which interface to use as the source and source address. You can override that choice by specifying the interface name as *if_name* (**inside**, for example). By default, the firewall sends five ICMP echo packets toward the destination, as shown in the following example:

```
Firewall# ping www.mycompany.com
Type escape sequence to abort.
Sending 5, 100-byte ICMP Echos to 10.7.2.27, timeout is 2 seconds:
!!!!!
```

```
Success rate is 100 percent (5/5), round-trip min/avg/max = 1/1/1 ms
Firewall#
```

TIP   Be aware that although the firewall transmits the ping packet (ICMP echo request), it does not necessarily allow the reply (ICMP echo reply) to return and terminate on its interface. If the **ping** command returns question marks, as in the following example, the firewall is not receiving or permitting the ICMP echo-reply packets.

```
Firewall# ping 10.10.10.10
Type escape sequence to abort.
Sending 5, 100-byte ICMP Echos to 10.10.10.10, timeout is 2 seconds:
?????
Success rate is 0 percent (0/5)
Firewall#
```

By default, PIX and ASA platforms permit inbound ICMP packets to terminate on their interfaces, but FWSM does not. In any event, make sure that the firewall is configured to permit at least the specific ICMP packet types that are useful for troubleshooting. You can use the following **icmp** commands to accomplish this:

```
Firewall(config)# icmp permit any echo if_name
Firewall(config)# icmp permit any echo-reply if_name
Firewall(config)# icmp permit any time-exceeded if_name
Firewall(config)# icmp deny any if_name
```

On an ASA or a FWSM, the **ping** command has been expanded to allow more options. This is similar to the same command in Cisco IOS Software. Further, you can enter the **ping** command without any arguments to perform an extended ping. The firewall prompts for each parameter that it needs. Extended pings are useful when you need to send a specific size ICMP packet,

In the following example, 50 ICMP echo packets are sent to destination 10.10.10.10. Each packet is 1000 bytes in size.

```
Firewall# ping
Interface: outside
Target IP address: 10.10.10.10
Repeat count: [5] 50
Datagram size: [100] 1000
Timeout in seconds: [2]
Extended commands [n]: y
Verbose? [no]:
Validate reply data? [no]:
Data pattern [0xabcd]:
Sweep range of sizes [n]:
Type escape sequence to abort.
Sending 50, 1000-byte ICMP Echos to 10.10.10.10, timeout is 2 seconds:
!!!!!!!!!!!!!!!!!!!!!!!!!!!!!!!!!!!!!!!!!!!!!!!!!!!
Success rate is 100 percent (50/50), round-trip min/avg/max = 1/2/10 ms
Firewall#
```

TIP	After you begin an extended ping, you have to wait until all of the ping packets are sent and replies are received. If the destination does not answer with an echo-reply, the firewall waits for a timeout period (default 2 seconds) before moving on to the next ping.
	If you select a very large repeat count (number of ping packets) and the destination does not reply, you could be waiting a very long time for the ping command to finish. You can break out of the ping process at any time by entering the **Ctrl-C** keystroke sequence.

Try sending pings from the firewall to a known host in each direction. If the pings are successful, the firewall can communicate with nearby hosts on the most basic level.

Now go to a host on each side of the firewall, and try to send ping packets toward the firewall. First, you can try to ping the firewall interfaces directly.

If that is successful, you might want to try sending pings from a host on one side of the firewall to a host on the other. This tests the full round-trip path out and back *through* the firewall. Make sure you have configured any access lists to allow inbound ICMP echo, echo-reply, and time-exceeded packet types on the firewall interfaces. This might need to be configured on each of the firewall interfaces along the path, depending on the firewall platform and whether an access list has been applied to the interfaces. In addition, ASA and FWSM offer an ICMP inspection engine that should be enabled so that ICMP traffic can be inspected and permitted.

TIP	You can also enable ICMP debugging on the firewall to get detailed information about how ICMP packets are being handled. Be careful, though, because any type of packet debugging can adversely load an already-busy firewall. Also, when you enable ICMP debugging, the firewall reports on *any* ICMP packet that arrives, is inspected, and is forwarded. This might result in much more information than you are expecting, especially when you are trying to test by pinging a single host.
	Use the following command to start ICMP debugging:
	`Firewall# `**`debug icmp trace`**
	Be sure to stop the debugging session as soon as you are finished with it. You can use the **no debug icmp trace** command, as well as **no debug all** or **undebug all**.
	For example, suppose host 192.168.199.100 on the inside of a firewall is trying to ping host 172.16.89.5 on the outside. The ICMP debug output is as follows:

	`Firewall# `**`debug icmp trace`**
	`ICMP trace on`
	`Warning: this may cause problems on busy networks`
	`Firewall# 1: ICMP echo-request from inside:192.168.199.100 to`
	`  172.16.89.5 ID=0 seq=1435 length=80`

```
2: ICMP echo-request: translating inside:192.168.199.100 to
   outside:172.16.89.161
3: ICMP echo-reply from outside:172.16.89.5 to 172.16.89.161 ID=0
   seq=1435 length=80
4: ICMP echo-reply: untranslating outside:172.16.89.161 to
   inside:192.168.199.100
Firewall# no debug icmp trace
ICMP trace off
```

Step 2: Check the ARP Cache

Like any host on a network, a firewall must have the basic mechanism to relate IP addresses (Layer 3) to MAC addresses (Layer 2). This is done by building and maintaining an ARP cache. Normally, when a host knows a destination's IP address, it sends an ARP request in the hope that the destination will send an ARP reply with its MAC address. The firewall can build its ARP cache by sending its own ARP requests or by listening to other ARP replies on its interfaces.

Connectivity through the firewall can be affected if the firewall has a stale or incorrect ARP entry. For example, the next-hop router on an interface might have just changed its IP address. A host on the local network of a firewall interface could also change its IP address. If the firewall has a previous ARP entry and does not hear an ARP reply with the new information, it continues to use the stale entry.

For example, consider a host that starts out with IP address 192.168.199.100. Later, it changes to 192.168.199.101. Here is the firewall ARP cache before and after the address change:

```
Firewall# show arp
        inside 192.168.199.100 0050.e2c6.f680
Firewall# show arp
        inside 192.168.199.101 0050.e2c6.f680
        inside 192.168.199.100 0050.e2c6.f680
Firewall# show arp timeout
arp timeout 14400 seconds
```

With the default ARP timeout value, the old ARP entry remains in the cache for up to 4 hours! (In ASA, the **show arp timeout** command is actually **show running-config arp timeout**.)

Now imagine the opposite case, in which a change in MAC addresses occurs. Suppose the hosts on a network have been using an existing router as their default gateway. The router has always been 192.168.199.1 (00d0.0457.3bfc). Now a firewall is being installed in the network, and it will become the default gateway for the internal hosts. Therefore, the firewall uses 192.168.199.1, and the change in gateway platforms is transparent to the end users.

For security reasons, Cisco firewalls try to stay silent and do not announce any information about themselves. As a result, they do not send gratuitous ARP requests on their interfaces. One side effect of this appears when a firewall replaces an existing router on the network. All the internal hosts still have an ARP cache entry for 192.168.199.1 as 00d0.0457.3bfc, which belonged to the router. The firewall comes up as 192.168.199.1, but with its own MAC address of 0090.276c.3d0a. Because it does not announce itself with a gratuitous ARP, the hosts never notice the change in MAC addresses, and they continue to use the old router MAC address until their ARP entries expire. In other words, none of the hosts can send packets to their default gateway (the firewall) until the old ARP entries are flushed.

You should also be aware of how a firewall maintains its own ARP cache. If an ARP cache entry exists for an IP-to-MAC address mapping, a new ARP reply has the following effect:

- If the MAC address is the same, but the IP address is different, a new ARP entry is added to the cache.

- If the IP address is the same, but the MAC address is different, the existing ARP entry is overwritten with the new information.

You can follow these steps to verify ARP cache information:

1. Display the ARP cache:

   ```
   Firewall# show arp
   ```
   Each ARP entry contains the station's MAC address, the corresponding IP address, and the firewall interface where the ARP reply was heard. A sample ARP cache is as follows:

   ```
   Firewall # show arp
           stateful 192.168.199.2 0030.8587.5432
           outside 172.16.11.71 0003.4725.2e23
           outside 172.16.11.67 00d0.01e6.6ffc
           inside 192.168.25.9 0003.4725.2e94
           inside 192.168.25.10 0003.a088.5769
           inside 192.168.254.2 0000.0c07.ac01
   ```

2. (Optional) Verify the ARP cache timeout value:

PIX 6.3	`Firewall# show arp timeout`
ASA, FWSM	`Firewall# show running-config arp timeout`

   Each ARP entry has an aging or persistence timer associated with it. By default, the firewall keeps an entry for 14,400 seconds (4 hours) before discarding it. If subsequent ARP replies are received for that entry before the timer expires, the timer is reset.

   TIP   To adjust the ARP persistence timeout value, you can use the **arp timeout** *seconds* configuration command.

   ---

3. (Optional) Flush the ARP cache:

   ```
   Firewall# clear arp
   ```

If an entry exists and the host changes its IP address, an ARP reply might not be received. The stale entry, with its now-outdated IP-MAC address mapping, continues to be used for up to 4 hours.

In this case, you should flush the stale ARP entry so that a new one can be created. It is not possible to flush just one entry; the entire ARP cache must be flushed at one time.

4. (Optional) Define a static ARP entry:

```
Firewall(config)# arp interface_name ip_address mac_address [alias]
```

Sometimes you might need to define a static ARP cache entry that will never expire. This can be handy if there is a host that only listens on its network interface and never sends an ARP reply. The static ARP entry is associated with the firewall interface named *interface_name* and binds *ip_address* to *mac_address* (dotted-triplet format as in xxxx.yyyy.zzzz).

You can add the **alias** keyword to create a static ARP cache entry that the firewall uses to generate proxy ARP replies. When other hosts send an ARP request for that address, the firewall uses the alias entry to send back an ARP reply.

Step 3: Check the Routing Table

A firewall maintains a routing table, much as a router does. The routing table is consulted when a packet has been inspected and is ready to be forwarded out a firewall interface. The firewall must have a route for the destination network in its routing table before a packet can be sent on its way.

You can verify the routing table contents with the **show route** command, as in this example:

```
Firewall# show route
O IA 192.168.167.1 255.255.255.255 [110/11] via 192.168.198.4, 0:00:01, inside
C    192.168.77.0 255.255.255.0 is directly connected, dmz
C    192.168.198.0 255.255.255.0 is directly connected, inside
C    10.1.0.0 255.255.0.0 is directly connected, outside
S*   0.0.0.0 0.0.0.0 [1/0] via 10.1.1.1, outside
Firewall#
```

Here, routes marked with **C** are directly connected to the firewall. In other words, they are subnets that are configured on the firewall interfaces. Routes marked with **O** have been learned through OSPF. The default route shown is labeled **S** because it has been statically configured on the firewall.

Verify that a destination network you are trying to reach through the firewall actually appears in the firewall's routing table. Obviously, if a specific subnet does not appear, the default route is used.

Step 4: Use Traceroute to Verify the Forwarding Path

Traceroute is a common tool you can use to discover the path from one host to another through the network. The originating host sends special packets toward the destination. Each router that is encountered along the way returns a message to the source, indicating that it was present on the path.

The host generating a traceroute sends packets toward the destination with the IP time-to-live (TTL) field incrementing from 1. The TTL field is a simple hop counter, specifying the maximum number of router hops that the packet is allowed to traverse.

The first traceroute packet has a TTL of 1; the first router to receive the packet must decrement the TTL (as all routers are required to do). The TTL is now 0, so the router drops the packet and returns an ICMP time-exceeded message to the source. The next traceroute packet has a TTL of 2, so the second-hop router returns an ICMP message, and so on.

As the ICMP time-exceeded messages are received at the traceroute source, the router IP address is displayed, along with the round-trip time. As soon as the destination host returns its ICMP message, a record of each router hop along the path is available.

Figure 11-21 illustrates this process. Host PC-A performs a traceroute to host PC-B. Each successive traceroute packet has a higher TTL and is returned by routers progressively further along the path. Notice that the firewall participates in the traceroute process only if ICMP packets are used as traceroute probes. Otherwise, the firewall only inspects and forwards the traceroute packets without modification and does not appear as a hop.

Figure 11-21   *Traceroute as a Progression of Probe Packets*

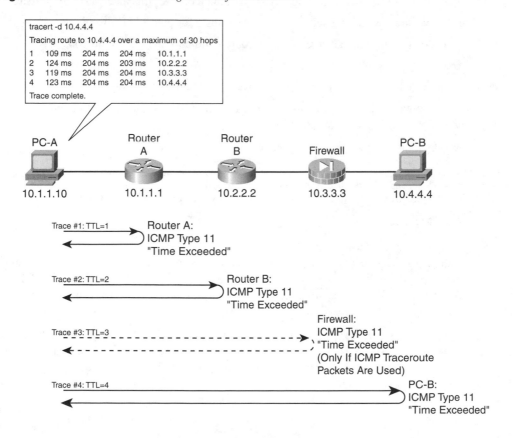

Using Traceroute on a Host

You can use traceroute on a host to troubleshoot or verify connectivity through a firewall. Be aware that the firewall itself might be missing from the traceroute hop information. If it is missing, UDP traceroute packets have been used; if it appears, ICMP traceroute packets have been used.

If the traceroute begins to time out before the destination host is reached, something along the way is preventing connectivity. This could be the firewall if it has not been configured to allow the traceroute packets in both directions.

When PCs perform a traceroute (the **tracert** command), they send ICMP echo-request packets with increasing TTL values. When Cisco routers and switches perform a traceroute (the **trace** IOS or **traceroute** CatOS command), they send UDP packets to port 33434 with increasing TTL values. (Some platforms use a port slightly greater than 33434, and others begin with 33434 and increase the port number with each packet sent.)

You should configure the firewall to permit the following types of packets through each of its interfaces along the traceroute path:

- **ICMP echo-request**—Traceroute packets sent from the source.

- **ICMP echo-reply**—When the target host is finally reached, it returns an echo-reply message.

- **ICMP unreachable**—Messages returned by distant hosts for path MTU discovery.

- **ICMP time-exceeded**—Messages returned by routers indicating a traceroute hop.

- **UDP**—Traceroute packets sent from Cisco devices.

- **DNS**—Used to look up domain names of each traceroute hop (if requested).

You can permit these packet types on the firewall by using the following template to configure an access list that will be applied to a firewall interface:

```
Firewall(config)# access-list acl_name permit icmp any any eq echo
Firewall(config)# access-list acl_name permit icmp any any eq echo-reply
Firewall(config)# access-list acl_name permit icmp any any eq unreachable
Firewall(config)# access-list acl_name permit icmp any any eq time-exceeded
Firewall(config)# access-list acl_name permit udp any range 32768 65535 any range
  33434 33523
Firewall(config)# access-list acl_name permit udp any dns_address eq domain
```

The fifth line, permitting UDP traffic, is optional and should be used only if you require UDP traceroute response from the firewall. You should use caution if you decide to include that command, because it gives open access from any host to any host over a wide range of UDP ports. The UDP port range must be kept wide because the traceroute UDP port tends to vary across router and switch platforms.

Finally, if you use ICMP traceroute probes and you want the firewall to return an ICMP message to declare its presence, you need one final configuration change. (The firewall does not accept any UDP traceroute probes, so it does not return any ICMP error messages about them. As a result, the firewall does not appear as a hop when UDP probes are used.)

By default, an FWSM firewall drops any ICMP packet destined for a firewall interface address, whereas PIX and ASA platforms permit them. To get the firewall to interpret the traceroute probe and send back an ICMP time-exceeded message, you should enable specific ICMP processing on the inbound firewall interface:

```
Firewall(config)# icmp permit source-address source-mask echo if_name
Firewall(config)# icmp permit source-address source-mask echo-reply if_name
Firewall(config)# icmp permit source-address source-mask time-exceeded if_name
Firewall(config)# icmp permit source-address source-mask echo if_name
```

TIP   On ASA and FWSM platforms, you should enable the ICMP inspection engine to examine any ICMP traffic passing through the firewall. You can do this with the **inspect icmp** command while configuring a policy map.

On any Cisco firewall platform, you should enable the fixup or inspection for ICMP error messages with the **inspect icmp error** command (ASA and FWSM) or **fixup icmp error** command (PIX 6.3). No stateful inspection is performed; instead, the firewall examines the ICMP error packets and translates the appropriate addresses in the original header portion of the error payload.

Using Traceroute on the Firewall

Beginning with ASA 7.2(1), you can perform a traceroute on the ASA itself. In a nutshell, the ASA sends packets out toward a destination address, where each successive packet has its TTL value incremented by one. You can start a traceroute with the following command:

```
Firewall# traceroute destination [source source] [timeout timeout] [probe probe_num] [ttl
min_ttl max_ttl] [port port_value] [use-icmp] [numeric]
```

The *destination* can be an IP address or a hostname. If a hostname is used, the ASA must also be configured to use a DNS to resolve the destination address.

If you enter the **traceroute** command with no other keywords, the ASA prompts for each value. The following traceroute parameters can be used:

- **source** *source*—The source address used in the traceroute packets can be identified by an IP address or interface name. If an IP address is given, it must be one that is already configured on an interface.

- **timeout** *timeout*—By default, the firewall waits 3 seconds to receive an ICMP time-exceeded message for each probe sent.

- **probe** *probe_num*—By default, three probes are sent for each successive TTL value or router hop. This lets you see the results of any path load balancing along the way.

- **ttl** *min_ttl max_ttl*—By default, the traceroute begins with a minimum TTL of 1 and ends when the destination is reached, up to a maximum TTL of 30. You can adjust the TTL range to skip nearby router hops or to probe more distant router hops.

- **port** *port_value*—By default, traceroute sends probe packets using UDP port 33434. This is consistent with Cisco IOS devices. You can select a UDP port value between 1 and 65535, if needed.

- **use-icmp**—Traceroute uses ICMP probe packets, rather than UDP probes.

- **numeric**—By default, traceroute attempts to resolve the hostname for each router hop that it detects. You can use the **numeric** keyword to prevent reverse DNS lookups, so that only the IP addresses of router hops are shown. This can be useful if you do not have DNS servers configured on your firewall, or if you do not want the firewall spending extra time resolving the names.

TIP   Be aware that traceroute depends on ICMP timeout-exceeded messages being returned from each router hop toward the destination. By default, the firewall denies any inbound ICMP messages arriving on any of its interfaces. You should enter the following configuration command to permit the ICMP time-exceeded messages on the interface where the destination is found:

Firewall(config)# **icmp permit any time-exceeded** *if_name*

As an example, a traceroute is started to verify the path from the ASA's outside interface to www.cisco.com (198.133.219.25). Notice that three response times are given for each router hop, as the results of the three probes sent to each TTL value.

```
Firewall(config)# icmp permit any time-exceeded outside
Firewall(config)# exit
Firewall#
Firewall#
Firewall# traceroute www.cisco.com
Type escape sequence to abort.
Tracing the route to 198.133.219.25
 1  128.163.66.2 0 msec 0 msec 0 msec
 2  192.168.253.49 0 msec 0 msec 0 msec
 3  128.163.110.67 0 msec 0 msec 0 msec
 4  128.163.55.130 0 msec 0 msec 0 msec
 5  pks2-04-pop2.net.uky.edu (128.163.221.52) 0 msec 0 msec 0 msec
 6  pks2-04-pop2.net.uky.edu (128.163.221.2) 0 msec 0 msec 0 msec
 7  atl-edge-19.inet.qwest.net (208.46.0.121) 20 msec 20 msec 20 msec
 8  atl-core-01.inet.qwest.net (205.171.21.125) 10 msec 20 msec 20 msec
 9  atl-brdr-03.inet.qwest.net (205.171.21.106) 20 msec 20 msec 10 msec
10  ggr2-p322.attga.ip.att.net (192.205.33.89) 50 msec 40 msec 40 msec
11  tbr2011101.attga.ip.att.net (12.123.20.206) 90 msec 90 msec 100 msec
12  tbr1-cl13.dlstx.ip.att.net (12.122.2.89) 90 msec 90 msec 80 msec
13  tbr1-cl20.la2ca.ip.att.net (12.122.10.50) 80 msec 80 msec 90 msec
```

```
14 gar1-p370.sj2ca.ip.att.net (12.122.2.249) 90 msec 100 msec 90 msec
15 12.118.124.10 90 msec 80 msec 80 msec
16 sjce-dmzbb-gw1.cisco.com (128.107.239.53) 80 msec 90 msec 90 msec
17 sjck-dmzdc-gw1-gig1-1.cisco.com (128.107.224.69) 80 msec 70 msec 70 msec
18  *   *   *
Firewall#
```

As the traceroute progresses, you can see any of the following characters displayed, each indicating a different condition:

- *nn* **msec**—The number of milliseconds elapsed from when a probe was sent until an ICMP time-exceeded reply was received

- *—No response was received before the timeout period expired

- !N—ICMP network unreachable was received

- !H—ICMP host unreachable was received

- !P—ICMP port unreachable was received

- !A—ICMP administratively prohibited was received

- ?—Unknown ICMP error was received

TIP   After you begin a traceroute, you have to wait until all of the TTL values are tried (up to 30 by default). If the firewall does not receive ICMP time-exceeded messages in reply, it waits for a timeout period (default 3 seconds) before moving on to the next probe.

In other words, you could be waiting a very long time for the traceroute command to finish. You can break out of the traceroute process at any time by entering the **Ctrl-C** keystroke sequence.

Step 5: Check the Access Lists

If you find specific hosts or types of traffic that cannot pass through the firewall, you should verify the access lists that are applied to the firewall interfaces.

In some cases, corporate security policies might dictate that the firewall should deny a certain type of traffic. In other cases, an access list might be misconfigured or might have an outdated configuration that denies traffic by mistake.

You can follow these steps to help pinpoint an ACL configuration that could be blocking traffic:

1. Identify which ACL is applied to an interface:

PIX 6.3	Firewall# **show access-group**
ASA, FWSM	Firewall# **show running-config access-group**

If your firewall has many access lists configured, you might not remember which one has been applied or bound to a particular interface or in which direction it was bound. You also might not remember the name of a certain access list. The output of this command shows which ACL is bound to which interface, as in this example:

```
Firewall# show running-config access-group
access-group acl_out_v19 in interface outside
access-group acl_inside in interface inside
access-group acl_temp_dmz in interface dmz
access-group mylist_3 in interface dmz2
Firewall#
```

2. (Optional) Check the ACL commands in the configuration:

```
Firewall# show run | {include | grep} matching_text
```

If large ACLs are defined, you can use the **include** or **grep** keywords to search for specific addresses or words in the ACL. This is a much more efficient way to find matching statements than just paging through the firewall configuration with **show running-config** or **write term**. You can quickly see any references to *matching_text* in the ACL configuration.

However, if object groups are defined and they are applied in the ACL, this method might not display intuitive results. In other words, the object groups and ACLs are configured separately, so this search displays matching text from either section of the configuration.

3. Check ACL activity:

```
Firewall# show access-list acl_name [| {include | grep} matching_text]
```

Each condition in the access list is shown, along with a count of the number of "hits" or times any packet has matched that condition on the interface. You can add an optional filter to search the ACL for specific *matching_text*. If your ACL is very large, you might want to use the | **include** filter to look for subnet or host addresses or specific protocol or port numbers within the ACL.

If you know the specific ACL rule that you are expecting to be active in permitting or denying traffic, you can check its hit count (**hitcnt**). If the hit count is 0, no packets have matched that condition; if the count is positive or rising, it is matching traffic.

In the following example, the first line shown permits public access to the 192.168.106.0/24 subnet using SQL, but no matching traffic has been seen. The second line allows public access to a web server, and almost 6 million matching packets have been seen.

```
access-list acl_outside line 720 permit udp any 192.168.106.0 255.255.255.0
  eq 1433 (hitcnt=0)
access-list acl_outside line 761 permit tcp any host 192.168.106.13 eq www
  (hitcnt=5997791)
```

TIP	If you have configured many object groups in your firewall, you might find it difficult to sort through both object group and access list definitions to find specific conditions. The **show access-list** command also expands any object group references in the ACL so that the object group contents are shown with their respective hit counts.

In this way, the firewall rules can be shown as they are interpreted. In the following example, an object group called web-servers has been configured and referenced in an ACL:

```
Firewall# show access-list acl_outside | begin web-servers
access-list acl_outside line 740 permit tcp any object-group web-servers eq
www
access-list acl_outside line 740 permit tcp any host 172.17.69.20 eq www
  (hitcnt=8743)
access-list acl_outside line 740 permit tcp any host 172.17.69.30 eq www
  (hitcnt=16432)
access-list acl_outside line 740 permit tcp any host 172.17.69.40 eq www
  (hitcnt=1711)
access-list acl_outside line 740 permit tcp any host 172.17.69.50 eq www
  (hitcnt=4913495)
[output deleted]
```

Notice that each line has the same ACL line number (740), indicating that the object group is referenced in that line of the ACL **acl_outside**. The object group has been expanded so that the ACL looks like it was written with separate rules for each web server. This makes it much easier to search for things without trudging through complex nested object groups and ACL statements.

Beginning with ASA 8.0(1) and ASDM 6.0(1), you can display live ACL hit counts from an ASDM session. This can be useful if you want to see a list of the most used ACE entries.

The firewall identifies each ACL line with a unique hex value, which can be seen at the end of each line in the ACL configuration. ASDM uses the hex values to correlate ACE entries with their respective hit counts. As an example, consider the following ACL configuration:

```
Firewall# show access-list acl_outside
access-list acl_outside; 9 elements
access-list acl_outside line 1 extended permit tcp any host 172.21.67.101 eq www
(hitcnt=1) 0x82c8336b
access-list acl_outside line 2 extended permit tcp any host 172.21.67.101 eq https
(hitcnt=5) 0x8e5901d0
access-list acl_outside line 3 extended permit tcp any host 172.21.67.101 eq smtp
(hitcnt=2) 0xe467c098
access-list acl_outside line 4 extended permit icmp any host 172.21.67.101 (hitcnt=0)
0x57e1887
access-list acl_outside line 5 extended permit icmp any host 172.21.67.101 echo (hitcnt=0)
0xf9492c4a
access-list acl_outside line 6 extended permit icmp any host 172.21.67.101 echo-reply
(hitcnt=0) 0xf068af69
access-list acl_outside line 7 extended permit icmp any host 172.21.67.101 time-exceeded
(hitcnt=0) 0x2317d4
```

```
access-list acl_outside line 8 extended permit udp any host 172.21.67.101 eq domain
(hitcnt=0) 0xaf08b276
Firewall#
```

ASDM uses the **show access-list** *acl_name* **brief** command to get a list of ACEs that have a non-zero hit count. The output consists of only the hex identifiers and a 16-digit hex value for the hit counts, as in the following example:

```
Firewall# show access-list acl_outside brief
access-list acl_outside; 10 elements
82c8336b 00000000 00000001
8e5901d0 00000000 00000005
e467c098 00000000 00000002
057e1887 00000000 00000001
Firewall#
```

Notice how ACE identifier 8e5901d0 has a hit count of 5, and that it corresponds to line 2 of the **acl_outside** ACL. Using the same example ACL, Figure 11-22 shows how ASDM can be used to display the most used ACE entries that are applied to the firewall interfaces. After ASDM is started, make sure the **Home** button is selected, and go to the **Firewall Dashboard** tab. The ACL activity can be seen in the upper-right portion of the ASDM window.

Figure 11-22 *Using ASDM to View Live ACL Hit Counts*

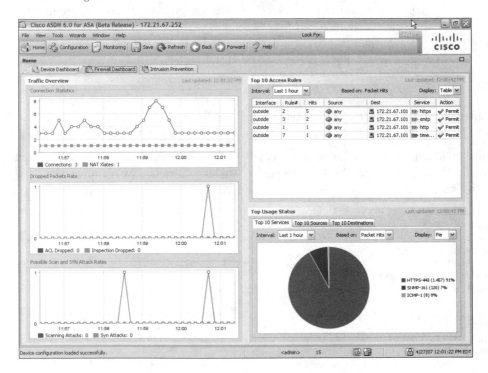

Step 6: Verify the Address Translation and Connection Tables

Before a host can send traffic through a firewall, the firewall must have the following items configured properly:

- Address translation, using **static** or **nat/global** commands (unless the **no-nat-control** command is configured)

- An access list that permits the traffic; this allows connections to be established

You can monitor the xlate and conn entries for specific hosts in several ways, as described in the following sections.

Monitoring Translations

You can see what (if any) address translations have been created for a host by using a form of the **show xlate** command:

PIX 6.3	Firewall# **show xlate** [**detail**] [**global** ∣ **local** *ip1*[*-ip2*] [**netmask** *mask*]] **lport** ∣ **gport** *port*[*-port*]] [**interface** *if1*[*,if2*][*,ifn*]] [**state static** [*,dump*] [*,portmap*] [*,norandomseq*] [*,identity*]] [**debug**] [**count**]
ASA, FWSM	Firewall# **show xlate** [{**global** ∣ **local**} *ip1*[*-ip2*] [**netmask** *mask*]] [{**lport** ∣ **gport**} *port*[*-port*]] [**interface** *if1*[*,if2*][*,ifn*]] [**state** {**static** ∣ **portmap** ∣ **identity** ∣ **norandomseq**}] [**debug**] [**detail**]

Remember with xlate entries, **global** represents the translated address on the lower-security interface, and **local** is the address on the higher-security interface. Use any of the following commands according to the IP address information you already know.

You can select a global or local address or a range of addresses. You can add a local port (**lport**) or global port (**gport**) or a range of ports. In addition, you can specify one or more firewall interfaces that are involved with the translation. You can specify the translation type as **static**, **portmap** (PAT), **identity** (identity NAT), or **noramdomseq** (no randomization of the TCP initial sequence number).

The command output is shown in a brief format (local and global addresses only) by default. The output can also be requested as **detail** (the default format plus the firewall interfaces and translation type) or as **debug** (the **detail** format plus the idle time).

To get a feel for the current number of xlate table entries, you can use the following command:

Firewall# **show xlate count**

TIP The **show xlate** commands covered in the following sections give basic information about the translated addresses, along with any port translation. Here is an example:

```
Firewall# show xlate local 172.27.112.26
18356 in use, 22368 most used
PAT Global 10.1.1.1(11104) Local 172.27.112.26(4685)
PAT Global 10.1.1.1(24560) Local 172.27.112.26(4695)
```

You can also display translation flags and timeout values by adding the **debug** keyword to each command:

```
Firewall# show xlate local 172.27.112.26 debug
18729 in use, 22368 most used
Flags: D - DNS, d - dump, I - identity, i - inside, n - no random,
       o - outside, r - portmap, s - static
TCP PAT from inside:172.27.112.26/4697 to outside:10.1.1.1/23228 flags
  r idle 0:03:19 timeout 0:00:30
TCP PAT from inside:172.27.112.26/4695 to outside:10.1.1.1/24560 flags
  r idle 48:06:38 timeout 0:00:30
```

Finding Xlate Entries Based on a Global Address

To find xlate entries based on a global address, use the following command:

```
Firewall# show xlate global global-ip [netmask mask] [gport global-port]
```

For example, the following output shows some of the PAT entries that have been created using global address 12.163.11.72:

```
Firewall# show xlate global 12.163.11.72
15624 in use, 26615 most used
PAT Global 12.163.11.72(10454) Local 172.21.40.111(1033)
PAT Global 12.163.11.72(10406) Local 172.21.96.91(1052)
PAT Global 12.163.11.72(10416) Local 172.21.100.59(2749)
[output omitted]
```

Finding Xlate Entries Based on a Local Address

To find xlate entries based on a local address, use the following command:

```
Firewall# show xlate local local-ip [netmask mask] [lport local-port]
```

For example, the following command is used to display the xlate entries for all local addresses using local port 123 (UDP 123 is used for NTP):

```
Firewall# show xlate lport 123
15630 in use, 26615 most used
PAT Global 128.1.10.72(190) Local 172.21.60.179(123)
PAT Global 128.1.10.72(108) Local 172.21.56.125(123)
PAT Global 128.1.10.72(122) Local 172.21.156.122(123)
PAT Global 128.1.10.72(116) Local 172.21.198.207(123)
[output omitted]
```

Finding All Static Xlate Entries

To find all static xlate entries, use the following command:

```
Firewall# show xlate state static
```

The following command displays some of the xlate entries that have been configured with the **static** command:

```
Firewall# show xlate state static
Global 10.16.98.118 Local 172.16.100.99
Global 10.16.98.101 Local 172.21.192.116
Global 10.16.98.105 Local 172.17.197.66
Global 10.16.98.111 Local 172.17.232.74
Global 10.16.98.107 Local 172.20.196.434.
```

Finding All PAT Entries (Dynamic Xlates)

To find all PAT entries (dynamic xlates), use the following command:

```
Firewall# show xlate state portmap
```

For example, the following command displays all the dynamic PAT entries that are currently in the xlate table:

```
Firewall# show xlate state portmap
15723 in use, 26615 most used
PAT Global 68.163.1.2(10452) Local 172.16.104.89(4499)
PAT Global 68.163.1.2(10454) Local 172.16.40.111(1033)
PAT Global 68.163.1.2(10406) Local 172.16.96.91(1052)
```

Finding All Identity Entries

To find all identity entries (global and local addresses are identical), use the following command:

```
Firewall# show xlate state identity
```

For example, the following command displays all identity xlate entries that are currently in use:

```
Firewall# show xlate state identity
1 in use, 12 most used
Global 192.168.198.17 Local 192.168.198.17
```

Monitoring Connections

You can see what (if any) UDP and TCP connections have been established for a host by using a form of the **show conn** command. The command has the following syntax:

```
Firewall# show conn [state state_type] [{foreign | local} ip1[-ip2] netmask mask]
  [long] [{lport | fport} port1[-port2]] [protocol {tcp | udp}]
```

With no additional keywords, **show conn** displays the entire conn table. On ASA and FWSM platforms, you can add the **all** keyword to show all connections in the table, including connections that terminate on the firewall itself.

For TCP connections, you can specify the connection state as **state** *state_type*, where the state type is one of the keywords listed in Table 11-14.

Table 11-14   *TCP Connection State Types*

Keyword	Flag	Description
up	U	The TCP connection is up and functional
finin	r	TCP FIN requested in the inbound direction and acknowledged
finout	R	TCP FIN requested in the outbound direction and acknowledged
http_get	—	HTTP GET connection
smtp_data	M	SMTP data connection
nojava	—	A connection that has Java applets blocked by the **java filter** command
data_in	I	Data has moved in the inbound direction
data_out	O	Data has moved in the outbound direction
rpc	R	SunRPC
h225	h	H.225
h323	H	H.323
sqlnet_fixup_data	q	SQL*Net
conn_inbound	B	Connection with the initial SYN originating from the outside
sip	T	SIP
mgcp	g	MGCP
ctiqbe	C	Computer Telephony Interface Quick Buffer Encoding (CTIQBE)
skinny	k	Cisco Skinny SCCP

You can also specify the foreign or local IP address (or range of addresses) used in the connections, as well as the local port (**lport**) or foreign port (**fport**) or a range of ports. The IP protocol can also be given as **tcp** or **udp**.

With connections, "foreign" represents the host on the lower-security interface, and "local" is the address of the host on the higher-security interface. Table 11-15 lists the possible display formats.

Table 11-15   *Display Formats Available with the **show conn** Command*

Keyword	Information Displayed
(Default)	Local and foreign IP addresses and ports, idle time, connection byte count, connection flags
detail	Default format plus firewall interfaces
long	**detail** format plus address translations

You can also display the current number of conn table entries with the following command:

Firewall# **show conn count**

The output from this command shows the total number of conn table entries, regardless of protocol. It is not possible to show a breakdown of entries by protocol (UDP and TCP, for example).

The **show conn** commands listed in the following sections display the protocol, foreign and local addresses and ports, connection idle time, connection data volume, and connection flags. Here is a brief example:

Firewall# **show conn foreign 10.10.39.14**
10449 in use, 577536 most used
TCP out 10.10.39.14:1033 in 192.168.29.37:524 idle 0:08:06 Bytes 11076 flags UIOB

You can also display similar information along with a listing of the connection flags by adding the **detail** keyword:

Firewall# **show conn foreign 10.10.39.14 detail**
10385 in use, 577536 most used
Flags: A - awaiting inside ACK to SYN, a - awaiting outside ACK to SYN,
       B - initial SYN from outside, C - CTIQBE media, D - DNS, d - dump,
       E - outside back connection, F - outside FIN, f - inside FIN,
       G - group, g - MGCP, H - H.323, h - H.225.0, I - inbound data, i -
  incomplete,
       k - Skinny media, M - SMTP data, m - SIP media, O - outbound data,
       P - inside back connection, q - SQL*Net data, R - outside acknowledged FIN,
       R - UDP RPC, r - inside acknowledged FIN, S - awaiting inside SYN,
       s - awaiting outside SYN, T - SIP, t - SIP transient, U - up
TCP outside:10.10.39.14/1033 inside:192.168.29.37/524 flags UIOB

Notice that the foreign and local host addresses are shown with the firewall interface names where they reside. If you are interested in which host (foreign or local) initiated the connection, you have to interpret the connection flags.

In the preceding example, you can determine the following facts from **flags UIOB**:

- **U**—The connection is up (fully established).

- **I**—Inbound data has been received from the foreign host.

- **O**—Outbound data has been sent from the local host.
- **B**—The initial TCP SYN flag came from the outside (foreign host). Therefore, the connection was initiated by the foreign host.

Because UDP is not connection-oriented, it is not possible to see which host initiated a UDP session.

Finding Conn Entries Based on a Foreign Address

To find conn entries based on a foreign address, use the following command:

```
Firewall# show conn foreign foreign_ip [netmask mask]
```

The foreign address *foreign_ip* is used to find all the relevant connections in the conn table. For example, you can use the following command to find all active conn table entries involving the foreign address 198.133.219.25 (http://www.cisco.com):

```
Firewall# show conn foreign 198.133.219.25
7046 in use, 57005 most used
TCP out 198.133.219.25:80 in 172.21.4.5:3050 idle 0:03:32 Bytes 10762 flags UIO
Firewall#
```

Finding Conn Entries Based on a Local Address

To find conn entries based on a local address, use the following command:

```
Firewall# show conn local local_ip [netmask mask]
```

For example, local address 172.16.193.187 is found to have the following open conn table entries:

```
Firewall# show conn local 172.16.193.187
17267 in use, 57005 most used
TCP out 147.208.14.61:80 in 172.16.193.187:4536 idle 0:00:03 flags UIO
TCP out 64.215.168.97:80 in 172.16.193.187:4538 idle 0:00:03 flags UIO
UDP outside:65.98.25.54:53 inside:172.16.193.187:51455 flags d
[output omitted]
```

Finding Conn Entries Based on Protocol Information

To find conn entries based on protocol information, use the following command:

```
Firewall# show conn protocol {tcp | udp} [fport foreign_port | lport local_port]
```

The following TCP connections using foreign port 1433 are currently in this firewall's conn table:

```
Firewall# show conn protocol tcp fport 1433
TCP out 64.191.149.170:443 in 172.16.1.10:1988 idle 0:00:55 Bytes 0 flags saA
TCP out 160.109.67.70:443 in 172.16.1.11:1173 idle 0:03:56 Bytes 157428 flags UIO
TCP out 64.73.28.116:443 in 172.16.1.12:1294 idle 0:01:06 Bytes 921 flags UIO
[output omitted]
```

Monitoring Specific Hosts

If you are looking for stateful inspection information for a particular host, you can spend time sifting through the xlate and conn tables. However, there is a much more direct way to get this information in a single command:

PIX 6.3	Firewall# **show local-host** [*ip_address*]
ASA, FWSM	Firewall# **show local-host** [*ip_address*] [**all**] [**detail**]

You can get information about any "local" host as long as it resides on a firewall interface with a security level greater than 0 and you know its IP address. In ASA and FWSM, a local host can reside on any firewall address, regardless of the security level. The firewall does all the table lookups for you and returns any information it finds. The output also includes any connection limits that might apply to the host.

If you do not specify an IP address, only a count of connections on each interface is displayed.

In the following example, information about the host at 172.18.10.10 is sought. This subnet has been defined as a static identity translation so that addresses 172.18.10.x on the inside also appear on the outside.

```
Firewall# show local-host 172.18.10.10
Interface inside: 15721 active, 15829 maximum active, 0 denied
local host: <172.18.10.10>,
    TCP connection count/limit = 1/unlimited
    TCP embryonic count = 0
    TCP intercept watermark = unlimited
    UDP connection count/limit = 0/unlimited
  AAA:
  Xlate(s):
    Global 172.18.10.10 Local 172.18.10.10
  Conn(s):
    TCP out 172.16.3.14:53957 in 128. 172.18.10.10:23 idle 0:00:03 Bytes 545
  flags UIOB
Firewall#
```

You can see the static identity xlate entry by the IP address appearing as both global and local under the **Xlate(s)** section. The local host had only one active connection—a Telnet session (indicated by ":23" for TCP port 23) from the foreign host 172.16.3.14.

The **show local-host** command is especially useful for local hosts that have dynamic xlate or PAT entries for outbound connections. In the following example, you are interested in the activities of the local host at 172.21.96.22. All inside local hosts are translated using the firewall's outside interface address and dynamic port information.

```
Firewall# show local-host 172.21.96.22
Interface inside: 15725 active, 15829 maximum active, 0 denied
local host: <172.21.96.22>,
    TCP connection count/limit = 176/unlimited
    TCP embryonic count = 11
```

```
    TCP intercept watermark = unlimited
    UDP connection count/limit = 0/unlimited
 AAA:
 Xlate(s):
   PAT Global 207.246.96.46(44112) Local 172.21.96.22(1168)
   PAT Global 207.246.96.46 (44120) Local 172.21.96.22(1176)
   PAT Global 207.246.96.46 (58859) Local 172.21.96.22(1293)
   PAT Global 207.246.96.46 (29899) Local 172.21.96.22(1339)
   PAT Global 207.246.96.46 (33585) Local 172.21.96.22(1469)
[output deleted]
 Conn(s):
   TCP out 217.123.215.64:6883 in 172.21.96.22:1168 idle 0:00:21 Bytes 15918696
 flags UIO
   TCP out 66.127.201.130:6881 in 172.21.96.22:1176 idle 0:00:22 Bytes 24003969
 flags UIO
   TCP out 219.111.75.71:6881 in 172.21.96.22:1293 idle 0:00:58 Bytes 730251
 flags UIO
   TCP out 156.34.72.34:6881 in 172.21.96.22:1339 idle 0:00:58 Bytes 4969
 flags UIO
   TCP out 200.104.11.50:6883 in 172.21.96.22:1469 idle 0:00:19 Bytes 4744
 flags UIO
[output omitted]
```

Here, you find that local host 172.21.96.22 has 176 active (and established) TCP connections to foreign hosts. As well, the firewall has tracked 11 TCP connections that are embryonic or half-opened. This can be a cause of concern if many embryonic connections are opened to the local host. The firewall is using its default settings and allowing an unlimited number of embryonic connections to be attempted.

The **show local-host** command has also conveniently summarized all xlate entries involving host 172.21.96.22 so that you can see all the local and foreign port number pairs being used. Below that, all its active connections are summarized, as if you had used the **show conn** command.

By default, the **show local-host** command does not display any connections that are active to or from the firewall itself. You can add the **all** keyword to display all the local host's active connections—including those that terminate or originate at the firewall. The firewall interfaces can be considered as local hosts too.

In the following example, a client (172.21.4.60) on the firewall's outside interface (172.16.1.1) has opened an SSH connection to the firewall. Notice that the firewall interface name **NP Identity Ifc** is displayed as the interface where the SSH connection terminates.

```
Firewall# show local-host 172.16.1.1 all
Interface dmz: 0 active, 0 maximum active, 0 denied
Interface inside: 0 active, 1 maximum active, 0 denied
Interface outside: 1 active, 14 maximum active, 0 denied
Interface NP Identity Ifc: 1 active, 2 maximum active, 0 denied
local host: <172.16.1.1>,
    TCP flow count/limit = 0/unlimited
    TCP embryonic count to (from) host = 0 (0)
    TCP intercept watermark = unlimited
    UDP flow count/limit = 0/unlimited
```

```
Conn:
    TCP out 172.21.4.60:3244 in 172.16.1.1:22 idle 0:00:00 bytes 621703 flags UIOB
Firewall#
```

Clearing Xlate Table Entries

On several occasions, the xlate table might contain stale or incorrect entries. This can happen if you make configuration changes to the **static**, **global**, or **nat** commands on a firewall or to an interface access list. As soon as that happens, it is likely that the xlate table has existing entries that use previous or outdated translations.

For example, if several hosts are using Telnet connections, and a new policy is added to an access list to deny the Telnet protocol, new Telnet connections are blocked. The existing connections remain open until the application closes them or until the firewall idles them out. Therefore, the xlate entries and the corresponding conn table entries for the active Telnet sessions remain active too. Those entries must be cleared manually if the policy needs to be enforced immediately.

You can clear xlate entries manually, either one at a time or the whole table at once. Use one of the following commands:

Firewall# **clear xlate global** global_ip [**netmask** mask] [**gport** global_port]	Clears an xlate entry based on a global address.
Firewall# **clear xlate local** local_ip [**netmask** mask] [**lport** local_port]	Clears an xlate entry based on a local address.
Firewall# **clear xlate interface** if_name_1[,if_name_2]	Clears xlate entries bound to a pair of firewall interfaces.
Firewall# **clear xlate**	Clears the entire xlate table.

Although this is a quick way to flush the entire xlate table, you should be careful. Any active connections using the address translations are dropped immediately. This means that users could see applications or sessions terminate in the middle of important work.

If you must clear the xlate table, do so at a time of low usage or during a downtime window.

Adjusting Table Timeout Values

You can also adjust various idle timers that affect address translations and connections maintained by the firewall. Use the following commands if you feel a timeout adjustment is needed:

- Xlate entry timer:

    Firewall(config)# **timeout xlate** hh[:mm[:ss]]

    By default, xlate entries involving TCP connections are be deleted after they have been idle (no data passed) for 3 hours. The minimum idle time is 1 minute, but the xlate idle timer cannot be set to a value that is less than the uauth timer (the default is 5 minutes).

Xlate portmap (PAT) entries created for UDP always idle out after 30 seconds. This idle timer cannot be configured.

- TCP conn entry timer:

  `Firewall(config)# ` **`timeout conn`** ` hh[:mm[:ss]]`

  Conn table entries for TCP connections idle out after 1 hour by default. The minimum idle period is 5 minutes. You can use a time value of **0:0:0** or **0** to indicate that TCP conn entries should never time out. In that case, TCP connections must close themselves when both hosts exchange FIN flags.

- TCP half-closed conn entry timer:

  `Firewall(config)# ` **`half-closed`** ` hh[:mm[:ss]]`

  A TCP connection is half-closed if only one of the pair of hosts signals a connection termination with its FIN flag. If the other host does not respond with its FIN handshake, the firewall goes ahead and closes the connection after an idle period.

  By default, half-closed connections are deleted after 10 minutes. The minimum idle time is 5 minutes.

NOTE   Half-open TCP connections (also called embryonic connections) result if only one of the pair sends the TCP SYN flag. The firewall automatically closes half-open connections if a fixed period of 2 minutes elapses before the three-way TCP handshake completes.

- UDP conn entry timer:

  `Firewall(config)# ` **`udp`** ` hh[:mm[:ss]]`

  UDP sessions, because they are connectionless, must simply time out. No mechanism exists for one host to close or terminate a UDP session. By default, a firewall deletes a UDP conn entry after it has been idle (no data passing) for 2 minutes. The minimum idle time is 1 minute.

Step 7: Look for Active Shuns

A Cisco firewall can shun (block) traffic coming from specific source addresses on an interface. This feature is useful when a host is generating malicious traffic and needs to be stopped. If you have manually added shuns to your firewall, or if another system has added them automatically, you might forget that they are in place.

In fact, when shuns are defined, they are dynamic in nature and are not added to the firewall configuration. If you are troubleshooting why a host is not receiving or sending any traffic, you might not find the reason by looking through the firewall configuration.

You can display a list of active shuns with the following EXEC command:

`Firewall#` **`show shun`** `[src_ip]`

If you provide a specific source address *src_ip*, only shuns involving that address are shown.

You can also look at shun activity and duration with the following command:

`Firewall#` **`show shun statistics`**

To delete a shun, you can use the following EXEC command:

`Firewall#` **`no shun`** `src_ip [dst_ip sport dport [protocol]]`

You must provide the source address (*src_ip*). The destination address (dst_ip), source and destination ports, and protocol are all optional. If they are omitted, 0s are assumed in those fields.

For example, suppose a user has called to report that her host at 172.21.196.38 cannot reach the public network. You have trouble locating the cause of the problem until you look at a list of the active shuns on the firewall:

```
Firewall# show shun
Shun 172.16.44.59 0.0.0.0 0 0
Shun 172.20.36.62 0.0.0.0 0 0
Shun 172.31.69.84 0.0.0.0 0 0
Shun 172.21.196.38 0.0.0.0 0 0
Shun 172.18.77.186 0.0.0.0 0 0
Shun 172.16.103.161 0.0.0.0 0 0
Shun 172.16.100.166 0.0.0.0 0 0
Shun 172.21.196.230 0.0.0.0 0 0
Shun 172.16.73.135 0.0.0.0 0 0
Firewall#
Firewall# show shun statistics
stateful=OFF, cnt=0
dmz2=OFF, cnt=0
outside=OFF, cnt=210499
inside=ON, cnt=2605814591
Shun 172.16.44.59 cnt=269, time=(392:44:35)
Shun 172.20.36.62 cnt=125493, time=(392:44:35)
Shun 172.31.69.84 cnt=49384, time=(392:44:35)
Shun 172.21.196.38 cnt=80694744, time=(392:44:35)
Shun 172.18.77.186 cnt=36524, time=(392:44:35)
Shun 172.16.103.161 cnt=1021, time=(392:44:35)
Shun 172.16.100.166 cnt=9835, time=(392:44:35)
Shun 172.21.196.230 cnt=52, time=(392:44:35)
Shun 172.16.73.135 cnt=321282, time=(392:44:35)Firewall#
```

The shun in question (shaded in the output) has been quite active, blocking 80,694,744 packets since it was defined more than 392 hours ago. When you have determined that it is safe to delete that shun, you can use the following command:

`Firewall#` **`no shun 172.21.196.38`**

TIP	Keep in mind that shun definitions are dynamic in nature. You should keep an offline list of all the shuns you add manually. If the firewall loses power or reloads, or a failover condition occurs, all the active shuns are lost. In other words, you have to reconfigure them as soon as you realize they are no longer active.
	As a long-term plan, you should consider converting the shuns into access list entries so that they become part of the firewall configuration. This makes them more permanent and leverages the firewall's capability to generate Syslog information about their activity.

Step 8: Check User Authentication

You can configure user authentication in several forms on a Cisco firewall. Refer to the information in the following sections to verify that authentication is working properly.

Authentication Proxy (Uauth)

If your firewall is configured as an authentication proxy, a loss of connectivity might be related to authentication problems. You can view the active authenticated users with the **show uauth** command. Any users who have successfully authenticated are shown, along with their IP addresses and uauth timeout values:

```
Firewall# show uauth
                         Current     Most Seen
Authenticated Users      1           1
Authen In Progress       0           1
user 'hucaby' at 192.168.199.33, authenticated
   absolute   timeout: 0:05:00
   inactivity timeout: 0:00:00
Firewall#
```

If a user is listed as **authenticated** but is unable to connect through the firewall, there might be a problem with authorization. For example, a AAA server could be downloading an authorization filter or ACL name associated with the user, but that ACL is not defined on the firewall. If this is the case, the Syslog server should show a message similar to this:

```
Feb 26 2004 21:55:42 Firewall : %ASA-3-109016: Can't find authorization ACL
   'engineering' on 'ASA' for user 'hucaby'
```

If you do find a problem with a user's authentication session, you can clear that person from the uauth table with the **clear uauth** *username* command.

If no users are being successfully authenticated through the firewall, you should look on a more fundamental level. Make sure the firewall can communicate with the proper RADIUS or TACACS+ server. You can use the **debug aaa authentication** command to watch debug messages on the firewall console or Telnet session as a user tries to authenticate.

For example, suppose a firewall is configured to query a RADIUS server (192.168.11.49) for user authentication. A user named hucaby is getting an authentication prompt from the firewall but is being rejected. The **debug aaa authentication** command produces the following output:

```
Firewall# debug aaa authentication
Firewall# 34: Received response: , session id 201242794
35: Making authentication request for host 192.168.11.49, user , session id:
  201242794
36: Processing challenge for user , session id: 201242794, challenge: Please
  register for access
Username:
37: sending challenge to user: , challenge: Please register for access
Username: , session id: 201242794
38: Received response: hucaby, session id 201242794
39: Making authentication request for host 192.168.11.49, user hucaby, session id:
  201242794
40: Processing challenge for user hucaby, session id: 201242794, challenge:
  Password:
41: sending challenge to user: hucaby, challenge: Password: , session id:
  201242794
42: Received response: , session id 201242794
43: Making authentication request for host 192.168.11.49, user hucaby, session id:
  201242794
44: Authentication failed for user :hucaby, pass :firewallzrc001, session id:
  201242794
45: retrying Authentication for user :hucaby, pass : firewallzrc001, session id:
  201242794
46: Received response: , session id 201242794
47: Making authentication request for host 192.168.11.49, user , session id:
  201242794
48: Processing challenge for user , session id: 201242794, challenge: Please
  register for access
Username:
49: sending challenge to user: , challenge: Please register for access
Username: , session id: 201242794
```

The user is being prompted for login credentials, and you can see how the firewall is communicating the userID and then the password to the RADIUS server. The highlighted message indicates that the RADIUS server has rejected the user's information because the password is incorrect. In fact, the password entered by the user is displayed in the debug output.

Content Filtering

Another area to look at is content filtering through Websense or N2H2. If one of these services denies a user's access to a URL, you should check the server's configuration for that user or user group.

At the most basic level, you should see evidence that the firewall is talking to the content-filtering server. You can use the **show url-server stats** command. If the counters shown are nonzero and are increasing with user traffic, the content-filtering communication is working properly, as shown in this example:

```
Firewall# show url-server stats

URL Server Statistics:
----------------------
Vendor                        websense
URLs total/allowed/denied     420691/363332/57359
HTTPSs total/allowed/denied   0/0/0
FTPs total/allowed/denied     0/0/0

URL Server Status:
------------------
192.168.204.17                UP

URL Packets Sent and Received Stats:
------------------------------------
Message                  Sent    Recieved
STATUS_REQUEST           310338  309198
LOOKUP_REQUEST           416011  414554
LOG_REQUEST              0       NA
------------------------------------
Firewall#
```

If the firewall is having trouble reaching the content-filtering server, you might see one of the following Syslog messages:

```
%ASA-2-304007: URL Server IP_address  not responding, ENTERING ALLOW mode.
%ASA-3-304003: URL Server IP_address  timed out URL url
%ASA-3-304006: URL Server IP_address  not responding
%ASA-6-304004: URL Server IP_address  request failed URL url
```

As soon as the content-filtering server again can be reached, you should see this Syslog message:

```
%ASA-2-304008: LEAVING ALLOW mode, URL Server is up.
```

Step 9: See What Has Changed

If you have installed, configured, and tested a firewall, trusted users should be able to pass through it according to the security policies. At the same time, the firewall should deny or drop all untrusted users and traffic. Suppose things have been working like this for some time, but one day users begin to call and complain.

One possible cause of a problem is that someone somewhere has changed something on your network. One good troubleshooting approach is to ask, "What changed during the time when problems began to occur?"

In the case of a firewall, it is entirely possible that someone has made a change to the configuration, especially if you work with a staff of other firewall administrators. How can you determine if a change was made and who made it?

1. Implement an orderly change-management process. If an administrator needs to alter a firewall configuration, the change should be announced in advance, approved by peer review, and performed at an expected time. Records of the change-management activity should be kept as an audit trail.

2. Keep copies of the firewall configuration archived. As each change is made, archive the new configuration. Not only will you have an additional audit trail, but you also will make a downgrade situation easier if you need to back out of a large configuration change.

3. Use AAA authentication for firewall management access. This forces each firewall administrator to have a unique user ID and password, which makes management access more secure.

    In addition, the firewall generates an audit trail each time a configuration change is made or a command is executed. AAA authentication should always be used in conjunction with Syslog collection for the sole purpose of maintaining a thorough audit trail.

    When AAA authentication is not used, firewall administrators and users take on the generic identity **enable_1** (privilege level 1) when they first log in. After using the enable command, users take on the generic identity **enable_15** (privilege level 15). Naturally, when AAA authentication is used, users appear as their own user IDs.

    If you were trying to sift through the Syslog records to see who made changes to a firewall configuration, which of these messages would be more useful?

    ```
    Feb 26 2007 08:06:30 Firewall-A : %ASA-5-111008: User 'enable_15' executed
      the 'clear xlate' command.
    Feb 26 2007 08:09:13 Firewall-A : %ASA-5-111008: User 'enable_15' executed
      the 'no access-list acl_outside' command.
    ```

    or

    ```
    Feb 26 2007 08:06:30 Firewall-A : %ASA-5-111008: User 'hucaby' executed the
      'clear xlate' command.
    Feb 26 2007 08:09:13 Firewall-A : %ASA-5-111008: User 'hucaby' executed the
      'no access-list acl_outside' command.
    ```

Clearly, you would like to track down user hucaby to see why he cleared the xlate table and deleted the ACL applied to the outside interface at the start of the business day.

Refer to the following sections for information about these topics:

- **12-1: Initially Configuring an ASA SSM**—Explains how to provide a bootstrap configuration so that a Security Services Module (SSM) can be used in an Adaptive Security Appliance (ASA) chassis.

- **12-2: Configuring the CSC SSM**—Discusses the steps needed to configure and use a Content Security and Control (CSC) module for content inspection features.

- **12-3: Configuring the AIP SSM**—Describes the steps needed to configure and use an Advanced Inspection and Prevention (AIP) module for intrusion protection features.

CHAPTER 12

ASA Modules

Most of the ASA platform models offer a Security Services Module (SSM) slot that can be used to house special purpose hardware. Only the ASA 5505 and 5550 do not have an SSM slot. The slot can accept one of the following modules:

- **4GE**—The 4-port Gigabit Ethernet SSM offers four 10/100/1000 TX RJ-45 ports, as well as four small form-factor pluggable (SFP) module ports.

- **AIP**—The Advanced Inspection and Prevention (AIP) module acts as an in-depth Intrusion Prevention System (IPS) that inspects traffic against an extensive set of IPS signatures to classify and prevent malicious traffic from affecting resources protected by the ASA. The AIP uses the same operating system and signature database as other Cisco IPS appliances.

- **CSC**—The Content Security and Control (CSC) module offers advanced content-based inspection that is offloaded from the normal ASA CPU. The CSC can provide anti-virus, anti-spyware, anti-spam, anti-phishing, mail tagging, file blocking, URL blocking and filtering, and content filtering.

The 4GE SSM offers only additional interfaces; it does not perform any advanced processing or inspection. Therefore, after you insert it into an ASA chassis, you can configure its interfaces right away, just as you would the built-in interfaces.

The AIP and CSC SSMs, however, do require additional configuration before they can be used. Each module runs its own operating system and requires a code image. In addition, the ASA that hosts the SSM must be configured to funnel traffic to the SSM for inspection. The necessary configuration steps are covered in the sections within this chapter.

The CSC SSM, in particular, is very dependent upon having connectivity to Trend Micro. The CSC's management port is used to communicate with the Trend Micro servers over the Internet to download regular content security database updates. Updated databases can be posted at least once a day.

The AIP is also dependent upon periodic updates to its signature database. However, it can download updated files from a local server or client machine.

Both the AIP and CSC modules require a support contract to be maintained as long as they are used, so that they can be kept up-to-date with constantly changing criteria that describes constantly changing exploit schemes.

12-1: Initially Configuring an ASA SSM

When you add an AIP or CSC SSM to an ASA chassis, you need to configure the ASA with some basic features so you can communicate with the SSM. Then, the SSM requires its own configuration to control how it inspects traffic and how it reacts to malicious or undesirable activity.

Each SSM has two communication paths:

- A 10/100 TX RJ-45 management Ethernet port
- A backplane connection to the ASA CPU

All SSM configuration is done through the management port. The SSM can be configured through a command-line interface (CLI) or through ASDM, or even through the Cisco Security Manager (CSM) application. In any case, the CLI and Adaptive Security Device Manager (ASDM) interfaces passes configuration information through the SSM's management port. This is important because administrative access is kept totally separate from the traffic inspection or control path.

Preparing the ASA for SSM Management Traffic

First, the ASA should be configured so that you can use ASDM to configure and monitor the AIP or CSC SSM. You must bootstrap the SSM configuration through its own management interface, but you can do the bulk of your administrative work through ASDM.

Refer to the section "ASDM/PDM Sessions" in Section "4-5: Managing Administrative Sessions," from Chapter 4, "Firewall Management," for information on configuring ASDM on the ASA.

Next, you should make sure your ASA is configured to use an accurate clock source. The ASA can derive its time and date information from an internal clock or a Network Time Protocol (NTP) server on the network. Using an NTP server is usually more accurate, as the clock is kept up-to-date based on very accurate and redundant sources.

The ASA should have an accurate clock because it can generate time stamps on logging messages, maintain time-based access lists, and validate digital certificates. The CSC and AIP modules should have an accurate clock because they use time stamps and time-oriented operations in their inspection and analysis functions. Time stamps can be important when you gather forensic information about suspicious activity or in an audit trail.

Like the ASA, the CSC and AIP modules each have their own internal clocks, derived from either the ASA's clock or an external NTP server. If you take time to configure the ASA so that it uses an accurate time source, it only makes sense to keep the CSC or AIP module in sync with the ASA's clock. In other words, you should need to configure only one clock for both devices.

Refer to Section "10-1: Managing the Firewall Clock," from Chapter 10, "Firewall Logging," for complete information on setting the ASA's clock and configuring it to use an NTP server.

Finally, you need to configure the SSM's dedicated Ethernet management port so that it can be used to configure the module, download new code images and inspection policy databases, and generate logging messages.

Connecting and Configuring the SSM Management Interface

As soon as the module is installed in the ASA chassis, you need to connect its management port to either of the following:

- An unprotected VLAN, along with the ASA outside interface
- An ASA demilitarized zone (DMZ) interface by using a crossover cable or an external switch

The most straightforward way to bring up the management interface is to connect it to the outside or public side of the ASA, as shown in Figure 12-1. This allows the module to communicate with outside resources such as ASDM sessions and Trend Micro servers (CSC module only) directly, without any other firewall configuration or intervention. However, this means the management interface is not protected by the firewall at all. In fact, the Cisco SAFE architecture recommends that the management interface be kept separated or isolated from any user networks.

Figure 12-1   *Connecting the SSM Management Port on the Outside*

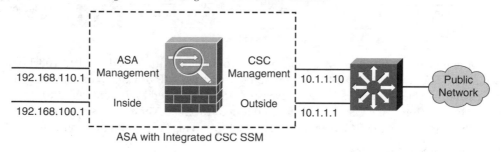

ASA with Integrated CSC SSM

This also means that untrusted hosts on the Internet might be able to communicate with your SSM management interface, too—something that you might not welcome.

You could also connect the SSM management interface to the same management network used by the ASA management interface. This keeps all of the management traffic isolated from other networks. If your management network is totally isolated from the Internet, this setup will not work because the CSC must have a way to contact the Trend Micro servers over the Internet.

Connecting the SSM management interface to a DMZ, as shown in Figure 12-2, offers the most robust solution. Because the SSM management traffic must pass through the firewall to reach external resources such as Trend Micro servers over the Internet, that traffic is protected by the firewall's stateful inspection. The firewall can also prevent outside hosts from discovering and attempting to exploit the module.

In the example from Figure 12-2, the ASA interfaces are configured with the following commands:

```
interface Ethernet0/0
 nameif outside
 security-level 0
 ip address 10.1.1.1 255.255.255.0
!
interface Ethernet0/1
 nameif inside
```

```
 security-level 100
 ip address 192.168.100.1 255.255.255.0
!
interface Ethernet0/2
 nameif dmz
 security-level 50
 ip address 192.168.110.1 255.255.255.0
```

Figure 12-2 *Connecting the SSM Management Interface to a DMZ*

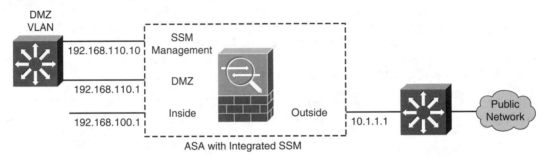

The SSM management interface will eventually be configured with IP address 192.168.110.10. This cannot be done from the ASA configuration because the AIP or CSC maintains its own management interface configuration. However, the ASA does need to be configured to support outbound connections for a CSC module to "call home" to Trend Micro for its updates. This can be done through a dynamic PAT operation, using the following ASA configuration commands:

```
global (outside) 1 interface
nat (dmz) 1 192.168.110.0 255.255.255.0
```

Here, the SSM management interface (192.168.110.10) would be translated to the outside interface address (10.1.1.1) during outbound connections. Keep in mind that you need to be able to connect to the SSM management interface to configure and monitor the module. The following ASA configuration commands enable outbound connections from a PC on the inside network toward the SSM on the DMZ network:

```
global (dmz) 1 interface
nat (inside) 1 192.168.100.0 255.255.255.0
```

One drawback to the preceding configuration is that you can only manage the SSM from the inside or DMZ networks. This is because dynamic PAT makes the SSM management interface appear as the ASA outside interface from the outside, using a dynamically assigned port number. To manage the module from the outside, the management interface must have a static address translation to an address that is reachable from the outside.

The following ASA configuration commands set up a static NAT so that the SSM appears as outside address 10.1.1.10. As well, an access list is created to permit inbound connections to the SSM management interface. With a CSC, all management connections use TCP port 8443; for an AIP, TCP port 443 would be used instead:

```
static (dmz,outside) 10.1.1.10 192.168.110.10 netmask 255.255.255.255
!
```

```
access-list acl_outside extended permit tcp any host 10.1.1.10 eq 8443
access-group acl_outside in interface outside
```

At this point, you should also consider whether you will be collecting e-mail or Syslog alerts from the SSM as it performs its functions. The CSC or AIP module itself will be configured in a later step, but the ASA should be configured separately to permit the e-mail or Syslog traffic coming from the SSM management interface address.

As an example, you can use the following ASA configuration commands to permit Syslog messages to the Syslog server located at inside address 192.168.100.15 and e-mail messages to any IP address:

```
access-list acl_dmz extended permit udp host 192.168.110.10 host 192.168.100.15 eq syslog
access-list acl_dmz extended permit tcp host 192.168.110.10 any eq smtp
access-group acl_dmz in interface dmz
```

12-2: Configuring the CSC SSM

The Content Security and Control (CSC) SSM was introduced with ASA release 7.1(1). The CSC is used in conjunction with the ASA to provide a variety of inspections and defenses based on traffic content.

The CSC communicates with the ASA over an internal backplane connection. Figure 12-3 shows how traffic is passed between the ASA and CSC. The ASA diverts traffic classified by a class map to the CSC module over the internal connection. The CSC inspects the traffic in both the forward and return directions so that it can block or modify the contents.

Figure 12-3   *Basic CSC SSM Operation*

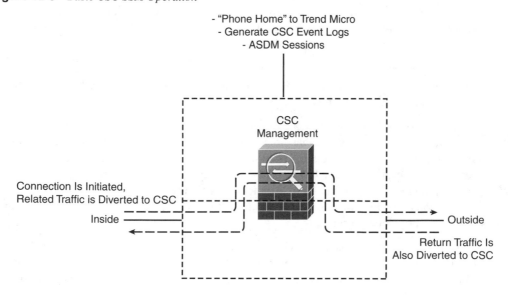

CSC SSM cannot support stateful failover because it does not maintain connection information about the traffic it inspects. Therefore, it cannot provide the failover unit with information necessary for stateful failover.

The connections that a CSC SSM is scanning are dropped upon failure of the security appliance in which the CSC SSM is installed. When the standby ASA becomes active, it forwards the scanned traffic to its own CSC SSM, and any existing connections are reset.

Configuring the ASA to Divert Traffic to the CSC SSM

As you work through initially installing and configuring your CSC SSM, keep in mind that the ASA and CSC SSM are essentially two independent pieces of hardware. Even though the CSC lives in an SSM slot on the ASA chassis, the two communicate over an out-of-band connection only for basic setup and status information. Even though the CSC SSM is installed and the ASA sees it as an active module, the ASA does *not* send any traffic to the CSC until you configure it to do so.

Any type of traffic traveling in any direction can be diverted to the CSC. For example, you can configure the ASA to send all traffic to the CSC for inspection. However, the CSC can inspect only the following types of traffic:

- **Simple Mail Transfer Protocol (SMTP)**—TCP port 25
- **Post Office Protocol version 3 (POP3)**—TCP port 110
- **Hypertext Transfer Protocol (HTTP)**—TCP port 80
- **File Transfer Protocol (FTP)**—TCP port 21

If you send any other types of traffic, the CSC is forced to look at those packets, discovers that they are not of the supported types, and ignores them. In other words, the CSC should not have to waste its time and resources looking at traffic it cannot inspect anyway.

Instead, you should identify only the types of traffic that can be inspected in your network setting. For example, if you have SMTP servers inside your network, then you should divert SMTP traffic to the CSC. If you do not have FTP servers, then do not divert FTP traffic to the CSC.

In addition, think about the direction that the inspected traffic is traveling. If you have an SMTP server inside your network, chances are that e-mail is reaching your users as SMTP packets traveling *inbound* to the server. Therefore, inbound SMTP should be diverted to the CSC so that inbound spam, viruses, and other malware can be detected on the way into your network. Most of the configuration examples shown in the Cisco documentation show only inbound SMTP diverted to a CSC. However, you might also want to divert outbound SMTP to the CSC, to detect and prevent any spam being sourced by your internal users.

Traffic is diverted to the CSC through a service policy that is applied to a firewall interface. As with any service policy, interesting traffic must be grouped into a traffic class, and a specific action must be taken. In this case, the traffic class is defined by an access list. The goal is to have one unique service policy applied to each firewall interface for traffic *entering* that interface. For example, you might have the following service policies:

Service Policy Name	Applied to Interface	Purpose
csc_inbound_divert	outside	Traffic entering the outside interface
csc_outbound_divert	inside	Traffic entering the inside interface
csc_dmz_divert	dmz	Traffic entering the DMZ interface

You can use the following steps to configure and apply a service policy on a firewall interface. Repeat these steps for other interfaces:

1. Identify traffic with an access list.

   Create an access list with an arbitrary name. You should permit traffic to be diverted to the CSC and deny traffic that does not need to be inspected. For inbound traffic on the outside interface, you can use the following template:

   ```
   Firewall(config)# access-list acl_name_inbound permit tcp any inside_subnet eq 80
   Firewall(config)# access-list acl_name_inbound permit tcp any inside_smtp_address eq 25
   ```

   For outbound traffic on the inside interface, you can use the following template:

   ```
   Firewall(config)# access-list acl_name_outbound permit tcp inside_subnet inside_mask
   any eq 80
   Firewall(config)# access-list acl_name_outbound permit tcp inside_subnet inside_mask
   any eq 25
   Firewall(config)# access-list acl_name_outbound permit tcp inside_subnet inside_mask
   any eq 110
   Firewall(config)# access-list acl_name_outbound permit tcp inside_subnet inside_mask
   any eq 21
   ```

2. Group traffic into a class.

   Create a class map with an arbitrary name. This class contains all traffic in one direction only. The class matches against the access list created in Step 1. Use the following configuration commands to create the class map:

   ```
   Firewall(config)# class-map class_map_name
   Firewall(config-cmap)# match access-list acl_name
   Firewall(config-cmap)# exit
   ```

3. Define a policy to divert traffic to the CSC.

   Create a policy map that references the class map created in Step 2. The policy map acts on traffic in one direction only. The traffic is diverted to the CSC with the **csc** command. Use the following configuration commands to create the policy map:

   ```
   Firewall(config)# policy-map policy_map_name
   Firewall(config-pmap)# class class_map_name
   Firewall(config-pmap-c)# csc {fail-close | fail-open}
   Firewall(config-pmap-c)# exit
   Firewall(config-pmap)# exit
   ```

Use the **fail-close** keyword to make the ASA stop forwarding traffic if the CSC module fails. Otherwise, you can use the **fail-open** keyword to make sure the ASA keeps forwarding traffic during a CSC failure.

4. Apply the policy to a firewall interface.

Finally, apply the policy map created in Step 3 to a firewall interface using the following configuration command:

```
Firewall(config)# service-policy policy_map_name interface interface_name
```

The following commands represent a complete example of the configuration commands needed to divert interesting traffic to the CSC. Inbound traffic arriving on the firewall's outside interface is matched with class map **csc_inbound** and handled by policy map **csc_inbound_policy.** Only inbound SMTP and HTTP traffic are diverted, assuming outside clients are sending mail and browsing web content on inside servers:

```
Firewall(config)# access-list csc_inbound_divert extended permit tcp 192.168.100.0
255.255.255.0 any eq smtp
Firewall(config)# access-list csc_inbound_divert extended permit tcp 192.168.100.0
255.255.255.0 any eq www
!
Firewall(config)# class-map csc_inbound
Firewall(config-cmap)# match access-list csc_inbound_divert
Firewall(config)# exit
!
Firewall(config)# policy-map csc_inbound_policy
Firewall(config-pmap)# class csc_inbound
Firewall(config-pmap-c)# csc fail-close
Firewall(config-pmap-c)# exit
Firewall(config-pmap)# exit
!
Firewall(config)# service-policy csc_inbound_policy interface outside
```

For outbound traffic arriving at the firewall's inside interface, class map **csc_outbound** matches traffic and policy map **csc_outbound_policy** handles the traffic. Here, only outbound SMTP, POP3, HTTP, and FTP connections are diverted, assuming inside users are heading toward outside servers.

```
Firewall(config)# access-list csc_outbound_divert extended permit tcp 192.168.100.0
255.255.255.0 any eq smtp
Firewall(config)# access-list csc_outbound_divert extended permit tcp 192.168.100.0
255.255.255.0 any eq pop3
Firewall(config)# access-list csc_outbound_divert extended permit tcp 192.168.100.0
255.255.255.0 any eq www
Firewall(config)# access-list csc_outbound_divert extended permit tcp 192.168.100.0
255.255.255.0 any eq ftp
!
Firewall(config)# class-map csc_outbound
Firewall(config-cmap)# match access-list csc_outbound_divert
Firewall(config-cmap)# exit
!
Firewall(config)# policy-map csc_outbound_policy
Firewall(config-pmap)# class csc_outbound
Firewall(config-pmap-c)# csc fail-close
```

```
Firewall(config-pmap-c)# exit
Firewall(config-pmap)# exit
!
Firewall(config)# service-policy csc_outbound_policy interface inside
```

Even though the CSC has not been configured at this stage, you should verify that the ASA is actually trying to divert traffic to it. You can do this by monitoring the access list counters, which are updated in real time. In the following example, the shaded output highlights the hit count for each access list entry, indicating the number of times a packet matched the condition:

```
Firewall# show access-list csc_outbound_divert
access-list csc_outbound_divert; 3 elements
access-list csc_outbound_divert line 1 extended permit tcp 192.168.100.0 255.255.255.0
any eq pop3 (hitcnt=479) 0x6dc20704
access-list csc_outbound_divert line 2 extended permit tcp 192.168.100.0 255.255.255.0
any eq www (hitcnt=1473) 0x94f0d51f
access-list csc_outbound_divert line 3 extended permit tcp 192.168.100.0 255.255.255.0
any eq ftp (hitcnt=16) 0x4f7313ea
Firewall#
```

Configuring the Initial CSC SSM Settings

The CSC SSM must be configured independently of the ASA. You can use several methods to connect to and configure the CSC. Most often, you use ASDM as your interface to the CSC, although other methods are discussed as they are needed. You should use the following steps to configure a CSC SSM:

1. Verify the CSC SSM status.

   After a CSC SSM is installed in an ASA chassis, you should verify that the module is powered up and available. You can do that with the **show module** ASA command, as shown in the following example. Here, the CSC SSM is listed as ASA module 1 in the "up" state.

   ```
   Firewall# show module

   Mod Card Type                                        Model               Serial No.
   --- -------------------------------------------- ------------------ -----------
     0 ASA 5510 Adaptive Security Appliance          ASA5510            JMX1014K070
     1 ASA 5500 Series Content Security Services Mo  ASA-SSM-CSC-10     JAF10252436

   Mod MAC Address Range                  Hw Version   Fw Version   Sw Version
   --- ---------------------------------- ------------ ------------ ---------------
     0 0016.c789.c8a4 to 0016.c789.c8a8   1.1          1.0(10)0     7.2(1)
     1 0018.7317.8eb3 to 0018.7317.8eb3   1.0          1.0(11)2     CSC SSM 6.1
                                                                    (Build#1519)

   Mod SSM Application Name         Status           SSM Application Version
   --- ---------------------------- ---------------- --------------------------
     1 CSC SSM                      Up               6.1 (Build#1519)

   Mod Status             Data Plane Status    Compatibility
   --- ------------------ -------------------- -------------
     0 Up Sys             Not Applicable
     1 Up                 Up
   Firewall#
   ```

2. Start the CSC Setup Wizard.

The CSC SSM must be configured with some initial information, such as an IP address, basic network settings, and license keys, before it can begin to operate. You should attempt to configure these settings through ASDM first, before trying any other methods.

Within ASDM, click on the **Configuration** tab at the top of the screen. Then click on the **Trend Micro Content Security** button on the left side of the screen. If the CSC SSM has never been configured before, you should see the CSC Setup Wizard window appear, as shown in Figure 12-4.

Figure 12-4 *The CSC Setup Wizard Begins the Initial Configuration*

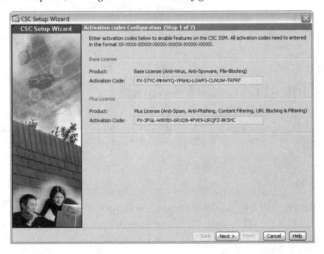

If you see a window titled Connecting to CSC..., as shown in Figure 12-5, instead of the CSC Setup Wizard, the CSC SSM has probably been previously configured. The ASDM fetches the last known management interface IP address from the CSC and offers to use it. If you do not recognize the management IP address, you need to reconfigure the IP address information. Refer to the section "Repairing the Initial CSC Configuration" in this chapter for more information.

Otherwise, the Connecting to CSC... window selects the default IP address that has been configured for the CSC's management interface. This is fine if your ASDM client can reach the management interface using that address. Suppose the management interface is located on a DMZ interface, but is translated to a different address on the outside of the ASA. In this case, you should select the **Other IP Address or Hostname** button and enter the translated IP address.

Figure 12-5 *A CSC with Preexisting IP Information*

After you are connected to the CSC, you can click on the **Wizard Setup** link to the left of the window and then on the **Launch Setup Wizard** button to launch the CSC Setup Wizard.

3. Enter the CSC activation codes.

A CSC SSM can have the following two license activation codes:

- **Base license**—Enables the Anti-Virus, Anti-Spyware, and File Blocking features
- **Plus license**—Enables the Anti-Spam, Anti-Phishing, Content Filtering, and URL Blocking/Filtering features

If your CSC module does not already have valid activation codes entered, you should enter them in the fields shown in Figure 12-4. You can obtain the activation codes by browsing to http:// www.cisco.com/go/license and entering the Product Activation Key (PAK) information that was included with the CSC module.

After the activation codes have been entered into the CSC Setup Wizard, click the **Next>** button.

4. Enter the IP Configuration.

The CSC Setup Wizard should open an IP Configuration window, as shown in Figure 12-6. Enter the CSC management interface IP address, subnet mask, and default gateway. You should also enter the IP addresses of a primary DNS and an optional secondary DNS. If your environment requires outbound connections to pass through a proxy server, you can also enter the IP address and port number of the proxy server.

5. Enter the CSC Host configuration.

In the window shown in Figure 12-7, you can enter a hostname and domain name that identifies the CSC SSM management interface. The CSC must also know about the e-mail domain used in your network so that it can examine incoming e-mail.

Figure 12-6 *Entering the CSC Management IP Configuration*

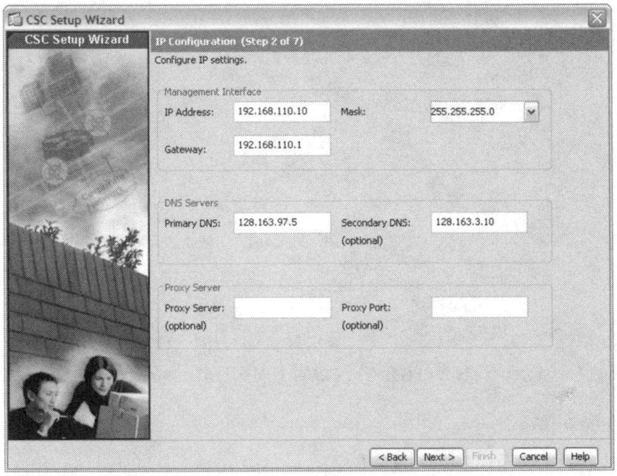

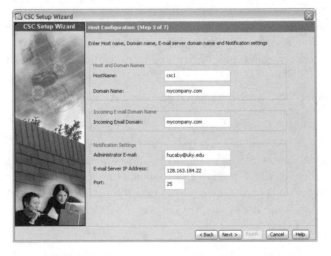

Figure 12-7 *Entering the CSC Host Configuration*

If you want the CSC SSM to send e-mail notifications as it operates, you should enter the e-mail address where those notifications should be sent. The notifications are sent using SMTP, so you should also enter the IP address of your local SMTP server, along with the TCP port used. By default, SMTP uses TCP port 25.

After you have entered the IP configuration information, click the **Next>** button.

6. Configure management access to the CSC.

You can limit access to the CSC management interface if your security policies require it. In the window shown in Figure 12-8, you can enter an IP address and a subnet mask that identify hosts that are permitted to access the CSC management interface. This can be a single host or an entire subnet. After you enter the address information, you can click the **Add>>** button to add it to the list of selected entries. By default, a host at any IP address is allowed to reach the CSC, as shown by the **0.0.0.0/0** entry in the list.

Figure 12-8 *Limiting Access to the CSC Management Interface*

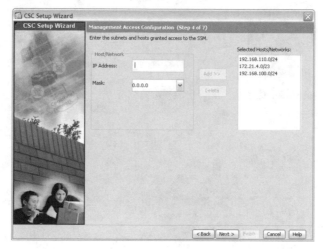

Click the **Next>** button to continue.

7. Configure the CSC management passwords.

After the initial configuration is completed, you are challenged to enter a password for all future connections to the CSC management interface. By default, the CSC uses password **cisco**. Because this is commonly known, you should change it now in the window shown in Figure 12-9. However, if you want to leave the password as it is, you can leave the password entries untouched and they will not be changed.

Click the **Next>** button to continue.

8. Identify traffic to be inspected.

By default, the CSC inspects HTTP, SMTP, POP3, and FTP traffic between any two hosts. You can configure more specific traffic in the window shown in Figure 12-10. Click the **Add** button to bring up the Specify Traffic for CSC Scan window, where you can enter source and destination addresses, as well as specific protocol and port numbers.

Figure 12-9 *Configuring the CSC Management Password*

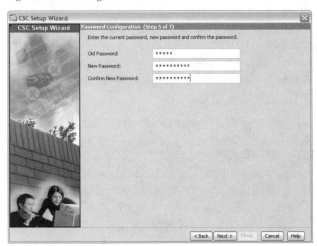

Figure 12-10 *Tuning the CSC Traffic Inspection*

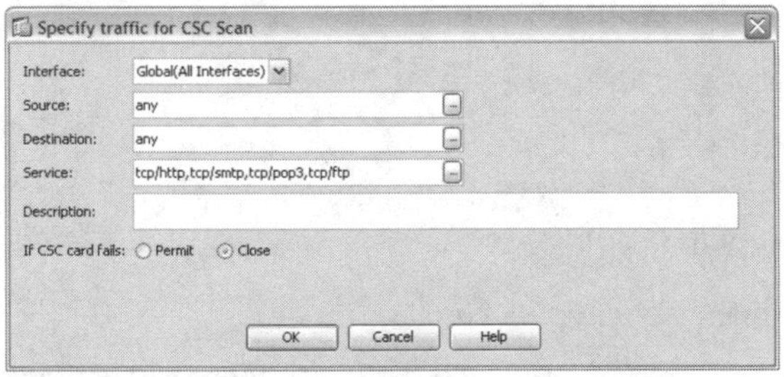

9. Complete the initial configuration.

   You should see a window showing a summary of each of the initial CSC configuration settings, as shown in Figure 12-11. At this point, ASDM automatically pushes the settings to the CSC, using an out-of-band connection.

At this point, the CSC management interface has been activated for use. From now on, you are prompted for a password when you try to monitor or configure the CSC.

Repairing the Initial CSC Configuration

If you notice that ASDM is trying to connect to the CSC management interface using an unexpected IP address, you need to repair the initial CSC IP configuration. To do this, first open a CLI-based connection to the ASA, using a console, Telnet, or Secure Shell (SSH) session.

Figure 12-11 *ASDM Updates the CSC with the Initial Configuration*

Then connect to the CSC SSM through the out-of-band connection it shares with the ASA by using the **session** command.

In the following example, the CSC is installed as module 1 in the ASA chassis. If you are unsure of the CSC's module number, use the **show module** ASA command.

The CSC module prompts for a username and password, rather than a password alone. By default, the username **cisco** can be used.

```
Firewall# session 1
Opening command session with slot 1.
Connected to slot 1. Escape character sequence is 'CTRL-^X'.

login: cisco
Password:
Last login: Tue Nov  7 10:51:14 from 127.0.1.1
     Trend Micro InterScan for Cisco CSC SSM Setup Main Menu
-------------------------------------------------------------
1. Network Settings
2. Date/Time Settings
3. Product Information
4. Service Status
5. Change Password for Command Line Interface
6. Restore Factory Default Settings
7. Troubleshooting Tools
8. Reset Management Port Access Control List
9. Ping
10. Exit ...
Enter a number from [1-10]:
```

You should use option **1** to change the initial network settings, as shown in the following example output:

```
Enter a number from [1-10]: 1

                        Network Settings
- - - - - - - - - - - - - - - - - - - - - - - - - - - - - - - - - - - - - - - -
IP              10.22.213.113
Netmask         255.255.255.192
Hostname        csc
Domain name     cisco.com
MAC address     00:18:73:17:8E:B3
Primary DNS     10.10.10.10
Secondary DNS   10.10.10.20
Gateway         10.22.213.65
No Proxy
Do you want to modify the network settings? [y | n]
```

If you continue with the previous scenario, the CSC management interface should have IP address 192.168.110.10—not 10.22.213.113 shown in the current network settings. Therefore, you should choose **y** to change the settings. In the following example, all of the initial network settings are changed to their appropriate values.

```
Do you want to modify the network settings? [y | n] y

                        Network Settings
- - - - - - - - - - - - - - - - - - - - - - - - - - - - - - - - - - - - - - - -
Enter the SSM card IP address: (default:10.22.213.113) 192.168.110.10
Enter subnet mask: (default:255.255.255.192) 255.255.255.0
Enter host name: (default:csc) csc
Enter domain name: (default:cisco.com) mycompany.com
Enter primary DNS IP address: (default:10.10.10.10) 128.163.97.5
Enter optional secondary DNS IP address: (default:10.10.10.20) 128.163.3.10
Enter gateway IP address: (default:10.22.213.65) 192.168.110.1
Do you use a proxy server? [y | n] (default:no)
Stopping services: OK
Applying network settings ...
Starting services: OK
Press Enter to continue ...
```

After the network settings have been corrected, you can go back to ASDM under the **Configuration** tab and the **Trend Micro Content Security** button. At that point, ASDM should open a window showing that it plans to connect to the correct CSC management IP address.

Connecting to the CSC Management Interface

After the CSC SSM has received its initial network configuration, you can connect to it through ASDM. When you select the **Configuration** tab and the **Trend Micro Content Security** button, ASDM announces that it is getting ready to connect to the CSC, as indicated by the window shown in Figure 12-12.

Figure 12-12   *Getting Ready to Connect to the CSC Management Interface*

By default, the last known IP address for the CSC management interface is used. In Figure 12-12, this address is 192.168.110.10, which is an address found on the DMZ interface of the ASA. This address can be used if your ASDM host is located on the inside or DMZ interfaces, where the ASA permits connections to that address.

However, if your ASDM host is located elsewhere, such as the outside ASA interface, you need to override the IP address. Select **Other IP Address or Hostname** and fill in the CSC management interface address as it is known on the outside network. In the example scenario, the ASA is configured to translate DMZ address 192.168.110.10 to outside address 10.1.1.10. Therefore, ASDM should connect to 10.1.1.10 using port 8443.

After ASDM completes the connection to the CSC management interface, it displays a list of configuration options under **Configuration > Trend Micro Content Security**. As well, you can view a snapshot of CSC activity by clicking the **Home** button and selecting the **Content Security** tab.

Configuring Automatic Updates

The CSC SSM must be able to retrieve periodic updates from Trend Micro so that it can stay up to date with current spam, spyware, and virus definitions. You should configure the update parameters next.

From ASDM, select **Configuration** and then the **Trend Micro Content Security** button. Log in to the CSC by entering the password at the prompt. In the list of configuration tasks, click on the **Updates** entry, which shows a summary of the scheduled updates, as shown in Figure 12-13.

Figure 12-13 *Getting Ready to Configure Automatic Updates*

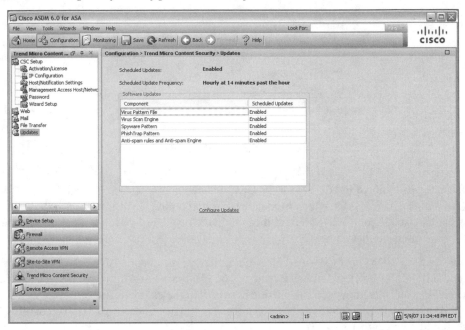

Now click on the **Configure Updates** link under the list of scheduled updates. This opens a new web session with the CSC management interface, using the Trend Micro InterScan for Cisco CSC SSM user interface. Enter the CSC management password at the prompt and click on the **Log On** button. You should see a browser page like the one shown in Figure 12-14.

In the left-hand list, make sure **Scheduled** is selected. In the **Scheduled Update** portion of the window, make sure the **Enable Scheduled Update** checkbox is checked. Then check each type of update you want to keep updated from the following list:

- **Virus pattern**—The database of virus signatures
- **Virus scan engine**—The virus scan software itself
- **Spyware pattern**—The database of spyware signatures
- **PhishTrap pattern**—The database of anti-phishing signatures
- **Anti-spam rules and Anti-spam engine**—The database of spam detection rules and known spam relays

Select the update schedule you would like to use, under **Update Schedule**. By default, updates occur every hour at 14 minutes past the hour. You can select intervals of every 15 minutes, every hour (at a specific minute), or every day (at a specific hour and minute). Click on the **Save** button to save the update configuration.

Figure 12-14 *Configuring Scheduled Update Parameters*

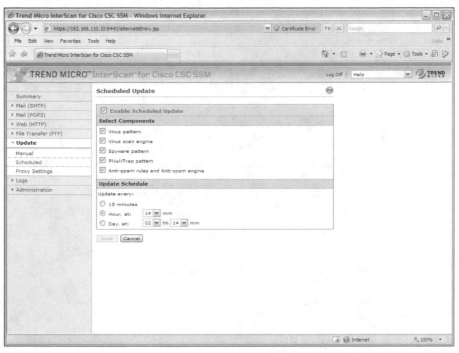

If your network environment uses a proxy server to control outbound connections, click on the **Proxy Settings** link and fill in the settings to define the proxy server address, port, and authentication. Click the **Save** button to save the proxy settings.

At this point, you should perform a test to verify that the CSC SSM can indeed get an update from the Trend Micro servers. Most likely, it will not be time for a scheduled update, so you have to force a manual update. In the Trend Micro InterScan for Cisco CSC SSM browser window, click on the **Manual** link under the **Update** category. The manual update begins as the CSC checks for the availability of new components from Trend Micro.

The manual update shows a list of current CSC components along with their version numbers. If newer versions of any of them are found, those are shown in the list with a checkbox and their version numbers in red, as shown in Figure 12-15.

Select each new component by checking their checkboxes and then click the **Update** button. The update process begins; while this is happening, you should not try to change any other settings on the CSC. If the update is successful, the components are shown in a list again, along with a timestamp when each was updated. The checkboxes are grayed out so that you cannot select them again.

Figure 12-15 *Setting Up a Manual Update*

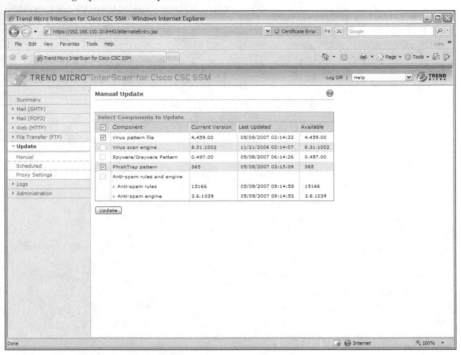

Configuring CSC Inspection Policies

You can configure the CSC SSM to inspect any of the following types of interesting traffic:

- **Web**—Specific URLs and known phishing sites can be blocked, access to websites can be restricted based on a category, file types can be blocked from downloading, and web page content and webmail content can be scanned for undesirable content.

- **Mail**—Incoming and outgoing SMTP traffic, as well as inbound POP3 traffic, can be scanned for undesirable content. Both SMTP and POP3 can be scanned for spam content and can be filtered according to text strings contained in the subject or body, and according to attachment size, filename, and file type.

- **File Transfer**—FTP traffic can be scanned for undesirable content. In addition, files downloaded by FTP can be filtered according to file type.

These categories are shown in ASDM under the **Configuration > Trend Micro Content Security** screen. When you click on any of the category names, ASDM shows a list of inspection types within that category. However, when you click on an inspection type to configure, ASDM starts up a new browser window using the Trend Micro InterScan for Cisco CSC SSM interface. After the InterScan session begins, you can do all inspection policy configuration from within the same interface without returning to ASDM.

In the Trend Micro InterScan for Cisco CSC SSM session, you can use the links listed on the left side of the screen to navigate to various policy configuration screens. These links are used in the sections that follow.

For HTTP, FTP, or e-mail-based file scanning, the CSC can use its IntelliScan feature to scan files based on a "true file type," which is determined by header information inside the files, rather than a filename extension. Otherwise, you can specify the filename extensions to be scanned.

Some files might be password-protected or compressed when they are downloaded. The CSC can attempt to scan these files too. You can choose whether to deliver or delete password-protected files. For compressed files, you can set limits on the extent of the file's compression process, to protect the CSC resources and the amount of time needed to download, uncompress, and deliver the files. Remember that the CSC has to download the complete file and then uncompress it before it can be delivered to the user.

By default, password-protected files are delivered. Compressed files are scanned only if they contain less than 200 internal files, are less than 30 MB, require more than three compression passes, or are more than 100 times the size when uncompressed. If the compressed files are not scanned, they are still delivered by default.

You can configure the CSC to scan files only if they are less than a certain size (50 MB by default). If files are too large to be scanned, they are delivered by default.

Configure Web (HTTP) Inspection Policies

If you plan to have the CSC SSM inspect web traffic for suspicious or unwanted content, you should configure the inspection policies discussed in the following sections.

Configuring URL Blocking

By default, the CSC SSM does not block any URLs that internal users attempt to view. You can configure a local list of strings to match against by selecting the **Via Local List** tab, as shown in Figure 12-16.

Under **Web (HTTP) > URL Blocking**, you can enter specific URLs in the **Match:** field. Click the **Block** button to add the URL to the block list or the **Do Not Block** button to permit the URL to be reached. URLs can be matched as specific website address prefixes, keyword matching, or specific hostname/file string matching. Click the **Save** button to save your changes.

The CSC SSM can also scan URLs to detect phishing sites, spyware sites, virus accomplice sites, and other sites that are known to have malicious purposes. From the **Web (HTTP) > URL Blocking** page, click on the **Via Pattern File (PhishTrap)** tab to see the window shown in Figure 12-17. By default, the CSC blocks users from reaching URLs that are known to have any of the listed types of activities. The database of URLs is maintained by Trend Micro and is automatically downloaded to the CSC during the scheduled updates. If you make any changes to the configuration, be sure to click the **Save** button.

Figure 12-16 *Blocking URLs by a Local List*

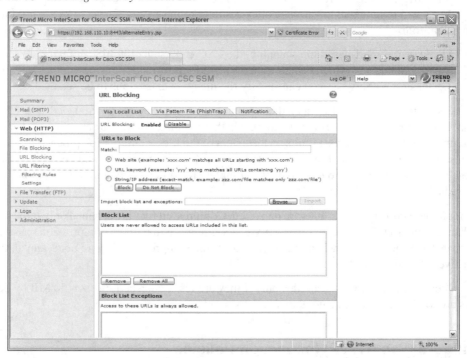

If you discover a website that seems to promote any of the Phish Trap categories is not blocked by the CSC, you can submit the URL to Trend Micro by filling in the URL and category in the bottom portion of the window. Add any notes that describe the website and its behavior to the **Note:** section and then click on the **Submit** button. The information you provide is automatically sent to Trend Micro for their analysis.

Finally, you should click on the **Notification** tab to review the action that the CSC takes when it blocks a user from reaching a URL. By default, the CSC returns the following message in the user's browser:

```
The URL you are attempting to access has been blocked.  Organization policy does not allow
access to this activity.
```

You can change that text by editing the **User Notification** field and clicking the **Save** button.

Configuring URL Filtering Rules

If your corporate policies warrant, you might want to control what web content your users can browse at different times of the day. The CSC SSM can use its URL Filtering feature to accomplish this automatically. Trend Micro maintains a database of URLs that are broken down into content categories. The CSC downloads this database during scheduled updates and can use it to categorize URLs as they are browsed.

Figure 12-17 *Blocking URLs by the Phish Trap Database*

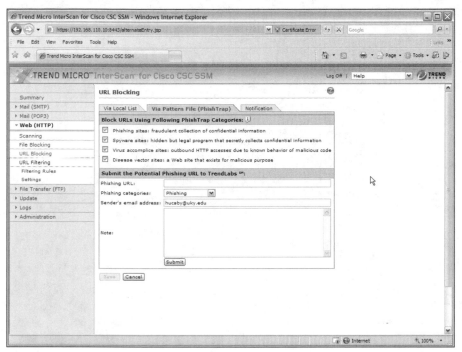

First, you must define some policies that the CSC can use to make decisions about whether a URL category is appropriate at any given time. Under the **Web (HTTP) > URL Filtering** section, go to the **Filtering Rules** link, as shown in Figure 12-18. Here, you can select whether to block any of the following categories during work time or leisure time (not work time).

- Company prohibited sites
- Not work related
- Research topics
- Business function related
- Customer defined
- Others

Clearly, these categories are rather broad and subjective. You define or tune the categories to meet your own needs as a second step. For now, you can make some broad assumptions based on the general category names. For example, Figure 12-18 shows how **Company prohibited sites** are blocked during work time and leisure time. That might make sense if your company policies state that users should do only work-related activities while they are at work or are using work-related equipment.

Figure 12-18   *Configuring URL Filtering Based on URL Category*

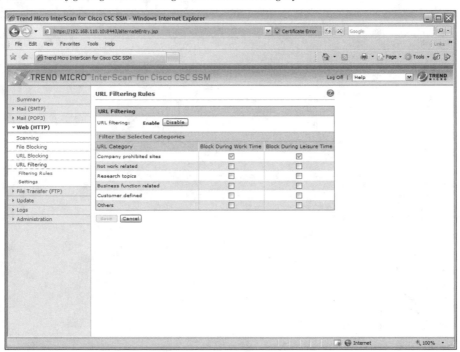

Configuring URL Filtering Settings

Next, you can begin to fine tune the URL categories to match your preferences or security policies. Under **Web (HTTP) > URL Filtering**, select the **Settings** link. This brings up a new window, as shown in Figure 12-19, with the following configuration tabs:

- **URL Categories**—Group specific web content sub-categories into the broad URL categories
- **URL Filtering Exceptions**—Match against URLs that are excluded from filtering
- **Schedule**—Define specific day and time ranges that are considered as "work time"
- **Re-classify URL**—Submit a URL to Trend Micro to request it be reclassified in a different category

Use the following steps to configure URL filtering:

1. Define URL categories.

   Trend Micro has defined a list of narrow "sub-categories" that describe web content that is available on the Internet. URLs are then mapped to sub-categories based on the content they contain. For example, if a URL presents a page showing people wearing intimate apparel or swimsuits, it might be tagged as belonging to the Intimate Apparel/Swimsuit sub-category.

Figure 12-19 *Configuring Settings for URL Filtering*

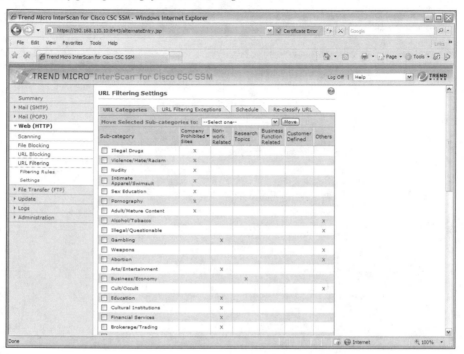

In turn, the CSC can map sub-categories into the broad URL categories that have URL filtering policies applied to them. The list of sub-categories and how they are mapped are shown in Figure 12-19.

By default, sub-categories like **Illegal Drugs** and **Violence/Hate/Racism** are mapped into the **Company Prohibited Sites** category, **Gambling** is mapped to **Non-work Related**, and **Weapons** into the **Other** category. You can change any of these mappings by selecting the checkboxes of sub-categories you want to move and then choosing a new category from the **Move Selected Sub-categories to:** drop-down list. Finally, you click on the **Move** button.

Remember that the sub-categories are mapped into categories, and the categories are enforced during work time and/or leisure time, according to the policies you define.

2. Identify any URL exceptions.

   If there are websites that should be exempt from URL filtering and should always be available to your users, you can specify them as filtering exceptions. Select the **URL Filtering Exceptions** tab under **Web (HTTP) > URL Filtering > Settings**, as shown in Figure 12-20. You can enter a specific URL as a website, or you can enter a keyword or a text string to match against. Be sure to click the **Add** button to add your entry to the list of exceptions. Finally, click the **Save** button to save the changes.

Figure 12-20 *Defining URLs That Are Exceptions to URL Filtering*

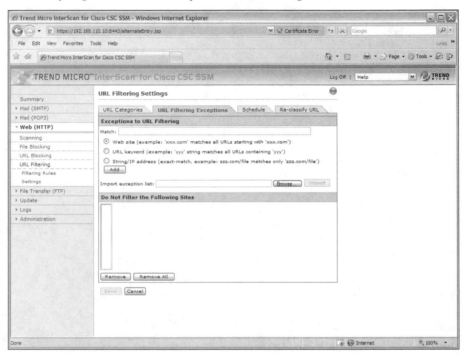

3. Define work time.

The CSC performs URL filtering based on a time schedule. All time is divided into "work time" and "leisure time" (not work time). Therefore, you should configure the CSC to have the correct concept of work time. Select the **Schedule** tab under **Web (HTTP) > URL Filtering > Settings**, as shown in Figure 12-21. By default, work time is defined as Monday through Friday, from **08:00** until **12:00**, and then from **13:00** until **17:00**. To change this, select the checkboxes for any days that contain work time. Then select morning and afternoon start and end times from the drop-down time menus. Be sure to click the **Save** button when you are finished making changes.

4. Submit a URL for reclassification.

If you find that a URL's content does not agree with the Trend Micro content category, you can submit the URL to Trend Micro for reclassification. If they agree, they put the URL into the category you suggest. To do this, select the **Re-classify URL** tab under **Web (HTTP) > URL Filtering > Settings**, as shown in Figure 12-22. Enter the URL, your e-mail address, and some notes to justify the category where you think the URL should belong. Click the **Submit** button when you are ready for the CSC to e-mail your request to Trend Micro.

Figure 12-21 *Defining the Work Time Schedule*

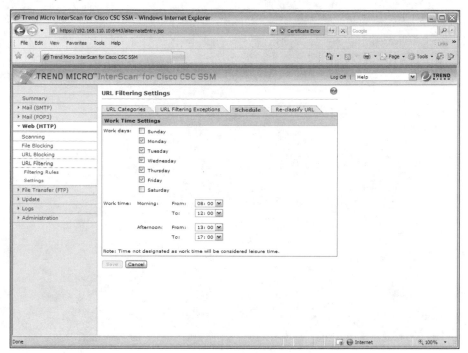

Configuring HTTP File Blocking

As users browse to websites, the CSC can block specific file types from being downloaded. To do this, select the **Target** tab under **Web (HTTP) > File Blocking**, as shown in Figure 12-23. Select the files types you want to be blocked from the list of audio/video, compressed, executable, images, Java, and Microsoft Office. You can also specify additional file extensions to be blocked by entering them in the **File extensions to block:** field and clicking the **Add** button. After all of your changes have been made, be sure to click the **Save** button.

Configuring HTTP Scanning

The CSC can scan files as they are downloaded as part of a web page or HTTP content. HTTP scanning can be done on all HTTP traffic (the default) or on webmail traffic only. To configure HTTP scanning, select the **Target** tab under the **Web (HTTP) > Scanning** link, as shown in Figure 12-24.

You can use the following sequence of steps to configure HTTP scanning on a CSC SSM:

1. Configure file scanning.

    First, choose the default type of file scanning. By default, the CSC scans all files as they are downloaded as part of a web page content.

Figure 12-22 *Requesting That a URL Be Reclassified in a Different Category*

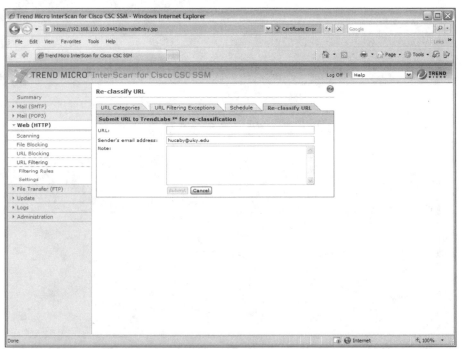

You can also specify individual types of spyware and grayware content to be detected during HTTP file scanning. By default, none of these types are detected. Be sure to click the **Save** button when you are finished configuring the **Target** tab.

2. Configure webmail scanning.

   To configure the CSC to scan webmail content, select the **Webmail Scanning** tab under the **Web (HTTP) > Scanning** link, as shown in Figure 12-25.

   By default, the CSC scans webmail content when users go to the Yahoo! Mail, AOL, MSN Hotmail, or Gmail sites using the URL patterns shown in Figure 12-25. You can add other specific URLs or keywords and text strings to match if your users go to webmail sites other than those listed. Enter a descriptive name in the **Name** field and a URL or match string in the **Match** field. Click the **Add** button to add the entries to the webmail scan list. Be sure to click the **Save** button after you are finished with the configuration.

Figure 12-23 *Specifying File Types to Block in HTTP Content*

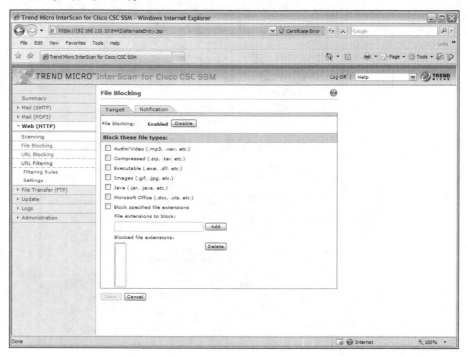

3. Specify an action.

    By default, the CSC attempts to clean files that it finds infected with a virus or malware. If a file cannot be cleaned, it is deleted from the HTTP content. Any spyware or grayware is deleted rather than delivered. You can change these policies by selecting the **Action** tab under the **Web (HTTP) > Scanning** link.

4. Define the notification.

    When the CSC detects an infected file that it also deletes, it posts the following message to the user's browser:

    ```
    The InterScan for CSC SSM has scanned the file you are attempting to transfer, and
    has detected a security risk - the file will not be transferred.
    ```

    You can change that message by editing the text under the **Notification** tab.

Configuring File Transfer (FTP) Inspection Policies

If you plan to have the CSC SSM inspect FTP traffic for suspicious or unwanted content, you should configure the inspection policies discussed in the following steps.

Figure 12-24 *Configuring HTTP File Scanning*

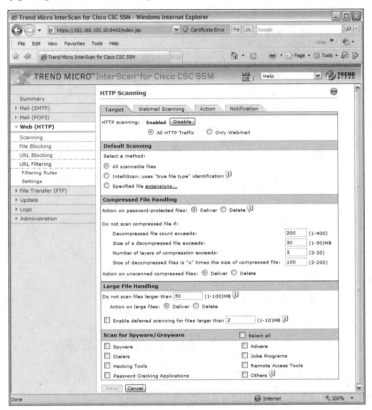

1. Configure inspection policies for file scanning.

   The CSC can scan files to detect undesirable content as the files are downloaded by FTP. This process and its configuration are very similar to HTTP scanning. To configure FTP file scanning, select the **Target** tab under the **File Transfer (FTP) > Scanning** link, as shown in Figure 12-26.

   First, choose the default type of file scanning. By default, the CSC scans all files as they are downloaded through an FTP connection.

   You can also specify individual types of spyware and grayware content that is detected during FTP file scanning. By default, none of these types are detected. Be sure to click the **Save** button when you are finished configuring the **Target** tab.

   By default, the CSC attempts to clean files that it finds infected with a virus or malware. If a file cannot be cleaned, it is deleted and not delivered to the end user. Any spyware or grayware is deleted rather than delivered. You can change these policies by selecting the **Action** tab under the **File Transfer (FTP) > Scanning** link.

Figure 12-25 *Configuring Webmail Scanning*

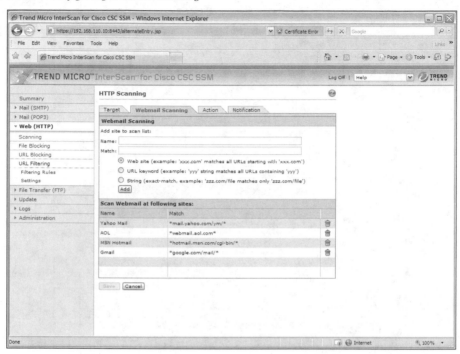

When the CSC detects an infected file that it also deletes, it posts the following message to the user's browser:

```
The InterScan for CSC SSM has scanned the file you are attempting to transfer, and
has detected a security risk - the file will not be transferred.
```

You can change that message by editing the text under the **Notification** tab.

2. Configure inspection policies for FTP file blocking.

As users attempt to download files by FTP, the CSC can block specific file types from being downloaded. To do this, select the **Target** tab under **File Transfer (FTP) > File Blocking**, as shown in Figure 12-27.

Select the files types you want to be blocked from the list of audio/video, compressed, executable, images, Java, and Microsoft Office. You can also specify additional file extensions to be blocked by entering them in the **File extensions to block:** field and clicking the **Add** button. After all of your changes have been made, be sure to click the **Save** button.

Configuring Mail (SMTP and POP3) Inspection Policies

If you plan to have the CSC SSM inspect e-mail traffic for suspicious or unwanted content, you should configure the inspection policies discussed in the sections that follow. The CSC can scan

Figure 12-26 *Configuring FTP File Scanning*

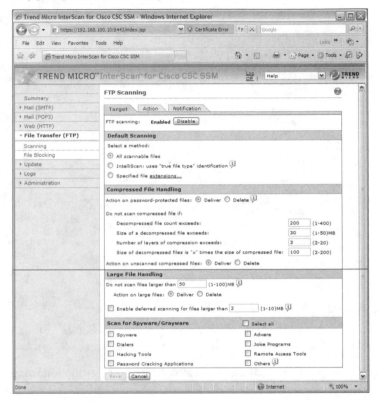

inbound traffic destined for SMTP servers, outbound traffic destined for SMTP servers, and inbound POP3 traffic destined for clients.

Also, the CSC can filter the content of e-mail messages, based on the file type and content of attachments. You can also configure the CSC to scan for spam e-mail and take action on offending messages.

Scanning SMTP Traffic

The CSC can scan SMTP messages to detect undesirable or malicious content. You can configure SMTP scanning by going to **Mail (SMTP) > Scanning** and then selecting either the **Incoming** or **Outgoing** link, depending on the direction that SMTP traffic is traveling in your network. If you have an SMTP server on the inside or DMZ interface of the ASA, configure incoming scanning to watch traffic coming in from external clients. Configure outgoing scanning to watch traffic being sent by internal clients:

1. Configure the scanning target.

Figure 12-27 *Specifying File Types to Block in FTP Content*

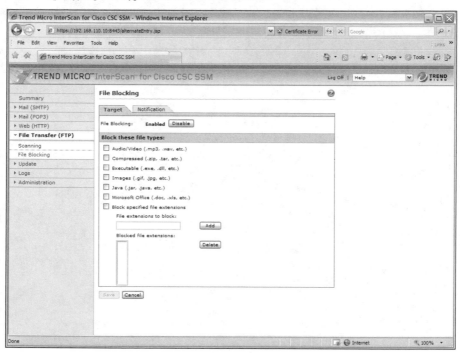

Select the **Target** tab, as shown in Figure 12-28. First, choose the default type of file scanning. By default, the CSC scans all attachment files as they are sent through an SMTP connection.

You can also specify individual types of spyware and grayware content to be detected during FTP file scanning. By default, none of these types are detected. Be sure to click the **Save** button when you are finished configuring the **Target** tab.

2. Configure the action.

Select the **Action** tab. If an attachment is found to have a virus or malware, it can be cleaned (the default). As an alternative, the CSC can deliver the message after the offending attachment has been deleted, or it can deliver the original message intact—offending attachment and all.

With spyware and grayware, you can configure the CSC to deliver the offending files or delete them (the default).

3. Configure the notification.

Figure 12-28 *Configuring SMTP Message Scanning*

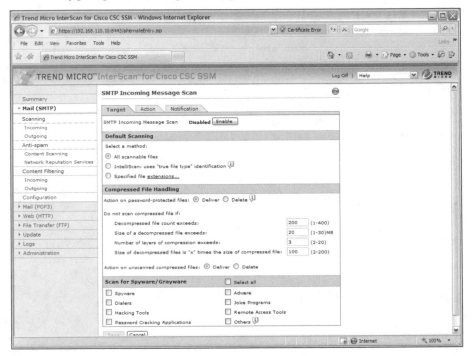

When the CSC detects suspicious content in an e-mail attachment file, it can send a notification. To configure this feature, select the **Notification** tab as shown in Figure 12-29. By default, no notifications are sent by e-mail. However, you can choose whether to send e-mail notices to the CSC administrator (the e-mail address you configured for CSC notifications), the e-mail message sender, and the e-mail message recipient.

By default, the CSC notifies the e-mail message recipient by inserting a descriptive message into the e-mail message text. You can also configure the CSC to insert a "risk free" message into the text of every message that has clean scanning results.

Filtering SMTP Content

You can configure the CSC to filter incoming or outgoing SMTP messages according to specific things that are found in the message itself. Under **Mail (SMTP) > Content Filtering**, choose the **Incoming** or **Outgoing** link (as shown in Figure 12-30), depending on the direction the target e-mail will be traveling in relation to the ASA.

Figure 12-29 *Configuring SMTP Message Scanning Notification*

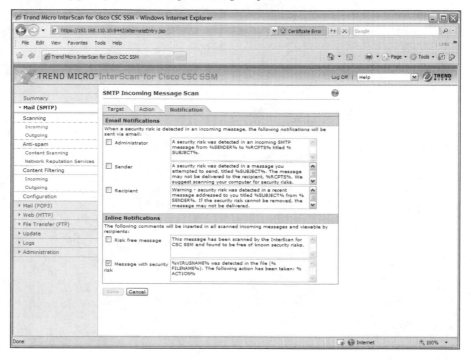

You can configure the CSC to filter out messages that are larger or smaller than a given size. This can be handy to filter out messages that contain very large attachments. The CSC can also filter messages if it finds specific words in the subject line or the message body text. To accomplish this, enter the words in the **Add words to subject filter** field or **Add words to body filter** field and click on the **Add** button.

You can also configure the CSC to filter messages according to the attributes of attachments. For example, you can enter specific words or character strings to match against the attachment filenames. You can also select attachment file types to filter out.

Under the **Action** tab, you can choose whether to delete or deliver (the default) messages that are filtered. You can also select a text message to insert in the mail message to alert the user of the filtered condition. Finally, the **Notification** tab allows an alert to be sent to the CSC administrator, the message sender, or the message recipient when a message has been filtered.

Detecting Spam SMTP E-mail

The CSC can detect spam e-mail by comparing information found in the message headers with a database maintained by Trend Micro. Anti-spam operation is independent of traffic direction—the CSC simply examines all e-mail messages as they pass through it.

Figure 12-30 *Configuring SMTP Message Content Filtering*

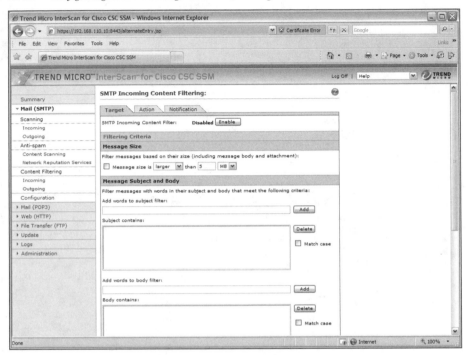

You can configure the following types of anti-spam detection:

- **Content scanning**—E-mail messages are examined as they are sent and are compared to a database of known spam patterns maintained by Trend Micro.

- **Network reputation services**—E-mail *senders* are examined and compared to a database of IP addresses known to produce spam. The sender's reputation of being a source of spam is used as the metric for spam detection. This makes identifying spam relays and known spam sources relatively easy and fast.

You can use the following steps to configure SMTP anti-spam operation.

1. Configure SMTP content scanning.

   Under the **Mail (SMTP) > Anti-spam > Content Scanning** link, select the **Target** tab, as shown in Figure 12-31. You can set the level of anti-spam detection in the **Filter Threshold** section. By default, the CSC uses a **Low** setting. The higher the setting, the more likely spam messages are detected. Also, you have a greater chance that the CSC triggers on false positives, or legitimate e-mail messages that it mistakenly labels as spam. If you find that a reasonable number of spam messages are getting through without detection, you can increase the filter threshold.

Figure 12-31 *Configuring SMTP Anti-Spam Content Scanning*

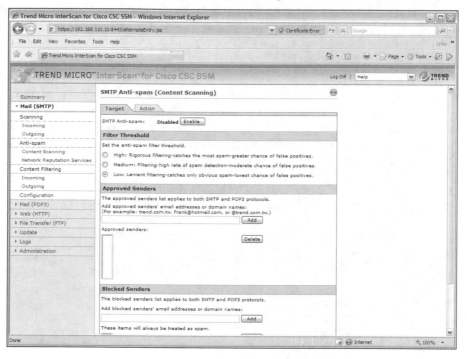

You can also add specific e-mail addresses or domain names to a list of approved senders or blocked senders. If the sender's address is found in the list of approved senders, the message is delivered without anti-spam detection. If the address is found in the list of blocked senders, all messages from that sender are dropped without delivery.

Under the **Action** tab, you can configure the action the CSC takes if it detects a spam message. By default, the message is "stamped" by having the text string **Spam:** added to the subject line. Stamping messages makes it easier for end users to create e-mail filters that can recognize the stamp string and take action automatically. Otherwise, you can configure the CSC to automatically delete spam messages before delivering them.

2. Configure Network Reputation Services.

   By default, SMTP anti-spam Network Reputation Services are enabled. The CSC can make use of the following two types of anti-spam services from Trend Micro:

   - **Real-Time Blackhole List (RBL+)**—Spam senders are identified by IP address from a list of known spam originators. This database is accurate and stable, but is not updated at the CSC in real time.

- **Quick IP List (QIL)**—Spam senders are identified using a dynamic exchange between the CSC and Trend Micro. New spam originators can be identified in real time because the CSC is constantly comparing sender addresses with the QIL content from Trend Micro. This database offers the most timely detection of new spam senders, but requires interactive communication with the Trend Micro servers.

You can set the level of anti-spam detection by going to the **Mail (SMTP) > Anti-spam > Network Reputation Services** link and selecting the **Target** tab, as shown in Figure 12-32. Under the **Set Service Level** section, you can choose **High** or **Low**. A setting of **High** uses the complete Trend Micro Network Anti-spam Service, which can identify known or likely spam senders by IP address, previous spam reputation, or current suspicious activity. A setting of **Low** uses a more basic Trend Micro database of known spam senders.

Figure 12-32 *Configuring SMTP Anti-Spam Network Reputation Services*

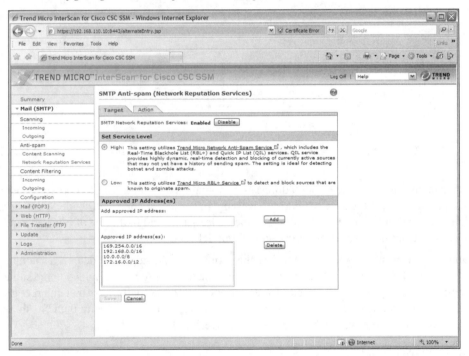

In the **Approved IP Address(es)** section, the CSC also keeps a list of addresses and subnets that it considers to be trusted or approved senders. Users sending SMTP messages from these addresses are approved to do so. By default, the following addresses are added to the approved list:

- 169.254.0.0/16
- 192.168.0.0/16

- 10.0.0.0/8
- 172.16.0.0/12

Notice that each of these subnets represents private address space as defined in RFC 1918. These addresses are not routable over the Internet and should be found only on an inside or protected interface of the ASA. In other words, the CSC considers your own internal users to have a good reputation in sending spam-free e-mail.

Under the **Action** tab, you can configure the action to take when e-mail senders are matched as spam senders. The actions are grouped according to the type of anti-spam detection: RBL+ or QIL match. By default, each type of match leads to **Intelligent action**, where the CSC denies the spam sender's SMTP connection and sends an SMTP error code. You can also choose to close the SMTP connection with no error code or to simply log the detection and deliver the spam message.

Configuring General SMTP Mail Handling

You can configure some basic policies that affect how the CSC handles SMTP content. Under the **Mail (SMTP) > Configuration** link, you can select tabs that correspond to the following configuration steps.

1. Configure the **Message Filter** tab.

   The CSC can flatly reject e-mail messages sent over SMTP if the messages are greater than a maximum size (default 20 MB) or if the messages contain more than a maximum number of recipients (default 100). You can adjust these values as shown in Figure 12-33.

Figure 12-33   *Configuring the SMTP Message Filter*

2. Configure the **Disclaimer** tab.

   By default, if the CSC does not detect any suspicious content and decides to deliver STMP e-mail messages, it does not make any changes to the message body. However, if your organization requires users to add a disclaimer to every message, you can configure the CSC to do this for all users automatically.

   In fact, you can use the disclaimer message to add any type of text to e-mail messages. For example, your organization might require certain warnings or cautions to be added to educate the mail recipients about specific company policies or legal actions that might be taken.

Using the parameters shown in Figure 12-34, select the **Add this disclaimer to all email messages** checkbox. Next, choose whether the CSC should add the disclaimer at the **beginning** or **end** of e-mail messages from the drop-down list. The CSC uses a default disclaimer text, but you can edit the text field if needed. Click the **Save** button to save your changes.

Figure 12-34   *Configuring the SMTP Disclaimer Message Parameters*

3. Configure the **Incoming Mail Domain** tab.

   The CSC must be able to determine whether SMTP mail is incoming or outgoing when it applies various content detection and blocking functions. If you have SMTP servers inside your organization, then SMTP traffic will be incoming from the Internet toward those servers. The CSC looks at the domain names of e-mail recipients in incoming messages as it examines the e-mail content.

   You should add any domain names that are used inside your organization for email purposes. For example, if your users have e-mail addresses of the form username@mycompany.com, then enter **mycompany.com** as an incoming mail domain, as shown in Figure 12-35.

Figure 12-35   *Configuring the SMTP Incoming Mail Domain Settings*

4. Configure the **Advanced Settings** tab.

   Malicious users can attempt to exploit SMTP connections as they set up an attack. The CSC can monitor the state of SMTP connections and take certain actions to mitigate an attack. You can configure the CSC to automatically time out idle SMTP connections after a time period (default 90 seconds) by adjusting the parameters shown in Figure 12-36.

Figure 12-36   *Configuring SMTP Advanced Settings*

You can also configure the CSC to close SMTP connections if any of the following conditions occur:

- Time elapses before a message is actually sent (default 45 seconds)

- A number of SMTP errors occur (default 3 errors)

- A number of SMTP reset commands are sent (default 3)

Scanning POP3 Traffic

The CSC can scan POP3 mail messages much like it scans SMTP mail. The main difference is that POP3 is used only when clients retrieve mail; SMTP is used when clients send mail. You can configure POP3 scanning by going to the **Mail (POP3) > Scanning** link and using the following steps:

1. Configure the scanning target

   Select the **Target** tab, as shown in Figure 12-37. First, set the maximum message size that the CSC allows. By default, messages larger than 20 MB are rejected. Next, choose the default type of file scanning. By default, the CSC scans all attachment files as they are sent through a POP3 connection. The CSC can also use its IntelliScan feature to scan files based on a "true file type," which is determined by header information inside the files, rather than a filename extension. Otherwise, you can specify the filename extensions to be scanned.

   Some attachments might be password-protected or compressed when they are downloaded. The CSC can attempt to scan these files, too. You can choose whether to deliver or delete password protected files. For compressed files, you can set limits on the extent of the file's compression process to protect the CSC resources and the amount of time needed to download, uncompress, and deliver the files. Remember that the CSC has to download the complete file and then uncompress it before it can be delivered to the user.

   By default, password-protected files are delivered. Compressed files are scanned only if they contain less than 200 internal files, are less than 20 MB, require more than 3 compression passes, or are more than 100 times the size when uncompressed. If the compressed files are not scanned, they are still delivered by default.

Figure 12-37 *Configuring POP3 Message Scanning*

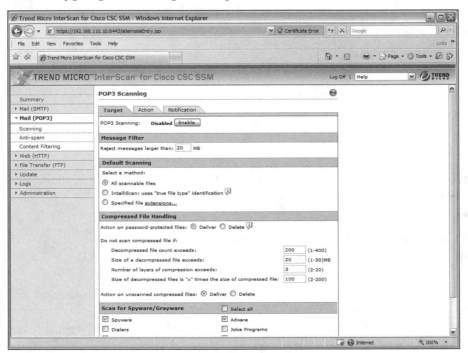

You can also specify individual types of spyware and grayware content to be detected during FTP file scanning. By default, none of these types are detected. Be sure to click the **Save** button when you are finished configuring the **Target** tab.

2. Configure the action.

   Select the **Action** tab. If an attachment is found to have a virus or malware, it can be cleaned (the default). As an alternative, the CSC can deliver the message after the offending attachment has been deleted, or it can deliver the original message intact—offending attachment and all.

   With spyware and grayware, you can configure the CSC to deliver the offending files or delete them (the default).

3. Configure the notification.

   When the CSC detects suspicious content in an e-mail attachment file, it can send a notification. To configure this feature, select the **Notification** tab. By default, no notifications are sent by e-mail. However, you can choose whether to send e-mail notices to the CSC administrator (the e-mail address you configured for CSC notifications), the e-mail message sender, and the e-mail message recipient.

By default, the CSC notifies the e-mail message recipient by inserting a descriptive message into the e-mail message text. You can also configure the CSC to insert a "risk free" message into the text of every message that has clean scanning results.

Detecting Spam in POP3 E-mail

The CSC can detect spam messages as they are retrieved through POP3 mail connections. Detecting spam in POP3 is a bit simpler than SMTP because e-mail messages are coming from a server toward the clients. With POP3, messages are always retrieved, so none of the parties involved can be a spam source; if spam exists, it is only as messages already queued for clients.

Under the **Mail (POP3) > Anti-spam** link, select the **Target** tab as shown in Figure 12-38. You can set the level of anti-spam detection in the **Filter Threshold** section. The higher the setting, the more likely spam messages are detected. However, the higher the setting also means a greater chance exists that the CSC triggers on false positives, or legitimate e-mail messages that it mistakenly labels as spam. If you find that a reasonable number of spam messages are getting through without detection, you can increase the filter threshold. Remember that POP3 anti-spam detection examines e-mail messages as they are *received*.

Figure 12-38 *Configuring POP3 Anti-Spam Content Scanning*

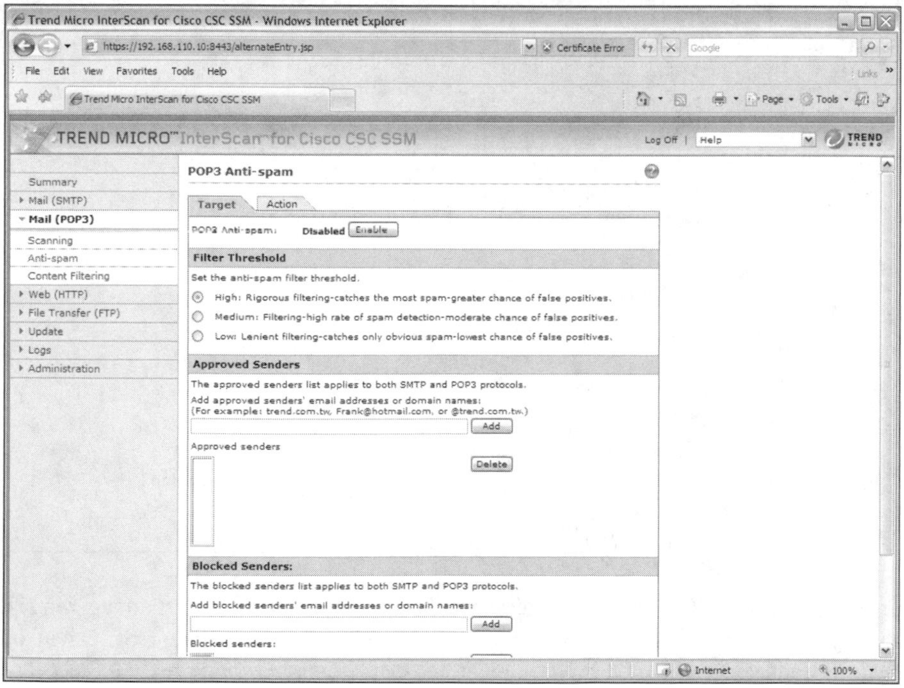

You can also add specific e-mail addresses or domain names to a list of approved senders or blocked senders. If the sender's address is found in the list of approved senders, the message is delivered without anti-spam detection. If the address is found in the list of blocked senders, all messages from that sender are dropped without delivery.

Under the **Action** tab, you can configure the action the CSC takes if it detects a spam message. By default, the message is "stamped" by having the text string **Spam:** added to the subject line. Stamping messages makes it easier for end users to create e-mail filters that can recognize the stamp string and take action automatically. Otherwise, you can configure the CSC to automatically delete spam messages before delivering them.

Filtering POP3 Content

You can configure the CSC to filter POP3 messages according to specific things that are found in the message itself. Click on the **Mail (POP3) > Content Filtering** link, as shown in Figure 12-39.

Figure 12-39 *Configuring POP3 Message Content Filtering*

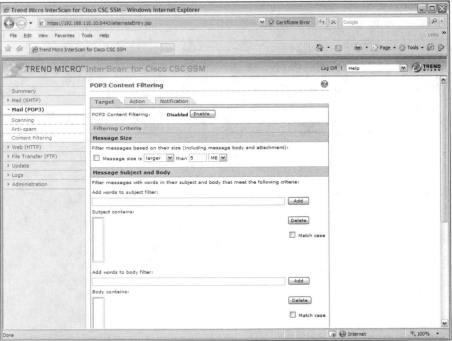

You can configure the CSC to filter out messages that are larger or smaller than a given size. This can be handy to filter out messages that contain very large attachments. The CSC can also filter messages if it finds specific words in the subject line or the message body text. To accomplish this, enter the words in the **Add words to subject filter** field or **Add words to body filter** field and click on the **Add** button.

You can also configure the CSC to filter messages according to the attributes of attachments. For example, you can enter specific words or character strings to match against the attachment filenames. You can also select attachment file types to filter out.

Under the **Action** tab, you can choose whether to delete or deliver (the default) messages that are filtered. You can also select a text message to insert in the mail message to alert the user of the filtered condition. Finally, the **Notification** tab allows an alert to be sent to the CSC administrator when a message has been filtered.

12-3: Configuring the AIP SSM

The Advanced Inspection and Prevention (AIP) SSM was introduced with ASA release 7.0(1). The AIP is used as a single Intrusion Protection System (IPS) in conjunction with the ASA to provide robust intrusion inspection functions based on a set of signatures.

Beginning with ASA release 8.0(1), and Cisco IPS 6.0 running on the AIP, you can configure more than one virtual sensor. The ASA can take advantage of the virtual sensors to inspect traffic on different interfaces, in different security contexts, and according to different policies. The ASA and AIP module can also perform anomaly detection to discover Internet worms that are scanning for targets to attack.

> **TIP**   For complete information about Cisco IPS sensors and their operation, you can refer to *Intrusion Prevention Fundamentals* by Earl Carter and Jonathan Hogue, Cisco Press, ISBN 1-58705-239-3.

Initially Configuring the AIP

After an AIP SSM has been installed in an ASA chassis, you need to connect to it and provide an initial configuration. This must be done through the AIP's management interface, according to the following steps:

1. Connect to the AIP from the ASA CLI.

   First, locate the AIP SSM within the chassis with the **show module** command. Then open a terminal session to the AIP's out-of-band channel with the **session** *slot_number* command, as in the following example:

```
Firewall# show module
Mod Card Type                                       Model            Serial No.
--- -------------------------------------------- ----------------- -----------
  0 ASA 5510 Adaptive Security Appliance           ASA5510          JMX1014K070
  1 ASA 5500 Series Security Services Module-10    ASA-SSM-10       JAB101300TZ
```

```
Mod MAC Address Range                  Hw Version   Fw Version   Sw Version
--- ------------------------------     -----------  -----------  ---------------
  0 0016.c789.c8a4 to 0016.c789.c8a8   1.1          1.0(10)0     8.0(1)18
  1 0015.c695.d461 to 0015.c695.d461   1.0          1.0(10)0     6.0(2)

Mod SSM Application Name               Status           SSM Application Version
--- ------------------------------     ---------------  ------------------------
  1 IPS                      Up                6.0(2)

Mod Status               Data Plane Status     Compatibility
--- -----------------    -------------------   -------------
  0 Up Sys               Not Applicable
  1 Up                   Up
Firewall#
Firewall# session 1
Opening command session with slot 1.
Connected to slot 1. Escape character sequence is 'CTRL-^X'.
login: cisco
Password:
```

By default, the AIP is configured with username **cisco** and password **cisco**. Because these defaults are well known, you should change them as soon as possible, as part of the initial setup in Step 2.

2. Run the initial setup.

As soon as you log in to the AIP through a terminal session the first time, the AIP prompts for the current username and password (both **cisco** by default), as well as a new password.

At this point, you are at a command prompt where you can enter the **setup** command. The AIP displays its current settings and then prompts you through a dialog to change the configuration.

As the AIP prompts for each network parameter, you can press the **Enter** key to accept the default value, or you can enter a new value. The setup process begins with a prompt to continue; press the **Enter** key to begin, as in the following example:

```
Current time: Mon May 14 08:39:16 2007
Setup Configuration last modified: Tue May 08 22:21:25 2007
Continue with configuration dialog?[yes]:
```

a.   Set the AIP hostname and prompt.

In the following example, the AIP is configured to have its prompt changed from the default **sensor** to **aip**:

```
Enter host name[sensor]: aip
```

b.   Set the management interface address.

The IP address, subnet mask (as a CIDR bit mask or the number of network bits), and default gateway are all configured on a single line, in the following format:

```
ip_address/bits,gateway_address
```

Be sure to separate the IP address and mask with a forward slash and the mask and gateway address with a comma. In the following example, the AIP management interface is assigned IP address 192.168.100.11, subnet mask 255.255.255.0 (/24), and default gateway 192.168.100.1:

```
Enter IP interface[10.1.9.201/24,10.1.9.1]: 192.168.100.11/24,192.168.100.1
```

c. Configure the Telnet server.

The AIP can accept Telnet connections on its management port, if they are needed. By default, Telnet is disabled. Because Telnet is not a secure protocol, you should keep it disabled by pressing the **Enter** key to accept the default:

```
Enter telnet-server status[disabled]:
```

d. Set the web server port number.

By default, the AIP allows SSL connections to its management interface over TCP port 443. You can accept the default port number by pressing **Enter**, or you can enter a new port number at the following prompt:

```
Enter web-server port[443]:
```

e. Identify addresses that can manage the AIP.

The AIP maintains an internal access list to limit which client IP addresses are allowed to connect to the management port. By default, all IP addresses are denied access. You should enter the IP subnets or addresses where trusted administrative users are located, so the AIP allows them to connect. Enter each IP address with a CIDR mask, as in the following example:

```
Modify current access list?[no]: yes
Current access list entries:
Delete:
Permit:  10.0.0.0/8
Permit:  192.168.1.0/24
```

You can keep adding one IP address/mask at each Permit prompt. Single IP addresses can be added with a **/32** mask (255.255.255.255). When you are finished adding addresses, press the **Enter** key by itself.

f. Configure the AIP clock.

By default, the AIP uses the ASA chassis as its time source. The AIP can also synchronize its time with an external NTP server, independent of the ASA chassis. The simplest solution is to configure the ASA chassis to use an NTP server and then the AIP can synchronize with the ASA.

Regardless, the AIP synchronizes only the date and current time (hours, minutes, seconds) with the ASA or NTP server. The time zone and summer time settings are all maintained independently on the AIP. If you want to use a time zone that is different from the default UTC, you have to configure the AIP accordingly. In the following example, the AIP is

Section 12-3

configured to use the ASA chassis (not NTP) with a recurring summer time or DST beginning on the second Sunday of March at 02:00:00 and ending on the first Sunday of November at 02:00:00:

```
Modify system clock settings?[no]: yes
  Use NTP?[no]:
  Modify summer time settings?[no]: yes
    Recurring, Date or Disable?[Recurring]:
    Start Month[april]: march
    Start Week[first]: second
    Start Day[sunday]: sunday
    Start Time[02:00:00]: 02:00:00
    End Month[october]: november
    End Week[last]: first
    End Day[sunday]: sunday
    End Time[02:00:00]: 02:00:00
    DST Zone[]: EDT
    Offset[60]:
  Modify system timezone?[no]: yes
    Timezone[UTC]: EST
    UTC Offset[0]: -5
```

Also, the AIP's time zone is called "EST" and is 5 hours behind UTC.

g. Identify sensor interfaces.

By default, no AIP interfaces are configured to accept traffic for inspection. You can assign interfaces to virtual sensors as a part of the initial configuration. However, you should take full advantage of the user interface in ASDM or IPS Device Manager (IDM) instead. In that case, choose the default **no** answer when you are prompted for interface/virtual sensor configuration.

```
Modify interface/virtual sensor configuration?[no]:
```

h. Configure default threat protection settings.

By default, the AIP is configured to provide threat detection on its virtual sensor vs0. Only high risk (risk ratings 90 through 100) are prevented. You can configure these settings in the initial setup here, if needed:

```
Modify default threat prevention settings?[no]:
```

However, you should consider doing this through the IDM interface instead. After the initial setup is done, IDM provides a much more robust management platform.

3. Reset the AIP.

Before the initial settings can be used, the AIP must be reset or rebooted. You can do this from the AIP session with the **reset** command.

Managing the AIP

You can manage the AIP from a GUI interface in two ways:

- Open a web browser to the AIP's management interface address as https://*aip-ip-address*
- Access the AIP through ASDM

Actually, both methods provide the same configuration and management tools in slightly different formats. The AIP web front end is called IPS Device Manager (IDM) and provides a native interface into the module's configuration. If you use ASDM, all of the same AIP functions are presented within the ASDM structure, providing a single management platform for all ASA-related features.

To access the AIP from within ASDM, select the **Configuration** tab and the **IPS** link in the left-hand column, as shown in Figure 12-40.

Figure 12-40 *Configuring an AIP from Within ASDM*

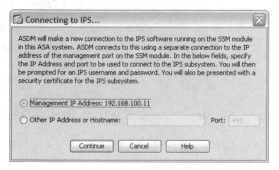

Section 12-3

TIP   The AIP uses a self-signed certificate, so your web browser will likely complain about its validity. The simplest workaround is to click on the **Continue to this website (not recommended)** link in your browser.

Updating the AIP License

The AIP cannot inspect traffic at all until it has a valid license. In addition, you will not be able to access new IPS signature databases or upload them to the AIP without an active license and Cisco support contract.

If you purchased a license and support contract, you can enter the license key in one of two ways:

- Directly from Cisco Connection Online (CCO, Cisco.com) or from ASDM/IDM
- Upload from the ASDM or IDM client

In ASDM, select the **Configuration** tab and then click on the **IPS** button in the left-hand column. You should see a window similar to that displayed in Figure 12-41.

Figure 12-41 *Updating the AIP License*

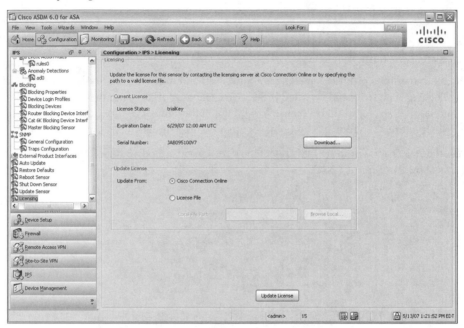

If you select the **Update from Cisco Connection Online** option, the AIP opens a connection to Cisco.com directly. It attempts to request and download a license automatically. If it is not successful, it gives you the option to request a 30-day trial license key.

If you received a license from Cisco in an e-mail, you can save the license as a file and upload it to the AIP. Select the **Update from License File** option and then click on the **Browse Local** button to locate the file. Finally, click on the **Update License** button to upload and install the license file.

Manually Updating the AIP Code or Signature Files

Occasionally, you might need to update the IPS code image or the signature database file on the AIP module. You can do this manually through the ASDM or IDM interface.

First, download the new file from Cisco.com and save it on a local server. The AIP can retrieve an image file from an FTP, HTTP, HTTPS, or Secure Copy (SCP) server. You can also download the file and save it locally on the ASDM client machine.

From ASDM, select the **Configuration** tab and then **IPS** in the left-hand column. In the IPS task list, select **Update Sensor**, as shown in Figure 12-42.

Figure 12-42 *Updating an AIP Image or Signature File*

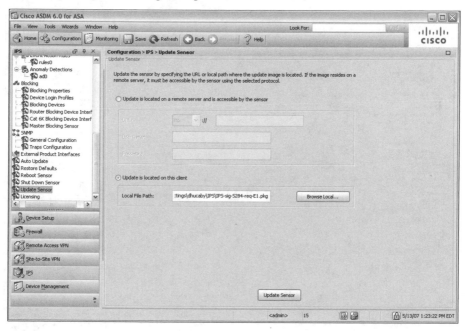

You can select **Update is located on a remote server and is accessible by the sensor** and supply the server type and URL, as well as a username and password. If you stored the image file on the local ASDM client machine, select **Update is located on this client** and click on the **Browse Local** button to locate the file.

Finally, click on the **Update Sensor** button to download the file to the AIP. If you updated the AIP image file, you also have to reboot the AIP to begin using the new code image. Signature database files, on the other hand, can be uploaded and used immediately without rebooting.

Automatically Updating AIP Image and Signature Files

Manually updating files on one AIP can be somewhat tedious, but updating files on many AIP modules can get out of hand. You can make use of the Auto Update feature to configure one or more AIPs to leverage a more automatic process. An AIP can poll an FTP or SCP server at regular intervals to see if new files are available. If so, the AIP downloads the new files and begins using them.

In ASDM, select the **Configure** tab and then **IPS**, followed by the **Auto Update** link in the scrolling list. You should see a window like that in Figure 12-43.

Figure 12-43   *Using Auto Update to Keep AIP Files Up to Date*

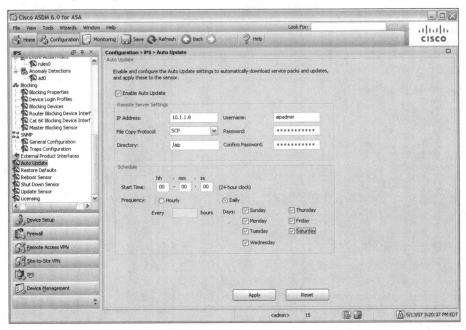

First, configure the AIP to begin polling the Auto Update Server (AUS) for new files. Click on the **Enable Auto Update** checkbox and then enter the IP address of the AUS machine, along with a valid username and password. Select the protocol to use for file copying (SCP or FTP) and the directory where the AIP files can be found.

Finally, enter the polling schedule that the AIP should use. Cisco can sometimes publish new IPS signature database files at least once a day, so you should consider selecting each day of the week for Auto Update. After you have entered all of the fields, click on the **Apply** button.

TIP	If you have a currently active IPS maintenance contract with Cisco, you can access the most up-to-date IPS image and signature database files.
	http://www.cisco.com/kobayashi/sw-center/ciscosecure/ids/crypto/index.shtml— Click on **Latest Signature Update** link.
	You can subscribe to the Cisco IPS Active Update Bulletin by going to http://www.cisco.com/offer/newsletter/123668_4 and filling in your information. The bulletins are sent each time a new IPS signature update is released.
	The Cisco Security IntelliShield Alert Manager service provides customized alerts of new vulnerabilities and threats. See http://www.cisco.com/go/intellishield for more information.

IPS Policies

An IPS sensor like the AIP performs all of its inspections and analysis based on a set of policies. The policies are built on three components:

- **IPS signatures**—A database of predefined signatures or ways to describe suspicious activity; signatures are based on characteristics of the data being passed.

- **Event actions**—The IPS sensor takes predefined actions on each signature that is detected in a traffic flow.

- **Anomaly detection**—The IPS sensor can detect traffic anomalies or suspicious activity related to Internet worm propagation.

By default, an AIP is preconfigured with a signature definition called sig0, a set of event action rules called rules0, and a set of anomaly detections called ad0. You can use the default policies or you can create your own through ASDM or IDM.

Working with Signature Definitions

From the ASDM, you can view the default signature definition sig0 by selecting the **Configuration** tab, then the **IPS** function, and then the **Signature Definitions** link under **Policies** in the scrolling list. Figure 12-44 shows a sample of sig0. Each signature has the following attributes:

- **A unique signature ID**—Each signature has a predefined identifier, shown in the **Sig ID** column

- **A descriptive name**—A text string that describes the purpose of the signature

- **A severity factor**—The severity factor is based on the following levels: Informational (25), Low (50), Medium (75), or High (100)

- **A fidelity rating**—A weighting (1–100) of how well the signature might perform without any prior knowledge of the traffic target

- **A base RR**—The base risk rating (1–100) or a composite index based on the severity level times the fidelity rating

- **An action**—The action taken by the AIP when the signature fires

You can use the default signature definition sig0 as-is, or you can make changes to individual signatures within sig0. Also, you can create your own customized signature definition based on sig0. To create a new definition, select **Signature Definitions** in the scrolling list and then select sig0 under **Policy Name**. You can click on the **Clone** button to make a copy of an existing signature definition or click on the **Add** button to create a new copy of **sig0** with an arbitrary name.

Working with Event Action Rules

Each signature used by the AIP has one or more specific actions defined. Whenever the signature fires or detects a specific behavior in the traffic, that action is taken. Basically, the actions are defined as one or more of the following:

- Deny some activity
- Generate a log

Figure 12-44 *The sig0 Signature Definition*

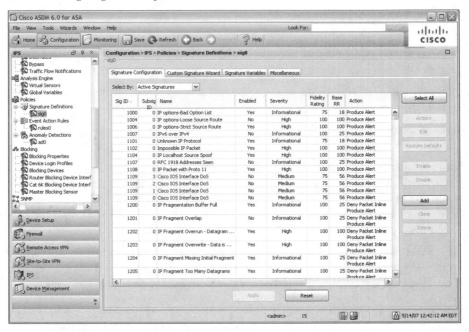

- Modify packets
- Generate an alert
- Request a reaction from a network device
- Reset the connection

Figure 12-45 shows the full set of actions that can be selected on a signature in the signature definition. The actions are predefined for each signature in the default sig0 definition, but can be overridden by configuring the signature.

The AIP has a default set of event action rules called **rules0** that can be used to override or set general parameters for actions. You can edit rules0 or define your own event action rule set by selecting the **Configuration** tab, then the **IPS** link, and then the **Event Action Rules** link in the scrolling list under **Policies**.

Working with Anomaly Detection Policies

Beginning with IPS 6.0 (and ASA release 8.0), an AIP has an anomaly detection engine that can detect worm-based activity on a network. A worm is an agent that begins on one host and propagates to as many other hosts as possible. Worms spread themselves automatically by looking for other potential vulnerable targets through network scans.

Figure 12-45 *Event Actions for an IPS Signature*

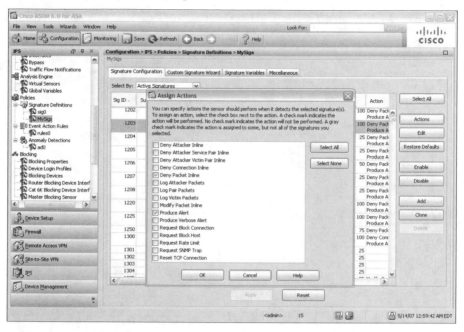

Anomaly Detection (AD) works by detecting large amounts of scanning traffic from single hosts to many others. AD looks for unidirectional User Datagram Protocol (UDP) traffic, where the worm-infected host is sending packets to many destination addresses using the same destination port, with little return traffic. With TCP, AD looks for many half-open or embryonic connections from one host to many others, using the same destination port.

The AD feature can operate in the following modes:

- **Inactive mode**—AD is disabled; anomalies or worm activities are not detected.

- **Learn mode**—AD listens to the network traffic, gathering a baseline of typical activity. This baseline is known as the *knowledge base*.

- **Detect mode**—The knowledge base is used as a threshold for worm-based activity. When the IPS sensor detects activity above the threshold, it sends alerts and takes action on the traffic. Detect mode also updates the knowledge base periodically, so it always has a current baseline of network traffic.

The AIP has a default set of anomaly detection policies called ad0. You can edit the defaults or add your own set of AD policies by selecting the **Configuration** tab, then **IPS**, and then **Anomaly Detections** in the scrolling list under **Policies** as shown in Figure 12-46.

Figure 12-46 *Anomaly Detection Settings*

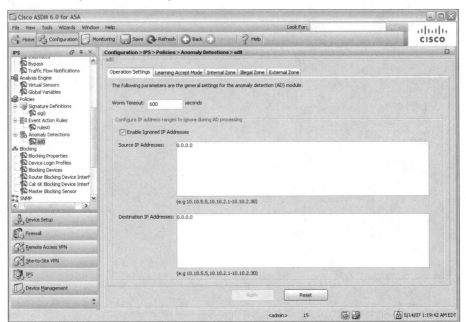

By default, the AIP runs AD in the detect mode, actively detecting and mitigating worm activity. When AD is first enabled on an IPS sensor, it runs for the first 24 hours in learn mode. After it gathers a baseline, it automatically moves to detect mode.

AIP Interfaces

The ASA and AIP are connected over the ASA chassis backplane by two hidden interfaces:

- **GigabitEthernet0/0**—Used only for command and control traffic between the ASA and AIP.

- **GigabitEthernet0/1**—Used for data transfer between the ASA and AIP; this is the only interface that can be monitored as a sensing interface by the AIP for IPS functions.

From the ASA, neither of these interfaces is available or configurable. The interfaces can be seen and used only from the AIP itself.

To perform IPS functions, an IPS platform must be able to monitor one or more of its interfaces. IPS sensor interfaces can be configured in any of the following ways:

- **Promiscuous monitoring**—A single interface is used to monitor traffic; the IPS sensor can make decisions on what to do with the packets, but the packets do not actually pass through the IPS.

- **Inline interface**—Usually two physical interfaces are configured as an inline pair, where the IPS sensor monitors traffic entering on one interface and exiting on the other.

  An AIP does not have multiple physical interfaces, so you can configure only a single interface in inline mode. Packets received from the ASA on the interface are examined by the AIP. If the AIP decides to permit a packet, the packet is returned to the ASA on the same interface for forwarding. If the AIP decides to block the packet, the packet is simply not returned to the ASA at all.

- **VLAN inline pair**—Two VLAN interfaces are configured as an inline pair, so that the IPS sensor examines traffic entering on one VLAN interface and exiting on the other.

  The ASA platform cannot use VLAN inline interface pairs because only one interface (GigabitEthernet0/1) connects the ASA and AIP over the backplane.

IPS Virtual Sensors

IPS 6.0 enables an IPS platform, such as the AIP, to define virtual sensors that can monitor traffic in a variety of ways. ASA 8.0 (1) is the first release to offer virtual sensor support in cooperation with an AIP running IPS 6.0. With virtual sensors, a single IPS hardware platform can run multiple IPS sensors, all operating independently.

An AIP can operate up to four different virtual sensors. Each of the virtual sensors must use the only interface available on the AIP—GigabitEthernet0/1. Reusing the same interface might seem to be a severe limitation. However, the AIP is able to isolate traffic to and from the virtual sensors even over the same interface.

Virtual sensors can be used in different policies within a policy map, and they can be allocated to one or more security contexts on an ASA. For example, you might customize one virtual sensor to meet the policies of a business unit and apply it to one security context. You could customize a different virtual sensor for another business unit, to be applied to a different context, and so on.

Each ASA context connects to the AIP over a different instance of backplane interface GigabitEthernet0/1. Remember that the virtual sensors are configured only on the AIP, so GigabitEthernet0/1 can be seen and manipulated only from the AIP—not from the ASA.

You can configure virtual sensors on the AIP with the following steps:

1. Configure IPS policies.

   The AIP is preconfigured with the default sig0 signature definition, rules0 event action rule set, and ad0 anomaly detection policies. You can use these policies as-is, or you can make changes to them as described in the section "IPS Policies" earlier in this chapter.

   The policies are applied to a sensor interface in Step 2.

2. Configure a virtual sensor.

   By default, one virtual sensor is preconfigured on an AIP. The virtual sensor is called vs0 and uses the GigabitEthernet0/1 backplane AIP interface. It also has the default policies sig0, rules0, and ad0 applied to it, as shown in Figure 12-47. Notice that the backplane interface is available to the virtual sensor, but has not been assigned to the sensor yet. This is done in Step 3.

Figure 12-47 *The Default vs0 Virtual Sensor*

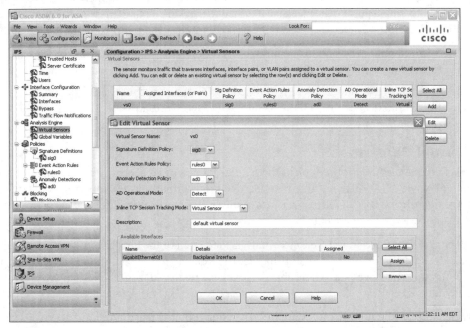

If your ASA is running in single-context security mode, you can use the default vs0 virtual sensor as it is already configured.

If your ASA is running multiple context mode and has more than one security context configured, you can use vs0 as well as any new virtual sensor that you configure in any of the contexts.

To configure a new virtual sensor, select the **Configuration** tab, then **IPS**, and then the **Virtual Sensors** link in the scrolling list under **Analysis Engine**. Click on the **Add** button and choose a name and policies for the sensor.

3. Assign an AIP interface to the virtual sensor.

   Before a virtual sensor can be used, you need to assign an AIP interface to it. Even the default vs0 virtual sensor does not have an interface assigned until you manually configure it.

   Select the **Virtual Sensors** link in the scrolling list under **Analysis Engine** and then select a virtual sensor. Next, click on the **Edit** button.

The Edit Virtual Sensor window is shown. Toward the bottom of the window, GigabitEthernet0/1 is shown as an available interface, but shown as **No** in the Assigned column. To assign the interface, click on the **Assign** button. (If you ever need to unassign an interface from a virtual sensor, click on the **Remove** button.)

In Figure 12-48, the default vs0 virtual sensor is being edited so that the GigabitEthernet0/1 interface can be assigned to it.

Figure 12-48 *Assigning a Sensing Interface to a Virtual Sensor*

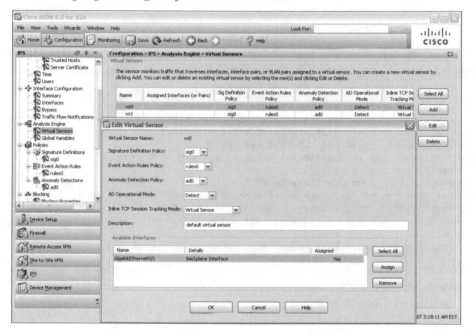

On an AIP, every virtual sensor is assigned to the GigabitEthernet0/1 backplane interface. Actually, the interface must be explicitly assigned to one virtual sensor; after that is done, it is implicitly assigned to the other virtual sensors.

Do not worry about duplicating the interface across the sensors—the ASA and AIP take care of keeping the sensors isolated to their security contexts.

4. Apply the virtual sensor to an ASA context.

    If the ASA is running in multiple context mode, the virtual sensor must be mapped to a security context. Use the following command in context configuration mode:

    ```
    Firewall(config-ctx)# allocate-ips sensor_name [mapped_name] [default]
    ```

    The virtual sensor named *sensor_name* is applied to the current context. By default, the sensor name also appears in the context configuration. If you do not want a context administrator to see the actual name of the sensor, you can supply an alias as *mapped_name* to be seen.

Section 12-3

> **TIP** The **allocate-ips** command is not available when the ASA is running in single context
> mode. In that case, the default virtual sensor vs0 is automatically applied to the ASA—
> even if other virtual sensors have been configured on the AIP. You can see the virtual
> sensor with the **show ips** command:
>
> ```
> Firewall# show ips
> Sensor Name      Sensor ID
> -----------      ---------
> vs0              1
> Firewall#
> ```

As an example, suppose virtual sensors vs0 and vs1 have been configured on the AIP and are to
be applied to security contexts Department1 and Department2, respectively. You can use the
following commands to apply the virtual sensors:

```
Firewall(config)# context Department1
Firewall(config-ctx)# allocate-interface Ethernet0/0
Firewall(config-ctx)# allocate-interface Ethernet0/1
Firewall(config-ctx)# allocate-ips vs0 ips-a
Firewall(config-ctx)# config-url disk0:/dept1.cfg
Firewall(config-ctx)# exit
Firewall(config)# context Department2
Firewall(config-ctx)# allocate-interface Ethernet0/2
Firewall(config-ctx)# allocate-interface Ethernet0/3
Firewall(config-ctx)# allocate-ips vs1 ips-b
Firewall(config-ctx)# config-url disk0:/dept2.cfg
Firewall(config-ctx)# exit
```

Notice that the virtual sensors are configured with mapped names ips-a and ips-b. In the
contexts, the administrators see only the mapped names:

```
Firewall/Department1# show ips
Sensor Name
-----------
ips-a
Firewall/Department1#
```

Also, you can allocate multiple virtual sensors across the contexts in any fashion, as in the
following example:

```
Firewall(config)# context Department1
Firewall(config-ctx)# allocate-interface Ethernet0/0
Firewall(config-ctx)# allocate-interface Ethernet0/1
Firewall(config-ctx)# allocate-ips vs0 ips-a
Firewall(config-ctx)# allocate-ips vs1 ips-b
Firewall(config-ctx)# config-url disk0:/dept1.cfg
Firewall(config-ctx)# exit
Firewall(config)# context Department2
Firewall(config-ctx)# allocate-interface Ethernet0/2
Firewall(config-ctx)# allocate-interface Ethernet0/3
Firewall(config-ctx)# allocate-ips vs1 ips-a
Firewall(config-ctx)# config-url disk0:/dept2.cfg
Firewall(config-ctx)# exit
```

5. Configure an ASA policy map to divert traffic to virtual sensor.

By default, the ASA does not send any traffic to an IPS virtual sensor. You need to configure a policy map that matches traffic to be inspected and then apply the policy map in a service policy.

In the policy map configuration, use the following command to divert traffic to the virtual sensor:

```
Firewall(config)# policy-map pmap_name
Firewall(config-pmap)# class cmap_name
Firewall(config-pmap-c)# ips {promiscuous | inline} {fail-close | fail-open} [sensor sensor_name]
Firewall(config-pmap-c)# exit
Firewall(config-pmap)# exit
```

The virtual sensor can be used in promiscuous or inline mode. In addition, you can configure the ASA to keep forwarding traffic normally (**fail-open**) or to block all traffic (**fail-close**) if the AIP fails.

You can give the virtual sensor name with the **sensor** keyword, as either the virtual sensor name or the mapped name used in the context. If you do not give the **sensor** keyword, the default sensor is used.

In the following example, all traffic passing through the ASA's outside interface is diverted to virtual sensor vs0.

```
Firewall(config)# class-map anything
Firewall(config-cmap)# match any
Firewall(config-cmap)# exit
!
Firewall(config)# policy-map MyPolicy
Firewall(config-pmap)# class anything
Firewall(config-pmap-c)# ips inline fail-close sensor vs0
Firewall(config-pmap-c)# exit
Firewall(config-pmap)# exit
Firewall(config)# service-policy MyPolicy interface outside
```

If you have configured more than one virtual sensor on the AIP, you can divert different traffic to each by referencing them with multiple **ips** commands in the policy map.

Well-Known Protocol and Port Numbers

This appendix presents tables of well-known TCP/IP information that can be used in firewall configuration. Only the protocol and port numbers that have corresponding Cisco firewall configuration keywords are shown. These tables should provide a quick reference when you need a keyword or when you need to decipher other information from a keyword given by the firewall.

TIP   All well-known or assigned TCP/IP information is registered with the Internet Assigned Numbers Authority (IANA). For the most current number assignment information, go to http://www.iana.org/numbers.htm.

Another very handy source of networking information is the *RFC Sourcebook*, maintained by Network Sorcery, Inc. This website is a one-stop quick reference directory for RFCs, IP protocols, UDP and TCP ports, and more. You can find it at http://www.networksorcery.com/enp/default.htm.

A-1: IP Protocol Numbers

A higher-layer protocol is identified with an 8-bit field called Protocol in an IPv4 packet. Figure A-1 shows the IPv4 packet header format, with the Protocol field shaded.

Figure A-1   *IPv4 Header Format Showing the Protocol Field*

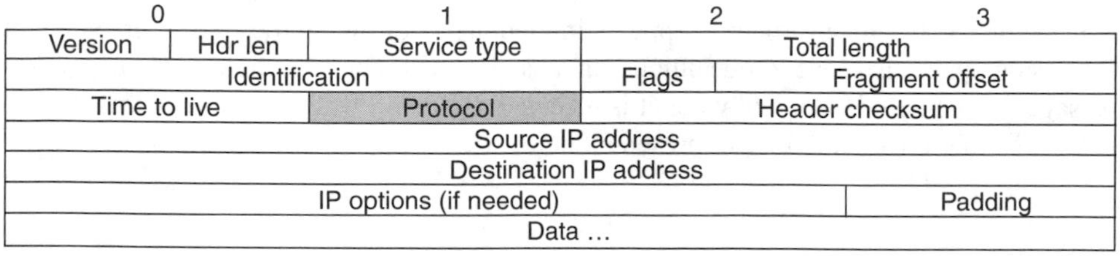

0		1	2	3
Version	Hdr len	Service type	Total length	
Identification			Flags	Fragment offset
Time to live		Protocol	Header checksum	
Source IP address				
Destination IP address				
IP options (if needed)				Padding
Data ...				

Cisco firewalls have keywords that can be used to specify certain IP protocols in access lists. These keywords are shown along with the IP protocol numbers in Table A-1.

Table A-1   *Cisco Firewall Keywords for IP Protocols*

Protocol Number	Firewall Keyword	IP Protocol Description
1	**icmp**	Internet Control Message Protocol (ICMP)
2	**igmp**	Internet Group Management Protocol (IGMP)
4	**ipinip**	IP-in-IP encapsulation
6	**tcp**	Transmission Control Protocol (TCP)
9	**igrp**	Interior Gateway Routing Protocol (IGRP)
17	**udp**	User Datagram Protocol (UDP)
47	**gre** or **pptp**	General Routing Encapsulation (GRE)
50	**esp** or **ipsec**	Encapsulating Security Payload (ESP)
51	**ah**	Authentication Header (AH)
58	**icmp6**	ICMP for IPv6
88	**eigrp**	Enhanced Interior Gateway Routing Protocol (EIGRP)
89	**ospf**	Open Shortest Path First (OSPF)
94	**nos**	Network Operating System (Novell NetWare)
103	**pim**	Protocol-Independent Multicast (PIM)
108	**pcp**	Payload Compression Protocol
109	**snp**	Sitara Networks Protocol

A-2: ICMP Message Types

Internet Control Message Protocol (ICMP) is used to transport error or control messages between routers and other devices. An ICMP message is encapsulated as the payload in an IP packet, as shown in Figure A-2. This information appears immediately following the IP header. Many of the ICMP message types also have a code number that can be used. The code field further specifies how the message type should be applied when it is received. Cisco firewalls cannot use the code field in access lists, so that information is not presented here.

Figure A-2   *ICMP Message Format*

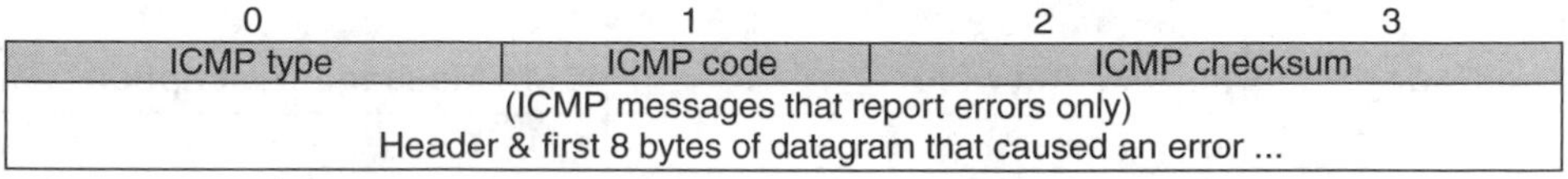

0	1	2	3
ICMP type	ICMP code	ICMP checksum	
(ICMP messages that report errors only)			
Header & first 8 bytes of datagram that caused an error ...			

Notice that in the case of an error condition, the first 8 bytes (64 bits) of the original datagram causing the error are included in the ICMP message. This provides the protocol and port numbers of the original message to be seen, making troubleshooting easier.

ICMP message type codes are registered with the IANA and can be found at http://www.iana.org/numbers.htm.

Table A-2 is a complete list of ICMP message types. It is reproduced with permission from the IANA. The Cisco firewall keywords were added to this list for quick reference.

Table A-2   *Well-Known ICMP Message Types*

ICMP MessageType	Firewall Keyword	ICMP Message Description
0	**echo-reply**	Echo reply
1	—	Reserved
2	—	Reserved
3	**unreachable**	Destination unreachable
4	**source-quench**	Source quench
5	**redirect**	Redirect
6	**alternate-address**	Alternate host address
7	—	Unassigned
8	**echo**	Echo request
9	**router-advertisement**	Router advertisement
10	**router-solicitation**	Router solicitation
11	**time-exceeded**	Time exceeded
12	**parameter-problem**	Parameter problem
13	**timestamp-request**	Timestamp request
14	**timestamp-reply**	Timestamp reply
15	**information-request**	Information request
16	**information-reply**	Information reply
17	**mask-request**	Address mask request

continues

Table A-2 *Well-Known ICMP Message Types (Continued)*

ICMP MessageType	Firewall Keyword	ICMP Message Description
18	**mask-reply**	Address mask reply
19	—	Reserved (for security)
20–29	—	Reserved (for robustness experiment)
30	**traceroute**	Traceroute
31	**conversion-error**	Conversion error
32	**mobile-redirect**	Mobile host redirect
33	—	IPv6 Where-Are-You
34	—	IPv6 I-Am-Here
35	—	Mobile registration request
36	—	Mobile registration reply
37	—	Domain name request
38	—	Domain name reply
39	—	SKIP algorithm discovery protocol
40	—	Photuris, security failures
41–255	—	Reserved

A-3: IP Port Numbers

Transport layer protocols identify higher-layer traffic with 16-bit fields called *port* numbers. A connection between two devices uses a source port and a destination port, both contained in the protocol data unit. Figure A-3 shows the User Datagram Protocol (UDP) header format, with the source and destination port fields shaded. Figure A-4 shows the Transmission Control Protocol (TCP) header format, with the source and destination port fields shaded.

Figure A-3 *UDP Datagram Format Showing Port Fields*

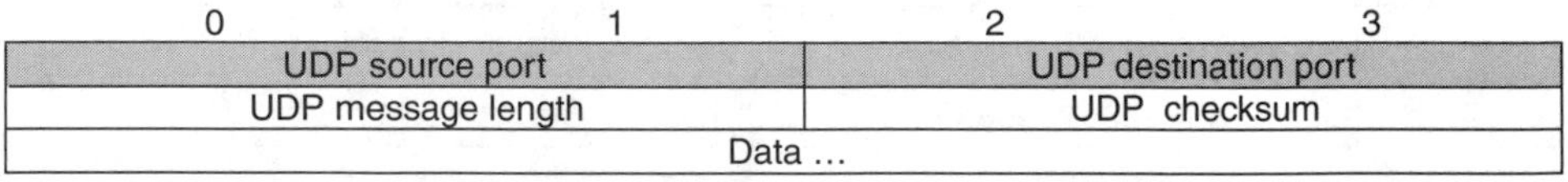

0	1	2	3
UDP source port		UDP destination port	
UDP message length		UDP checksum	
Data ...			

Figure A-4 *TCP Segment Format Showing Port Fields*

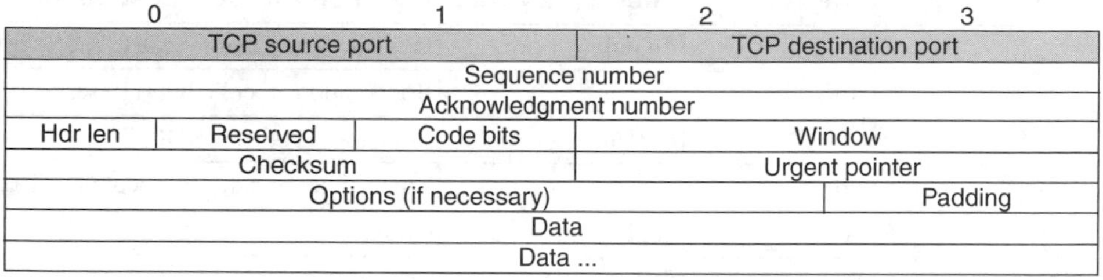

0	1	2	3
\multicolumn{2}{TCP source port}		\multicolumn{2}{TCP destination port}	

0		1		2		3
TCP source port			TCP destination port			
Sequence number						
Acknowledgment number						
Hdr len	Reserved	Code bits		Window		
Checksum			Urgent pointer			
Options (if necessary)				Padding		
Data						
Data ...						

Both UDP and TCP use port numbers that are divided into the following ranges:

- Well-known port numbers (0 through 1023)
- Registered port numbers (1024 through 49151)
- Dynamic or private port numbers (49152 through 65535)

Usually, a port assignment uses a common port number for both UDP and TCP. A connection from a client to a server uses the well-known port on the server as a *service contact port*, while the client is free to dynamically assign its own port number. For TCP, the connection is identified by the source and destination IP addresses, as well as the source and destination TCP port numbers.

Cisco firewalls have keywords that can be used to specify certain IP ports in access lists. Table A-3 shows these keywords, along with the IP port numbers.

Table A-3 *Cisco Firewall Keywords for IP Ports*

Port	UDP	TCP	Firewall Keyword	UDP/TCP Protocol Description
7	Yes	Yes	**echo**	Echo
9	Yes	Yes	**discard**	Discard
13	No	Yes	**daytime**	Day time, RFC 867
19	No	Yes	**chargen**	Character generator
20	No	Yes	**ftp-data**	File Transfer Protocol (FTP), data port
21	No	Yes	**ftp**	File Transfer Protocol (FTP), control port
22	No	Yes	**ssh**	Secure Shell (SSH)
23	No	Yes	**telnet**	Telnet, RFC 854
25	No	Yes	**smtp**	Simple Mail Transport Protocol (SMTP)
37	Yes	No	**time**	Time protocol
42	Yes	No	**nameserver**	Host Name Server
43	No	Yes	**whois**	Who Is
49	Yes	Yes	**tacacs**	Terminal Access Controller Access Control System Plus (TACACS+)

continues

Table A-3 *Cisco Firewall Keywords for IP Ports (Continued)*

Port	UDP	TCP	Firewall Keyword	UDP/TCP Protocol Description
53	Yes	Yes	**domain**	Domain Name System (DNS)
67	Yes	No	**bootps**	Bootstrap Protocol (BOOTP) server
68	Yes	No	**bootpc**	Bootstrap Protocol (BOOTP) client
69	Yes	No	**tftp**	Trivial File Transfer Protocol (TFTP)
70	No	Yes	**gopher**	Gopher
79	No	Yes	**finger**	Finger
80	Yes	Yes	**www** **htttp**	Hypertext Transfer Protocol (HTTP)
101	No	Yes	**hostname**	Host name server
109	No	Yes	**pop2**	Post Office Protocol (POP), version 2
110	No	Yes	**pop3**	Post Office Protocol (POP), version 3
111	Yes	Yes	**sunrpc (rpc)**	Sun Remote Procedure Call (RPC)
113	No	Yes	**ident**	Ident authentication service
119	No	Yes	**nntp**	Network News Transfer Protocol (NNTP)
123	Yes	No	**ntp**	Network Time Protocol (NTP)
137	Yes	No	**netbios-ns**	NetBIOS Name Service
138	Yes	No	**netbios-dgm**	NetBIOS Datagram Service
139	No	Yes	**netbios-ssn**	NetBIOS Session Service
143	No	Yes	**imap4**	Internet Message Access Protocol (IMAP), version 4
161	Yes	No	**snmp**	Simple Network Management Protocol (SNMP)
162	Yes	No	**snmptrap**	Simple Network Management Protocol (SNMP) trap
177	Yes	No	**xdmcp**	X Display Manager Control Protocol (XDMCP)
179	No	Yes	**bgp**	Border Gateway Protocol (BGP)
194	No	Yes	**irc**	Internet Relay Chat (IRC) protocol
195	Yes	No	**dnsix**	DNSIX Session Management Module Audit Redirector
389	No	Yes	**ldap**	Lightweight Directory Access Protocol (LDAP)
434	Yes	No	**mobile-ip**	MobileIP-Agent
443	No	Yes	**https**	Hypertext Transfer Protocol over SSL/TLS

Table A-3 *Cisco Firewall Keywords for IP Ports (Continued)*

Port	UDP	TCP	Firewall Keyword	UDP/TCP Protocol Description
445	Yes	Yes	cifs	Microsoft Common Internet File System (CIFS)
496	Yes	Yes	pim-auto-rp	Protocol-Independent Multicast (PIM) autodiscovery
500	Yes	No	isakmp	Internet Security Association and Key Management Protocol (ISAKMP; UDP only)
512	Yes	No	biff	New mail notification for UNIX-based mail systems
512	No	Yes	exec	Remote process execution
513	No	Yes	login	Remote login
513	Yes	No	who	Who
514	No	Yes	cmd	Remote process execution with automatic authentication
514	Yes	No	syslog	System log
515	No	Yes	lpd	Line Printer Daemon (LPD)
517	Yes	Yes	talk	Talk
520	Yes	No	rip	Routing Information Protocol (RIP)
540	No	Yes	uucp	UNIX-to-UNIX Copy Program (UUCP)
543	No	Yes	klogin	KLOGIN
544	No	Yes	kshell	Korn Shell
636	No	Yes	ldaps	Lightweight Directory Access Protocol (LDAP) over SSL/TLS
750	Yes	Yes	kerberos	Kerberos
1352	No	Yes	lotusnotes	IBM Lotus Notes
1494	No	Yes	citrix-ica	Citrix Independent Computing Architecture (ICA)
1521	No	Yes	sqlnet	Structured Query Language (SQL) Network
1645	Yes	No	radius	Remote Authentication Dial-In User Service (RADIUS) authentication; obsolete; moved to 1812
1646	Yes	No	radius-acct	Remote Authentication Dial-In User Service (RADIUS) accounting; obsolete; moved to 1813
1720	No	Yes	h323	H.323 call signaling
1723	No	Yes	pptp	Point-to-Point Tunneling Protocol (PPTP)

Table A-3   *Cisco Firewall Keywords for IP Ports (Continued)*

Port	UDP	TCP	Firewall Keyword	UDP/TCP Protocol Description
2049	Yes	Yes	**nfs**	Network File System (NFS)
2748	No	Yes	**ctiqbe**	Computer Telephony Interface Quick Buffer Encoding (CTIQBE)
5060	Yes	Yes	**sip**	Session Initiation Protocol (SIP)
5190	No	Yes	**aol**	America Online (AOL)
5510	Yes	No	**secureid-udp**	SecureID over UDP
5631	No	Yes	**pcanywhere-data**	pcAnywhere data
5632	Yes	No	**pcanywhere-status**	pcAnywhere status

Security Appliance Logging Messages

This appendix covers all the possible messages a firewall can generate. It can serve as a quick reference so that you can look up messages that are associated with the different severity levels.

Cisco firewall logging messages are listed in this section grouped according to their default severity level (1 to 7):

- **1**—Alerts
- **2**—Critical messages
- **3**—Errors
- **4**—Warnings
- **5**—Notifications
- **6**—Informational messages
- **7**—Debugging messages

Severity level 0, Emergencies, exists but is never used by Cisco firewalls. Historically, these messages have been associated with UNIX systems and are sent only when a system is unstable and can no longer operate properly. That extreme condition is not applicable with a firewall platform.

All syslog messages have a default severity level, which is listed in the following tables. You can reassign each message to a new severity level if needed.

The logging messages listed here are based on FWSM, ASA, and PIX platforms.

You can use the information presented in this appendix when you want to choose a severity level for a logging destination. Make sure the level you choose will generate the messages you need to see.

> **NOTE** When you choose a severity level, remember that logging messages from that level and all lower-numbered levels are sent. Only the messages from a higher-numbered level are not sent.

Figure B-1 shows each of the logging severity levels, along with a general list of the types of messages generated. Notice that each level also includes every level below it. The higher the severity level, the more types of messages that are included.

Figure B-1   *Syslog Severity Levels and Their Messages*

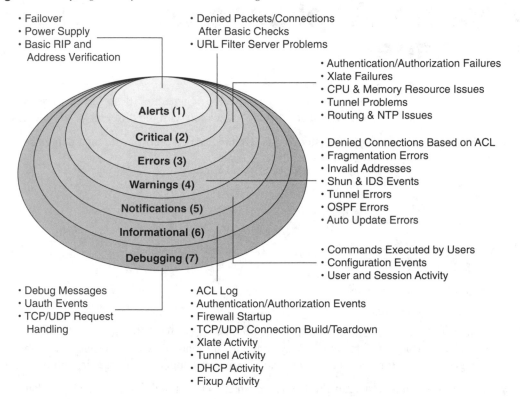

NOTE   In the tables in this appendix, the six-digit logging messages are listed in numerical order. When a firewall generates a logging message, it adds a prefix that usually indicates its hardware platform. For example, **%PIX** denotes the PIX Security Appliance platform, **%FWSM** denotes the Firewall Service Module (FWSM), and **%ASA** denotes the Adaptive Security Appliance (ASA).

For the purpose of this book, where all firewall platforms are covered, the messages are simply shown with a **%ASA** prefix.

B-1: Alerts—Syslog Severity Level 1 Messages

Table B-1 lists all the severity level 1 logging messages, along with their message numbers and text. All the messages supported by FWSM, ASA, and PIX are shown.

Table B-1 *Severity 1 (Alerts) Logging Messages*

Level and Message Number	Message Text
%ASA-1-101001	(Primary) Failover cable OK.
%ASA-1-101002	(Primary) Bad failover cable.
%ASA-1-101003	(Primary) Failover cable not connected (this unit).
%ASA-1-101004	(Primary) Failover cable not connected (other unit).
%ASA-1-101005	(Primary) Error reading failover cable status.
%ASA-1-102001	(Primary) Power failure/system reload other side.
%ASA-1-103001	(Primary) No response from other firewall (reason code = *code*).
%ASA-1-103002	(Primary) Other firewall network interface *interface_number* OK.
%ASA-1-103003	(Primary) Other firewall network interface *interface_number* failed.
%ASA-1-103004	(Primary) Other firewall reports this firewall failed.
%ASA-1-103005	(Primary) Other firewall reporting failure.
%ASA-1-103006	(Primary/Secondary) Mate version is not compatible with ours.
%ASA-1-103007	(Primary/Secondary) Mate version is not identical with ours.
%ASA-1-103011	Unknown message text.
%ASA-1-104001	(Primary) Switching to ACTIVE (cause: *string*).
%ASA-1-104002	(Primary) Switching to STNDBY (cause: *string*).
%ASA-1-104003	(Primary) Switching to FAILED.
%ASA-1-104004	(Primary) Switching to OK.
%ASA-1-105001	(Primary) Disabling failover.
%ASA-1-105002	(Primary) Enabling failover.
%ASA-1-105003	(Primary) Monitoring on interface *interface_name* waiting.
%ASA-1-105004	(Primary) Monitoring on interface *interface_name* normal.
%ASA-1-105005	(Primary) Lost failover communications with mate on interface *interface_name*.
%ASA-1-105006	(Primary) Link status 'Up' on interface *interface_name*.
%ASA-1-105007	(Primary) Link status 'Down' on interface *interface_name*.
%ASA-1-105008	(Primary) Testing interface *interface_name*.
%ASA-1-105009	(Primary) Testing on interface *interface_name* {Passed	Failed}.

continues

Table B-1 *Severity 1 (Alerts) Logging Messages (Continued)*

Level and Message Number	Message Text
%ASA-1-105011	(Primary) Failover cable communication failure.
%ASA-1-105020	(Primary) Incomplete/slow config replication.
%ASA-1-105021	(Failover unit) Standby unit failed to sync due to a locked context config.
%ASA-1-105031	Failover LAN interface is up.
%ASA-1-105032	LAN failover interface is down.
%ASA-1-105033	Unknown message text.
%ASA-1-105034	Receive a LAN_FAILOVER_UP message from peer.
%ASA-1-105035	Receive a LAN failover interface down message from a peer.
%ASA-1-105036	PIX dropped a LAN failover command message.
%ASA-1-105037	The primary and standby units are switching back and forth as the active unit.
%ASA-1-105038	(Primary) Interface count mismatch.
%ASA-1-105039	(Primary) Unable to verify the interface count with mate. Failover may be disabled in mate.
%ASA-1-105040	(Primary) Mate failover version is not compatible.
%ASA-1-105041	Unknown message text.
%ASA-1-105042	(Primary) Failover interface OK.
%ASA-1-105043	(Primary) Failover interface failed.
%ASA-1-105044	(Primary) Mate operational mode *mode* is not compatible with my mode *mode*.
%ASA-1-105045	Primary) Mate license (*number* contexts) is not compatible with my license (*number* contexts).
%ASA-1-105046	(Primary | Secondary) Mate has a different chassis.
%ASA-1-105047	Mate has an *io_card_name1* card in slot *slot_number* that is different from my *io_card_name2*.
%ASA-1-105048	Unknown message text.
%ASA-1-106004	Unknown message text.
%ASA-1-106005	Unknown message text.
%ASA-1-106008	Unknown message text.
%ASA-1-106021	Deny protocol reverse path check from *source_address* to *dest_address* on interface *interface_name*.
%ASA-1-106022	Deny protocol connection spoof from *source_address* to *dest_address* on interface *interface_name*.
%ASA-1-106101	The number of ACL log deny-flows has reached limit (*number*).

Table B-1   *Severity 1 (Alerts) Logging Messages (Continued)*

Level and Message Number	Message Text
%ASA-1-107001	RIP auth failed from *IP_address*.
%ASA-1-107002	RIP pkt failed from *IP_address*.
%ASA-1-108001	Unknown message text.
%ASA-1-109004	Unknown message text.
%ASA-1-111002	Begin configuration: *IP_address* writing to *device*.
%ASA-1-111111	*error_message*. (System or infrastructure error has occurred)
%ASA-1-415001	:*internal_sig_id* HTTP Tunnel detected—*action tunnel_type* from *src_ip* to *dest_ip*.
%ASA-1-415002	:*internal_sig_id* HTTP Instant Messenger detected—*action instant_messenger_type* from *src_ip* to *dest_ip*.
%ASA-1-415003	:*internal_sig_id* HTTP Peer-to-Peer detected—*action instant_messenger_type* from *src_ip* to *dest_ip*.
%ASA-1-415004	:*internal_sig_id* Content type not found—*action* Content Verification Failed from *src_ip* to *dest_ip*.
%ASA-1-415006	:*internal_sig_id* Content size *size* out of range—*action mime_type* from *src_ip* to *dest_ip*.
%ASA-1-415007	:*internal_sig_id* HTTP Extension method illegal—*action* '*method_name*' from *src_ip* to *dest_ip*.
%ASA-1-415008	:*internal_sig_id* HTTP RFC method illegal—*action* '*method_name*' from *src_ip* to *dest_ip*.
%ASA-1-415009	:*internal_sig_id* HTTP Header length exceeded. Received *length* byte Header—*action* header length exceeded from *src_ip* to *dest_ip*.
%ASA-1-415010	:*internal_sig_id* HTTP protocol violation detected—*action* HTTP Protocol not detected from *src_ip* to *dest_ip*.
%ASA-1-415011	:*internal_sig_id* HTTP URL Length exceeded. Received *size* byte URL—*action* URL length exceeded from *src_ip* to *dest_ip*.
%ASA-1-415012	:*internal_sig_id* HTTP Deobfuscation signature detected—*action* HTTP deobfuscation detected IDS evasion technique from *src_ip* to *src_ip*.
%ASA-1-415013	:*internal_sig_id* HTTP Transfer encoding violation detected—*action Xfer_encode* Transfer encoding not allowed from *src_ip* to *dest_ip*.
%ASA-1-415014	:*internal_sig_id* Maximum of 10 unanswered HTTP requests exceeded from *src_ip* to *dest_ip*.
%ASA-1-709003	(Primary) Beginning configuration replication—Receiving from mate.
%ASA-1-709004	(Primary) End Configuration Replication (ACT).
%ASA-1-709005	(Primary) Beginning configuration replication—Receiving from mate.

continues

Table B-1 *Severity 1 (Alerts) Logging Messages (Continued)*

Level and Message Number	Message Text
%ASA-1-709006	(Primary) End Configuration Replication (STB).
%ASA-1-713900	*Descriptive_event_string*. (A message with several possible text strings describing a serious event or failure)
%ASA-1-715039	Unexpected cleanup of tunnel table entry during SA delete.

B-2: Critical—Syslog Severity Level 2 Messages

Table B-2 lists all the severity level 2 logging messages, along with their message numbers and text. All the messages supported by FWSM, ASA, and PIX are shown.

Table B-2 *Severity 2 (Critical) Logging Messages*

Level and Message Number	Message Text
%ASA-2-106001	Inbound TCP connection denied from *IP_address/port* to *IP_address/port* flags *tcp_flags* on interface *interface_name*.
%ASA-2-106002	Protocol connection denied by outbound list *acl_ID* src *inside_address* dest *outside_address*.
%ASA-2-106006	Deny inbound UDP from *outside_address/outside_port* to *inside_address/inside_port* on interface *interface_name*.
%ASA-2-106007	Deny inbound UDP from *outside_address/outside_port* to *inside_address/inside_port* due to DNS {Response | Query}.
%ASA-2-106012	Deny IP from *IP_address* to *IP_address*, IP options hex.
%ASA-2-106013	Dropping echo request from *IP_address* to PAT address *IP_address*.
%ASA-2-106016	Deny IP spoof from (*IP_address*) to *IP_address* on interface *interface_name*.
%ASA-2-106017	Deny IP due to Land Attack from *IP_address* to *IP_address*.
%ASA-2-106018	ICMP packet type *ICMP_type* denied by outbound list *acl_ID* src *inside_address* dest *outside_address*.
%ASA-2-106020	Deny IP teardrop fragment (size = *number*, offset = *number*) from *IP_address* to *IP_address*.
%ASA-2-106024	Access rules memory exhausted.
%ASA-2-108002	SMTP replaced string: out *source_address* in *inside_address* data: *string*.
%ASA-2-108003	Terminating ESMTP/SMTP connection; malicious pattern detected in the mail address.
%ASA-2-109011	Authen Session Start: user '*user*', sid *number*.

Table B-2   *Severity 2 (Critical) Logging Messages (Continued)*

Level and Message Number	Message Text
%ASA-2-112001	(string: dec) PIX Clear complete.
%ASA-2-201003	Embryonic limit exceeded nconns/elimit for *outside_address/outside_port* (*global_address*) *inside_address/inside_port* on interface *interface_name*.
%ASA-2-204001	Unknown message text.
%ASA-2-204002	Unknown message text.
%ASA-2-211002	Unknown message text.
%ASA-2-214001	Terminating manager session from *IP_address* on interface *interface_name*. Reason: incoming encrypted data (*number* bytes) longer than *number* bytes.
%ASA-2-215001	Bad route_compress() call, sdb= *number*.
%ASA-2-217001	No memory for string in string.
%ASA-2-304007	URL Server IP_address not responding, ENTERING ALLOW mode.
%ASA-2-304008	LEAVING ALLOW mode, URL Server is up.
%ASA-2-304009	Ran out of buffer blocks specified by url-block command.
%ASA-2-316001	Denied new tunnel to *IP_address*. VPN peer limit (*platform_vpn_peer_limit*) exceeded.
%ASA-2-709007	Configuration replication failed for command *command*.
%ASA-2-709008	Configuration may be out of sync between Active Standby units.
%ASA-2-713078	Temp buffer for building mode config attributes exceeded: bufsize *available size*, used *value*.
%ASA-2-713175	Unknown message text.
%ASA-2-713176	*Device_type* memory resources are critical, IKE key acquire message on interface *interface_number*, for Peer *IP_address* ignored.
%ASA-2-713183	Unknown message text.
%ASA-2-713187	Tunnel Rejected: IKE peer does not match remote peer as defined in L2L policy IKE peer address: *IP_address*, Remote peer address: *IP_address*.
%ASA-2-713901	*Descriptive_event_string*. (This might be the result of a configuration error on the headend or remote-access client.)
%ASA-2-717008	Insufficient memory to *process_requiring_memory*.
%ASA-2-717011	Unexpected event.

B-3: Errors—Syslog Severity Level 3 Messages

Table B-3 lists all the severity level 3 logging messages, along with their message numbers and text. All the messages supported by FWSM, ASA, and PIX are shown.

Table B-3 *Severity 3 (Errors) Logging Messages*

Level and Message Number	Message Text
%ASA-3-105010	(Primary) Failover message block alloc failed.
%ASA-3-106010	Deny inbound protocol src *interface_name*: *dest_address*/*dest_port* dst *interface_name*: *source_address*/*source_port*.
%ASA-3-106011	Deny inbound (no xlate) string.
%ASA-3-106014	Deny inbound icmp src *interface_name*: *IP_address* dst *interface_name*: *IP_address* (type dec, code dec).
%ASA-3-108003	Terminating ESMTP/SMTP connection; malicious pattern detected in the mail address from *src_ifc*:*src_ip*/*src_port* to *dst_ifc*:*dst_ip*/*dst_port*. Data:*string*.
%ASA-3-109010	Auth from *inside_address*/*inside_port* to *outside_address*/*outside_port* failed (too many pending auths) on interface *interface_name*.
%ASA-3-109013	User must authenticate before using this service.
%ASA-3-109016	Cannot find authorization ACL *acl_ID* on 'PIX' for user '*user*'.
%ASA-3-109018	Downloaded ACL *acl_ID* is empty.
%ASA-3-109019	Downloaded ACL *acl_ID* has parsing error; ACE string.
%ASA-3-109020	Downloaded ACL has config error; ACE.
%ASA-3-109023	User from *src_IP_address*/*src_port* to *dest_IP_address*/*dest_port* on interface outside must authenticate before using this service.
%ASA-3-109026	[aaa protocol] Invalid reply digest received, shared server key may be mismatched.
%ASA-3-109032	Unable to install ACL, downloaded for user, Error in ACE.
%ASA-3-113001	Unable to open AAA session. Session limit [*limit*] reached.
%ASA-3-113018	User: unsupported downloaded ACL Entry.
%ASA-3-201002	Too many connections on {static l xlate} *global_address*! econns nconns.
%ASA-3-201004	Too many UDP connections on {static l xlate} *global_address*! *udp conn limit*.
%ASA-3-201005	FTP data connection failed for *IP_address*.
%ASA-3-201006	RCMD backconnection failed for *IP_address*/*port*.
%ASA-3-201008	The PIX is disallowing new connections.
%ASA-3-201009	TCP connection limit of *number* for host *IP_address* on *interface_name* exceeded.

Table B-3 *Severity 3 (Errors) Logging Messages (Continued)*

Level and Message Number	Message Text
%ASA-3-201011	Connection limit exceeded *cnt/limit* for *dir* packet from *sip/sport* to *dip/dport* on interface *if_name*.
%ASA-3-202001	Out of address translation slots!
%ASA-3-202005	Nonembryonic in embryonic list *outside_address/outside_port inside_address/ inside_port*.
%ASA-3-202011	Connection limit exceeded for air packet from source_address.
%ASA-3-208005	(function: line_num) pix clear command return code.
%ASA-3-210001	LU SW_Module_Name error = *number*.
%ASA-3-210002	LU allocate block (bytes) failed.
%ASA-3-210003	Unknown LU Object number.
%ASA-3-210005	LU allocate connection failed.
%ASA-3-210006	LU look NAT for *IP_address* failed.
%ASA-3-210007	LU allocate xlate failed.
%ASA-3-210008	LU no xlate for *inside_address/inside_port outside_address/outside_port*.
%ASA-3-210010	LU make UDP connection for *outside_address: outside_port inside_address: inside_port* failed.
%ASA-3-210020	LU PAT port reserve failed.
%ASA-3-210021	LU create static xlate *global_address* ifc *interface_name* failed.
%ASA-3-211001	Memory allocation error.
%ASA-3-211003	CPU utilization for *number* seconds = *percent*.
%ASA-3-212001	Unable to open SNMP channel (UDP port *port*) on interface *interface_number*, error code = *code*.
%ASA-3-212002	Unable to open SNMP trap channel (UDP port *port*) on interface *interface_number*, error code = *code*.
%ASA-3-212003	Unable to receive an SNMP request on interface *interface_number*, error code = *code*, will try again.
%ASA-3-212004	Unable to send an SNMP response to IP address *IP_address* port *port* interface *interface_number*, error code = *code*.
%ASA-3-212005	Incoming SNMP request (*number* bytes) on interface *interface_name* exceeds data buffer size, discarding this SNMP request.
%ASA-3-212006	Dropping SNMP request from *src_ip/src_port* to *ifc_name:dst_ip/dst_port* because: *reason*.

continues

Section B-3

Table B-3 *Severity 3 (Errors) Logging Messages (Continued)*

Level and Message Number	Message Text
%ASA-3-213001	PPTP control daemon socket io string, errno = *number*.
%ASA-3-213002	PPTP tunnel hashtable insert failed, peer = *IP_address*.
%ASA-3-213003	PPP virtual interface *interface_number* is not opened.
%ASA-3-213004	PPP virtual interface *interface_number* client ip allocation failed.
%ASA-3-216001	Unknown message text.
%ASA-3-217001	No memory for *string* in *string*.
%ASA-3-302007	Unknown message text.
%ASA-3-302008	Unknown message text.
%ASA-3-302019	H.323 *library_name* ASN Library failed to initialize, error code *number*.
%ASA-3-302302	ACL = deny; no sa created.
%ASA-3-303001	Unknown message text.
%ASA-3-304003	URL server *IP_address* timed out URL *url*.
%ASA-3-304006	URL server *IP_address* not responding.
%ASA-3-305005	No translation group found for protocol src *interface_name*: *dest_address/dest_port* dst *interface_name*: *source_address/source_port*.
%ASA-3-305006	Regular translation creation failed for protocol src *interface_name*: *source_address/source_port* dst *interface_name*: *dest_address/dest_port*.
%ASA-3-305008	Free unallocated global IP address.
%ASA-3-306001	Unknown message text.
%FWSM-3-309001	Denied manager connection from *IP_address*.
%ASA-3-310001	Unknown message text.
%ASA-3-311005	Unknown message text.
%ASA-3-313001	Denied ICMP type=*number*, code=*code* from *IP_address* on interface *interface_name*.
%ASA-3-313002	Unknown message text.
%FWSM-3-315001	Denied SSH session from *IP_address* on interface *interface_name*.
%ASA-3-315004	Fail to establish SSH session because PIX RSA host key retrieval failed.
%ASA-3-316001	Denied new tunnel to *IP_address*. VPN peer limit (*platform_vpn_peer_limit*) exceeded.
%ASA-3-317001	No memory available for *limit_slow*.
%ASA-3-317002	Bad path index of number for *IP_address*, number *max*.

Table B-3 *Severity 3 (Errors) Logging Messages (Continued)*

Level and Message Number	Message Text
%ASA-3-317003	IP routing table creation failure—*reason*.
%ASA-3-317004	IP routing table limit warning.
%ASA-3-317005	IP routing table limit exceeded—*reason*, *IP_address netmask*.
%ASA-3-318001	Internal error: *reason*.
%ASA-3-318002	Flagged as being an ABR without a backbone area.
%ASA-3-318003	Reached unknown state in neighbor state machine.
%ASA-3-318004	Area string lsid *IP_address* mask *netmask* adv *IP_address* type *number*.
%ASA-3-318005	lsid *IP_address* adv *IP_address* type *number* gateway *gateway_address* metric *number* network *IP_address* mask *netmask* protocol *hex* attr *hex* net-metric *number*.
%ASA-3-318006	if *interface_name if_state number*.
%ASA-3-318007	OSPF is enabled on *interface_name* during idb initialization.
%ASA-3-318008	OSPF process number is changing router-id. Reconfigure virtual link neighbors with our new router-id.
%ASA-3-319001	Acknowledge for arp update for IP address *dest_addr* not received (*number*).
%ASA-3-319002	Acknowledge for route update for IP address *dest_addr* not received (*number*).
%ASA-3-319003	ARP update for IP address *address* to NP*n* failed.
%ASA-3-319004	Route update for IP address *dest_addr* failed (*number*).
%ASA-3-320001	The subject name of the peer cert is not allowed for connection.
%ASA-3-322001	Deny MAC address *mac-address*, possible spoof attempt on interface *interface*.
%ASA-3-322002	ARP inspection check failed for arp {request I response} received from host *mac-address* on interface *interface*. This host is advertising MAC address *mac-address-1* for IP address *ip-address*, which is {statically I dynamically} bound to MAC address *mac-address-2*.
%ASA-3-322003	ARP inspection check failed for arp {request I response} received from host *mac-address* on interface *interface*. This host is advertising MAC address *mac-address-1* for IP address *ip-address*, which is not bound to any MAC address.
%ASA-3-323001	Module in slot *slotnum* experienced a control channel communication failure.
%ASA-3-323002	Module in slot *slotnum* is not able to shut down, shut down request not answered.
%ASA-3-323003	Module in slot *slotnum* is not able to reload, reload request not answered.
%ASA-3-324000	Drop GTPv *version* message *msg_type* from *src_ifc*:*src_ip*/*src_port* to *dest_ifc*:*dest_ip*/*dest_port* Reason: *reason*.

continues

Table B-3 *Severity 3 (Errors) Logging Messages (Continued)*

Level and Message Number	Message Text
%ASA-3-324001	GTPv0 packet parsing error from *src_ifc*:*src_ip*/*src_port* to *dest_ifc*:*dest_ip*/*dest_port*, TID: *tid_value*, Reason: *reason*.
%ASA-3-324002	No PDP[MCB] exists to process GTPv0 *msg_type* from *src_ifc*:*src_ip*/*src_port* to *dest_ifc*:*dest_ip*/*dest_port*, TID: *tid_value*.
%ASA-3-324003	No matching request to process GTPv *version msg_type* from *src_ifc*:*src_ip*/*src_port* to *dest_ifc*:*dest_ip*/*dest_port*.
%ASA-3-324004	GTP packet with version %d from *src_ifc*:*src_ip*/*src_port* to *dest_ifc*:*dest_ip*/*dest_port* is not supported.
%ASA-3-324005	Unable to create tunnel from *src_ifc*:*src_ip*/*src_port* to *dest_ifc*:*dest_ip*/*dest_port*.
%ASA-3-324006	GSN *ip_address* tunnel limit *tunnel_limit* exceeded, PDP Context TID *tid* failed.
%ASA-3-324007	Unable to create GTP connection for response from *src_ifc*:*src_ip*/0 to *dest_ifc*:*dest_ip*/*dest_port*.
%ASA-3-325001	Router *ipv6_address* on *interface* has conflicting ND (Neighbor Discovery) settings.
%ASA-3-326001	Unexpected error in the timer library: *error_message*.
%ASA-3-326002	Error in *error_message* : *error_message*. (IGMP process)
%ASA-3-326003	Unknown message text.
%ASA-3-326004	An internal error occurred while processing a packet queue. (IGMP)
%ASA-3-326005	MRIB notification failed for (*addr*,*addr*).
%ASA-3-326006	Entry-creation failed for (*addr*,*addr*).
%ASA-3-326007	Entry-update failed for (*addr*,*addr*).
%ASA-3-326008	MRIB registration failed.
%ASA-3-326009	MRIB connection-open failed.
%ASA-3-326010	MRIB unbind failed.
%ASA-3-326011	MRIB table deletion failed.
%ASA-3-326012	Initialization of *string* functionality failed.
%ASA-3-326013	Internal error: *string* in *string* line %d (%s).
%ASA-3-326014	Initialization failed: *error_message error_message*.
%ASA-3-326015	Communication error: *error_message error_message*.
%ASA-3-326016	Failed to set un-numbered interface for *ifname*.
%ASA-3-326017	Interface Manager error—*string* in *string* : *string*.
%ASA-3-326018	Unknown message text.

Table B-3   *Severity 3 (Errors) Logging Messages (Continued)*

Level and Message Number	Message Text
%ASA-3-326019	*string* in *string* : *string*. (PIM)
%ASA-3-326020	List error in *string* : *string*. (PIM)
%ASA-3-326021	Error in *string* : *string*. (PIM)
%ASA-3-326022	Error in *string* : *string*. (PIM)
%ASA-3-326023	*string—addr* : *string*. (PIM)
%ASA-3-326024	An internal error occurred while processing a packet queue.
%ASA-3-326025	*string*. (PIM)
%ASA-3-326026	Server unexpected error: *error_messsage*.
%ASA-3-326027	Corrupted update: *error_messsage*.
%ASA-3-326028	Asynchronous error: *error_messsage*.
%ASA-3-326029	Unknown message text.
%ASA-3-403501	PPPoE—Bad host-unique in PADO—packet dropped. Intf: *interface_name* AC: *ac_name*.
%ASA-3-403502	PPPoE—Bad host-unique in PADS—dropping packet. Intf: *interface_name* AC: *ac_name*.
%ASA-3-403503	PPPoE: PPP link down: *reason*.
%ASA-3-403504	PPPoE: No 'vpdn group' for PPPoE is created.
%ASA-3-403505	PPPoE: PPP—Unable to set default route to *IP_address* at *interface_name*.
%ASA-3-403506	PPPoE: Failed to assign PPP *IP_address* netmask *netmask* at *interface_name*.
%ASA-3-404102	ISAKMP: Exceeded embryonic limit.
%ASA-3-407002	Embryonic limit neconns/elimit for through connections exceeded. *outside_address/outside_port* to *global_address* (*inside_address*)/*inside_port* on interface *interface_name*.
%ASA-3-414001	Failed to save logging buffer using file name *file_name* to FTP server *ftp_server_ip* on interface *interface_name*: [*fail_reason*].
%ASA-3-414002	Failed to save logging buffer to flash:/syslog directory using file name: *filename*: [*fail_reason*].
%FWSM-3-605001	HTTP daemon interface *interface_name*: Connection denied from *IP_address*.
%ASA-3-610001	NTP daemon interface *interface_name*: Packet denied from *IP_address*.
%ASA-3-610002	NTP daemon interface *interface_name*: Authentication failed for packet from *IP_address*.
%ASA-3-611313	VPNClient: Backup Server List Error: *reason*.

continues

Table B-3 *Severity 3 (Errors) Logging Messages (Continued)*

Level and Message Number	Message Text
%ASA-3-620002	Unsupported CTIQBE version: *hex*: from *interface_name:IP_address/port* to *interface_name:IP_address/port*.
%ASA-3-702302	Replay rollover detected.
%ASA-3-710003	{TCP | UDP} access denied by ACL from *source_address/source_port* to *interface_name*: *dest_address/service*.
%ASA-3-713002	Unknown message text.
%ASA-3-713003	Unknown message text.
%ASA-3-713004	*Device* scheduled for reboot or shutdown, IKE key acquire message on interface *interface num*, for Peer *address* ignored.
%ASA-3-713008	Key ID in ID payload too big for pre-shared IKE tunnel.
%ASA-3-713009	OU in DN in ID payload too big for Certs IKE tunnel.
%ASA-3-713011	Unknown message text.
%ASA-3-713012	Unknown protocol (*protocol*). Not adding SA w/spi=*SPI value*.
%ASA-3-713013	Unknown message text.
%ASA-3-713014	Unknown Domain of Interpretation (DOI): *DOI value*.
%ASA-3-713015	Unknown message text.
%ASA-3-713016	Unknown identification type, Phase *1 or 2*, Type *ID Type*.
%ASA-3-713017	Identification type not supported, Phase *1 or 2*, Type *ID Type*.
%ASA-3-713018	Unknown ID type during find of group name for certs, Type *ID Type*.
%ASA-3-713019	Unknown message text.
%ASA-3-713020	No Group found by matching OU(s) from ID payload: *OU value*.
%ASA-3-713021	Unknown message text.
%ASA-3-713022	No group found matching *peer ID or address* for pre-shared key peer *address of peer*.
%ASA-3-713032	Received invalid local Proxy Range *IP address-IP address*.
%ASA-3-713033	Received invalid remote Proxy Range *IP address-IP address*.
%ASA-3-713042	IKE Initiator unable to find policy: Intf *interface number*, Src: *IP address*, Dst: *IP address*.
%ASA-3-713043	Cookie/peer address *IP address* session already in progress.
%ASA-3-713046	Unknown message text.
%ASA-3-713047	Unsupported Oakley group: Group *Diffie-Hellman group*.

Table B-3 *Severity 3 (Errors) Logging Messages (Continued)*

Level and Message Number	Message Text
%ASA-3-713048	Error processing payload: Payload ID: *id*.
%ASA-3-713051	Terminating connection attempt: IPSEC not permitted for group (*group name*).
%ASA-3-713053	Unknown message text.
%ASA-3-713054	Unknown message text.
%ASA-3-713055	Unknown message text.
%ASA-3-713056	Tunnel rejected: SA (*SA name*) not found for group (*group name*)!
%ASA-3-713057	Unknown message text.
%ASA-3-713058	Unknown message text.
%ASA-3-713059	Tunnel Rejected: User (*username*) matched with group name, group-lock check failed.
%ASA-3-713060	Tunnel Rejected: User (*username*) not member of group (*group name*), group-lock check failed.
%ASA-3-713061	Tunnel rejected: Crypto Map Policy not found for Src: *IP address*, Dst: *IP address*!
%ASA-3-713062	IKE Peer address same as our interface address *IP address*.
%ASA-3-713063	IKE Peer address not configured for destination *IP address*.
%ASA-3-713064	Unknown message text.
%ASA-3-713065	IKE Remote Peer did not negotiate the following: *proposal attribute*.
%ASA-3-713069	Unknown message text.
%ASA-3-713070	Unknown message text.
%ASA-3-713072	Password for user (*username*) too long, truncating to *number* characters.
%ASA-3-713077	Unknown message text.
%ASA-3-713080	Unknown message text.
%ASA-3-713081	Unsupported certificate encoding type *encoding type*.
%ASA-3-713082	Failed to retrieve identity certificate.
%ASA-3-713083	Invalid certificate handle.
%ASA-3-713084	Received invalid phase 1 port value (*port number*) in ID.
%ASA-3-713085	Received invalid phase 1 protocol value (*protocol value*) in ID payload.
%ASA-3-713086	Received unexpected Certificate payload Possible invalid Auth Method (*Auth method (auth numerical value)*).
%ASA-3-713088	Set Cert filehandle failure: no IPScc SA in group *group name*.
%ASA-3-713089	Unknown message text.

continues

Table B-3 *Severity 3 (Errors) Logging Messages (Continued)*

Level and Message Number	Message Text
%ASA-3-713090	Unknown message text.
%ASA-3-713091	Unknown message text.
%ASA-3-713093	Unknown message text.
%ASA-3-713095	Unknown message text.
%ASA-3-713098	Aborting: No identity cert specified in IPSec SA (*SA name*)!
%ASA-3-713100	Unknown message text.
%ASA-3-713102	Phase 1 ID Data length *number* too long—reject tunnel!
%ASA-3-713105	Zero length data in ID payload received during phase *1 or 2* processing.
%ASA-3-713106	Unknown message text.
%ASA-3-713107	IP address request attempt failed!
%ASA-3-713109	Unable to process the received peer certificate.
%ASA-3-713110	Unknown message text.
%ASA-3-713111	Unknown message text.
%ASA-3-713112	Failed to process CONNECTED notify (SPI *SPI value*)!
%ASA-3-713116	Terminating connection attempt: L2TP-over-IPSEC attempted by group (*group name*) but L2TP disabled.
%ASA-3-713118	Detected invalid Diffie-Helmann group descriptor *Group number*, in *IKE area*.
%ASA-3-713119	PHASE 1 COMPLETED.
%ASA-3-713120	Unknown message text.
%ASA-3-713122	Keep-alives configured *keepalive type* but peer *IP address* support keep-alives (type = *keepalive type*).
%ASA-3-713123	IKE lost contact with remote peer, deleting connection (keepalive type: *keepalive type*).
%ASA-3-713124	Received DPD sequence number *rcv sequence #* in *DPD Action, description expected seq #*.
%ASA-3-713125	Unknown message text.
%ASA-3-713126	Unknown message text.
%ASA-3-713127	Xauth required but selected Proposal does not support xauth, Check priorities of ike xauth proposals in ike proposal list.
%ASA-3-713128	Connection attempt to VCPIP redirected to VCA peer *IP address* via load balancing.
%ASA-3-713129	Received unexpected Transaction Exchange payload type: *payload id*.

Table B-3 *Severity 3 (Errors) Logging Messages (Continued)*

Level and Message Number	Message Text
%ASA-3-713132	Cannot obtain an IP address for remote peer.
%ASA-3-713133	Mismatch: Overriding phase 2 DH Group (DH group *DH group id*) with phase 1 group (DH group *DH group number*).
%ASA-3-713134	Mismatch: P1 Authentication algorithm in the crypto map entry different from negotiated algorithm for the L2L connection.
%ASA-3-713138	Group *group name* not found and BASE GROUP default preshared key not configured.
%ASA-3-713140	Split Tunneling Policy requires network list but none configured.
%ASA-3-713141	Client-reported firewall does not match configured firewall: *action* tunnel. Received—Vendor: *vendor(id)*, Product *product(id)*, Caps: *capability value*. Expected—Vendor: *vendor(id)*, Product: *product(id)*, Caps: *capability value*.
%ASA-3-713142	Client did not report firewall in use, but there is a configured firewall: *action* tunnel. Expected—Vendor: *vendor(id)*, Product *product(id)*, Caps: *capability value*.
%ASA-3-713146	Could not add route for Hardware Client in network extension mode, address: *IP address*, mask: *network mask*.
%ASA-3-713149	Hardware client security attribute *attribute name* was enabled but not requested.
%ASA-3-713150	Unknown message text.
%ASA-3-713151	Unknown message text.
%ASA-3-713152	Unable to obtain any rules from filter *ACL tag* to send to client for CPP, terminating connection.
%ASA-3-713153	Unknown message text.
%ASA-3-713159	TCP Connection to Firewall Server has been lost, restricted tunnels are now allowed full network access.
%ASA-3-713161	Remote user (session Id—*id*) network access has been restricted by the Firewall Server.
%ASA-3-713162	Remote user (session Id—*id*) has been rejected by the Firewall Server.
%ASA-3-713163	Remote user (session Id—*id*) has been terminated by the Firewall Server.
%ASA-3-713165	Unknown message text.
%ASA-3-713166	Headend security gateway has failed our user authentication attempt—check configured username and password.
%ASA-3-713167	Remote peer has failed user authentication—check configured username and password.
%ASA-3-713168	Re-auth enabled, but tunnel must be authenticated interactively!

continues

Section B-3

Table B-3 *Severity 3 (Errors) Logging Messages (Continued)*

Level and Message Number	Message Text
%ASA-3-713174	Hardware Client connection rejected! Network Extension Mode is not allowed for this group!
%ASA-3-713181	Unknown message text.
%ASA-3-713182	IKE could not recognize the version of the client! IPSec Fragmentation Policy will be ignored for this connection!
%ASA-3-713185	Error: Username too long—connection aborted.
%ASA-3-713186	Invalid secondary domain name list received from the authentication server. List Received: *list_text* Character *index* (*value*) is illegal.
%ASA-3-713188	Unknown message text.
%ASA-3-713189	Attempted to assign network or broadcast IP address, removing (*IP_address*) from pool.
%ASA-3-713191	Unknown message text.
%ASA-3-713193	Received packet with missing payload, Expected payload: *payload_id*.
%ASA-3-713194	*IKE	IPsec* Delete With Reason message: *termination_reason*.
%ASA-3-713195	Tunnel rejected: Originate-Only: Cannot accept incoming tunnel yet!
%ASA-3-713198	User Authorization failed: *username* User authorization failed.
%ASA-3-713203	IKE Receiver: Error reading from socket.
%ASA-3-713205	Could not add static route for client address: *IP address*.
%ASA-3-713206	Tunnel Rejected: Conflicting protocols specified by tunnel-group and group-policy.
%ASA-3-713208	Cannot create dynamic rule for Backup L2L entry *rule id*.
%ASA-3-713209	Cannot delete dynamic rule for Backup L2L entry *rule id*.
%ASA-3-713210	Cannot create dynamic map for Backup L2L entry *rule id*.
%ASA-3-713212	Could not add route for L2L peer coming in on a dynamic map. address: *IP address*, mask: *network mask*.
%ASA-3-713214	Could not delete route for L2L peer that came in on a dynamic map. address: *IP address*, mask: *network mask*.
%ASA-3-713217	Skipping unrecognized rule: action: *action* client type: *client type* client version: *client version*.
%ASA-3-713218	Tunnel Rejected: Client Type or Version not allowed.
%ASA-3-713226	Connection failed with peer, no trustpoint defined in tunnel-group.
%ASA-3-713902	Unknown message text.
%ASA-3-717001	Querying keypair failed.

Table B-3 *Severity 3 (Errors) Logging Messages (Continued)*

Level and Message Number	Message Text
%ASA-3-717002	Certificate enrollment failed for trustpoint *trustpoint_name*.
%ASA-3-717009	Certificate validate failed. *reason_string*.
%ASA-3-717010	CRL polling failed for trustpoint *trustpoint_name*.
%ASA-3-717012	Failed to refresh CRL cache entry from the server for trustpoint at time_of_failure.
%ASA-3-717015	CRL received from issuer is too large to process.
%ASA-3-717017	Failed to query CA certificate for trustpoint from enrollment _url.
%ASA-3-717018	CRL received from issuer has too many entries to process.
%ASA-3-717019	Failed to insert CRL for trustpoint.

B-4: Warnings—Syslog Severity Level 4 Messages

Table B-4 lists all the severity level 4 logging messages, along with their message numbers and text. All the messages supported by FWSM, ASA, and PIX are shown.

Table B-4 *Severity 4 (Warnings) Logging Messages*

Level and Message Number	Message Text
%ASA-4-106023	Deny protocol src [*interface_name*:*source_address*/*source_port*] dst *interface_name*:*dest_address*/*dest_port* [type {*string*}, code {*code*}] by *access_group acl_ID*.
%ASA-4-106027	Failed to determine the security context for the *packet*:*vlansource Vlan#*:*ethertype* src *sourceMAC* dst *destMAC*.
%ASA-4-106101	Maximum number of ACL denied flows reached.
%ASA-4-109017	User at *IP_address* exceeded auth proxy connection limit (*max*).
%ASA-4-109022	Exceeded HTTPS proxy process limit.
%ASA-4-109027	[aaa protocol] Unable to decipher response message Server = *server_IP_address*, User = *username*.
%ASA-4-109028	aaa bypassed for same-security traffic from ingress interface.
%ASA-4-109030	Autodetect ACL convert wildcard did not convert ACL access_list source I dest netmask.
%ASA-4-109031	NT Domain Authentication Failed: rejecting guest login for username.
%ASA-4-109035	Authentication failed for user username as the password expired.

continues

Section B-4

Table B-4 *Severity 4 (Warnings) Logging Messages (Continued)*

Level and Message Number	Message Text
%ASA-4-109036	Teardown protocol connection session_id due to Uauth timeout.
%ASA-4-109037	Authentication cannot be done for the user since auth_proto client is too busy.
%ASA-4-109039	Func_ID: Uauth Unproxy Failed due to the reason: Failed_Reason.
%ASA-4-209003	Fragment database limit of *number* exceeded: src = *IP_address*, dest = *IP_address*, proto = *protocol*, id = *number*.
%ASA-4-209004	Invalid IP fragment, size = *bytes* exceeds maximum size = *bytes*: src = *IP_address*, dest = *IP_address*, proto = *protocol*, id = *number*.
%ASA-4-209005	Discard IP fragment set with more than *number* elements: src = *IP_address*, dest = *IP_address*, proto = *protocol*, id = *number*.
%ASA-4-302025	Unable to Pre-allocate H323 GUP Connection.
%FWSM-4-307004	Telnet session limit exceeded. Connection request from *IP_address* on interface *interface_name*.
%ASA-4-308002	Static *global_address inside_address* netmask *netmask* overlapped with *global_address inside_address*.
%FWSM-4-309004	Manager session limit exceeded. Connection request from *IP_address* on interface *interface_name*.
%ASA-4-313003	Invalid destination for ICMP error.
%ASA-4-313004	Denied ICMP type=*icmp_type*, from *src_IP_address* on interface *interface_name* to *dest_IP_address*:no matching session.
%FWSM-4-315005	SH session limit exceeded. Connection request from *IP_address* on interface *interface_name*.
%ASA-4-325002	Duplicate address *ipv6_address/mac_address* on *interface*.
%ASA-4-400000-%ASA-4-400051	IDS: *signature_number signature_message* from *IP_address* to *IP_address* on interface *interface_name*.
%ASA-4-401000	Unknown message text.
%ASA-4-401001	Shuns cleared.
%ASA-4-401002	Shun added: *IP_address IP_address port port*.
%ASA-4-401003	Shun deleted: *IP_address*.
%ASA-4-401004	Shunned packet: *IP_address* ==> *IP_address* on interface *interface_name*.
%ASA-4-401005	Shun add failed: unable to allocate resources for *IP_address IP_address port port*.
%ASA-4-402101	Decaps: rec'd IPSEC packet has invalid spi for destaddr=*dest_address*, prot=*protocol*, spi=*number*.

Table B-4   *Severity 4 (Warnings) Logging Messages (Continued)*

Level and Message Number	Message Text
%ASA-4-402102	Decapsulate: packet missing {AH I ESP}, destadr=*dest_address*, actual prot=*protocol*.
%ASA-4-402103	Identity doesn't match negotiated identity (ip) dest_address= *dest_address*, src_addr= *source_address*, prot= *protocol*, (ident) local=*inside_address*, remote=*remote_address*, local_ proxy=*IP_address/IP_address/port/port*, remote_ proxy=*IP_address/IP_address/port/port*.
%ASA-4-402104	Unknown message text.
%ASA-4-402106	Rec'd packet not an IPSEC packet (ip) dest_address= *dest_address*, src_addr= *source_address*, prot= *protocol*.
%ASA-4-402107	Unknown message text.
%ASA-4-403101	PPTP session state not established, but received an XGRE packet, tunnel_id=*number*, session_id=*number*.
%ASA-4-403102	PPP virtual interface *interface_name* rcvd pkt with invalid protocol: *protocol*, reason: *reason*.
%ASA-4-403103	PPP virtual interface max connections reached.
%ASA-4-403104	PPP virtual interface *interface_name* requires mschap for MPPE.
%ASA-4-403106	PPP virtual interface *interface_name* requires RADIUS for MPPE.
%ASA-4-403107	PPP virtual interface *interface_name* missing aaa server group info.
%ASA-4-403108	PPP virtual interface *interface_name* missing client ip address option.
%ASA-4-403109	Rec'd packet not a PPTP packet. (ip) dest_address= *dest_address*, src_addr= *source_address*, data: *string*.
%ASA-4-403110	PPP virtual interface *interface_name*, user: *user* missing MPPE key from aaa server.
%ASA-4-403505	PPPoE:PPP—Unable to set default route to *IP_address* at *interface_name*.
%ASA-4-403506	PPPoE: Failed to assign PPP *IP_address* netmask *netmask* at *interface_name*.
%ASA-4-404101	ISAKMP: Failed to allocate address for client from pool string.
%ASA-4-405001	Received ARP {request I response} collision from *IP_address/mac_address* on interface *interface_name*.
%ASA-4-405002	Received mac mismatch collision from *IP_address/mac_address* for authenticated host.
%ASA-4-405101	Unable to Pre-allocate H225 Call Signalling Connection for *foreign_address outside_address*[*/outside_port*] to *local_address inside_address*[*/inside_port*].
%ASA-4-405102	Unable to Pre-allocate H245 Connection for *foreign_address outside_address* [*/outside_port*] to *local_address inside_address*[*/inside_port*].

continues

Table B-4 *Severity 4 (Warnings) Logging Messages (Continued)*

Level and Message Number	Message Text
%ASA-4-405103	H225 message from *src_ip/src_port* to *dest_ip/dest_prot* contains bad protocol discriminator *hex_value*.
%ASA-4-405104	H225 message received from *outside_address/outside_port* to *inside_address/inside_port* before SETUP.
%ASA-4-405105	H323 RAS message AdmissionConfirm received from *source_IP_ address/source_port* to *destination_IP_address/destination_port* without an AdmissionRequest.
%ASA-4-405201	ILS *ILS_message_type* from *inside_interface:source_IP_address* to *outside_interface:/destination_IP_address* has wrong embedded address *embedded_IP_address*.
%ASA-4-406000	Unknown message text.
%ASA-4-406001	FTP port command low port: *IP_address/port* to *IP_address* on interface *interface_name*.
%ASA-4-406002	FTP port command different address: *IP_address(IP_address)* to *IP_address* on interface *interface_name*.
%ASA-4-407001	Deny traffic for local-host *interface_name:inside_address*, license limit of *number* exceeded.
%ASA-4-407002	Embryonic limit neconns/elimit for through connections exceeded: *outside_address/outside_port* to *global_address (inside_address)/inside_port* on interface *interface_name*.
%ASA-4-407003	Established limit for RPC services exceeded *number*.
%ASA-4-408001	IP route counter negative—reason, *IP_address* Attempt: *number*.
%ASA-4-408002	*ospf process id route type* update *address1 mask1* [*distance1/metric1*] via *source IP:interface1 address2 mask2* [*distance2/metric2*].
%ASA-4-409001	Database scanner: external LSA *IP_address* netmask is lost, reinstalls.
%ASA-4-409002	db_free: external LSA *IP_address netmask*.
%ASA-4-409003	Received invalid packet: *reason* from *IP_address*, *interface_name*.
%ASA-4-409004	Received reason from unknown neighbor *IP_address*.
%ASA-4-409005	Invalid length number in OSPF packet from *IP_address* (ID *IP_address*), *interface_name*.
%ASA-4-409006	Invalid lsa: *reason* Type *number*, LSID *IP_address* from *IP_address*, *IP_address*, *interface_name*.
%ASA-4-409007	Found LSA with the same host bit set but using different mask LSA ID *IP_address netmask* New: Destination *IP_address netmask*.

Table B-4 *Severity 4 (Warnings) Logging Messages (Continued)*

Level and Message Number	Message Text
%ASA-4-409008	Found generating default LSA with non-zero mask LSA type : *number* Mask : *IP_address* metric : *number* area : *string*.
%ASA-4-409009	OSPF process number cannot start. There must be at least one up IP interface, for OSPF to use as router ID.
%ASA-4-409010	Virtual link information found in non-backbone area: string.
%ASA-4-409011	OSPF detected duplicate router-id *IP_address* from *IP_address* on interface *interface_name*.
%ASA-4-409012	Detected router with duplicate router ID *IP_address* in area string.
%ASA-4-409013	Detected router with duplicate router ID *IP_address* in Type-4 LSA advertised by *IP_address*.
%ASA-4-409023	Attempting AAA Fallback method *method_name* for *request_type* request for user *username* :Auth-server group *server_tag* unreachable.
%ASA-4-410001	UDP DNS packet dropped due to domain name length check of 255 bytes: actual length:*n* bytes.
%ASA-4-411001	Line protocol on interface *interface_name* changed state to up.
%ASA-4-411002	Line protocol on interface *interface_name* changed state to down.
%ASA-4-411003	Configuration status on interface *interface_name* changed state to downup.
%ASA-4-411004	Configuration status on interface *interface_name* changed state to up.
%ASA-4-412001	MAC *mac-address* moved from *interface-1* to *interface-2*.
%ASA-4-412002	Detected bridge table full while inserting MAC *mac-address* on interface *interface*. Number of entries = *num*.
%ASA-4-413001	Module in slot *slotnum* is not able to shut down. Module Error: *errnum message*.
%ASA-4-413002	Module in slot *slotnum* is not able to reload. Module Error: *errnum message*.
%ASA-4-413003	Module in slot *slotnum* is not a recognized type.
%ASA-4-415012	:internal_sig_id More than HTTP Deobfuscation signature detected – IPS evasion technique from source_address to dest_address.
%ASA-4-415014	:internal_sig_id More than 10 unanswered HTTP requests exceeded from source_address to dest_address.
%ASA-4-416001	Dropped UDP SNMP packet from *source_interface:source_IP/source_port* to *dest_interface:dest_IP/dest_port*; version (*version*) is not allowed through the firewall.
%ASA-4-417001	Unexpected event received: *number*.

continues

Table B-4 *Severity 4 (Warnings) Logging Messages (Continued)*

Level and Message Number	Message Text
%ASA-4-417002	Unknown message text.
%ASA-4-417003	Unknown message text.
%ASA-4-417004	Filter violation error: conn *number* (*string*:*string*) in *string*.
%ASA-4-417005	Unknown message text.
%ASA-4-417006	No memory for *string* in *string*. Handling: *string*.
%ASA-4-417007	Unknown message text.
%ASA-4-418001	Through-the-device packet to/from management-only network is denied: *prot_str* from *ifc_name ip* (*port*) to *ifc_name ip* (*port*).
%ASA-4-500004	Invalid transport field for protocol=*protocol*, from *source_address*/*source_port* to *dest_address*/*dest_port*.
%ASA-4-507001	Terminating TCP-Proxy connection from *ifc_in*:*sip*/*sport* to *ifc_out*:*dip*/*dport*— reassembly limit of *limit* bytes exceeded.
%FWSM-4-605002	HTTP daemon connection limit exceeded.
%ASA-4-612002	Auto Update failed:*filename*, version:*number*, reason:*reason*.
%ASA-4-612003	Auto Update failed to contact:*url*, reason:*reason*.
%ASA-4-620002	Unsupported CTIQBE version: hex: from *interface_name*:*IP_address*/*port* to *interface_name*:*IP_address*/*port*.
%ASA-4-710004	TCP connection limit exceeded from *source_address*/*source_port* to *interface_name*:*dest_address*/*service*.
%ASA-4-713154	DNS lookup for *peer description* Server [*server name*] failed!
%ASA-4-713157	Timed out on initial contact to server [*server name or IP address*] Tunnel could not be established.
%ASA-4-713207	Unknown message text.
%ASA-4-713903	*Descriptive_event_string*.
%ASA-4-716007	Group *name* User *user* WebVPN session terminated. Maximum time exceeded.
%ASA-4-716022	WebVPN filter setup has returned an error *acl*.
%ASA-4-716023	Group *name* User *user* Session could not be established: session limit of *max_sess* reached.
%ASA-4-720001	(VPN unit) Failed to initialize with Chunk Manager.
%ASA-4-720007	(VPN unit) Failed to allocate chunk from Chunk Manager.
%ASA-4-720008	(VPN unit) Failed to register to High Availability Framework.
%ASA-4-720009	(VPN unit) Failed to create version control block.

Table B-4   *Severity 4 (Warnings) Logging Messages (Continued)*

Level and Message Number	Message Text
%ASA-4-720011	(VPN unit) Failed to allocate memory.
%ASA-4-720013	(VPN unit) Failed to insert certificate in trustpoint.

B-5: Notifications—Syslog Severity Level 5 Messages

Table B-5 lists all the severity level 5 logging messages, along with their message numbers and text. All the messages supported by FWSM, ASA, and PIX are shown.

Table B-5   *Severity 5 (Notifications) Logging Messages*

Level and Message Number	Message Text
%ASA-5-109012	Authen Session End: user '*user*', sid *number*, elapsed number *seconds*.
%ASA-5-109029	Parsing downloaded ACL: string.
%ASA-5-111001	Begin configuration: *IP_address* writing to device.
%ASA-5-111002	Begin configuration: IP_address reading from device.
%ASA-5-111003	*IP_address* Erase configuration.
%ASA-5-111004	*IP_address* end configuration: {FAILED | OK}.
%ASA-5-111005	*IP_address* end configuration: OK.
%FWSM-5-111006	Console Login from user at *IP_address*.
%ASA-5-111007	Begin configuration: *IP_address* reading from device.
%ASA-5-111008	User *user* executed the command *string*.
%ASA-5-199001	PIX reload command executed from telnet (remote *IP_address*).
%ASA-5-199006	Orderly reload started at *when* by *whom*. Reload reason: *reason*.
%ASA-5-199007	IP detected an attached application using port *port* while removing context.
%ASA-5-199008	*Protocol* detected an attached application using local port *local_port* and destination port *dest_port*.
%ASA-5-303004	FTP cmd_string command unsupported – failed strict inspection, terminating connection.
%ASA-5-304001	User *source_address* accessed {JAVA URL | URL} *dest_address*: *url*.
%ASA-5-304002	Access denied URL url SRC *IP_address* DEST *IP_address*: *url*.
%ASA-5-321001	Resource *var1* limit of *var2* reached.

continues

Table B-5 *Severity 5 (Notifications) Logging Messages (Continued)*

Level and Message Number	Message Text
%ASA-5-321002	Resource *var1* rate limit of *var2* reached.
%ASA-5-415001	HTTP Tunnel detected.
%ASA-5-415002	HTTP Instant Messenger detected.
%ASA-5-415003	HTTP Peer-to-Peer detected.
%ASA-1-415005	Content type does not match specified type—Content Verification Failed.
%ASA-5-415007	HTTP Extension method detected.
%ASA-5-415008	HTTP RFC method detected.
%ASA-5-415010	HTTP protocol violation detected.
%ASA-5-415013	HTTP Transfer encoding violation detected.
%ASA-5-500001	ActiveX content modified src *IP_address* dest *IP_address* on interface *interface_name*.
%ASA-5-500002	Java content modified src *IP_address* dest *IP_address* on interface *interface_name*.
%ASA-5-500003	Bad TCP hdr length (hdrlen=*bytes*, pktlen=*bytes*) from *source_address/source_port* to *dest_address/dest_port*, flags: *tcp_flags*, on interface *interface_name*.
%ASA-5-501101	User transitioning priv level.
%ASA-5-502101	New user added to local dbase: Uname: *user* Priv: *privilege_level* Encpass: *string*.
%ASA-5-502102	User deleted from local dbase: Uname: *user* Priv: *privilege_level* Encpass: *string*.
%ASA-5-502103	User priv level changed: Uname: *user* From: *privilege_level* To: *privilege_level*.
%ASA-5-502111	New group policy added: name: *policy_name* Type: *policy_type*.
%ASA-5-502112	Group policy deleted: name: *policy_name* Type: *policy_type*.
%ASA-5-503001	Process number, *Nbr IP_address* on *interface_name* from *string* to *string*, *reason*.
%ASA-5-504001	Security context *context-name* was added to the system.
%ASA-5-504002	Security context *context-name* was removed from the system.
%ASA-5-505001	Module in slot *slotnum* is shutting down. Please wait...
%ASA-5-505002	Module in slot *slotnum* is reloading. Please wait...
%ASA-5-505003	Module in slot *slotnum* is resetting. Please wait...
%ASA-5-505004	Module in slot *slotnum* shutdown is complete.
%ASA -5-505005	Module in slot *slotnum* is initializing control communication. Please wait...
%ASA -5-505006	Module in slot *slotnum* is Up.
%ASA-5-505007	Module in slot *slotnum* is recovering. Please wait...

Table B-5   *Severity 5 (Notifications) Logging Messages (Continued)*

Level and Message Number	Message Text
%ASA-5-506001	*event_source_str event_str.* (Status of a file system has changed)
%ASA-5-507001	Terminating TCP-Proxy connection.
%ASA-5-611103	User logged out: Uname: *user.*
%ASA-5-611104	Serial console idle timeout exceeded.
%ASA-5-612001	Auto Update succeeded:*filename*, version:*number.*
%ASA-5-713005	Unknown message text.
%ASA-5-713006	Failed to obtain state for message Id *id*, Peer Address: *address.*
%ASA-5-713010	*IKE area*: failed to find centry for message Id *id.*
%ASA-5-713041	IKE Initiator: *new or rekey* Phase *1 or 2*, Intf *interface number*, IKE Peer *IP address* local Proxy Address *IP address*, remote Proxy Address *IP address*, Crypto map (*crypto map tag*).
%ASA-5-713045	Unknown message text.
%ASA-5-713049	Security negotiation complete for *Tunnel type* type (*group name*) *Initiator/ Responder*, Inbound SPI = *SPI*, Outbound SPI = *SPI.*
%ASA-5-713050	Connection terminated for peer *IP address*. Reason: *termination reason* Remote Proxy *IP address*, Local Proxy *IP address.*
%ASA-5-713067	Unknown message text.
%ASA-5-713068	Received non-routine Notify message: *notify type* (*notify value*).
%ASA-5-713071	Unknown message text.
%ASA-5-713073	Responder forcing change of *Phase 1/Phase 2* rekeying duration from *larger value* to *smaller value* seconds.
%ASA-5-713074	Responder forcing change of IPSec rekeying duration from *larger value* to *smaller value* Kbs.
%ASA-5-713075	Overriding Initiator's IPSec rekeying duration from *larger value* to *smaller value* seconds.
%ASA-5-713076	Overriding Initiator's IPSec rekeying duration from *larger value* to *smaller value* Kbs.
%ASA-5-713087	Unknown message text.
%ASA-5-713092	Unknown message text.
%ASA-5-713115	Client rejected NAT enabled IPSec request, falling back to standard IPSec.
%ASA-5-713130	Received unsupported transaction mode attribute: *attribute id.*
%ASA-5-713131	Received unknown transaction mode attribute: *attribute id.*

Section B-5

continues

Table B-5 *Severity 5 (Notifications) Logging Messages (Continued)*

Level and Message Number	Message Text
%ASA-5-713135	message received, redirecting tunnel to *IP address*.
%ASA-5-713136	IKE session establishment timed out [*IKE state name*], aborting!
%ASA-5-713137	Reaper overriding refCnt [*refcnt #*] and tunnelCnt [*tunnel cnt #*]—deleting SA!
%ASA-5-713139	*group name* not found, using BASE GROUP default preshared key.
%ASA-5-713144	Ignoring received malformed firewall record; reason—*error reason* TLV type *attribute value correction*.
%ASA-5-713148	Terminating tunnel to Hardware Client in network extension mode, unable to delete static route for address: *IP address*, mask: *network mask*.
%ASA-5-713155	DNS lookup for Primary VPN Server [*server name*] successfully resolved after a previous failure. Resetting any Backup Server init.
%ASA-5-713156	Initializing Backup Server [*server name* or *IP address*].
%ASA-5-713158	Client rejected NAT enabled IPSec Over UDP request, falling back to IPSec Over TCP.
%ASA-5-713178	IKE Initiator received a packet from its peer without a Responder cookie.
%ASA-5-713179	IKE AM Initiator received a packet from its peer without a *payload_type* payload.
%ASA-5-713180	Unknown message text.
%ASA-5-713196	Remote L2L Peer *IP_address* initiated a tunnel with same outer and inner addresses. Peer could be Originate Only—Possible misconfiguration!
%ASA-5-713197	The configured Confidence Interval of *seconds* seconds is invalid for this *tunnel_type* connection. Enforcing the *second* second default.
%ASA-5-713199	Reaper corrected an SA that has not decremented the concurrent IKE negotiations counter (*counter_value*)!
%ASA-5-713200	Unknown message text.
%ASA-5-713201	Unknown message text.
%ASA-5-713202	Unknown message text.
%ASA-5-713216	Rule: *action Client type* : *version* Client: *type version is/is not* allowed.
%ASA-5-713229	Auto-Update Notification to client of update.
%ASA-5-713904	*Descriptive_event_string*.
%ASA-5-717013	Removing a cached CRL to accomodate an incoming CRL.
%ASA-5-717014	Unable to cache a CRL received from CDP due to size limitations.
%ASA-5-718002	Create peer *IP_address* failure, already at maximum of *number_of_peers*.
%ASA-5-718005	Fail to send to *IP_address*, port *port_number*.

Table B-5   *Severity 5 (Notifications) Logging Messages (Continued)*

Level and Message Number	Message Text
%ASA-5-718006	Invalid load balancing state transition.
%ASA-5-718007	Socket open failure *failure_code*.
%ASA-5-718008	Socket bind failure *failure_code*.
%ASA-5-718009	Send HELLO response failure to *IP_address*.
%ASA-5-718010	Sent HELLO response to *IP_address*.
%ASA-5-718011	Send HELLO request failure to *IP_address*.
%ASA-5-718012	Sent HELLO request to *IP_address*.
%ASA-5-718014	Master peer *IP_address* is not answering HELLO.
%ASA-5-718015	Received HELLO request from *IP_address*.
%ASA-5-718016	Received HELLO response from *IP_address*.
%ASA-5-718018	Send KEEPALIVE request failure to *IP_address*.
%ASA-5-718020	Send KEEPALIVE response failure to *IP_address*.
%ASA-5-718024	Send CFG UPDATE failure to *IP_address*.
%ASA-5-718028	Send OOS indicator failure to *IP_address*.
%ASA-5-718031	Received OOS obituary for *IP_address*.
%ASA-5-718032	Received OOS indicator from *IP_address*.
%ASA-5-718033	Send TOPOLOGY indicator failure to *IP_address*.
%ASA-5-718042	Unable to ARP for *IP_address*.
%ASA-5-718043	Updating/removing duplicate peer entry *IP_address*.
%ASA-5-718044	Deleted peer *IP_address*.
%ASA-5-718045	Created peer *IP_address*.
%ASA-5-718048	Create of secure tunnel failure for peer *IP_address*.
%ASA-5-718050	Delete of secure tunnel failure for peer *IP_address*.
%ASA-5-718052	Received GRAT-ARP from duplicate master.
%ASA-5-718053	Detected duplicate master, mastership stolen.
%ASA-5-718054	Detected duplicate master *MAC_address* and going to SLAVE.
%ASA-5-718055	Detected duplicate master *MAC_address* and staying MASTER.
%ASA-5-718056	Deleted Master peer, IP *IP_address*.
%ASA-5-718057	Queue send failure from ISR, msg type *failure_code*.
%ASA-5-718060	Inbound socket select fail: context=*context_ID*.

continues

Table B-5 *Severity 5 (Notifications) Logging Messages (Continued)*

Level and Message Number	Message Text
%ASA-5-718061	Inbound socket read fail: context=*context_ID*.
%ASA-5-718062	Inbound thread is awake (context=*context_ID*).
%ASA-5-718063	Interface *interface_name* is down.
%ASA-5-718064	Admin. interface *interface_name* is down.
%ASA-5-718065	Cannot continue to run (public=*up/down*, private=*up/down*, enable=*LB_state*, master=*IP_address*, session=*Enable/Disable*).
%ASA-5-718066	Cannot add secondary address to interface *interface_name*, ip *IP_address*.
%ASA-5-718067	Cannot delete secondary address to interface *interface_name*, ip *IP_address*.
%ASA-5-718068	Start VPN Load Balancing in context *context_ID*.
%ASA-5-718069	Stop VPN Load Balancing in context *context_ID*.
%ASA-5-718070	Reset VPN Load Balancing in context *context_ID*.
%ASA-5-718071	Terminate VPN Load Balancing in context *context_ID*.
%ASA-5-718072	Becoming master of Load Balancing in context *context_ID*.
%ASA-5-718073	Becoming slave of Load Balancing in context *context_ID*.
%ASA-5-718074	Fail to create access list for peer *context_ID*.
%ASA-5-718075	Peer *IP_address* access list not set.
%ASA-5-718076	Fail to create tunnel group for peer *IP_address*.
%ASA-5-718077	Fail to delete tunnel group for peer *IP_address*.
%ASA-5-718078	Fail to create crypto map for peer *IP_address*.
%ASA-5-718079	Fail to delete crypto map for peer *IP_address*.
%ASA-5-718080	Fail to create crypto policy for peer *IP_address*.
%ASA-5-718081	Fail to delete crypto policy for peer *IP_address*.
%ASA-5-718082	Unknown message text.
%ASA-5-718083	Unknown message text.
%ASA-5-718084	Public/cluster IP not on the same subnet: public *IP_address*, mask *subnet_mask*, cluster *IP_address*.
%ASA-5-718085	Interface *interface_name* has no IP address defined.
%ASA-5-718086	Fail to install LB NP rules: type *rule_type*, dst *interface_name*, port *port_number*.
%ASA-5-718087	Fail to delete LB NP rules: type *rule_type*, rule *rule_ID*.
%ASA-5-719014	Email Proxy is changing listen port from old_port to new_port for mail protocol.

Table B-5   *Severity 5 (Notifications) Logging Messages (Continued)*

Level and Message Number	Message Text
%ASA-5-720016	(VPN unit) Failed to initialize default timer.
%ASA-5-720017	(VPN unit) Failed to update LB runtime data.
%ASA-5-720018	(VPN unit) Failed to get a buffer from the underlying core high availability subsystem.
%ASA-5-720019	(VPN unit) Failed to update cTCP statistics.
%ASA-5-720020	(VPN unit) Failed to send type timer message.

B-6: Informational—Syslog Severity Level 6 Messages

Table B-6 lists all the severity level 6 logging messages, along with their message numbers and text. All the messages supported by FWSM, ASA, and PIX are shown.

Table B-6   *Severity 6 (Informational) Logging Messages*

Level and Message Number	Message Text
%ASA-6-103012	Unknown message text.
%ASA-6-106012	Deny IP from *IP_address* to *IP_address*, IP options *hex*.
%ASA-6-106015	Deny TCP (no connection) from *IP_address/port* to *IP_address/port* flags *tcp_flags* on interface *interface_name*.
%ASA-6-106025	Failed to determine the security context for the *packet:sourceVlan:sourceIP destIP sourcePort destPort protocol*.
%ASA-6-106026	Failed to determine the security context for the *packet:sourceVlan:sourceIP destIP sourcePort destPort protocol*.
%ASA-6-106100	(PIX 6.3) access-list *acl_ID* {permitted	denied	est-allowed} protocol *interface_name/source_address(source_port)* -> *interface_name/ dest_address(dest_port)* hit-cnt *number* ({first hit | number-second interval}).
%ASA-6-106102	access-list *id action* url *url* hit-cnt *hits*.
%ASA-6-106103	access-list *id action* tcp *interface ip-addr port interface ip-addr port* hit-cnt hits.
%ASA-6-109001	Auth start for user *user* from *inside_address/inside_port* to *outside_address/ outside_port*.
%ASA-6-109002	Auth from *inside_address/inside_port* to *outside_address/outside_port* failed (server *IP_address* failed) on interface *interface_name*.

continues

Table B-6 *Severity 6 (Informational) Logging Messages (Continued)*

Level and Message Number	Message Text
%ASA-6-109003	Auth from *inside_address* to *outside_address*/*outside_port* failed (all servers failed) on interface *interface_name*.
%ASA-6-109005	Authentication succeeded for user *user* from *inside_address*/*inside_port* to *outside_address*/*outside_port* on interface *interface_name*.
%ASA-6-109006	Authentication failed for user *user* from *inside_address*/*inside_port* to *outside_address*/*outside_port* on interface *interface_name*.
%ASA-6-109007	Authorization permitted for user *user* from *inside_address*/*inside_port* to *outside_address*/*outside_port* on interface *interface_name*.
%ASA-6-109008	Authorization denied for user *user* from *source_address*/*source_port* to *destination_address*/*destination_port* on interface *interface_name*.
%ASA-6-109009	Authorization denied from *inside_address*/*inside_port* to *outside_address*/*outside_port* (not authenticated) on interface *interface_name*.
%ASA-6-109015	Authorization denied (acl=*acl_ID*) for user '*user*' from *source_address*/*source_port* to *dest_address*/*dest_port* on interface *interface_name*.
%ASA-6-109024	Authorization denied from *source_IP_address*/*src_port* to *dest_IP_address*/*dest_port* (not authenticated) on interface *interface_name* using *protocol*.
%ASA-6-109025	Authorization denied (acl=*acl_ID*) for user '*user*' from *source_address*/*source_port* to *dest_address*/*dest_port* on interface *interface_name* using protocol.
%ASA-6-110001	No route to *dest_address* from *source_address*.
%ASA-6-113002	Unknown message text.
%ASA-6-113003	AAA group policy for user *username* is being set to *policy_name*.
%ASA-6-113004	AAA user *aaa_type* Successful : server = *server_IP_address*, User = *username*.
%ASA-6-113005	AAA user authentication Rejected : reason = *reason* : server = *server_IP_address*, User = *username*.
%ASA-6-113006	User *user_name* locked out on exceeding *number* successive failed authentication attempts.
%ASA-6-113007	User *user_name* unlocked by *administrator*.
%ASA-6-113008	AAA transaction status ACCEPT: user.
%ASA-6-113009	AAA retrieved default group policy for user.
%ASA-6-113010	AAA challenge received for user from server.
%ASA-6-113011	AAA retrieved user specific group policy for user.
%ASA-6-113012	AAA user authentication successful: local database: user.
%ASA-6-113013	AAA unable to complete the request Error: reason.

Table B-6 *Severity 6 (Informational) Logging Messages (Continued)*

Level and Message Number	Message Text
%ASA-6-113014	AAA authentication server not accessible.
%ASA-6-113015	AAA user authentication rejected.
%ASA-6-113016	AAA credentials rejected: reason: server: user.
%ASA-6-113017	AAA credentials rejected: reason: local database: user.
%ASA-6-199002	PIX startup completed. Beginning operation.
%ASA-6-199003	Reducing link MTU dec.
%ASA-6-199005	PIX Startup begin.
%ASA-6-201010	Embryonic connection limit exceeded *cnt/limit* for *dir* packet from *sip/sport* to *dip/dport* on interface *if_name*.
%ASA-6-210022	LU missed number updates.
%ASA-6-302003	Built H245 connection for foreign_address *outside_address/outside_port local_address inside_address/inside_port*.
%ASA-6-302004	Pre-allocate H323 UDP backconnection for *foreign_address outside_address/outside_port to local_address inside_address/inside_port*.
%ASA-6-302009	Rebuilt TCP connection number for *foreign_address outside_address/outside_port global_address global_address/global_port local_address inside_address/inside_port*.
%ASA-6-302010	Connections in use, connections most used.
%ASA-6-302012	Pre-allocate H225 Call Signalling Connection for faddr *ip address/port* to laddr *ip address*.
%ASA-6-302013	Built {inbound	outbound} TCP connection number for *interface_name:real_address/real_port* (*mapped_address/mapped_port*) to *interface_name:real_address/real_port* (*mapped_address/mapped_port*) [(*user*)].
%ASA-6-302014	Teardown TCP connection number for *interface_name:real_address/real_port* to *interface_name:real_address/real_port duration time bytes number* [*reason*] [(*user*)].
%ASA-6-302015	Built {inbound	outbound} UDP connection number for *interface_name:real_address/real_port* (*mapped_address/mapped_port*) to *interface_name:real_address/real_port* (*mapped_address/mapped_port*) [(*user*)].
%ASA-6-302016	Teardown UDP connection number for *interface_name:real_address/real_port* to *interface_name:real_address/real_port duration time bytes number* [(*user*)].
%ASA-6-302017	Built {inbound	outbound} GRE connection *id* from *interface:real_address* (*translated_address*) to *interface:real_address/real_cid* (*translated_address/translated_cid*)[(*user*).

continues

Table B-6 *Severity 6 (Informational) Logging Messages (Continued)*

Level and Message Number	Message Text
%ASA-6-302018	Teardown GRE connection *id* from *interface*:*real_address* (*translated_address*) to *interface*:*real_address*/*real_cid* (*translated_address*/*translated_cid*) duration *hh:mm:ss* bytes *bytes* [(*user*)].
%ASA-6-302020	Built {inbound | outbound} ICMP connection for faddr {*faddr* | *icmp_seq_num*} gaddr {*gaddr* | *cmp_type*} laddr *laddr*.
%ASA-6-302021	Teardown ICMP connection for faddr {*faddr* | *icmp_seq_num*} gaddr {*gaddr* | *cmp_type*} laddr *laddr*.
%ASA-6-302022	Built IP protocol connection.
%ASA-6-302023	Teardown IP protocol connection.
%ASA-6-302024	Pre-allocated H323 GUP connection.
%ASA-6-303002	*source_address* {Stored | Retrieved} *dest_address*: *mapped_address*.
%ASA-6-303003	FTP *cmd_name* command denied, terminating connection from *src_if*:*src_ip*/*src_port* to *dest_if*:*dest_ip*/*dest_port*.
%ASA-6-304004	URL Server *IP_address* request failed URL *url*.
%ASA-6-305007	addrpool_free(): Orphan IP *IP_address* on interface *interface_number*.
%ASA-6-305009	Built {dynamic | static} translation from *interface_name* [(*acl-name*)]:*real_address* to *interface_name*:*mapped_address*.
%ASA-6-305010	Teardown {dynamic | static} translation from *interface_name* [(*acl-name*)]:*real_address* to *interface_name*:*mapped_address* duration *time*.
%ASA-6-305011	Built {dynamic | static} {TCP | UDP | ICMP} translation from *interface_name* [(*acl-name*)]:*real_address*/*real_port* to *interface_name*:*mapped_address*/*mapped_port*.
%ASA-6-305012	Teardown {dynamic | static} {TCP | UDP | ICMP} translation from *interface_name* [(*acl-name*)]:*real_address*/{*real_port* | *real_ICMP_ID*} to *interface_name*:*mapped_address*/{*mapped_port* | *mapped_ICMP_ID*} duration *time*.
%FWSM-6-307001	Denied Telnet login session from *IP_address* on interface *interface_name*.
%FWSM-6-307002	Permitted Telnet login session from *IP_addr*.
%FWSM-6-307003	Telnet login session failed from *IP_address* (*num* attempts) on interface *interface_name*.
%ASA-6-308001	PIX console enable password incorrect for *number* tries (from *IP_address*).
%ASA-6-309002	Permitted manager connection from *IP_address*.
%ASA-6-311001	LU loading standby start.
%ASA-6-311002	LU loading standby end.

Table B-6 *Severity 6 (Informational) Logging Messages (Continued)*

Level and Message Number	Message Text
%ASA-6-311003	LU recv thread up.
%ASA-6-311004	LU xmit thread up.
%ASA-6-312001	RIP hdr failed from *IP_address*: cmd=*string*, version=*number* domain=*string* on interface *interface_name*.
%ASA-6-314001	Pre-allocate RTSP UDP backconnection for *foreign_address outside_address/ outside_port* to *local_address inside_address/inside_port*.
%FWSM-6-315002	Permitted SSH session from IP_address on interface *interface_name* for user "*user_id*".
%FWSM-6-315003	SSH login session failed from *IP_address* on (*num* attempts) on interface *interface_name* by user "*user_id*".
%ASA-6-315011	SSH session from *IP_address* on interface *interface_name* for user *user* disconnected by SSH server, reason: *reason*.
%ASA-6-321003	Resource *var1* log level of *var2* reached.
%ASA-6-321004	Resource *var1* rate log level of *var2* reached.
%ASA-6-403500	PPPoE—Service name 'any' not received in PADO. Intf:*interface_name* AC:*ac_name*.
%ASA-6-415006	Content size out of range.
%ASA-6-415009	HTTP Header length exceeded.
%ASA-6-415011	HTTP URL length exceeded.
%ASA-6-602101	PMTU-D packet number bytes greater than effective mtu number dest_addr=*dest_address*, src_addr=*source_address*, prot=*protocol*.
%ASA-6-602102	Adjusting IPSec tunnel mtu.
%ASA-6-602201	ISAKMP Phase 1 SA created.
%ASA-6-602202	ISAKMP session connected.
%ASA-6-602203	ISAKMP session disconnected.
%ASA-6-602301	SA created.
%ASA-6-602302	Deleting SA.
%ASA-6-603101	PPTP received out of seq or duplicate pkt, tnl_id=*number*, sess_id=*number*, seq=*number*.
%ASA-6-603102	PPP virtual interface *interface_name*—user: *user* aaa authentication started.
%ASA-6-603103	PPP virtual interface *interface_name*—user: *user* aaa authentication status.
%ASA-6-603104	PPTP Tunnel created, tunnel_id is *number*, remote_peer_ip is *remote_address*, ppp_virtual_interface_id is *number*, client_dynamic_ip is *IP_address*, username is *user*, MPPE_key_strength is *string*.

continues

Table B-6 *Severity 6 (Informational) Logging Messages (Continued)*

Level and Message Number	Message Text
%ASA-6-603105	PPTP Tunnel deleted, tunnel_id = *number*, remote_peer_ip= *remote_address*.
%ASA-6-603106	L2TP Tunnel created, tunnel_id is *number*, remote_peer_ip is *remote_address*, ppp_virtual_interface_id is *number*, client_dynamic_ip is *IP_address*, username is *user*.
%ASA-6-603107	L2TP Tunnel deleted, tunnel_id = *number*, remote_peer_ip = *remote_address*.
%ASA-6-603108	Built PPTP Tunnel at *interface_name*, tunnel-id = *number*, remote-peer = *IP_address*, virtual-interface = *number*, client-dynamic-ip = *IP_address*, username = *user*, MPPE-key-strength = *number*.
%ASA-6-603109	Teardown PPPOE Tunnel at *interface_name*, tunnel-id = *number*, remote-peer = *IP_address*.
%ASA-6-604101	DHCP client interface *interface_name*: Allocated ip = *IP_address*, mask = *netmask*, gw = *gateway_address*.
%ASA-6-604102	DHCP client interface *interface_name*: address released.
%ASA-6-604103	DHCP daemon interface *interface_name*: address granted *MAC_address* (*IP_address*).
%ASA-6-604104	DHCP daemon interface *interface_name*: address released.
%FWSM-6-605003	HTTP daemon: Login failed from *IP_address* for user "*user_id*".
%ASA-6-605004	Login denied from {*source_address/source_port*	serial} to {*interface_name:dest_address*/service	console} for user "*user*".
%ASA-6-605005	Login permitted from {*source_address/source_port*	serial} to {*interface_name:dest_address*/service	console} for user "*user*".
%ASA-6-606001	PDM session number *number* from *IP_address* started.
%ASA-6-606002	PDM session number *number* from *IP_address* ended.
%ASA-6-606003	PDM logging session number *id* from *ip* started *id* session ID assigned.
%ASA-6-606004	PDM logging session number *id* from *ip* ended.
%ASA-6-607001	Pre-allocate SIP *connection_type* secondary channel for *interface_name:IP_address/port* to *interface_name:IP_address* from string *message*.
%ASA-6-608001	Pre-allocate Skinny *connection_type* secondary channel for *interface_name:IP_address* to *interface_name:IP_address/port* from string *message*.
%ASA-6-609001	Built local-host *interface_name:IP_address*.
%ASA-6-609002	Teardown local-host *interface_name:IP_address* duration *time*.
%ASA-6-610101	Authorization failed: Cmd: *command* Cmdtype: *command_modifier*.

Table B-6 *Severity 6 (Informational) Logging Messages (Continued)*

Level and Message Number	Message Text
%ASA-6-611101	User authentication succeeded: Uname: *user*.
%ASA-6-611102	User authentication failed: Uname: *user*.
%ASA-6-611301	VPNClient: NAT configured for Client Mode with no split tunneling: NAT addr: *mapped_address*.
%ASA-6-611302	VPNClient: NAT exemption configured for Network Extension Mode with no split tunneling.
%ASA-6-611303	VPNClient: NAT configured for Client Mode with split tunneling: NAT addr: *mapped_address* Split Tunnel Networks: *IP_address/netmask IP_address/netmask* ...
%ASA-6-611304	VPNClient: NAT exemption configured for Network Extension Mode with split tunneling: Split Tunnel Networks: *IP_address/netmask IP_address/netmask* ...
%ASA-6-611305	VPNClient: DHCP Policy installed: Primary DNS: *IP_address* Secondary DNS: *IP_address* Primary WINS: *IP_address* Secondary WINS: *IP_address*.
%ASA-6-611306	VPNClient: Perfect Forward Secrecy Policy installed.
%ASA-6-611307	VPNClient: Head end: *IP_address*.
%ASA-6-611308	VPNClient: Split DNS Policy installed: List of domains: string *string* ...
%ASA-6-611309	VPNClient: Disconnecting from head end and uninstalling previously downloaded policy: Head End : *IP_address*.
%ASA-6-611310	VNPClient: XAUTH Succeeded: Peer: *IP_address*.
%ASA-6-611311	VNPClient: XAUTH Failed: Peer: *IP_address*.
%ASA-6-611312	VPNClient: Backup Server List: *reason*.
%ASA-6-611314	VPNClient: Load Balancing Cluster with Virtual IP: *IP_address* has redirected the PIX to server *IP_address*.
%ASA-6-611315	VPNClient: Disconnecting from Load Balancing Cluster member *IP_address*.
%ASA-6-611316	VPNClient: Secure Unit Authentication Enabled.
%ASA-6-611317	VPNClient: Secure Unit Authentication Disabled.
%ASA-6-611318	VPNClient: User Authentication Enabled: Auth Server IP: *IP_address* Auth Server Port: port Idle Timeout: *time*.
%ASA-6-611319	VPNClient: User Authentication Disabled.
%ASA-6-611320	VPNClient: Device Pass Thru Enabled.
%ASA-6-611321	VPNClient: Device Pass Thru Disabled.
%ASA-6-611322	VPNClient: Extended XAUTH conversation initiated when SUA disabled.

continues

Table B-6 *Severity 6 (Informational) Logging Messages (Continued)*

Level and Message Number	Message Text
%ASA-6-611323	VPNClient: Duplicate split nw entry.
%ASA-6-613001	Checksum Failure in database in area *string* Link State Id *IP_address* Old Checksum *number* New Checksum *number*.
%ASA-6-613002	interface *interface_name* has zero bandwidth.
%ASA-6-613003	*IP_address* netmask changed from area *string* to area *string*.
%ASA-6-614001	Split DNS: request patched from server: *IP_address* to server: *IP_address*.
%ASA-6-614002	Split DNS: reply from server:*IP_address* reverse patched back to original server:*IP_address*.
%ASA-6-615001	VLAN number not available for firewall interface.
%ASA-6-615002	VLAN number available for firewall interface.
%ASA-6-616001	Pre-allocate MGCP *data-channel* connection for *inside_ifc*:*inside_ip address* to *outside_ifc*:*outside_ipaddress*/*port* from *message_type message*.
%ASA-6-617001	GTPv *version msg_type* from *src_ifc*:*src_ip*/*src_port* not accepted by *dest_ifc*:*dest_ip*/*dest_port*.
%ASA-6-617002	Removing v1 PDP Context with TID *tid* from GGSN *ip_address* and SGSN *ip_add*, Reason: *reason* or Removing v1 {primary	secondary} PDP Context with TID *tid* from GGSN *ip_address* and SGSN *ip_add*, Reason: *reason*.
%ASA-6-617003	GTP Tunnel created from *src_ifc*:*src_ip*/*src_port* to *dest_ifc*:*dest_ip*/*dest_port*.
%ASA-6-617004	GTP connection created for response from *src_ifc*:*src_ip*/0 to *dest_ifc*:*dest_ip*/*dest_port*.
%ASA-6-620001	Pre-allocate CTIQBE {RTP	RTCP} secondary channel for *interface_name*:*outside_address*[/*outside_port*] to *interface_name*:*inside_address*[/*inside_port*] from *CTIQBE_message_name message*.
%ASA-6-621001	Interface *ifname* does not support multicast, not enabled. (PIM)
%ASA-6-621002	Interface *ifname* does not support multicast, not enabled. (IGMP)
%ASA-6-621003	The event queue size has exceeded *number*.
%ASA-6-621004	Unknown message text.
%ASA-6-621005	Unknown message text.
%ASA-6-621006	Mrib disconnected, (*addr,addr*) event cancelled.
%ASA-6-621007	Bad register from *ifname*:*addr* to *addr* for (*addr, addr*).
%ASA-6-622001	Built BGP peering session, BGP _PEER_SES_ESTABLISH.
%ASA-6-622002	Teardown BGP peering session, BGP_PEER_SES_TEAR_DOWN.

Table B-6 *Severity 6 (Informational) Logging Messages (Continued)*

Level and Message Number	Message Text
%ASA-6-713038	Unknown message text.
%ASA-6-713145	Detected Hardware Client in network extension mode, adding static route for address: *IP address*, mask: *network mask*.
%ASA-6-713147	Terminating tunnel to Hardware Client in network extension mode, deleting static route for address: *IP address*, mask: *network mask*.
%ASA-6-713172	Automatic NAT Detection Status: Remote end {is I is not} behind a NAT device This end {is I is not} behind a NAT device.
%ASA-6-713177	Received remote Proxy Host FQDN in ID Payload: Host Name: *host_name* Address *IP_address*, Protocol *protocol_value*, Port *port_number*.
%ASA-6-713184	Client Type: *Client_type* Client Application Version: *Application_version_string*.
%ASA-6-713211	Adding static route for L2L peer coming in on a dynamic map. address: *IP address*, mask: *network mask*.
%ASA-6-713213	Deleting static route for L2L peer that came in on a dynamic map. address: *IP address*, mask: *network mask*.
%ASA-6-713215	No match against Client Type and Version rules. Client: *type version is/is not* allowed by default.
%ASA-6-713219	Queueing KEY-ACQUIRE messages to be processed when P1 SA is complete.
%ASA-6-713220	De-queueing KEY-ACQUIRE messages that were left pending.
%ASA-6-713905	*Descriptive_event_string*.
%ASA-6-716001	Group *group* User *user* WebVPN session started.
%ASA-6-716002	Authentication successful, Group *group*, User *user*, Session Type *type*.
%ASA-6-716003	Group *group* User *user* WebVPN session not allowed. WebVPN ACL parse error.
%ASA-6-716004	Group *group* User *user* WebVPN session terminated. User requested.
%ASA-6-716005	Group *name* User *user* WebVPN session terminated. Administrator reset.
%ASA-6-716006	Group *name* User *user* WebVPN session terminated. Idle timeout.
%ASA-6-716009	Group *name* User *user* WebVPN access denied for this URL *url*.
%ASA-6-716038	Authentication: successful, group = *name* user = *user*, Session Type: WebVPN.
%ASA-6-716039	Authentication: rejected, group = *name* user = *user*, Session Type: WebVPN.
%ASA-6-716040	Reboot pending, new sessions disabled. Denied user login.
%ASA-6-717003	Certificate received from Certificate Authority for trustpoint *trustpoint_name*.
%ASA-6-717004	PKCS #12 export failed for trustpoint *trustpoint_name*.
%ASA-6-717005	PKCS #12 export succeeded for trustpoint *trustpoint_name*.

continues

Section B-6

Table B-6 *Severity 6 (Informational) Logging Messages (Continued)*

Level and Message Number	Message Text
%ASA-6-717006	PKCS #12 import failed for trustpoint *trustpoint_name*.
%ASA-6-717007	PKCS #12 import succeeded for trustpoint *trustpoint_name*.
%ASA-6-717016	Removing expired CRL from the CRL cache.
%ASA-6-718003	Got unknown peer message *message_number* from *IP_address*, local version *version_number*, remote version *version_number*.
%ASA-6-718004	Got unknown internal message *message_number*.
%ASA-6-718013	Peer *IP_address* is not answering HELLO.
%ASA-6-718027	Received unexpected KEEPALIVE request from *IP_address*.
%ASA-6-718030	Received planned OOS from *IP_address*.
%ASA-6-718037	Master processed *number_of_timeouts* timeouts.
%ASA-6-718038	Slave processed *number_of_timeouts* timeouts.
%ASA-6-718039	Process dead peer *IP_address*.
%ASA-6-718040	Timed-out exchange ID *exchange_ID* not found.
%ASA-6-718051	Deleted secure tunnel to peer *IP_address*.
%ASA-6-719001	Email proxy session could not be established: session limit of maximum_sessions has been reached.
%ASA-6-719003	Email proxy session pointer resources have been freed.
%ASA-6-719004	Email proxy session pointer has been successfully established.
%ASA-6-719010	Email proxy feature is disabled on interface.
%ASA-6-719011	Email proxy feature is enabled on interface.
%ASA-6-719012	Email proxy server listening on port for mail protocol.
%ASA-6-719013	Email proxy server closing port for mail protocol.
%ASA-6-719025	Email proxy DNS name resolution failed for hostname.
%ASA-6-719026	Email proxy DNS name hostname resolved to IP_address.
%ASA-6-720002	(VPN unit) Starting VPN stateful failover subsystem.
%ASA-6-720003	(VPN unit) Initialization of VPN stateful failover component completed successfully.
%ASA-6-720004	(VPN unit) VPN failover main thread started.
%ASA-6-720005	(VPN unit) VPN failover timer thread started.
%ASA-6-720006	(VPN unit) VPN failover sync thread started.
%ASA-6-720010	(VPN unit) VPN failover client is being disabled.

Table B-6   *Severity 6 (Informational) Logging Messages (Continued)*

Level and Message Number	Message Text
%ASA-6-720012	(VPN unit) Failed to update IPsec failover runtime data on the standby unit.
%ASA-6-720014	(VPN unit) Phase 2 connection entry contains no SA list.
%ASA-6-720015	(VPN unit) Cannot find Phase 1 SA for Phase 2 connection entry.

B-7: Debugging—Syslog Severity Level 7 Messages

Table B-7 lists all the severity level 7 logging messages, along with their message numbers and text. All the messages supported by FWSM, ASA, and PIX are shown.

Table B-7   *Severity 7 (Debugging) Logging Messages*

Level and Message Number	Message Text
%ASA-7-106100	access-list acl_ID {permitted I denied I est-allowed} protocol interface_name/ source_address(source_ port) -> interface_name/dest_address(dest_ port) hit-cnt number ({first hit I number-second interval}).
%ASA-7-109014	*uauth_lookup_net* fail for uauth_in().
%ASA-7-109021	Uauth null proxy error.
%ASA-7-109026	[*aaa protocol*] Invalid reply digest received; shared server key may be mismatched.
%ASA-7-111009	User *user* executed cmd:*string*.
%ASA-7-199907	IP detected an attached application using port *port* while removing context.
%ASA-7-199908	*Protocol* detected an attached application using local port *local_port* and destination port *dest_port*.
%ASA-7-199909	ICMP detected an attached application while removing a context.
%ASA-7-304005	URL Server *IP_address* request pending URL *url*.
%ASA-7-304009	Ran out of buffer blocks specified by url-block command.
%ASA-7-701001	alloc_user() out of Tcp_user objects.
%ASA-7-701002	alloc_user() out of Tcp_ proxy objects.
%ASA-7-702201	ISAKMP Phase 1 delete received.
%ASA-7-702202	ISAKMP Phase 1 delete sent.
%ASA-7-702203	ISAKMP DPD timed out.
%ASA-7-702204	ISAKMP Phase 1 retransmission.
%ASA-7-702205	ISAKMP Phase 2 retransmission.

continues

Table B-7 *Severity 7 (Debugging) Logging Messages (Continued)*

Level and Message Number	Message Text
%ASA-7-702206	ISAKMP malformed payload received.
%ASA-7-702207	ISAKMP duplicate packet detected.
%ASA-7-702208	ISAKMP Phase 1 exchange started.
%ASA-7-702209	ISAKMP Phase 2 exchange started.
%ASA-7-702210	ISAKMP Phase 1 exchange completed.
%ASA-7-702211	ISAKMP Phase 2 exchange completed.
%ASA-7-702212	ISAKMP Phase 1 initiating rekey.
%ASA-7-702301	Lifetime expiring.
%ASA-7-702303	sa_request.
%ASA-7-703001	H.225 message received from *interface_name:ip_address/port* to *interface_name:ip_address/port* is using an unsupported version number.
%ASA-7-703002	Received H.225 Release Complete with newConnectionNeeded for *interface_name:ip_address* to *interface_name:ip_address/port*.
%ASA-7-709001	FO replication failed: cmd=*command* returned=*code*.
%ASA-7-709002	FO unreplicable: cmd=*command*.
%ASA-7-710001	TCP access requested from *source_address/source_port* to *interface_name:dest_address/service*.
%ASA-7-710002	{TCP | UDP} access permitted from *source_address/source_port* to *interface_name:dest_address/service*.
%ASA-7-710004	TCP connection limit exceeded from *source_address/source_port* to *interface_name:dest_address/service*.
%ASA-7-710005	{TCP | UDP} request discarded from *source_address/source_port* to *interface_name:dest_address/service*.
%ASA-7-710006	Protocol request discarded from *source_address* to *interface_name:dest_address*.
%ASA-7-711001	debug_trace_msg.
%ASA-7-711002	Task ran for *elapsed_time* msecs, process = *process_name*.
%ASA-7-711003	Unknown/Invalid interface identifier.
%ASA-7-712001	Unknown message text.
%ASA-7-712002	Unknown message text.
%ASA-7-712003	Unknown message text.
%ASA-7-713001	Unknown message text.
%ASA-7-713007	Unknown message text.

Table B-7   *Severity 7 (Debugging) Logging Messages (Continued)*

Level and Message Number	Message Text
%ASA-7-713023	Unknown message text.
%ASA-7-713024	Received local Proxy Host data in ID Payload: Address *IP address*, Protocol *protocol value*, Port *port number*.
%ASA-7-713025	Received remote Proxy Host data in ID Payload: Address *IP address*, Protocol *protocol value*, Port *port number*.
%ASA-7-713026	Transmitted local Proxy Host data in ID Payload: Address *IP address*, Protocol *protocol value*, Port *port number*.
%ASA-7-713027	Transmitted remote Proxy Host data in ID Payload: Address *IP address*, Protocol *protocol value*, Port *port number*.
%ASA-7-713028	Received local Proxy Range data in ID Payload: Addresses *IP address-IP address*, Protocol *protocol value*, Port *port number*.
%ASA-7-713029	Received remote Proxy Range data in ID Payload: Addresses *IP address-IP address*, Protocol *protocol value*, Port *port number*.
%ASA-7-713030	Transmitted local Proxy Range data in ID Payload: Addresses *IP address-IP address*, Protocol *protocol value*, Port *port number*.
%ASA-7-713031	Transmitted remote Proxy Range data in ID Payload: Addresses *IP address-IP address*, Protocol *protocol value*, Port *port number*.
%ASA-7-713034	Received local IP Proxy Subnet data in ID Payload: Address *IP address*, Mask *network mask*, Protocol *protocol value*, Port *port number*.
%ASA-7-713035	Received remote IP Proxy Subnet data in ID Payload: Address *IP address*, Mask *network mask*, Protocol *protocol value*, Port *port number*.
%ASA-7-713036	Transmitted local IP Proxy Subnet data in ID Payload: Address *IP address*, Mask *network mask*, Protocol *protocol value*, Port *port*.
%ASA-7-713037	Transmitted remote IP Proxy Subnet data in ID Payload: Address *IP address*, Mask *network mask*, Protocol *protocol value*, Port *port*.
%ASA-7-713039	Send failure: Bytes (*number of bytes*), Peer: *IP address*.
%ASA-7-713040	Could not find connection entry and cannot encrypt: Msgid—*ID*.
%ASA-7-713044	Unknown message text.
%ASA-7-713052	User (username) authenticated.
%ASA-7-713066	IKE Remote Peer configured for SA: *SA name*.
%ASA-7-713079	Unknown message text.
%ASA-7-713094	Cert validation failure: handle invalid for *Main/Aggressive Mode Initiator/ Responder*!
%ASA-7-713096	Unknown message text.

continues

Table B-7 *Severity 7 (Debugging) Logging Messages (Continued)*

Level and Message Number	Message Text
%ASA-7-713097	Unknown message text.
%ASA-7-713099	Tunnel Rejected: Received NONCE length *number* is out of range!
%ASA-7-713101	Unknown message text.
%ASA-7-713103	Invalid (NULL) secret key detected while computing hash.
%ASA-7-713104	Attempt to get Phase 1 ID data failed while *hash computation*.
%ASA-7-713108	Unknown message text.
%ASA-7-713113	Deleting IKE SA with associated IPSec connection entries. IKE peer: *IP address*, SA addr: *internal SA address*, tunnel count: *count*.
%ASA-7-713114	Connection entry (*conn entry internal address*) points to IKE SA (*SA internal address*) for peer *IP address*, but cookies don't match.
%ASA-7-713117	Received Invalid SPI notify (SPI *SPI Value*)!
%ASA-7-713121	Keep-alive type for this connection: *keepalive type*.
%ASA-7-713143	Processing firewall record. Vendor: *vendor*(*id*), Product: *product*(*id*), Caps: *capability value*, Version Number: *version number*, Version String: *version text*.
%ASA-7-713160	Remote user (session Id—*id*) has been granted access by the Firewall Server.
%ASA-7-713164	The Firewall Server has requested a list of active user sessions.
%ASA-7-713169	IKE Received delete for rekeyed SA IKE peer: *IP address*, SA addr: *internal SA address*, tunnelCnt: *tunnel cnt*.
%ASA-7-713170	IKE Received delete for rekeyed centry IKE peer: *IP_address*, centry addr: *internal_address*, msgid: *id*.
%ASA-7-713171	NAT-Traversal sending NAT-Original-Address payload.
%ASA-7-713173	Unknown message text.
%ASA-7-713187	Tunnel Rejected: IKE peer does not match remote peer as defined in L2L policy IKE peer address: *IP_address*, Remote peer address: *IP_address*.
%ASA-7-713190	Got bad refCnt (*refcnt_value*) assigning IP address (*IP_address*).
%ASA-7-713192	Unknown message text.
%ASA-7-713204	Adding static route for client address: *IP address*.
%ASA-7-713221	Static Crypto Map check, checking map = *crypto map tag*, seq = *seq #*...
%ASA-7-713222	Static Crypto Map check, map = *crypto map tag*, seq = *seq #*, ACL does not match proxy IDs src:*address* dst:*address*.
%ASA-7-713223	Static Crypto Map check, map = *crypto map tag*, seq = *seq #*, no ACL configured.
%ASA-7-713224	Static Crypto Map Check by-passed: Crypto map entry incomplete!

Table B-7 *Severity 7 (Debugging) Logging Messages (Continued)*

Level and Message Number	Message Text
%ASA-7-713225	[IKEv1], Group = *group_name*, IP = *ip_address*, Static Crypto Map check, map *map_name*, seq = *sequence_number* is a successful match.
%ASA-7-713906	*debug_message.* (VPN)
%ASA-7-714001	*Description of event or packet.* (IKE)
%ASA-7-714002	IKE Initiator starting QM: msg id = *message_ID_value*.
%ASA-7-714003	IKE Responder starting QM: msg id = *message_ID_value*.
%ASA-7-714004	IKE Initiator sending 1st QM pkt: msg id = *message_ID_value*.
%ASA-7-714005	IKE Responder sending 2nd QM pkt: msg id = *message_ID_value*.
%ASA-7-714006	IKE Initiator sending 3rd QM pkt: msg id = *message_ID_value*.
%ASA-7-714007	IKE Initiator sending Initial Contact.
%ASA-7-714008	Unknown message text.
%ASA-7-714009	Unknown message text.
%ASA-7-714010	Unknown message text.
%ASA-7-714011	Description of received ID values.
%ASA-7-715001	Descriptive statement.
%ASA-7-715002	Unknown message text.
%ASA-7-715003	Unknown message text.
%ASA-7-715004	*subroutine name*() Q Send failure: RetCode (*return code*).
%ASA-7-715005	*subroutine name*() Bad message code: Code (*message code*).
%ASA-7-715006	IKE got SPI from key engine: SPI = *SPI value*.
%ASA-7-715007	IKE got a KEY_ADD msg for SA: SPI = *SPI value*.
%ASA-7-715008	Could not delete SA *SA address*, refCnt = *number*, caller = *calling subroutine address*.
%ASA-7-715009	IKE Deleting SA: Remote Proxy *IP address*, Local Proxy *IP address*.
%ASA-7-715010	Unknown message text.
%ASA-7-715011	Unknown message text.
%ASA-7-715012	Unknown message text.
%ASA-7-715013	Tunnel negotiation in progress for destination *IP address*, discarding data.
%ASA-7-715014	Unknown message text.
%ASA-7-715015	Unknown message text.

continues

Section B-7

Table B-7 *Severity 7 (Debugging) Logging Messages (Continued)*

Level and Message Number	Message Text
%ASA-7-715016	Unknown message text.
%ASA-7-715017	Unknown message text.
%ASA-7-715018	Unknown message text.
%ASA-7-715019	IKEGetUserAttributes: *Attribute name* = *Attribute value.*
%ASA-7-715020	construct_cfg_set: *Attribute name* = *Attribute value.*
%ASA-7-715021	Delay Quick Mode processing, Cert/Trans Exch/RM DSID in progress.
%ASA-7-715022	Resume Quick Mode processing, Cert/Trans Exch/RM DSID completed.
%ASA-7-715023	Unknown message text.
%ASA-7-715024	Unknown message text.
%ASA-7-715025	Unknown message text.
%ASA-7-715026	Unknown message text.
%ASA-7-715027	IPSec SA Proposal # *chosen proposal*, Transform # *chosen transform* acceptable Matches global IPSec SA entry # *crypto map index.*
%ASA-7-715028	IKE SA Proposal # 1, Transform # *chosen tranform* acceptable Matches global IKE entry # *crypto map index.*
%ASA-7-715029	Unknown message text.
%ASA-7-715030	Unknown message text.
%ASA-7-715031	Unknown message text.
%ASA-7-715032	Unknown message text.
%ASA-7-715033	Processing CONNECTED notify (MsgId *message ID*).
%ASA-7-715034	*action* IOS keep alive payload: proposal=*time 1/time 2* sec.
%ASA-7-715035	Starting IOS keepalive monitor: *seconds* sec.
%ASA-7-715036	Sending keep-alive of type *notify type* (seq number *number*).
%ASA-7-715037	Unknown IOS Vendor ID version: *major.minor.variance.*
%ASA-7-715038	*action Spoofing information* Vendor ID payload (version: *major.minor.variance*, capabilities: *capabilities value*).
%ASA-7-715040	Deleting active auth handle during SA deletion: handle = *internal authentication handle.*
%ASA-7-715041	Received keep-alive of type *keepalive_type*, not the negotiated type.
%ASA-7-715042	IKE received response of type *failure_type* to a request from the IP address utility.
%ASA-7-715043	Unknown message text.

Table B-7   *Severity 7 (Debugging) Logging Messages (Continued)*

Level and Message Number	Message Text
%ASA-7-715044	Ignoring Keepalive payload from vendor not support KeepAlive capability.
%ASA-7-715045	ERROR: malformed Keepalive payload.
%ASA-7-715046	Constructing *payload_description* payload.
%ASA-7-715047	Processing *payload_description* payload.
%ASA-7-715048	Send *VID_type* VID.
%ASA-7-715049	Received *VID_type* VID.
%ASA-7-715050	Claims to be IOS but failed authentication.
%ASA-7-715051	Received unexpected TLV type *TLV_type* while processing FWTYPE ModeCfg Reply.
%ASA-7-715052	Old P1 SA is being deleted but new SA is DEAD, cannot transition centries.
%ASA-7-715053	MODE_CFG: Received request for *attribute_info*!
%ASA-7-715054	MODE_CFG: Received *attribute_name* reply: *value*.
%ASA-7-715055	Send *attribute_name*.
%ASA-7-715056	Client is configured for *TCP_transparency*.
%ASA-7-715057	Auto-detected a NAT device with NAT-Traversal. Ignoring IPSec-over-UDP configuration.
%ASA-7-715058	NAT-Discovery payloads missing. Aborting NAT-Traversal.
%ASA-7-715059	Proposing/Selecting only UDP-Encapsulated-Tunnel and UDP-Encapsulated-Transport modes defined by NAT-Traversal.
%ASA-7-715060	Dropped received IKE fragment. Reason: *reason*.
%ASA-7-715061	Rcv'd fragment from a new fragmentation set. Deleting any old fragments.
%ASA-7-715062	Error assembling fragments! Fragment numbers are non-continuous.
%ASA-7-715063	Successfully assembled an encrypted pkt from rcv'd fragments!
%ASA-7-715064	IKE Peer included IKE fragmentation capability flags: Main Mode: *true/false* Aggressive Mode: *true/false*.
%ASA-7-715065	IKE *state_machine subtype* FSM error history (struct *data_structure_address*) *state*, *event*: *state/event* pairs.
%ASA-7-715066	Can't load an IPSec SA! The corresponding IKE SA contains an invalid logical ID.
%ASA-7-715067	QM IsRekeyed: existing sa from different peer, rejecting new sa.
%ASA-7-715068	QM IsRekeyed: duplicate sa found by *addr*, deleting old sa.
%ASA-7-715069	Invalid ESP SPI size of *SPI_size*.

continues

Table B-7 *Severity 7 (Debugging) Logging Messages (Continued)*

Level and Message Number	Message Text
%ASA-7-715070	Invalid IPComp SPI size of *SPI_size*.
%ASA-7-715071	AH proposal not supported.
%ASA-7-715072	Received proposal with unknown protocol ID *protocol_ID*.
%ASA-7-715073	Unknown message text.
%ASA-7-715074	Could not retrieve authentication attributes for peer *IP_address*.
%ASA-7-715075	Group = *group_name*, Username = *client*, IP = *ip_address* Received keep-alive of type *mess_type* (seq number *seq#*).
%ASA-7-716008	Group *name* User *user* WebVPN access granted to URL: *url*.
%ASA-7-716010	Group *name* User *user* browse *path* failed. Unable to contact server.
%ASA-7-716011	Group *name* User *user* browse *path* failed. Unable to contact server.
%ASA-7-716012	Group *name* User *user* create file *path*.
%ASA-7-716013	Group *name* User *user* close file *path*.
%ASA-7-716014	Group *name* User *user* rename *old* to *new*.
%ASA-7-716015	Group *name* User *user* remove file *path*.
%ASA-7-716016	Group *name* User *user* create directory *path*.
%ASA-7-716017	Group *name* User *user* remove directory *path*.
%ASA-7-716018	WebVPN ACL parsed *acl*.
%ASA-7-716019	WebVPN ACL parse error in *acl*: cannot resolve *host*.
%ASA-7-716020	WebVPN ACL setting filter ID to *id*.
%ASA-7-716021	WebVPN ACL parser error invalid destination mask in *acl*.
%ASA -7-716024	Group *name* User *user* Unable to browse the network. Error: *description*.
%ASA -7-716025	Group *name* User *user* Unable to browse domain *domain*. Error: *description*.
%ASA -7-716026	Group *name* User *user* Unable to browse directory *directory*. Error: *description*.
%ASA -7-716027	Group *name* User *user* Unable to view file *file*. Error: *description*.
%ASA-7-716028	Group *name* User *user* Unable to remove file *file*. Error: *description*.
%ASA-7-716029	Group *name* User *user* Unable to rename file *file*. Error: *description*.
%ASA-7-716030	Group *name* User *user* Unable to modify file *file*. Error: *description*.
%ASA-7-716031	Group *name* User *user* Unable to create file *file*. Error: *description*.
%ASA-7-716032	Group *name* User *user* Unable to create folder *folder*. Error: *description*.
%ASA-7-716033	Group *name* User *user* Unable to remove folder *folder*. Error: *description*.

Table B-7   *Severity 7 (Debugging) Logging Messages (Continued)*

Level and Message Number	Message Text
%ASA-7-716034	Group *name* User *user* Unable to write to file *file*. *description*.
%ASA-7-716035	Group *name* User *user* Unable to read file *file*. *description*.
%ASA-7-716036	Group *name* User *user* File Access: User *username* logged into the *server* server.
%ASA-7-716037	Group *name* User *user* File Access: User *username* failed to log into the *server* server.
%ASA-7-718017	Got timeout for unknown peer *IP_address* msg type *message_type*.
%ASA-7-718019	Sent KEEPALIVE request to *IP_address*.
%ASA-7-718021	Sent KEEPALIVE response to *IP_address*.
%ASA-7-718022	Received KEEPALIVE request from *IP_address*.
%ASA-7-718023	Received KEEPALIVE response from *IP_address*.
%ASA-7-718025	Sent CFG UPDATE to *IP_address*.
%ASA-7-718026	Received CFG UPDATE from *IP_address*.
%ASA-7-718029	Sent OOS indicator to *IP_address*.
%ASA-7-718034	Sent TOPOLOGY indicator to *IP_address*.
%ASA-7-718035	Received TOPOLOGY indicator from *IP_address*.
%ASA-7-718036	Process timeout for req-type *type_value*, exid *exchange_ID*, peer *IP_address*.
%ASA-7-718041	Timeout [msgType=*type*] processed with no callback.
%ASA-7-718046	Create group policy *policy_name*.
%ASA-7-718047	Fail to create group policy *policy_name*.
%ASA-7-718049	Created secure tunnel to peer *IP_address*.
%ASA-7-718058	State machine return code: *action_routine*, *return_code*.
%ASA-7-718059	State machine function trace: state=*state_name*, event=*event_name*, func=*action_routine*.

Section B-7

INDEX

Symbols & Numerics

C

G

H

M

Q-R

S

W

X-Y-Z

Safari®

BOOKS ONLINE

ENABLED

THIS BOOK IS SAFARI ENABLED

INCLUDES FREE 45-DAY ACCESS TO THE ONLINE EDITION

The Safari® Enabled icon on the cover of your favorite technology book means the book is available through Safari Bookshelf. When you buy this book, you get free access to the online edition for 45 days.

Safari Bookshelf is an electronic reference library that lets you easily search thousands of technical books, find code samples, download chapters, and access technical information whenever and wherever you need it.

TO GAIN 45-DAY SAFARI ENABLED ACCESS TO THIS BOOK:

● Go to **http://www.ciscopress.com/safarienabled**

● Complete the brief registration form

● Enter the coupon code found in the front of this book before the "Contents at a Glance" page

If you have difficulty registering on Safari Bookshelf or accessing the online edition, please e-mail customer-service@safaribooksonline.com.

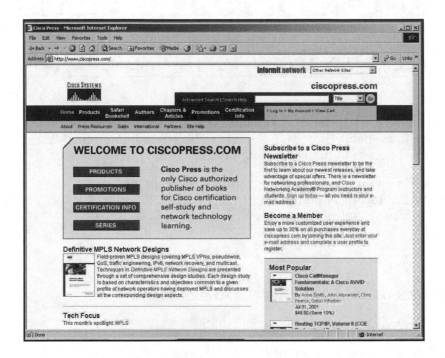

CISCO SYSTEMS

Cisco Press

3 STEPS TO LEARNING

STEP 1

STEP 2

STEP 3

First-Step

Fundamentals

Networking Technology Guides

STEP 1   **First-Step**—Benefit from easy-to-grasp explanations.
No experience required!

STEP 2   **Fundamentals**—Understand the purpose, application,
and management of technology.

STEP 3   **Networking Technology Guides**—Gain the knowledge
to master the challenge of the network.

NETWORK BUSINESS SERIES

The Network Business series helps professionals tackle the
business issues surrounding the network. Whether you are a
seasoned IT professional or a business manager with minimal
technical expertise, this series will help you understand the
business case for technologies.

Justify Your Network Investment.

Look for Cisco Press titles at your favorite bookseller today.

Visit **www.ciscopress.com/series** for details on each of these book series.

SEARCH THOUSANDS
OF BOOKS FROM
LEADING PUBLISHERS

Safari® Bookshelf is a searchable electronic reference library for IT professionals that features more than 2,000 titles from technical publishers, including Cisco Press.

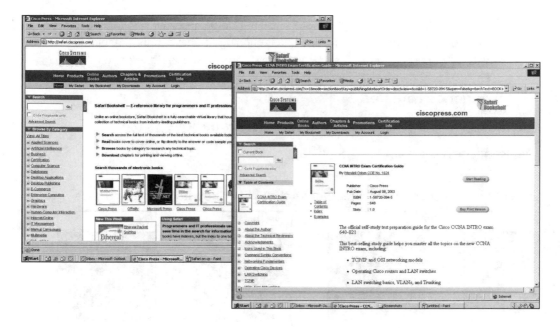

With Safari Bookshelf you can

- **Search** the full text of thousands of technical books, including more than 70 Cisco Press titles from authors such as Wendell Odom, Jeff Doyle, Bill Parkhurst, Sam Halabi, and Karl Solie.

- **Read** the books on My Bookshelf from cover to cover, or just flip to the information you need.

- **Browse** books by category to research any technical topic.

- **Download** chapters for printing and viewing offline.

With a customized library, you'll have access to your books when and where you need them—and all you need is a user name and password.

TRY SAFARI BOOKSHELF FREE FOR 14 DAYS!

You can sign up to get a 10-slot Bookshelf free for the first 14 days.
Visit **http://safari.ciscopress.com** to register.